GARDEN GUIDE

GARDEN GUIDE

44th Edition

FULLY REVISED AND UPDATED

HarperCollins*Publishers*

Acknowledgments
We wish to thank the following for assisting with this book:
Allen Gilbert, Judy Horton, Sam and Michael Yates,
Donald Coles, Margaret Hanks, Bayer Australia Ltd, Kevin Handreck,
Jim Fogarty, Annette McFarlane, Murray Hook and Geoff Miers.
Historical photographs and material are used by kind permission
of the Yates family and the Yates archives except where otherwise credited.
Picture research by Jennifer Blau.
Illustrations by Nicola Oram.
Index by Don Jordan, Antipodes Indexing.

HarperCollins*Publishers*

First published in Australia in 1895 by Arthur Yates & Co.
This edition published in Australia in 2015
by HarperCollins*Publishers* Australia Pty Limited
ABN 36 009 913 517
www.harpercollins.com.au

HarperCollins*Publishers*
Level 13, 201 Elizabeth Street, Sydney NSW 2000, Australia
Unit D1, 63 Apollo Drive, Rosedale, Auckland 0632, New Zealand
A53, Sector 57, Noida, UP, India
1 London Bridge Street, London SE1 9GF, United Kingdom
2 Bloor Street East, 20th floor, Toronto, Ontario M4W 1A8 Canada
195 Broadway, New York NY 10007, USA

National Library of Australia Cataloguing-in-Publication data:

Yates garden guide.
44th ed.
ISBN 978 0 7322 8987 4 (paperback)
Includes index.
Gardening – Australia.
Arthur Yates & Co.

635.0994

Cover design by HarperCollins Design Studio
Cover images: Woman gardening by sanjeri / Getty Images; all other images by shutterstock.com
Endpapers: Image by shutterstock.com
Original internal design by Melanie Calabretta and Judi Rowe/HarperCollins Design Studio
Typeset by HarperCollins Design Studio in Sabon 8/10.5pt
Colour reproduction by Graphic Print Group, South Australia
Printed and bound in China by RR Donnelley

9 8 7 6 5 4 3 2 1   15 16 17 18 19

Foreword

Now well into its second century, *Yates Garden Guide* has become an essential part of Australian gardening.

As our world changes, gardening habits change. Gardening fashions change, too, just as fashions do in any other part of life. *Yates Garden Guide* records, reflects and reacts to these changes, keeping each edition of the book new and up to date. Although the book has been a bestseller since its first publication in 1895, the challenge has been to keep it fresh and relevant for succeeding generations. We are proud that the book's continuing popularity proves that we have achieved success in this endeavour.

The book has grown from its initial ninety pages but it can't continue to grow – and it can't include everything. Hence, another challenge has been deciding what to include and what to leave out.

While pledging to change with the times, *Yates Garden Guide* also upholds the original philosophy espoused by Arthur Yates in 1895. This sees it committed to remaining a practical book that is of value to everyday homeowners, whether they garden on acreage, on a balcony or on a kitchen windowsill. The mark of our achievement is that this book can offer something of value to all. If *Yates Garden Guide* stays true to these aims it is sure to still be in publication into its third century – whether in the original print form or in a digitised version.

The temptation for today's authors, in this international world, is to write books that offer general information that can be loosely translated to any part of the world. This would, we think, be contrary to Arthur's original aim and to the values that have made the book such a success. We want the book to remain essentially Australian and to continue to rejoice in its Australianness.

Contents

Introduction

The Yates story began in Manchester in 1826 when George Yates, son of a cotton manufacturer, opened a grocery and seed shop. The seed side of the business became so successful that, three years later, George opened a second shop exclusively for selling seeds, and put his eldest son, Samuel (aged only fifteen at the time), in charge. Samuel's trade grew rapidly and he soon moved to larger premises. After his father's death, Samuel took over the business and, in turn, brought his own sons into the firm.

In 1879 Arthur, the second son, an asthmatic with a weak chest, was sent to New Zealand in the hope that the climate would prove beneficial to his health. He kept a detailed diary during the three months he spent travelling from Liverpool on the emigrant ship SS *Auckland*.

Arthur landed in New Zealand on 23 December 1879. He worked for a few years as a farmhand and shepherd but, with his entrepreneurial family background, he could not help but see that this new land offered great opportunities for a young seedsman with good trade connections back in Europe.

On 1 June 1883, Arthur opened a small shop in Auckland. As he had gained some experience in the family business before leaving England, he knew the importance of keeping good financial records. On his first day his takings were 1/6 and his expenditure 2/6 but, despite this inauspicious start, trade rapidly improved and he soon began taking orders from all over the country.

In 1886, Arthur visited Australia where he appointed an agent to take orders for seeds in NSW and Victoria. Then, in 1887, he leased premises in Sussex Street, Sydney. The same year his brother Ernest arrived in New Zealand from Manchester, and this allowed Arthur to leave Auckland and move across to Sydney where he felt the climate suited him better. In 1888 Arthur returned to England and married Miss Caroline Davies. After a European honeymoon, the young couple settled in a gracious, two-storey, brick home in the Sydney suburbs.

In 1893, Arthur launched his range of packet seeds which were, for the first time, illustrated with images of the desired results. These were very well received. And with the development of an affluent middle class and the growing popularity of the suburban quarter-acre block, business continued to flourish.

Arthur's next venture was to write the first *Yates' Gardening Guide*, further helping Yates to become a household name. The book has been adapted many times over the years and, as a

Yates display in a Hobart shop window in 1922.

result, has succeeded in establishing a following with each new generation.

Arthur and Ernest ran the company together until, in 1906, they agreed to an amicable split, with each retaining the name Arthur Yates and Co on their respective sides of the Tasman.

As the company expanded in Australia it became clear that larger premises were required and an imposing, five-storey, purpose-built warehouse was constructed. Then, at the turn of the century, Yates acquired a property at Exeter in the NSW Southern Highlands. In this cool, pleasant climate, this location became not only trial and breeding grounds for seeds and bulbs, but a favourite spot for family holidays (by 1904 Arthur and Caroline had six children). The four sons all joined the family business.

Arthur died in 1926 but the business continued to grow and the *Guide* had, by the time of his death, become an established institution in Australian life. In the next year, 1927, it was released in its seventeenth edition. The twenty-sixth edition came out in 1956, the thirty-eighth in 1992 and the

Centennial (thirty-ninth) edition in 1995. A major update for the fortieth edition, released in 1998, saw *Yates Garden Guide* take on a new lease of life in preparation for the twenty-first century.

The various editions of *Yates Garden Guide* reflect and help create trends in gardening activities and garden design and chart the changing relative importance of various elements in the Australian garden (such as the backyard, the bushhouse, the lawn, display flower beds and kitchen gardens). These books, and the comprehensive calendars, seasonal reminders, catalogues and specialist publications that were produced by Yates through the twentieth century, form a collection that has become an important resource in preserving the story of Australian gardening. They record the great world events that affected gardening – the wars, the Great Depression and the growing affluence of society after the Second World War. They chronicle the ever-growing ripples of concern about pesticide use that followed the publication of Rachel Carson's *Silent Spring* in 1962. They reflect the profligate water consumption of the years from the 1960s to the 1990s and the drought that brought this era to an end (the fortieth edition was the first to include a chapter on 'The Water-Saving Garden'). The waves of migrants from Europe and, later, Asia, the shrinking backyard and the negative effects on gardening of the harried, hurried lifestyles of Australians in the early twenty-first century are all found depicted in the Yates archives. And, as a backdrop to these changes, is the ongoing dichotomy over whether Australians should accept and applaud a native landscape that's so well adapted to our variable climate, or try to reshape their outdoor spaces into some kind of Arcadian ideal (usually inspired by English gardens).

Yates itself continued to change and adapt as it entered its second century. The Yates family ceased to be involved with the company in the 1980s and this saw Yates come under the control of a succession of owners. But there have been two constants: the company has remained a leader in Australian gardening, and it has continued to

First edition of Yates' Gardening Guide.

be Australian-owned, In recent years Yates has become part of DuluxGroup, an Australian public company that prides itself on guardianship of some of Australia's most trusted brands.

Testing the growth of seeds in 1900.

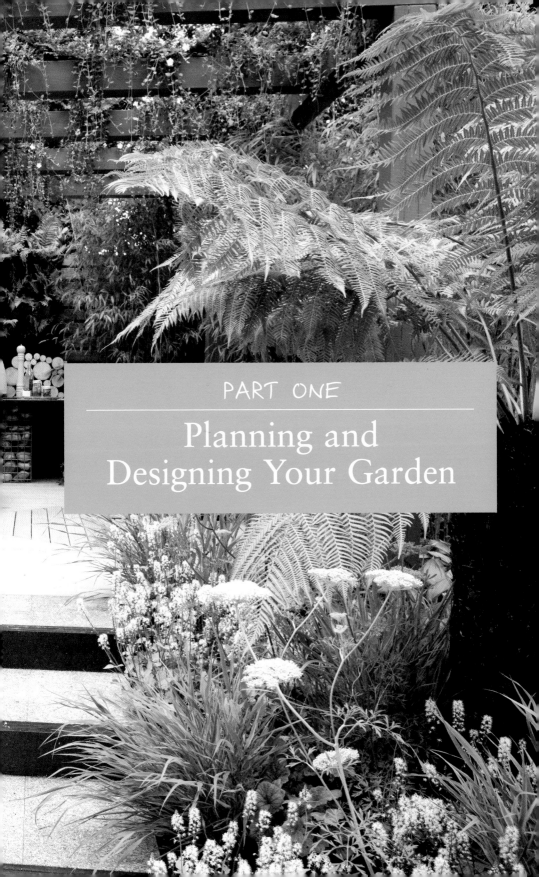

PART ONE

Planning and Designing Your Garden

Australian Gardening through the Years

For more than 40,000 years on this continent the indigenous people lived with the environment and made use of the plants around them. Very few of them gardened in the traditional European sense, however, so when the First Fleet arrived in 1788 the newcomers were largely unimpressed by the untamed native bush, even though naturalists Banks and Solander had enthusiastically collected plant specimens from Botany Bay when they arrived on the *Endeavour* in 1770.

The First Fleet carried a range of seeds and plants for the new settlement but the first few years were difficult. The soil around Port Jackson (now Sydney Harbour) was poor, plant varieties were unsuited to the climate and the seasons were reversed, so that many crops failed simply because they were planted at the wrong time of year. Things improved a little when farms were established west of Sydney in the more fertile land to be found in the Parramatta and the Hawkesbury River areas.

The early years of cultivation were characterised by the desperate need to grow food and it wasn't until food supplies were reliable that the settlers' attention turned to growing ornamental gardens. The first government houses in Sydney and Parramatta featured ornamentals among the fruit trees and vegetable beds. Layout of these early gardens tended to feature straight lines and clipped hedges. Scant attention was paid to the native plants, although these continued to be the cause of great interest in Britain. Fortunately, with the establishment of the Sydney Botanic Gardens in 1816, serious attempts began to be made to collect and cultivate native plants and to send specimens to other botanic gardens around the world.

As the nineteenth century progressed, gardening became a much more popular pastime. By 1820 Elizabeth Farm, first started by John and Elizabeth Macarthur in 1793, was described as being surrounded by 'pleasure grounds' in the style of an English country house. In 1826 Alexander Macleay received a land grant of 54 acres at Elizabeth Bay, east of Sydney town, where he began to create a grand garden that saw native plants were blended with specimens from around the world. Settlers in other colonies were also establishing their own estates. For Georgiana Molloy in Western Australia, her garden was a source of joy that relieved homesickness. Georgiana became a gifted amateur botanist who collected indigenous plant specimens that were sent to excited recipients in England. Anna Wickham of Newstead House in Brisbane enjoyed exchanging plants with her Macarthur cousins in NSW. Ornamental gardens flourished in the gentler conditions found in Victoria and Tasmania and the wool and gold wealth of the mid 1800s meant that gardens became status symbols of the newly rich.

This interest in horticulture was reflected in the larger populace, with cottage gardens being created around the smallest of dwellings. And, as prosperity became more widespread, home owners were able to devote time and energy to the ornamental garden, as well as to the ever-important productive vegetable patch and home orchard.

By the time Arthur Yates set up business in Australia in 1887, it was in a more formal Victorian era. Gardens at the turn of the nineteenth century featured distinctly segmented areas. Special 'picking beds' or 'garden borders' featured plants such as roses, dahlias and perennials which were specifically grown for cut flowers to decorate the parlour and other rooms of the house. Kitchen gardens were grown for the cultivation of fruit and vegetables for the table. Other areas included shrubberies of mixed ornamental shrubs and trees and, in larger gardens, even 'wooded' areas. Lawns were grassed areas scythed higher than what we are presently accustomed to and designed to link garden spaces.

Influenced by trends in 'the old country' where the prevailing climate allowed limited time outside, the Victorians, even in Australia, filled their homes with indoor plants. In keeping with the notion of bringing the garden inside, pot plants such as aspidistras and palms were placed on stands in darker rooms and hallways. Larger houses sometimes included 'garden rooms' or attached conservatories where large plants such as ferns and palms, which were very fashionable at the time, were nurtured, along with exotic and more decorative flowering species such as passionflower or other specific plant collections. However, maintaining these spaces was costly and labour intensive and so they eventually fell from favour.

Modest homes had glass- or hot-houses providing an opportunity for gardeners to grow small collections of a particular plant family which interested them. Seedlings and cuttings were propagated in these structures prior to planting out in the garden. Edible species such as tomatoes, cucumbers and even grapevines were also grown there to enable an early supply of vegetables and fruit for the household. These structures were often beset by problems with pests and diseases as they needed careful attention to sanitation. They became less popular once women took on other work, especially in times of war.

In those early days, Sydney alone had more than 100 seed companies competing for business. Growers later started selling seedlings from wooden seed trays – the retailer removed the required number of young plants and wrapped them in used newspaper for customers. This tradition lived on until the 1960s when different seeding techniques and plastic punnets were introduced.

During the following years, gardens were influenced by many factors, including available land and water, architectural styles, transport, world events such as wars and financial downturns, pests and diseases, labour and gardening knowledge. Trends in gardening, as in architecture, have always been cyclical with people seeking something fresh or new, though not always revolutionary.

THE FEDERATION GARDEN

The beginning of the twentieth century marked the Edwardian era and, in Australia, a new architectural style, the Federation house. The garden was characterised by timber paling fences on the rear and side boundaries. Side fences supported fragrant climbing species such as jasmine or *Mandevilla* spp. or were softened with a row of pencil pines, depending on the aspect. A gently curving pathway led to the front door. This was often paved with tessellated tiles or painted cement bordered by bricks laid on edge. A narrow ribbon-like garden followed the path and was usually planted with annuals. Circular or geometric-shaped beds were sometimes placed in lawn areas on either side of the path. These were filled with roses and edged with annuals to complement those planted along the path. The annuals were usually grown from seed sown in wooden boxes by the gardener and later pricked out into the garden beds. Open lawns surrounded the house, often sloping, with rolled edges between differing levels and rarely terraced. On larger properties, specimen trees such as Atlas cedars (or even the now-maligned camphor laurels) were planted on the lawn in the front of the house.

Features in the garden included grand steps or staircases constructed of stone or brick, complementing the materials used on the house. The car access was narrow, in most cases leading to a single garage situated behind the dwelling. The driveway consisted simply of twin concrete strips, bricks or stone flagging with grass or a bed of a low-growing species in between.

BETWEEN THE WARS

During the inter-war period, the style of gardens did not change much from that of the Federation period and generally followed the earlier Gardenesque style. The designs were, however, influenced by a number of fashions which were led by economic boom and depression, as well as the availability of plants provided by the nursery trade. Social changes at this time also brought a huge decline in the number of larger gardens cared for by hired help and an increase in those that were smaller, more manageable and maintained mostly by their owners.

Most gardens were humble. They were usually laid out with straight edges and often featured low hedges or close-boarded side and rear fences. Functional plantings of fruit trees and vegetables were grown in the backyard while the front was predominantly lawn. Herbaceous plants such as agapanthus, dahlias, gladioli and carnations, and annuals such as marigolds, anemones, ranunculus, along with bulbs and ferns, were all favoured. Jacarandas also proliferated in many gardens.

The garden became a great play area for children with extensive lawns and trees to hang a swing from, or to climb. It was common to have chooks, not only to harvest eggs but also for meat for the dinner table on festive occasions. The poultry often had free range in the backyard which helped keep pests in the garden at bay.

During the period spanning the two world wars several styles emerged in the design of houses and gardens.

Arts and Crafts

The Arts and Crafts movement, from 1900 to 1920, featured timber paling fences and fretted timber screens to separate properties. Cottage style and woodland gardens appeared. These were planted with the increasingly popular jacaranda, herbaceous side gardens, iris and agapanthus. Ferns were also favoured and structures housing collections of them often featured in gardens at this time.

The Californian Bungalow

The Californian Bungalow style prevailed from about 1916 to the 1930s. Its painted front fence was quite low and often constructed from sturdy posts and metal tube rails with infill panels of wire mesh. A matching gate was built into the fence and it was in many cases positioned asymmetrically to one side of the frontage. On street corner properties the gate was often placed on a chamfered angle at the junction of the streets. In the front garden, a single large weeping standard rose featured in a circular garden bed, and was under-planted with perennials and annuals. Other species in the garden included other roses, herbaceous plants and often a purple-foliaged flowering ornamental plum which was fashionable at the time.

This house dates back to the inter-war period and displays a mix of Arts and Crafts and Californian Bungalow styles.

Formal, carefully arranged plantings in a Georgian Revival style garden.

Georgian formality

During the Georgian Revival period in the 1920s to 1930s, designers created formal garden designs using symmetry in layouts by including geometric axes, vistas and focal points. Sometime the focal point was highlighted with the placement of a large urn, often containing a box or conifer specimen. Straight lines were created with paths and hedges of trimmed privet or abelia. Timber pergolas were also often used to create axes.

Landscape features such as loggias and low walls were built from masonry or stonework and paved terraces were often circular. Faux stonework appeared as capping to low walls on front verandas and was repeated on walls and gate pillars in the garden. Wrought iron was used for balustrades for steps and staircases. Timber Chinoiserie features were incorporated into tea houses, moon gates and used as trim to other structures in the garden.

Larger properties sometimes featured tennis courts. Pairs of Lord Howe Island or fan palms and Roman cypress were all used to accentuate the formality of the period. Other plants in the garden included plumbago, lavender and rosemary while large trees such as white cedars, jacarandas, peppercorn trees and robinias were commonly seen.

Spanish Mission

Late in the 1920s to the 1950s, the Hollywood/Spanish Mission style arrived in Australia. Garden walls, rendered to match those of the house, were built to separate patios, courtyards and terraced gardens. These areas were all adorned with feature steps, pools and fountains. Hedges of species such as escallonia or abelia formed structural parts of the planting design while exotic species such as New Zealand cabbage trees, tall conifers and palms were used as accents. Plants such as bananas and bird of paradise also made bold statements, while citrus, oleanders, hibiscus and geraniums (many potted specimens) were found throughout the garden.

Stockbroker Tudor

The period in the late 1920s to the 1930s also included the formal old English/Stockbroker Tudor style of architecture and landscaping. It featured saw-tooth brick edging, stonework walls and paving. Hedges of box, lavender and rosemary were common and other popular plants of the time were flowering cherries, Japanese maples, camellias and roses set out in formal beds. Both house and garden walls were sometimes softened with Virginia creeper which gave a dramatic effect in the autumn.

Streamline Moderne

The P&O/Streamline Moderne style of architecture from the 1930s to 1950s brought with it curved walls to houses. Structures and outbuildings had art deco detailing and steel-pipe and wrought-iron balustrades were used on steps and patios. Sharply defined edging, coloured concrete, crazy paved terraces and lily ponds with goldfish featured in many gardens of this time. Mosaic-tile highlights were often used for ornamentation throughout the garden.

In many cases, dwellings were two-storeyed; some had flat roofs. Plantings of pencil pines and other exotic species such as cacti, bananas and bird of paradise complemented the design of the homes. Dahlias, which had been very popular 100 years earlier in colonial days, had a revival.

Edna Walling

From the late 1920s, Edna Walling emerged as one of Australia's most important garden designers. Her first gardens reflected a cottage style with simple layouts, low-sitting walls, generous pergolas and garden rooms. These gardens were lushly planted with trees, shrubs, many perennials and shrub roses and, somewhat notably, rarely included annuals.

Although she often used large eucalypts as background plantings, it was not until the early 1950s that she completely embraced native plants in her landscape designs – something of a revolutionary idea in a country that, before then, was more inclined to fence out the bush. She became passionate about preserving the natural environment.

POST-WAR GARDENS

During wartimes, backyards had sizeable vegetable plots and these edible species often replaced annuals in other garden beds. Citrus and other fruit trees were also planted to supplement the family's food supply during times of rationing. After the Second World War, shortages of materials led to a new flat-roofed architectural style and people began to experiment with roof gardens. However, they were hard to maintain, especially in exposed locations. Later on, with better supplies, pitched roofs became fashionable once again and roof gardens almost disappeared – until recent years when they have had a resurgence in the higher-density inner-city environment.

The Hills Hoist

The arrival of the Hills Hoist in the 1940s played a big influence on the layout of the backyard, with some becoming almost 'shrines' to the clothesline which was commonly placed centre stage and often set on an axis or path leading from the back door of the house. Up until then, clotheslines usually consisted of a couple of wires strung between two posts with a crudely adjustable wooden prop positioned at mid point to tension the wires. When not in use, this arrangement somewhat blended into the backyard without making too much of a statement. In more recent times, our drying arrangements have become more sophisticated, using configurations that are

Vegetable gardens became a popular way to supplement food rationing during the war.

The Hills Hoist became a dominant feature of the backyard garden design, from the 1940s.

less intrusive than the more dominant circular unit.

European influences

Throughout the post-war years a flourish of immigrants, such as Italians, Greeks and, later, Hungarians, arrived in Australia bringing with them more variety in edible plants. Much to the surprise of some people, these were not only grown in the backyard but sometimes in the front garden as well. However, this practice, while common in areas settled by these new citizens, did not really set a general trend.

The Italians, in particular, also brought ornamental features such as statuary and fountains for their properties, all of which were reminders of their home country. Other new settlers from Europe also introduced a more ornate style of masonry and tile paving, and the use of pebbled areas in lieu of other hard surfaces.

THE GREAT AUSTRALIAN DREAM

In the 1950s, many of the earlier design influences prevailed but the ideal of owning your own home, surrounded by garden on a quarter-acre block, really took hold. The backyard was usually open and it was in most cases very utilitarian. It had areas designated as lawn, always with clothes-drying facilities, very often a large vegetable garden, sometimes a glasshouse and, of course, it always contained a back shed. Outdoor living areas were not so usual in this era although some gardens did have small paved areas to accommodate a seat or bench to sit and enjoy or contemplate the garden.

The land in front of the house consisted mainly of lawn, sometimes with small geometric-shaped feature beds planted out with seasonal annuals. However, the invention of the Victa rotary motor-mower soon brought on the demise of such garden beds. Feature mowing strips appeared where previously the 'spade edge' defined areas of grass. Pieces of bush rock, set vertically in cement, were common for this purpose. Sometimes rock was removed during the excavation of platforms for houses built on concrete slabs. This rock was also purchased and brought in where the rock was not available on site as the trend became more popular.

Front boundaries were often defined by low brick or stone walls constructed with materials matching those used on the dwellings. Sometimes these walls had inset panels of wrought iron along with a matching gate. Metal letterboxes were often

This flower-filled garden in Queensland was an entrant in a gardening competition in 1955.

set into low pillars built as gate posts. Behind these walls, gardeners displayed collections of classic and new varieties of hybrid tea roses, usually in varying colours, and inter-planted with annuals for seasonal interest.

Timber paling fences were usually used on side boundaries, and taller plants, shrubs and perennials were planted alongside.

The 1950s were also notable for a very special garden feature the tyre swan – sculpted literally from an old tyre – which was included in many domestic and commercial landscapes around this time. Sadly, this truly Australian species, which brought with it a sense of fun, has now become extinct due to the change in the construction of the modern tyre.

Japanese influences

For the more adventurous, Japanese-themed areas within gardens became fashionable. These featured expanses of raked gravel, large rocks and reflective ponds, sometimes including ornate bridges leading to small islands.

Species such as maples, small conifers and azaleas were planted. Larger plants were placed alone expressly for their beauty of form, their seasonal interest when blooming or clad in autumn leaves, or even for their tracery of bare branches in winter.

Bamboo was not only used for planting but for its dried stems which were used for screening and landscape decoration – sometimes in the form of items such as deer frighteners (water spouts). Covered timber gateways, often decorated with bamboo stem panels, separated these themed areas from other parts of the garden. Lanterns made from granite or imitation stone provided focal points in these fairly minimalist landscapes.

The modern garden

The 1960s brought houses that had larger areas of glass, and sliding doors which encouraged people to create gardens which they could enjoy from both the indoors and outdoors. Gardening magazines published articles showing new ideas originating from America which inspired readers to create a more modern and less formal look to their properties. Trends included fretwork concrete block or timber screens providing

Japanese garden featuring a lantern and pond.

courtyards and patios with intimate areas. Very often these areas appeared on the street side of the home if it faced the right aspect. Square-shaped stepping stones linking paving through lawns and garden beds became a new trend.

Increasing numbers of swimming pools started appearing in backyards and they were surrounded with plantings of palms, philodendrons and other warm-climate plants to give a casual tropical ambience. Cabanas and paved alfresco-eating areas complemented the pools. Timber decks extended living spaces, especially in gardens with steeper slopes.

The car port, usually attached to the dwelling, became commonplace and it was certainly less intrusive than a freestanding garage, which had been the norm up until this time. Many homes had one or two garages built into or under the house and excavation for driveways and sets of steps impacted on the landscape.

The 'tin fence' appeared and it was about this time that front and side fences in many new subdivisions disappeared altogether. In the latter scenario, letterboxes became

Modern houses in the 1960s had larger windows opening out to the garden which extended the living areas outdoors. Side and front fences often disappeared.

features that sat in small, island beds on the street front, often incorporating a few bush rocks, sometimes a dwarf nandina or a small conifer. Roses remained as popular as ever, with different tones such as Blue Moon being introduced and the newer, more floriferous floribunda varieties appeared in greater numbers.

Some eschewed the new modernity, however, and reproduction colonial homes also became popular at this time. This style of home brought with it a return to cottage garden plantings, including old-fashioned roses, shrubs, perennials, bulbs and annuals.

THE NATIVE GARDEN

Along with a movement which embraced the natural-look, native gardens became the new theme of choice in the 1970s. Ellis Stones, Australia's first popular landscape architect and protégé of Edna Walling, very cleverly incorporated natural elements such as rock

and recycled timbers along with a wide range of native plants into his garden designs — a style which many gardeners soon copied.

Groundcover plants complemented the natural theme and helped achieve the so-called low maintenance of gardens fashionable at this time. Mulches also became widely used in many gardens to control weeds. The mulch was spread over areas of black polythene sheeting and later over a 'weed mat'.

Organic forms were preferred where at all possible and curved or kidney-shaped swimming pools became a very common feature in the backyard. Bush houses were often used to grow shade-loving plants or species more delicate than those growing elsewhere in the garden. These structures were sometimes also used for outdoor entertaining and relaxing. To complete the look, brush fences enclosed courtyards and sometimes entire lots.

Often a native tree such as *Eucalyptus nicholii* or a silver dollar gum featured in the front lawn but, now, many have disappeared from suburbia as they became too big for many gardens. Palms continued to be used for a tropical ambience and it was at this time that the cocos palm, now considered a weed in many areas, was planted extensively.

Houses were often constructed from rustic brickwork and featured lashings of 'mission brown' facings. The return of women to the workforce in the '90s saw many families invest in two cars and more garage space, and this, along with subdivisions of smaller blocks, brought a reduction in actual garden area. Driveways and paths featured generous areas of recycled bricks or 'tumbled' coloured cement pavers.

Plants with yellow foliage, such as golden conifers like Cripps Golden Cypress, 'Swanes Golden' pencil pine and golden robinias, became widespread. While these plants contrasted well with the buildings of the era, their over-use led to their demise in favour of upcoming trends and new species.

THE FORMAL GARDEN

The 1980s saw a return to a more formal look to gardens and, with overseas travel a common practice, gardeners enjoyed creating a little bit of their favourite destination in their own garden on their return home.

The Tuscan garden with box hedges and species such as lavender and rosemary became a new trend that quickly distinguished itself from the more natural gardens of the previous decade. Gardens featured statuary and other ornamentation including water features. Often grand fountains, typically ornate, were installed in larger gardens while more modest examples, simple wall fountains or large pots of water, were placed into smaller gardens and more intimate spaces. Structures such as garden

Unstructured native garden featuring low groundcover plants, gravel and recycled timber steps.

The Tuscan garden featured box hedges, ornate water features and a return to formal design.

walls and gazebos were rendered or 'bagged' to match the colour of the walls to the main dwelling, further emphasising the Italianate look.

It was also popular, at this time, to design the garden into a series of 'rooms' with particular colour schemes, such as The White Garden as seen at Sissinghurst in England or 'green gardens', which were often very structured and layered with varying plant species and hedges of differing heights. Conifers made a big return to the garden, predominantly in the form of hedging but also as accent plants in the case of pencil pines or conical junipers. Topiary, which originated in Italy in the 1600s, also became fashionable and it featured in all shapes and sizes.

There was also a re-emergence of Federation architecture in the 1980s and 1990s but the homes were now larger, usually set on much smaller blocks than in the past, and they often had up to three garages,

leaving less space for lawns and gardens. While the gardens were planted in a sympathetic manner to the homes, they were often more formal in nature than their earlier counterparts. Screen planting and hedges of species such as Leyland cypresses and murraya separated and enclosed areas of gardens. Edges to garden beds featured mondo grass, agapanthus and box hedges while infill plantings included azalea, gardenia and clivea. Standard roses (commonly white Iceberg) lined pathways and garden borders with groundcovers or annuals mass-planted underneath. Standardised specimens and other topiary available at the time were also incorporated into the design as focal points and highlights. Climbers such as wisteria and the very hardy star jasmine were extensively planted for screening or softening, echoing the use of jasmine in the Federation era.

A move to the more disciplined or formal plantings in the late 1990s was seen to complement the neoclassical look of many new homes being built or renovated at this time. A variety of hedges continued to be used as prominent landscape features and many gardens were separated into a series of intimate spaces or rooms, using these elements.

Over the years the media, especially radio shows, educated the public with new ideas, ideal plant selection and better gardening habits. Television programs showcasing gardening introduced a wider audience to design layouts with an emphasis on the placing, the repetition and 'drift' planting of a particular species rather than the more random or 'stud' positioning of plants in many gardens of the past.

GARDENING IN A HOT LAND

Water has always featured in our gardens with dams or small lakes on country properties providing water for stock, a source of irrigation for the land, and the garden. This water has also provided a habitat for wildlife, as well as to give reflective vistas in the landscape. In urban areas, smaller gardens have often incorporated fish or lily ponds but over the years these have lost popularity due to maintenance and safety considerations, and other sorts of water features such as fountains have become more prevalent.

The prolonged drought of recent times led to a new interest in the use of succulents in the garden. Large agave and aloe species were used as dramatic feature plants while smaller varieties such as sedums and echeveria provided ground cover. However, this trend has not been a widespread success. In areas where the climate has seen a return to more inclement periods, many of these species have suffered root rot and fungal leaf problems. In addition, hail damage can affect large fleshy leaf varieties which take some time to regain their original splendour.

The growing of hardy grass species such as purple fountain grass and native lomandra and dianella varieties became invaluable where low-water-usage plantings were necessary in times of low rainfall. The popularity of these plants continues especially with the introduction of new varieties of the latter two species. The foliage of these grasses adds interesting texture to other garden plantings as well as requiring little water to survive.

With the 'dry river bed' a feature in many landscapes in the drought, this look can be applied to the garden, particularly those designed with a natural theme.

In many parts of Australia, authorities have allowed and even encouraged the installation of rainwater tanks on properties, so many varied containers have been incorporated into the garden in the last twenty years giving additional water in times of shortages.

Tropical gardens have been an ongoing trend of the last couple of decades. Emphasis on the shape, colour and texture of leaves has become important in garden design and has emerged as significant criteria when selecting species. Asian influences, such as Balinese pavilions used for outdoor entertaining and relaxation, have become very popular, along with other ornamentation such as rustic gates and oriental statuary.

Interesting effects can be created with succulents and they are ideal in a hot climate.

A Buddha statue in an Asian-style garden.

This rooftop garden makes good use of vertical space.

A NEW CENTURY OF GARDENS

The ongoing trend from the 1990s through the 2000s has been one of a shrinking garden with a growing dominance of larger houses now taking up almost the whole block with little space for lawn. The trend to higher-density housing in the city has also meant that more people are restricted to creating smaller gardening spaces, such as container gardens on balconies, roof gardens, small outdoor rooms and courtyards. Vertical gardens that take up little horizontal space are popular, but careful plant choice and appropriate care regimes are critical to success.

In the last few decades there has been an emergence of houses with wide sliding or, more recently, folding, glass doors which give the illusion of a seamless barrier between the indoors and outdoors. These doors have allowed us to take the indoors out into the garden, allowing it to become a functional area for entertaining, with separate structures incorporating bars, kitchens, eating and living spaces.

The post-modern architectural design trend in the 1990s and 2000s has brought gardens with sleek, minimalist designs. Accent plants with strappy leaves, the use of hedging and simple topiary specimens have been used to make a design statement. This has been seen as a welcome trend since flowers are not wholly relied on for interest in the garden.

While subtler colour tones are still popular, there has been a change to stronger and bolder colour schemes. Foliage, particularly in red tones, has become fashionable – the 'new yellow' of the past. Plants with white flowers remain very much in style and are often used as focal points in the garden. Species with silver foliage have become valued for providing contrast and interest in the design of gardens. Older, tougher plant species such as osmanthus and newer varieties of other stalwarts like loropetalum are making a welcome return in many new landscape plantings.

In recent times there has been increasing interest in the growing of edible species and an emphasis on organic and permaculture principles with ornamental and edible species

A lush and vibrant garden can be created by container gardening in smaller garden spaces.

often found growing together, sometimes in the guise of companion planting. Composting facilities, worm farms and even chooks are increasingly being included in the backyard.

Native-plant growers are introducing a greater range of interesting new varieties. It is increasingly recommended to include native species in our new plantings to encourage native fauna to our gardens and, by growing plants best adapted to the local environment, use less water.

From trends emerging overseas in the future we may see a return to a more natural style of landscaping which will be easier to maintain as our lives get busier and we find that we are more and more conscious of budget restraints.

Native plants save on water and maintenance.

Starting a Community or Co-op Garden

While allotment (shared) gardens have never been as popular in Australia as in the UK – perhaps because the individual quarter acre has (until now) been an easily achievable Australian dream – with more families moving to inner city or high density living, the idea of sharing garden space has taken on greater appeal. Local councils are leading the way, but many other groups are also active. If you want to get involved in a community garden, your local council is a good place to start – hopefully you may be able to join an existing group. If you can't, the council should be able to give you some direction or guidelines for starting up a new group.

And if the idea of joining a larger community garden group isn't your thing, a few families or households can get together to form their own, smaller scale, vegie-growing co-op. There are many benefits to be derived from these more casual arrangements, such as:

- You can garden without leaving your own home, but enjoy the company of a larger group.

It's much easier to get the whole family involved if other families are doing the same thing. This applies particularly to kids who enjoy sharing experiences with friends but aren't so excited about doing things with mum and dad.

You can pool knowledge so that the more experienced members of the group provide guidance for the novices.

If the co-op gardens are close together, it's simple and cost-effective to arrange bulk deliveries of soil, building materials, manure and mulches.

Individual garden plots can be devoted to one type of crop, but the harvest can be shared by all. This makes it easier to care for a particular crop. For example, if you are the carrot grower of the group, you only need to worry about fertilising carrots. And if you're only growing lettuces, you'll know they do best if they are regularly fed with a liquid, high-nitrogen food like Thrive Soluble All Purpose.

When it comes to purchasing larger items, you can increase your buying power. If you are buying a number of expensive items, such as compost tumblers, you're in a much better position to negotiate a discount.

Similarly, if you want to hire some equipment, the usage time and costs can be allocated across all the members of the co-op.

The co-op garden can become the basis for great learning experiences for children. Encourage them to write, record and photograph their gardening story. A tech-savvy person can set up a blog for the group.

Final advice: before setting up your co-op, get together to agree on the ground rules that everyone will commit to following. And make sure that each household checks its insurance cover!

2
Garden Design

Many of us have visited gardens which we admire and maybe even draw inspiration from. But what is it about these gardens that grabs our attention? Is it simply the style of the garden, or is it the layout, the colour scheme, the way the plants or 'soft landscape' blend with the paths, patios, walls or 'hard landscape': the way a gardener has blended design with nature?

There can be many ways to achieve a great garden but a well-designed garden is usually one which uses the hard landscape as a frame, allowing the plant selection to become the focal point. A great garden also encourages you to 'move' through it, exploring all the different vistas it has to offer. A badly designed garden is often one-dimensional: all laid out in front of the viewer with no hint of surprise. Think of the many back yards where nothing more is on show than a large slab of lawn and a thin strip of garden bed around the perimeter. There is no sense here of the romance and curiosity of a well-thought-out garden.

Gardens are about interaction between humans and plants. We experience plants through touch, sight, sound, taste and smell. A good garden is one which offers a multitude of pleasures: a place to relax by yourself or with friends, bounty to cook and eat, or even just a piece of living artistry to contemplate from the couch on a rainy day. Designing such a place is the ultimate challenge in working with nature.

PRINCIPLES OF GARDEN DESIGN

When designing a garden, there are several key principles which will help you understand the challenge of your task ahead:

- Utilising and dealing with space
- Creating unity; linking the whole design so there is a relationship between elements
- Working with scale; achieving pleasing proportions between one thing and another
- Using the third dimension; changing space by changing levels (elevations, steps, terracing, roof lines)
- Combining hard and soft landscape features
- Maximising views and vistas
- Identifying style
- Establishing a foundation for mood and response
- Allowing interaction with people; using the senses of sight, smell, touch, hearing and taste
- Making a garden attractive
- Creating a functional space
- Making the garden suit your lifestyle

In creating your garden there are five main steps towards achieving a successful design.

1. Selecting a garden style
2. Design concept
3. Hard landscape design
4. Soft landscape design
5. The final plan

HINT

All gardeners should be encouraged to include in their design an area which is just for them. This space should have a theme based on a particular love or passion — fragrant plants, herbs, a certain colour scheme, or whatever is important to that particular gardener.

PRUE SMITH
GARDEN WRITER

HINT

Gardening becomes so much more enjoyable when you grow only those plants suited to your conditions. Any plant which, in spite of the best culture, continues to struggle, should be put out of its misery.

JOHN STOWAR

LANDSCAPE CONSULTANT AND
HORTICULTURAL JOURNALIST

SELECTING A GARDEN STYLE

You may already have a vision of your ideal garden but there are several factors which may influence the style of garden you ultimately choose to design.

- Architecture and style of house. This is very important as the design of your garden should always complement the style of your house.
- Surrounding or neighbouring landscapes. Look at other gardens in your area and take note of which type of plants thrive the best. Consider blending your garden with the surrounding landscape so it doesn't look out of place, especially if you live near natural bushland.
- Environmental requirements. Many subdivisions have strict guidelines about planting new gardens and these may have a strong impact on the style of garden you choose. For instance, if a native plant list for your garden is required, then it makes sense to select a native or Australian garden style.
- Council requirements. These may range from plant selection described above to laws regarding heritage overlay areas, protection of existing trees and vegetation, water run off and limits to hard surfacing of new gardens.
- Family requirements. The needs of children, other members of your family, and pets may influence many aspects of your garden. It is important to remember that these needs are likely to change over

time as children grow up, and where possible, this should be considered in your planning.
- Family heritage. There may be some key cultural or traditional aspects which may have an influence on the design of your garden. If you have European heritage, you may want to create a garden based around family entertainment, with areas allocated for growing vegetables and fruit trees. If you have English heritage, you may want to create an English-style garden with lots of flowering perennials.
- Lifestyle choices. Do you want to use your garden for sport, entertaining or simply to relax?
- Time. Are you a busy person with little time to devote to gardening or are you a keen gardener? How long do you have to transform and maintain your garden?
- Financial considerations. What sort of budget do you have for a garden makeover? How much do you want to invest in your property? What might potential auction results be?
- Colour preferences. Do you prefer softer, natural-looking colours or do you prefer bright, modern colours?
- Plant preferences. Do you prefer colourful flowers, large trees or structural foliage plants?

Contrasting bright colours and strong lines feature in this formal style vegetable garden.

This Balinese-inspired garden, with a pavilion set among lush foliage plants, is an ideal place to relax in a hot climate.

- Traditional or modern design principles. Which best reflects your house? Which appeals to you? Or are you seeking a combination of both?
- Formal or informal style. This may be determined by the style of house and its interior, and by the needs of children or pets.
- Travel experiences. You may want to create a style influenced by places you have visited when travelling.

HINT

Always remember to take photos of your garden from time to time, or just before you start a new job in it. When you look back at them, it will give you a lift when you see just how much progress has been made since they were taken.

LORNA ROSE M.A.I.H.

HORTICULTURAL PHOTOGRAPHER

There are many garden styles to choose from, drawing on influences from places as diverse as Bali and Morocco to aesthetics ranging from formal minimalist gardens to bush gardens and permaculture. Features of several popular styles are described in the boxes on pages 22–23 and may provide inspiration for your garden design.

If you are unsure about which style of garden to choose, the most important thing is to blend the style of garden with the style of house. There is more likelihood of failure if these are mismatched.

Many professional garden designers will do consultations, and it may be worthwhile employing a professional even just for some initial verbal advice. Alternatively, speak to your architect if your house is new or you have just had a renovation done. Reading books, magazines and watching television can all give inspiration and ideas. Try to involve members of your family and close friends for comments, and an objective opinion.

Basic Garden Styles

Australian style

Australian style gardens showcase the many wonderful trees and shrubs indigenous to our part of the world. Gardens can be located in any geographic region from the coast to the bush and from tropical to the cooler climates of south-eastern Australia. Blending with their natural surroundings, they feature local native plantings, attract a variety of birds and other wildlife, are drought tolerant and environmentally conscious.

Design style may be informal or formal, but often uses curved lines to replicate natural contours and employs earthy, bush colours. Consider incorporating feature rocks, gravel, pebbles and local stone, grasses and grass trees, wildflowers and billabong-style ponds. Grafted gums are useful for small gardens.

Resort style

Resort style gardens are inspired by tropical garden styles characteristic of Bali and other parts of South East Asia. Resort style gardens are perfect for areas in Australia with subtropical and tropical climates; however, with proper plant selection, it is possible to also adapt this style for cooler parts of Australia.

Emphasising relaxation, resort gardens often have flowing lines, lounges, bamboo, rattan or timber furniture, market umbrellas, barbecue and entertainment areas. In hot climates, shade, water features, pools and spas all cool things down. Consider using design elements such as paving, decking, boardwalks and ropes, pebbling and stone slabs. Typical plantings are close together and include foliage plants, palm trees and bromeliads.

Mediterranean style

Mediterranean style gardens depict many of the popular Mediterranean regions from Spain, southern France, Italy and Greece, and are inspired by their lifestyle and culture. Tending to be drought tolerant, they are suitable in many parts of Australia.

Provincial style gardens are informal, rustic, and have an aged-farmhouse look using natural stone paving and lime-washed walls. Shaded outdoor areas with pergolas and climbing plants are ideal for alfresco dining. Olive trees and home-grown fruit and vegetables along with picking flowers are characteristic.

Formal Italian style may also include wall-mounted water features, courtyards and piazzas using cobblestone paving, pebbling, mosaics and tiling.

Natural style

Natural style gardens include coastal and bush gardens. They are similar to Australian style gardens but may blend both Australian and exotic plants. Exotic species are selected for their aesthetic input into garden bed displays as well as their ability to grow in Australian conditions.

Informal in design and sympathetic to the surrounding landscape, natural style gardens use curved lines to replicate nature and are inspired by Australian bush colours. Typical plantings include grasses mixed with exotics such as succulents, wildflowers, proteas and picking flowers. Consider using natural stone paving and walls, exposed timbers, decking, shade sails and market umbrellas in neutral colours and natural style water features.

Basic Garden Styles (cont'd)

English style

English style gardens stem back to the heritage of many of our earlier settlers and are still popular today.

Formal English gardens are best suited to Georgian style architecture or formal houses. Design principles are based on square, rectangular and circular shapes in paths and lawns, and the use of axes and symmetry. Gardens are neat with clipped hedges, topiary, coppiced and espaliered trees and minimal flowering plants. Paved areas incorporating urns and fountains are common.

Informal gardens use curved lines and create elements of curiosity. There is more emphasis on colour and fragrance with flowers, herbs, fruit trees, vegetable gardens and lawns. Arbours and pergolas can be attractive features.

DESIGN CONCEPT

Having decided on your basic garden style you next need to consider how to incorporate all the features you desire in your garden and decide how to do this in a way that is pleasing to the eye.

The design of a garden begins with the concept stage. Concept drawings are basic layouts which help to locate essential items in a garden. These drawings are an ideal way to enable adequate involvement of all people associated with a garden, to express their ideas, needs and desires. Concept drawings are not detailed in content; they are basic outlines of the location of all the components of a garden. Examples of these drawings are on pages 31–33.

What to consider

Before you put pencil to paper, there are many questions and considerations in addition to those that influenced your initial choice of garden style.

- Linking the garden with the interior of the house. Do you want to construct a deck? How can you best maintain views and vistas from doorways and windows?
- Entertainment area. Do you want this adjoining the house or by a swimming pool? Do you require a covered area to provide shelter?
- Garden bed layout. What shape should these be and how large?
- Size of lawn. While a large lawn may be appealing for children, consider the time that it will take to mow and care for.
- Requirements of children. Do you want to incorporate swings, a sandpit or a cubby house?
- Pets. Do you need space for a dog to run around?
- Service area requirements. How much space is required for a shed, clothes line, compost, firewood, kids' toys, bikes, etc?
- Swimming pool or spa.
- Water feature or pond.

- Features. Feature plants, furniture, urns and statues create interest in the garden and help to define your garden style.
- Fences, walls and retaining walls. Will you require split levels and steps?
- Paved surfaces. What type and colour do you want? How extensive will these be? Do you want a small pathway or a larger paved area instead of a lawn?
- Plant selection and climate. It is critically important to choose plants that suit your climate. In gardening, rainfall and temperature are the most important factors. The highest and lowest temperatures are more critical than the average temperature because it is the extremes that cause problems with plant growth. Australia has three very broad climate zones: tropical/subtropical, temperate, and cold (these zones are illustrated in the map on pages 500–501), but many local variations and microclimates.
- Aspect, sun and shade. Many plants require full sunlight, but others tolerate shade in varying degrees. The preferred aspect for most Australian houses and gardens is northeast so that sun is received

HINT

Never plant evergreen trees on the north side of your house if you want to take advantage of the winter sun.

MELANIE KINSEY
HORTICULTURAL JOURNALIST

in the early morning and for most of the day. A northeast slope is even better, because it is warmer and protected from cold southerly and southwest winds. It is possible to build a house on almost any block of land so that the garden gets sufficient sunlight. Many people prefer the front of the house to face south so that they can have the main garden and outdoor living areas at the back of the house for more privacy.

- Wind protection. Plants grow better and people enjoy outdoor living more if they are sheltered from strong winds. In the southern part of Australia, where most of us live, the worst winds are the cold southerlies of winter and early spring and

Lawn has been dispensed with in favour of rockpools and a stone path leading to a quiet table at the back of the garden.

HINT

When designing a garden, be aware that beds containing annuals and perennials need more maintenance than hard surfaces, such as paving.

ROD McMILLAN

PUBLISHER, TOUR LEADER, DIRECTOR — ADLAND HORTICULTURAL

the hot westerly winds of summer. Northeast winds may be a problem in exposed areas on the eastern coast.

Existing trees, plants and other features. Established plants such as native trees can be a great asset to a garden but a new design can also give you the opportunity to banish inappropriate plants. Rocky outcrops can become attractive features. Even a low-lying wet area may be useful as the basis for an ornamental pool. Decide what you want to keep and consider how best to work it into your new design.

Soil type and drainage. Heavy clay soils are more fertile than light sandy soils, but invariably cause drainage problems. Sandy soils will often have a clay subsoil, or a rock layer close to the surface which traps water, even on sloping ground. On very steep slopes, surface run-off water may be excessive, requiring terracing of the slope with retaining walls.

Apart from practical considerations about what to include in your concept, you will also need to consider the colour balance of your garden and how to lay it all out.

Line and form

Consider the emotional effect that the use of line and form achieve. A garden with gentle, free-flowing, curved lines that mirror nature allows the eye to move slowly around the garden giving rise to a relaxed and peaceful response. A garden constructed with hard-edged straight lines that lead the eye quickly from point to point tends to be more forceful and structured. Form is related to shape and structure of plants and other objects in the garden. Consider which shapes appeal to you and how to achieve unity between various elements in the garden.

Selecting colours

Creating the perfect atmosphere in a garden comes down to selecting the right colour scheme. To create an Australian garden, for example, colours such as browns and silver, with hard surfacing in natural stone colours, will help to create the scene you want to achieve.

Consider the interior colour scheme of your house as well as the exterior trim and roof colours. Draw inspiration from these colours to create a relationship between indoor and outdoor living spaces.

Best results can be obtained by keeping the colour palette as simple as possible. Try not to contrast too many primary colours as this will look messy and unattractive to the eye. A simple colour scheme will have more impact.

The final choice of colour comes down to personal preference. But if you have any doubts, consider using a colour consultant to guide you with your final selection.

Using axes in design

In gardening terms, an axis is an imaginary line running between view points in a garden. For example, a front garden's axis will usually run from the front door to the street. A back garden's axis will run from the back of the house towards the main view.

The eye is drawn to an urn at the end of this pathway framed by clipped box and an archway with runner beans and hollyhocks.

Individual axes run down the sides of the house where windows view onto side fences. Although there is one major axis in a garden, you may consider creating various minor axes to aid you when designing a garden. Although the dictionary defines an axis as a straight line, curved lines can be drawn off a straight axis and this is exactly how you can create an element of curiosity in your garden.

Focal points

The key is defining the origin of an axis and then determining the outcome of this axis. The outcome of an axis may well be a feature or focal point. This might include the use of water, an urn, a garden seat, sculpture or simply a defining plant to create the focal point of the axis.

Focal points are used sometimes as a more subtle attraction to draw you through a garden. It may be a statue partly hidden behind foliage, a striking plant in flower or perhaps an archway that frames the entrance to a new part of the garden. By drawing you closer, other focal points can in turn be used to lead you further through the garden.

Drawing the eye

Moving the eye along an axis is important in design. For example, using steppers on lawn may not only be practical, but also help to direct your vision to a focal point at the end of the axis. By designing the line of the axis, you can affect the vision by slowing it down (curved lines) or speeding it up (straight lines) and therefore you can create very formal focal points or more subdued discreet focal points depending on the mood you want to create.

Framing the view

Framing an axis defines the line of sight in a garden. Anything from low hedges to tall trees are ideal for framing an axis. Coloured border plantings can also be used for framing an axis. Create straight or curved garden beds and plant in themes for effect.

HARD LANDSCAPE DESIGN

Hard landscaping components of a garden include paved areas, driveways, walls, swimming pools, water features, timber decks, fences and entertainment areas. These

HINT

Create 'focal' or 'viewing' points in the garden by positioning specimen or architectural plants, either centrally or in pairs, to frame feature walls, doorways, seats or views.

COLIN BARLOW
GARDEN WRITER, DESIGNER, HORTICULTURALIST AND TV PRESENTER — *HOME IN WA*

features, and their construction, are covered in more detail in Chapter 3. The design of the hard landscape is integral as it forms the backbone and structure of a garden. These aspects are therefore usually constructed before planting begins.

Using local materials

If you are unsure about what sort of materials to use in your hard landscape design, consider the availability of local materials such as stone, and recycled products such as timber. Try your nearest garden supplier or quarry for types of stone. Timber recyclers often stock interesting hard woods, perfect for decking or screens in a garden and already seasoned by many years of exposure to the elements. Using local materials will ensure your design style suits the environment your garden is in.

The subconscious designer

Moving around a well-designed garden should be something you do without thinking about it. Apart from looking attractive, good design makes your garden functional, comfortable and easy to use. One area in which the sub-conscious mind plays an important part is in determining heights for features of the hard landscape.

Perfect sitting heights

When constructing seating in the garden, bear in mind that an ideal seat height is 450 mm. However, for more informal seating such as on stools, or perhaps on a retaining wall, an ideal height is 680 mm.

Vision lines

A vision line or eye line is the horizontal line drawn at eye height. This is important for determining the placement height of focal points such as water features. If you are mounting an animal- or human-headed water feature on a wall, and you mount it higher than average eye line, the water feature will seem very intimidating; however, if too low, it will seem subordinate. It is therefore desirable to mount it so that the eyes of the feature are horizontal with the average human eye line.

If you take the height of a human to be 182 cm (6 feet), then the eye line would be approximately 160 cm. If your eye line is lower than this, calculate the best height for your water feature by adding your eye-line height (x) to this eye-line height and divide by 2 (i.e. x + 160 cm, divided by 2 = average eye line height for you). This ensures the eye line of the water feature suits not only you, but other people who may enjoy the garden.

If your wall-mounted water feature is not an animal- or human-headed feature, take the main focal point of the feature to be the eye-line location. Alternatively, locate the height two-thirds of the way up the water feature as the appropriate eye-line height. This, of course, works for any wall-mounted features.

Paving design

Clever paving design can also tap into our subconscious minds and impact on the way we respond and move in a garden. Straight lines in paving can speed us up. Curved lines can slow us down. Square areas can stop us while round areas provide a more relaxed place to wander around. Cobbled surfaces will have slower traffic than smooth bitumen surfaces. As a rule, we do not like to look along grout lines in paving, so always try to run lines across the main view.

SOFT LANDSCAPE DESIGN

Once you have created the hard landscape as a framework for your garden, it is time to consider your planting design and select trees and shrubs.

Planting style

Your style of planting should run in the theme of the garden you have selected. As a general rule you should always select plants that grow in similar habitats. For instance, don't mix tropical plants with dry-tolerant plants. Keeping a similar theme of plants will unify your garden. If you want to use different styles of planting, try segmenting the garden into different areas so you can differentiate your plant selection.

The best inspiration often comes from nature. A brick-paved path creates the hard landscape while an abundance of Australian native plants forms the soft landscape in this Western Australian bush garden.

Aspect

Different parts of the garden will have different requirements. Consider areas that are prone to full sun and select suitable plants, rather than those that are suited to full shade. Windy areas will need plants tolerant to those conditions. Planting wind breaks will help reduce the impact on other plants in the garden.

Colour

Selecting colour of plants can be a challenge as there are many colours of flowers to consider when designing a planting scheme. Apart from considerations due to the style of garden and the colour scheme of your house, the best inspiration is nature. Often it's the simplest colour schemes that are most striking. Try to keep hues to a mix of three to five rather than having every colour of the rainbow; this will look very messy and confusing to the eye.

Foliage

Selecting foliage for colour is also crucial. Foliage can vary greatly in shape, type and colour. Avoid mixing lush, thick-leaved plants with dry, thin, grey-leaved or grassy plants. Some foliage plants make great architectural plants and are perfect for using in pots or in garden beds to make a statement.

Rhythm

To help create a flow through your garden, plant certain plants at intervals to create rhythm. This may be clipped balls or architectural foliage plants or it may even be feature trees. Rhythm will help bounce the eye through a garden and unify it so it appears 'designed'. For example, you may plant balls at 2 m spacing around a curved garden bed or perhaps alternate two different plants along a pathway.

Balance

A well-designed planting scheme will have balance in the shapes of plants selected. Consider mixing a blend of plants that are round, horizontal, columnar, spiky and low to the ground. Getting the balance right is the key. Avoid selecting plants that all fit into the one category of shape.

Perspective

Deeper garden beds will make your garden seem bigger. Avoid the temptation to run your beds around the perimeter of your fence line. This locks a garden in and will actually make it seem smaller and uninviting. Try to plant taller plants at the back of beds and lower plants at the front. This will also help with the perspective of having a bigger garden. Planting shade-tolerant flowering plants in the back of shady beds will make your bed look deeper. Bright colours will bring a garden closer to you, softer hues will push the garden away. Consider these tricks of perspective when designing your planting schemes.

Lawns

If your garden includes lawns, think carefully about the best position for them. This may depend on soil types in your garden, as well as the sunlight and shelter available in various positions. Placing lawns in shady areas will result in bare patches and muddy or mossy areas of grass. It may be better to make your garden beds deeper to include these shady areas, and plant shade-tolerant plants, rather than have problem areas of lawn.

Trees

Garden trees should be chosen carefully. The size of a tree after ten or twenty years is an important consideration. Choose trees that will grow to a suitable size rather than trees that have to be regularly pruned to keep them within reasonable bounds. Some other considerations when selecting trees are: the vigour and extent of spread of root systems; deciduous or evergreen habit; the type of foliage; and flowering habit, time and colour. A poor choice might adversely affect the other plants in the garden through root competition and shading.

Shrubs

Shrubs can be used very effectively for boundary planting. Decide on the ultimate height desired and choose shrubs that will reach that height at maturity. Pruning and trimming to size can then be avoided and the plants will be free to follow their natural growth form.

A garden with shrubs as the only feature would be easy to maintain but visually rather monotonous. Low-growing perennials used along shrubbery frontages will give a changing pattern of colour and shape. Evergreen perennials will produce the best effect but deciduous species (plants such as bulbs that die back in winter) can be tucked in to give some variation.

There is a tendency to over-plant with shrubs in a new garden because there seems to be room for lots of them, but space for the shrubs to spread is essential. Shrubs in large pots or tubs should not be overlooked when garden plans are being made because, to some extent, these shrubs are mobile. The containers might be brought to where the plants can be seen to best effect when in flower, and relegated to a minor position at other times. Permanently placed container-grown shrubs are very useful for softening paved areas.

Flowers

Flowering plants used to be considered essential in the garden, but many modern gardens rely on the form, foliage colour and texture of plants to create interest. Flowers can be useful when a massed colour effect is desired or when the greens of the garden need a lift. It's often best to have a basic planting of perennials with additional clumps of flowering annuals to add seasonal interest and to provide blooms for cutting. Annuals grow in many shapes and sizes and a wide range of colours.

Climbers

Do not overlook climbing plants. Because of their vertical habit they don't take up much room in the garden and can be used to soften or add colour to walls, fences and pergolas. However, regular maintenance of climbers is most important. Too often they can outgrow their welcome and become messy or woody.

THE FINAL PLAN

After you have considered all the features of the block, both good and bad, the next step is to make a plan to scale. Use stiff white paper or graph paper for the base plan, with several sheets of tracing paper for translucent overlays.

House and site plans are drawn on a metric scale of 1:100 (a line 1 cm long on the plan will represent 1 m on the ground). Pads of graph paper are available from stationers, measuring 18 cm x 30 cm, a suitable size for an average block with a frontage of 15–18 m and a depth of 30 m. Use two sheets joined together for larger blocks.

Make the base plan very clear so it can be seen through the tracing paper on which you will draw your garden designs. On the base plan show the boundaries of the land, the position of the house and existing features such as trees and shrubs. It is also a good idea to indicate the general contours or slope and note the position of steep areas, low-lying spots and shallow soil over rocky sections, because these may influence future planting schemes. Mark in the positions of all services, including electricity cables, gas, telephone, water (with tap positions), sewerage or septic systems.

Outside the boundary show compass points to give you an idea of sun and shade areas, and mark in the prevailing wind direction. Also indicate any unsightly aspects to be screened, or pleasant views to be retained. Use the first overlay of see-through paper to broadly define suitable areas for different purposes or activities. Further sheets can be used to plan the various areas in more detail.

Next draw in your hard landscape design such as paving, retaining walls, and outdoor structures. Draw elevation drawings so you can familiarise yourself with the heights of the garden. Consider all the details of the hard landscape selection. Accurate quantities of materials required can then be calculated from these drawings.

Once you have drawn your hard landscape, select suitable plants and design your garden beds and planting schemes. Consider how big each plant grows at maturity so you can quantify how many plants you will need. Use a good resource book for guidance. Make a list and consult your nearest garden centre for supply.

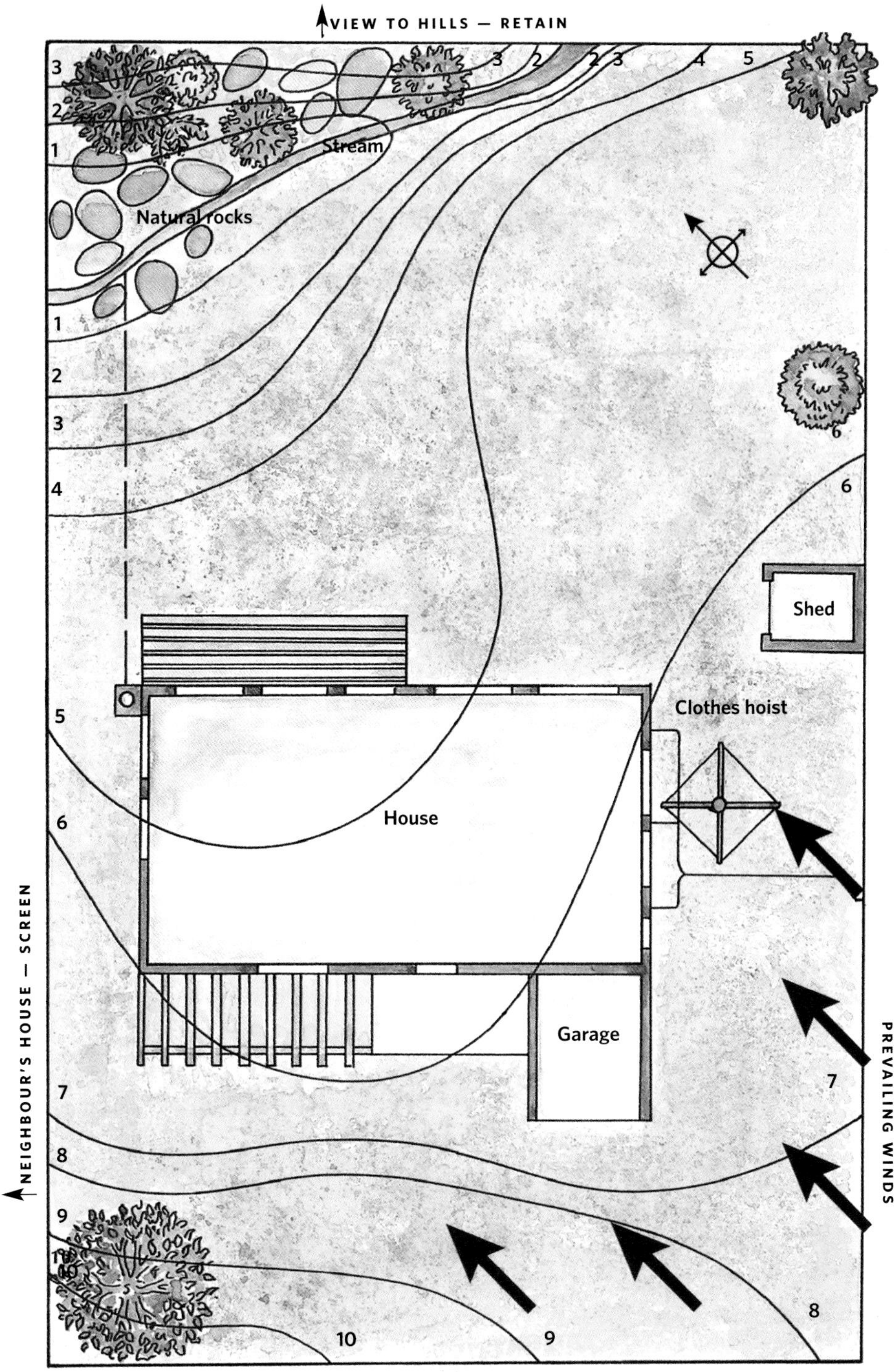

Base plan for a new garden.

VIEW TO HILLS — RETAIN

3
2
1

Stream

Natural rocks

1
2
3
4

6

Shed

5

Clothes hoist

6

House

NEIGHBOUR'S HOUSE — SCREEN

7

8

9

Garage

7

8

10

9

PREVAILING WINDS

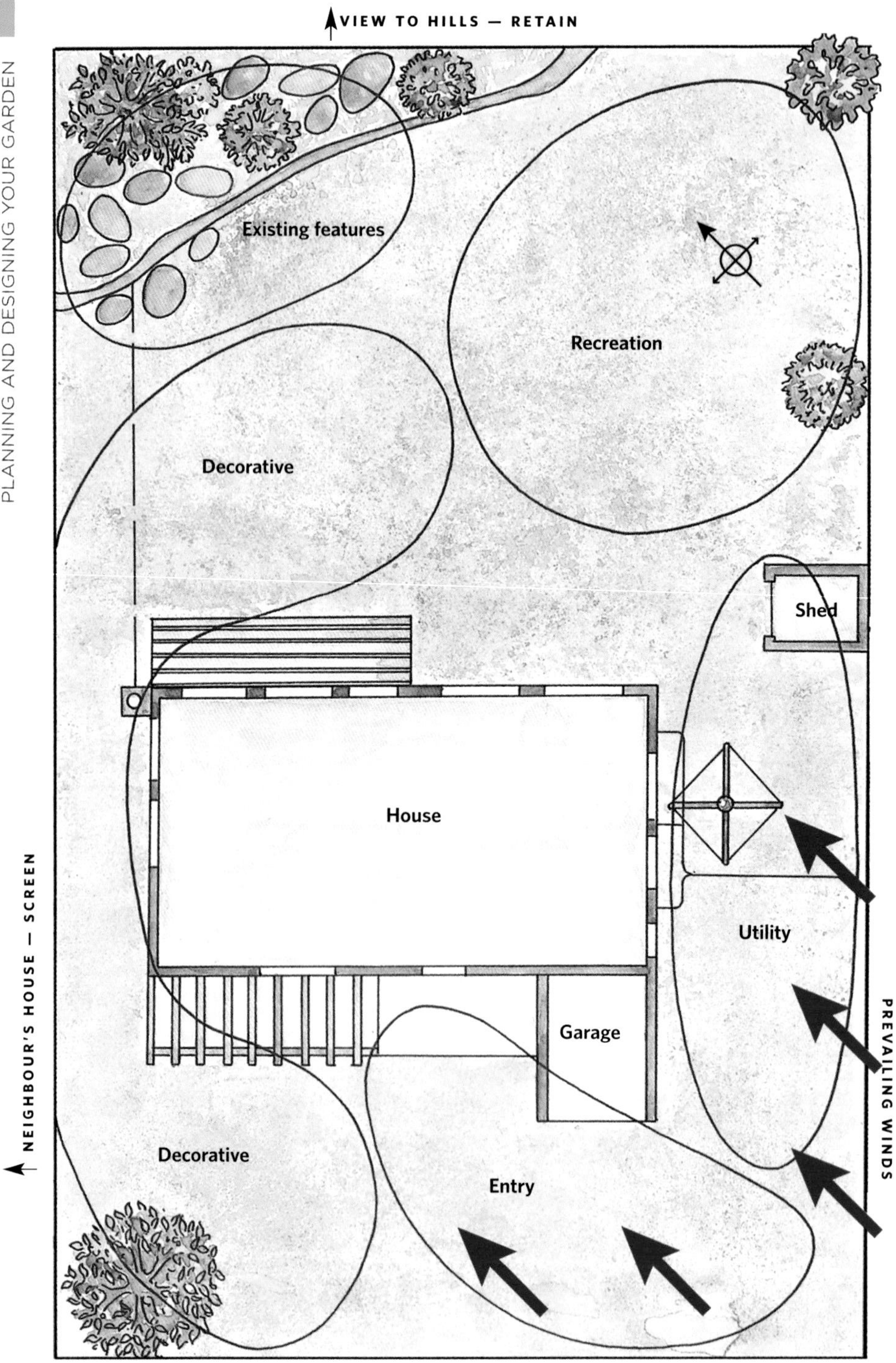

↑VIEW TO HILLS — RETAIN

Existing features

Recreation

Decorative

Shed

NEIGHBOUR'S HOUSE — SCREEN

House

Utility

Garage

Decorative

Entry

PREVAILING WINDS

First garden plan overlay showing main purpose and activity areas.

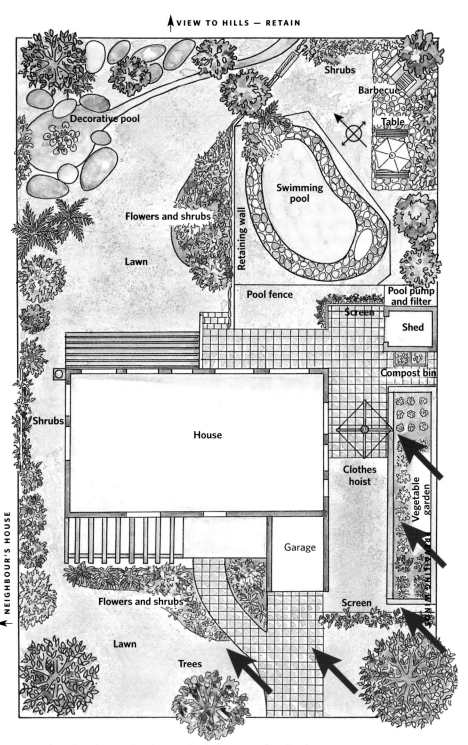

↑ VIEW TO HILLS — RETAIN

Shrubs

Barbecue

Table

Decorative pool

Swimming pool

Flowers and shrubs

Retaining wall

Lawn

Pool fence

Pool pump and filter

Screen

Shed

Compost bin

Shrubs

House

Vegetable garden

RETAINING WALL

NEIGHBOUR'S HOUSE

Clothes hoist

Garage

Flowers and shrubs

Screen

Lawn

Trees

Second garden plan overlay showing final planting and garden layout.

The Low-allergen Garden

The plants we grow in our gardens are not always beautiful and harmless. The months from August until March can mean sneezing, itchy eyes, a runny nose and extreme fatigue in people who are sensitive to pollen. Others may suffer seasonal asthma, or find that their asthma becomes worse during these months.

These symptoms can be significantly reduced with some careful planning of your garden. The plants which cause most trouble are very often in our own backyards. Many wind-borne pollens only travel short distances, so controlling pollen sources in your garden, especially near your windows, is important.

CREATING A LOW-ALLERGEN GARDEN

The most significant step you can take in planning a low-allergen garden is to choose bird- or insect-pollinated plants rather than wind-pollinated ones. Plants pollinated by birds and insects produce only small amounts of pollen. Many native trees and shrubs are pollinated by birds and insects.

Lawns can also produce a lot of wind-borne pollen. Choose native species or low-pollinating introduced species such as Greenlees Park couch or buffalo. When mowing a lawn, protect your eyes, nose and mouth with a mask and goggles, or mow while the dew is still on the lawn.

Grow windbreaks or build high, climber-covered fences to reduce the amount of wind-borne pollen reaching your garden from neighbouring properties.

THANKS TO THE ASTHMA FOUNDATION OF NEW SOUTH WALES FOR THIS INFORMATION

Weeds produce airborne pollen as well as taking valuable nutrients from the soil. Mulching helps to control weeds, but it is important that you use an inorganic mulch, since organic mulch like straw and hay may harbour moulds which are allergenic for some people. A suitable ground cover is a good substitute for mulch.

Lightly scented plants are preferable to strong scents, as these can act as an irritant and cause symptoms similar to those caused by breathing in pollen or mould spores.

OTHER THINGS YOU CAN DO

It is a good idea to stay indoors on hot, still days when pollen counts are high, or on very windy days. The best time to garden is in the early morning, before temperatures rise and the breezes increase, and also on cool, cloudy days.

Watch out for areas that may harbour moulds, such as shaded and southern sides of houses, and avoid digging in compost heaps, as these contain mould spores which could aggravate asthma or other irritations.

Be aware that washing that is dried outside may pick up pollen and cause allergic symptoms in the very pollen-sensitive person.

WHAT TO AVOID

The following plants should be avoided by those who suffer from asthma:
- asteraceae family (daisies, chrysanthemums, calendulas, marigolds)
- most introduced grasses • wattles
- alder • ash • birch • she-oak • cypress
- elm • liquidambar • maple • white cedar
- oak • olive • poplar • privet • walnut
- willow

The following plants may cause a painful rash if touched:
- primula • common or English ivy
- poinsettia • rhus tree • *Grevillea* 'Robyn Gordon' and other cultivars • many bulbs

CHOOSING SUITABLE PLANTS

Low-allergy plants include those that are pollinated by insects or birds only, or that are propagated by cuttings or grafting. Some plants you might like to try are:

GRASSES AND GROUND COVERS
- rice or weeping grass • kangaroo grass
- buffalo • kidney weed (dichondra)
- snow-in-summer • low-growing cotoneaster • native violet

CLIMBERS
- clematis • Chilean jasmine • passionfruit
- banksia rose • star jasmine

SHRUBS
- azalea • rhododendron • camellia
- gardenia • rosemary • heath banksia
- bottlebrush • silky tea tree

TREES
- magnolia • sweet bay • citrus
- flowering almond, apricot and cherry
- scribbly gum • silky oak • lillypilly
- cabbage tree palm

FLOWERS
- alyssum • aquilegia • foxglove
- impatiens • lobelia • nasturtium • petunia
- snapdragon

For a full list of suitable low-allergen plants, contact your local nursery or the website of the Asthma Foundation in your state.

3
Features for Your Garden

A gardener with imagination and ingenuity can introduce many special features to make a garden more interesting and attractive. A garden provides plenty of opportunities for creative thinking. Many garden features can be created by the home gardener and there is a wealth of landscaping materials from which to choose. A do-it-yourself job may take a little longer, but it will give much more satisfaction than calling in a landscape consultant or contractor. This chapter aims to give you some first principles for the design and construction of garden features.

PATIOS AND TERRACES

Patio is a Spanish word meaning the inner court of a house. A terrace is defined as a promenade or place for leisurely walking. In the Australian garden scene, both words have come to mean an area which is an extension of the house with access from the living room, dining room or kitchen. Often these areas are uncovered, but in warm climates an overhead framework for creepers, shade cloth or clear sheeting can be a useful addition. The cover provides some shade, reduces glare, and allows the area to be used during hot or wet seasons. Enclosure on at least one side by a trellised vine can increase privacy.

It is best if a patio or terrace faces east, northeast or north in order to trap sun from early morning to mid-afternoon. Patios and terraces are ideal for outdoor meals. On flat sites it is usual to build them flush with garden beds or lawn, or with one or two shallow steps to the garden. A railing or low wall is needed on sloping sites, especially if young children are around.

The patio or terrace is ideal for outdoor pot and tub plants which need open sunlight and extra warmth. Container-grown vegetables and herbs are also popular.

The paving surface of the patio or terrace should be smooth (for walking and for the placing of outdoor tables and chairs) and easy to sweep and clean. Brick paving, which can be laid in many patterns, is popular, but may absorb stains. A less expensive alternative is pre-cast concrete paving blocks or slabs. Quarry tiles, which come in a wide variety of colours, shapes and textures, give a more formal appearance but must be laid on a concrete base. These tiles do not absorb stains and are easy to clean. Large split sandstone slabs need careful laying for an even surface, but dressed (sawn) slabs make one of the best paving materials. These have an attractive, non-slip, easy-to-clean surface which dries quickly after rain. Where the paving is set on a sand base, ants sometimes bring sand to the surface along joints. Weeds may germinate there too. Ants and weeds can be removed with one of the several suitable commercial products.

HINT

When designing your garden the first thing to do is write a wish list of everything you would like to have in your garden. Once you've decided what you want, it's much easier to work out where each area fits best before starting to dig and plant.

DEBBIE McDONALD
GARDEN WRITER, EDITOR
AND HORTICULTURIST

COURTYARDS

Courtyards by their very nature need more careful planning than larger garden areas. They generally flow on from the house and are frequently used as an extension of the living area of the house. Where they comprise the total outdoor area of a dwelling, they should reflect in some degree the style of the house, or at least have an overall theme. If the courtyard is a transitional area between the house and a garden beyond, there should be some thought given to tying the courtyard planting in with the garden so that one flows seamlessly into the other.

You should consider the main use of the area. If you entertain a lot, then you will need to allocate adequate space for a table and chairs before deciding how to decorate the area with plants. If the courtyard is to be used primarily for restful recreation, then thought will need to be given to seating. Think about what kind of atmosphere you want to create, whether it be calm and relaxing or bright and stimulating. Many people like to incorporate a pond, fountain or other water feature to add the sight and sound of water.

Courtyards are usually open to the sky and are really an outside room. Some people prefer a covered courtyard – a vine covering a pergola, a clear or opaque roof – as protection against direct sunlight. You can build a courtyard in a very small space, between the house and garage or between the house and a boundary fence or wall. In warm climates, the zone between the house and the garage or carport can be roofed but left open at the ends. Known as breezeways, these areas protect car travellers arriving or leaving during rain, but can also be used as an airy, shaded retreat in hot weather. Breezeways can be planted as is suggested for shady courtyards.

Choose courtyard plants carefully. Plants for shade or semi-shade are usually the most suitable but one side of the courtyard may be sunny at some times of the year. Low-growing shrubs are best in the sunniest parts. Ground-cover plantings could include ferns, plants with small foliage and some flowering plants. Paved courtyards need the relief provided by plants in tubs or pots. Climbing or clinging plants can be effective in reducing the starkness of walls. For further planting suggestions see Chapter 21.

DECKS

A deck or timber platform offers another alternative for outdoor living. It is a natural choice for steep or rocky sites where flat land

Stepped timber decking and the use of gravel and pebbles create an interesting alternative to lawn or paving.

is scarce. It is less expensive to build a deck than to level the ground and erect a massive retaining wall.

You can use low-level decks on flat sites as an alternative to paving. This way you can extend the house at floor level, provide a non-slip surface adjacent to a swimming pool, or make a shady dining area around the trunk of a large tree. High-level decks need a safety rail. Decks of stained or treated timber are simple to maintain. Small gaps between decking boards allow quick drainage after rain and easy sweeping. Many do-it-yourself enthusiasts can build simple low-level decks, but a high-level deck is usually a job for an experienced carpenter. The foundation area must be well drained to carry water away from the posts or piers supporting the deck.

Container-grown plants soften and decorate open decks and the roofed verandahs which are features of many Queensland houses. Choice of specimens for a container planting on a deck is influenced by the amount of sunlight reaching the flooring. Open decks are suitable for small, sun-hardy shrubs, while covered verandahs require plants for semi-shade. Check local council requirements before beginning construction.

BARBECUES AND SWIMMING POOLS

For many families the barbecue and swimming pool are the centres of outdoor entertaining and family recreation. These facilities can be used to best advantage if they are near each other. It is preferable to have the pool and barbecue sites in close proximity to the house. This makes the outdoor living areas an extension of the patio or terrace and the indoors. Also, from a practical point of view, the kitchen and bathroom are within easy reach.

The swimming pool itself should receive full sunlight for much of the day. This can be achieved to some extent by attention to another matter, namely, siting the pool where tall trees can't continually shed leaves into it. Shelter from wind can be provided by the house, shrubberies, hedges or vine-covered trellises. Pools need a surround of concrete tiles or other non-slip and waterproof material. Beyond the pool surrounds, a lawn

is ideal, providing an area for outdoor furniture that will serve both pool and barbecue.

Trees take several years to reach a size where they will throw worthwhile shade, and many species have root systems that may cause problems for older pools. A creeper-covered pergola may be a much better means of providing shade near the pool. Trees need not be excluded, but they should be chosen from the list of trees of limited height, appropriate to the locality, and then planted as far from the pool as is practicable.

In most areas it is mandatory to have a safety fence around a swimming pool. Tall shrubs grown for windbreaks, screening for privacy, or visual effects outside a pool safety fence must be far enough away to prevent their use as aids to scaling the fence. Use lower shrubs, perennials and flowering annuals within the fenced section.

Essential pool equipment, such as the filter and pump, can be screened by low hedges. Abelia, box, murraya, and blue plumbago are examples of suitable shrubs that can be clipped to make a dense screen.

There is so much variation in climate zones in Australia that it must be left to individual home owners to work out the most appropriate plantings for their pool and barbecue areas. The use of tall species of strelitzia, philodendrons, palms and gingers of various kinds, which warm-climate gardeners use to such good effect, would not be possible in cool–temperate regions. Checking your neighbourhood to see which plants grow well is probably the best starting point when planning what and where to plant.

Shrubs and a spreading tree will screen and shade a barbecue area. With that as a basis, more detailed plantings can be made according to individual preferences, microclimates and garden design.

Views towards other parts of the garden from outdoor living spaces should always be retained. A decorative pond and its surrounding plants, or a big tree on a far boundary, should not be looked on as separate entities but rather as integral parts of the whole garden. The objective should be to have them all visible from various points both inside the house and in the garden.

Designing Outdoor Entertainment Spaces

The key to a well-designed garden is locating an entertainment area to increase the use of your living space outdoors. This will partly depend on the aspect of your garden, and how much sun and shade it gets in different seasons. Use the following checklist when designing the area:

Location. Select the area in your garden in which you would most like to sit and entertain. Pick a spot in a sheltered situation out of the wind and on reasonably level ground. Consider privacy from neighbours and easy access to the house and kitchen.

Steps. Avoid major changes of level and steps if possible. While steps are often required, they can become dangerous so consider this carefully during the planning process. Consult a designer if you need help.

Outlook. Identify key views and possible sites for water features, focal plants or sculpture. The sound of water can be very useful for blocking out background traffic noise.

Shelter. Consider shelter from sun and rain. Depending on your budget, covered roof pergolas, shade sails, umbrellas, climbing plants or shade trees will provide protection.

Privacy. To create a sanctuary, enclose the entertainment space by using screens of timber, metal, cloth or plants. People will relax if they feel safe and secure.

Cooking facilities. Think carefully about the type of barbecue you want and if you select a gas barbecue, consider getting a plumber to connect it to the gas mains to save changing gas bottles.

Water supply. For cooking purposes it can be handy to have a water supply close by, so consider placing a tap within reach or, even better, install a sink.

Power. Most outdoor areas will need some sort of power source so speak to an electrician about getting outdoor power points installed.

Music. Consider installing outdoor speakers for music.

Lighting. Garden lighting is essential for any entertainment area both for illumination and ambience and is well worth the investment.

Colour scheme. Try to reflect your lifestyle in the colour scheme you use. For a loud, showy entertainment area, go for bright vibrant colours. For more subdued, cooler effects stick to natural colours and materials. The style of your garden may also impact on your colour scheme.

Bench space. You can never have too much bench space for food platters and glasses.

Seating. Consider how many people you want to be able to seat. If you have raised beds, you may be able to make use of the tops of the walls for additional seating. (See page 27 for ideal sitting heights.)

Outdoor furniture. Invest in good quality and comfortable furniture that you will be happy to keep for years to come. Remember to allow ample space around the table for movement of chairs. If you want to be able to move the furniture around, take its weight into consideration.

Pot plants. Grow herbs and vegetables in pots to allow easy access to a fresh salad or garnish.

DECORATIVE PONDS

Decorative ponds introduce movement and sparkling light to a garden and give a sense of coolness during the hotter part of the year. Informal ponds can be located in shady places, although that makes it impossible to grow plants like water lilies which require full sunlight. For part shade there are aquatic plants that are tolerant of partial sun. In the vicinity of a shaded pond the microclimate is such that shade-tolerant vegetation flourishes. Tree ferns, palms of limited size, variously sized foliage plants of many species, small ferns and club mosses introduce a rainforest atmosphere, especially if there are overhanging trees and background shrubs.

Plantings around decorative ponds should not be in a narrow band close to the edge of the pond. Make plantings up to several metres away from the poolside, using a variety of plants that are compatible with one another in size, foliage type and the form and colour of the leaves. A fairly open foreground, using mainly low-growing plants, puts the pond and its surrounding vegetation into a pleasant perspective. Ponds need fish in them to control the aquatic larvae of pest insects, especially mosquitoes. The bright colours of goldfish enhance a pond's appearance, but remember that fish need projecting rocks or some other kind of shelter from predatory birds.

For informal ponds, ready-made fibreglass liners are available in various shapes and sizes. Excavate a hole, slip in the fibreglass shell and you have an instant pond. More popular are the do-it-yourself ponds which are constructed by lining an excavation of your own design with black polythene or flexible waterproof sheeting. Suitable grades of sheeting can be bought at nurseries and hardware stores. Also available are pond-making kits, with instructions and diagrams.

Having decided on the shape and size of your pond, you should allow enough flexible lining for the sloping sides, plus about 20 cm overlap all around so you can anchor it down. If you wish to keep and breed fish (which keep the pond clean and free of mosquito wrigglers) you will need to excavate part of the pool to a depth of about 45 cm. Ensure that this deep part is overhung with rocks or vegetation.

Some of the excavated soil can be used to form a rocky mound behind the pond or to build up the edges on the low sides. In the latter case, tread the soil down firmly. Lay the liner loosely, anchoring the edges with small stones, and fill with water. This gives firm contact between the sheet and the base, and allows you to check water levels accurately at all points. Build up low spots and shave off high spots as required.

Now lap the edges with stones to cover and anchor the liner in place. Use thinner stones at the front and wider slabs overhanging the water at the back. One or two large stones can project well over the water, but make sure they are counter balanced in case someone stands on them. All stones and edges should be firm and well settled at this stage. When you are happy with the effect, siphon out the water and apply a 2.5 cm layer of cement (one part cement to three parts sand) as a permanent protection to the polythene. Keep the cement mix fairly dry. Starting at the lowest point, gradually spread the cement upwards and tuck under the stones. For easier working, place a hessian sack, an old mat or piece of carpet on the cemented bottom so you can stand on this without causing damage. When almost dry, smooth the cement by rubbing with a piece of hessian.

When completed, blend the pond into the surroundings with scattered rocks, boulders, pebbles or gravel. Ferns, Nile grass (*Cyperus papyrus*), New Zealand flax, irises and native grasses are good subjects for pond surrounds. Do not plant large trees close by because the roots may damage the pond.

Formal ponds, which may be circular, oval, square or rectangular, are often more

HINT

Several strands of fishing line zigzagged across the fish pond will keep fish-eating birds at bay, without causing injury to the birds.

GEOFF MIERS

GEOFF MIERS GARDEN SOLUTIONS

ALICE SPRINGS, NORTHERN TERRITORY

appropriate in small gardens, especially in paved areas. The surround can be built in brickwork on a concrete slab, and can be topped with a coping slab. The brickwork can be cement-rendered with a mix of one part cement to three parts sand to which a waterproofing compound has been added. If the edge of the pond is built up 40–50 cm above ground level the coping slab can be used as a seat. A high surround presents a deterrent for small children but should never be regarded as childproof. Formal ponds may be located in open places so that the structure and texture of the pond materials are displayed. Plantings around formal ponds are usually restrained in order to give the pond plants themselves greater prominence.

In both informal and formal ponds, pockets of brick or stone on the bottom can hold aquatic plants, or plants can be grown in sunken pots or wire baskets. Waterlilies (*Nymphaea* spp.) are the most popular, but there are many other attractive and useful oxygenating plants which will keep the water clean and fresh. Among them are sacred lotus (*Nelumbo nucifera*), arrowhead (*Sagittaria sagittifolia*), water thyme (*Anachris canadensis*), pickerel weed (*Pontederia cordata*), and marsilea, a native fern. If water plants become too rampant, as some species may do, thin them out before they take over the pool completely. Some floating plants, notably water hyacinth and salvinia, have been declared noxious weeds in some states. They must not be used in garden ponds.

FROG PONDS

A frog pond can be easily made by sinking a plastic container with sloping sides into a shaded part of the garden. Fill with water and after a few days the chlorine in the water will have dissipated. Don't attempt to introduce frogs – let them move in naturally. You can add some native fish but it's best to consult an expert as to suitable fish species – you don't want them to predate on the tadpoles. A solar powered light sited near the pond will attract some of the insects that the frogs love to eat.

Waterlilies grow in this extensive pond which is a dominant feature of this formal garden.

The solid structure of this pergola is both aesthetically pleasing and functional.

PLAY AREAS

A playground is a great asset. It encourages youngsters to play out of doors and gives them a feeling of ownership of their own small part of the garden. For toddlers, a sandpit is a must. Locate it where spilled sand does not matter and construct it on a base of unmortared bricks or concrete pavers for good drainage after rain. A removable cover that keeps out visiting cats can also be a good idea. A surround of concrete blocks or dressed timber (no splinters) can be used. Seesaws and swings suit older children but make sure they are soundly built and unlikely to cause mishaps. Swings should always have plastic seats. Smooth timber logs are quite attractive and kids will invent their own games climbing over or around them. For children who are old enough, a rope ladder on the limb of a large tree is a great attraction, especially if it leads to a cubby house. Play areas should be carpeted with rough lawn. Lawn is soft enough for jumping and falling on and good for rough-and-tumble games. If the area is too shady for grass, use pine bark, or even artificial grass, to soften falls.

PERGOLAS

A pergola was originally an arbour or covered walk at the bottom of the garden. Today, a pergola is commonly an extension of the house over a patio or terrace. In many respects it has taken over from the verandah of colonial days. A well-designed pergola is not only an attractive addition to your house but a structure to support vines or creepers and hanging baskets.

The structure must be strong if it is to carry a heavy creeper like wisteria or grape vine. Remember that a vine's growth will be limited if it is confined to a pot. Wooden posts 100 mm square, with load-bearing rails of 100 mm x 50 mm timber on edge and 75 mm x 50 mm cross-rails on edge, are standard in such constructions. You can use pine posts and rails for a more rustic look. Posts can also be brick piers or moulded concrete. Roofing is not necessary but some people use timber slats, shade cloth or translucent polycarbonate sheets.

SCREENS

Building sites are likely to become smaller, rather than larger, in future. This means that privacy from the street or from your neighbours is often at a premium. Trees, shrubs and hedges come to mind immediately, but in some situations there is not sufficient space for them to grow, and structured screens are a useful substitute.

There are many kinds of screen: brick, concrete blocks, stone, slatted timber, lattice, translucent polycarbonate sheets and toughened glass panels. Don't forget that screens must look good from both sides, your own and your neighbour's! Check with the neighbour first, then check local council regulations to see how high and how close to the boundary your screen can go. Many screens will support attractive, useful creepers and vines. (See Chapter 18.)

For full and permanent screening, choose species which are evergreen. Consider, too, the type of foliage, because some climbers are less than beautiful except when in flower. Aspect is critical. If the vine doesn't have sufficient sunlight the flowers and growth may all end up on your neighbour's side. The weight of the vine when it has covered the

HINT

If you are short on garden space, use vertical space to maximise your growing area. Hanging baskets, wall-mounted pots, tiered pot stands, wall trellises and window boxes are ideal for this purpose.

JOHN MASON
GARDEN AUTHOR, PRINCIPAL
– ACS DISTANCE EDUCATION

screen is important, too. Some plants (such as wisteria) develop thick, woody stems and foliage in great abundance. They become too bulky and too heavy as time passes. Climbers with thin and flexible stems (e.g. *Pandorea* spp) are easily trained over a screen and are still relatively lightweight when fully grown.

A lattice screen is softened by climbing roses.

Top five fast-growing trees

VIRGILIA

'A short life but a gay one' is a truism for this rapid-growing South African tree. Virgilia is sometimes called 'tree-in-a-hurry' and has soft, finely divided leaves and mauve-pink spring pea blossoms. A great choice for a small garden.

GUM TREE

The most Australian of all trees, gum trees have more than 600 species, so there's one to suit every garden. Hybrids of the spectacular Western Australian flowering gum, which is most noticeable when it produces showy red blossoms, are now being grafted onto hardy rootstocks. This greatly extends the range of areas where it can be grown.

FIDDLEWOOD

This very fast-growing tree has the peculiar habit of getting some autumn colouring in early summer before losing many of its leaves.

WATTLE

Many wattles make wonderful 'nurse' trees. They provide shelter and protection for slower-growing plants.

CASUARINA

There's a casuarina for every situation, from the seaside to the desert edge. On most species the fine, weeping branchlets droop gracefully.

GUM TREE

WATTLE

HINT

Try creating dramatic plantings by contrasting silver-foliaged plants with red, black, purple and yellow flowers and foliage. Bordered by a green lawn, these colour schemes can look stunning.

COLIN BARLOW

GARDEN WRITER, DESIGNER, HORTICULTURALIST AND TV PRESENTER

— HOME IN WA

GARDEN TREES

A garden without trees lacks the tall plants that give balance to the shrubs. There are trees whose natural growth pattern achieves a mature height of 6–8 m, which is quite enough for most suburban gardens. Big trees are best used only in large gardens. Several small trees planted near one another will, in time, enmesh their canopies.

The provision of shade in summer is one of the most important roles that trees play in a garden. In cool climates, deciduous trees may be preferable to evergreens so that summer shade will be replaced by sunlight in winter.

Whatever the type of tree, there will be a shaded area beneath for at least several months each year. This raises some difficulties with underplantings. The usual lawn grasses do not thrive, and weeds that favour shady places often flourish under trees. Laying paving under the tree and growing some plants in containers is one way of improving these difficult areas. An alternative solution is to plant lots of shade-tolerant plants under the tree. Some paving stones and a garden seat will work well in this shady spot. Plants with large leaves are often used because they impart an air of luxuriant tropical vegetation and because these types of leaves have evolved to make the most of the available light. Several species of gingers, philodendron and monstera, aspidistra (an excellent plant for the deepest shade), dracaena, cordyline, the dwarf palms, curcuma and ctenanthe, plus the colour of balsams, impatiens, vinca, iresine (bloodleaf) and coleus, and the fine foliage of ferns – these are only some of the plants that can suit difficult spots under trees. Where there is a group of shade

Brightly flowering annuals and bulbs provide a blaze of colour.

trees, a mini-rainforest effect can be achieved, especially if some light climbing plants are placed where it becomes possible for them to cling to the lower parts of tree trunks. Rainforest effects need not be confined to the tropics and subtropics. Densely planted areas with meandering paths can be developed using cool-climate plants too.

USE OF FLOWERING ANNUALS

Annual flowering plants (those that grow, bloom and die in one season) are some of the easiest ways to have garden colour but they need regular maintenance. Garden beds in full sun that are devoted largely to annuals can create outstanding floral displays but a small number of annuals will grow in less than full sunlight. The most shade tolerant are cinerarias, primulas, torenia, lobelia, bedding begonias, impatiens and dwarf marigolds. Alyssum, torenia, portulaca, French marigolds, petunias and phlox are low-growing plants with a spreading habit that makes them suitable for foreground plantings, for sunny parts of rock gardens, or for use as edgings or ribbons of colour. Most gardens can make use of flowering annuals outside the formal flowerbeds. Even a few brightly flowering annuals grouped in clumps can change a garden's appearance quite markedly.

TERRACING SLOPES

On level sites, a terrace garden can serve the same purpose as a retaining wall.

Terraces can be created with rocks, railway sleepers or treated pine logs. If building a rock garden, use ripped rather than bush rock. Collecting bush rock causes environmental damage and destroys the habitat of many tiny creatures.

On slopes, rocks are used to form pockets of terraced beds. Bury their large ends (to about one-third of their depth) in soil. Always use the largest rocks at the bottom of the mound or slope. Prostrate plants can cover rocks placed as water barriers. The plants will reduce the speed of flowing water while the underlying rocks, plus the plants' roots, will hold the soil.

Many terraces are over-planted in a desire to have an instant garden, but often end up as a shapeless mass of greenery. A happier approach is to plant alternate pockets with suitable perennials or clump-forming plants and keep the remaining pockets for colourful annuals to give a more interesting and varied effect throughout the year.

There are hundreds of suitable low-growing and prostrate plants, including hardy natives such as prostrate grevilleas, creeping boobialla and scaevola (fan flowers) cultivars.

DRIVEWAYS, PATHS AND STEPPING STONES

Driveways are a strictly utilitarian part of the garden but ideally should blend with the general design. There are many practical considerations to keep in mind. Keep the driveway as short as possible and, for convenience and safety, avoid sharp curves. The angle of approach to or from the street should not be too sharp, nor should the entrance be obscured by large trees or shrubs. If possible, provide a turning area in the garden so you don't have to back your car into the street. A turning area can also be used to wash the car, for a children's play area or just as parking space for a visitor's car. Sloping sites present special problems for driveways. The construction of a driveway and garage may call for excavating, filling and wall-building. On very steep slopes falling away from the street, a suspended car ramp may be the answer.

Driveways need solid foundations to prevent cracking and sinking. Split sandstone slabs or bricks can be bedded on a 10 cm sand base. Gravel in various colours is quite a good surface, but is prone to weed invasion and to erosion on slopes. A bitumen driveway is best constructed by a contractor; you need an area of about 60 square metres to make it an economical proposition. Pavers are popular for driveway surfaces but must be laid on a well-prepared bed. They are relatively easy to lay, are easy to maintain and are available in quite a range of colours.

Concrete is cheap and needs minimal after-care. There are many different kinds of concrete available including coloured concrete, stencilled concrete giving the illusion of paving, and seeded and exposed aggregates which are concretes with pebbles or stones embedded, giving an interesting textured finish. Concrete tracks are the least expensive solution. In warm to hot localities, turf growing between concrete car tracks is preferable to the pebbles or gravel that are sometimes used in cool climates.

A path need not be the shortest distance between two points except between house and utility areas, clothes hoist, garbage bin, garage or carport. A curved path is more interesting, provided the garden scene is attractive and inviting. Planning and building some paths can often be deferred until the

An informal path made of bricks set in a well-maintained bed of decorative gravel.

garden is well established, when the best positions can be decided.

There are many materials for paths. The surface should be safe and easy to walk on, but foundations need not be as solid as for driveways and large paved areas. Gravel of many grades and shades is popular and may be contained by a brick or concrete border adjacent to lawn or flowerbeds. In localities where there is heavy rain from time to time, gravel tends to wash down slopes. Some paths can be informal to the extent that ground covers spill onto them from one or both sides.

Stepping stones may form a sufficient path across a lawn. The dotted-line effect is often more pleasing than a solid one, and does not divide the lawn into separate sections. Set flagstones or concrete paving slabs flush with the lawn on a sand base 4 cm deep. An occasional trim around the edges will keep them neat and tidy. Informal paths can be made by laying pebbles, gravel or pine bark. Another option is to use stabilised sand (ten parts sand to one part cement).

STEPS AND RETAINING WALLS

Both steps and retaining walls are almost inevitable on sloping land. Steps can be an attractive garden feature as well as giving access to a change in level. They should be wide and shallow for ease of walking up and down, especially for older people and very young children.

The riser (vertical part) should not exceed 15 cm in height, and the tread (horizontal part) should not be less than 30 cm deep. For brick steps, two courses for the riser and a tread as wide as one brick length plus one brick width is a comfortable combination.

Deep steps are often necessary on steep slopes. For long flights, incorporate a landing every ten to twelve steps. The landing can also be used as a place to change direction. A handrail is an asset where steps are steep. Steps are awkward to negotiate with lawnmowers and wheelbarrows, so a ramp may be a practical alternative. Ramps, however, take much more space to give an easy grade.

Split or dressed stone steps are popular. Bricks, concrete blocks, pavers or slabs are used in more formal situations. Horizontal logs, sawn timber decking, railway sleepers and

Treated logs have been used to build a solid retaining wall on a steep slope.

large hardwood discs blend with informal or bush settings.

HINT

Make paths to the front door smooth, direct, evenly graded and at least one metre wide so guests know where they're going, and goods and furniture are easy to move in and out.

CATHERINE STEWART
GARDENDRUM

Retaining walls resist the downhill thrust of earth behind them. Again, brick, stone, concrete and timber may be used. Dry walls, any form of packed stone walling, whether cement is used or not, are more attractive and quite stable if they are less than 1.5 m high. The face can be sloped slightly backwards for greater stability. Drainage is important, too. If the wall is not to become a dam, provide weep holes every 2.5–3 m along the base of the wall.

HINT

Decorative pebbles are very popular in modern gardens. They can add style to a landscape but remember, it is incredibly hard to keep loose pebbles clean in an area where you get a lot of fallen leaves and other debris.

HELEN MOODY

HORTIMEDIA FREELANCE WRITER
AND PR CONSULTANT

Lay the largest rocks or stones at the bottom, bedding them in the soil. Between each row of stones distribute a 4 cm layer of soil and bring the filling soil up behind them. Then lay another row of stones and repeat the process. Each row of stones should be slightly behind the row below to make the batter or backward slope, about 5 cm for every 30 cm of height.

If trailing or rockery plants are to be grown in the 'wall garden', plant them as the wall is built, spreading their roots into the soil in the crevices. If the construction materials allow it, recesses which can be filled with soil to act as planting points should be provided. The best soil is a loam which can be easily spread and worked into crevices. Soil should be damp enough to hold together, but not wet. Sandy soils are difficult to use for this job and tend to flow out of the cracks when dry.

SHADEHOUSES

There are many good reasons for constructing a shadehouse in the garden. A collection of orchids or container-grown ferns and foliage plants is one justification for having a shadehouse. A shadehouse is desirable when a number of potted indoor plants are in use. House plants benefit from having a spell outside in the shadehouse environment because they are then in better, brighter, circumambient light. Another use for a shadehouse is to make it an open-

This garden shadehouse has been built as an extension to the main house.

A small glasshouse is all that's required to give plants a good start in a cold climate.

fronted annexe to a patio or terrace. This is a particularly desirable arrangement in tropical and subtropical regions where relief from glare and, perhaps, additional shade from one side may make the environment more pleasant. Plants grown in tubs, troughs or pots on the patio become an extension of the shadehouse.

A shadehouse reduces direct sunlight, provides a cool, moist atmosphere and protects plants from hot, dry winds. When you build a shadehouse you create a microclimate for plants which may not survive in the open. Select a sunny aspect: a shadehouse should not be dark and dismal.

The size of the structure will depend on your enthusiasm for shadehouse plants and ferns. The frame must be solid – treated timber or steel tubing is best – and the uprights should be set solidly in concrete footings. The floor can be concrete too, but ashes, gravel, metal dust or pine bark are less expensive alternatives.

Lattice, wooden slats, or 10 cm wire netting threaded with tea-tree pieces can be used for shadehouse walls and roof, but shade cloth is an effective and long-lasting modern substitute. It comes in a number of colours and gives different percentages of shade ranging from 32 per cent to 92 per cent. Choose a grade which allows more, rather than less, sunlight – 32 per cent and 50 per cent are both good. A tap for watering should be located near the door. Overhead mist sprinklers are more professional, but observe water restrictions.

The most popular shadehouse plants are orchids (see Chapter 23) and ferns, but there are many other species that have brilliant flowers, or coloured or variegated leaves, which are suitable and attractive. Larger garden centres and those specialising in shade plants usually have a wide range from which to choose.

GLASSHOUSES

In Australia, glasshouses are popular in cold-climate zones, especially Victoria and Tasmania. If your hobby is growing delicate tropical and warmth-loving plants you will need some winter protection for them.

The construction of a glasshouse is not difficult and the use of standard glasshouse fittings simplifies the job considerably. The frame is made from 75 mm x 50 mm timber, or an all-steel structure can be made using galvanised pipe and pressed metal fittings. Width, length and height should be multiples of standard glass sheets plus an allowance for glazing bars. Building a small lean-to glasshouse on a blank wall of the house is an easier option. In this case, make sure the glasshouse is in a position to receive a reasonable amount of sun. In warm areas some shade cover for your glasshouse may be needed during the summer months.

Perfumed plants add an extra dimension to the garden by stimulating your sense of smell. Daphne and gardenias have long been popular for their fragrance but try also osmanthus, sarcococca, magnolias and michelias, ginger lilies, wintersweet, luculia, alocasia, Stephanotis, brugmansia and philadelphus.

TEENA CRAWFORD
GARDEN WRITER AND CONSULTANT

Visit gardens and nurseries whenever you feel there is the need for improvement in an area of your own garden. You may not be wishing to plant immediately, but notes can be made of plants that are attractive in foliage, flower or fruit at that particular time of the year, so that appropriate plants can be selected for future inclusion in your garden.

GWEN ELLIOT AM
GARDEN WRITER AND BROADCASTER

Before planting, place the plants where you want them to go. Check their spacing and position and when you're happy, start digging!

COLIN BARLOW
GARDEN WRITER, DESIGNER AND
HORTICULTURALIST, TV PRESENTER *HOME IN WA*

There was a time when Brownie points were scored for growing rare or 'hard-to-grow' plants, even if they were sickly looking and perhaps plagued with pests and disease. Commonplace plants, grown well and occasionally with flair, produce a much better garden.

JOHN STOWAR
LANDSCAPE CONSULTANT AND HORTICULTURAL
JOURNALIST

Plan a garden for the future, but expect it to evolve and need changing, despite your well-laid-out plans. Such is the temperament of Mother Nature.

MEREDITH KIRTON
AUTHOR OF *DIG, PLOT, AN HOUR IN
THE GARDEN*
WWW.GROWHARVESTCOOK.COM.AU

When you're creating a new garden bed, use a garden hose to outline the shape, moving it around until you're completely satisfied. Because the hose stands out against bare soil or grass, it gives you a much better picture of how your bed shapes will work.

ANDREW SECCULL
GARDEN DESIGNER

Your own ideas are as good as everyone else's. Make yourself happy by planting the garden that you want.

LINDA ROSS
2GB GARDEN CLINIC, TOUR LEADER –
ROSS GARDEN TOURS, GARDEN DESIGN WRITER

To have an ongoing love affair with your garden throughout the year, there are a few golden rules to follow:
- Gardening should always be fun, so only garden when you feel like it.
- To have success with your plants, always try and source as much advice and information as you can about the ones that are thriving in your area.
- Don't try the difficult and exotic. There's plenty of time for them later. Also, ask the more senior gardeners in the community for a few tips or even join a garden club in your area.
- Get to know your local nursery personnel. They have the knowledge

and they really care about what advice they offer you as a valued long-term customer.

- Plan some cogitating time to enjoy your garden, however grand or humble it may be. You'll be surprised how much you love your garden after all.

PRUE AND MICHAEL KEELAN
RADIO 5AA AND CHANNEL NINE ADELAIDE

It's important to have individuality in gardening. Most people can't afford to have their gardens designed by professionals and have to rely on their own reading and ideas. I am also a great believer in planting things that thrive in the conditions the gardener has to offer. One reason is that our lives are just so ridiculously busy. Another is the increasing cost of water, and a third is that suitable plants always look so much healthier and perform so much better. If you join and support local garden clubs or horticultural groups, your knowledge, experience and confidence will grow. Have a go at developing your own ideas. If you surround yourself with plants in a design that suits you, that's a wonderful achievement.

PRUE SMITH
GARDEN WRITER

No single sort of garden suits everyone. Shut your eyes and dream of the garden you'd most love – then open your eyes and start planting. Loved gardens flourish, boring ones are hard work.

JACKIE FRENCH
GARDEN WRITER, BROADCASTER, COLUMNIST,
AUSTRALIAN CHILDREN'S LAUREATE 2014 2015 AND
SENIOR AUSTRALIAN OF THE YEAR

Stop doing dumb things. If plants fail to thrive after trying them (or their replacements) in two or three different situations, don't persist. Mother Nature is telling you something: these plants are too particular for your situation, soil and climate.

TREVOR NOTTLE
GARDEN WRITER AND CONSULTANT

The secret behind a good garden is first in its preparation. Best results come from understanding soil requirements (checking pH, adding organic matter, using appropriate fertilisers), installing an irrigation system and ensuring drainage is adequate. Then choose plants with characteristics that suit your garden, and they'll flourish!

KERAN BARRETT
EDITOR, THEGARDENINGMAGAZINE.COM.AU

Repetition of plants in the garden is not unadventurous! When, by experience, you find certain plants that really thrive in your garden, be bold enough to group them or repeat them as much as you like, within a good design layout. After all, Mother Nature is dropping the hint and who are we to argue?

ELWYN SWANE
GARDEN AUTHOR AND HORTICULTURAL
CONSULTANT – GARDEN TALK GLFM AREA RADIO

Use hardwood timber decking off living spaces as it is easier on the feet and can form a visual contrast to areas of paving. If you want seating under a feature tree and don't want to damage the roots, decking is the answer.

PETER FUDGE
GARDEN DESIGNER
WWW.PETERFUDGEGARDENS.COM.AU

How many gardeners do you have? Before you start out to create that vision of earthly paradise that is sitting quietly in your imagination, try to work out accurately how much work you will be prepared to put into the garden of your dreams. Be honest. You may just want to keep on bowling, fishing, shopping, reading, promenading, taking coffee, listening to music, playing with the grandchildren, chatting to friends and neighbours, etc. Will it be just you alone? Will your partner help out? Will your teenagers help regularly? Do you have the skills, fitness and energy? How much paid work can you afford? What skills will your garden need to keep it going? Sissinghurst is all very well, so is the National Botanic Garden, but the maintenance consumes hundreds of hours of expensive skilled work. Working out what your dream will need to make it come true is but the first step.

TREVOR NOTTLE
GARDEN WRITER AND CONSULTANT

When designing or redesigning a garden, ask yourself the purpose of the area under consideration. When you know why you want something, it's easy to plan for it.

FIONA OGILVIE
GARDEN WRITER – THE LAND

Buying one of each colour is folly as far as bulbs are concerned, and just as bad when choosing roses, azaleas, rhododendrons, camellias and tulips. More can never be a bore when big blocks of colour are needed to make the greatest impact. Whether you want a pale-pink colour scheme or a screaming orange one, one pink hyacinth or one orange ranunculus will never be convincing. Don't be afraid of too much colour; it will always be toned down, if not dominated, by green. Give it the works and take no notice of people who say they can't abide strong colours in a garden.

TREVOR NOTTLE
GARDEN WRITER AND CONSULTANT

The fastest way to get a garden growing is with plants suited to the local climate. Once they are established you can start pushing the boundaries.

FIONA OGILVIE
GARDEN WRITER – THE LAND

As gardens are growing smaller and smaller, resist the temptation to think that the small garden requires small plants. As boundaries close in around us, it is even more critical to have a balancing amount of 'green'. Far better to have one or two really decent-sized plants as a substantial presence in the garden – perhaps plants that go up more than they go out – than a low 'carpet of colour'.

MICHAEL McCOY
GARDEN DESIGNER

A minimum of 2 m is a good 'rule of thumb' for paths and bed widths. This rule must be strictly observed, especially for exuberant planters, to ensure ease of access to all parts of your garden and to avoid savage and ongoing cutting back. It is also a good height for walls and privacy hedges.

JOHN STOWAR
LANDSCAPE CONSULTANT AND HORTICULTURAL JOURNALIST

After playing with colour for many years, attempting very carefully contrived colour schemes, the conclusion I came to was this: as long as the garden is packed full to overflowing with plants and foliage of all shapes and sizes, you can pretty much get away with murder. The vigour and vivacity of the plants are far more important than the match of their colours.

MICHAEL McCOY
GARDEN DESIGNER

Work with the plant and the weather to save energy. How many people put the banksia rose in a tiny arbour to find they have to spend lots of time trying to keep it small enough? If a plant is a different size to that expected, try to move it to somewhere more suitable rather than keep on having to cut it.

SUE TEMPLETON
SALVIA SPECIALIST

One of the hardest things for keen gardeners to accept is that good garden design depends primarily on creating pleasant and memorable spaces. Plants must be subservient to them, which makes their selection and placement so important.

JOHN STOWAR
LANDSCAPE CONSULTANT AND
HORTICULTURAL JOURNALIST

A digital camera is one of the best tools gardeners can own. Hone your landscape design skills by taking pictures of your own garden and carry the camera with you when visiting other gardens. It's amazing how much you pick up when the images are downloaded to the computer, often missed when walking around the garden. Whether it's an urn in the wrong place or a bush that needs pruning or moving, it's surprising what the camera reveals.

CHRISTINE REID
AUSTRALIAN COUNTRY STYLE MAGAZINE

When planting deciduous trees, underplant with evergreen shrubs in groups of threes and fives to provide glossy green foliage. This avoids the bare look in winter and adds visual impact to the garden.

SUSAN MONTGOMERY
GARDEN DESIGNER

When purchasing an established garden, try to observe it over four seasons and in all weather conditions before embarking on changes. Hasty action is often regretted later.

JOHN STOWAR
LANDSCAPE CONSULTANT AND
HORTICULTURAL JOURNALIST

Gardens that I have enjoyed visiting the most are always those that have provided all-year-round seasonal interest. To maximise the potential of any garden, the gardener must use a palette of plants that not only flower at different periods in the year, but also have a variety of interesting textures and shapes within their composition.

MATTHEW LUNN
CURTIN FM 100.1

One of my favourite plant combinations is clivias mixed with maidenhair fern. The vivid green, dancing leaves of the maidenhair brighten up and fill the gaps between the dark green strappy clivia leaves.

DEBBIE McDONALD

GARDEN WRITER, EDITOR
AND HORTICULTURIST

Fit a ball float on the edge of your pond. Connect this to a water supply. When the water level drops due to evaporation the ball falls and opens a valve (just like in the cistern of a toilet), and automatically fills the pond. This will protect butyl liners from cracking in the sun.

PETER DE WAART

HORTICULTURIST

From the very beginning, don't forget to assess any drainage problems that may exist. Careful choice of landscaping style and plant types can overcome most difficult situations.

JOHN MASON

GARDEN AUTHOR, PRINCIPAL —
ACS DISTANCE EDUCATION

If you are unsure about what plants to choose when designing a planting scheme, select one large shrub, one medium shrub, one round-shaped plant, one plant with strappy foliage, one plant with horizontal foliage, one ground cover with vertical (grassy) foliage, and one ground cover with rounded foliage. This is a simple recipe for creating a planting scheme of your own. If you have too many varieties and colours of plants the beds will look messy. Stay with only a

couple of main colours and select maybe six plants to repeat through the beds. When you get more confidence then you can add some more plants for statement.

JIM FOGARTY

GARDEN DESIGNER
WWW.JIMFOGARTYDESIGN.COM.AU

DIY low-voltage garden lighting is a safe and economical way to illuminate your outdoor areas. Use spotlights to highlight water features, trees and statuary. Solar lights make use of our abundant sunshine and offer a low cost solution to outdoor lighting.

COLIN BARLOW

GARDEN WRITER, DESIGNER AND
HORTICULTURIST, TV PRESENTER –
HOME IN WA

Use cheap gutter guard to cover a row of small succulents like echeveria while they take root and the birds won't disturb them.

MELANIE KINSEY

HORTICULTURAL JOURNALIST

Spend 'time-out' with your garden and touch base with the plants. Don't be afraid to transplant or remove any which are struggling in unhappy marriages.

ANNE THOMSON

GARDEN DESIGNER – THE GARDEN DESIGN STUDIO

When you are doing work in your garden, don't restrict your creativity – experiment with colour and texture combinations. Avoid following mundane so-called 'fashions' and don't let neighbours, friends or relatives deter you from being innovative in your approach to gardening.

RICK ECKERSLEY
PRINCIPAL DESIGNER – ECKERSLEY STAFFORD
LANDSCAPE DESIGN

Avoid placing plants that have invasive roots near buildings, paved areas, water features, drains and septic tanks. Such plants include willows, poplars, birches, liquidambars and many eucalypts.

JOHN MASON
GARDEN AUTHOR, PRINCIPAL —
ACS DISTANCE EDUCATION

In garden areas with minimal space – for example, the narrow garden close to the neighbour's fence – use climbers to cover walls and strap-leaved plants to fill contained garden beds. Strap-leaved plants do not send out cross branches which can crowd out other plants or obstruct walkways.

RICK ECKERSLEY
PRINCIPAL DESIGNER – ECKERSLEY STAFFORD
LANDSCAPE DESIGN

Many practices that have been adopted by Aussie gardeners are entirely inappropriate to Australian conditions. We should be thinking not only of plants that are suited to our conditions, but also of water-wise gardening. We can draw inspiration from countries with similar climates, such as the Mediterranean, South Africa and even the Middle East (not the desert, but parts of Iran and Iraq, where some of the most beautiful gardens, such as the Gardens of Babylon, first developed).

PRUE SMITH
GARDEN WRITER

Consider how big each plant is likely to grow. You should allow sufficient space for future growth, and avoid planting large trees in places where they will eventually shade out lawns, damage buildings or create other problems.

JOHN MASON
GARDEN AUTHOR, PRINCIPAL —
ACS DISTANCE EDUCATION

Be careful of what you plant near the front door if you don't have time to continually sweep the path. A messy gum tree whose leaves fall every day, or a climbing rose over an arbour are better in an informal spot where the mess they make doesn't matter so much.

SUE TEMPLETON
SALVIA SPECIALIST

In a cool climate, make yourself a warm winter nook. Protect it from winter winds with a wall or thick hedge, use dark-coloured paving to absorb and reradiate heat, and underprune trees so winter sun can penetrate. In warmer zones, keep yourself cooler with shade structures that vent, by pitching roofs to spill out hot air or, even better, planting a spreading tree or a vine to cover the pergola.

CATHERINE STEWART
GARDENDRUM

Get your ground shaping right first (and therefore your drainage), before embarking on planting. This minimises the need for planting changes down the track after your plants are well established.

JOHN STOWAR
LANDSCAPE CONSULTANT AND
HORTICULTURAL JOURNALIST

Flowers come and go so it is a false economy to select plants for your garden purely on the basis of flowers. The enduring qualities of foliage, texture and bark create more interesting possibilities within the design palette.

ANNE THOMSON
GARDEN DESIGNER – THE GARDEN DESIGN STUDIO

For a change, plant for tapestries of green (foliage) rather than for splashes of colour (flowers).

ANNE LATREILLE
GARDEN WRITER

Dividing a garden, even with just one wall or hedge with an opening, immediately makes it look bigger.

FIONA OGILVIE
GARDEN WRITER – THE LAND

When planning your garden, make sure there is a pleasant spot for a comfortable garden seat. This seat will beckon you in spare moments to come contemplate and enjoy your outdoor space.

LIBBY CAMERON
GARDEN WRITER

You can extend the hours of enjoyment you derive from your garden by installing garden lighting; you don't need much to illuminate a small area.

JOHN GABRIELE
GARDEN WRITER – ILLAWARRA MERCURY
WEEKENDER MAGAZINE, GARDENING PRESENTER
ABC ILLAWARRA 97.3FM

Learn gardening from books, magazines, radio and TV, but talk to other gardeners at garden clubs and open gardens for the real nitty gritty.

CATHERINE STEWART
GARDENDRUM

A great garden does not have to be a 'weed-free showpiece' or even a 'riot of colour'. Far more desirable is a peaceful retreat: your sanctuary.

JOHN STOWAR
LANDSCAPE CONSULTANT AND
HORTICULTURAL JOURNALIST

Tree and shrub plant labels generally underestimate the height the plant will grow to. Because plants can't read, they often keep growing beyond the height mentioned on the label! Rule of thumb – double any height listed on a plant label for a more accurate mature height.

DAVID YOUNG OAM
FORMER WRITER, TV AND RADIO PRESENTER

A garden journal, even one kept in a desultory fashion like mine, is a font of useful information. And because I can easily imagine how much more useful it would be if I'd kept it for years, diligently filling in details about plants and their growth habits and favourite partners, and occasional setbacks; and about the weather; and great plans, and little ideas; and jobs lists and plant lists. If I were able to give advice to my younger self just starting to get dirty in the garden, it would be this: take notes.

ROBIN POWELL
GARDEN WRITER, *SYDNEY MORNING HERALD*

Looking for plant varieties that will thrive at your place? Start by looking over the fence and down the street to see what is performing well. While the internet may have opened up an exciting realm of seemingly endless plant information, local intel like this, along with speaking with local garden centre staff is priceless – literally!

MATTHEW CARROLL
HORTIMAN™ – WWW.HORTIMAN.COM
[FOLLOW @HORTIMAN]

If you are new to gardening, start your endeavours modestly, before moving on to bigger and better things. It is important that you enjoy the time you spend in the garden, not feel overwhelmed by taking on too much too quickly. Remember, you have to learn to crawl before you can run!

SIMON RICKARD
PASSIONATE GARDENER, PLANTSMAN AND AUTHOR OF *HEIRLOOM VEGETABLES: A GUIDE TO THEIR HISTORY AND VARIETIES*

Never throw away old toothbrushes. Use them to scrape aphids from rose shoots and buds or to remove soft scale and mealy-bugs from pot plants and the soft new stems of shrubs. Brushes with tapered heads are good for getting into the bases of orchid leaves. Scouring bird droppings from decks and outdoor furniture can be laborious, even when using the hose in jet mode, but a toothbrush will remove the hard outer ring of each splatter. And use a toothbrush to pull spiderwebs out of the rims of plant pots.

JULIA BERNEY
HORTICULTURAL–AGRICULTURAL FREELANCE EDITOR

Overgrown citrus trees can be rejuvenated by heavy pruning in spring; but their bark is very easily sunburnt. Protect by painting the whole thing with whitewash, made by stirring half a cup of hydrated or builder's lime into half a litre of water, using a plastic (never metal) bucket, measuring cup and spoon, and adding a teaspoonful or two of white oil or pest oil to make it stick. (Dry lime is dangerously corrosive, so wear old clothes, rubber gloves, and a face mask.) The wash will last long enough for the new growth to shade the old branches, but it will be two or three years before your next crop of fruit.

ROGER MANN
LANDSCAPE ARCHITECT AND AUTHOR OF YATES ROSES AND NAMING THE ROSE

To make picking fallen leaves out of plants like Clivias or Bromeliads a lot easier, especially those that are under the trees, use an old pair of long metal kitchen tongs. Your back will thank you for it.

MARIANNE CANNON
PRESENTER, *REAL WORLD GARDENER* ON 2RRR AND ACROSS AUSTRALIA ON THE COMMUNITY RADIO NETWORK

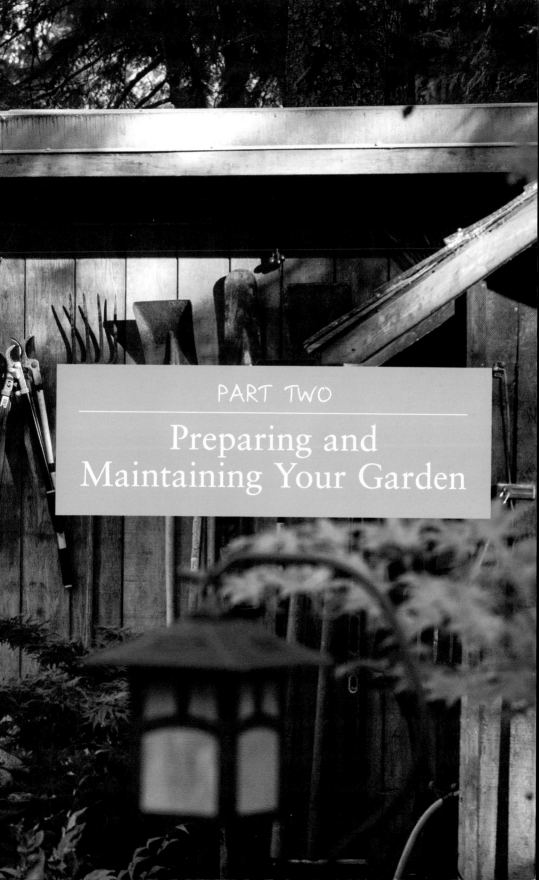

PART TWO

Preparing and
Maintaining Your Garden

4
Soils, Compost and Worms

To know your soil you should first understand how plants grow and manufacture food. Plants – from the smallest seedlings to the largest trees – are factories which take raw materials from the air, water and soil to build carbohydrates, proteins and fats. To do this they need a constant supply of raw materials and a source of energy – sunlight – to form roots, leaves, stems, flowers, fruits and seeds. Each part of the plant has a special job to do, but its performance depends on the cooperation of every other part.

Leaves and young stems are the real manufacturing sections. They contain a green pigment called chlorophyll which, in the presence of light, allows them to produce sugars from carbon dioxide from the air and water from the soil. This sugar production is called photosynthesis and is the starting point for more complex substances such as starches and cellulose. The plant proteins and amino acids which are so important for both human and animal nutrition are nitrogenous compounds synthesised in the plant tissues from nitrogen absorbed from the soil water. Other plant nutrients are also absorbed from the soil.

HOW ROOTS DO THEIR WORK

Roots anchor a plant in the soil. Some plants have a long, strong taproot with smaller lateral roots. Others have a branched fibrous root system. Whatever form it takes, the root system absorbs water and dissolved nutrients from the soil through the root hairs (elongated cells just behind the root tip) and passes them to conducting tissue in the root, then on to the stem and other parts of the plant. Roots must respire (or breathe) to perform their task of absorbing and conducting efficiently, so a soil must be able to provide oxygen as well as water and nutrients.

SOIL TYPES

Some soils are better for growing plants than others. The terms rich and poor, good and bad, fertile and infertile are commonly used to describe these differences. The quality of the soil in your garden largely depends on the type of parent rock from which it is formed, on the influence of climate over hundreds of thousands of years and on what your house builder and previous owners have done to it. It is remarkable how much poor soils can be improved if you learn to manage them properly.

Soil is made up of mineral particles which vary in shape, size and chemical composition. Sand particles are quite large because they break down slowly. Other minerals break down more quickly into clay particles. These are extremely small – many thousands of times smaller than coarse sand – and they have an important effect on the physical and chemical properties of the soil. The size of the particles – coarse sand, fine sand, silt and clay – and the proportions in which they occur determine soil texture.

Sandy soils

Sandy soils have large particles with large spaces, called pore spaces, between them. They drain readily, have good aeration and are easy to cultivate. For this reason they are often called 'light' soils. However, very sandy soils are less effective at retaining water and nutrients than other soil types.

When slightly moist, good loam soil will stay together when shaped into a ball.

Clay soils

Clay soils have small particles and little pore space. They store water well, often too well for good drainage and aeration, and retain plant nutrients. Clay particles attract and hold nutrients on their surface. Clay soils can be difficult to cultivate and are often called 'heavy'.

HINT

Only dig over your soil when it is damp — never when bone dry or soaking wet as you will destroy its structure.

MELANIE KINSEY

HORTICULTURAL JOURNALIST

Loams

All soils between the extremes of sand and clay are referred to as loams. They are mixtures of coarse and fine particles. They are divided into such categories as sandy loam (more sand than clay) and clay loam (more clay than sand). You can identify the soil in your garden by the feel in your hand when the soil is slightly moist.

Sandy soil does not stick together and is coarse and gritty.

Sandy loam sticks together, is friable (easily crumbled) and slightly gritty.

Loam sticks together, is friable and not gritty.

Clay loam sticks together, is slightly friable but plastic.

Clay soil sticks together, is not friable, but rather it is plastic and sticky.

ORGANIC MATTER AND SOIL STRUCTURE

All soils contain some organic matter. Organic matter consists of the remains of plants and animals and the organisms (earthworms, slaters, beetles, bacteria, fungi, and so on) that are decomposing them.

Of the various components of plant remains, the proteins and carbohydrates are quickly broken down into simple chemicals that can be absorbed by both plants and bacteria, but the more resistant bits of organic matter remain as small fragments which form a dark brown material called humus. Particles of humus attract and hold nutrients on their surface in the same way as clay colloids. Humus particles bind mineral particles (especially fine sand, silt and clay) into aggregates or crumbs. These crumbs have relatively large pore spaces between them which help drainage and aeration. The addition of humus to heavy soils makes them easier to cultivate.

HOW TO IMPROVE SOILS

The water- and nutrient-holding ability of sandy soils can be improved by adding organic matter. Animal manure, leaf mould, spent mushroom compost, garden compost and green manure crops are all excellent additives when dug into the soil.

Animal manures are probably the best because they contain useful quantities of nutrients as well (see pages 82–83). Animal manures and mushroom compost are readily available in bags and sometimes in bulk. Composted 'green wastes' are also readily available, or you can make your own compost. Green manure crops are also a good source of organic matter but few home gardens have space to grow them nowadays. Peat moss is a good moisture-holding material but it contains negligible quantities of plant nutrients. There are concerns about the non-renewable nature of peat moss so cocofibre peat is an environmentally responsible substitute.

All organic materials will eventually decompose in soil and therefore must be renewed from time to time, especially in annual flower and vegetable beds that are continually cultivated.

Clay soils benefit from organic matter too, because it improves their structure by binding clay particles into crumbs. This allows better air and water movement. By adding coarse sand to heavy soils you can make a permanent improvement in their texture. Spread the sand to a depth of 5–8 cm, then mix well into the topsoil to a depth of 15–20 cm. Gypsum can be incorporated into a clay soil and in most cases will help the soil to function more effectively. Add gypsum at a rate of about 0.5–1 kg per square metre of soil.

The crumb structure of clay and clay loam is destroyed if they are dug when too wet. Allow the soil to dry out for a day or two before digging. When cultivating any soil, only dig the topsoil. Do not dig so deeply as to bring subsoil (especially clay) to the surface.

SOIL WATER AND SOIL AIR

If a soil is saturated, the pore spaces are full of water and there is no room for air. As the soil drains, excess water, called 'gravitational water', moves downwards, leaving a film of water around each soil particle. The soil is now at 'field capacity', that is, it is holding as much water as it can against gravity. Sandy soils have a very low field capacity. Clay soils may have a field capacity ten times as great.

Some plants (especially vegetables with large leaves, like cabbage, cauliflower, lettuce and some vine crops) wilt readily in very hot weather. This is because they are losing water faster than the roots can take it up. Provided the soil is moist enough, the plants recover in the cool of the evening and the leaves are back to normal the following morning.

DRAINAGE

Too much water is also harmful to plants. In saturated soil, root respiration slows down due to a lack of oxygen. Soil bacteria and other soil organisms also need oxygen to function, so organic decay is restricted in wet soil. Another harmful aspect of wet soil is a decrease in soil temperature. Well-drained, friable soils are warmer than wet soils. A warm soil increases root respiration and plants grow faster. Bacterial activity also increases.

Fortunately, many garden soils have good natural drainage. Soils which have a high proportion of sand seldom present a drainage problem unless there is a clay subsoil or rock layer close to the surface. On heavy soils, drainage improvement of some kind is usually needed. To check the need for drainage, dig a few test holes to a depth of 40–50 cm and inspect after heavy watering or rain. If water remains in the holes for 24

Structure of soil

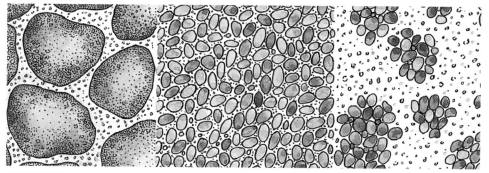

SANDY SOIL: *large air spaces between particles allow free drainage but do not hold water or nutrients well.*

CLAY SOIL: *fine particles are tightly packed together, so drainage and aeration are poor.*

IMPROVED CLAY SOIL: *particles are aggregated into clumps, improving air space and drainage.*

Even the poorest soil can be improved – so don't despair. With attention given to drainage and nutrients, and the addition of earthworms, the worst of soils can usually be rescued.

JOHN MASON

GARDEN AUTHOR, PRINCIPAL —

ACS DISTANCE EDUCATION

hours, some artificial drainage is required.

On sloping sites, a rubble drain running diagonally at the top of the slope to divert run-off water or seepage away from the garden may be sufficient. Dig the trench 40–50 cm deep and fill with rough stones to a depth of 15–20 cm. Cover with a layer of aggregate or gravel and replace the topsoil.

Another simple drainage method is to raise garden beds 15–20 cm above the surrounding surface. The sides of the beds should slope at 45–60 degrees. If gardens are surrounded by stone or brickwork, make provision for weep holes at the bottom of the surround.

If drainage is a major problem, a permanent herringbone system made of slotted polythene pipes may be needed. Set the drains 6–9 m apart and dig trenches about 60 cm deep with a fall of not more than 1 in 200 so that the pipes are self-cleaning. Line trenches with geofabric. Pipes should be bedded in porous material such as aggregate, gravel or coarse sand. In very wet situations, it may be best to consult a drainage expert.

WATERING AND MULCHING

How much and how often you water plants depends on the soil type of your garden, the kind of plants you grow, your general climate and the time of the year. Microclimatic factors, such as slope, aspect or exposure to wind, will also affect loss of water from plants and soil. It is difficult to lay down rules for watering, but there are a few general principles worth knowing.

Sandy soils generally need more frequent watering than clay soils, but less water should be applied each time. Whatever the soil type, do not let plants reach wilting point before you water again. Plants do not thrive on such 'on and off' treatment. Remember, a good soaking encourages deep rooting and soil stays moist for a long time. Light sprinkling, no matter how often you do it, encourages roots to stay at the surface. The subsoil gets drier and drier and becomes difficult to wet again without a lot of heavy soaking. Early morning or evening is considered the best time for watering, because evaporation rates are likely to be lower than in the middle of the day. In humid areas, however, evening watering over plants that are susceptible to fungal diseases will encourage such diseases to flourish, and therefore should be avoided. In the morning it is usually less windy, too, so the water spray goes where you want it. In very dry weather, morning watering may help pollination and seed-setting in some vegetables, particularly sweet corn and beans.

Mulching is a good way of conserving soil moisture, especially in summer. A mulch is any soil covering which protects surface roots and reduces evaporation. It also helps maintain an even soil temperature and discourages many weeds from growing.

The best mulches are loose materials that allow most rain or irrigation water to run through to the soil. They must also allow free access of air to soil and roots. The depth of

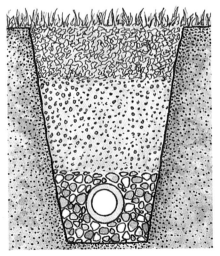

Drainage pipes must be bedded in porous material such as gravel or coarse sand before the subsoil and topsoil are replaced.

the mulch should vary with its coarseness, from shallow for the finest to thicker for the coarsest (2–6 cm). Garden compost, leaf mould, dry lawn clippings, well-rotted animal manure, straw, tan and pine bark, lucerne hay and sawdust are common mulching materials. Do not dig mulches into the soil (especially bark materials and sawdust). All will eventually decompose naturally and become integrated with the topsoil. Mineral substances, stones, pebbles, gravel and sand are used as permanent mulches in gardens planted with trees and shrubs. Woven weed mats, too, are available by the metre from garden suppliers. These effectively suppress weeds while still allowing oxygen and moisture to penetrate the soil. In ornamental situations they need to be anchored in place and disguised by a more attractive layer of organic mulch.

Over-watering is wasteful because it washes out plant nutrients. A common mistake is to over-water in winter when plant growth rate is reduced. (In the case of deciduous shrubs and trees, the plants are dormant.) Over-watering in winter often happens with summer-growing lawns like couch grass. If a plant is not growing actively, little or no water is needed.

HINT

Think of Goldilocks when adding mulch to garden beds. Not too thin, otherwise the gold of the sun will reach the soil and weeds will germinate. Not too thick, otherwise it locks out the water. But just right when it s about 5 cm deep for most organic mulches.

ROD McMILLAN

PUBLISHER, TOUR LEADER, DIRECTOR –
ADLAND HORTICULTURAL

Wet soil may also favour the spread of some fungal diseases, so it is best to keep mulch a few centimetres away from the stems of plants or the trunks of shrubs and trees. Such a moist area may encourage root rots to attack the plant at or near soil level.

Top five flowers for alkaline soil

GLADIOLI

Gladioli, which usually flower about 100 days after planting the bulbs, can be grown in a wide range of climates.

HYACINTH

One of the best features of hyacinth flowers is their delightful perfume.

SWEET PEA

Sweet peas will grow most happily in soil with a pH between 7 and 8. This is why it is often recommended that soil be limed before planting.

LILAC

Lilac flourishes in harsh conditions, as long as the winters are cold.

GYPSOPHILA

Baby's breath is known as 'chalk plant' because it grows naturally on chalky limestone soils. It makes a splendid cut flower.

Top five vegies for acid soil

POTATO

Grow potatoes to help break up the soil in a new garden. The crop will be a bonus.

PUMPKIN

Pumpkins are so tolerant that they'll grow just about anywhere – even out of your compost heap!

CUCUMBER

Like pumpkins, cucumbers have separate male and female flowers. Only the female flowers will develop fruit.

BEANS

Because they can make use of nitrogen from the atmosphere, bean plants will actually enrich the soil in your garden.

SWEET CORN

The only member of the grass family that is grown as a vegetable, sweet corn has spread from its original home in the Americas to become a staple food in many parts of the world.

PUMPKIN

BEANS

WATERING METHODS

There are dozens of kinds of sprays and sprinklers for watering gardens. Those which give a fine spray are generally preferred because large drops of water tend to pack the surface of heavy soils. Fine sprays also generally have a lower watering rate, which gives better penetration and less run off on sloping sites. However, be aware that fine sprays allow greater evaporation.

A soaker hose, with small holes less than 30 cm apart, is useful for slow watering but must be handled carefully in a crowded garden of shrubs or annuals. The small holes may become blocked and this needs watching. Porous hoses made from recycled rubber allow water to seep through the tiny holes in the structure of the hose walls.

HINT

If soils with high levels of organic matter are allowed to totally dry out they can become water-repellant. To overcome this, add a soil-wetting agent. Once the soil has become thoroughly moistened, cover the area with a layer of mulch and make sure it gets watered at least once per week during the summer months.

JOHN MASON

GARDEN AUTHOR, PRINCIPAL –
ACS DISTANCE EDUCATION

Ordinary garden hose has stood the test of time and is as popular as ever. Nozzles adjustable for spray width and droplet size can be hand-held or attached to a stand. A water-breaker nozzle or wand is excellent for watering seed beds, small seedlings and plants in pots. It delivers a full volume of water in a soft and even spray, which does not damage the fragile plants.

Irrigation systems are reasonably priced and readily available. A system can be designed for individual needs and installed by a handyperson, or professional advice and installation may be preferred. Some systems incorporate automatic timing devices that switch lines on or off according to a predetermined pattern and time span. Drip irrigation systems are preferred when water is in short supply.

COMPOSTING

Mention the word composting to any keen gardener or hobby farmer and you can be assured of a lengthy discussion about materials, methods, special techniques with even secret recipes obtained from distant ancestors thrown in for good measure.

Some people will say that to produce good compost you only have to throw all your rubbish in a heap and let it rot. This is perhaps the oldest method of making compost and it will work eventually, provided that you have a good mixture of different materials in the composting heap. Actually, any material of plant or animal origin can be used to make compost.

This 'rubbish heap' method can be very slow, however, and, although the usual range of micro-organisms act in converting the rubbish to compost, conditions are often not ideal and the heap can take ten or eighteen months to mature.

Sometimes anaerobic (without oxygen) conditions develop, creating a wet and smelly heap; these heaps are eventually worked on by worms to complete the composting process. With this method you actually end up with a compost comprised of very rich worm casts (vermicast).

If you have only one product in the compost heap, for example a high carbon source such as sawdust, it will not compost at all until a nitrogen source such as animal manure or grass clippings is thoroughly mixed into the heap.

The carbon–nitrogen ratio (C/N) is very important. Simply explained, it means that a mix of both high carbon and high nitrogen materials must be placed in the compost pile. This is the food supply for all the micro-organisms that produce the compost, and a correct mix allows efficient and fast compost production.

Examples of high carbon materials are paper, wheat straw, sawdust and chipped wood products. Some high nitrogen sources

Well-rotted compost provides food for plants.

are animal manures, including poultry and pigeon manure, urine, grass clippings and green prunings from garden plants. Some materials have a reasonable C/N ratio and under ideal conditions will compost readily; examples of these are lucerne straw and grass clippings.

One composting mixture described by Kevin Handreck in *Gardening Down-Under* (published by Landlinks Press, VIC) is for leaves, sawdust and animal manure to be used in a volume to volume ratio of 1:1:3. Using a wheelbarrow as the measure, Handreck suggests you use one barrowload of leaves, one barrowload of sawdust and three barrowloads of manure. You may use any equivalent measuring implement at hand if no wheelbarrow is available or if that amount is too large for you to handle. The important thing to remember is that no matter what size heap you build, the ratio of materials should give you a good C/N ratio.

Other factors that aid the composting process are temperature, moisture, oxygen supply and the particle size of the material in the compost heap. The organisms that break down the organic material in the compost heap must also be available; these can be

HINT

A dial-type thermometer with a long probe is a valuable tool for good compost production. Temperatures at the centre of the pile need to be between 40°C and 60°C. If this is achieved the compost will 'cook' much faster and produce well-matured, usable product in a short time. At high temperatures weed seeds will be deactivated and disease-causing pathogens destroyed.

JOHN MASON

GARDEN AUTHOR, PRINCIPAL —
ACS DISTANCE EDUCATION

introduced by adding commercially available compost activators, animal manures, one spadeful of organically active soil, or a handful of compost from your previous compost pile.

A correct temperature range is necessary for composting. Positioning the compost pile or compost bin in a place where it will obtain plenty of sunlight can help, especially in areas with cold winters. But if your heap is large enough and is made correctly it should generate its own heat. Make sure that the heap does not become too dry during the initial activation period and in hot summer periods.

Once activated, a composting heap goes through various temperature changes. This is because different organisms are present in the various temperature regimes. These organisms have high rates of multiplication and can cause compost heaps to reach temperatures above 60°C, a temperature high enough to kill many weed seeds. However, since all parts of the heap may not reach these temperatures, it is just as well to keep weed seeds out of composting material.

Moisture is essential for the organisms in the compost pile. When building a compost heap it is important to moisten each layer as it is placed on the heap. If the compost gets too dry the microbial activity will cease; conversely, the compost must not get too wet

and cold as the activity will also cease. Therefore, protect open heaps from rain during wet weather and check the compost heap regularly.

Adequate aeration is needed to provide the organisms in the compost heap with oxygen. There are many ingenious ways to add air to your compost heap.

Place an open-layered design of bricks at the base of the heap so as to provide air channels.

Tie stakes together or make tubes of plastic, reinforcement mesh or rolled-up chicken wire to form tubes. Place these vertically into the heap.

Use plastic piping with holes drilled in a spiral design along the full length of the pipe. These can be inserted vertically into the heaps and are particularly useful in compost bins because the extra air speeds up the composting process.

Turning over the compost heap at least once every day will greatly enhance the composting process and aerate the heap.

The smaller the size of the individual pieces of materials placed in your compost heap, the faster it will mature. Small pieces of material have a relatively larger surface area than big pieces, so organisms within the compost have a larger area to work on and will break down the material into compost at a much faster rate than would occur in compost heaps built with large pieces of material. To break down the materials you can use mulching machines, which are available in a large range of sizes (and prices). Some city councils provide a service where they mulch the material for you to take home for composting. Mulching can be done with other cutting implements, such as rotary mowers with or without catchers.

The way the materials are placed in the compost heap will influence its successful operation. Materials with high moisture content, such as wet grass and fresh vegetable matter, should be mixed with other materials that can absorb the excess moisture – for example, shredded paper, straw, or sawdust. If large pieces of materials are used they should be spread evenly through the heap, or placed at the base of the compost heap if you are using an open-air composting method.

Generally, compost heaps are built by having successive layers of materials (each

100–250 mm thick) interspersed with layers of organic fertiliser (manure) or a material with a high nitrogen content. Some methods suggest mixing all the materials together, then building the compost heap. Rotary bins are designed to mix the material every time the bin is rotated and are more efficient because of this feature.

Many compost designs incorporate the use of lime on each layer. This is unnecessary if you build the heap to provide good aeration; however, you may wish to sprinkle some lime into the compost to provide extra calcium. A number of compost recipes suggest the layering of soil on each layer of material that is placed into the compost heap. Soil will provide organisms, but commercial compost activators, animal manures, or one handful of compost from a previous heap will provide most of the organisms necessary. Placing layers of soil within your compost heap is not recommended; too many home gardeners destroy their compost heaps this way and end up with a smelly, compressed, wet mix that will take a very long time to break down into compost. A layer of material such as sawdust can be used as an alternative to soil to seal the heap to prevent odours.

To have a nutrient-rich compost you should put nutrient-rich materials into the compost heap. Sprinkle on some fertiliser to add nutrients to your heap. In addition, moisturising the heap with a diluted seaweed product will help to provide micronutrients. Some forms of seaweed have been found to contain nearly all the free elements known to exist – including gold!

There are many different kinds of compost bins which can be effectively used. Here are some of them:

  Recycled plastic bins and 200-litre drums
  Home-made wire mesh bins (place recycled paper, cardboard or plastic around the outside of these bins to enable them to compost quickly in cool weather)
  Bins made of polycarbonate or long-lasting plastic
  Kit bins
  Wooden bins
  Rotating bins
  Ordinary plastic bags and thick, industrial-strength bags
  Rubbish bins converted to compost bins by cutting out the base
  Composting toilets, which are highly recommended as they do not contribute to ground-water and soil pollution like septic tank systems

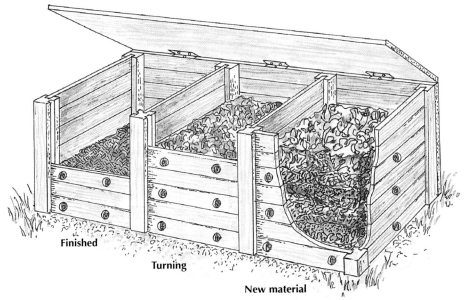

Finished

Turning

New material

If you have a number of bins, you can make use of completed compost while other heaps are at different stages of decomposition.

HINT

The compost bin needs to be secure to prevent it from becoming home to mice and other vermin trying to find food and shelter. It is also important to protect your compost pile from becoming saturated by heavy rains.

JOHN MASON

GARDEN AUTHOR, PRINCIPAL —
ACS DISTANCE EDUCATION

Do not use galvanised containers as they can supply toxic amounts of zinc to the compost.

All of the abovementioned bins have advantages and disadvantages. Compost bins which absorb heat, have good aeration, or are designed to be easily turned are more efficient, but providing you have the correct C/N ratio, moisture, warmth, and material that is of a small particle size, it is possible to compost in an ordinary plastic bag and obtain compost within a few weeks, even in winter.

There is no reason for anyone not to compost their kitchen and garden waste; 40 per cent of municipal waste can be turned into compost and up to 80 per cent of kitchen waste can be converted to compost. Many councils are now subsidising the cost of compost bins to ratepayers. This idea is likely to spread Australia-wide, as it reduces the cost of waste collection and disposal.

You should encourage your local council to aid in the recycling and composting of community waste. Any person building a new toilet system, replacing the old, or installing a second unit, should think about installing a composting toilet. Compost from composting toilets is ideal and can be used directly on the garden. Health authorities now approve of these systems.

When compost is used in the garden it improves soil structure, provides nutrients and humus to the soil and plants, reduces water use by acting as an 'organic sponge' reservoir within the soil and provides you with the material for organically growing vegetables and fruit. Compost can be used to build a 'no-dig' garden which is easily maintained, is ideal for people of all ages, and is environmentally friendly (see pages 74–75).

WORMS

There are actually thousands of species of worms, ranging from the tiniest eelworms that can only be seen with the aid of a microscope with a magnification power of 300 000:1, to the gigantic Gippsland earthworms that can grow to several metres in length.

The most common of all worms are the earthworms, those found living in the soil, under forest litter, or in rotting vegetation. Earthworms have been described as 'the living gut of this planet', an apt description since without earthworms it is very likely that there would be no life forms (as we know them) on this earth today. All plants and animals rely on worms, because worms mine the soil and recycle nutrients.

Earthworms burrow in the soil, aerating the soil structure and thus providing oxygen for billions of bacteria, fungi and other micro- and macro-organisms. These in turn provide the environment for plants to grow. Each day every worm digests about half its own weight of soil. This works out to be somewhere near 40–50 g dry weight per year. If you have 200 worms per square metre, then that population can shift an incredible 80–100 tonnes of soil per hectare per year. Worms concentrate the minerals in the soil as it passes through their gut, so that the resulting worm casts can contain up to six times the available nitrogen, seven times the available phosphorus, twelve times the available potassium, and also increased availability of many of the minor elements such as calcium, magnesium and sulfur. In fact, worm casts can be said to be the complete plant food. You cannot put too much on your plants – worm casts won't burn plant roots or foliage.

Many worms mix organic matter into the soil, thus improving the structure of that soil. This can be seen as a dark area spreading down into the soil layer.

Taken a step further, by increasing the air supply to the soil, worms actually facilitate a massive build-up of soil organisms, which also allows roots of plants to grow deeper into the lower soil depths. Improved root growth gives better crop yields and reduces the demand for water due to surface evaporation around roots. Most organic gardeners and farmers rely heavily on the action of worms to implement their sustainable systems.

Growing your own worms

Worm bins can be constructed from bath tubs, tin cans, boxes, old fish tank frames, bricks and wooden planking. Providing the container is about 25–30 cm deep, it will do as a starter. The bin should be placed in a position where it does not get too hot during the summer months. Home-garden worm farms made from recycled plastic are popular for disposing of household vegetable waste. Containers of worms are available for purchase but it is important to be aware that the species of worms that do the best job of breaking down organic material in bins and worm farms do not survive well in soils.

To breed worms successfully you must supply them with food which is high in nitrogen, such as kitchen waste, bread, straw, leaves, grass clippings, herbs and animal manure. Bran is often used too. In other words, worms thrive on anything you would customarily put in your compost heap.

The moisture content of a worm farm is important, since worms require water but

Plastic worm farms with pre-structured layers are compact and convenient.

dislike waterlogged soils. Each worm farm should have a removable cover to prevent waterlogging of the worm bed during periods of rain. The bed should be kept moist but not saturated. Placing wet bags on the surface will reduce evaporation losses and create the darkness required by the worms. The contents of your bin should consist of about 5 cm of loamy soil, then about 10 cm of the ingredients mentioned above, then another 5 cm of loamy soil. Check the worm bin weekly for moisture content and food supply.

HINT

If you are too busy to maintain a worm farm, simply place scraps in a covered bucket and when it is half full, top up with water. Dig a hole somewhere in your garden, tip in the waste and water and cover with soil. Each time choose a different position. Earthworms will break down the waste within four to six weeks. Avoid using meat and fats.

MARGARET SIRL

ABC GARDENING, SOUTH EAST NSW, GARDEN CONSULTANT AND DESIGNER

Worms can hasten the breakdown of organic matter into useful compost.

No-dig Gardening

A no-dig garden is just that – a garden bed made up of layers of organic materials that does not require backbreaking digging and tilling. Esther Deans, inventor of the 'no-dig' garden, recommends her method for all gardeners but says it is particularly useful for those physically unable to dig in the traditional fashion. Children, older gardeners, handicapped people or those confined to a wheelchair will find this method practical and toil-free.

WHERE TO PUT A NO-DIG GARDEN

A no-dig garden can go almost anywhere. It can be situated on a section of lawn or existing garden. It can be built over hard, rocky ground or even on top of a concrete slab. It is also possible to adapt the method to create an elevated garden. Use any type of frame or container, set at a convenient level, and line it with heavy-duty plastic punched with drainage holes and make the garden within the frame.

MAKING A NO-DIG GARDEN

On the ground

1. Select a site, preferably in a sunny position.
2. Build a box frame with boards or bricks.
3. Place a 5- to 10-mm thick layer of newspaper (not cardboard or glossy magazine paper) in the bottom of the frame. Overlap the paper so there are no gaps.
4. Cover with pads of lucerne hay as they come off the bale.

CONSTRUCTING THE BED

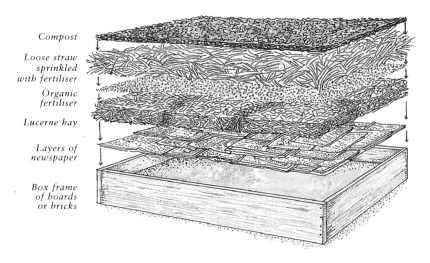

Compost

Loose straw sprinkled with fertiliser

Organic fertiliser

Lucerne hay

Layers of newspaper

Box frame of boards or bricks

5. Sprinkle on a dusting of organic fertiliser.
6. Cover with 20 cm of loose straw.
7. Scatter some fertiliser onto this layer.
8. Tip a circle of rich compost 10 cm deep and about 45 cm in diameter in places where seeds are to be planted.

On rocky ground or concrete

1. Build a box frame with boards or bricks.
2. On the bottom spread a layer of decaying leaves, small sticks and pieces of seaweed to a depth of 10 cm.
3. Layer the organic materials as in the method above.

TENDING YOUR GARDEN

Do not dig a no-dig garden. It is both unnecessary and detrimental to the unique process. Simply replace new layers of compost, manure, lucerne and newspapers when necessary.

Rotate your crops. For example, when leafy summer crops have been harvested the layers of the garden will have composted down and merged into each other. Add another layer of compost and plant autumn seeds such as carrots, onions, cauliflower or cabbage.

Water during the early morning when evaporation is at its lowest.

Weeding will be minimal because the organic materials added to the garden should be weed-free.

WHAT TO PLANT

Vegetable seeds and seedlings, flowering annuals, herbs, bulbs and strawberries all thrive in a no-dig garden. Use the following vegetable-growing schedule as a guide to obtaining a rich seasonal bounty from your no-dig garden.

VEGETABLE SOWING GUIDE

This is a guide for temperate regions. Consult an advisor at your local nursery if you live in a different climatic region.

SPRING

Sow seeds of French, climbing or scarlet runner beans, beetroot, carrot, corn, melon,

pumpkin, radish and summer squash. Sow seeds or plant seedlings of cabbage, capsicum, celery, cucumber, eggplant, lettuce, marrow, silver beet, tomato and zucchini. Set in potato tubers.

SUMMER

Sow seeds of French beans, carrot, corn, beetroot and radish. Sow seeds or plant seedlings of Brussels sprouts, cabbage, cauliflower, capsicum, celery, tomato, leek, lettuce, silver beet, tomato and vine crops.

AUTUMN

Sow seeds of broad beans, bok choy, carrot, Chinese cabbage, peas, radish and spinach. Sow seeds or plant seedlings of broccoli, kohlrabi, leek, lettuce and onion.

WINTER

Sow seeds of pea, snow pea and spinach. Sow seeds or plant seedlings of lettuce and onion. Plant garlic cloves.

5
Plant Nutrients and Fertilisers

It was not until 1840 that the German chemist Justus von Liebig proved that carbon came from carbon dioxide in the air and not from humus in the soil. He proved too that other nutrients were absorbed by plant roots as simple chemicals dissolved in soil water.

Great strides in the study of plant nutrition have been made in the last 150 years. We now know that, apart from carbon, hydrogen and oxygen, which plants get from air and water, about a dozen nutrients or elements are essential for plant growth. These nutrients are contained in the minerals and organic matter in the soil. The organic matter must be decomposed so that plant roots can absorb the dissolved nutrients as simple chemicals or parts of molecules called 'ions'.

We can supplement these sources of nutrients through applications of suitable fertilisers. It makes no difference whether plants obtain nutrients from decomposed matter or from fertilisers. Plants grow best when a combination of organic matter and fertilisers is available to them.

The nutrient elements that are essential to the growth of all plants can be divided into three groups. The major elements are needed in larger amounts than are the secondary elements, which in turn are required more than the trace (or minor) elements. In the following list, the names of the elements are followed by their symbols (as seen listed on fertiliser packages).

Major elements
nitrogen (N), phosphorus (P), potassium (K)
Secondary elements
calcium (Ca), magnesium (Mg), sulfur (S)
Minor elements
iron (Fe), manganese (Mn), copper (Cu),
zinc (Zn), boron (B), molybdenum (Mo)

A number of other elements, including chlorine, nickel, sodium and silicon, are also needed by at least some plants. None is likely to be deficient in home garden soils.

MAJOR ELEMENTS

Nitrogen, phosphorus and potassium, often called 'the big three', are the most important elements required by plants. Each is needed in large amounts and the presence or absence of any one of them has a dramatic effect on plant growth.

Nitrogen (N)

Nitrogen is an essential part of the proteins in plant (and animal) cells. It is also a necessary part of chlorophyll, the green pigment in plants, and is extremely important to leaf growth. Plants deficient in nitrogen are stunted, with pale green or yellow leaves, often with reddish tints.

Soil bacteria break down protein in organic matter into nitrogen-rich ammonium ions. Another group of bacteria lives in nodules or swellings on the roots of legumes (peas, beans, lupins, clovers, lucerne, acacias, cassia and many others). These bacteria are able to 'fix' nitrogen in the air between the soil particles. The 'fixed' nitrogen is used by the host plant but, when the roots die, the nodules disintegrate and release nitrogen which can then be used by crops. (See 'Green manure crops' on page 83 in this chapter.)

Most powdered and granular fertiliser mixtures contain sulfate of ammonia as the source of nitrogen.

HINT

Topsoil is almost always nonexistent on a housing development lot. When building a new garden, it is important to take time to improve the soil structure. Fork gypsum into heavy clay soils, add plenty of organic matter and mulch beds thickly with lucerne hay to add nitrogen, potassium and calcium and to encourage worm activity.

ELWYN SWANE

GARDEN AUTHOR AND HORTICULTURAL
CONSULTANT – GARDEN TALK GLFM
AREA RADIO

Urea (46 per cent N) is a soluble, quick-acting form of nitrogen which is widely used in water-soluble fertiliser mixtures such as powdered Thrive and Aquasol. When applied as a spray, some urea is absorbed through the leaves. Most, however, is washed into the soil and converted into nitrate nitrogen.

Potassium nitrate (13 per cent N) is a quick-acting source of nitrogen and potassium (36 per cent K). It is commonly used in water-soluble fertiliser mixtures.

Phosphorus (P)

Phosphorus forms part of the nucleoproteins in plant cells, so it is important in growing tissue where the cells are actively dividing. It promotes the development of seedlings, root growth, flowering and the formation of fruits and seeds. A deficiency of phosphorus leads to poor root development, stunted growth and often a purplish discolouration of the leaves. Most soils in Australia originally had enough phosphorus for our native plants but not enough for most of our exotic and garden crops plants. Additions need to be made to garden soils for most plants except those that are sensitive to phosphorus (banksias, grevilleas, proteas and many native pea flowers). However, many garden soils come to have very high phosphorus levels

from additions of mixed fertilisers and poultry manures.

Superphosphate (9 per cent P) is the most common phosphorus fertiliser and is used in most powdered and granular mixtures. It is not completely soluble. It is a mixture of calcium phosphate and calcium sulfate, so it provides useful quantities of calcium (22 per cent Ca) and sulfur (11 per cent S) as well as phosphorus.

Phosphorus can move rapidly through some soils (particularly sandy soils) and may pollute waterways and encourage algal blooms under certain conditions. Therefore, there are now restrictions on the level of P in home garden fertilisers in Western Australia.

Potassium (K)

Potassium promotes chlorophyll production and plays an important part in the strength of cells and the movement of water in plants. It also helps plants resist disease and improves the quality of flowers, fruits and seeds.

Plants deficient in potassium have weak stems; their leaves, especially the older ones, may be floppy, with yellow or brown tips or scorched margins. Sandy soils in high rainfall areas are most likely to be deficient.

Potassium chloride (50 per cent K), also known as muriate of potash, is the most widely used of all potassium fertilisers. Its application should be avoided in areas where the water is salty.

Potassium sulfate (42 per cent K) also contains sulfur (18 per cent S) but is more expensive than potassium chloride. It is preferred for some crops, for example strawberries and potatoes. It is widely used in water-soluble fertiliser mixtures.

SECONDARY ELEMENTS

Calcium (Ca)

Calcium is important in the construction and strength of cell walls in plants in a similar way as it is to the bones of animals. It also promotes proper functioning of growing tissue, especially in root tips.

Calcium neutralises acids in the cell sap and when applied to soil as lime plays an important part in reducing soil acidity. Calcium as a nutrient is rarely deficient unless the soil is extremely acid.

Magnesium (Mg)

Magnesium is a crucial part of the chlorophyll molecule so is important in photosynthesis. Lack of magnesium causes leaf yellowing, especially on the older leaves of plants, because magnesium, like potassium, is mobile in the plant and young leaves have first call on these two nutrients.

Most Australian soils provide adequate amounts of magnesium. The exceptions are those that have received excessive applications of poultry manures; the potassium in these can interfere with magnesium supply to plants. Some powdered fertilisers, and all water-soluble ones contain adequate quantities of magnesium sulfate or Epsom salts (10 per cent Mg). Dolomite (3–8 per cent Mg) is a poor source of magnesium. It must be applied in large quantities and is slowly released over two or three years.

Sulfur (S)

Sulfur forms part of many plant proteins. It does not occur in chlorophyll but it is involved in its production. Sulfur deficiency shows up as yellowing of leaves and stunting of shoots, with symptoms similar to those of nitrogen deficiency. Australia has some sulfur-deficient soils in parts of the highlands of the Great Dividing Range. In garden soils a deficiency is extremely unlikely because superphosphate (11 per cent S), sulfate of ammonia (24 per cent S) and all powdered and granular mixtures contain sulfur in adequate quantities. Organic matter also contains sulfur, but like nitrogen it is only available following bacterial breakdown to the sulfate form. In districts where sulfur deficiencies are known to occur, gypsum or calcium sulfate (15 per cent S) can be used.

TRACE ELEMENTS

Minor or trace elements are important but they are needed only in minute quantities. Their excessive use may do more harm than good to the plants in your garden. In a normal garden situation, trace element deficiencies are not common.

All organic materials – animal manures, blood and bone, bone dust, compost and leaf mould – contain trace elements. Even superphosphate, which is made from rock phosphate, contains useful amounts. Trace elements are added to some proprietary fertiliser mixtures and also to water-soluble mixtures (e.g. Thrive and Aquasol) in small but adequate quantities. It is easier and safer to use these ready-prepared products than to mix your own. Trace elements act as growth regulators or enzymes (starters) in building chemical compounds inside plant cells.

Iron (Fe)

Iron is not a part of the chlorophyll molecule but small quantities must be present for its formation. Symptoms of iron deficiency include yellowing of younger leaves, because iron is relatively immobile in the plant. A deficiency is more likely in alkaline soils. All neutral and acidic soils naturally supply enough iron to most plants. If extra iron is needed, iron chelates release quickly but they last only a short time in alkaline soils.

HINT

When buying fertiliser, always read the label to see what percentage of nitrogen, phosphorus and potassium it contains and relate this to its price. In some cases you get very little for your money. It is also worth remembering that you get the best value by buying in bulk.

PETER VALDER

BOTANIST, WRITER – *BURKE'S BACKYARD* MAGAZINE

Manganese (Mn)

Manganese plays a similar role to iron but is needed to form proteins. Deficiency symptoms – again, more likely on alkaline soils – are yellowing of younger leaves, especially between the veins. Plants may also be stunted. An excess of manganese may produce toxic effects on very acid soils. These effects are overcome by liming to raise pH above pH 5.5. (See page 85.)

Copper (Cu) and Zinc (Zn)

Both copper and zinc are enzyme activators. Lack of either element leads to leaf mottling, and yellowing in younger leaves.

In citrus trees zinc deficiency causes an abnormality called 'little leaf'. Copper and zinc deficiencies are more likely on very acid, sandy coastal soils but may sometimes also occur on 'black earth' soils in dry inland districts.

Boron (B)

Boron is important to growing tissue in young shoots, roots, flower buds and fruits. A deficiency leads to breakdown of internal tissue and corkiness, especially in apples, beetroot and turnips – often called 'brown heart'.

Tissue breakdown may also occur in the stems of celery and silverbeet and in the flower buds of cauliflower and broccoli. Boron deficiency is more likely in alkaline soils or in those which have been limed heavily. There is a narrow span between not enough boron and too much.

Molybdenum (Mo)

Molybdenum is needed for the conversion of nitrogen gas into plant protein. Deficiencies are most prevalent in high rainfall areas on acid soils. Very often an application of lime will release sufficient soil molybdenum to correct a deficiency. As little as 25 g per hectare of molybdenum will correct deficiencies. Molybdenum deficiencies are common in cauliflowers, Brussels sprouts and other members of the cabbage family, causing the disease known as 'whiptail'. In home gardens, the use of one of the water-soluble fertilisers – all of which contain molybdenum in adequate quantities – will correct most deficiencies.

INORGANIC FERTILISERS

The analysis of fertiliser materials is expressed as the percentage of nitrogen, phosphorus and potassium they contain, often called the N.P.K. ratio. Home gardeners will usually find it easier to use mixed 'complete' N.P.K. fertilisers than the separate compounds listed above, but the separate compounds are sometimes useful if only one or two nutrient elements are needed (for example, when there is already an ample supply of phosphorus in the soil).

N.P.K. mixtures come in powdered, granular and water-soluble form. There are dozens of brands and many formulations. Some powdered mixtures contain blood and bone as well as inorganic chemicals. Granular mixtures have the advantage of being free-running and of not setting hard in storage, so you can buy them in large quantities and have them on hand when you need them.

Powdered and granular fertilisers

These are often formulated to suit particular groups of plants although some with a balanced N.P.K ratio (often called All Purpose) are designed to feed a wide range of plants. Others have much more specific applications. Granular lawn fertiliser, for example, will have a high proportion of nitrogen to promote green, leafy growth. Rose food and citrus food will contain higher levels of nutrients such as potassium that encourage growth, flowering and production.

Because granular fertilisers are high in salts they should only ever be applied to moist soil and should be watered in well afterwards. Avoid application to foliage or close to plant stems, as this could cause salt burn.

Water-soluble fertilisers

Thrive Soluble and Aquasol are well-known, Australian-developed and made, water-soluble fertilisers. The main ingredients are urea, mono-ammonium phosphate and potassium sulfate or potassium nitrate. Each one also contains a balanced trace element mix. The ingredients dissolve completely in water, so it is easy to apply them in dilute solutions by watering can or through a hose-spray attachment. They can be used safely as nutrient boosters for flowering annuals, vegetables, shrubs, indoor and outdoor pot plants – in fact, for every plant in the garden. The N.P.K. analysis of both is higher, especially in nitrogen, than for powdered or granular fertilisers. The approximate analysis of Thrive is N.P.K. 27:5:9. A special formulation, Thrive Flower & Fruit, with an N.P.K of 15:4:26, is specially formulated to meet the needs of flowering and fruiting plants.

Potassium, copper and zinc are essential for healthy citrus trees.

HINT

The best way to apply controlled- release fertiliser to larger-growing shrubs and trees is to create fertiliser holes around the plant. First of all, deep water the area, then insert a crowbar or similar-sized instrument deeply into the soil – preferably 60 cm or more – at the drip line. Continue this process right around the drip line of the plant. The holes should be spaced at 1 m intervals.

Dribble the required amount of fertiliser into the holes, and it will be taken up by the roots far more effectively and quickly than when scattered on the topsoil, without any loss to the elements.

VALERIE AND GERRY ZWART
GARDEN WRITERS, QUEENSLAND

Slow-release fertilisers

There is nothing really new about slow-release fertilisers. We have been using them for years: bone dust, blood and bone, animal manures and compost. All these organic materials must be decomposed before the nutrients are available. Pelletised manures like Dynamic Lifter also act as slow-release fertilisers, because it takes some time before the nutrients dissolve out of them and become available to the plants.

Some inorganic fertilisers release nutrients over a longer period because they are covered with a special coating or in a chemical form that slows this process. Yates Lawn Master, which feeds for three months, is a good example of nutrients that release slowly due to their specific chemical structure.

Controlled-release fertilisers

In slow or controlled-release fertilisers the soluble fertiliser particle is protected with an exterior coating. Some coatings dissolve slowly, others expand to allow the fertiliser in

solution to leach through the membrane. Paraffins, waxes, resins, polythene and sulfur have been used as coating materials. One of the most widely used in commercial plant nurseries is Nutricote controlled-release fertiliser.

Nutricote has a polymer resin coating which acts as a membrane. Water penetrates the membrane to dissolve the nutrients, which then diffuse out slowly through the plastic membrane and into the soil. When all the nutrients are released the shell gradually breaks down.

The rate of nutrient release depends on soil temperature. This is appropriate because plants grow faster and take up more nutrients in warm soils. Release is not influenced by soil acidity or alkalinity or by bacterial activity in any way.

Controlled-release fertilisers are recommended for adding to soil mixtures for seed beds, boxes and punnets, for a wide range of container-grown plants and for plants growing in restricted spaces.

Home gardeners often find controlled-release fertilisers, and combinations of controlled-release and compound fertiliser nutrients, the most convenient way to feed potted plants.

ORGANIC FERTILISERS

These fertilisers include animal manures and animal or vegetable by-products. Animal manures contain small quantities of nitrogen, phosphorus and potassium, which vary with the kind of animal, its diet and the amount of straw or litter mixed with the manure. They are first-class materials for improving the structure of soils, but they must be added in large quantities to benefit the soil in this way. Spread them to a depth of 5–7 cm over the surface and dig them into the topsoil. Animal manure containing a lot of straw may cause a temporary nitrogen deficiency because bacteria decomposing the straw have first call and plants may suffer. So add extra nitrogen or, better still, a complete fertiliser which contains at least 10 per cent nitrogen plus phosphorus and potassium.

Liquid organics

Liquid animal manure watered onto leafy vegetables every week or two is an excellent fertiliser. The liquid is made by suspending a permeable bag filled with fresh manure in a large cask or drum of water. After a week the liquid is diluted with water (one part to three parts) for use. There are many convenient, commercially-available, organic-based liquid fertilisers such as fish emulsion and other blends. They combine the advantages of guaranteed nutrient availability with natural components that stimulate soil microbial activity.

Seaweed tonics are also included in this group although it's important to remember that they aren't fertilisers. Rather, they contain natural hormones that stimulate root growth and build plant defences against stress.

Green manure crops

Green manuring is another relatively inexpensive way of adding organic matter to the soil, but the system is usually confined to vegetable gardens when empty beds are lying idle in winter. In our climate, because there are many vegetables which can be grown in winter, there is often little space left over for a green manure crop.

However, if you do have an empty bed

there are several green manure crops you can use. Seeds of wheat, barley or oats can be broadcast at 30–60 g per square metre in autumn to provide a large bulk of material to dig into the soil in spring. Legume crops which add nitrogen through nodule bacteria in their roots are usually preferred. Suitable crops for autumn planting are field peas and vetches. The recommended seed rate is 15–30 g per square metre. Dig the crops in when they begin to flower in spring. Good summer-growing legume crops for warm northern climates include dolichos (lab lab bean) and cow peas. These are sown in spring and dug in by mid-summer when they flower. A complete fertiliser must be broadcast at one-third of a cup per square metre when sowing all green manure crops.

Water the crops a day or two before digging them in. If the crop is very tall, flatten it and chop up with a sharp spade. After digging, keep the soil damp but not wet, then after three weeks dig the soil over again. It will take another three or four weeks for the organic matter to decompose. If there is any sign of yellowing in the following crop, give side dressings of a nitrogen fertiliser.

Analysis of Organic Manures and Organic By-products

MANURE OR FERTILISER	APPROXIMATE NUTRIENT CONTENT %		
	NITROGEN (N)	PHOSPHORUS (P)	POTASSIUM (K)
ANIMAL MANURE			
Cow	1.0	0.4	0.5
Chicken	2.1	1.6	1.0
Chicken (pelleted slow-release)	3	2	1.5
Horse	0.7	0.4	0.5
Pig	1.1	0.7	0.1
Sheep	1.8	0.4	0.5
ORGANIC BY-PRODUCTS			
Bone dust	3.0	10.9	—
Blood and bone	6.0	7.0	—
Castor meal	5.5	0.8	0.9
Cotton-seed meal	6.0	1.3	0.9
Linseed meal	3.0	0.4	1.7

Commercial organic fertilisers

Easy-to-handle organic fertilisers are now readily available, with pelleted, slow-release poultry manure being the most popular. Products such as Dynamic Lifter pellets are widely used to fertilise plants in the ground and in containers, both in domestic and commercial situations.

Dynamic Lifter variants fortified with extra nutrients are available for lawns and plants with special needs such as roses and fruit trees. Each pellet contains inorganic and organic fertiliser blended together.

Organic by-products of animal origin include bone dust, bone meal and blood and bone. Most of these fertilisers contain higher quantities of nitrogen and phosphorus than animal manure, but very little potassium. Nutrients are released slowly. Spread them at 125–250 g per square metre and dig into the topsoil.

LIME AND pH

Even if all essential elements are present in a soil, it cannot be taken for granted that they are all available to plants. Availability depends very much on the acidity or alkalinity (amount of lime) in the soil. Just as we can measure temperature with a thermometer, so we can measure whether a soil is sour (acid) or sweet (alkaline). Acidity or alkalinity (sometimes called 'soil reaction') is measured on a scale of pH units. This scale ranges from

HINT

Try adding wood ash in moderation to your compost bin as an alternative to using lime to increase the pH. It makes a great defensive wall or barrier to keep out an array of crawling pests from the vegetable garden. However, don't use wood ash in the garden if your soils are alkaline as it will increase the alkalinity.

GEOFF MIERS

GEOFF MIERS GARDEN SOLUTIONS
ALICE SPRINGS, NORTHERN TERRITORY

pH units 0.0 (the most acid) to pH 14.0 (the most alkaline). The halfway mark, pH 7.0, is neither acid nor alkaline. Distilled water has a pH of 7.0. In soils, the pH ranges from pH 4.0 (strongly acid) to pH 10.0 (strongly alkaline), so soils can be rated accordingly.

If soil pH is too high or too low, some elements may not be available. This is shown in the diagram opposite in which the width of the horizontal bars gives the relative availability of each element at different pH levels. On strongly acid soils (pH 4.0–5.0) all of the major elements – nitrogen, phosphorus, potassium, calcium, magnesium and sulfur, and the trace element molybdenum – are poorly available to plants. As soil pH increases into the 7.5–8.0 range, phosphorus availability decreases, as do the availabilities of the other five trace elements. In soils which are in the slight to medium alkaline range (pH 7.5–8.5), phosphorus again becomes unavailable, and so do the other five trace elements: iron, manganese, boron, copper and zinc. All plant nutrients are available between pH 6.0 and pH 7.0, with the best availability at pH 6.5 – a soil which is very slightly acid.

How plants react to pH

Most plants grow happily if the soil pH is between 6.0 and 7.0, but there are exceptions. Lime-intolerant (acid-loving) plants – such as azaleas, camellias, ericas, gardenias and rhododendrons – prefer strongly acid soil (pH 5.0–5.5). Some others prefer a medium acid soil (pH 5.5–6.0). These include hippeastrum, cineraria, clematis, cyclamen, dianthus, ferns, fir trees, junipers, lupins, magnolias, orchids, veronicas and most bulbs. We could add many Australian native shrubs and trees to this group.

Most vegetables and herbs thrive on soils with a pH between 6.0 and 7.0. Exceptions are potato, sweet potato and watermelon (pH 5.0–5.5). Many other garden plants will also tolerate a medium acid soil. Blueberries prefer acidic conditions.

How to check pH

In Australia, most soils in high rainfall districts on the coast and eastern highlands are naturally acid. Soils in these districts usually have a pH between 5.0 and 6.5, with

Influence of pH on Nutrient Availability

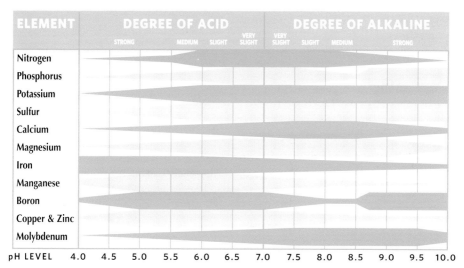

some as low as pH 4.0. In drier inland areas, the pH of soils approaches the neutral point and some are in the slight to medium alkaline range (pH 7.5–8.5).

This means that most soils in or near Australian capital cities will be in the medium to slightly acid range, as will be many large towns in the eastern states. The exceptions are Adelaide, and towns in low-rainfall districts where soils are neutral or alkaline. The colour of hydrangeas growing in your neighbourhood is a good guide – blue flowers in acid soils, pink flowers in alkaline soils – but there is no real way of knowing what has happened to the soil in a particular garden. The best approach is to have your soil pH tested. Many garden centres offer this service.

There are several colour-chart pH testing kits available from nurseries and garden stores. The most reliable of these testing kits are those in which a liquid indicator is mixed with a small soil sample to form a paste. The colour of the indicator changes according to the pH of the soil. A second chemical (barium sulfate powder) is puffed onto the wet soil so that the colour can be easily seen. This colour is then compared to the colours on the chart supplied in the kit. The colours range from orange (pH 2.0) through yellow, lemon, green, to violet (pH 10.0), at 0.5 unit intervals. One popular kit also contains a useful list of recommended pH ranges for flowers, ornamental shrubs, trees, vegetables and fruit.

How to raise pH

Lime contains calcium, one of the base or 'alkali' elements, and is used to raise the pH of acid soils.

Agricultural lime (Calcium carbonate) is finely ground, but takes some time to react with the acidity in the soil. Some fast-acting liquid limes are now available. All limestones contain some magnesium, but the dolomitic limestones and dolomite contain higher proportions. These are preferable for liming soils that have received heavy applications of poultry manures.

Hydrated lime or slaked lime (calcium hydroxide) can also be used. It is quick-acting in raising soil pH but should not be applied at the same time as fertilisers. A given weight of hydrated lime is equivalent to about 1.3 times that weight of agricultural lime.

Gypsum (calcium sulfate) is often used to improve soils containing high levels of sodium. It contains 23 per cent calcium and 15 per cent sulfur but it is not a liming material – in fact, it has a neutral or very slightly acid effect on soil. However, by displacing sodium, gypsum will improve the structure of soil.

Agricultural lime (or dolomite) can be applied at any time of the year and watered into the topsoil. The quantity required depends on soil type – sand, loam or clay – and the amount of organic matter in the soil. It is best to raise pH slowly rather than apply massive doses. The following quantities of agricultural lime are a guide to raising pH by one unit, say from pH 5.5 to pH 6.5.

In gardens where the soil is known to be acid, lime is often applied at the above rates every year or two. This maintains a desirable pH, especially in annual flowerbeds and vegetable plots which are usually cropped continuously throughout the year.

SOIL TYPE	QUANTITY OF LIME (GRAMS PER SQUARE METRE)
Sandy soil	150–200
Loam	200–280
Clay soil	280–450

There is no practical evidence that lime binds sand or clay particles into crumbs in a direct way. However, it does have an effect on soil chemistry, favouring bacterial activity and the decomposition of organic matter. The formation of humus particles, in turn, promotes a good crumb structure.

How to lower pH

The best acidifying agent to lower pH on alkaline soils is sulfur. Be aware, however, that for all practical purposes it is not possible to lower the pH of soils with a pH above 8.3. Sulfates such as aluminium sulfate (alum) and iron sulfate are sometimes recommended. Yates Soil Acidifier, which contains liquid sulfur, will lower pH if applied as recommended. Sulfate of ammonia also has an acidifying effect if used over a long period. Peat moss will also lower pH, but the results are less predictable. The following quantities of sulfur are a guide for lowering the pH by one unit, say from pH 7.5 to pH 6.5.

When making soil tests, always record the area from which samples were taken, and the date of the test. If lime or sulfur is applied to correct pH levels, make a note of how much and when it was applied.

SOIL TYPE	QUANTITY OF SULFUR (GRAMS PER SQUARE METRE)
Sandy soil	30–60
Loam	60–90
Clay soil	90–120

HYDROPONICS

Hydroponics is a system of growing plants without soil. If there is sufficient light, the right temperature, air to supply carbon dioxide to leaves and oxygen for the plant and its roots, we should be able to feed them water and nutrients for healthy growth.

Many experiments have been carried out in laboratories using water-culture methods. These gave precise information on the effect of each nutrient on plants. In true water culture, roots dip into a nutrient solution through which air is bubbled regularly so roots can breathe. More often, plants are grown in a combination of free-draining sand or gravel and an inert moisture-holding material like vermiculite, and fed with a nutrient solution.

Carnations, lettuce and strawberries and a number of other crops have been successfully grown commercially in hydroponic beds.

Growing plants in this way has special appeal to people living in flats or home units where there is a sunny balcony or patio but no outside garden.

Hydroponics is much the same as growing plants in tubs or pots – but without soil. Containers must have free drainage and plants must be watered and fed regularly. Several kits for hydroponic beds and planter boxes are available.

The advantages of hydroponics are that it involves no digging, few weeds grow, and very little maintenance is required, apart from regular watering and feeding. If you want to try your hand at hydroponics, fill a polystyrene trough with a mixture containing two parts coarse river sand, one part crushed charcoal and one part vermiculite, plus a tablespoon of granular, all-purpose fertiliser per bucket of mix. Sow three rows of baby carrots and water them regularly.

A comparatively easy and economical hydroponic nutrient solution can be made by mixing one part of Aquasol with one part of nitrate of potash and a half part of Epsom salts. Dissolve at the rate of 5 g (a level measuring spoon) to 5 litres of water and feed every few days as required. Before sowing or planting, work superphosphate into the growing medium at the rate of 1 kg per 10 square metres of surface (top) area.

This will encourage stronger root growth and also supply calcium. Flush with clean water every week to prevent salt build-up. Repeat the application of superphosphate at monthly intervals.

Many nutrient mixtures for hydroponic gardening are made up to special formulas. A hydroponic supplier will be able to give advice on these mixtures.

Delicious tomatoes can be grown hydroponically.

6
Organic Gardening

There has been increasing interest in the subject of organic gardening in recent years. It is now commonplace to find organic fruit and vegetables for sale at your local greengrocer and organic food is widely acclaimed for not only its health benefits, but also for its superior taste. However, organic gardening is not just about growing fruit and vegetables. It represents a major shift in attitude towards gardening and embraces a wider philosophy of how we take care of the earth and its resources – the ethics and practice of this approach form the basis of permaculture. Organic gardening uses natural soil improvement techniques to build healthy soil and grow strong, pest- and disease-resistant plants that are climatically suitable and do not need to be maintained by constant spraying.

Making compost, building no-dig gardens and growing green manure crops are all common organic practices. A range of fertilisers and soil additives based on animal manures, blood and bone, mushroom compost, seaweed, fish waste and legume plants such as lucerne and pea straw are permitted within organic growing regimes. Your local garden centre can provide and advise you about suitable products.

Using these ingredients increases the levels of organic matter and humus in the soil, providing balanced plant nutrition and attracting organisms such as beneficial soil fungi and worms to the garden. In both flower and vegetable gardens, organic growers favour open pollinated seeds and heirloom varieties. The use of genetically engineered crops is not permitted. Organic gardeners use organic seeds that have not been treated with chemical fungicides such as those included in the Yates organic seed range. Organic gardeners also plant locally adapted fruiting and ornamental species as well as native plants that provide habitat for bird life. One of the main aims in organic gardening is to encourage resident populations of birds, beneficial insects, spiders, small reptiles and other animals to help bring about natural pest control and create a self-sustaining ecosystem.

CERTIFIED ORGANIC GROWERS

Certification standards set down by the Australian Quarantine Inspection Service (AQIS) under the National Standards for Organic and Biodynamic Produce apply to commercial growers who wish to market their produce as organic. The standards that apply to commercial growers also provide a useful guide to the techniques and inputs that you can use at home.

START WITH THE SOIL

You may think you have no decent soil to work with, but it is amazing what can be achieved by adding organic matter to rock-hard ground, sticky clay or pure sand. Collect raw materials to build a no-dig garden (see pages 74–75) or use this more traditional approach.

Start simply by improving a small patch only. Chip away any grass and weeds in the area where you intend to create the garden. Break up the soil using a mattock or strong garden fork. Add generous amounts of gypsum to clay soil. Water the area well.

Next, add at least one full wheelbarrow of compost or decomposed animal manure per square metre of garden area. The relative nutrient values of various types of organic manures and organic by-products are detailed on pages 82–84.

If the soil is too hard or heavy to work, spread your organic matter over the top and cover with mulch. In the coming weeks this material will begin to work magic on your soil. Over time you will gradually be able to incorporate this material into the soil with relative ease.

If you find it difficult to access sufficient supplies of organic matter, you can try growing your

Top five companion plants

TOMATOES AND BASIL

Not only do these help each other to grow well, their flavours are complementary.

GARLIC AND ROSES

Garlic keeps insect pests away from roses and is also said to improve their perfume.

CLIMBING BEANS AND SWEET CORN

The Native American Indians began this planting association. Climbing beans add nitrogen to the soil for the corn and, in return, the corn stalk becomes a support for the beans.

ROSEMARY AND SAGE

Each helps the other to grow well. Rosemary also promotes healthy cabbages and carrots.

BEETROOT AND LEAFY GREEN VEGETABLES

Beetroot gets on well with most plants but goes particularly well with leafy vegetables such as lettuce, spinach and silver beet.

TOMATOES AND BASIL

own green manure crop. (See page 83.) If you have a large garden this can be a less expensive way of obtaining organic matter.

Keep working the soil over, adding extra organic matter until you have broken up the soil to at least a spade depth. When worms begin to appear you are ready to plant.

Off-the-shelf soil improvement

You will obtain better results if you concentrate on generously enriching the soil in one small area and expand the garden as materials and time allow. A wide range of organic soil improvement products are available through nurseries. National organic standards permit the use of:

- compost, composted animal manures, blood and bone, hoof and horn meal and other animal waste by-products
- natural crushed rock, dolomite, gypsum, lime, rock and guano phosphate, rock potash and sulfate of potash, sulfur and bentonite
- seaweed, fish meal and fish waste extracts
- lucerne, pea straw, coir peat and other plant by-products
- wood ash and wood products such as sawdust and bark from untreated sources
- worm castings and liquid from worm farms
- zeolite, Epsom salts, trace elements and natural chelates

COPING WITH WEEDS

When it comes to weed control, organic gardeners are not limited to laborious hand weeding. The first line of defence is in

HINT

Some organic gardeners create special algae ponds that are quite shallow, and to the water they add animal manures. The liquid mix is removed as required from the pond and diluted and then used as a liquid fertiliser.

GEOFF MIERS

GEOFF MIERS GARDEN SOLUTIONS

ALICE SPRINGS, NORTHERN TERRITORY

prevention using soil-improving, plant-based mulch materials such as lucerne, pea straw, lab lab and other legumes to inhibit germination of weed seeds. These materials break down fairly rapidly and require regular replacement. However, as they decompose they provide food for soil organisms and help to enrich the soil and improve its structure and texture.

Mowing and the use of biodegradable weed mats are also permitted under organic growing regimes. Where gardeners keep animals such as chickens and ducks, these can be used in a mobile run to prepare an area or clear away the remains of a vegetable harvest prior to replanting.

Solarisation is a technique that uses the heat of the sun to kill weeds and is obviously most effective during the warmest months of the year. Prepare the area for planting by incorporating green manure, compost or other organic matter. Rake the bed level ready for planting and water well. Cover the area with clear plastic and seal the edges by weighing them down with soil, rocks or timber.

The heat of the sun will raise the temperature of the soil immediately beneath the plastic by up to 15 degrees above air temperature. During the heat of summer when the daytime temperature may reach 35°C, the top few centimetres of soil beneath the plastic will reach 50°C, killing off many harmful bacteria and weed seeds that do manage to germinate.

After two to three weeks of treatment, remove the plastic and plant the bed with as little disturbance as possible. Water the plants in and mulch the area well.

Commercial organic producers use gas-fired flame weeders and steam weeders to burn weeds out. Organic herbicides based on pine oil, coconut oil or vinegar may also be used to control weeds.

A weedmat helps to control weeds in this bed of young corn plants.

Marigolds, chicory and fennel are excellent companion plants.

CLEAN OUT THE GARDEN SHED

Converting to organic gardening may require you to rid yourself of some unsuitable garden products. Never be tempted to dispose of products by pouring them down the sink or putting them out with other household garbage.

Many government agencies, local shires and councils have facilities to collect and dispose of unwanted and out-of-date insect sprays, weedkillers and fertilisers. Contact your local authority for advice as to your nearest collection point, before gathering together the products you no longer require.

MANAGING PESTS

There are occasions when certain pest and disease problems create havoc in all gardens. Fortunately for organic gardeners there are now plenty of low-toxic products available whose use is permitted under national organic certification.

Off-the-shelf pest and disease control

Organic gardeners aim to grow strong pest-resistant plants. They also establish a diverse range of plant species and create natural habitats that support a range of beneficial organisms to help bring about natural pest control. When pest or disease outbreaks do occur, national organic standards permit the use of:

- biological controls using naturally occurring cultured organisms such as Yates Nature's Way Caterpillar Killer Dipel Bio-insecticide (*Bacillus thuringiensis var. Kurstaki*)
- copper oxychloride such as Yates Leaf Curl Copper Fungicide
- fruit fly baits in enclosed traps
- exclusion fabrics including cloth and paper fruit fly control bags
- boracic acid for cockroach control
- iron-based products such as those used in organic snail bait
- light mineral oil such as PestOil
- lime products including dolomite, garden lime and agricultural lime
- lime sulfur-based products including Yates Lime Sulfur Spray
- powdered or wettable sulfur
- natural pyrethrum
- plant oils such as vegetable oil, neem and garlic
- potassium permanganate (Condy's Crystals)
- potassium-based soap sprays such as Natrasoap
- plant-derived products including rotenone

as found in Yates Vegetable Derris Dust
- vinegar
- seaweed, seaweed meal and seaweed extracts
- sodium silicate and sodium bicarbonate
- horticultural insect barrier glues and sticky traps

COMMON MISCONCEPTIONS

Many people believe that organic gardening is a 'do nothing approach' that just lets nature takes its course. The reverse is often the case.

When you first adopt organic gardening techniques you will need to put in extra work making compost, improving your soil, mulching, planting, creating an appropriate habitat and adopting other techniques that reduce your reliance on fertilisers and sprays.

Some people are under the mistaken belief that to become organic you must devote your entire garden to vegetable production. Organic growing techniques are applicable to both ornamental gardens as well as productive plantings of herbs, vegetables and

Nasturtiums grow in beds well mulched with straw.

fruit trees. You can garden organically even if you do not grow edible crops as the soil improvement and pest-control techniques are equally applicable to roses, herbaceous perennials, flowering annuals and native plants.

ORGANIC STATUS

When conventional primary producers change to organic techniques they go through a transition period of at least two years before they achieve certified organic status. Home gardeners converting to organic growing should expect to go through a similar transition.

During the transition period, it is common to suffer increased pest and disease problems and lower production. This is because it takes time and effort to build up the levels of organic matter in the soil, grow strong pest and disease resistant plants and surround yourself with insects, lizards, birds and other animals that will help to keep potential problems at bay.

The length of the transition period in your development of an organic garden will depend on factors such as:
- How extensively fertilisers and sprays have been used in the past
- Your existing soil type and the level of organic matter it contains
- The style of gardens around you and the habitat they create
- How much time and effort you are prepared to put into the garden
- Your access to resources such as animal manure, grass clippings, legume mulches and general composting materials
- Your gardening experience and knowledge
- Your willingness to remove less suitable plant species that support pest populations

Despite the initial time and effort in establishing an organic garden, there is something extraordinarily satisfying about getting back to nature and harvesting fruit, vegetables and flowers from your own garden. A floral bouquet, fresh garden herbs, crisp salad greens, sun-ripened tomatoes or home-grown lemons – all this, and more, can be produced using organic methods whether you garden in pots on a patio or on a large suburban block.

PERMACULTURE

Permaculture is a design philosophy that uses nature as its model. Originally developed by Bill Mollison and David Holmgren, gardens, homes, communities and even entire cities have been developed using permaculture principles.

Organic gardening practices are the centrepiece of permaculture. However, permaculture looks at more than just gardening. It also considers sustainability in how we design and build our homes and cities, the resources we use and how we care for the natural environment.

Permaculture values all living organisms, no matter how small or seemingly insignificant. This is based on the belief that everything is connected and that all organisms play their part in maintaining our complex ecosystem. It encourages people to take care of the earth and its resources and care for one another by limiting our consumption and becoming more self-reliant. One strategy is to grow fruit and vegetables in our own back yards and neighbourhood community gardens.

APPLYING PERMACULTURE PRINCIPLES

It is possible to put permaculture into practice in your home and garden by following a few simple principles.

Maximise potential

Try to consider at least three functions for every plant or structure in your garden in

Flowers and vegetables grow in every usable space and an old Hills Hoist supports a grape vine in this community garden.

order to utilise everything to its fullest potential. If you intend planting a lemon tree, consider planting it close to the kitchen where you can access the fruit easily. The blossoms of a lemon tree are highly scented and the yellow fruit are very attractive, so plant the tree where it can be appreciated. Most lemons grow into medium-sized trees. The evergreen foliage can provide summer shade, so utilise this feature when positioning the tree.

Consider how the garden shed can do more than just store tools. Could it support a passionfruit vine, collect rainwater for the garden or screen the compost area?

Mutual benefit

Good design groups items according to their relationship to one another. Position a compost bin close to the vegetable garden. Waste from the garden can be placed into the bin and, once processed, the compost can be returned to the garden to grow more vegetables. Strongly aromatic herbs could be planted close to a citrus tree to help repel pests and occupy a space that might otherwise be taken over by weeds. There are many ways in which you can group plants and structures for mutual benefit.

Energy efficiency

In an energy-efficient garden, if you need a sprig of parsley, it should be within easy reach of the back door or be able to be plucked from a hanging basket or window box. To plan a permaculture garden, create a series of concentric rings or zones around your home. Plants that need close attention or regular harvesting such as vegetables and herbs should be planted in zone one. Plants that need less attention such as native species or nut trees can be planted in an outer zone.

Garden intensively to make the best use of space. To save personal energy, mulch instead of weeding, plant gardens instead of mowing and divert water run off from pathways into the garden rather than watering.

Renewable biological resources

Reduce the materials you import to grow and maintain your garden. Save your own seed. Grow plants from cuttings. (See Chapter 10.)

Select plants that can be regularly pruned to provide compost ingredients or mulch. Grow nitrogen-fixing legume plants as companions to fruit trees. Harvest comfrey leaves and steep them in water to make your own liquid fertiliser.

On-site recycling

Consider all the inputs used in your home and garden and the waste you generate. Grow a green manure crop and make your own compost. Keep a few chickens and collect the manure to reduce your need to buy fertiliser.

Reduce waste by refusing unnecessary packaging. Recycle your grey water, compost your kitchen waste or feed it to some chickens. Utilise waste paper beneath mulch layers. Any items that cannot be used on site should be recycled.

Mimic nature

Nature does not follow straight lines or demand trimmed perfection. Permaculture mimics nature by grouping plants with similar soil and water needs together. Nature utilises every niche, so include plants, rocks and water features that provide habitat for animals.

Legume plants produce their own nitrogen and can be specifically planted to improve poor soil and prepare the ground for future crops. In nature, this process is known as succession planting.

Plant densely using productive tuberous-rooted plants, ground covers, understorey shrubs, small trees and a selection of taller tree species. This strategy, known as 'plant stacking', mimics the multiple layers within a forest. By adopting this approach and choosing productive plants it is possible to achieve a diverse yield.

Maximise biodiversity

Disaster-proof your garden through diverse planting. This way if a pest or disease occurs, only a limited number of susceptible species will fall victim. Maximising plant biodiversity also ensures a diverse range of insects, birds and reptiles will be attracted to your garden. You will be rewarded with the additional source of interest as well as providing them with a much needed habitat.

Chooks in the Garden

Many gardeners are wary about introducing chooks into the garden. Chooks have a bad reputation for scratching up the garden and eating your most precious plants. But, by your choosing the right techniques, chooks can be safely integrated and can bring some major benefits to the garden. They eat pests, produce manure and scratch out weeds.

CHOOK PENS

Housing your chooks is the first consideration and should be well thought out before purchasing or acquiring birds. 'Chook tractor' is the whimsical name for a portable cage that is moved around the garden, settling on one area at a time. The tractor has an open base that allows the chooks to scratch the soil beneath. The tractor can be easily moved from one place to another to take advantage of fresh scratching sites.

Fixed pens are the traditional method of housing. These work well if they're large enough. If not, it's best to let the chooks out each day – they'll find their own way back before nightfall. Make sure the pen is secure from dogs, cats, lizards and foxes, both on top and at ground level. This may entail digging netting in well below ground so that foxes and dogs can't dig their way in. Chook houses can be built up on stilts to raise them above the dangers of digging canines.

Letting chooks out can be risky for the garden. Chooks can easily dislodge soft plants such as annuals and perennials. And vegetable beds are irresistible. But if chooks are allowed onto a vegetable bed once a crop is finished, they'll do an excellent job of stirring the soil, destroying pests, and incorporating manure and old plant matter.

An established orchard is a great space for chooks to scratch and peck. At the same time, they'll inadvertently help with control of pests such as fruit fly and codling moth. The root systems of young fruit trees can be protected with a layer of stones that will make a surprisingly good mulch, keeping the roots cool and moist.

STARTING OUT

It's best to purchase point-of-lay pullets from a reputable supplier. If you start with younger chickens, some are sure to turn out to be roosters which, of course, won't lay eggs and can be so noisy they are banned in most local-council areas. Don't be too ambitious: start with a small number of hens and add to the flock as your poultry-keeping skills improve.

FEED

Feed with a proprietary mixed poultry food but supplement with vegie scraps from the kitchen. Chooks are very useful for getting rid of leftovers – they've even been known to get rid of pizza crusts. Try to keep their food away from rodents.

WATER

A supply of clean water is essential. Make sure it's changed regularly.

For more information, see *The Contented Chook* and *Happy Hens*, from ABC Books.

7
The Water-saving Garden

In this, the world's driest continent, we have come to realise that water is our most precious resource, one that should never be taken for granted. Over the last one hundred years Australians have developed very effective water storage facilities and, for many gardeners, especially those near the coast, this has meant that we have become accustomed to having ample supplies of water for gardens.

A gardening tradition that was largely imported from England has given many Australian gardeners ambitions to develop a lush, green garden that is full of plants with high water needs. As the Australian population has expanded it has become more and more evident that the number of water storage facilities cannot keep on increasing (there are many environmental considerations involved that prohibit the building of new dams and their support infrastructure), and home gardeners must learn to garden with less water. Many water authorities now charge by usage and this 'hip pocket' message has really helped to emphasise the importance of not wasting water on the garden.

Gardening with less water requires some thought and planning, and changes to old habits. Here are a few simple hints that will help you cut down your use of water, while protecting the substantial investment you have put into that valuable asset: your garden.

MAKING THE MOST OF YOUR WATER

Water in the morning or evening. This gives moisture time to penetrate so that it doesn't evaporate before it gets down into the soil.

Train your plants in good water habits. Less frequent, deep soakings will train the roots to grow down into the soil. Light sprinklings (especially with a hand-held hose) are therapeutic for the gardener, but create problems for plants. They encourage the roots to stay near the surface where they are more vulnerable to heating up and drying out.

Train yourself – and your kids – in good water habits. Don't leave garden taps dripping, don't use hose water to clean paths and driveways; you can do just as good a job with a broom and some muscle!

Water the roots of your plants, not the leaves. Don't let your precious H_2O blow away in the breeze. Use a soaker hose, a watering system, or direct the water into a plastic tube that carries the water straight down to the roots of the plants. (Hint: an empty soft drink bottle makes a great watering system for an individual plant. Fill with water, punch two small holes in the lid and upend the bottle beside a small plant. The water will gradually seep into the soil.)

Mulch around your plants to conserve moisture in the soil, making sure there is moisture in the soil before you apply mulch. Use old grass clippings, manure, compost, newspaper, rocks, rice hulls or whatever else you can get hold of. Don't allow mulch to touch the plant's trunk and don't use grass clippings that have been sprayed with a weedkiller. (See the section entitled 'Mulching' on page 110 in this chapter.)

Top five drought-tolerant shrubs

OLEANDER

Nerium oleander Reliable summer colour in shades of red, pink, salmon and white. Although these plants are renowned for their poisonous characteristics, their bitter taste is usually an effective deterrent to ingestion.

SILVER CASSIA

Senna artemisioides Native to dry parts of Australia, the bright silver foliage of silver cassia contrasts with its golden-yellow flowers.

GERALDTON WAX

Chamelaucium uncinatum A popular cut flower, Geraldton wax must have perfect drainage and may be short-lived in humid areas.

JAPONICA

Chaenomeles japonica Also known as flowering quince, this great survivor produces a dense mound of thorny branches that sport pretty spring blooms.

COASTAL ROSEMARY

Westringia fruticosa Rosemary-like leaves and small, lipped flowers over a long period. Good salt tolerance.

OLEANDER

TIPS TO USING LESS WATER

Group your plants according to their water needs. Put the plants that need the most water together in one part of the garden. If you have just one plant with high water requirements in a garden bed, it will mean that all the other plants in that bed will receive more water than they need.

Give your plants the best chance of surviving dry periods: don't be tempted to grow plants that prefer shade in full sun. A vulnerable shrub in a hot, dry position will need much more watering to keep it in good condition.

Fertilise your plants using liquid fertiliser. Dry fertilisers take water from the soil but soluble fertilisers like Thrive or Aquasol, which are applied in liquid form, will encourage plant growth without raising salt levels in the soil.

Control weeds in the garden. Weeds are great competitors and they will fight with your garden plants for every precious drop. Use a glyphosate-based herbicide, such as Zero which won't affect the soil. Make sure that the herbicide doesn't contact your garden plants.

Reduce lawn areas. Lawns can consume more water than many other parts of the garden. Instead of lawn, a water-saving garden could use paving, pebbles, or drought-tolerant ground covers such as grevilleas, myoporum, snake vine (*Hibbertia scandens*), dusky coral pea (*Kennedia rubicunda*) or succulents.

Train your lawn in good water habits, in the same way as you would train your other garden plants. Once the lawn is well established, give long soakings rather than short, light waterings. This will encourage a deeper, more hardy root system.

Grow grasses that need less water: couch, kikuyu, Queensland blue couch, carpet grass, buffalo and tall fescues. Tall fescue is the best choice in cool climates because it stands up well to winter cold. Its resistance to drought is dependent on an established root system, so try to plant this grass in autumn, to allow time for the roots to establish before summer.

During very dry periods let the lawn die off completely – it is easier to replace lawn than trees and shrubs when the rain eventually falls again. When mowing, leave the grass longer than normal. Longer grass means a deeper root system, and the long blades shade the soil, which also helps keeps the soil temperature down.

GROWING DROUGHT-TOLERANT PLANTS

There is a wide range of plants that are attractive, hardy and well suited to dry conditions. Many Australian natives have evolved to handle periods of water stress but there are also introduced species that make good choices for a water-saving garden. Look for plants with small leaves, hard leaf surfaces or hairy leaf coverings. Exotics such as Californian, Mediterranean and South African plants are often well adapted to a dry climate.

Succulents and cacti are also obvious choices as they have evolved to handle low rainfall periods by developing water-storing stems and leaves or, in the case of most cacti, no leaves at all (plants lose most water through their leaves).

When selecting plants, it is important to check with your local council or plant supplier for possible weed potential in your area.

Refer to the front flap of this book for a key to abbreviations.

NATIVE TREES

Flowering gum

(*Corymbia cultivars*) E, FS, H 5 m, W 3 m. Newer hybrids (such as 'Summer Red') are grafted onto hardy rootstocks and produce stunning flower clusters in pink, cream, orange and red.

Coast banksia

(*Banksia integrifolia*) E, FS or HS, H 3–5 m, W 2–3 m. Upright, bird-attracting cream flowers are followed by woody seed pods. Salt tolerant. Leathery, white-backed leaves.

Bottlebrush

(*Callistemon* 'Harkness') E, FS or HS, H 5 m, W 3 m. Also known as 'Gawler Hybrid', this bottlebrush is one of the most reliable for flower performance.

Once they are well established in the garden, many Australian natives, such as these toothbrush-flowered grevilleas, can handle periods of water stress.

The 'Giant Candles' cultivar of Banksia ericifolia *makes a spectacular display.*

Silky Oak

(*Grevillea robusta*) E, FS, H 12–15 m, W 6 m. The 'tree' grevillea has one-sided combs of golden-yellow flowers in early summer.

Snow in summer

(*Melaleuca linariifolia*) E, FS, H 10 m, W 5 m. This slow-growing paperbark has small, fine leaves and is crowned by fluffy white summer blooms.

Kurrajong

(*Brachychiton populneus*) E, FS, H 6–9 m, W 4–6 m. Small, bell-shaped, cream flowers in summer among the deep-green leaves. The foliage is used as emergency stock feed in times of extreme drought. Tolerates limestone soils.

White cedar

(*Melia azedarach*) D, FS, H 10–15 m, W 8–10 m. Fast-growing tree is native to Australia through to parts of Asia. Pretty lilac flowers. Leaves may be damaged by native caterpillars.

INTRODUCED TREES

Irish strawberry

(*Arbutus unedo*) E, FS or HS, H 5–6 m, W 3–4 m. Rounded head of dense foliage with small, white flowers followed by attractive balls of fruit.

Honey locust

(*Gleditsia triacanthos* 'Sunburst') D, FS, H 10–15 m, W 5–7 m. Large deciduous tree. Fine foliage emerges yellow, matures to green and colours yellow in autumn. Excellent shade tree.

Norfolk Island hibiscus

(*Lagunaria patersonia*) E, FS, H 9 m, W 4 m. Upright tree with grey, salt-resistant leaves and pretty pink bell flowers. Watch out for irritant hairs in seed pods.

Judas tree

(*Cercis siliquastrum*) D, FS, H 5–8 m, W 3–5 m. Very hardy deciduous tree. Rosy pink to purple flowers.

Osage orange

(*Maclura pomifera*) D, FS, H 10–15 m, W 7 m. Deciduous shade tree with curious, orange-sized inedible fruit on female trees.

SMALL NATIVE SHRUBS

Bottlebrush 'Little John'

(*Callistemon* 'Little John') E, FS or HS, H 1 m, W 50 cm. Grey-green leaves contrast well with deep-crimson flowers.

Eriostemon

(*Philotheca myoporoides*) E, HS or SS, H 1.2 m, W 90 cm. Native waxflower. Narrow, scented, mid-green leaves with pink-budded, white, winter to spring, starry flowers.

Woolly grevillea

(*Grevillea lanigera*) E, FS to HS, H 1 m, W 1.2 m. Red spider flowers sit amongst short, stubby leaves. Look for 'Mt Taboritha' form.

Native fuchsia

(*Correa reflexa*) E, HS to S, H 1 m, W 1 m. Many cultivars with pendulous, tube-shaped

HINT

One of the best methods to cut down water evaporation from the soil is to simply cover as much of the ground as possible with plants. This has the added benefit of cutting down the amount of mulch needed and of course, you will save money and time.

LORNA ROSE M.A.I.H.

HORTICULTURAL PHOTOGRAPHER

flowers. Good plants for dry shade under established trees.

Rice flower

(*Pimelea ferruginea*) E, FS to HS, H 1 m, W 1 m. Neatly shaped shrub studded with balls of deep-pink flowers in late winter and spring.

SMALL INTRODUCED SHRUBS

Lavender

(*Lavandula* spp.) E, FS, H 30 cm–1 m, W 50 cm. Old favourites. Numerous cultivars, all with perfumed blooms.

Mexican orange blossom

(*Choisya ternata*) E, FS, H 1.2 m, W 1 m. White perfumed flowers in spring. Glossy, three-part leaves.

Glossy abelia

(*Abelia x grandiflora*) E, FS or HS, H 2–3 m W 1–2m. Arching stems from base. Small, white bell flowers followed by long-lasting coloured calyces.

Dusty miller

(*Centaurea cineraria*) E, FS, H 1.2 m, W 1 m. Silvery leaves and small, purple-mauve flowers. Needs full sun and good drainage.

Mexican tree poppy

(*Romneya coulteri*) D, FS, H 1.5 m–2 m, W 3 m. Upright stems with large spring flowers. Grey-green leaves and white, yellow-centred blooms. Prefers sandy soils.

LARGE NATIVE SHRUBS

Banksia 'Giant Candles'

(*Banksia ericifolia*) E, FS to HS, H 3–4 m, W 2–3 m. Large, bird-attracting, upright winter flower cones.

Hop bush

(*Dodonaea viscosa* 'Purpurea') E, FS, H 3 m, W 1.5 m. Upright shrub with long, red-coloured leaves. Insignificant flowers are followed by showy seed pods.

Bottlebrush

(*Callistemon citrinus* and other species) E, FS or HS, H 2–6 m, W 2–5 m. Renowned for their brush-like cylindrical blooms in red, pink and white shades. Very adaptable.

Native hibiscus

(*Alyogyne huegelii*) E, FS, H 2.5 m, W 1.5 m. Upright growth, finely cut, slightly furry leaves. Beautiful purple/blue flowers.

Bracelet honey myrtle

(*Melaleuca armillaris*) E, FS, H 3–5 m, W 3–5 m. Very fine foliage, white fluffy flowers. Watch for leaf-eating grubs.

Native hibiscus is known for its vivid purple flower.

LARGE INTRODUCED SHRUBS

Laurustinus

(*Viburnum tinus*) E, FS to HS, H 3 m, W 1.5 m. Good hedge plant with clusters of white winter flowers. Can be affected by sap-sucking thrips (causing silvery foliage) in dry conditions.

Bay tree

(*Laurus nobilis*) E, FS to HS, H 5 m, W 2.5 m. Source of bay leaves that have culinary and medicinal value. Upright habit.

Chinese fringe flower

(*Loropetalum chinense*) E, HS to SS, H 1–2 m, W 1–2 m. Horizontal layers of growth. Finely cut pink or white spring flowers. Slow.

Indian hawthorn

(*Rhaphiolepis umbellata*) E, FS to HS, H 1.5–3 m, W 1–1.5 m. Tough leaves and fragile-looking pink or white flowers. Cut back after flowering to prevent seed dispersal problems. Slow.

Sacred bamboo

(*Nandina domestica*) E, FS to SS, H 2 m, W 1 m. Bamboo-like appearance. Upright growth, useful for narrow spaces. Small, white flowers, red berries.

LOW NATIVE PLANTS AND GROUND COVERS

Native sarsparilla

(*Hardenbergia violacea*) E, FS or HS, H 20 cm, W 2–3 m. Climber/ground cover with pea-shaped purple flowers in late winter and early spring. New cultivars.

Grevillea 'Royal Mantle'

(*Grevillea* 'Poorinda Royal Mantle') E, FS or HS, H 20 cm, W 2 m. Almost horizontal growth habit, can be grown to drape vertically. Toothbrush flowers. Other cultivars.

Paper daisies

(*Xerochrysum bracteatum*) E, FS or HS, H to 1 m, W 50 cm. Also called strawflowers. Valued for adding flower colour in the garden.

Sturt's desert pea

(*Swainsona formosa*) E, FS, H 80 cm, W 1.5 m. Short-lived, grey-leaved plant. Striking red and black flowers. Requires excellent drainage.

Red coral pea

(*Kennedia rubicunda*) E, HS, H 10 cm, W 1–2 m. Climbing plant will grow as a ground cover if not supported.

Paper daisies.

INTRODUCED LOW PLANTS AND GROUND COVERS

Snow in summer
(*Cerastium tomentosum*) E, FS, H 10 cm, W 50 cm. Grey-leaved spreading ground cover with small, white flowers.

Thyme
(*Thymus serpyllum*) E, FS, H 10 cm, W 25 cm. Edible herb with Mediterranean origins.

African daisy
(*Osteospermum* cultivars) E, FS, H 60 cm, W 1 m. Known as 'freeway daisy' in the US because of its hardiness. Tolerates a wide range of conditions. Flowers close in low light. Closely related to *Dimorphotheca* spp.

Indian blanket
(*Gaillardia x grandiflora*) E, FS, H 40 cm, W 30 cm. Useful ground cover produces sunset-coloured daisies for months on end.

Lamb's ears
(*Stachys byzantina*) E, FS to SS, H 20 cm, W 30 cm. Leaves are thickly coated with fine grey hairs which give protection from water loss. Upright spikes of mauve blooms.

NATIVE STRUCTURAL PLANTS

Spiny mat rush
(*Lomandra longifolia* and cultivars) E, FS to SS, H to 1 m, W to 1 m. Grass-like clumps of shiny leaves. Tolerates a wide range of conditions. Newer cultivars.

Blue flax lily
(*Dianella* spp. and cultivars) E, FS to S, H to 1 m, W 60 cm. Vertical foliage clump, many cultivars with green or grey-blue leaves. Small blue flowers followed by blue berries.

Kangaroo grass
(*Themeda australis*) E, FS to HS, H 50 cm, W 50 cm. Native grass with brownish tinge. Red-brown, spiky seed clusters.

Kangaroo paw
(*Anigozanthos* cultivars) E, FS, H to 1.2 m, W to 1 m. Clumping foliage and curious flowers. Newer cultivars have improved disease resistance.

Lepidozamia
(*Lepidozamia peroffskyana*) E, HS to S, H 2 m (very slow), W 2 m. Cycad with long, glossy leaves from central base. Gradually forms trunk. Best grown in light shade.

INTRODUCED STRUCTURAL PLANTS

Yucca
(*Yucca filamentosa*) E, FS, H 75 cm–8 m, W 50 cm–3 m. Strappy foliage, each leaf ending in a sharp point. Late-summer flower spike supports white, egg-shell-shaped blooms.

Sago palm
(*Cycas revoluta*) E, FS to HS, H 1–3 m, W 1–2 m. Traditional cycad, useful for a formal effect. Slow-growing rows of leaves develop from the centre clump.

Dragon tree
(*Dracaena draco*) E, FS to SS, H 10 m, W 4 m (very slow). Sword-shaped leaves. Eventually develops a branched, tree-like form.

Bird of Paradise
(*Strelitzia reginae*) E, FS, H 1.2 m, W 1.5 m. Hardy clump with narrow, paddle-shaped leaves. Bird-like flowers.

The striking Bird of Paradise flower.

Renga renga lily

(*Arthropodium cirrhatum*) E, FS to SS, H 50 cm, W 50 cm. Grey-leafed clumper from New Zealand with sprays of small, white flowers. Dislikes summer humidity.

THE WATER-SAVING VEGETABLE GARDEN

Vegetables must have adequate water to crop successfully so they can be some of the most difficult plants to grow in drought periods or when water's in short supply. There are, however, some strategies that can be followed to help vegetables survive dry times:

- Select the right vegetables (see below).
- Group vegetables with similar watering requirements together as you would with other plants, or even consider planting them among ornamental plants that need about the same amount of water.
- Position vegetables that need most water closest to the source of water.
- Build up the soil with plenty of organic matter. Build your compost bin in the vegetable patch so that garden waste can be added quickly and compost is easy to spread when it's ready.
- Mulch vegetables with organic mulch. As with mulching any other plants don't put the mulch hard up against the stem or base of the plant and make sure there is plenty of moisture in the bed before mulching.
- Create windbreaks around vegetable beds. This cuts down on water loss from the soil and from the leaves of plants.

WATER REQUIREMENTS FOR VEGETABLE CROPS	
Low water use	turnips, parsnips, beetroot, carrots, onions, shallots, swedes, Jerusalem artichokes, asparagus, rhubarb, silver beet
Moderate water use	beans, cauliflower, cabbages, tomatoes, radishes, zucchini, leeks
High water use	lettuce, celery, sweet corn, Chinese cabbages

- Keep vegetable beds free of weeds. Weeds will always compete with the vegetables for water.
- Start vegetable seedlings indoors or under shelter and transplant them outside when they're well established. Larger plants are less vulnerable to heat stress and are easier to mulch.
- Construct portable shade panels that can be moved to protect vegetable beds during extremely hot weather.
- Fertilise vegetables regularly as they have especially high nutrient requirements. During dry periods feed with an organic plant food (such as Dynamic Lifter pellets) or soluble or liquid foods. Avoid dry granular fertilisers because, unless there's sufficient soil moisture, they can cause burning.
- Install a drip irrigation system that waters at ground level.
- Apply water beneath mulch.
- Consider trench watering, a method that has been used for centuries. Build trenches around beds and flood them when water is available. Then allow the water to soak slowly into the soil.
- Half submerge one or more tin cans (with holes punched in the base to allow drainage) or plastic plant pots into the soil next to the plant. Fill with water and allow it to seep into the soil.
- Build raised beds from timber or bricks, or use open-bottomed metal or plastic drums. Line the sides with sheets of newspaper and fill them with compost-enriched soil. Some resourceful gardeners even use cat litter made from compressed recycled newspaper to add water-retaining bulk.

THE WATER-SAVING ORCHARD

Like vegetables, most fruit trees need ample water to crop well, but some have evolved in dry climates and, once established, will handle dry conditions with little adverse effect on their productivity.

Some of the best fruiting plants for dry climates are the loquat (*Eriobotrya obliqua*), mulberry (*Morus nigra*), pomegranate (*Punica granatum*), olive (*Olea europea*) and feijoa (*Acca sellowiana*).

Other fruiting plants, such as grapevines or citrus, have good drought resistance if they are well mulched. In order to crop successfully, they may need supplementary watering during flowering and fruit development periods.

WATER-SAVING CONTAINER PLANTINGS

Container plantings can work well in a water-saving garden. It's easy to attend to the special needs of containerised plants and they can be positioned in obvious spots where they are difficult to overlook. Don't forget, though, that containers dry out much more readily than garden soil – regular watering is essential.

These are general rules for success with low-water-use containers:

- Pots should be as large as possible and should be grouped together to keep them cooler.
- For maximum moisture retention select a potting mix that carries the premium Australian Standards Mark.
- If using a general purpose potting mix, add water-storage crystals to the mix before planting.
- If a plant is already growing in the pot, spoon pre-moistened crystals into vertical

holes in the mix and top off with more mix.
- Spray the insides of porous pots with Yates Pot-A-Seal or line the sides with a few sheets of newspaper before filling with mix.
- Apply Waterwise soil wetters to the top of the mix.
- Mulch with an organic layer of mulch (avoiding direct contact with the plant).

GREY WATER

Grey water is the term used for waste water from the bathroom, kitchen or laundry. (Water from the toilet, however, is known as black water.) Some local authorities may prohibit the harvesting of grey water so it's wise to check with your water supplier before you start.

Untreated grey water can be applied to the root area of plants if care is taken to use suitable low-sodium and low-phosphorus detergents and to make sure that kitchen water does not contain oils, fats or visible solids. The laundry and bathroom (not the toilet) are the best sources of grey water but any water that is likely to contain faecal matter (e.g. water that has been used to wash babies' nappies) should be avoided. If applying grey water through an irrigation system, use underground drippers. Mini-sprinklers should

These home-made mini-hothouses help to prevent water loss in the vegetable garden.

HINT

If you are using grey water from your washing machine you should use a washing powder that is low in sodium (salt) and phosphorus and that is pH neutral. Liquid detergents are best in this regard. It is a good idea to use fresh water on the garden every now and then to help prevent a build-up of salts and other nutrients that may be present in the grey water.

HELEN MOODY

HORTIMEDIA – FREELANCE WRITER

AND PR CONSULTANT

be avoided because they may increase the risk of contaminants spreading.

Some adjustments will have to be made to your existing waste-water disposal system in order to harvest grey water. Grey water diverters and filtering systems are available. Refer to a plumber, irrigation specialist or water authority for advice. Most elaborate grey water systems will include a clearly marked tank that regulates the water flow into the garden. This is not intended as a storage tank and should be emptied as soon as possible.

Grey water can have some potential health risks so should always be used with care. Follow these precautions:

- If using untreated grey water from the bathroom or laundry it's best to only use rinse water.
- Don't use grey water on edible plants.
- Try to spread the application of grey water around different parts of the garden.
- Allow grey water to cool before applying it to the garden.
- Keep children and pets away from grey water.
- Apply grey water at ground level.
- Allow grey water to percolate through mulch to remove any solid matter.
- If applying grey water through a watering system, make sure the system is below surface level.

- Don't store grey water in tanks or other containers.
- Don't allow grey water to run off your property.

WATER HARVESTING

Water harvesting is logical, can suit any garden, is economical in the long run, is sustainable and will greatly benefit your garden.

Harvest water by catching, holding and using any rainwater that falls on your block. Apart from reducing your water bill, you'll find a good soaking rain, where all water is captured and used, also helps to flush salts out of the topsoil and is like a tonic to plants.

Sumps and trenches can also be created in the garden to divert water to places of high usage (e.g. citrus trees). These sumps and trenches can be backfilled with rocks, rubble or sand to disguise, but still allow for, many hundreds or thousands of litres to be stored. Water diverted to a dry waterhole will collect there after moderate rain and slowly permeate the soil over several days. By incorporating hollows and natural creek beds into the landscape design, water harvesting methods can become integral to the overall garden design without becoming obvious.

RAINWATER TANKS

After being prohibited for many years water tanks are now not only permitted, but also encouraged, by many authorities, particularly for supplementing garden water supply. Ensuring that tank water is clean and free of bacterial impurities has always been a major concern, but if tank water is reserved for use on the garden, water purity is less of an issue.

What size tank?

Sydney Water recommends a minimum tank size of 2000 litres for a small garden and up to 5000 litres for a larger garden. If space is limited there are options such as bladder tanks that fit horizontally under the house, or 'water walls' that fit vertically outside the house.

Types of water tanks

Polyethylene

These are deservedly popular because they can be moulded to shape, are light, don't corrode and are UV-stabilised. The water wall is a system of slim poly-tanks that can fit into very narrow spaces.

Metal
Galvanised tanks are the old-style 'corrugated iron' tanks. These are preferred by traditionalists but larger sizes take up a lot of space. Colorbond (polymer-coated steel) will last longer without rusting.

Concrete
Concrete tanks are expensive and heavy, but very long lasting.

Fibreglass
Fibreglass tanks are lightweight and resistant to corrosion. Make sure that they are light-proof.

Bladder or flexible sac
The water sac can go into the unused space under a floor. Standard sizes are available or sacs can be custom-built to fit a required space.

Planning for a water tank
Start by contacting local council and water authorities to find out about regulations. These can cover matters such as potential effect on neighbours, whether a licensed plumber is required for installation, and the structural soundness of any tank stand. By contacting appropriate authorities you will also find out about any rebates that are available.

HINT
Water tanks come in many shapes and sizes; there are even designer-conscious tanks in bright colours and underground storage tanks. But whichever you choose, go for the largest size you can afford or accommodate. In dry times you will be glad you chose a bigger tank.

HELEN MOODY

HORTIMEDIA – FREELANCE WRITER
AND PR CONSULTANT

It's simplest to keep tank water quite separate from mains water. This avoids any regulatory issues and cuts down on installation costs.

Check to see where you'll fit a water tank. The roof will usually be the most important source of water, so be sure that roof drainage has access to the tank and that the roofing material won't contaminate the water. Remember that unless a tank is on a stand, it's likely that a pump will be required to extract the water.

WATER-SAVING PRODUCTS

Water-storing crystals
There are many new products available to the home gardener that will help reduce water use in the garden. Water-storing polymer crystals are polymer 'sugars' that can hold hundreds of times their weight in water. Either mix the dry crystals into the soil before planting or, preferably, leave them to sit in water for a few hours before use. During this time they will swell up and change from their crystalline form into a soft gel. The gel provides a reserve of moisture for the plants' roots to draw on during dry periods.

Anti-transpirants
DroughtShield is another polymer product. DroughtShield is sprayed over the plant surfaces. This thin film of polymer provides a flexible outer coating that allows the plant to function normally, but protects it from sunburn and reduces water loss by as much as 50 per cent. Use DroughtShield in situations where you are growing plants that might be slightly out of their climatic range, especially plants that would prefer a cooler climate.

When transplanting, spray a film of DroughtShield over the plant before moving it from its original position. Even if the plant loses some roots during the move, the layer of DroughtShield will help it to survive until the root system has had a chance to regrow.

Soil wetters
Soil wetters break the surface tension of the soil and allow the water to penetrate deeply. If soil or potting mix has dried out, or become compacted – as often happens with a frequently used lawn – it can actually repel

A combination of good mulching and careful plant selection makes a successful water-saving garden. Here we see border plantings of lamb's ear Stachys byzantina.

water and shed it from the surface. Treatment with a soil wetter can often remedy this situation.

Above all, you should always keep in mind that mulching can reduce the amount of water you use on your garden by 50 per cent and, as it also provides many other benefits to your garden, it is one of the best measures to employ.

MULCHING

It is important, especially in Australia, to recognise the value of mulching materials as they can protect soils from the harsh sun, add organic matter to depleted soils, preserve moisture, reduce the need for irrigation, improve crop production, increase soil microbial activity, alleviate the effects of soil pollution, correct past bad farming practices, give plants humus, aid weed control, help in recycling waste material and build good soil structure. Mulch can be used to begin an easy, work-free garden area, control weeds in your garden, or help you build a no-dig vegetable garden (see pages 74–75).

Materials used for mulching include the following:

Sawdust, wood shavings and wood pulp

Before using as a mulch these common components of potting mixes are best composted for two to eight weeks, preferably with animal manure. If fresh material is used without adding some nitrogen in the form of fertiliser or animal manure, you may see yellow leaves on plants, which is a sign of nitrogen deficiency. Fresh wood or bark chips or material from council mulchers will usually be mixed with some moist, green plant material containing nitrogen. This mulch will need to be composted before use.

Bark chips and pine bark

Some eucalypt bark, for example redgum and blackbutt, and pine bark chips contain resins which must be leached from the bark before it is used. Two weeks of leaching, composting or constant wetting with water will get rid of these plant-retardant resins. These make excellent, long-lasting mulches.

Gravel, stones, quartz and scoria

These are often used for special landscape effects, for colour and form. It is not advisable for those gardeners who want to dig the soil in garden beds, as very often stones 'stray' from these areas and can ruin mower blades or mechanical equipment. Gravel is often used for driveways, small garden areas, or in pots.

Plastic sheeting

Used extensively in landscaping during the 1950–70s period as the answer to all weed problems, plastic sheeting is no longer recommended since plastic builds up warmth, encouraging surface root growth, and thus plants are susceptible to being blown out of the ground by strong winds. Moisture builds up under the plastic, and little if any oxygen is allowed to permeate into the soil. If you use plastic sheeting it should be perforated to allow soil aeration, but it is much better to buy specially manufactured 'weedmats' that are made from woven synthetic material.

HINT

Before planting tubestock, soak the plants and a bucket of rainsaver crystals in a seaweed solution. Once you have dug your holes, take out the plants and place them in the hole with a handful of the jelly-like seaweed-soaked crystals and plant as usual. Mulch and water the plants with seaweed solution only twice more within a month. I haven't lost one this year since doing this.

TIM JACKSON
FREELANCE GARDEN WRITER

Weedmat

Specially formulated woven mesh is used for weed control and to allow water to penetrate to plant roots. The open mesh also allows oxygen to permeate into the soil. It is sold by the metre in varying widths. It can be useful for smothering persistent weeds such as oxalis.

Pasture hay

This is wonderful material, especially if obtained from an old, disused haystack. However, new hay can be the source of grass seeds and weed seed, and should be composted before use, or covered with other mulching material to suppress weed seedling growth. It is readily obtained in small bales, in very large round bales (some biodynamically grown without using chemicals), or loose from disused or old haystacks.

Crop straw

This is ideal mulch. Usually with no weed seeds, it is high in carbon and only needs nitrogen added to it to help decomposition. Crop straw is often used to protect strawberries and vegetables from soil-borne diseases such as botrytis, thus preventing fruit rots developing. It is usually available either in small bales or loose.

Top five drought-tolerant ground covers and perennials

BABY SUN ROSE

Aptenia cordifolia Succulent ground cover with low (to 5 cm), spreading stems and heart-shaped leaves. Small, pink or red daisy-like summer flowers.

SPINY MAT RUSH

Lomandra spp. With its clumps of grass-like foliage, lomandra's tough constitution has made it a favourite roadside planting.

PROSTRATE ROSEMARY

Rosmarinus officinalis 'Prostrate' This toughie has the bonus of flavoursome leaves that can be harvested for culinary uses.

SWAN RIVER DAISY

Brachyscome spp. There are annual and perennial species of this hardy genus. Plant breeders are expanding the availability of flower colours beyond the common mauve-blue.

CREEPING BOOBIALLA

Myoporum parvifolium Prostrate spreader with semi-succulent leaves and small, white summer flowers.

SPINY MAT RUSH

A thick layer of crop straw mulch will retain soil moisture and reduce weed competition for this citrus tree.

Lucerne hay

Renowned as a fantastic mulch, it has its own carbon/nitrogen composition. It is very nutritious, composts well, and is used for no-dig gardens. An excellent activator for compost, it will compost quickly with the addition of compost accelerator to encourage microbial activity. It is usually available in small bales or chopped up in bags and is relatively expensive. Compressed cubes of lucerne hay are also available.

Pea straw

This soft material breaks down quickly, and is an ideal mulch, though it will contain some pea seeds that may self-germinate. These are easily weeded out, or plants can be left to grow to provide nitrogen to the soil. Adding activators such as milk may help decomposition. It is available in small-bale form.

Pelletised mulch

Compressed pellets of finely chopped lucerne hay, wheat straw and pea straw are placed in a single layer onto garden beds and, once watered, swell up to many times their original size. This is an excellent, organically rich mulch that maintains moisture levels in the soil and, as it breaks down, improves and enriches the soil.

HINT

Be waterwise. Keep an empty, unrinsed 2-litre plastic milk bottle with a handle on the kitchen sink. Run tap water into it as you wait for the temperature you need. Strain water from cooked vegetables, pasta or rice into the bottle. Then use the liquid to water your outdoor potted plants.

SUSAN PARSONS
KITCHEN GARDEN WRITER

Eucalyptus leaves

Eucalyptus leaves make a very good mulch which is slow to decompose. The leaves give a natural look to those areas planted with Australian native plants, and will decompose faster if shredded with a mulching machine before application. Because whole leaves 'fit' into each other, only thin layers are needed for good weed control. Eucalyptus leaves are sometimes available in large wrapped bales.

Peat moss

Large-scale use of peat is environmentally unsound because of the finite nature of peat resources. Where possible use coco-fibre peat. Peat moss from sphagnum peat bogs is expensive but can be an ideal mulch. Usually very acid, it can be used around acid-loving plants. It is used also to correct the pH of highly alkaline soils.

Grass clippings

Fresh grass has a high nitrogen and moisture content and will compost well if high carbonaceous materials such as straw are mixed with it. It is ideal for mulch if allowed to dry out in the sun before applying to soil or around plants.

Compost

Any well-prepared, nutrient-rich compost is excellent to use in the garden. It provides humus and food for plants, will not burn plant roots and is an ideal material to help build up the micro-organisms in the soil.

Mushroom compost

A very good material, mushroom compost is excellent for plant growth, but check pH as some samples have high pH or high salt content, which will retard plant growth. Always obtain mushroom compost from a reliable source.

Recycled waste

Many municipal councils are concerned about waste disposal and pollution of the environment by waste products. Waste authorities are now recycling some of this resource, partly by composting and mulching organic material and then selling this back to the general public or direct to farmers.

Sewage waste

Sewage is now also being recycled in many cities and towns to prevent pollution of waterways, ground water and the ocean. After composting, the sewage material is recycled as compost and fertiliser, incorporated into soil mixes or sold to farmers to help rejuvenate soils. One inherent problem with many forms of sewage waste is the heavy metal components, but this problem may be solved in future years.

Worm casts

The best material available of all the mulching products, worm casts are available from worm farmers. Casts are reasonably high in plant food value, cannot burn plant roots, can be spread to any depth desired, and build up biological activity in your soil. Compost produced in home worm farms also makes a rich soil-improving mulch for small areas.

Hessian

Plants are planted through the hessian, or it can be used as a base for sowing grass seed. Hessian is an ideal material for this, as the fibres will rot away within a few months.

Tan bark

A by-product of the tanning industry, the bark is from acacia (wattle tree) species. Expensive, but sometimes sought for its landscape effect (it has a very dark colour), it is an acidic material with some residual resins that impede weed growth.

Seaweed

Seaweed is an ideal mulch, but it will take a long time to decompose. Seaweed gathered from the shoreline should be washed,

Your own home-made compost makes one of the best mulches. Not only does it hold moisture, it also improves and enriches the soil.

especially if this mulch is used very frequently in the garden. Various forms are available, such as sea grass and kelp. Check with your local council or government department representative for permission to collect from the shore. A 'gel' can be made by placing cut and dried pieces of kelp in a drum with water. Add some fertiliser, manure, or urine. This forms a gel that can be spread around plants or diluted with water and used as liquid fertiliser. Seaweed is nutritious and various species have been found to contain nearly all the elements known. Seaweed provides nutrients and plant growth substances. Many organic growers use seaweed foliar or granular applications to provide micronutrients and a balanced food supply. Seaweed extracts are also thought to be beneficial in reducing the incidence of pests and diseases.

Sugar cane waste

This by-product from sugar cane production is readily available. Sugar cane waste is a very good, cheap material which has some nutritional value for plants.

Paper

Shredded paper or sheets of paper can be used as mulch. This material is ideal for

Fallen leaves are nature's mulch. Don't waste them: spread them directly onto garden beds or add them to compost.

Leaflitter provides a natural mulch that suits informal gardens.

preventing weed growth around newly planted trees, to use under other mulch material (usually 1–5 cm thick), or as the base for a no-dig garden. Note that newsprint does contain very small amounts of heavy metals. Paper has a high carbon content and will need a high nitrogenous material, such as grass clippings or animal manure, to help break it down.

Rice hulls

Rice hulls, from dehusked rice, are available very cheaply from rice mills. Taking a long time to break down, rice hulls make a long lasting mulch and can sometimes be used as an ingredient in potting mixes. Straw or some heavy mulch material should be layered over rice hulls in areas that experience high winds.

Animal manures

All manures make great mulches and provide plants with food. Fresh manures must be used cautiously as they can burn plant roots. Used fresh, manures are spread to a thickness of 1–2 cm only, but if the manure is mixed with straw, wood shavings, sawdust or other material it can be spread to twice this depth. If the manure has been composted for one or two months or more, or has been weathered for many months, then it can be spread to a depth of 5 cm. Some manures, such as sheep manure, may contain lots of weed seeds; composting sheep manure before use will kill these seeds.

HINT

Different mulches should be put on at various thicknesses to ensure water gets through to the soil. Coarse mulches can be put on 6 cm thick, medium mulches 4 cm thick, while fine mulches should only be put on 2 cm thick.

KEVIN WALSH

AUTHOR – WATERWISE GARDENING

Carpet underlay

A material recommended by permaculturists to prevent weed growth, carpet works well with blackberries. A readily available mulch source in urban areas, it can be laid and then holes or slits cut into the material so that plants can be planted through it. Use carpet made from natural materials.

Natural mulch

Trees such as peppercorns often have accumulated leaf mulch under them that can be utilised as a garden mulch. Deciduous trees also shed copious amounts of leaf litter that can be collected to make a natural-looking and effective mulch. Don't collect from reserves or parks.

Dried pine needles

Though slightly acidic, pine needles can be used as a mulch. Applied around strawberry plants to improve strawberry fruit flavour, the needles are long-lasting. They will, however, break down quickly if chopped up and composted with manure and a little lime.

Kitchen waste

Many products found in the kitchen and home can be used as mulch, for example tea leaves, coffee grounds, hair clippings, rags (shredded), egg shells, shells from nuts, stone fruit seeds (crushed) and old telephone books (shredded).

Industry by-products

Many products such as bagasse (a by-product of the sugar-making process), spent hops, feathermeal, or vegetable trash from greengrocers or market places can make useful mulch. Keep in mind that material normally sent to the rubbish tip can be recycled, even if it may need composting before using as a mulch.

Overlapped sheets of newspaper are excellent for suppressing weeds. Once in place, cover them with an attractive mulch layer.

8
Pests, Diseases and Weeds

You need not be an expert on pests, diseases and weeds to have a clean, healthy garden which will grow top-quality flowers, fruit and vegetables. Most garden problems are easily controlled if detected in the early stages. The quick reference chart at the end of this chapter (see pages 134–137) tells you what pests and diseases attack your plants, how to identify them or their symptoms and the most effective, low-toxic control.

It is important to know the normal, healthy appearance of plants so that problems caused by pests or diseases can be detected quickly. Early recognition of a problem gives you a good start in overcoming it. But it is not always a pest or disease which makes a plant unhealthy.

Inadequate watering may be the cause. If you allow soil to dry out to a depth of 5–10 cm below the surface, subsequent light watering, however frequent, will not let the water soak in to reach plant roots. The best way to overcome this is to water thoroughly until the soil is evenly moist throughout its depth. Over-watering and bad drainage can also be the cause of unhealthy plants. Overly wet conditions can impair root efficiency by preventing air (for respiration) from reaching them.

Low levels of nutrients or lack of fertiliser, and in some cases a deficiency of trace elements, may be the cause of poor growth. But soil analysis is complicated and does not always give a cut-and-dried answer to the problem of unhealthy plants. The simplest strategy is to use a mixed fertiliser which contains the major nutrients (nitrogen, phosphorus and potassium) plus animal manure, if available, or compost. (See Chapters 4 and 5.) However, never use fertilisers in excess of the quantities recommended.

CHEMICALS FOR THE HOME GARDEN

There is a wide range of chemicals available for ridding the garden of pests and diseases. Some of these are specific in their action while others are broad-spectrum chemicals and will control more than one pest or disease. Multi-purpose sprays are available, which contain one or more insecticides to control pests, combined with one or more fungicides to control diseases. These sprays can be useful, especially when there is some doubt as to the cause of the problem.

Whatever garden chemicals are used, it is important to stress that they should be used with care. Fortunately, modern garden chemicals are far less toxic or persistent than their predecessors. Most garden chemicals can be used with safety if directions are followed and simple precautions are taken:

Read directions carefully before using and use only for the purpose stated on the label.

Avoid contact of spray or dust with skin.

Avoid breathing fumes from sprays or dusts.

Avoid spraying or dusting on windy days. A calm day is best for spraying.

Avoid eating or smoking when spraying or dusting.

Rinse spray equipment after use and wash face and hands with soap and water.

Store sprays and dusts out of reach of children or in a locked cupboard.

Do not harvest vegetable and fruit crops earlier than the withholding period (the time from when control is applied until crop can be picked).

DUSTS OR SPRAYS?

Whether you use dusts or sprays, it is important to apply them so that all parts of the plant are covered. Dusts do not need mixing and are simple to apply. But dusts can be difficult to apply to larger plants and are easily washed off by rain or overhead watering.

Generally, spraying gives a better and more even coverage of the plant surfaces, and therefore more effective control. Many home gardeners find the pressure sprayers, such as the Yates Garden Sprayer, the most convenient. For small balcony gardens, pot plants and glass or shadehouses a plastic atomiser will prove adequate.

HINT

Bug juice sprays can be most effective against garden pests. Collect a handful of the target pests, place in a container, crush or pulp them into a mush and add 500 ml of warm water and some soap or white oil to help it stick. Allow to cool, strain and paint onto the affected area or dilute further and spray over the entire plant.

GEOFF MIERS

GEOFF MIERS GARDEN SOLUTIONS
ALICE SPRINGS, NORTHERN TERRITORY

For correct strength of sprays, always follow the manufacturer's directions exactly. Do not be tempted to put in a little extra for good measure – it is unnecessary and can even be harmful. Most garden chemicals can be used in the same container, providing the container, hose and nozzle are washed out thoroughly immediately after use. Extra care must be taken to wash weedkillers from any containers or spray equipment used.

PESTS

Most garden pests are members of the insect world – beetles, bugs, caterpillars, aphids or thrips – but also include tiny sap-sucking mites.

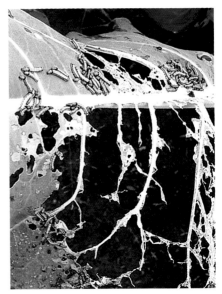

Many leaf-eating caterpillars can be controlled with Dipel, a bio-insecticide.

Snails and slugs are not insects but probably do as much damage as other pests.

Pests are controlled by insecticides, miticides and snail baits. Before we describe these pests in detail we will divide them into two broad groups: chewing and sap-sucking pests.

Chewing pests actually eat plant tissues – that is, leaves, stems, buds, flowers or fruits. Beetles, caterpillars, codling moth, cutworms, grasshoppers and fruit fly (grubs or larvae) are included in this group. They are controlled by contact insecticides or stomach poisons. Snails and slugs are usually included in this group too because they can be controlled by stomach baits in the same way as chewing insects.

Sap-sucking insects are those which suck sap from young shoots, flower buds, leaves and stems. They do not actually eat plant tissue so a contact or systemic insecticide (absorbed by plants into the sap stream) is needed to control them. The sap-suckers include aphids, thrips, leaf hoppers, mites and several kinds of bugs and scale insects.

Most sap-suckers feed by inserting their sharp mouthparts (or beaks) into plant tissue and extracting the sap. This kind of feeding causes collapse of plant cells, destruction of

Not all leaf-eating insects are caterpillars. In this case, the culprit is a beetle.

Beetles, weevils, grasshoppers and crickets

Beetles and other insects which chew leaves and stems may not need to be controlled. However, black beetles are a serious pest in lawns and also attack other plants. The adult beetles do some damage but most damage is caused by the larvae in mid-summer to early autumn. Yates Complete Lawn Insect Control will take care of them in their curl grub or adult beetle stage. The best time for treatment is mid-spring to mid-summer, which is peak egg hatch season, but if beetles are seen at other times of the year treat the lawn immediately. Lawn grubs in spring and summer, and army worm in autumn, may cause serious damage to turf grasses. The grass dies in patches for no apparent reason and the grubs occasionally come to the surface. Close inspection of the soil is advisable to confirm the presence of these pests. Again, Yates Complete Lawn Insect Control is a recommended treatment.

tissues and wilting. Many virus diseases of plants are transmitted from one plant to another by sap-sucking insects.

Chewing insects

Caterpillars

There are many types of caterpillars which are usually the larval (caterpillar or grub) stage of moths such as cabbage moth, potato moth, cabbage white butterfly or tomato moth. The moths lay their eggs on the underside of leaves. The larvae of caterpillars hatch from the eggs and then feed on the leaves or fruit. Caterpillars can be controlled by Yates Mavrik Chewing and Sucking Insect Killer, Pyrethrum, Success Ultra or Baythroid. Yates Nature's Way Caterpillar Killer contains Dipel, a bio-insecticide with low human toxicity which controls leaf-eating caterpillars in the moth and butterfly family.

Cutworms

Another kind of caterpillar is the cutworm, which is brown or green (or sometimes striped) and mostly feeds at night. These caterpillars cut through the stems of seedlings or transplants. Spray plants with Yates Baythroid Lawn Grub & Garden Insecticide in the late afternoon or early evening.

HINT

Erect a fine mesh net over your brassica vegetables to prevent cabbage white butterflies laying eggs on your plants. Prevention is always better than trying to control caterpillar pests after they have started chewing holes in your plants.

DENIS CRAWFORD

AUTHOR, *GARDEN PESTS, DISEASES AND GOOD BUGS*

Codling moth

Codling moth may cause serious damage in apples, pears and quinces. The moths lay their eggs on leaves and the developing fruit as flowering finishes. When the eggs hatch, the caterpillars burrow into the fruit. Apply Success Ultra from early flowering onwards and destroy any affected fruit. Trap migrating caterpillars in corrugated cardboard bands wrapped around the tree trunk.

Codling moth damage in an apple.

Pittosporum leafminer damage.

Fruit fly

Fruit fly attacks most kinds of summer fruit, including peaches, plums, nectarines, apples, pears and citrus. It is also a serious pest of tomato, capsicum and eggplant, especially in coastal and some inland areas. The wasp-like fly lays eggs in the developing fruit, which is most susceptible to attack a few weeks before harvesting.

The eggs hatch quickly and the larvae (maggots) burrow through the fruit and make it inedible. Yates Nature's Way Fruit Fly Control is a lure that attracts and kills the fly before she lays her eggs in the fruit. There is no need to apply the product directly on fruit. It can instead be sprayed on the lower trunk or foliage. Hormone-based lures, for example, Dak-pots, which attract male fruit flies, are useful indicators of fruit fly activity. Garden hygiene is also important in controlling fruit fly. All infected fruit should be gathered and destroyed by burning or boiling. These measures are compulsory in most states. In South Australia, householders suspecting the presence of fruit fly should ring the Fruit Fly Hotline 1300 666 010 so that Biosecurity SA

can take the necessary steps to identify the pest and eradicate it.

Bean fly

Bean fly may be a serious pest of French beans (both dwarf and climbing) in warm, subtropical and tropical areas. The small, adult fly lays eggs on the leaves and the larvae or maggots tunnel into the young stems which swell and break. Destroy damaged leaves at first sign. Don't plant beans in the same bed every year.

Leafminers

Leafminers are larvae that tunnel through the leaves leaving scribble-like white markings, especially in cinerarias, nasturtiums, marguerites, spinach and silver beet. Remove and put affected leaves in the bin. Citrus leafminer is a problem in some parts of Australia. It can be effectively controlled by using Yates White Oil or PestOil.

Borers

Borers attack fruit trees and a number of ornamental trees and shrubs. The grubs tunnel into the trunk or branches, leaving a mass of sawdust or gum oozing from the hole. Probe the hole with a piece of wire to destroy the grub. Improve the plant's growing conditions by fertilising, mulching and watering.

Snails and slugs

Blitzem or Baysol are very effective against snails and slugs. Scatter the baits (as directed on the package) where seeds have been sown or seedlings transplanted. These pests are more active in cool, wet weather, so it is wise to spread baits in these conditions, especially under shrubs and hedges where snails and slugs shelter and breed.

Some plants, in particular begonias, nasturtiums, lilies, and other strap-leaved plants, are favourite breeding spots. Most snail baits contain a pet deterrent for added safety to domestic pets but it is important to read and follow the directions carefully.

Sap-sucking insects

Aphids

Aphids are small, soft-bodied insects which usually cluster on young shoots and flower buds or underneath leaves. There are many different species which vary in colour – yellow, bronze, green, brown, pink, grey and black. Aphids attack fruit trees (including citrus trees), roses, camellias, chrysanthemums and other ornamentals, a wide range of vegetables, flowering annuals, bulbs and even weeds. Woolly aphids give a white, fleecy appearance on the branches of apples, pears, crab apples and hawthorns and other trees. Aphids also transmit virus diseases such as broad bean wilt (on broad beans and sweet peas), potato mosaic and

HINT

To control codling moth in fruit trees, hang a couple of open-necked jars half filled with sweet sherry in your apple and pear trees around late September. This will attract the moths and they will die happily in the sherry before laying any eggs near your fruit. Change the sherry on a regular basis for best results.

MORRIS HOLMES
HORTICULTURAL CONSULTANT
AND GARDEN DESIGNER

A cross-section of a branch shows how borer has attacked a citrus tree.

Although it looks like a slug, pear and cherry slug is actually a leaf-eating grub.

mosaic virus of stocks. Some weeds are alternative hosts for virus disease. Because aphids are small and often collect on the underside of foliage, they are frequently undetected. Small colonies multiply rapidly and can develop into a heavy infestation in a matter of days. Systemic sprays are most effective in controlling aphids. Confidor is excellent for shrubs, flowers and ornamentals because it persists in the sap for several weeks. For vegetables, Baythroid, Natrasoap, Bug Gun or Confidor are recommended. Always observe the withholding period (time from spray to harvest).

Pyrethrum sprays (for example Bug Gun) and Derris Dust also provide some control but have short residual effect and plants can be reinfested in a few days.

Leaf hoppers

Leaf hoppers are small, quick-flying insects, sometimes called jassids. They are usually green or brown and their feeding causes mottling of the leaves. They attack many

HINT

Build-up of aphid populations can be reduced by simply spraying the plant with a short, sharp jet of water. For small or delicate plants place your hand behind that part of the plant to be sprayed as this will limit potential damage to the plant.

GEOFF MIERS

GEOFF MIERS GARDEN SOLUTIONS

ALICE SPRINGS, NORTHERN TERRITORY

plants and can also transmit virus diseases. Control as for aphids.

Whiteflies

These small, white-winged, sap-sucking flies have become very prevalent in recent years. They usually attack annuals and vegetables,

Aphids are sap-sucking insects that can rapidly build up numbers when conditions are favourable.

Although thrips are tiny insects, they can seriously disfigure flowers like roses. They are especially attracted to light-coloured blooms.

Bronze orange bugs grow larger and darker in colour as they progress through several nymphal stages.

especially tomato, bean and vine crops. Control as for aphids.

Thrips

Thrips are small insects about 1 mm long and just visible to the naked eye. They vary in colour from white through yellow and brown to black. Thrips attack the flowers, fruit and foliage of vegetable crops and ornamental plants. Roses, fruit trees, azaleas, gladioli, tomatoes, onions and beans are regular victims of thrip invasion. They also feed on a wide range of weeds. During hot weather, weeds dry up and the insects migrate to more attractive plants. Certain kinds of thrips transmit spotted wilt virus which may seriously affect tomato, lettuce and dahlias in summer. Thrips are often most difficult to control because the eggs are laid inside the plant tissue and the pupae and adults often feed on unopened flower buds. This prevents sprays and dusts from reaching the insects. Regular spraying with Confidor or Natrasoap will control them. A pyrethrum spray such as Bug Gun is recommended for small pot plants and indoor plants.

Bugs

These large insects are often called shield bugs because of their shape and tough exterior. They can be serious pests in summer.

The green vegetable bug is bright green in colour and about 1 cm long in adulthood, but more rounded and black and white or black and red in younger stages. It attacks beans, tomatoes, potatoes, sweet corn, vine crops, grapes, sunflowers, and other ornamentals.

The bronze orange bug, which is actually orange-brown or black when mature, and twice as large, attacks citrus trees, causing wilting of the young shoots and flower stalks.

The Rutherglen bug is a smaller, grey-brown insect which damages a wide range of plants and may reach plague proportions in hot, dry summers.

Lace bugs are small, soft-bodied insects with rather large, lacy wings. They cling to the underside of leaves and their feeding causes mottling and bronzing. They are serious pests of azaleas. Control with Confidor.

Harlequin bug is a large, reddish-black bug which attacks a wide variety of plants, including melons, pumpkins, tomatoes, rhubarb and fruit trees such as apples, figs and oranges. It also attacks ornamentals such as dahlias and violets.

Bugs can be controlled by using any of several insecticides but are always more effectively treated in the early stages. Confidor is an effective systemic spray.

Mealybugs

Mealybugs are small insects covered with a white mealy coating; some have white hairs attached to their bodies. Heavy infestations can occur on citrus trees, daphne and other ornamental plants. Orchids and ferns, especially in shadehouses, can become infested too. They may also attack bulbs in storage and the roots of some plants such as polyanthus, liliums and callas. Confidor will control mealybugs, but use it in a ready-to-use formulation on soft plants in a shadehouse. This also applies to indoor pot plants.

Mites

The two-spotted mite (red spider) attacks a wide range of fruit trees (apples, pears, peaches), vegetables (tomato, beans, vine crops) and ornamentals (azalea, roses, marigolds). Symptoms of two-spotted mite are bronzing or dull-grey mottling of the leaves. In heavy infestations leaves may drop. The tiny pinkish-red mites cluster on the underside of the leaves, often producing a mass of fine webbing. The two-spotted mite has become problematic because the use of insecticides has decreased the number of natural insect enemies, such as ladybirds. Tomato mite and red-legged earth mite (a winter pest of peas and other vegetables) are other pests of this group. They can be controlled by Natrasoap, a low-toxic insecticide, or by the insecticide Mavrik. Sulfur and lime sulfur, both of which are often used to control fungus diseases, will also give some protection against mites.

Scale insects

The most common scale insect is white wax scale. This insect is easily recognised by the presence of large patches of waxy materials along the stems and shoots of citrus trees, gardenias, pittosporum and other ornamental shrubs. The wax covers the insects which are feeding on the sap. Scrub off plants or spray with Yates White Oil, preferably in summer

Mealybugs love to gather in protected parts of the plant, like the underside of leaves.

Two-spotted mites discolour the foliage of affected plants.

Scale insects build themselves a protective covering.

when scale insects are breeding. Spray oils in the cool of the day on well-watered plants. Scale Gun is convenient, as it combines white oil and insecticide. Red scale, brown scale and white louse scale are related insects. They can be controlled in the same way as white wax scale. Confidor controls soft scale on ornamentals.

HINT

For severe outbreaks of scale insects, spray with a heavy dose of white oil in the evening as temperatures cool and wash off the following morning before the sun hits the plants. White oil left on the plant in sunshine will cause foliage burn and leaf drop.

GEOFF MIERS

GEOFF MIERS GARDEN SOLUTIONS
ALICE SPRINGS, NORTHERN TERRITORY

DISEASES

Plant diseases are mainly caused by parasitic organisms called 'plant pathogens'. The pathogen may be a fungus, a bacterium, a virus or a nematode. In addition, there are non-parasitic diseases that will sometimes need to be controlled.

Fungal diseases

Most plant diseases are caused by fungi which may be carried in the seed, in the soil or on other plants or weeds. They spread quickly, especially in warm, humid weather, by means of microscopic spores which are distributed by wind or water. Rain or water-splash favours their spread. Fungal diseases fall into four main groups: mildews, rusts, leaf spots, and stem and root rots.

Mildew

Powdery mildew is a fungus which spreads a white or ash-grey film over the upper and lower surfaces of the leaves of plants – usually the older leaves. Powdery mildew is a common disease of roses, crepe myrtles, dahlias, zinnias, calendulas, sweet peas, and vine crops. The systemic fungicide in Rose Shield will control this disease on ornamentals. Also effective is an application of Mancozeb Plus Garden Fungicide or Fungus Gun.

Downy mildew is often more widespread in younger plants and is recognised by downy, whitish tufts or spores on the underside of the leaves. Downy mildew is common on grapes, vine crops, cabbages and other crucifers, onions, lettuce and stocks. Spray with Mancozeb Plus Garden Fungicide. Regular application of the spray is necessary during rainy weather.

Rust

Rust fungus is easily identified by the many orange or red pustules on leaves or stems which break open and release masses of spores. Rust is a common disease of calendulas, snapdragons, geraniums, gerberas and beans. It has become a serious disease of frangipani and poplar trees. Good control can be obtained with sulfur, lime sulfur and Mancozeb Plus and Yates rose sprays.

Leaf spots

Leaf spots are easily seen and may be serious on roses (black spot and anthracnose). Leaf spots and blights are also common on tomato, potato, capsicum, carrot, parsnip, beet and silver beet, polyanthus, iris and many shrubs. Leaf spots are usually more serious in wet conditions. Sprays of Liquid Copper or Mancozeb will control most leaf spots.

On roses use Rose Gun Advanced or Rose Shield, as these products control a number of fungi and insect pests.

Yates Mancozeb Plus Garden Fungicide controls both powdery and downy mildew as well as leaf spots and rust.

Stem rots and root rots

The causes of stem rots, root rots and collar rots are not easily determined but most are due to fungal pathogens which attack the conducting tissues of the plant, causing it to wilt and finally collapse.

Sclerotinia is a widespread fungus which attacks many soft-stemmed plants, including beans, lettuce, nemesias, linarias and other

Powdery mildew on a cucurbit leaf.

Azalea petal blight is a widespread fungal disease.

annuals. The stem rot and the fungus then form small, hard-fruiting bodies called sclerotia which fall to the ground. These develop a mycelium and, later, small toadstool-like structures which shed spores to restart the cycle.

Petal blight of azaleas has a similar life cycle. Keep flowers as dry as possible (water at base) and spray from expanded bud stage with Yates Zaleton to prevent and control infection.

Some fungal pathogens attack the stems or crowns of plants at ground level. These fungi are more active in damp conditions and poorly drained soils. Root rot or collar rot is common in delphiniums, carnations, gerberas, strawberries, cabbages and other crucifers. Citrus, avocado and other fruit trees and shrubs (especially Australian natives such as grevillea) may also be attacked. While dampness and poor drainage encourage these root and crown rots, some control and protection can be achieved by spraying with Yates Anti-Rot Phosacid Systemic Fungicide.

'Damping off' is a fungal disease of seeds and young seedlings. The fungus causing this disease is soil-borne and most active under

damp, cold conditions. To prevent seedlings falling over at soil level, spray with Mancozeb Plus as directed.

Bacterial diseases

Bacterial diseases are not common in the home garden, which is fortunate because there are virtually no chemicals available to control them efficiently. Black rot of cabbage and other crucifers is seen occasionally and there are also a few bacterial leaf spots of tomato and zinnia and a leaf and pod spot of beans (halo blight). Yates Liquid Copper is a helpful preventative treatment. None of these diseases is usually serious. Many bacterial diseases are seed-borne, but careful attention to hygiene in seed production and treatment by seed companies makes this source of infection unlikely.

HINT

If you find aphids on your plants, wait a week or so to give parasites and predators a chance to control them for you. You can tell if aphids are parasitised when they swell up into 'mummies' and die.

DENIS CRAWFORD

AUTHOR, *GARDEN PESTS, DISEASES AND GOOD BUGS*

Viral diseases

Viral diseases are often found in the home garden. Spotted wilt of tomatoes, necrotic yellow of lettuce and broad bean wilt of broad beans and sweet peas can be quite devastating. Other viral diseases, like those causing striping in tulips and stocks and the greening of aster and gerbera flowers, do not usually affect the vigour of the plants.

Some other viral diseases gradually reduce the vigour and productiveness of the plants they attack, especially perennials. Good examples are 'woody' fruit of passionfruit, crinkle leaf of strawberries, leaf-roll virus of potatoes, spotted wilt of dahlias and mosaic virus of orchids. No chemicals will control the viral diseases of plants, so garden hygiene is most important in controlling infection. Plants suspected of viral infection should be removed and destroyed. It is worthwhile to remove all weeds from the garden and surrounds because many weeds are alternative hosts for viral diseases. And finally, remember that viral diseases are transmitted from one plant to another by sap-sucking insects such as aphids, jassids and thrips. If you control these pests, the battle against viral disease is almost won.

Diseases caused by nematodes

Nematodes or eelworms are minute, soil-inhabiting worms, some of which are useful in decomposing organic matter and others of which are parasites attacking the roots of plants and causing large swellings or galls. They are more prevalent on sandy soils than heavy soils. Tomatoes, beetroots, carrots, lettuces, cabbages, carnations and gardenias are susceptible to attack. Do not grow susceptible plants in that part of the garden for one or two seasons. Adding organic matter to the soil will help reduce nematode infestation.

Leaving the soil completely free of plants (including weeds) from spring to autumn is also a useful method of reducing nematode populations.

Another important nematode is the leaf nematode of chrysanthemums. Leaves show large, triangular dead patches and die off from the base upwards. The leaf nematode is often prevalent from late summer to early autumn when accompanied by extended rain periods. Reduce this problem with good garden hygiene and by minimising watering of foliage.

Non-parasitic diseases

Poor growth of plants is not always caused by parasitic organisms. Environmental factors either in the atmosphere or in the soil may be the reason for unhealthy plants. These so-called diseases would more correctly be described as physiological disorders.

The influence of the atmosphere in which plants grow is important. Excessive cold often causes purple or red pigments to develop in the leaves of roses and many plants. Chlorosis (yellowing) of leaves occurs in others. In other cases, flower buds do not form properly or flowers are not pollinated. Low temperatures are the main cause of poor pollination in tomatoes and capsicum, especially in spring and early summer. This often leads to misshapen fruit called 'catface'. Vine crops often fail to set fruit at low temperatures or in cloudy weather, due to the absence of bees.

On the other hand, excessive heat, which is often combined with a dry atmosphere, causes wilting, scorching of leaves (tip burn) and other tender tissues (sunscald of tomato and capsicum), blossom drop in tomatoes and capsicums and faulty pollination in beans and sweet corn (pollen blast).

Cold winds slow down growth and hot winds increase moisture loss from plants and soil. Strong winds cause structural injury to leaves, stems, flowers and fruits.

Insufficient light results in soft, spindly growth, especially in seedlings, and may reduce flowering and fruiting in older plants.

In industrial areas of cities and towns, chemical pollutants such as sulfur dioxide and the exhaust fumes of motor vehicles produce hydrocarbons and oxides of nitrogen which can have toxic effects on plants. Fluorine, ozone and ethylene are other harmful gases which may cause yellowing of leaves or interfere with flowering and fruit formation.

Dust and smoke from factories can cause damage by blocking the stomates (breathing pores) of leaves and forming a film which prevents light from reaching the leaf surface. Some plants are more resistant to gases and dusts in the atmosphere, so gardeners who are unfortunate to live near these sources of pollution should restrict their plants to those which can best resist it. Your local nursery will be able to assist you with your selection. An application of lime will often correct the problem as it allows soil molybdenum to become more available to the plants.

The influence of soil factors on the growth of plants has been mentioned in the opening paragraphs of this chapter and also in Chapters 4 and 5.

The importance of adequate watering cannot be stressed too strongly. Insufficient water not only causes wilting; a disturbance in the even supply of moisture can be responsible for blossom fall in sweet peas and tomatoes and early fruit drop in citrus trees. Lack of water can also lead to the accumulation of salt (mostly as chlorides) in the soil, especially in gardens in inland irrigation districts or those exposed to salt spray near the coast. Excess chlorides in the soil cause severe leaf scorch, especially on the

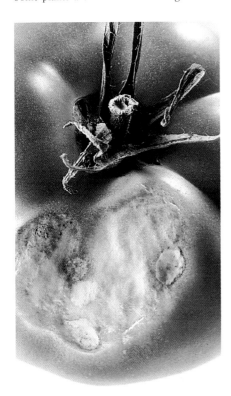

Sunscald on a tomato.

Cold damage on a butternut pumpkin.

Cold conditions have caused pigmentation in the leaves of these cabbages.

leaf margins, and may eventually result in the death of a plant. Plants susceptible to this problem are beans, cabbages, cauliflowers, lettuces, onions, tomatoes, citrus trees, peaches, apricots, bananas and grapevines.

On very acid soils, all the important plant nutrients – nitrogen, phosphorus, potassium, calcium, magnesium and sulfur – are usually in short supply. (See Chapter 5.) A common disorder in tomatoes is blossom-end rot in which the fruit becomes sunken and blackened. This condition is caused by lack of calcium in the developing fruit. Blossom-end rot is aggravated by moisture stress in very hot weather, so regular watering and mulching of the surface will help control the problem. Over-watering should be avoided, however, because root absorption may be less efficient. An application of lime or gypsum (calcium sulfate) to the bed before planting will lessen the incidence of this disorder. Tip burn of cabbage and blackheart of celery are similar kinds of calcium deficiency.

A deficiency of magnesium shows symptoms of yellowing between the leaf veins, especially on the older leaves. It is not uncommon on acid soils. Susceptible plants are citrus trees, apples, bananas, grape vines, beetroots, tomatoes and members of the cabbage family.

The trace element molybdenum is also deficient in acid soil and causes a disorder called whiptail in broccoli, Brussels sprouts, cabbages and cauliflowers. The leaf blades become narrow and the margins of the leaves thickened and distorted. The application of water-soluble fertilisers – all of which contain molybdenum – will usually overcome this problem. Molybdenum deficiencies have also been recorded in lettuces, tomatoes and vine crops when these are grown on acid soil.

On alkaline soils, other elements are likely to be unavailable. This shortage applies particularly to iron and manganese, the lack of which causes chlorosis in young leaves of azaleas, rhododendrons, camellias and other acid-loving plants. Deficiencies of manganese can also occur in citrus trees, beetroots and tomatoes, especially in inland areas or on heavily limed soil. On the other hand, excess manganese (manganese toxicity) has been found to cause yellowing in crops of beans and pineapples on acid soils on the coast of New South Wales and Queensland.

Boron is another trace element which may be deficient on alkaline soil. Symptoms are usually associated with growing tissue such as shoots, buds, fruits and storage roots. Susceptible plants are apples (internal browning), broccoli and cauliflowers (hollow stems), beetroot (heart rot), silver beet and celery (stem cracking), swedes and turnips (brown heart).

Deficiencies of copper and zinc are not common but have been recorded on very acid, sandy, coastal soils and also on fertile, inland 'black earth' soils. Symptoms occur in the younger leaves, which are chlorotic and stunted. The disorder has been called little leaf or rosette in apples, peaches, apricots and citrus trees. Bananas and maize (which includes sweet corn) are also susceptible to zinc deficiency.

While trace elements are an interesting facet of plant nutrition, deficiencies of these are not common in a home garden where organic matter and mixed fertilisers are used. In addition, the water-soluble fertilisers – Thrive and Aquasol – and some granular fertilisers contain trace elements in small but balanced quantities. Because trace elements are required in such small amounts by plants, their correct application is essential. The use of 'complete' fertilisers is an easy and safe way to correct many trace element deficiencies.

Pests and diseases of fruit trees

Apples, pears and quinces are attacked by codling moth and fruit fly. Aphids can also do damage and woolly aphid can be a serious pest in apples. Stone fruits (peaches, plums, nectarines and apricots) are attacked by fruit fly but not by codling moth. Tip moth and green and black peach aphids are often a problem, especially in inland districts. (See previous sections under relevant headings for control of these pests.)

Black spot (apple scab) and powdery

Careful plant selection can ensure that plants are healthy, even when growing in difficult situations like this exposed coastal garden.

mildew of apples are controlled by sprays such as Yates Mancozeb Plus. Apply when leaf buds show green tips, at pink bud stage and then after full bloom. Bitter rot of apples can be checked by sprays of Mancozeb. Apply when leaf buds show green tips.

With stone fruits, a clean-up spray is necessary while the trees are still dormant in June or early July. Spray with Leaf Curl Spray or lime sulfur at early bud swell. Any dried-up fruit ('mummies') should be collected from around the base of the tree and destroyed.

Spray stone fruit with Mancozeb to control rust three weeks after flower fall and repeat at three-week intervals. Peach leaf-curl and shot hole of stone fruits are controlled by winter clean-up sprays. A further spray in autumn at leaf fall is advisable. Brown rot is a destructive disease of stone fruits. The clean-up spray in winter helps to control brown rot, but this should be followed by spraying with Mancozeb Plus Fungicide at full bloom, petal fall and then every three weeks until two weeks before harvest. Collect and destroy any fruit affected with brown rot.

Pests and diseases of citrus trees

The important pests of citrus trees are scale insects (white wax, red, brown and white louse scale), bronze orange bug, aphids, citrus leaf miner and fruit fly. Control measures for leaf miner are given in previous pages. One other serious pest is the citrus gall wasp. This small wasp, about 6 mm long, lays eggs in soft stems in spring. The larvae tunnel through the stems, forming swellings or galls. There is no chemical control. Remove any stems or twigs with galls, cutting well behind them. Remove them before the end of August because a new generation of wasps emerges from the galls about this time. Seal pruned galls in a plastic bag and dispose of in the rubbish. Citrus leaf miner is a serious pest in New South Wales, Queensland, Western Australia and parts of Victoria. It may be controlled by spraying with white oil or PestOil.

Black spot, a fungal disease, disfigures rose leaves and eventually leads to excessive leaf drop.

A serious disease of citrus trees in coastal districts is lemon scab. Spray with copper oxychloride and white oil when trees commence flowering in spring, followed by a second spray in summer after flowering has finished. Melanose is also a common citrus disease causing rotting of the fruit at the stem end and diebacks of branches and twigs. The sprays used to control lemon scab should also control melanose.

Sooty mould is caused by a black fungus which covers the leaves of citrus. It does very little damage, as the fungus survives on the sugary secretions from aphids or scale insects. If these pests are controlled, the sooty mould will disappear.

Collar rot attacks the trunks of citrus trees just above soil level. Yellowing leaves and cracking bark are the usual symptoms. Spray foliage with Yates Anti-Rot Phosacid. Susceptible trees (especially lemons) should be given a preventative spray with Anti-Rot twice a year. Yellowing and dwarfing of leaves may also be due to lack of nitrogen and perhaps trace element deficiencies. See Chapter 5 for fertiliser recommendations.

Lawn problems

Black beetles, cockchafer grubs, army worms, ants and mole crickets are the main pests of lawns. For control, see previous section under the heading 'Beetles, weevils, grasshoppers and crickets' (page 119). The main diseases of lawns are brown patch and dollar spot. Both are caused by a fungus and usually occur in late spring, summer and autumn when the weather is warm and humid. Brown patch starts with small discoloured patches of grass which later spread to form irregular dead patches a metre or more in diameter. Bent grass is very susceptible. Dollar spot is very similar in appearance but the spots usually remain small and circular. Both bent grass and Queensland blue couch are susceptible. A number of turf fungicides are available to control both diseases. The most commonly available one, Mancozeb Plus, controls brown patch and dollar spot. Zaleton controls anthracnose, brown patch, winter fusarium, helminthosporium, leptosphaerulina, curvularia and dollar spot. Lawns should

Sooty mould grows on the excretions from sap-sucking insects.

always be watered in the morning so that they dry well before nightfall.

Fairy ring forms a ring of green grass surrounded by an outer ring of dead grass with mushroom-like growths appearing occasionally in the affected area. The fungus responsible for fairy rings is very deep in the soil and the only complete cure is to remove the turf and soil to a depth of 20 cm from the affected area.

Algae (a green or black scum) and moss are usually problems in shaded, over-wet or badly drained sections of the lawn. If these conditions are alleviated the grass will again cover the area. Slime moulds form small, steel-grey or black mounds on leaves and stems of grass in warm, moist weather. These are not parasites and do not injure the grass, although they may look unsightly. Slime moulds can be brushed off the lawn with a stiff broom. Moss may be controlled with sulfate of iron.

Garden Problem Solver

LAWN

PROBLEM		SOLUTION
Black Beetle		**Yates Complete Lawn Insect Control** Hint: Black beetle damages roots, causing dead brown patches in the lawn. Birds pecking at your lawn may also indicate their presence.
Curl Grubs		**Yates Complete Lawn Insect Control** Hint: Curl grubs and other scarab larvae chew grass roots. When used as directed *Complete Lawn Insect Control* treats these and other lawn pests.
Bindii		**Yates BuffaloPro** Hint: It is important to control bindii when plants first appear and before the barbed seeds develop.
Clover		**Yates Bindii & Clover Weeder** Hint: *Yates Bindii & Clover Weeder* is an economical way to treat clover; 500 ml treats more than 330 sqm of lawn.
Dandelions		**Yates Weed 'n' Feed** Hint: *Weed 'n' Feed* not only controls dandelions and flatweeds but also bindii and clover. It speeds up results by also fertilising your lawn.
Onion Weed		**Yates Zero Rapid 1-Hr Action Weedkiller** Hint: After treatment tiny side bulbs will detach themselves and begin to grow. Follow-up treatments with *Zero* will be necessary.
Paspalum		**Yates Zero Rapid 1-Hr Action Weedkiller** Hint: Paspalum can take over your lawn if left untreated. Spot-spray regularly with *Yates Zero Rapid 1-Hr Action Weedkiller* to wipe out weeds. Avoid contacting lawn grass with herbicide.

FRUIT TREES AND CITRUS

PROBLEM	SOLUTION
Brown Rot	**Yates Triforine Fungicide** Hint: Remove all rotted or dry fruit and prune deciduous trees before spraying. A late-winter spray with *Yates Lime Sulfur* will also help in control.
Codling Moth	**Success Ultra Insect Control** Hint: To control codling moth begin spray program at petal fall. Clean up fallen fruit from beneath the tree.
Grape Vine Caterpillar	**Yates Nature's Way Caterpillar Killer Dipel** Hint: *Dipel* is a natural insecticide based on a bacteria, and can be used to control many different moth and butterfly caterpillars.
Peach Leaf Curl	**Yates Liquid Copper** Hint: Spray with *Liquid Copper* in late winter when buds just start to swell. Good coverage is essential.
Citrus Collar Rot	**Yates Anti Rot** Hint: As well as controlling citrus collar rot, *Anti Rot* helps prevent root rot in susceptible plants such as daphnes, grevilleas, avocados and banksias.
Citrus Leaf Miner	**PestOil** Hint: *PestOil* forms a protective layer over the leaves, so spray new growth every few weeks.
Scale	**PestOil** Hint: Scales suck nutrients from plants and can cause unsightly sooty mould. Spraying with *PestOil* will control both problems.

VEGETABLES AND ORNAMENTALS

PROBLEM	SOLUTION
Tomatoes – Tomato Caterpillar	**Yates Success Ultra** Hint: Grubs can spoil your home-grown tomatoes. To protect them, start spraying early in the season with *Success Ultra*.
Tomato Disease	**Yates Tomato & Vegetable Dust** Dust regularly to protect tomatoes from pests and diseases.
Whitefly	**Yates Pyrethrum** Hint: Whitefly are tiny white insects that hide underneath foliage and fly around when disturbed.
Caterpillars	**Yates Success Ultra** Hint: *Success Ultra* is a caterpillar control that is derived from a naturally occurring soil organism. Alternatively use *Dipel*.
Hibiscus Flower Beetle	**Bayer Confidor** Hint: Look out for holes in your hibiscus petals – a sure sign that your plant has hibiscus flower beetles. Flowers may drop prematurely.
Snails & Slugs	**Yates Blitzem Snail & Slug Pellets** Hint: Snails and slugs love to hide in strappy-leafed plants like agapanthus. Sprinkle *Blitzem Snail & Slug Pellets* at the base of the plant.
Two-Spotted Mite	**Yates Nature's Way Vegie & Herb Natrasoap** Hint: Two-spotted mites (also known as red spider mites) are only just visible.

CAMELLIAS AND AZALEAS

PROBLEM	SOLUTION
Thrips/Lace Bug	**Bayer Confidor** Hint: Start spraying new growth in early spring to prevent the silvery mottled leaves caused by thrips and lace bug.
Two-Spotted Mite	**Yates Nature's Way Vegie & Herb Natrasoap** Hint: Discourage two-spotted mites by regularly mist-spraying leaves with water from a hose or atomiser.

CAMELLIAS AND AZALEAS (CONTINUED)

PROBLEM	SOLUTION
Aphids	**Yates Pyrethrum RTU** Hint: Aphids love soft new shoots, so be on the alert during growth periods.
Soft Scale	**Bayer Confidor** Hint: Dried scale coverings can remain on leaves after treatment but eventually they will flake off.
Sooty Mould	**Bayer Confidor** Hint: Sooty mould is caused by sap-sucking insects like soft scale. After *Confidor* has killed scale, sooty mould will gradually flake off.

ROSES

PROBLEM	SOLUTION
Aphids	**Bayer Confidor** Hint: Aphids suck nutrients from new growth and spread damaging virus diseases. *Confidor* gives long-lasting protection from aphids.
Thrips	**Yates Baythroid** Hint: Thrips are very active in spring. The tiny insects cause browning of petals, especially on light-coloured roses.
Two-Spotted Mite	**Yates Rose Gun Advanced** Hint: Mites are almost invisible to the naked eye. They cause most problems during dry weather.
Rose Scale	**Yates Scale Gun** Hint: An application of *Yates Lime Sulfur* immediately after pruning can also help with control of rose scale.
Black Spot	**Yates Rose Gun Advanced** Hint: *Yates Rose Gun Advanced* combines two insecticides, a miticide and a systemic fungicide. For larger gardens use concentrated *Yates Rose Shield*.
Rust	**Yates Rose Shield** Hint: Reduce the risk of rose disease by watering plants at the base in the early morning.
Powdery Mildew	**Yates Rose Gun Advanced** Hint: To control powdery mildew in larger gardens use *Yates Rose Shield* or *Yates Triforine*.

Guide to Common Terms Relating to Plant Protection

Active constituent (ai)	**The component in the product that actually does the job.**
Systemic	**The active constituent enters and moves around in the plant's sap and water system. This means it can affect pests that attack the plant while it is active within the plant.**
Contact	**The product works by directly contacting the pest.**
Stomach poison	**Affects leaf chewers and suckers that ingest plant material.**
APVMA	**Australian Pesticides and Veterinary Medicines Authority. Controls and registers pesticides in Australia.**
Registration	**The product can be sold for the purpose claimed on the packaging.**
Withholding period	**The time that must pass after application of a pesticide before crops can be harvested.**
Signal heading	**The message above the product name that gives some indication of the toxicity of the product.**

Weeds

Weeds in the garden, especially annual weeds, can be eliminated to a great degree if they are prevented from flowering and forming seed. They can be controlled by hand weeding or hoeing, preferably when they are quite small, or by spot weeding with a glyphosate herbicide.

An extremely effective weedicide, glyphosate is commonly sold as Zero. This is a non-selective chemical which is ideal to control persistent weeds like paspalum, couch grass, nutgrass and sorrel. The chemical is translocated from the above-ground parts of the plant to the persistent underground parts. The chemical is relatively safe to use but it is important to take care to prevent spray or drift spray from reaching wanted plants. Glyphosate breaks down rapidly in soil or water.

Weeds near fences, trees and borders

Weeds, both grasses and others, are a nuisance if they trail over fences, around trunks of woody shrubs and trees or across borders and edges of gardens. Try to establish a clear line of control, taking care not to contact wanted plants.

Weeds in paths and driveways

On areas such as paths, driveways, courtyards or tennis hardcourts, total weedkillers can be used. There are many brands, such as Once-A-Year Pathweeder. It is important to stress that this has a residual effect on the soil – usually for at least six months – and that on slopes in the period after application there may be some leaching of the chemicals into adjacent areas.

Perennial woody weeds

Large woody weeds like blackberry, lantana, briars, scrub and trees can be killed with specific herbicides for this purpose. Overall sprays control blackberries and other woody weeds. For trees and larger scrub growth, the chemical can be sprayed into holes bored in the trunk or into a frill ring cut around the trunk. The spray may drift in the wind and damage nearby plants, so take care to spray on a calm day.

HINT

If a plant suddenly appears in your garden that you didn't put there, it's not a welcome gift – even if it's pretty.
It's a weed that will soon be everywhere. Keep a small bucket with a weeder and gloves near the back door ready for a quick weeding session when you can.

CATHERINE STEWART
GARDENDRUM

Weeds in lawns

The best way to prevent weeds in lawns is to have healthy, vigorous turf which resists weed invasion. This is achieved by correct application of fertilisers, adequate watering and other maintenance practices. However, weeds may still be a problem and a wide range of selective weedkillers is available to control them. Lawn weeds can be divided into four groups.

GRASSY WEEDS

Any grass which differs from the grass composing the lawn can be considered a weed. Some common grassy weeds are paspalum, summer grass, winter grass and Mullumbimby couch. In fact, couch grass in a bent lawn or carpet grass in a couch lawn could be regarded as a weed. Such weeds should be removed by hand or carefully treated with glyphosate, using a Zero Weeding Brush. Avoid touching desirable grasses with the brush.

Clumping grasses such as paspalum or Parramatta grass can be 'crowned' at the soil surface with a hoe or sharp knife. There is no need to remove the root system. Sedges can be discouraged by the installation of better drainage.

Blackberry is a perennial woody weed that is best controlled by a herbicide spray.

Weedkillers for Specific Applications

LOCATION/ PROBLEM	WEEDKILLER	COMMENTS
Broadleaf weeds and bindii in lawns (except buffalo).	Bindii & Clover Weeder, Yates Weed 'n' Feed Granular, Yates Weed 'n' Feed Liquid Hose On	Selective control of broadleaf weeds in turf. Does not control grassy weeds. Read directions carefully before purchase.
Broadleaf weeds in buffalo lawns.	BuffaloPro, Bindii and Broadleaf Weeder, BuffaloPro Weed 'n' Feed Hose On	Suitable for application to buffalo lawns (and other grass lawns).
Driveways, paths, fencelines.	Zero Glyphosate	Kills a wide range of plants, including grasses, with repeated applications required on some hard-to-kill weeds such as tradescantia. No residual effect on soil. Do not allow spray to contact with wanted plants.
Unwanted woody plants.	Yates Tree & Blackberry Killer	Controls blackberry, lantana and sapling weeds.

BROADLEAF WEEDS

Marshmallow, dandelion, cat's ear, lamb's tongue, cudweed and chickweed are some of the common broadleaf weeds found in lawns. Products such as BuffaloPro, Weed 'n' Feed and Bindii & Clover Weeder are effective in eradicating them but read and follow instructions carefully.

CLOVER-LIKE WEEDS

Clovers, medics and creeping oxalis are the main weeds in this group. BuffaloPro and Bindii & Clover Weeder will control clovers and the broadleaf weeds.

FINELEAF WEEDS

Carrot weeds and bindii are the main fineleaf weeds found in lawns. Control can be achieved with a number of products specific They include BuffaloPro, Bindii & Clover Weeder (MCPA and Dicamba) and Bindii & Broadleaf Lawn Weed Spray (MCPA and Bromoxynil).

The weedkillers listed in the last three sections can be used on most lawn grasses. They should not be used on lawns composed of mixtures that include strawberry clover or white clover. Buffalo lawns are easily damaged by weedkillers, so exercise caution and read the label carefully before application. Be sure to only use products such as BuffaloPro which are safe for use on buffalo lawns.

HINT

The best way to rid your lawn of those annoying and unsightly weeds is to feed them first! Apply a lawn fertiliser high in nitrogen, and then watch the weeds grow. Two weeks later use a selective lawn herbicide such as Bindii & Clover Weeder. You will be amazed at the results as more herbicide is absorbed by the weeds, giving them a knockout blow.

COLIN BARLOW

GARDEN WRITER, DESIGNER AND HORTICULTURALIST, TV PRESENTER – *HOME IN WA*

HINT

To prevent weed spray from drifting onto nearby plants, cut off the top and neck of a soft-drink bottle and tape it to the end of the pressure sprayer wand to create a 'hood'. Spray over the top of the weed, close to the ground.

ROB PELLETIER

ABC RADIO VICTORIA, COLUMNIST WEEKLY TIMES FARM MAGAZINE

The use of sulfate of ammonia, or lawn foods which contain it, will discourage weeds, especially broadleaf weeds and clovers. The herbicide effect is increased if the fertiliser is applied dry to a lawn which is damp with dew. Lawn sand – a mixture of equal parts of sulfate and ammonia, sulfate of iron and sand – is another method of lawn weed control. The mixture is applied dry at

4 kg per 100 square metres and the lawn should not be watered for a day or two. The grass may suffer a temporary burn but will recover rapidly. Yates Weed 'n' Feed Granular is a dry product similar to lawn sand. Liquid Weed 'n' Feeds are convenient hose-on applications both to fertilise lawn grasses and control broadleaf weeds.

Pesticides mentioned in this chapter are generally available throughout Australia. For advice on specific treatment of pests in your district, consult your state's Department of Agriculture. Before buying or using any pesticide read the label carefully.

HINT

When installing a new raised garden bed place damp newspaper, about 10 sheets thick, over the ground first. This will help to reduce weeds growing up through the bed for a few months.

ANGIE THOMAS

YATES GARDENING EXPERT

Five bulbs that can become weeds

WATSONIA

These do particularly well in sandy soil and in drier climates, and can become great invaders.

TRITONIA (MONTBRETIA)

This indestructible plant is also known as Crocosmia, but, whatever it's called, it can be bad news in bushland.

FREESIA

The dainty Freesia refracta 'Alba' is often seen growing wild on roadsides.

LILIUM FORMOSANUM

Who would think that any of the stately liliums could become pests? Unfortunately, this variety is such a survivor that, under the right conditions, it can take on weedy proportions.

ARUM

Because they have a rhizomatous rather than a bulbous rootstock, arum lilies are not always classed as bulbs, but there's no doubt that they can become weeds, especially in damp spots.

Many gardeners complain that they have no soil suitable for bedding plants and so avoid growing them altogether. It's a great pity as nothing can match the all-year-round colour they can provide. Establish raised beds of just 200 mm using bricks or timber and fill with two parts triple-washed sand to one part recycled green organics and your annual beds will never look back.

MALCOLM CAMPBELL
ABC RADIO 891 PRESENTER AND WEEKLY
COLUMNIST FOR NEWS LIMITED IN ADELAIDE

Don't leave half empty bags of potting mix open and in the sun. Ensure potting mix is stored in a cool dry place such as the shed, roll the top of half-used bags and seal with a clothes peg. This will prevent the mix from drying out. When using potting mix, be sure to open the bag when out in the fresh air.

KAREN SMITH
EDITOR, *HORT JOURNAL*

Spring is the ideal time to mulch the soil at least 10–15 cm thick with an organic soil conditioner. This helps improve the water holding capacity and drainage of the soil while adding beneficial micro-organisms and bacteria at the same time. Apply a wetting agent after mulching to ensure that you do not waste any water and your plants will survive this summer.

COLIN BARLOW
GARDEN WRITER, DESIGNER AND
HORTICULTURALIST, TV PRESENTER –
HOME IN WA

Coarse wood mulch works well on beds of shrubs and herbaceous perennials because, after a few months, the large particles meld to form a barrier that prevents most weeds establishing. The one disadvantage comes when you want to plant a new shrub after a year or so. It's hard to dig through the surface, and chips of old mulch fall into the planting hole where, being so dry, they may draw moisture from the new shrub's roots. Remove the old mulch first, and chuck the chips in the bin as they can harbour tiny, superficial weeds. Oxalis is an example: it manages to thrive quite happily in the mulch layer.

JULIA BERNEY
HORTICLTURAL–AGRICULTURAL FREELANCE
EDITOR

Instead of composting, which a lot of gardeners find troublesome, why not build a small enclosure to house a couple of chickens who will happily do all your composting for you. Every bit of available green waste, prunings, kitchen scraps, grass clippings – in fact any organic waste – can simply be thrown to the chickens who will scratch it and eat it and turn it over and poop on it until it's ready to be raked up and spread around the garden. Inside their overnight enclosure, a layer of straw or lucerne will catch their nightly droppings, and this again will turn into a fantastic mulch for garden beds. And you will have the added bonus of wonderfully fresh eggs from your own backyard.

MARY MOODY
GARDEN AND TRAVEL WRITER

We all know the importance of mulching the garden to hold moisture around the root zone. However, just adding mulch without cultivating the soil is not wise because on uncultivated soil the rain and water find it hard to penetrate. The run-off from uncultivated soil means that at least half the water is not reaching the roots of your plants.

Cultivate the soil, water it well, cultivate again then add mulch. If your plants need fertiliser or manure, then now is a good time to add them.

After mulch has been added, water the area again.

KEVIN HEINZE 1928–2008
INAUGURAL RECIPIENT OF THE HORTICULTURAL MEDIA ASSOCIATION SILVER LAUREL 'HALL OF FAME' AWARD

If your soil is becoming 'tired' and not properly producing those 'gems' you just had to buy, it's time to get out the fork and start digging then raking. Go fairly deep with the fork (spades kill worms), then rake the soil from different angles. This will develop a soil with a fine tilth, as loved by all plants, particularly carrots. Incorporate matured garden compost and manures, and, in our water-short country, add some coco peat to help retain moisture levels.

BILL GREER d. 2013
GARDENING COLUMNIST – *WARWICK DAILY NEWS* QUEENSLAND.

Collect soft autumn leaves and place in a large plastic bag. Sprinkle a little cow manure through the leaves, moisten and place the bag in the sun. Within a short time you will have rich leaf mould. Alternatively, create a special compost heap only for soft autumn leaves. Blend leaves with sprinkles of animal manure and water lightly to make the best compost or soil conditioner.

GEOFF MIERS
GEOFF MIERS GARDEN SOLUTIONS, ALICE SPRINGS, NT

Never give up on a clay soil. If you keep on working at it and introduce plenty of liquid gypsum, it's amazing what nutrients you can unlock. Apply a lot initially, then top up on a regular yearly basis. Adding compost will improve the quality of the soil, and mulching will protect against damage from heavy rain.

TONY FAWCETT
GARDEN WRITER – SATURDAY *HERALD SUN HOME MAGAZINE*

The great miscalculation gardeners make is to concentrate their efforts on the plants instead of the soil in which they plant them. Never lose sight of the old adage 'the answer lies in the soil'. Attend to its needs by conditioning, mulching, enriching, feeding and moisturising.

ANNE THOMSON
GARDEN DESIGNER – THE GARDEN DESIGN STUDIO

I sometimes think a metal detector is a necessary tool in the garden shed. After losing tools in garden compost and mulched garden beds, I now paint the handles a bright yellow. It makes gardening more cheerful as well.

SUSAN MONTGOMERY
SUSAN MONTGOMERY DESIGNS

Worm 'wee' (liquid castings) collected from a worm farm can be easily applied to the garden by placing the wee concentrate in an empty 'clip-on-the-hose' container. Make sure there are no lumps as these will block the inlet pipe! Turn the hose on and water flowers, vegetables and shrubs with the right concentration of wee.

DAVID YOUNG OAM

FORMER WRITER, TV AND RADIO PRESENTER

To help get new plants established, especially in dry weather or sandy soil, cut a piece of polypipe the same depth as the pot the plant came from, and poke it down the side of the planting hole. You can then direct the hose into the pipe and deliver water straight to the base of the hole where most roots are, instead of spraying it on the soil surface where much of it can be lost through evaporation.

JULIA BERNEY

HORTICLTURAL–AGRICULTURAL FREELANCE EDITOR

Reduction of water use in gardens is often necessary when restrictions on supplementary watering are introduced. If possible it is best to avoid suddenly turning off drip systems, regular sprinklers or other water sources. Any recent soft new growth will need continued moisture to avoid wilting or death of young stems. It is better to gradually reduce watering, allowing time for plants to become hardened and adjust to the change.

GWEN ELLIOT AM

GARDEN WRITER AND BROADCASTER

Be prepared to accept a few munched leaves as part of the perfect garden – invertebrate company, both good and bad, is all part of the environment you are creating in your back yard. When you do find a suspect pest, examine the plant damage, don some garden gloves and manually remove the culprit. If a pesticide is necessary to control an infestation, apply it with intelligence and care – you don't want to kill all your beneficial bugs just to get rid of a few pests. There may be a little collateral plant damage but if you want butterflies and ladybirds, you have to put up with a few caterpillars and – gasp – aphids!

JANE DAVENPORT

ARTOMOLOGIST – IMAGINALITY STUDIOS, WWW.JANEDAVENPORT.COM

August is the best time to kill those pesky African black beetles that chew the roots of the grass and cause brown patches in your lawn during spring and summer. Use chemicals that are safe and have a low toxicity such as Confidor Hose-on Lawn Insecticide, an easy and effective solution as it catches the beetle larvae or 'curl grubs' when they are at the most vulnerable stage of their life cycle.

COLIN BARLOW

GARDEN WRITER, DESIGNER AND HORTICULTURALIST, TV PRESENTER – *HOME IN WA*

The underside of bird's nest fern fronds can be host to many 'little white things' that have the appearance of shredded desiccated coconut. They are Coconut or Fern Scale and they can severely damage plants. These scale insects can be difficult to control.

Badly infested fronds should be removed immediately. Other fronds can be sprayed on a cool day with white oil at half the recommended rate. This application may need to be repeated at fortnightly intervals until all the insects are killed. Avoid using white oil sprays on soft, young fern fronds.

RODGER ELLIOT AM
CO-AUTHOR *ENCYCLOPAEDIA OF AUSTRALIAN PLANTS*

Plant yellow-flowering plants such as marigold, sunflower and calendula to attract beneficial insects such as hoverflies, which love to feed on aphids.

PETER DE WAART
HORTICULTURALIST

Always water your plants in the morning; plants, like us, need a good breakfast. The sun activates the water, generating the food that the plant will draw on throughout the day.

MARK HAY
GARDEN CENTRE PROPRIETOR, FORMER TV AND RADIO TALKBACK HORTICULTURAL HOST, GARDEN ADVISER

This spray is good for controlling black spot and powdery mildew on roses; use first in spring when leaves are full size and then continue weekly throughout the year.

Mix well three teaspoons of bicarbonate of soda, two and a half tablespoons of PestOil and 4.5 litres of water. Spray two times in three weeks.

Continue to spray weekly to help prevent black spot and powdery mildew. Saturate the whole plant each time you spray (i.e. spray to run off). This spray recipe comes from the American Rose Society. An added benefit is the PestOil will also help to control aphids (and other insects).

ELIZABETH SWANE
ABC RADIO GARDENER

To counter the problem of blackbirds scratching mulch willy nilly all over the garden, try cutting 45 cm strips of galvanised chicken wire and lay them length-wise along the leading edges of all garden beds, buried just beneath the top layer of mulch. If necessary, the wire can be pinned down with small cleft sticks pushed into the soil through corner holes. With the wire in place, the birds are unable to scratch through the mesh and so push off to next door! Best of all, after more than thirty years it's still working!

NEIL WILLIAMS
GARDEN WRITER – EDITOR AND FREELANCE HORTICULTURAL CONSULTANT

Home-made garlic, nettle, soap, eucalyptus, nicotine, rhubarb, tomato and basil sprays are all effective against aphids.

GEOFF MIERS
GEOFF MIERS GARDEN SOLUTIONS, ALICE SPRINGS, NT

If ant numbers have become impossible, pour boiling water down ant holes. This will reduce numbers to an acceptable level without devastating the entire population. Ants provide many benefits to the garden. To deter white cabbage butterfly place golf balls or white egg shell halves throughout the garden. Wash the egg shells as, unwashed, they will attract unwanted cats in to the garden.

GEOFF MIERS
GEOFF MIERS GARDEN SOLUTIONS,
ALICE SPRINGS, NT

To control a range of pests moving up into large trees, consider placing a barrier band around the tree trunk. Use aluminium foil and mould it into the trunk and then paint with thick axle grease. Nothing will pass this barrier. The aluminium allows you to really mould it into the cracks in the bark, thus preventing the pests slipping in under the barrier.

GEOFF MIERS
GEOFF MIERS GARDEN SOLUTIONS,
ALICE SPRINGS, NT

There are alternatives to using chemicals to control pests in the garden. There are many insects and mites that do not damage plants but will actually attack the pests that do. Many of the beneficial insects that feed on, or parasitise, pest insects are attracted to flowering plants. By placing flowering plants in and around the vegetable patch you can help increase the numbers of these good bugs. You can also buy some beneficial insects to help boost the numbers in the garden and to take on particular pests. There are 'biological controls' available for red spider mite, aphids, mealybugs, white fly and scale insects. The suppliers can be contacted through this website: www.goodbugs.org.au

ANDY RYLAND
INTEGRATED PEST MANAGEMENT CONSULTANT

When watering the garden with a hose, place the nozzle in a partly-filled watering can, near to where you want to start watering. Then turn on the tap. This way the hose won't 'snake' all over the garden and wet everyone and everything, and won't waste water.

TIM NORTH 1921–2011
GARDEN WRITER

Birds are brilliant at keeping an insect balance in the garden, so encourage them with shallow ponds and birdbaths. Wattlebirds and whipbirds particularly love a daily splash. Put large, shallow terracotta bowls of water on the terrace, in clear space, so birds can spot an approaching predator, but also near bush cover which they can quickly fly to. Place a birdbath in the centre of the vegetable garden, and one or two more in quiet corners.

FRANCES HUTCHISON
GARDENING AUTHOR AND EDITOR

Coffee lovers share their passion with earthworms. Sprinkle coffee grounds around the garden near vegetables and roses to encourage earthworms. The grounds also repel insects and provide nutrients.

FRANCES HUTCHISON
GARDENING AUTHOR AND EDITOR

When using pesticides for controlling garden pests and diseases, ensure that you read all label information carefully. Always use protective clothing when spraying, including a hat, gauntlet-length rubber gloves, protective glasses and a respirator suitable for agricultural chemicals.

JOHN GABRIELE
GARDEN WRITER *ILLAWARRA MERCURY WEEKENDER* MAGAZINE, GARDENING PRESENTER ABC ILLAWARRA 97.3FM

Slaters are a sign of a healthy, organic-based garden, but sometimes they can get out of hand. To protect seedlings, cut the top and bottom off a milk carton, slip it over the seedling and push it into the soil. Slaters will not climb over the barrier. The carton breaks down by the time seedlings are large enough to be unattractive to the slaters.

JOHN 'GREENFINGERS' COLWILL
GARDEN WRITER AND BROADCASTER

Encourage beneficial fungi such as mycorrhiza in your garden by limiting the use of fungal sprays. Wherever possible, aim to strengthen the plant first by improving the soil. This will give your plants better disease and pest resistance and resilience.

PAUL PLANT, FAIH, RH
GARDENING WRITER, EDITOR, PHOTOGRAPHER AND BROADCASTER

Wetting agents are essential with potting mixes, but they work for only about 6 months, so you must apply them every 6 months.

DON BURKE
BURKE'S BACKYARD

It is a good idea to use a wetting agent when spraying herbicide; it helps the spray droplets stick to the weeds. If you haven't any wetting agent use Yates White Oil or dishwashing liquid.

MARK HAY
GARDEN CENTRE PROPRIETOR, FORMER TV AND RADIO TALKBACK HORTICULTURAL HOST, GARDEN ADVISER

Keep all pesticides in their original containers with labels intact. Decanting chemicals into alternative containers is against the law and extremely dangerous.

JOHN GABRIELE
GARDEN WRITER *ILLAWARRA MERCURY WEEKENDER* MAGAZINE, GARDENING PRESENTER ABC ILLAWARRA 97.3FM

Don't let the weeds get away from you. They're so easy to scratch out when they are small and weedy, so daunting when they're full-grown and covered with prickles, spines or seeds! Have you noticed, when weeds are tiny they're a brighter green? This makes them easier to spot.

ANNE LATREILLE
GARDEN WRITER

Before sowing fern spores pour boiling water on the propagating mix. This pasteurises the surface, controlling fungi and algae, and greatly improves germination.

JERRY COLEBY-WILLIAMS RHS, NEBSM, MAIH
DIRECTOR – SEED SAVERS FOUNDATION AND PRESENTER – ABC *GARDENING AUSTRALIA*

A useful propagating device for soft-stemmed cuttings can be made by corking the hole of a small terracotta pot, placing it inside a bigger one then filling the in-between space with growing mix to hold the cuttings. Fill the small empty pot with water to allow it to seep into the mix. Keep topped up.

DIANA O'BRIEN
GARDEN WRITER – *THE CHRONICLE*, ACT

Water cuttings and newly planted seedlings with a seaweed solution to help them to grow and develop.

JENNIFER STACKHOUSE
EDITOR, *GREENWORLD* MAGAZINE

Ever wondered what to do with all that used potting mix you're left with when repotting container plants? It can be scattered about the garden or added to the compost bin, but I usually re-use it by blending it with fresh mix (one part by volume 'old' mix to two parts of new). Leave it open to the air for a couple of months, keep moist and turn regularly so the sun will disinfect it, then add some slow release fertiliser before mixing it with the fresh potting mixture.

NOELLE WEATHERLEY
GARDEN WRITER AND EDITOR

Trace elements are like the chains on a bicycle: if one chain-link breaks, it's impossible to ride up the hill. Trace elements may only be needed in small quantities but if they're missing they can limit the growth and productivity of your garden plants.

PAUL PLANT FAIH, RH
GARDENING WRITER, EDITOR, PHOTOGRAPHER
AND BROADCASTER

To get new plants off to a great start, mix a 'cocktail' of plant starter, soil tonic and liquid wetting agent together (at the recommended dilution rates) in a watering can and use the solution to water in after repotting or transplanting. Your plants will jump away!

NOELLE WEATHERLEY
GARDEN WRITER AND EDITOR

Cultivating a new garden bed will often bring dormant weed seeds to the surface. If you are intending to sow vegetable or flower seeds in this bed, make sure you allow time for the weed seeds to germinate first and treat them either by hand removal or spraying. You may need to do this a few times over a two or three week period. If you don't, the weeds may germinate and prevent the seeds that you have sown from germinating.

KAREN SMITH
EDITOR, *HORT JOURNAL*

Aptenia cordifolia 'Red Apple'. This commonly grown, widespread ground cover has as many positives as it has negatives. A luxuriant green ground cover for sunny or shady areas, it can suppress weeds and control erosion, and is popular with bees when flowering almost year round. A big negative is that it can smother large areas relatively fast, but you can tuck or fold the spreading perimeter under itself to slow its growth, spread and root activity, making a tidy and appealing edge.

ATTILA KAPITANY
SUCCULENT EXPERT & AUTHOR

If you find yourself without any powdered rooting hormone or Formula 20, try these substitutes.

- Vegemite contains vitamins that can aid root formation. Dissolve a teaspoon of Vegemite in a large jar of water and soak cuttings in it for at least an hour.
- Harness the growth factors in willows to make a homemade rooting hormone. Boil a saucepan of water, turn off the heat and drop in a handful of split willow stems cut into 3 cm segments. Steep overnight then soak cuttings in the cooled liquid for a few hours. The liquid can be kept in a bottle in the fridge for a few days.
- For a more direct approach, dip the end of cuttings in neat honey and plant into coarse sand or propagating mix.

PAUL URQUHART
GARDEN WRITER

Cabbage white butterfly shapes cut out of weatherproof white plastic (e.g. empty margarine containers) and stapled to cabbage, cauliflower and broccoli leaves will fool visiting butterflies into believing one of their kind has already visited your plants. The butterflies won't lay their eggs as competition with other larvae may result in their offspring not surviving.

DAVID YOUNG OAM
FORMER WRITER, TV AND RADIO PRESENTER

Identify plants with a durable label - e.g. a metal tag inscribed with the point of a nail. It is especially useful for deciduous shrubs, roses and climbers such as Clematis which may appear to be dead in mid winter. Knowing the name of the plant and its flowering time is an invaluable aid for winter

pruning - one of the secrets of successful gardening.

DIANA O'BRIEN
GARDEN WRITER, THE CHRONICLE, ACT

Mosquitoes need water as much as plants do. Excess water pooled in a saucer under a pot will provide a wonderful place for mosquitoes to breed. Check ponds and make sure there are some fish present that eat mosquito larva. Also check around the garden for anything else that may hold water after rain or watering and fix any sagging guttering. Rectify the situation or be prepared to buy lots of mosquito repellent.

DAVID YOUNG OAM
FORMER WRITER, TV AND RADIO PRESENTER

In South Australia, the simple act of adding temporary shade in the garden holds the key to preventing significant plant damage caused by an ever-increasing number of summer heatwaves. Shading can drop air temperatures in and around the plant's canopy by 15°C to 20°C and drop topsoil temperatures (where most roots grow) by 10°C to 15°C. When mulching is added to shading, you can drop topsoil temperatures a further 5°C to 10°C. Collectively, these measures will go a long way to preventing plant stress.

JON LAMB
SA GARDEN WRITER AND ABC 891 SATURDAY TALKBACK GARDENER

PART THREE

Propagating Plants

9
Seeds and Seedlings

Seeds are formed in the flowers of plants by male pollen cells fertilising the female ovules or egg cells. Most plants have male and female parts in the one flower. Some, like sweet corn and vine crops, have male and female flowers on different parts of the same plant. Asparagus, date palms, papaws and some other plants have male flowers on one plant and female flowers on another.

Many annual plants are cross-pollinated, with the pollen being transferred by wind or insects (mostly bees) to other plants. The other plants may be of the same variety, of a different variety or sometimes of a different, but closely related, species. For this reason, plants grown from the seed of cross-pollinated plants may not be true to type unless special care is taken by seedsmen to prevent 'crossing'. Plant breeders use controlled cross-pollination to develop new varieties and F1 (first filial generation) hybrids. Hybrid flowers and vegetables have special qualities of uniformity, vigour and tolerance to unfavourable conditions. Many hybrids also have greater disease resistance. Hybrids produce seed in the same manner as any other plant, but the seed of hybrid plants may not necessarily grow true to type in the next generation so may not be worth sowing.

SEED STRUCTURE AND SEED LIFE

All seeds have two parts: an embryo, in which the shoot and root of the new plant are already formed; and storage tissue to feed the embryo when germination starts. The seeds you buy may look dry and lifeless but they do contain some moisture (8–10 per cent), and respiration (breathing) is going on at a slow rate, very much like a motor idling.

Like all living things, seeds will eventually die. They die faster when stored in warm, humid conditions, so it is difficult to keep them alive in tropical climates. Even in a mild climate like Sydney, short-lived seeds (aster, carnation, gerbera, onion, parsley and parsnip) will begin to lose germination vigour in eighteen months or less. Seedsmen have overcome this storage problem by drying seeds to a low moisture content (4–7 per cent) and sealing them in moisture-proof packets. This way, respiration is slowed down further, and seeds maintain germination vigour for many years. Long-lived seeds (lupins, sweet peas, zinnias, capsicum, tomato and vine crops such as pumpkins and cucumbers) maintain germination for several years under favourable conditions. However, to keep them in peak condition they too are sold in foil packets. If you are storing seeds at home, whether in foil or paper packets, always keep them in a cool, dry place. An insulated container makes a good storage container and desiccant packs (such as supplied with many new shoes) can help absorb excess moisture within the container.

HOW SEEDS GERMINATE

Water and air

Seeds must absorb 40–60 per cent of their weight in water to trigger germination. When germination starts they respire faster, so they need more air as well. When you sow seeds in soil, they take up moisture from the film of water surrounding the soil particles. The space between the particles (pore space) supplies the air. If the pore spaces are very small, as in silty or clay soils, there is too much water and not enough air. Sandy soils have large pore spaces and a good air supply but hold moisture badly. If you add moisture-holding materials (peat moss, vermiculite, compost or seed-raising mixture) to sandy soils, then you have the ideal combination for seeds to germinate: sufficient water and sufficient air.

A seed carries its own food source for the growing seedling.

Temperature

Soil temperature is important, too. Most garden seeds will germinate if the soil temperature reaches 20°C. As the soil temperature decreases, germination becomes slower. There are some exceptions, however. A few spring-flowering annuals, such as alyssum, cornflower, gypsophila, larkspur, linaria, nemesia, polyanthus, poppy (Iceland) and primula, germinate well at 15°C. Spinach (not silver beet) also germinates best in cool soil.

HINT

Store part-sown packets of seeds in Glad 'Snap-lock' bags. There won't be any spillage or spoilage and the bags even have a label on which to write the name of the contents.

TIM NORTH 1921–2011

GARDENING WRITER

Many summer-flowering annuals, such as amaranthus, celosia, coleus, gerbera, petunia, portulaca, salvia and zinnia, need a soil temperature of 25°C to germinate quickly. This also applies to warm-season vegetables such as beans, capsicum, sweet corn, tomato and vine crops. For example, bean seedlings may take between two and three weeks to emerge if seed is sown in early spring, but they will emerge in seven to ten days if the seeds are sown a few weeks later when the soil is warmer.

Light

Many seeds will germinate successfully, regardless of the amount of light they receive but some seeds have evolved to have very special light requirements. Some large seeds need darkness for germination, while others must be contacted by light. Those in this last category are usually quite small and should be thinly scattered onto the surface of the mix. They should then be pressed gently into the mix so that they are in contact with the moisture, but still exposed to the light. They can be left uncovered, although vermiculite is useful for covering these tiny seeds. It is translucent and allows light to reach the seed, while at the same time retaining moisture. Fine seeds should be watered carefully with a light misting or by immersing the seed tray in water. It is best to cover the seed tray with plastic wrap or glass to retain moisture around the seeds.

Time for germination

Quite apart from temperature, some seeds germinate much faster than others, so it is important to know when to expect seedlings from the seeds you sow. Under good conditions, seedlings of aster, marigold, zinnia, beans, peas, lettuce, vine crops and the cabbage family emerge in six to ten days (often less). Slow starters include begonia, cineraria, coleus, cyclamen, delphinium, larkspur, pansy, polyanthus, primula, verbena, parsley and parsnip. Seedlings of these may take three to four weeks to show, so keep the soil damp, but not wet, for this length of time. Seeds of Australian native plants are notoriously slow to germinate. Some, such as boronia and Sturt's desert pea, may take two to three months to emerge. The number of days for the seedlings of vegetables and flowers to emerge is given in the Sowing Guides in Chapters 11 and 15.

HINT

If saving money is a reason to grow your own vegies, always start with seeds – they are way cheaper than buying little plants. (See pages 224-7 for seed sowing timetable.)

GEOFFREY BURNIE

GARDENING JOURNALIST

SOWING SEEDS DIRECT INTO GARDEN BEDS

Many seeds can be sown direct into their garden situation. Direct sowing avoids double handling. Plants are usually more vigorous, because 'transplant shock' (damage to roots followed by temporary wilting) is avoided too. If you are running late with your plantings of flowers or vegetables, direct sowing can often make up for lost time.

Most plants recommended for direct sowing have relatively large seeds, but all have vigorous seedlings which can cope with conditions in the open garden. Popular flowers for direct sowing are alyssum, aster, balsam, calendula, celosia, larkspur, linaria, marigold, mignonette, nasturtium, nemesia, phlox, stock, sweet pea, sunflowers, verbena and zinnia.

Vegetables with large seeds (beans, broad beans, peas and sweet corn), and root crops such as beetroot, carrots, parsnip and turnip (all of which transplant badly), are direct sown. Many others, such as cabbage, Chinese cabbage, lettuce, onion, silver beet and spinach, prefer this method too. You can sow late crops of tomato, capsicum and vine crops direct, too, but many gardeners prefer to raise early plants in punnets or pots.

Preparing soil and applying fertiliser

When sowing direct, prepare the garden bed a week or two beforehand. Always cultivate the soil when in a dark, damp condition to preserve a good crumb structure.

Preparing the garden bed a week or two before using it stimulates the germination of those weed seeds which are inevitably present in the soil. By removing these weeds the gardener is then able to sow into a relatively weed-free seed bed. It is important that the

The first leaves to open on a developing seedling are called the 'seed leaves'.

PROPAGATING PLANTS

HINT

Long time gardeners swear
that a sprinkle of salt along a
row of newly sown beetroot
seed is a sure fire way to
achieve germination.

DIANA O'BRIEN

GARDEN WRITER, *THE CHRONICLE*, ACT

germinating seed has as little competition
from weeds as possible.

Young weeds can be sprayed with
glyphosate herbicide (e.g. Zero). After
spraying, wait until the weeds have died
before cultivating again.

Before sowing, add a complete, balanced
fertiliser. An organic fertiliser like Dynamic
Lifter is safer as it is less likely to burn the
seeds if they come into direct contact with the
pellets. If sowing seeds in rows or a definite
pattern it is possible to use a dry, granular
fertiliser by scattering the granules in a band
15-20 cm wide either beneath the row or
along either side of it.

Large seeds (beans, broad beans, peas,
sweet peas and sweet corn) are liable to burn
if in direct contact with fertiliser, so it is best
to apply fertiliser in a band to the side of their
seed row or just below it. There are two ways
of doing this:

1. If applying fertiliser beneath the row,
   create a furrow, scatter fertiliser along its
   base, cover with soil and then sow seeds
   on top at the correct depth. By the time
   the roots grow down, the fertiliser will be
   well blended with the soil.
2. If applying on the side, create two
   furrows on either side of the line where
   the seed is to be sown. Scatter fertilise
   along the furrow and cover in. Then sow
   seeds as directed in a line in the middle of
   the two fertiliser bands.

Another method of direct sowing is to sow
seeds in clumps or stations at the required
distance apart. Scatter fertiliser in a band and
rake in as before, or scatter the fertiliser at
each position where seed is to be sown and
mix it with the topsoil. Make saucer-shaped

depressions at each station and sow a few
seeds in each. Many bedding plants,
including nemesia, phlox, stock and zinnia,
can be sown in clumps about 20 cm apart.
Usually, all seedlings can be retained without
thinning to give a denser mass of colour.
Seeds of lettuce, silver beet, spinach, and late
sowings of tomato, capsicum and vine crops,
can be sown in clumps (three to five seeds to
each) in the same way. Thin each clump to
the strongest seedling. With tomato and vine
crops, retain two seedlings. Sweet corn is
often sown in pairs and the weaker seedling
removed after germination.

Sowing depth

Sowing depth depends on seed size: the
smaller the seeds, the shallower they are
sown. As discussed, some actually need light
to trigger germination. Others need to be
kept in the dark.

When sowing direct, sow seeds of
medium size in rows 12 mm deep. They can
be covered with soil, but it is far better to
cover with vermiculite, compost, peat moss,
or seed-raising mixture. These light-textured
materials hold moisture but have large
spaces between particles to provide good
aeration. Vermiculite is so light it can be
used to cover even very small seeds. An easy
way to apply dry vermiculite evenly is to fill
a jug with the material and pour it along the
row, or over the seeds at each station.
Vermiculite also acts as a marker for the
position where seedlings will emerge. A very
light mulch of grass clippings or chopped
sugar cane mulch over the entire bed can
help to retain moisture and prevent the soil
from caking.

Large seeds (beans, peas, sweet peas, vine
crops, etc.) can be sown more deeply, at
25–50 mm. Always sow them into dark,
damp soil at the bottom of the furrow. Then
cover the furrow with soil and lightly tamp
down with the back of the rake or the flat of
your hand. Covering with compost or
vermiculite is not necessary unless the soil is
extremely heavy. Lightly rake the whole bed
and spread a light mulch of grass clippings. If
the seeds are pressed into dark, damp soil,
further watering is usually not required until
seedlings emerge. Too much moisture for
these large seeds, especially in the first day or

two, can be harmful to germination because water is trapped beneath the seed coat and excludes air for respiration. For this reason, do not soak beans, peas, broad beans or sweet peas in water overnight before sowing.

Spacing seeds

The spacing of seeds, especially for those sown in rows or clumps, depends on the kind of seed to be sown. This is given in the cultivation notes on the reverse side of each packet. It is also shown in the Sowing Guide in Chapter 15 (see pages 286–295).

Sowing seed thinly can be difficult for home gardeners but, like most things, it is simple once you know how. First, make a V-shaped crease in the packet as a 'track' for the seeds. Then take the packet between thumb and fingers, but leave the index finger free to tap the packet. As you tap, seeds will shuffle along the crease and fall onto the soil. With a little practice you can tap out one or two seeds at a time. Alternatively, empty a quantity of seeds into the palm of the hand. Take a pinch of seeds between thumb and forefinger and sprinkle along the row or drop a few seeds at each station. Tiny seeds can also be mixed with a small amount of fine sand and sprinkled along the furrow.

Moisture control and early care

Apart from large seeds, which usually do not require extra water before seedlings emerge, most seeds must be kept damp, but not wet, until seedlings show through. This is most important for seeds which may take three to four weeks (or more in cool weather) to emerge. If you have used compost or vermiculite to cover the seeds, plus a grass clipping mulch on the beds, you will have ideal conditions for retaining moisture, making water penetration easy and preventing surface soil from caking.

When seedlings have emerged, continue watering, but rather more thoroughly and

Always water young seedlings with a fine, gentle spray.

HINT

To encourage fine seed to germinate, mark out rows about half a centimetre deep with the handle of a rake, lightly cover, gently water the seed then place an old fence paling over the seed row. Check regularly after three or four days; once the seed has germinated, remove the paling.

MORRIS HOLMES

HORTICULTURAL CONSULTANT AND
GARDEN DESIGNER

less frequently, to encourage deep rooting. As a general guide, a seedling 2.5 cm high may have its roots at a depth of 5–7 cm, so there is not much benefit to be had from a light sprinkling which wets the surface soil only. For watering seeds and seedlings, always use a fine hose spray, a water-breaker nozzle or a watering can with a fine rose.

Slugs and snails love young seedlings. Scatter Blitzem or Baysol pellets over the bed a day or two after you sow the seed. Repeat the treatment when seedlings emerge, or sooner if the bait disintegrates in heavy rain. Or put a physical barrier, such as a toilet paper cardboard roll, around each seedling.

RAISING SEEDLINGS

Seeds of many plants are best raised in seed beds, seed boxes, punnets and pots. The main reason is that the seeds are small and the seedlings lack the vigour and rapid growth of larger seeds. In raising seedlings, you have much better control over early growing conditions, light, temperature, soil mix, water and nutrients. Begonia, cineraria, coleus, cyclamen, poppy (Iceland), petunia, polyanthus and primula are good examples of seeds that are best raised in this way. For example, petunia seedlings may take three or four weeks to reach a height of 2.5 cm, whereas marigold seedlings grow to that height in a week. Some flower seeds are expensive, so it is important to raise as many seedlings as possible.

There are, of course, many flower seeds which can be sown direct or raised as seedlings, just as you choose. This gives greater flexibility to your planting program. For example, you may have a bed of petunia or phlox still flowering well in late summer. Rather than sacrifice this colour display for an empty bed, raise seedlings of, say, nemesia, which will be ready for transplanting when the summer flowers are finished.

It is often more convenient to raise the seedlings of some vegetables, especially when you need only a few plants. This is particularly true of broccoli, cabbage, cauliflower, and of early plants of capsicum, eggplant, tomato and all the vine crops. Sow the seed in punnets and prick out seedlings into 10 cm plastic pots to grow on for another four weeks or more.

Soil mixtures and seedlings

Packaged seed-raising mix from a reputable manufacturer is suitable for growing most seedlings, but you can also make your own. You will need a mix which is open, friable and well drained. Sand, preferably coarse river sand, is the best material to meet this requirement. Do not use beach sand unless it has been thoroughly washed to remove salt. You will need a good moisture-holding material too. Choose from vermiculite, spent mushroom compost, garden compost or peat moss. Vermiculite is one of the best materials because the tiny root hairs of the seedlings penetrate the particles to provide a built-in moisture supply. When seedlings are transplanted, the young roots cling to the particles and so take moisture with them to the new spot in the garden.

For a start, try a soil mix containing one part garden soil, one part coarse sand and one part vermiculite, compost or peat moss (you will have to dampen the peat moss before adding to the mix). Add 30 g of a pre-sowing fertiliser and 90 g of lime to each bucket of mix. The mix must be free-flowing and should not compress in the hand when damp. If your garden soil is very sandy, you will need less sand and more moisture-holding material. If your garden soil is heavy or contains a lot of organic matter, you will need more sand. Test the mix by filling a seedling tray or punnet and watering it with a fine spray. The mix should absorb moisture quickly, in a few seconds, and drain freely. If it does not, add a little more sand.

Seed beds

A permanent seed bed is a good idea in a large garden or if you wish to raise large numbers of seedlings. Select a sunny, sheltered spot in the garden, build it up 15–20 cm for drainage and contain it with boards or a brick surround. An area 1 m square is a convenient size. To sandy soils add liberal quantities of vermiculite or other moisture-holding material. On clay soils spread a 5 cm layer of coarse sand as well. Then add the mixed fertiliser at one-third of a cup per square metre and lime at one cup per square metre. Dig the bed over to mix the ingredients thoroughly to a depth of about 10 cm.

You will need some protection for young seedlings in an open seed bed. A frame of 50 mm x 25 mm timber, covered with flyscreen wire or 32 per cent shade cloth, is suitable. Make wooden legs at each corner or rest it on upright bricks. Use the frame to protect young seedlings from direct sunlight during the hottest part of the day. Don't keep seedlings covered all the time, otherwise they become soft and lanky. Give the seedlings more sun and less shade as they grow. The frame is useful for covering the seed bed in heavy rain, too.

Seed trays, punnets and pots

These are shallower than a seed bed and so do not hold as much moisture. They have the advantage, however, of being able to be moved about easily to give seedlings the required conditions of shade or sunlight. After sowing, the containers can be kept indoors to provide a rather higher and more even temperature (especially in winter), and moved outside as soon as the seedlings emerge. Plastic trays, punnets and mini-punnets are already provided with good drainage, are easy to wash and clean, and can be used over and over again. You can fill these containers with soil mix, sow seeds and prick out seedlings while standing or sitting at a workbench – easier than squatting at the seed bed.

A more recent innovation is the introduction of a variety of cell containers formed in the shape of an inverted cone.

Plastic wrap helps retain moisture around seeds during the germination period.

Seedlings started in peat moss pellets suffer no transplant shock.

They are useful for raising seedlings from seed, as the seedling is easily removed from them with little or no damage to the root system of the plant, thus minimising transplanting shock. The shape of the cone concentrates the development of the roots downward.

Fill the container of your choice with seed-raising mix to the top of the container. With

HINT

If the weather is hot, shelter new seedlings with twigs cut from bushy shrubs in the garden. Push one or two prunings in beside each seedling. They will give some shade for a few days before the leaves start to drop off. This gradually habituates the seedling to more sun.

SHIRLEY STACKHOUSE
GARDEN WRITER

a flat board, firm the mix to a level 6–12 mm below the rim of the container. (You can use the bottom of an empty tray or punnet for firming the mix, because the bottom is slightly smaller in area than the top.) Another method is to almost fill the container with some dry mixture, dump it on the bench to level it and then water well with a fine spray until water seeps from the drainage holes. Alternatively, stand containers in shallow water until moisture seeps to the surface. With both these methods the soil mix is often too wet for immediate use, so leave for a day or two before sowing.

Another method of raising seeds favoured by many home gardeners and commercial growers is planting the seed in peat pellets. These are pellets of compressed peat moss which, when expanded by adding water, make a block of peat moss suitable for raising seeds or cuttings. When the plant is of suitable size for transplanting, the peat block, complete with plant, is put into the permanent position in the garden and no 'transplant shock' is encountered.

Sowing seed

When sowing in seed beds, mark out shallow rows or drills about 6 mm deep and 5–7 cm apart with the edge of a flat board or dowel stick. Scatter seed thinly along the rows by tapping seeds from the packet. Do not crowd seeds in the row. For every 2.5 cm of row, sow five to seven small seeds like primula or three to four medium-sized seeds such as aster, pansy or stock. Then sprinkle vermiculite to the required depth over the surface. Make sure the material you use is free-flowing and spreads evenly. This covering allows water to penetrate, forms a mulch to stop the surface drying out and protects seeds from washing away. Water well with a fine hose spray or a watering can with a fine rose. For plastic seed trays, mark out shallow rows or drills with a board or dowel stick as described for seed beds. Sow seed, cover with moisture-holding material and water gently as before.

An alternative method is to use a 'marking board'. This is a flat board, slightly smaller in area than the tray, with 100 evenly spaced flat-headed nails driven into it. The heads of the nails are approximately 12 mm in diameter and protrude from the board about 6 mm. Press the board firmly into the damp soil surface, leaving 100 shallow holes. If the soil is too dry, the holes will fill with loose soil. Tap out between two and four seeds into each hole. Then cover the whole tray with vermiculite or compost to a depth of 3 mm. Water well with a fine spray as previously.

Plastic punnets are ideal for very small seeds like petunia, begonias and primula. Your seed-raising mix should be damp and free from lumps or clods. Sprinkle seed over the surface and firm down with a board or the bottom of an empty punnet. Water very gently. A thin layer of vermiculite over the seeds will keep them moist and allow light to reach them.

Punnets and mini-punnets are good for vegetable seedlings when you only need a few plants. Scatter about twenty seeds to a punnet or about ten seeds to a mini-punnet. This number will give you about a dozen or half a dozen seedlings respectively of broccoli, cabbage or tomato. Press into the damp mix with the bottom of an empty punnet, cover and water gently. For large seeds of pumpkin, cucumber, zucchini, marrow and other vine crops, use eight seeds to a punnet or four seeds to a mini-punnet. Press seeds into mix point down. Vine crop seeds of the cucumber family are prone to rotting so do not over-water them.

General care of seedlings

You must keep seeds moist but not wet until seedlings emerge. This may be seven to ten days for fast-germinating seeds but two to four weeks or more for slow starters. Check the Sowing Guides in Chapters 11 and 15 for approximate times.

Although the covering of moisture-holding material may appear dry on top, the soil underneath can be quite damp. Test this by scraping some of the covering away with your finger and feeling the dampness of the mix underneath. The same rule applies to seedlings once they are started. Keep them damp but not wet. As they grow stronger, thorough but less frequent watering is needed. Morning, rather than evening, watering is recommended. Seedlings require

Top five flowers to grow from seed

SWEET PEAS

These blooms offer everything – fragrance, colour, ease of cultivation. To top it off, they make great cut flowers.

NASTURTIUM

Pots, hanging baskets, banks, borders: all can be brightened up with the cheerful colours of nasturtiums – and, as a bonus, they're edible!

MARIGOLD

These grow best in warmer weather, but in frost-free areas the smaller-flowered varieties will perform year round.

SUNFLOWER

Sunflowers seem to capture the colour and cheerfulness of the sun. The bright-yellow blooms add warmth to the summer garden.

DAHLIA

Dahlias are members of the daisy family that bloom during the hotter months. They develop a curious, potato-like tuber and can last for years.

DAHLIA

some shade when very young but, as they grow, they need more sunlight. This way, they become more accustomed to conditions in the open garden. Too much shade makes soft, lanky seedlings which transplant poorly.

For extra warmth, especially in winter, you can cover seed beds with glass or clear plastic until seedlings emerge. Remove the cover immediately seedlings break the surface. Don't use these coverings in direct sunlight – the temperature increases so much that the seedlings 'cook' as they break the surface. Trays and punnets may also be covered with glass or enclosed in clear plastic bags or cling wrap to increase temperature and prevent evaporation (both indoors and outdoors), but remove these coverings when seedlings emerge. In very cold districts you may consider an electrically heated tray which fits under a miniature greenhouse or invest in a heated glasshouse.

Control slugs and snails by scattering Blitzem or Baysol pellets on or around seed beds, trays or containers. If you don't do this you may wake up one morning to find no seedlings at all! Damping off can occur in seedlings after they have emerged, especially

Plastic wrap keeps seeds warm while they are germinating.

STEP 1

Fill a small container with potting mix when seedlings grown in seed containers get their first true leaves.

STEP 2

Lift the seedlings, holding them by their leaves. Gently tease out the roots of individual plants.

STEP 3

Make holes in which to transplant the seedlings using an old pen or pencil (often called a 'dibble').

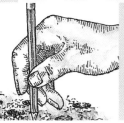

STEP 4

Place seedlings in holes, firm the mix down and water. Keep out of direct sunlight for a week.

if the weather is humid and the seeds are sown thickly. If some of your seedlings start to topple over at soil level, immediately spray them with a solution of Mancozeb Plus.

As soon as seedlings have their true leaves (after the first two seed leaves have emerged), begin fertilising with a soluble plant food, such as Thrive or Aquasol, at half strength.

Pricking out

This is a way to remove crowded seedlings when they are quite small (about 12 mm tall) to a larger container. Fill the seedling tray with potting mix then gently prise out a few seedlings with a pointed knife.

Separate the seedlings on a flat, clean surface. Take a seedling (gently but firmly) between thumb and forefinger in one hand and with the other use a dibble or a pencil to make a small hole in the mix. Lower the seedling roots into the hole and push a little soil mix around them with the dibble to firm the seedling. When the tray is full, gently water and keep in shade or under a fly screen or shade cloth frame for a few days until seedlings are well established. Grow seedlings on until they are 7–10 cm high and then transplant to garden beds.

Transplanting

Prepare the bed to receive seedlings two or three weeks before transplanting by adding mixed fertiliser. Blend well into the soil. Level the bed and water well so the soil is dark and damp. The day before transplanting, water the seedlings as well.

Mark out the position for each seedling. Make a hole in the soil with a trowel or your hand, 7–10 cm deep and wide enough to accommodate the seedling. Gently ease out seedlings from seed bed or container, taking as much soil as possible with each one. Lower the seedling into the hole and press soil around it, making a small depression at the same time to direct water to the roots. For seedlings in individual pots, simply tap the pot to remove the seedling and plant it slightly deeper than it was in the pot.

If you have garden compost or dry grass clippings available, spread some around each plant in an area about 30 cm in diameter. Then water each plant well with a gentle spray to settle soil around the roots.

It is best to transplant seedlings in the late afternoon or evening. If planting during the day, provide protection with pieces of brush or shadecloth that's supported on stakes, especially in hot weather.

Scatter snail and slug baits over the bed to protect the young plants and repeat application if heavy rain falls.

SEEDS WITH SPECIAL NEEDS

Seeds that need light to germinate:
 ageratum, alyssum, aquilegia, begonia, coleus, impatiens, lettuce, petunia, primula, snapdragon

Seeds that need darkness to germinate:
 calendula, coriander, cyclamen, delphinium, gazania, larkspur, nasturtium, nemesia, pansy, schizanthus (poor man's orchid), verbena, vinca, viola

Seeds that are sensitive to low temperatures:
 aster, calendula, beans, capsicums, carrots, celosia, coleus, cucumbers, eggplant, marigold, parsley, petunia, pumpkin/squash, salvia, tomato, verbena, zinnia

Seeds sensitive to high temperatures:
 alyssum, candytuft, coriander, cress, dahlia, freesia, gazania, larkspur, lettuce, nasturtium, nemesia, peas, phlox, poppy, spinach

Begonia seeds need light to germinate.

Nasturtium seeds need darkness to germinate.

Checklist to Germination Trouble

Too wet	Seed needs to be damp, not wet, for germination. Excess water prevents oxygen getting to the seed. Poorly drained soils may also have a high incidence of soil fungus diseases. The condition of wet soils can be improved with the addition of peat and compost and by raising the beds above the surrounding levels. To improve the germination of seeds, sow them in a band of seed-raising mix.
Too dry	A certain amount of water is essential for germination, so maintaining constant moisture during the germination period is vital. Cover containers with glass or paper to prevent drying.
Too cold	Cold temperatures result in slow, uneven germination; disease becomes prevalent and seedlings may be injured. Each species has a different optimum temperature for germination. Do not sow summer plants too early, e.g. beans, tomatoes, sweet corn, pumpkins, melons, cucumbers, petunia, portulaca and zinnia.
Too hot	High temperatures result in excessive drying and injury to seedlings.
Planting too deep	This will result in delayed emergence. Seeds may not be able to grow sufficiently to reach the surface on the limited food reserve within the seed. Soil temperature is also lower with depth. As a guide, sow seed to a depth equal to twice the thickness of the seed. Very fine flower seed, e.g. begonia and petunia, is best just pressed into the surface. In dry weather, seed can be planted a little deeper as the surface may dry out.
Planting seeds too shallow	Shallow planting can cause seeds to dry out.
Seed beds too loose	Mix which has not been firmed down results in too much air surrounding the seeds; they will not absorb moisture, and are likely to dry out.
Seed beds too firm	Firming mix down too hard prevents oxygen getting to the seed. Drainage is also impeded.
Presence of soil fungus diseases	Seeds may rot or seedlings topple. Over-watering, poor drainage and lack of ventilation will increase the incidence. Sow seeds in sterilised seed-raising mix and ensure containers are clean. Plan a rotation of crops to prevent the build-up of soil disease (leaf crops followed by root crops). Spray seeds of ornamentals with Mancozeb Plus.
Slugs and snails	During late autumn, winter and spring, slugs and snails may destroy seedlings as soon as they appear. Apply Baysol or Blitzem Snail & Slug Pellets or create a physical snail/slug barrier.
Birds, cats, dogs, insects	Animals are often responsible for destroying seeds and seedlings. Cover seed beds with a fine-meshed netting. Seeds can be damaged or eaten by insect pests. Spray with a suitable insecticide.
Fertiliser burn	Seed in direct contact with fertiliser can be burnt. Fertiliser should be worked into soil several weeks before sowing seed, or placed in a band below or beside the seed. Seedlings in the presences of high soluble salts are also more prone to 'damping off' diseases.
Seed viability and storage	Always use fresh seed. Some seeds such as parsnip and lettuce have a short life once the foil packet is opened. Seed deteriorates quickly if stored in a damp place, or exposed to high temperature. Always treat and handle seed with care to prolong its life. As a general guide, once the foil sachet has been opened the seed should be used within six months.

Thrifty Gardening

A beautiful garden need not cost the earth. Propagating plants from seeds or cuttings is both an economical and satisfying way to expand your stocks of garden material. Self-propagation also allows you to indulge in some of the more unusual plants not available through regular channels. Commercial seed packets, plant networks, mail order nurseries and friends are good sources of new plant material.

One of the best ways to import quick colour into a garden is with flowering annuals. Propagating annuals from seed is an extremely inexpensive way to supply plants for the garden. The number of seeds per packet varies with seed size, but for an outlay of only a few dollars you will often receive from between 250 to 1000 of the smaller flower seeds.

Expert advice on fleshing out a garden with perennials always calls for planting in drifts. Drifts require several plants of the one type to be used. Select and purchase one perennial plant; it will clump up quickly and can then easily be divided into several plants to fill out garden space.

If the budget doesn't stretch to buying a whole row of shrubs for a hedge or low edgers, buy one plant and take cuttings – you'll have a whole row in no time.

Stem cut lines

Internodal cut lines

SMART SEED SOWING

When using old pots and punnets for propagating, firstly clean them with soapy water, then sterilise them with bleach or antiseptic.

Use a commercial seed-raising mix or make up your own mix using peat moss, coarse sand and perlite.

Some seeds remain viable after being kept for a long period of time: tomatoes, eucalypts and grevilleas may germinate after being stored for ten years or more. Others don't. Check the use-by date on the seed packet and sow prior to that date.

TYPES OF CUTTINGS

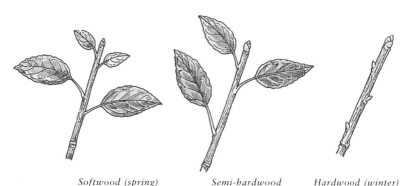

Softwood (spring)   *Semi-hardwood*   *Hardwood (winter)*
                             (summer/autumn)

have older wood at the base. To wound, use a sharp knife or razor blade. Scrape off a little of the outer tissue on either side of the bottom of the stem. Dip into hormone rooting powder and pot up, several cuttings to a pot, using a mixture of sand and peat moss.

Softwood cuttings

Soft, succulent new spring growth can be taken from plants in spring or summer. fuchsia, abelia, azalea and philadelphus (mock orange) are readily propagated from softwood cuttings.

Semi-hardwood cuttings

Take cuttings of new growth which has begun to harden up for murraya, *Choisya ternata*, camellia, daphne, gardenia and *Buxus* (box).

Hardwood cuttings

Hardwood cuttings of the previous season's growth can be taken in winter for hydrangea, grapes, crepe myrtle, roses and wisteria.

FIVE NEVER-FAIL CUTTINGS

- impatiens • Marguerite daisy
- fuchsia • pelargonium • coleus

Avoid overcrowding seeds. The root system of each emerging seedling needs room to grow to its full capacity and take up the available nutrients in the soil.

Sow seeds at the depth recommended on the pack. If the seeds are sown too close to the surface of the soil they may dry out or become dislodged when watering. If seeds are sown too deeply, they are literally buried and will be deprived of light and oxygen.

FIVE NEVER-FAIL SEEDS

- nasturtium • alyssum • sunflower
- cosmos • Mexican sunflower

TOOLS OF THE TRADE

- seed-raising mix • tamper (to press the mix down firmly) • punnets and pots
- labels and indelible marker • seeds
- plastic bag cloches or mini-greenhouse
- secateurs • rooting hormone powder

CUTTING TO MAKE MORE

Some plants are harder to strike than others. Knowing the age of wood to use will help. See the three types opposite. Make sure the section of stem being used has at least one bud. Cut just below a node and remove the bottom leaves. Wounding the stem is particularly useful for those species difficult to root and those which

10
New Plants from Old

Vegetative propagation means causing plants to multiply by means other than seeds. Two advantages of this process are that gardeners are certain that new plants will be identical to old ones, and that they will have a usable plant in less time than one grown from seed. In some cases, plants set seed poorly or not at all, so one must use vegetative methods. With others, you have a choice – you can sow seed or propagate vegetatively.

Examples of vegetative propagation in the garden are easy to find. Strawberries have stolons or runners which form new shoots and roots at every node or joint. Common mint has underground stems called rhizomes. These make a dense mat and each small piece can become a new plant. Potatoes have swollen underground stems or tubers. Each bud or eye on a potato is a potential potato plant. Bulbs and corms provide other examples of the ability of plants to multiply and grow. Unfortunately, many of our most troublesome weeds also have this ability.

All forms of vegetative reproduction depend on small regions of tissue which produce new plant cells. Growing tissue, where cells are actively dividing, is located in the tips of stems and roots and in lateral buds. Stems and roots increase in diameter too, especially in larger plants. To achieve growth in diameter there is another area of growing tissue called the cambium layer. It is best described as a thin, unbroken cylinder of dividing cells which connects every part of the plant. The cambium layer splits off new cells from both its inside and outside layers.

The cambium layer is the vital part of any plant when taking cuttings, or in layering, budding or grafting. For this reason, cuttings are taken just below a node or joint in the stem, or below a leaf axil, where one finds the greatest concentration of dividing cells which heal the wound ('form a callus') from which new roots will grow. In budding and grafting, the cambium layers of the two plants are placed in contact. This allows the bud or graft (the scion) to draw on food from the growing plant (the stock), and the two plants join together.

PLANT DIVISION

With the exception of taprooted plants, all perennials which form clumps of roots, shoots and foliage can be lifted and divided into a number of pieces for replanting. This is a quick and simple way to get new plants. Some clumps divide easily, but in others you must be more ruthless and use a spade or a sharp knife. Often you can cut off pieces with sufficient root without lifting the parent plant. Division is a useful method for herbaceous perennials (which die down in winter and regrow in spring) like phlox, Michaelmas daisy, gerbera, chrysanthemum and dahlia, and also for true perennials such as agapanthus, iris, canna, strelitzia, violet, nandina, New Zealand flax and ornamental grasses. Many perennial plants become too large and overcrowded and benefit from division every two or three years.

LAYERING

Layering is another easy method of propagation. It has the advantage that the 'layer' is not completely cut from the parent plant and continues to draw nourishment from it. Layering is a good way to multiply many small trees and shrubs, including azalea, rhododendron, magnolia, gardenia and daphne. Carnations, sometimes rather difficult as cuttings, take to this treatment too.

When layering small trees or shrubs, select a thin, supple branch close to the ground. Bend the branch towards the soil and make a slanting cut 5–7 cm long with a sharp knife on the underside of the branch. Finish the cut at a node, but take care not to cut more than halfway through the branch.

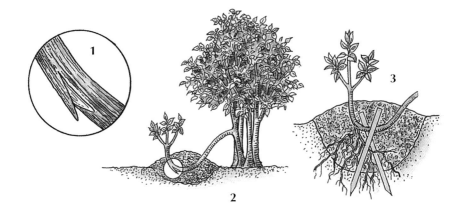

Layering (sometimes called 'serpentine layering') is an easy method of propagation. (1) Make a slanting cut 5–7 cm long on the underside of a branch, finishing the cut at a node. (2) Bend the branch towards the ground and cover with soil. (3) Anchor the branch in the soil with wire in the shape of a 'U'. When a good root system is formed, cut the layer from the parent plant.

The cut can be kept slightly open with a matchstick or a sliver of wood and the cut portion dusted with hormone cutting powder.

HINT

When planning a hedge that requires many plants, seek out the owner of another such hedge and ask if you can obtain the clippings when it is next clipped. Then use them as cuttings to produce your own plants. This is particularly easy with plants such as lavenders and box.

TONY FAWCETT

GARDEN WRITER – SATURDAY *HERALD SUN* *HOME* MAGAZINE

Now bury the cut portion of the branch in the soil and anchor it with a piece of stout wire bent to form a 'U'. If the soil is hard and lumpy, scrape it away and replace it with lighter soil or, preferably, a mixture of sand and compost or leaf mould. The end of the branch can be kept in an upright position by tying it to a small stake.

You can, of course, layer a number of branches at once. Keep the soil damp, but not wet, to encourage roots to form. If the branch is layered in late winter or early spring, roots are usually formed by the following autumn. You can gently scrape away the soil occasionally to check if roots are showing. When a good root system has formed, cut the branch from the parent plant. Leave the new plant for three or four weeks to adjust to its independent status, then lift it carefully and replant in its new position.

Much the same method can be used for carnations, but start layering in December or January. The rooted plants will be ready for planting in April or May. Remove the lower leaves (next to the parent plant), leaving a tuft of leaves at the end of the stem. These leaves can be shortened slightly.

Many climbing and trailing plants are layered easily. Bend down well-ripened stems and peg them in the ground so that one or two nodes are covered with soil. Cutting the stems from the parent plant is rarely necessary.

AIR-LAYERING

If branches or stems are too large and stiff to bend to the ground, air-layering (sometimes called 'marcotting') is an alternative method. Make a slanting cut in the stem, finishing at a node. Keep the cut open with a sliver of wood. Then wrap the cut with damp sphagnum moss and cover with aluminium

HINT

When fast-growing plants like marguerite daisies, geraniums and pelargoniums start to look woody, take soft-tip cuttings. These cuttings should make roots in three to four weeks. Once the new plants are growing well, dig out the old plant and start afresh. You may do this every two to three years.

MARGARET HANKS

HORTICULTURIST

foil or plastic tied in place with string or budding tape. This keeps the cut moist. Some gardeners ringbark the branch completely to encourage rooting. Inspect periodically to ascertain whether the roots are well developed and the time has come to cut it from the parent plant. Air-layers need careful attention for the first few weeks after removal until the plants have become adjusted to relying on their new root system. Air layers are often used to propagate fruit

trees but are also useful for growing woody plants such as magnolias.

CUTTINGS

Many garden plants are grown from cuttings. A cutting is a piece of stem, leaf or root which, when planted under favourable conditions, produces another plant. You can collect, prepare and grow cuttings without too much effort, and little space or gardening skill is needed.

Cuttings fall into three main groups: stem cuttings, leaf cuttings and root cuttings. Stem cuttings are further divided into three subgroups depending on the type of wood used: softwood, semi-hardwood and hardwood cuttings. But before you start, there are a few other aspects to consider.

Tools and equipment

You need a good quality knife for a start. A razor blade with one edge covered with insulating or adhesive tape is useful for small cuttings. A good pair of secateurs should be kept in top condition by regular sharpening. A plastic collection bag for cuttings is useful to prevent them drying out and wilting, especially for softwood cuttings or if you are collecting cuttings away from home.

Low-growing branches of azaleas will sometimes layer and form roots where they contact the soil.

Top five plants to grow from cuttings

ABELIA

Useful, hardy shrub with clusters of small white bells in summer.

AZALEA

Some modern varieties flower for months.

FUCHSIA

Grows easily from tip cuttings taken either in early summer or mid-winter.

PHILOTHECA (syn. *Eriostemon*)

These natives do best if new plants are started every few years.

GARDENIA

All types of gardenias readily form roots on tip cuttings with firm bases.

ABELIA

FUCHSIA

ERIOSTEMON

Containers and rooting mixtures

The best containers are plastic pots, punnets or trays. These are easy to clean, so wash thoroughly before using. All containers must have free drainage. The rooting mix must be as free as possible from disease, insects and weed seeds. Leading nurseries sterilise the rooting medium and the containers they use, but this sophisticated treatment is difficult for the average home gardener.

The materials recommended below are relatively sterile and relatively free of these problems. Good-quality seed-raising mixtures (such as Yates Seed Raising Mix) are suitable. Coarse river sand is often used but dries out quickly. Try a mix containing two parts of coarse sand and one part of peat moss or vermiculite. A mix which holds more moisture is one part of coarse sand and one part of peat moss or vermiculite. Charcoal, when crushed and screened, may be added to keep the mixture clean and more open. A suggested mix is two parts coarse sand, one part peat moss or vermiculite and one part charcoal.

Root-promoting hormones

Hormone 'cutting' powders or gels can help cuttings form a callus and make roots quickly. There are a number of proprietary brands, including Yates Cutting Powder and Clonex Root Hormone Gels. Dip the cleanly cut ends into the powder or gel before planting. Full directions are given on the pack. Cutting powders are also useful for dusting the cut surfaces of stems for layering (see pages 169–171).

Protection for cuttings

Successfully striking cuttings depends a lot on providing a suitable microclimate. High humidity to prevent moisture loss is important. A mini-greenhouse with a clear plastic lid can be useful if you grow a lot of cuttings. An inverted glass jar, base of a clear plastic bottle or a clear plastic bag supported on a wire frame placed over a pot of cuttings offer simple solutions. Large boxes (with the bottoms knocked out) or frames with glass or plastic covers are good for a number of pots. Stand them on a 2–3 cm layer of moisture-holding material – peat moss, charcoal, pine bark – so water will evaporate continuously. Boxes and frames should not be too deep; about 50 cm is sufficient. This allows about 15 cm between the top of the cuttings and the cover. Provide some shade because direct sunlight will build up too much heat. Most cuttings strike best at a temperature of 20–25°C, so keep your pots in a shady spot or place newspaper or shade cloth over the top of your box or frame for a week or so. Then harden them to direct sunlight. Ventilation is also needed, so prop the jar up slightly, open the plastic bag, or raise the frame cover a little.

The three main groups of cuttings are as follows. Stem cuttings are divided into three further subgroups according to the type of wood used.

HINT

Beware if people are pulling up large sections of plant to give you. It might be an invasive pest in your garden too!

SUE TEMPLETON
SALVIA SPECIALIST

Stem cuttings
Softwood cuttings

These are taken in spring from shrubby plants with soft green shoots. Because the plants are in active growth, take care to prevent cuttings wilting before you plant them. Take softwood cuttings early in the morning when the plant is full of sap. If they start to dry out, cover them with moist newspaper. There are exceptions to this rule – very sappy plants like geraniums, succulents and cactus will tolerate wilting even for a day or two. This gives the cut section time to dry out and start to heal.

With tip cuttings, remove the leaves from the stem where the cut is to be made. Make a clean cut at a slight angle just below a node or leaf axil. For plants with large leaves, remove all but a few top ones. These can be reduced to about half their length.

Tip cuttings are usually 5–10 cm in length and have four to six nodes. This method suits azaleas, gardenias and similar evergreens with large leaves. Heel cuttings are good for conifers and many other plants. Take off side shoots so that a small heel of the older branch is attached. Trim off any excess bark.

Semi-hardwood cuttings

Take cuttings 10–15 cm long from evergreen trees and shrubs where the stems have started to mature into firmer brown or grey wood. These cuttings can be side shoots with a heel or a section of the lower, more mature part of the stem with the cut just below a node. Again, reduce the number or size of the leaves to avoid excessive moisture loss.

Hardwood cuttings

These are taken from deciduous trees or shrubs in winter when they are dormant. Select wood about 6–20 mm in diameter and about 20 cm long, with four to six nodes on each cutting. These cuttings usually root easily, in the same way that branches of mulberries, willows, poplars and coral trees will grow when simply pushed into the ground. To avoid planting hardwood cuttings upside down, make a slanting cut at the bottom just below the node and a straight cut about 6–12 mm above the top node. This way you will be reminded to plant the cutting point down.

Leaf cuttings

These are used for many indoor plants. The leaves of Rex begonia, for example, can be cut in sections and laid on a moist rooting medium, or a single leaf can be laid flat and the veins cut with a sharp knife or razor blade. For propagating African violets, remove a mature leaf with about 25 mm of petiole (leaf stem) and bury the petiole in the rooting mix. Shoots and roots develop from the base of the leaf. Sansevieria (mother-in-law's tongue) can be propagated from 5 cm sections of leaf. The bases of these sections are placed vertically in a rooting medium.

Root cuttings

This is not a common method of propagation in the garden but some plants can produce buds from their thick, fleshy roots. Root

Transplanting Tips

It's often desirable to move a plant from one part of the garden to another but make sure you think carefully before you rush in with your spade. Transplanting always involves risk for the plant, so don't do it unless you're prepared to take that risk. Of course, in some cases, such as when the plant's on the site of a new building, it will have to be moved.

Your chances of success when transplanting depend very much on the size of the plant. Generally, the smaller the plant, the easier it will be to move with minimal root disturbance.

Select a gentle time of year – when it's not too hot or too cold – to move evergreen shrubs and small trees. That usually means spring or autumn. Deciduous plants, those that lose their leaves in winter, are best moved in the colder months when they are dormant.

When it comes to larger trees and shrubs, you'll be limited by the weight you can lift. A root ball that measures one metre across can be surprisingly heavy and it may require at least four people to lift it. If the root ball is larger than you can physically handle, you'll have to cut the roots back to a manageable size, which could cause irreparable damage. In this case it may be better to consult an expert arborist for advice.

Despite these qualifications, there are many things you can do to improve your chances of success at transplanting time, including:

- Prepare the new position well beforehand. Dig organic matter and some gentle Dynamic Lifter pellets into the soil. Add water-storing crystals if required. Check drainage, aspect etc.

- If the plant has a large root system and you can wait a couple of months to make the move, look at the plant and assess the diameter of root ball you think you can handle. Then use a sharp spade to cut vertically down into the soil around this circle. Push the spade in as deeply as possible. This will encourage new roots to grow inside this area during the coming weeks.

- Choose a cool day to move. Water the root ball and the new planting spot and allow both to drain.

- Spray the foliage of the plant with Yates DroughtShield.

- Move with care, digging to extract the root ball with minimal disturbance. Wrap with plastic sheet or hessian to hold the root ball together.

- Position plant in its new spot so it's facing the same aspect as before. And don't plant any deeper in the soil than the plant was beforehand.

- Trim any damaged shoots. Apart from this, these days most experts suggest it's best not to cut back the foliage.

- Backfill gently and water to settle soil around the roots.

- Apply some Yates Waterwise Soil Saturator to the root area to encourage water to move easily into the roots.

- Make sure the root ball stays moist, especially in the vital first weeks.

- An application of a seaweed tonic will boost the growth of new roots and help the plant to re-establish as quickly as possible.

- If hot weather arrives unexpectedly, rig up some temporary shade.

- If the plant is unstable or in a windy spot, consider putting in some support stakes. Use figure of eight soft ties to loosely attach the plant, allowing room for a small amount of movement.

Coloured-leaf begonias grow readily from leaf cuttings.

sections 8–10 cm long and 12 mm in diameter are covered with 1–2 cm of rooting mix. Perennial phlox, albizia, bouvardia, crepe myrtle and wisteria have been propagated by this method.

Planting cuttings

Pot up cuttings as soon as possible. Fill the pots with a rooting medium, which should be slightly damp. Dip the cut surface into water and then into hormone powder or gel. Make

HINT

An old metal ironing board, with covers removed, makes an ideal potting bench. Soil falls through the holes, you can set it to the height you want (including a low setting for kids) and, when you've finished, it packs neatly against the garage wall.

BRODEE MYERS-COOKE

EDITOR-IN-CHIEF TASTE.COM.AU

holes with a dibble or pencil about 5 cm apart in the damp mix around the edge of the pot. Set the cuttings in the holes about one-third of their length deep. Firm the mix around them and water the pots gently. Protect cuttings as described above for the first week or two, and then allow more sun and ventilation. Always keep pots moist but not wet. Roots take time to develop. It may be many weeks before they will support the new plant, so do not try to move cuttings too early. It is best to transfer rooted cuttings to individual 7–10 cm pots and grow them on until the root system is well advanced.

BUDDING AND GRAFTING

These methods of propagation involve the union of a cut portion of one plant (the scion) with a stem or branch of a growing plant (the stock). In other words, the cambium layers of both scion and stock must be in contact. Both methods are used by nurseries, especially when a selected variety is budded or grafted onto a more vigorous or disease-resistant root stock.

Budding and grafting are really tasks for the specialist, and most home gardeners have neither the skill or expertise to undertake such

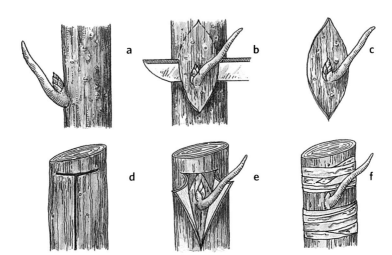

*Shield budding is the method used for grafting fruit trees, citrus and roses. Diagrams **a**, **b** and **c** show how the bud is sliced from the scion. **d**. A T-shaped cut is made in the stock. **e**. The bud is inserted in the stock, closing the bark flaps over the edges of the shield. **f**. Tie the shield firmly to the stock with plastic grafting tape, but take care not to cover the bud.*

methods successfully. Hence, only a brief summary with diagrams is given here. Those who wish for more detail should consult one of the books available on this subject.

Shield budding

Shield budding is mostly used for propagating citrus trees, deciduous fruit trees and roses. Spring or early autumn, when the plants are in active growth, are suitable times for budding.

1. To prepare the stock, make a T-shaped cut in the bark on one- or two-year-old wood. The flaps of bark should lift easily from the wood.
2. Cut the bud from a pencil-thick shoot of the scion. Use a very sharp knife to slice an oval-shaped piece of bark and wood with the bud in the centre. Make the shield 2–4 cm long. Remove the piece of wood behind the shield if it will lift out easily.
3. Place the shield into the T-shaped cut, closing the bark flaps over its edges. Trim off surplus bark at the top of the shield.
4. Starting at the bottom, use budding tape to tie the shield firmly to the stock along its full length. Take care not to cover the bud.
5. After about three weeks, cut the tape away. If the shield is still green and the bud plump, it has taken.

6. If budded in spring, cut off the stock above the bud when binding is cut. If budded in autumn, the bud remains dormant until early spring when the stock is cut back.

Whip-tongue graft

This method is used when the scion and the stock are of the same diameter – to about 2.5 cm thick.

1. Cut the top of the stock and the bottom of the scion with a slanting cut 4 cm long. The scion should be about 10 cm long.
2. Cut along the grain on both faces, one-third of the length from the tips to a depth of 6 mm.
3. Fit scion to stock so that the tongues interlock and the cambium layers match on at least one side.
4. Bind the graft carefully with budding tape to make it firm and airtight.

Crown or rind graft

This method is used for one or more scions on a trunk or branch of stock over 2.5 cm in diameter.

1. Saw off the stock at right angles. Smooth the cut surface with a sharp knife.
2. Make a vertical cut 5–7 cm long for each scion. The knife should penetrate the

bark to the wood, but not further.

3. Prepare 15 cm scions with a long, slanting cut to the base to form a tapered wedge.

4. Slip the thin end of the wedge between the bark and the wood of the stock and push down until the cut surface of the scion fits snugly against the exposed tissue of the stock.

5. When all scions are in position, bind them with budding tape and, if possible, cover the whole cut surface with grafting wax to exclude air and rain.

TISSUE CULTURE

Plant tissue culture is essentially a laboratory technique. It is the vegetative propagation of plants on artificial nutrient under aseptic (sterile) conditions.

The main objectives of plant propagation under the tissue culture system are: the rapid regeneration of plant specimens ensuring genetic homogeneity; the multiplication of important plant species which are difficult to propagate by conventional means (for example, orchid hybrids); and the elimination of viruses from infected plants.

The plant parts which are suitable for plant tissue culture range from plant organs, plant tissue, diminutive shoot tips, seeds, anthers, pollen grains and plant cells.

The general method employed for cultivating larger plant tissue is to sterilise the surface of the tissue and place it on a sterile nutrient base under aseptic conditions for exclusion of micro-organisms, such as fungi and bacteria. The cultured tissue and nutrient are usually maintained in a flask or bottle and are incubated under artificially controlled conditions of light and temperature.

Plants which are commonly regenerated by plant tissue culture for commercial or scientific purposes are strawberries, forest trees, azaleas, ferns, rice, sugar cane, grapes, tobacco, carnations, chrysanthemums, roses and several foliage plants. Tissue culture has enabled the introduction of many new plant types into the Australian garden.

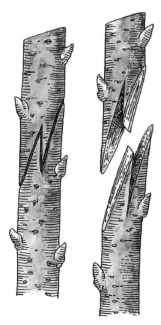

Whip-tongue grafting is useful when both scion and stock are the same thickness. The diagram shows how the cuts are made and fitted together before binding with insulating or grafting tape.

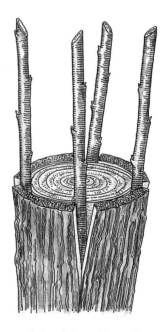

Crown or rind graft is used for grafting one or more scions into a thick trunk or branch of the stock. Slits are made in the bark of the stock, and scions cut to tapered wedges are inserted and held in place with budding tape.

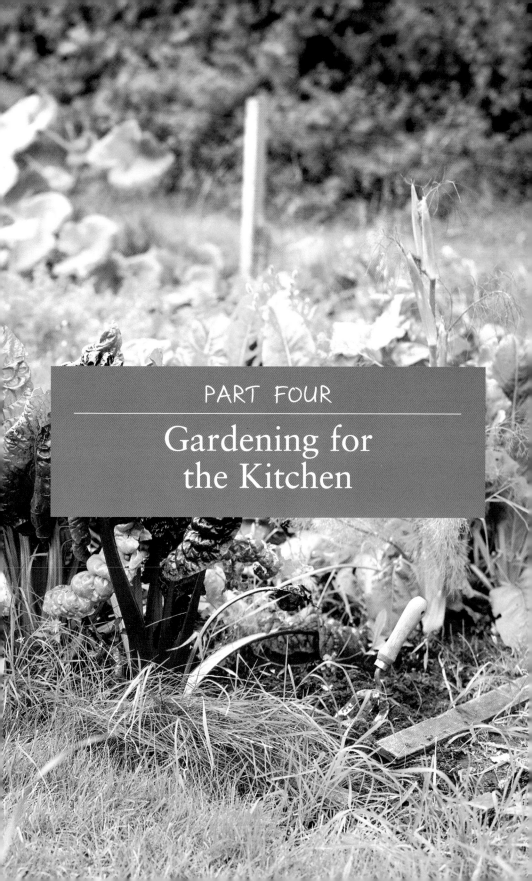

PART FOUR

Gardening for
the Kitchen

11
Vegetables

Of all gardening activities, being able to harvest your own fresh, vitamin-packed vegetables is arguably one of the most rewarding.

Vegetables are often divided into three groups depending on the part of the plants we usually eat:

1. Fruit and seed vegetables, such as beans, peas, capsicum, eggplant, tomato, sweet corn and vine crops (cucurbits, like pumpkins, squash and zucchini).
2. Leaf and stem vegetables, such as cabbage, celery, lettuce, rhubarb, silver beet and spinach. Broccoli and cauliflower are usually included in this group, too, although the part we eat is the flower bud and not the leaves or stems.
3. Root and bulb vegetables, such as beetroot, carrots, onions, parsnips, potatoes, radishes and turnips.

You do not need different soil for different vegetables. If you can grow good tomatoes there is no reason why you cannot grow good beans, cabbages or carrots, too. However, the grouping of vegetables into fruit, leaf and root plants does give good guidelines for fertiliser use. Fruit and root vegetables need larger quantities of potassium and phosphorus in fertiliser, because these elements stimulate flowers, fruits and seeds and root development. Fertilisers high in nitrogen may produce too much leaf growth and reduce yields of fruits and seeds. On the other hand, nitrogenous fertilisers are needed in greater quantities by leafy vegetables like cabbage, chicory, lettuce, silver beet and spinach.

Growing vegetables gives best results if you plan a program of small, successive sowings and plantings throughout the year. To do this, you should know when and how to grow different vegetables, how long each takes to reach maturity and what yield to expect.

COOL- AND WARM-SEASON VEGETABLES

Most vegetables prefer to grow in a specific temperature range and are disappointing if planted out of season.

Cool-season vegetables grow best at low temperatures of 10–20°C, but they tolerate even colder conditions and are usually frost-resistant. This group, which includes broad beans, broccoli, Brussels sprouts, cauliflower, onions, peas, spinach and turnips, are sown to grow during the cooler months of the year. Warm-season vegetables grow best at a temperature of 20°C or above. They perform poorly in cool weather and are susceptible to frost. This group includes beans, capsicum, eggplant, potato, sweet corn, sweet potato, tomato and all the vine crops. In most parts of the country they are sown in spring or early summer to grow during warmer months.

A third group has intermediate temperature requirements and grows best at 15–25°C. This group includes beetroot, cabbage, carrot, celery, leek, lettuce, parsnip, radish and silver beet. It is important to sow them at the correct time of the year for your climate because they tend to 'bolt', or run to seed, if they are sown too early or too late (especially in areas that have very hot or very cold extremes). Root crops, like beetroot, carrot and parsnip, may run to seed if sown too late in autumn or winter. Silver beet, a close relative of beetroot, may do this too, although newer varieties are more tolerant. Some varieties of lettuce run to seed if sown in warm weather, so choose those that have been selected for growing in summer. The best months for sowing each kind of vegetable in each climate zone – tropical, subtropical, temperate and cold – are shown in the Sowing Guide on pages 224–227. A map of climate zones in Australia is shown on pages 500–501.

NEED FOR SUNLIGHT

An open, sunny site is a must for your vegetable garden. To grow well, vegetables need as much sunlight as possible, especially in winter when days are shorter. If possible, select a part of the garden facing north to northeast to catch the morning sun and at least four or five hours of direct sunlight each day. Make allowance for longer shadows in winter. Try to avoid shade from buildings, fences, or large trees and shrubs. Trees and shrubs with large root systems will compete for moisture and nutrients, as well as light. A level site is best and easiest to manage, with both beds and rows running north–south. This way each plant in the row receives maximum sunlight. On sloping sites, garden beds should run across the slope with a retaining wall on the downhill side to prevent erosion and loss of soil. In this case it may be best for rows to run across the beds instead of along them.

SHELTER FROM WINDS

Vegetables need some protection from wind. Cold winds slow down growth, and hot, dry winds cause water to evaporate from soil and leaves. Strong winds also damage leaves and stems and may loosen and weaken roots. Windbreaks of trees, shrubs or hedges growing on the south or west of the vegetable garden do not create shade problems and can be planted well back from the garden to give good wind protection. Artificial windbreaks of lattice, slatted timber or light brush fences make excellent wind-barriers. They reduce wind velocity without creating turbulence. Brick or concrete walls with about 50 per cent opening have this effect too. Wind-barriers on the south offer a bonus by providing support for climbing beans and cucumbers in summer, and climbing peas in winter.

SIZE AND LAYOUT

Available space and your own enthusiasm will dictate the size of your vegetable plot. Generally, it is best to have beds 150 cm wide and paths 30–40 cm between each bed. This allows you to work from both sides. This width is doubly convenient because it will accommodate three plants of broccoli, cabbage or tomato across the bed, or three rows of beans, peas or sweet corn. With smaller, more upright growers – such as beetroot, carrots, lettuce and silver beet – you

Vegetables to Grow in Winter

VEGETABLE	SUGGESTED VARIETY	SOW COOL DISTRICT	SOW WARM DISTRICT
Broccoli	Winter Harvest	January-February	February-March
Cabbage	Eureka	January-March	March-May
Cauliflower	Mini, Phenomenal Early	January-March	February-March
Carrots	All Seasons, Topweight	January-March	March-May
Lettuce	Winter Triumph	March-April	April-May
Leeks	Welsh Wonder	January-February	April-June
Parsnips	Hollow Crown	January-March	April-May
Silver beet	Fordhook Giant	February-March	March-May
Spinach	Winter Queen	February-April	March-May
Broad Beans	Coles Dwarf	April-May	April-June

can fit in five or six rows across the bed. Beds may be of any length, but 9 m is a convenient length because it can be divided into 3 m sections for successive plantings. To provide year-round vegetables for a family of four you need about six beds, each 9 m by 1.5 m, a total area of about 100 square metres. For new gardeners, a smaller area of three beds is suggested.

HINT

Growing colourful lettuce, parsley, rainbow chard and chives in flowerbeds is an excellent idea for gardeners who do not have the space for a vegetable garden. The plants are all attractive, and can create extra interest.

VALERIE AND GERRY ZWART

GARDEN WRITERS, QUEENSLAND

It is better to look after a small garden well than to have a large garden which may be too hard to manage. You can always increase the area by adding extra beds or making them longer. Raised vegetable beds made of corrugated iron or timber are popular in gardens with limited space. They also reduce the amount of bending required to tend them.

There is a modern trend to grow vegetables among flowers and in ornamental garden beds, especially using attractive plants like red-stemmed silver beet, parsley, coloured and frilly-leaved lettuce and borders of chives.

SOIL FOR VEGETABLES

Soil for vegetables should have a loose, crumbly structure which is capable of absorbing and holding water and nutrients, but it should be well aerated and drain easily.

As described in Chapter 4, you can improve sandy soils easily by adding moisture-holding materials such as animal manure, mushroom compost, garden compost, vermiculite or peat moss. The structure of heavy soils also benefits from organic matter and their texture is improved by adding coarse sand. Always dig heavy soil

when damp but not too wet. For most vegetables, including root crops, dig soil to 25–30 cm deep but do not bring subsoil to the surface. Extra drainage is usually necessary on heavy soils. Raise each bed 15–20 cm by shovelling soil from the pathway onto beds on either side. Slope the edge of the beds to between 45 and 60 degrees. This allows downward and sideways movement of water. Beds can also be contained by flat boards held in position with stout pegs, or surrounded by bricks or concrete, but remember to make provision for weep holes or leave gaps for drainage.

FERTILISERS

It is best to apply a pre-sowing or pre-planting mixed fertiliser for each vegetable crop you grow. Broadcast the fertiliser, apply in bands or dig into the soil before planting. Root and bulb vegetables, once established, will often produce a good crop without side-dressings of additional fertiliser. Leaf vegetables demand extra nitrogen in the form of liquid feeds of Thrive or Aquasol every ten to fourteen days during the growing period.

Lime and pH

Most vegetables and herbs grow successfully in soil which is slightly or very slightly acidic (pH 6.0–7.0). A few vegetables, such as potatoes, sweet potatoes and watermelons, will tolerate a strongly acidic soil. In high rainfall districts near the coast it is a good idea to add agricultural lime or dolomite (lime with extra magnesium) to vegetable beds every year or two, but there is no need to apply lime before every crop. Too much lime can be harmful (see section on pH and lime in Chapter 5). A good time to apply lime is after summer crops have finished and before cool-season crops are established.

CROP ROTATION

The main reason for crop rotation in the vegetable garden is to prevent the spread of diseases (or insect pests) which may attack vegetables belonging to the same family or group. If disease in any crop is serious, it's unwise to plant a closely related crop in the same bed. Complicated charts and diagrams for crop rotation are rather confusing and seldom work out as planned. In Australia, there is a natural rotation between warm- and cool-season crops. Providing you apply fertiliser and organic matter and are aware of the possibility of related plants contracting a disease from a previous crop, you need not be overly concerned about crop rotation. Try, if possible, to grow successive crops that are unrelated (e.g. don't follow summer beans by peas or broad beans).

WATERING AND MULCHING

The general principles of watering and mulching have been discussed in Chapter 4. To grow quickly, vegetables need adequate water at all times. Most of the water they absorb is passed through the plant and is evaporated or transpired by the leaves. In hot, dry weather, leaf vegetables may lose several times their weight in water each day. Once vegetables are established, a soaking will encourage deep roots. This helps them to withstand dry conditions for longer periods.

HINT

Using vegetables as a decorative border can be pleasing to the eye and a joy to the stomach. Best root candidates are carrots, which have lovely lacy foliage, and red-leafed beetroot. Leaf lettuces, which come in colours of green, pink and purple, look almost too good to pick and can rival many annual flowering plants.

DERYN THORPE

GARDEN WRITER, *THE WEST AUSTRALIAN* NEWSPAPER AND *GARDENING AUSTRALIA* MAGAZINE

Lavender and other flowering ornamentals will attract pollinating bees into your vegetable patch.

Depending on water restrictions, vegetable beds can be watered with sprinklers or drippers. A slow application rate is best for vegetables. Soaker hoses or micro-irrigation systems are also useful for slow watering and can be laid between the rows. Furrow irrigation is suitable for flat beds, or for those with a gentle slope, especially for watering tomatoes, potatoes and other crops where it is desirable to keep the leaves dry to reduce the risk of developing and spreading leaf diseases. Make a deep furrow, with a gradual fall to one end, between the rows of plants. Water with a slow-running hose until the furrow is completely filled with water.

Mulching vegetable beds, especially in summer, will greatly reduce loss of soil moisture. It also provides a more even temperature and discourages weeds. The best mulching materials for vegetable beds are organically–derived such as garden compost, well-rotted animal manure or lucerne hay. The mulch can be dug into the soil when preparing for the next crop.

CHOOSING YOUR CROPS

Naturally you will choose vegetables that you and your family enjoy eating, but some give better value than others. Yield for the area occupied is a good reason for growing a particular vegetable. Climbing beans, climbing peas and cucumbers growing on a trellis use vertical space but little ground level space. Tomatoes and capsicum give high yields for space occupied. The cut-and-come-again vegetables – broccoli, celery (pick green outside leaves progressively), loose-hearted types of lettuce, rhubarb and silver beet – are good value for extended harvesting. Salad vegetables and leaf crops, which lose quality quickly after harvest, are excellent in the home garden because of their extra flavour and freshness.

New dwarf or bush varieties of some vegetables are now available, for example dwarf or mini tomatoes, bush pumpkin and baby carrots and beetroot. They take up little garden space and many can be grown in tubs or large pots on a sunny balcony.

Some of the most productive home-garden vegetables are: beans (dwarf and climbing), broccoli, Brussels sprouts, cabbage (especially Chinese cabbages), capsicum, carrot, cauliflower, cucumber (on trellis), lettuce, baby squash, onion, parsnips, peas (climbing), pumpkin (bush), radish, rhubarb, silver beet, spinach, tomato and turnip.

GENERAL HINTS FOR VEGETABLE GROWING

Successive sowings

For a continuous satisfactory supply of home-grown vegies, make small successive sowings or plantings. Try to always have an empty bed or section of bed in preparation for the next sowing or planting.

Tall vegetables

Plant tall crops (tomatoes, sweet corn, broad beans) on the southern end of beds to prevent shading of low-growing vegetables. If making successive sowings of any crop in the one bed – say, dwarf beans or sweet corn – use the southern end first so that subsequent sowings get full sunlight.

Grouping vegetables

If possible, try to group vegetables which grow to the same height and mature about the same time (carrots, leeks and parsnips). This gives each a fair share of sunlight and, after harvest, the whole section can be dug and prepared for the next crops. Root and bulb crops are usually easier to handle in long rows of 2–3 m.

Long-standing crops

Plant perennial crops such as asparagus and rhubarb in a separate section or at one end of a bed where they can grow undisturbed. Don't forget that crops with an extended harvest period (capsicum, celery and silver beet) will continue occupying space for two or three months after your first picking.

HINT

Thyme is a must in the vegetable garden as it will attract bees to the area to pollinate your crops.

JUNE TAYLOR
GARDEN WRITER

Pest and Disease Control for Vegetables

PLANT	PEST OR DISEASE	SYMPTOMS	CONTROL
Broad beans	Black aphids	Small black insects on underside of leaves and shoots.	Natrasoap, Pyrethrum, Bug Gun
French and runner beans	Two-spotted mite	Bronzing and unthriftiness of foliage.	Natrasoap
	Bean fly	Larvae burrow into stalks and stems.	Remove affected pods
	Green vegetable bug	Large green shield bugs.	Baythroid
	Rust	Red-brown blisters on leaves and pods.	Mancozeb Plus
Broccoli, Brussels sprouts, Cabbage, Cauliflower	Larvae of cabbage moth and white butterfly	Holes in leaves.	Success Ultra, Baythroid, Derris, Dipel, Mavrik, Pyrethrum, Bug Gun
	Grey aphids	Small grey insects on underside of leaves.	Natrasoap, Pyrethrum, Confidor
	Cutworms	Seedlings eaten at ground level.	Success Ultra, Baythroid
Capsicum	Fruit fly	Larvae burrow through fruit.	Nature's Way Fruit Fly Control
Carrot	Aphids	Small insects usually underneath leaves.	Natrasoap, Pyrethrum, Bug Gun
Celery	Leaf spot	Brown spots over leaves.	Mancozeb Plus
Cucumber	Powdery mildew	Powdery white film on leaves.	Lime Sulfur
	Downy mildew	Leaf spots and downy tufts underneath.	Liquid Copper
	Whitefly	Small, white, moth-like insects.	Confidor
Eggplant	Thrips	Discoloured foliage.	Confidor
Lettuce	Aphids	See Carrots.	
	Downy mildew	Leaf spots and downy mildew tufts underneath.	Mancozeb Plus, Liquid Copper
Marrows (zucchinis), Melon, Squash	See powdery mildew	Powdery white film over leaves.	Lime Sulfur
Onion	Thrips	White flecks on foliage.	Natrasoap
	Downy mildew	Leaves die from tips and downy tufts on leaves.	Mancozeb Plus, Liquid Copper

PLANT	PEST OR DISEASE	SYMPTOMS	CONTROL
Parsnip	Powdery mildew	See Marrows	
Peas	Mites	See Beans	
Potato	Potato moth	Leaves or tubers infested.	Tomato & Vegetable Dust
	Late blight	Large black areas on leaves.	Liquid Copper
Pumpkin	See Marrows		
Seeds and seedlings	Damping off	Seeds fail to germinate or seedlings fall over at soil level.	Mancozeb Plus
Silver beet, Spinach	Leaf spot	Small brown spots on foliage.	Mancozeb Plus
Sweet corn	Corn ear worm	Caterpillar in top of cob.	Pyrethrum
Tomato	Tomato caterpillar	Caterpillar attacks fruit at stalk end.	Success Ultra, Pyrethrum, Mavrik
	Spotted wilt	Browning of young foliage.	Remove infected plants and control thrips – see Onion
	Fruit fly	See Capsicum.	
	Root eelworm	Swellings on roots.	Increase organic matter in soil
	Leaf spot	Brown target-like spots on foliage and fruit.	Tomato & Vegetable Dust, Liquid Copper

HINT

Get into the habit of sowing a 'mixed punnet' of in-season vegie seeds each fortnight. It only takes a few minutes and will give you a continuous supply of seedlings for a delicious, year-long harvest.

ANGIE THOMAS

YATES GARDENING EXPERT

Making way for new crops

Always pull out and compost crops that are past their best as soon as possible. Why keep a whole row of beans or peas for just a few pods?

HOW TO GROW INDIVIDUAL VEGETABLES

Artichokes

The globe artichoke is a grey-green thistle-like plant that grows to a height of 1 m or more. It takes up a lot of space in the vegetable garden but is dramatically attractive so many like to find a spot in the ornamental garden where it can flourish undisturbed for three or four years. A few artichoke plants can be grown in sunny spots in the flower garden. The best climate is one with a mild winter (ideally, frost free) and a cool summer.

Seeds of globe artichoke may be sown in spring. Plants can also be started from shoots or suckers. Plant these in late winter in cool districts, or in autumn where it is warmer. Shoots should be about 30 cm in length with well-developed roots. Plant them 1 m apart and rake in a small handful of fertiliser in a circle around each plant.

The globe-shaped buds appear in early spring and plants keep bearing until November. After flowering, keep plants watered and mulched through summer. In autumn, cut plants back to 30 cm high and apply a side-dressing of mixed fertiliser. Add a mulch of animal manure or compost to help maintain good soil structure. Prune back to the four or five strongest shoots in winter for buds next spring. Plants will bear well for three or four years, after which they should be divided and replanted. Harvest buds when 5–10 cm in diameter and still tight and tender. For larger main buds, prune out lateral buds when about the size of a golf ball. Three to five plants should be sufficient for an average family.

The unrelated Jerusalem artichoke is really a large sunflower with tuberous roots like a potato. It is a perennial, but is grown as an annual from tubers planted in late winter or early spring. Plant tubers 10–15 cm deep and 50–60 cm apart with a pre-planting fertiliser scattered in a circle around each. The plants produce yellow flowers in summer, but it's best to pinch them out in the bud stage. Tubers are ready four to six weeks after buds appear, but can be left in the ground until plants die down in winter if necessary. Nine to twelve plants should be sufficient for the average family.

Asparagus

Once established, asparagus plants are very long-lived and can go on producing for twenty years or more. Asparagus is best suited to mild or cold climates. Frosts are no problem because the plant (often called asparagus fern) dies off each winter to produce new shoots (called spears) in spring.

Light soils, through which the spears can easily push, are preferred.

Sow asparagus seed in spring in a seed bed in a corner of the vegetable garden. Seedlings should be two years old before planting out in their permanent position. Asparagus has male and female flowers on separate plants. Male plants produce bigger and better spears, so female plants (which develop red berries in the second autumn from sowing) should be discarded. Most gardeners prefer to buy two-year-old crowns from nurseries in winter. 'Mary Washington' is the standard variety but there are also purple-stemmed cultivars.

Before planting crowns, prepare the bed to spade depth and add fertiliser plus liberal quantities of organic matter to improve soil structure. Acidic soils should be dressed with a small amount of garden lime. Set crowns 15–20 cm deep and 30–50 cm apart along the bottom of a trench. Cover with about 5 cm of soil, filling in the remainder of the trench as the fern grows. Do not completely cover new shoots. Water regularly and feed every couple of weeks throughout summer with high-nitrogen Thrive plant food. Do not cut any spears in the first spring after planting. Cut down the dry, yellow fern in winter to ground level and rake it up for composting. Fertilise again in late winter to encourage spears in spring. Cutting can increase each year as plants grow older and reach full bearing in four or five years. Each year, start cutting when spears appear (August or September, depending on district). Harvest every day or two and continue cutting for eight to ten weeks.

'Green' asparagus is cut from level beds when spears are 15–20 cm long and before the tips open. For 'white' or 'blanched' asparagus (whose stems are deliberately deprived of sunlight), hill the soil over the row to a depth of 25–30 cm in late winter. As the tip of the spear breaks the surface, push a sharp knife through the soil to cut the spear about 15 cm below. Hills may be levelled when the fern is removed in winter. Cultivate and fertilise, then rebuild the hills before spring. Whether you grow green or white asparagus, 20–25 plants is ample for the average family. Spears keep well for several days in the crisper tray of the refrigerator or, after washing and blanching (immersing vegetables in boiling water) for three minutes, can be packaged for the home freezer.

Beans

Great for beginners, beans are among the most popular of all vegetables for growing in home gardens. They produce outstanding yields for the space they take up. Beans are warm-season vegetables that are susceptible to frost. They can be grown all year round in warm northern regions. In temperate areas the growing season is five to six months, but in cold climates only three or four months. Beans do best on well-drained soils, but may suffer on very sandy soils, so add old organic matter to improve water-holding capacity. Mulching with compost or grass clippings is recommended in very hot weather but avoid direct contact with the bean plants. Beans are also susceptible to wind damage, so protect them with windbreaks. Dwarf beans are ready to pick in eight to ten weeks. Climbing beans are great space-savers, and yield more pods over a longer period, but take ten to twelve weeks to reach picking stage. Cultivation methods for both dwarf and climbing beans are the same.

After soil has lost its winter chill, sow dwarf beans into pre-moistened soil in rows 50–60 cm apart, spacing seeds 7–10 cm along the row. A row 3–5 m long at each sowing is suitable for the average family. Make the next sowing when plants in the previous crop develop their first true leaves.

Top five beans

'BLUE LAKE'

Everyone's favourite climbing bean, 'Blue Lake', performs well during the warm part of the year in any climate. It's great beside a fence or against a wall.

'BORLOTTI'

Choose this bean if you want to dry the seeds for winter stews. 'Borlotti' has pretty pink-speckled pods and cream seeds.

'SNAPBEAN'

This tender green bean has a fashionable white seed and is stringless. It's tender enough to be eaten raw, or you can cook it for just a couple of minutes in the microwave.

'BOUNTIFUL BUTTER'

Butter beans produce waxy yellow pods on a dwarf bush. Because of their mild flavour, they're excellent in stir fries.

'SCARLET RUNNER'

'Scarlet Runner' has attractive flowers. The large beans taste wonderful but plants will really only bear reliably in areas with cool summers.

'BLUE LAKE'

'BORLOTTI'

'SCARLET RUNNER'

Sow climbing beans to grow on a fence or trellis, spacing seeds 10–15 cm apart. You can make a simple trellis by stretching two wires between steel droppers or timber posts, with the bottom wire at 15 cm and top wire at 2 m. Use garden twine between the bottom and top wires for the bean plants to climb. A row 2–3 m in length is suitable for the average family. Another way to grow climbing beans is to form a tripod or A-frame of garden stakes and sow two or three seeds at the bottom of each stake.

When sowing dwarf or climbing beans, always apply a pre-planting fertiliser in a band, as suggested for sowing large seeds direct in Chapter 9. Be careful not to allow bean seeds to directly contact the fertiliser as they're susceptible to fertiliser burn. If you press bean seeds into damp soil they absorb sufficient moisture to germinate. Avoid watering for a day or two after sowing and do not soak seeds in water overnight – this may hinder, rather than help, germination.

Bean plants don't usually need much extra fertilising as they grow, but liquid feeds of low nitrogen, water-soluble fertilisers (e.g. Thrive Flower & Fruit), applied when flowering commences, will increase yield and quality. Always pick beans when young and tender, before the seeds swell to make the pods lumpy. After the first picking the pods mature quickly, so pick them every three to five days. This will prolong flowering and production. Use the beans when as fresh as possible. They're best if picked and cooked the same day, although they keep well in the refrigerator for a few days. For quick freezing, wash and prepare pods as for cooking, blanch for three minutes, drain and package.

Solving Problems with Beans

PROBLEM	CAUSE	SOLUTION
Excessive leaf growth.	Too much nitrogen fertiliser	Use a balanced N.P.K. fertiliser such as Thrive Flower & Fruit.
Stem and stalks swollen and cracked. Young plants wilt, old plants break easily.	Bean fly	Remove affected pods.
Fine yellow mottling of upper leaves. Masses of small insects fly from plant when disturbed.	Whitefly	Natrasoap, Pyrethrum.
Pods twisted and distorted, may be lumpy and have rusty marks near stalk end.	Blossom thrips	Spray blossoms with Natrasoap early in the day before bees are active.
Angular spots with wide halo around them on leaves. Leaves may be pale green with dark veins. Plants wilt.	Halo blight	Remove and destroy affected plants. When conditions favour the disease (wet and/or windy) spray crop with Liquid Copper every 10–14 days.
Yellowish-orange pustules on leaves which yellow and fall.	Rust	Mancozeb Plus at first sign of problem.

Dwarf string beans

'Brown Beauty' is a good hot-weather variety and bears a heavy crop over a period of three weeks or more when picked regularly. 'Hawkesbury Wonder' is also popular. It sets pods in cooler weather and is excellent for sowing late in the season. All varieties of string beans are almost stringless when picked young; the pods need 'topping and tailing' only.

Dwarf stringless beans

'Pioneer' is an excellent-quality fleshy bean which is recommended for successive sowings throughout the season. It is resistant to bean rust, a fungus disease which attacks susceptible varieties in hot, humid weather. 'Snapbean' has round, stringless pods even when mature. Pods are often cross-cut rather than sliced. 'Snapbean' is cold-sensitive, so avoid sowing this variety early in the season. 'Gourmet's Delight' is a rust-resistant, stringless variety that is better suited to sowing early or late in the season. 'Bountiful Butter' is a dwarf waxpod (butter) bean. The tender, fleshy pods are rich yellow in colour.

Climbing beans

'Purple King' is an old garden favourite. The long, dark-purple, rather flat pods turn green when cooked. The plant bears over a long period but is rather susceptible to rust in warm, humid weather. 'Blue Lake' is the best stringless climbing bean and is renowned for its flavour. It bears a heavy crop of long, round pods and is especially suited to cool, highland climates and southern states. Snake bean is another stringless bean that is best suited to tropical or warm–temperate conditions. It belongs to a separate species closely related to cow peas and is often called 'Yard Long' or 'Asparagus Bean' because the light-green, rounded pods grow to 40 cm long or more. Pods are stringless but must be picked young. There are climbing and dwarf varieties of snake bean.

Climbing runner beans

Runner beans are perennial plants that die back after cropping in summer but grow again from the crown the following spring. The pods are broader and shorter with a rough texture but are tender when cooked. They are popular in cool districts and are

A wigwam of garden stakes or sturdy bamboo poles can be used to support climbing beans.

grown extensively in Victorian and Tasmanian home gardens. The flowers are large and ornamental. The most popular variety is 'Scarlet Runner', which has brilliant-red flowers. Although they will still flower profusely, runner beans will not set fruit in high temperatures.

Dried beans

Most varieties of beans can be used as dried beans. Allow pods to ripen on the bush or vine. When dry, shell the seeds. These can be used in soups, stews and bean salads. Two varieties of French beans grown specifically for this purpose are 'Borlotti' (Italian or cooker bean) with speckled yellow and red seeds, and 'Cannellini' (white kidney bean). Other beans in this dried bean group include lima bean (harvested before the seeds ripen and shelled like peas) and soybeans, which are used (particularly in Asian countries) to make sauces and beverages, and as a milk or cheese substitute. Soybeans have very high protein content.

Vegetables

WHAT TO LOOK FOR	NUTRITION	STORAGE	PREPARATION	METHOD OF COOKING
BEANS Firm. Long straight beans, crisp enough to snap. Good green colour.	Small mineral and vitamin content, particularly vitamin C. Some fibre. 126 kilojoules per 100 grams.	Wash, drain and store in vented plastic bag in refrigerator. Use soon after harvest.	Wash, top and tail and remove strings. Slice diagonally or leave whole.	Steam or boil. May be lightly tossed in butter to glaze. Do not overcook.
BROCCOLI Compact flower heads with no sign of yellow. Leaves and stems should show no sign of ageing.	Good source of folic acid. Excellent source of vitamin A and vitamin C. Fair source of calcium and fibre. 147 kilojoules per 100 grams.	Keep dry. Handle as little as possible as flowers bruise. Store in vented plastic bag in refrigerator. Use within 1–2 days.	Wash. Steam flowers whole in bunches. Stems may be sliced and served as a separate vegetable.	Steam, boil or oven-bake. May be served raw if finely sliced. Remember, stems take longer to cook than flowers.
BRUSSELS SPROUTS Firm and compact with no limp leaves.	Excellent source of vitamin C. Good source of folic acid and fibre. 205 kilojoules per 100 grams.	Wrap in plastic. Store in refrigerator.	Wash. Trim stalk. Remove any poor-quality leaves.	Steam or boil. May be deep-fried in batter after initial cooking.
CABBAGES Firm head. Outer leaves should be strongly coloured and not limp.	Good source of vitamin C. Some calcium and fibre. 109 kilojoules per 100 grams.	Trim lightly and remove outer leaves. Wrap in plastic and store in refrigerator. Use within a week of harvest.	Remove any poor-quality leaves. Wash. Remove rib if desired. Slice finely or leave whole.	Drop a whole walnut into the water while cooking cabbage to minimise odour. May be boiled, steamed or stir-fried.
CAPSICUMS Well-shaped, thick-walled and firm, with a uniform glossy colour (yellow, red or bright green).	Very good source of vitamin C. Fair source of vitamin A. 109 kilojoules per 100 grams.	Store in plastic bag in refrigerator. Use within 5 days.	Simply wash and remove all seeds.	Delicious raw in salads. May be stuffed and baked or used in soups and casseroles.
CARROTS Firm, smooth and well formed. Deep orange to red in colour.	Outstanding source of vitamin A. Some fibre. 151 kilojoules per 100 grams.	Store in plastic bag in refrigerator.	Wash and scrape lightly. May be left whole, sliced or diced for cooking.	Steam, boil, braise or shred. Delicious raw or cooked.
CAULIFLOWERS Should not have a ricey appearance or obvious flowers. Look for firm white compact heads without spots or bruises.	Very good source of vitamin C, fair source of folic acid and fibre. 109 kilojoules per 100 grams.	Remove all leaves as they absorb moisture from head. Store in plastic bag in refrigerator. Use before heads turn brown.	Wash and break into flowerets or leave whole.	Steam or boil and top with cheese sauce. Use raw in salads and soup.

WHAT TO LOOK FOR	NUTRITION	STORAGE	PREPARATION	METHOD OF COOKING
CELERY Crisp, firm, well-coloured stalks with no blemishes or limp leaves.	Small mineral content, some fibre. 75 kilojoules per 100 grams.	Wash and store in plastic bag in refrigerator.	Remove leaves, wash stalks and cut to desired length. Remove any loose fibres.	Eat fresh, braise or stir-fry. May be added for flavour to stews or soups.
CUCUMBERS Should be green with no yellow colouring. Firm and fresh looking.	Low energy, high water content. 59 kilojoules per 100 grams.	Store in crisper in refrigerator. Use within a few weeks.	Wash and slice. Remove rind if desired.	Boil, steam or bake with filling. Most often eaten raw.
EGGPLANTS Dark purple to purple-black colour with glossy skin. Firm to touch.	High water content. Small amounts of most minerals and vitamins. Some fibre. 105 kilojoules per 100 grams.	Keep for about 7 days in refrigerator crisper.	Wipe over. Not necessary to remove skin. Discard stalk. Slice and leave sprinkled with salt for 20 minutes to extract bitter juice. Rinse prior to cooking.	Bake, boil, fry or mash.
LETTUCE Choose firm, green heads with crisp, blemish-free leaves.	Some potassium, fibre and folic acid. 71 kilojoules per 100 grams.	Perishable. Store in plastic bag in refrigerator crisper and use as soon as possible.	Remove core, wash under running water, drain. Tear rather than cut leaves.	Usually eaten fresh. May be braised, stir-fried or added to soup.
MUSHROOMS Look for firmness, white or creamy colour and unbroken shape. Avoid withered mushrooms.	Good source of niacin and riboflavin. Excellent source of potassium. 92 kilojoules per 100 grams.	Perishable. Store in paper bag in refrigerator. Use within 2–3 days.	Do not peel. Wipe over cap. Only remove stem if desired. Do not wash under running water.	Can be eaten raw, baked with a filling or sautéed in butter. Cook only lightly.
ONIONS Firm, with clear outer skin, no dark patches or signs of sprouting.	Small amounts of vitamins and minerals. Rich in sugars. 147 kilojoules per 100 grams.	Store in cool, dry and dark area. May be stored in refrigerator.	Peel and cut in required style, e.g. rings, quarters, etc.	Sauté, boil, bake, cream or fry.
PEAS Pods should be bright green in colour. Very firm and full pods indicate over-maturity.	Some protein and iron. Fair source of thiamin and folic acid. Good source of dietary fibre. 335 kilojoules per 100 grams.	Store in plastic bag in refrigerator. Use as soon as possible.	Remove shell and discard, unless using snow peas.	Boil, steam, or braise with lettuce.
POTATOES Firm and unbroken skin with no green tinge. There should be no dark spots or green shoots.	Fairly good source of vitamin C. Good source of potassium and dietary fibre. Some protein. 335 kilojoules per 100 grams.	Store in cool, dry and dark area. Do not store in refrigerator.	Do not soak in water. Only peel if necessary.	Bake, boil, fry, steam or mash.

WHAT TO LOOK FOR	NUTRITION	STORAGE	PREPARATION	METHOD OF COOKING
PUMPKINS Firm, bright and well-coloured flesh.	Good source of vitamin A. Some fibre. 130 kilojoules per 100 grams.	Cool, dark storage until cut. Then remove seeds, wrap in plastic bag, and store in refrigerator.	Wipe over. Cut into suitably sized pieces, remove seeds, stringy pieces and skin if desired.	Bake, boil, steam or mash.
ROCKMELONS Smell is a good indication of flavour and ripeness. Avoid soft spots and look for a clean stem scar.	Excellent source of vitamin C. Good source of vitamin A. Fair source of dietary fibre. Some iron. 105 kilojoules per 100 grams.	Ripen at room temperature for finer flavour. Wrap cut melon in plastic bag and store in refrigerator away from butter and milk.	Tends to flavour other foods when cut. Remove seeds and serve chilled. Slice as required.	Use in fruit salad, eat alone or with ice cream. Ideal as an entree, sliced and served with prosciutto, or filled with port.
SILVER BEET Glossy, bright-green leaves that show no sign of limpness.	Excellent source of vitamin A. Good source of folic acid and vitamin C. Fair source of calcium and iron. Some fibre. 96 kilojoules per 100 grams.	Pick on day required. Store in plastic bag in refrigerator. Highly perishable.	Wash carefully. Tear rather than cut leaves. Stems may be served as a separate vegetable.	Eat raw in salad, steam or boil. Use as a wrapper for fillings.
SWEET CORN Husks fresh and green in colour. Kernels well-filled, tender, milky, and pale yellow in colour.	Some protein and vitamin A. Good source of dietary fibre. 406 kilojoules per 100 grams.	Wrap in vented plastic bag and keep refrigerated.	Remove corn silk and outer leaves.	Boil, bake or steam.
TOMATOES Free of blemishes, firmly fleshed. Should weigh heavy in the hand.	Good source of vitamin C, some vitamin A. 88 kilojoules per 100 grams.	Only refrigerate when over-ripe. Always remove from refrigerator 1 hour before eating to improve flavour.	Wash, dry and remove stalk. Remove skin only if necessary by plunging into boiling water.	Use fresh or stew, bake, sauté, stuff, or prepare as a sauce.
WATERMELONS Large, well-coloured, bright fruit that is heavy in the hand. A yellowish underside is a good guide to ripeness.	Fair source of vitamin C. Some vitamin A. 113 kilojoules per 100 grams.	Store in cool place in refrigerator. When cut, use promptly.	Wipe skin, serve chilled in slices or wedges. Use a melon baller for a quick dessert.	Great for picnics and in fruit salad, jams and pickles. Rind can be steamed and served with butter and nutmeg. Lovely as a refreshing drink.
ZUCCHINI Well shaped with firm, glossy skin and good colour.	Low energy, high water content. 66 kilojoules per 100 grams.	Place in plastic bag in refrigerator.	Wash or wipe over. Use unpeeled, sliced or halved or cut in strips.	Boil, steam, bake or eat raw.

Beetroot

Beetroot is an attractive and tasty vegetable for cooked dishes, salads and pickling. Beetroot is adaptable to all climate zones but plants may bolt (run to seed) if sown out of season. Sow seed from July to March in temperate climates but only from September to February where colder. In warm or tropical areas beetroot can be sown for much of the year, although sowing during the wet season can be risky.

The 'seed' is a cluster of two to four true seeds in a corky coating that absorbs water slowly, so it is a good idea to soak seed for a few hours before sowing. Apply a pre-planting fertiliser in a band where the seed is to be sown and rake into the soil. Sow seed in drills 20–30 cm apart and 12 mm deep. Cover seeds with compost or vermiculite and spread a light mulch of grass clippings over the bed. Keep damp with light watering until seedlings emerge in ten to fourteen days. Thin seedlings (two or three seedlings may emerge from each cluster) early to 5–8 cm apart. Roots are ready to pull about ten weeks after sowing. Start pulling alternate roots early. This spreads the harvest, and roots left in the soil have room to gain in size. Roots grow at, or slightly above, soil level so do not cover them with soil when cultivating between rows. Beetroot is best when grown quickly and responds to liquid feeds of Thrive and Aquasol. Sow successive rows 2–3 m long every four to six weeks during the season. Beetroot keeps well in open storage for a few weeks but it can remain in reasonable condition for two or three months when stored in the refrigerator.

Varieties

'Derwent Globe' is a deep, red, round beet with flesh of good texture and flavour. 'Baby' is a small variety with good colour and flavour. It matures quickly and pulling can commence six to seven weeks after sowing. Pull alternate plants unless harvesting the whole row. 'Cylindra', as its name suggests, has a cylindrical shape which makes it excellent for slicing.

Borecole

Borecole (also called Scotch kale or curly greens) is a loose-leafed member of the cabbage group of plants. It is widely used in the British Isles and Northern Europe. It is very cold hardy and withstands severe winter conditions, but is not grown to any extent in Australia. Borecole is grown in exactly the same way as cabbage. It can be used by harvesting the outside leaves progressively, like silver beet, or by cutting the whole plant at once.

Broad beans

Unlike other beans, broad beans are cool-season vegetables that provide meals in spring and early summer when other vegetables are often scarce. They are useful legumes for soil improvement too. Broad beans are best suited to mild–temperate and cool climates and are sown from early autumn to late winter in most districts.

Broad beans are a tall leafy crop that needs plenty of space to grow. Sow seeds in rows 60–75 cm apart after banding a pre-planting fertiliser alongside. Another way is to sow double rows 25–30 cm apart with 75–90 cm between each pair of rows. Dusting seed with fungicide before sowing can be helpful. Press the large seeds into damp soil at the bottom of a furrow about 5 cm deep, spacing them 15–20 cm apart. Cover with soil, press down and very lightly rake surface. If sown in damp soil, more water is not needed until seedlings emerge in ten to fourteen days.

Extra fertiliser is usually unnecessary while the crop is growing. Too much fertiliser, especially fertiliser high in nitrogen, promotes leaf growth at the expense of

HINT

Avoid beginners' mistakes in vegetable planting. Don't plant seeds too deep, over-fertilise, make a too-big vegie patch that is hard to look after, or sow seeds too thickly. Use a seed sower, or mix seeds with sand or radish seeds to spread them out.

FRANCES HUTCHISON
GARDENING AUTHOR AND EDITOR

flowers and pods. Plants of broad beans may need some support. An easy way is to use garden twine stretched between stakes at each end of the row. Flower-drop is a common problem in early spring and is due to low temperatures. Pod setting improves with warmer weather and greater bee activity. You can pick pods when young and slice them like French beans, or leave them to fill before shelling the half-ripe seeds. A 5–6 m row is usually sufficient for one sowing for the average family.

Varieties
'Early Long Pod' grows to 2 m tall with pods 20–25 cm long. 'Coles Dwarf' or 'Dwarf Prolific' grows to 1 m with smaller pods. A dwarf variety is often preferred by home gardeners as the plants are more compact and less liable to wind damage.

Broccoli
Broccoli is an excellent cool-season vegetable for use in late autumn, winter and early spring, although newer varieties are more tolerant to heat. It is a close relative of cauliflower but the tightly packed heads are green. The large centre head may reach 20 cm in diameter. When this is cut, new shoots with smaller heads form in the leaf axils, so a single plant will bear for many weeks. Broccoli does best in temperate and cold climates but is adaptable to all climates with a cool winter. In cold districts, sow seed in December or even November. Early sowing allows plants to grow a large frame before cold weather. In temperate and warmer climates, sow from late summer to autumn. Successive sowings may be made. Usually nine to twelve plants at each sowing, four to six weeks apart, is sufficient for the average family.

Broccoli is usually raised as seedlings in small pots. Sow seed into seed raising mix, prick out seedlings early into individual 10 cm pots and grow on until 7–10 cm high. Transfer plants to a well-prepared bed to which plenty of organic matter and a pre-planting fertiliser have been added. Seeds may also be sown direct in clumps or stations spaced 45–60 cm apart. Thin each station to one seedling. Broccoli, like all leafy crops, needs to be grown quickly and responds to side-dressing with nitrogen-rich fertilisers or

liquid feeds of Thrive. Use dusts or sprays to control caterpillars and aphids. (See Chapter 8.)

Cut the centre head when still tightly packed and before the individual flower buds open. Take about 10 cm of main stem with a slanting cut. This prevents water lodging in the stem and causing rotting. Cut side shoots as they develop, again taking 10 cm of stem. Centre heads and side shoots store well in the crisper tray of the refrigerator for several days, or can be prepared as for cooking, or can be prepared as for cooking, blanched 3–4 minutes, packaged and deep-frozen.

Varieties
'Winter Harvest' broccoli is the best choice for growing into the colder months when other varieties do not thrive. It has firm, dome-shaped heads with an attractive green colour. Some new cultivars of broccoli have been bred with greater heat tolerance. 'Summer Green' is a heat-tolerant variety that can be grown in the warmer months. Chinese broccoli does not develop a large head and is usually picked when a few of the flowers have opened.

Broccoli 'Romanesco' looks somewhat like a light green cauliflower with the head formed in unusual spiraling whorls.

Brussels sprouts
Brussels sprouts are another cool-season crop but they are less adaptable than broccoli. They do best in mild–temperate and cold districts and are not really suited to warm northern climates. Make sowings from October to early February in cold districts and from December to late February in mild–temperate areas. Brussels sprouts are usually raised as seedlings in the same way as broccoli. Transplant seedlings at the same size into a prepared, well-manured and fertilised bed. The plants need more space to grow than broccoli, so allow 60–75 cm between plants. Apply side-dressings of nitrogen-rich fertiliser or liquid feeds regularly from transplanting onwards. Hill soil around plants as they grow to lessen wind damage. Dust or spray to control caterpillars and aphids. For the average family, six to nine plants are usually sufficient for one sowing.

Brussels sprouts are ready to harvest four or five months after transplanting. The cabbage-shaped sprouts form in the leaf axils of the main stem and mature progressively from bottom to top. When bottom sprouts are quite small, start stripping lower leaves with a sideways pull. This allows sprouts to develop more easily. Pick the sprouts with a downward and sideways action. Discard any fluffy sprouts at the bottom of the stem. Continue stripping leaves and pick sprouts as they become usable. Modern varieties, especially hybrids, tend to form sprouts from bottom to top about the same time. If plants are well grown, cut the main stem at ground level and pick all sprouts at once. This makes harvesting easier but you may have to sacrifice a few small sprouts at the top of the stem. Sprouts store well in the refrigerator for seven to ten days or they can be washed, trimmed of loose outside leaves, blanched for four to five minutes, packaged and deep-frozen.

Varieties

'Drumtight' is adaptable to a wide range of climatic conditions, is vigorous and very uniform. Harvest sprouts when they are hard and tight.

Cabbage

Cabbages are very adaptable to climatic conditions. In warm northern areas they are sown during most months of the year, although they may be difficult to grow well in the wet season. In temperate and cold districts they can be sown from early spring to autumn. Some old varieties tend to 'burst' or run to seed if sown out of season, but modern varieties are more reliable. Like other leaf crops, cabbages like plenty of moisture and fertiliser, so the soil must have excellent

Flowers and vegetables can grow together as companions. The flowers attract pollinators and friendly insects for the vegetables while benefiting from the good soil and plentiful sunshine.

structure (apply plenty of organic matter) and use a pre-planting fertiliser when preparing the bed.

Cabbage plants can be raised as seedlings in the same way as broccoli, or sown direct in clumps in the garden bed and later thinned to one seedling. Plant spacing depends on variety. Space small varieties 40–50 cm apart each way but give more room (60–75 cm) for large cabbage varieties.

Plenty of water (but good drainage) and regular side-dressings of nitrogen fertiliser or liquid feeds of water-soluble fertiliser every two to three weeks will promote quick growth and crisp heads. Dust or spray regularly to control caterpillars and aphids. (See Chapter 8.)

You can make successive sowings of cabbage over a long period. Usually nine to twelve plants is sufficient at each sowing for the average family. Make next sowing when seedlings of previous batch are 15–20 cm tall. Start cutting the first plants from each sowing when the heads are firm but quite small. Hybrid varieties have an advantage here because they 'hold' well in the garden and are slower to burst or run to seed. Cabbages store well in the refrigerator for a week.

Varieties

'Sugarloaf' has conical heads weighing up to 2–3 kg. 'Eureka' is an early-maturing, medium-sized, globe-shaped cabbage of excellent quality, weighing to about 4 kg. It has good holding ability and disease resistance. It performs best when sown to mature in summer, autumn or early winter. 'Savoy Hybrid' is a very large cabbage with dark-green, blistered leaves. It is not as popular as it used to be because it's a bit too large for modern, small families.

Cape gooseberry

Cape gooseberry, also known as ground cherry, husk tomato or Chinese lantern plant, is grown for its small, globe-shaped, yellow or red fruits that are enclosed in papery husks. The fruit may be eaten fresh but is more often used to make jams or jellies. Cape gooseberry is a warm-season plant. In frost-free, warm and tropical climates, the bushes are perennial and reach a height of 1 m or more. In cool–temperate climates cape

gooseberry is grown as an annual during summer. It needs a warm, sheltered position. In suitable areas it may be grown as an ornamental shrub.

Generally, the cultivation of Cape gooseberry is very similar to that of capsicum. Sow seeds in punnets in spring when the weather is warm. Transplant seedlings to the garden when 8–10 cm tall, spacing them 1 m apart. For the average family two to three plants should be ample. Plants take five or six months before fruit is ready for picking. In warm, frost-free districts cut plants back hard after fruiting to induce new growth for the next year's crop. Plants may bear well for three or four years.

Capsicum

There are two kinds of capsicum or pepper. The sweet (mild) ones are eaten raw in salads or used in cooked dishes, soups and stews. The hot pepper or chilli is used fresh or dried as a flavouring and for sauces and pickles. Whether sweet or hot, capsicums are warm-season plants like tomatoes, and in warm tropical/subtropical climates you can grow them almost all year round. In temperate zones sow seed from August to December and, in cold climates, September to November only. In frost-free areas, capsicums will die back over winter and shoot again in spring, but they are most successfully grown as annuals.

You can sow seed direct but, because of the short growing season in most districts, it is best to raise seedlings in a warm spot for transplanting to the open garden as soon as the soil is warm enough. You only need a small number of plants – four to six well-grown plants is sufficient for the average family. There is hardly time, even in a mild climate like Sydney's, for successive sowings. Seedlings transplanted in mid-September will bear fruit about Christmas and keep bearing until autumn. In warm northern areas, providing there are no frosts, successive sowings every eight to ten weeks will give a continuous supply. It is easy to raise seedlings in plastic punnets. Keep the punnets indoors until seedlings emerge, then prick them out into 10 cm pots to grow on in a sunny, sheltered spot until about 15 cm tall. Transfer them to a bed well prepared beforehand with

Chillies are hottest when ripe and fully coloured.

HINT

To improve germination of carrot seeds water them lightly after sowing then lay hessian, shade cloth or cardboard over the rows, which helps keep the seeds moist. It's important to check them every day and remove the cover as soon as the first seedling emerges.

ANGIE THOMAS

YATES GARDENING EXPERT

organic matter and pre-planting fertiliser. Space plants 50–60 cm apart.

Capsicums have a fairly deep root system and are adaptable to both heavy and light soils, but they need regular watering. Do not force plants, especially with high-nitrogen fertilisers, in the early stages. This will make too much leaf growth. After flowering has started, a side-dressing of mixed fertiliser scattered around each plant will promote good fruiting. Fertilisers formulated for growing tomatoes will be ideal for capsicums. Repeat every four or five weeks while the plants are bearing. Capsicums rarely need staking, but well-grown plants may need support if carrying a heavy crop and exposed to wind. Drive in a stake close to each plant and tie the main stems to it with garden twine. Capsicums can be useful and ornamental when grown in large pots or tubs on a sunny terrace or patio. A pot 40 cm in diameter and the same depth will grow a good-sized plant, but pay special care to watering because pots dry out quickly.

You can pick sweet capsicums at any stage; there is no need to wait till they are full size. Frequent picking encourages more flowers and fruits. Hot capsicums (chillies) can be picked when immature or left on the bush until full-coloured and shrivelled.

Varieties

'Giant Bell' ('Californian Wonder' type) is a popular variety of sweet capsicum with large, bell-shaped, dark-green fruits turning red as they mature. 'Colour Salad Collection' contains both green and yellow varieties. Hot chillies have rather small, green fruit that turn red at full maturity. 'Hot Pepper', 'Jalapeno', 'Inferno' and 'Cherry Bomb' are typical names of some of the most popular varieties. Handle with care and wash hands well afterwards.

Carrots

Carrots are an adaptable crop in the home garden and give a good yield for the space they require. In warm northern zones, you can sow carrot seed almost any month of the year, although mid-summer sowings are often avoided. Best months to sow in temperate zones are July through to March and, in cold districts, August to February. Sowings in late autumn or winter may run to seed without forming roots.

Deep sandy soil or heavy soils with good structure allow roots to grow and expand quickly. On clay soils, add coarse sand to improve texture, and organic matter to improve structure. Organic matter in the soil can cause the roots to be forked and misshapen; avoid this by mixing it evenly through the soil. For carrots, you will need a well-prepared bed for direct sowing with firm soil below and a loose, crumbly surface. After scattering pre-planting fertiliser in a band where seed is to be sown, mark out shallow furrows 20–30 cm apart and sow seeds 6 mm deep by tapping the seeds from the packet as described in Chapter 9. Cover with compost, vermiculite or seed-raising mixture and water gently. Seedlings may take two to three weeks to emerge, so keep the bed damp until they do. A light sprinkling of grass clippings makes a good mulch. Some growers suggest laying a wooden plank on top of the row to help retain moisture around the seed. Lift regularly and remove as soon as there are signs of germination.

When seedlings are 5 cm high, thin them to 2–3 cm apart. Later, when 15 cm high, thin again to 5 cm apart. The removed seedlings will have tender roots that are large enough to eat. While thinning, remove weed seedlings too. If space between rows is then cultivated and mulched, further weeding is seldom needed. The base fertiliser applied before sowing may be sufficient to grow a good crop, but liquid feeds every few weeks will promote faster growth. Do not overfeed, especially with high-nitrogen fertilisers.

Most varieties take three to four months from sowing to harvest. For the average family a row 4–6 m long is sufficient for each sowing. Make further sowings at four- to six-week intervals during the season. Pests and diseases are usually not a serious problem. Start pulling early to spread the harvest and allow remaining roots to grow larger. Carrots keep well in open storage (remove tops) but even better in the refrigerator crisper tray.

Solving Problems with Carrots

SYMPTOM	CAUSE	SOLUTION
Branched and misshapen roots.	Stones, clods or lumps of bulky organic manure in soil, or pythium fungus in soil.	Prepare a deep, crumbly, well-drained soil which allows roots to expand and grow quickly.
Pale colour.	Pale variety, or strongly acidic soil, or excess nitrogen, or high temperature during growth.	Plant deeply coloured carrots such as 'Chantenay', or add lime to soil and avoid nitrogen fertiliser. Potash increases intensity of colour.
Seedlings burn off.	Hot, sunny weather at tender stage of growth.	Sprinkle with water, keep soil moist. Erect temporary shade.
Green tops on carrot roots.	Sunlight on exposed crowns.	Pile earth up to cover crowns during growth.
Roots cracked or split.	Interior of carrot grows faster than skin; caused by heavy rain following a dry spell, or over-fertilising.	Mulch to retain even moisture levels in soil.
Bolting – running to seed prematurely without forming roots.	Seedlings subject to cool weather during early spring growth.	Sow at a more suitable time of year.
Excessive leaf growth.	Excess nitrogen.	Avoid nitrogenous fertilisers, and use balanced ones.

Varieties

'Topweight' has a strong top with long, tapering roots of good colour. 'Western Red' is another popular long-rooted variety. 'All Seasons' is similar to 'Topweight' but has a deeper colour. All three varieties are resistant to virus disease. 'Majestic Red' is bred for Australian conditions and has tapering roots of a good colour and flavour.

Shorter, stump-root varieties are often preferred in the home garden and are better suited to shallow soils. 'Early Chantenay' has excellent colour and has been a favoured home-garden variety for a number of years. Its broad 'shoulders' taper quickly down to a pointed base. 'Manchester Table' is a very popular old variety with a cylindrical shape and deep-orange flesh.

'Baby' is a sweet, tender, finger-sized carrot which is ready for harvest in ten to twelve weeks from sowing. It can be sown more thickly in rows 10–15 cm apart and rarely needs thinning when grown in light, friable soil. Because of its fast maturity it can be sown later in autumn than other varieties and is suitable for growing in pots or troughs in a sunny, sheltered position.

Cauliflower

Cauliflower, like broccoli, is a valuable winter vegetable but is not so adaptable to climate. Cauliflower takes longer to grow – 14–24 weeks, depending on variety – and there is only one head per plant. Cauliflowers are best grown in cool to cold climates but can also be successful in mild–temperate areas on the coast. Most varieties available in Australia are doubtful propositions in tropical zones. Cauliflowers need low temperatures for flower heads (called 'curds') to form, so they must be sown from mid-summer to autumn to develop a good-sized plant before cold weather sets in. The best months to sow them are shown in the sowing guide in this chapter. You can have an extended harvest of cauliflower by sowing two varieties of different maturity at the one time.

Cauliflower seeds, like those of broccoli, Brussels sprouts and cabbage, are usually sown in pots or punnets and the seedlings transplanted when 7–10 cm high. Space the plants 50–75 cm apart. Late varieties need rather more space than early varieties. Like other leafy plants in this group, cauliflowers are hungry plants. Prepare the bed with plenty of organic matter and a ration of pre-planting fertiliser as described previously for broccoli. Give regular side-dressings of nitrogen fertiliser every two to three weeks, or liquid feeds every ten to fourteen days. Dust or spray regularly to control caterpillars and aphids.

Cut the curds when tight and solid for best quality; do not wait until they become soft and fuzzy. Protect the white curds from direct sunlight (and yellow discolouration) by breaking outside leaves inward or by tying the ends of longer leaves together with string to form a shady tent over the centre. Start cutting some plants early to extend the harvest. Curds store well in the refrigerator crisper for up to a week.

Varieties

All varieties produce top-quality curds when grown quickly and harvested at the correct time. The main difference in varieties is the time they take to mature. The most popular traditional cauliflower variety is 'Phenomenal Early' which matures within fourteen to eighteen weeks. Newer hybrid cauliflowers can reach maturity as early as fifteen weeks and can be sown all year round in warmer districts, although it would be wise to avoid heatwave periods.

Broccoflower is an unusual cauliflower with green curds. The heads resemble broccoli but have a true cauliflower taste. There are, of course, other varieties which may be available as seedlings from nurseries.

Celery

Celery is a very good home garden vegetable, especially if the outside stems are picked like silver beet. These green stems give a continuous harvest over two or three months for use in salads, soups, stews or as a cooked vegetable. If you prefer white celery, blanch the stems by excluding sunlight. Celery prefers a mild to cool climate (where it's sown in spring) but grows well in warmer areas in late summer and autumn. Raise seedlings in pots or punnets in much the same way as other vegetable seedlings. Seeds are small and it may take two to three weeks for the seedlings to emerge. Seedlings grow slowly, too, and it is best to prick them out into small pots or mini punnets to grow on until large enough (eight to ten weeks) for planting out in the garden.

Prepare the bed with liberal amounts of compost or animal manure, if available, and add some pre-planting fertiliser as well. Space plants 30–40 cm apart and water well. Celery is shallow-rooted and regular watering is needed every day or two in hot weather. Plants need generous feeding to grow quickly, otherwise stems become coarse and stringy. Hence, give liquid feeds of fertilisers like Thrive every two weeks or so. Leaf spot disease may be troublesome but can be controlled with a copper fungicide spray. (See Chapter 8.)

For green celery, simply pick outside stems with a sideways pull to break them off at ground level, but leave as many younger leaves as possible for regrowth. You can 'blanch' celery plants three to four weeks before harvesting by wrapping black polythene or a few thicknesses of newspaper around the stems from ground level to about 40 cm high, and tying loosely with string. Empty milk cartons work well in a home garden situation. A scattering of snail bait will deter snails and slugs from sheltering inside the cover. The old method of blanching by setting seedlings in a trench and covering with soil as they grow is not recommended because of increased risk of disease problems.

Celery keeps well in the refrigerator crisper for up to a week, or you can trim off the leaves, chop stems into 5 cm lengths, blanch for three minutes and freeze for later use. Leaves can also be dried until brittle and chopped or crushed into small pieces to use for flavouring in the same way as dried herbs. 'Green Crunch' celery is stringless, has good flavour and a crisp texture.

Celeriac

Celeriac (turnip-rooted celery) is grown in the same way as celery. The tops may be used as green celery. The tuberous roots, which may reach a diameter of 5–8 cm and the same length, can be grated for salads or used in soups and stews.

Chicory

Chicory, or witlof, is not widely grown in home gardens in Australia. To make witlof, chicory roots can be dug up in late summer and buried upright in damp sand, peat moss or vermiculite with an 8–10 cm covering of the material on top. New growth forms plump white shoots called 'chicons' which can be used for winter salads. Chicory roots can be dried, ground and used as a coffee substitute.

Radicchio is a form of chicory that has become a popular salad component. Sow radicchio in the same way as lettuce, and thin seedlings to the same distance. Fertiliser and cultivation requirements are almost identical. Good watering and fertilising will encourage rapid growth which will prevent the piquant leaves from becoming bitter.

Chillies
See Capsicum.

Chinese cabbage

Chinese cabbage is a close relative of European cabbage but is a different species. It is widely grown in Asian countries where it is called pe-tsai, pak choy, bok choy, Hong Kong, michili, kim chee and other names. There are many different varieties available. Generally, plants of Chinese cabbages are smaller than European cabbages. Plants are more upright, and may have looser heads. The leaves often have a texture like lettuce, and a sweeter flavour.

Chinese cabbage is grown in the same way as cabbage, but is best sown to grow when temperatures are mild (preferably autumn or spring). Chinese cabbages tend to run to seed when temperatures are cold. They can also perform poorly when temperatures are high. Seed is best sown direct in clumps 30–40 cm apart and seedlings thinned to the strongest. For the average family, six to nine plants is usually sufficient for each sowing.

Protect plants by dusting or spraying against caterpillars and aphids. (See Chapter 8.) Chinese cabbages, like other leaf crops, need generous feeding, so follow the same program as for cabbages. Plants grow quickly and are ready for harvest eight to ten weeks from sowing. Chinese cabbage can be used in salads or coleslaws or cooked in the same way as cabbage.

Varieties

Seeds of Chinese cabbage have been sold under many of the Chinese names they have been given such as 'Pe-tsai', 'Wombok' or 'Chinese Great Luck'. Another variety is 'Pak Choy', which does not form a head. It has mid-green leaves and pale green stalks, not unlike silver beet. The outside leaves can be picked separately or the whole plant cut at ground level.

Choko

Choko, also known as chayote, is a vigorous vine crop that grows in mild–temperate and subtropical zones. It is frost-susceptible and needs a warm growing season of five to six months. The pear-shaped fruits have a texture and flavour rather like marrow or summer squash. The choko vine is best grown on a fence or trellis in an out-of-the-way part of the garden where it can run wild. The vine is started from a single sprouted fruit but it is important to select a well-matured fruit with a smooth skin free of prickles. Keep the fruit indoors until it sprouts.

Prepare soil well by adding organic matter and a pre-planting fertiliser. Plant the choko into damp soil with the shoot and top of the fruit just above soil level. One well-grown vine is sufficient for the average family but plant two or three fruits about 1 m apart in case of failure. While the vine grows, give side-dressings of high-nutrient fertiliser such as citrus food every five or six weeks. Plants started in spring will flower in late summer to bear fruit in autumn. In winter, cut the old vines down, leaving two to four young shoots for the next crop. Cultivate around the plants in early spring and work in organic matter and fertiliser in the same way as for starting a new vine. Keep well watered while growing.

Pick the fruit when lime-green and 5–7 cm long. If left on the vine too long, the fruit becomes coarse and loses flavour. Chokoes store well in the refrigerator crisper for a week or more. They aren't suitable for freezing as the flesh becomes soggy on thawing out.

Cucumber

Cucumber is a warm-season vegetable that is adaptable to all climate zones.

In tropical/subtropical areas, sow any month from July to March. In temperate areas, best months for sowing are September to January. In cold districts, with a short growing season, October to December.

You can sow seed direct into a well-prepared bed with added compost or animal manure plus a pre-planting fertiliser. Soil must be warm, 20°C or above, for good germination. Good drainage is essential, as cucumber seeds (and those of all vine crops) are liable to damp off. Press four or five seeds into 'dark damp' soil at each clump or station, spaced about 1 m between rows and 40–50 cm between clumps. Thin seedlings to the two strongest. Although clumps are often called 'hills', they should really be volcano-shaped so that water is directed to plant roots. To save space, cucumbers can be grown on a fence or trellis. The vines need some help to climb when young, so tie the stems to the wire support. Later, tendrils cling to the wire quite well.

For early cucumbers, sow seeds in punnets. Prick out seedlings at the cotyledon (double seed leaf) stage before they form the first true leaves and transplant into 10cm plastic pots to grow on before planting in the garden. This way they can be easily handled without root damage.

Cucumbers and other vine crops like 'good going'. Thorough soil preparation with organic matter and pre-planting fertiliser will see the plants through to flowering; after flowering commences, scatter a mixed fertiliser around the base of the plants. Repeat this side-dressing at four- to five-week intervals while plants are bearing. For the average family, four to six plants is sufficient. These will continue to fruit well into autumn. The worst enemies of cucumbers and other vine crops are mildews. Some varieties are resistant to mildew but refer to Chapter 8 for control of these diseases.

You can pick long, green varieties as gherkins when 5–10 cm long, to use fresh or for pickling. For high-quality salad use, pick green varieties when 15–20 cm long, or round (apple-shaped) cucumbers when no larger than a cricket ball. Early and regular picking promotes further flowering and fruit-setting. Like all vine crops, female flowers are pollinated by bees after visiting the male (pollen) flowers. Failure to set fruit is often due to cold weather or the absence of bees. Fruit-setting will improve in warm, sunny weather.

Varieties

Green cucumbers are long and thin, sometimes rather oval-shaped. They start bearing eight to ten weeks from sowing. The best green variety is 'Burpless'. It is tolerant to downy and powdery mildew and has long, thin fruit which may grow to 40 cm but is still fleshy and tender. This is an excellent home-garden variety especially suitable for trellis growing. 'Pickling' or 'Gherkin' have tender, crisp fruit which may be picked when less than 5 cm in length and produce a heavy crop or left to reach 15–18 cm if larger fruit is preferred.

Lebanese cucumber has dark-green fruit that should be picked and eaten when small, approximately 10 cm in length. The sweetly flavoured burpless fruit may be eaten whole or sliced for salads. Occasionally there are male and female flowers on separate plants – so always sow a good range of seeds.

Round or apple-shaped cucumbers have a lime-green, cream or white skin. They take ten to twelve weeks to fruiting but are extremely prolific.

There are many other cucumber varieties. One of the most unusual is 'African Horned', a novelty variety that has almost oval fruit with prominent spines on the greenish skin. When the skin yellows, the flesh becomes sweet.

Eggplant

Eggplant or aubergine is closely related to potato but is grown for its (mostly) purple, egg-shaped or pear-shaped fruits which vary in length from 10 to 25 cm. It is a native of Africa and southern Asia so needs a long, warm growing season. In tropical/subtropical climates, sow seed from September to March. In mild–temperate climates like Sydney's, sow from September to December. In cold districts, sow eggplants only in the period from October to November because the plants take fourteen to sixteen weeks to bear.

You can grow eggplants in the same way as capsicums. In areas with a short growing season, it is best to raise plants in punnets or pots before pricking out seedlings into individual pots and transferring them to the garden bed when the weather is warm. Plants grow 60–90 cm tall, so space them 60–75 cm apart, and may need to be staked for support. For the average family, four to six plants is usually sufficient. Harvest fruit when the skin is smooth and rich purple in colour. If the skin has started to wrinkle with maturity, the flesh will be coarse and tough. The fruit stalks are hard and woody so cut them with a pair of secateurs to avoid damaging the plants. When well grown, you can expect six to eight fruits on each plant.

Varieties

'Blacknite' has a traditional oval shape and dark-purple fruit.

Dwarf eggplant varieties produce smaller fruit that is ready in about eleven weeks from sowing. Unusual white varieties are now available.

Endive

Endive is closely related to chicory but is grown for its serrated, frilled leaves that form a loose heart and add an interesting taste to salads. It is similar in appearance to lettuce and is grown in much the same way. Endive is usually sown in late summer and early autumn for winter harvest. In warm northern zones it can be sown from autumn to spring. For the average family six to nine plants is sufficient. The leaves may have a slightly bitter taste which can be removed by blanching. To do this, cover plants with large plastic pots or a thick layer of straw about three weeks before cutting. 'Green Curled' is the most popular variety.

Kale

Regarded as a 'superfood' because of its high levels of nutrients and tryptophan, an amino acid that helps in the formation of mood-lifting serotonin, kale has become such a popular vegetable that it is occasionally in short supply. Fortunately kale is very easy to grow in the home garden in similar conditions to the related cabbages and broccoli and kale plants are attractive enough to be planted in the ornamental garden. In fact some coloured leaf kales (often called flowering cabbages) are grown strictly as ornamentals (see page 314).

HINT

Harvest mature leeks by cutting off the stems below ground. The still-in-place root base will produce a crop of new seedlings which can then be transplanted in an ongoing growth cycle. As the stems develop, heap some straw mulch around their bases. This will help stop dirt from washing between the leaves and will ensure that the bottom section remains desirably white.

DIANA O'BRIEN

GARDEN WRITER, *THE CHRONICLE*, ACT

Kale is a fast growing, cool season crop that can be started in late summer or early autumn in most districts. Sow seeds into pots for later transplanting or direct into the garden bed if conditions aren't too hot and dry. Baby kale leaves can be ready for harvest in as little as seven weeks. Kale has better flavour if picked just before use.

Prepare soil well before planting by digging in some organic matter and some all-purpose vegetable fertiliser.

Varieties

'Curly Kale' has attractive, much-crinkled, deep green leaves. Leaf colour is stronger in cooler conditions.

'Cavolo nero', also called Tuscan kale or black cabbage, has dark-coloured upright leaves growing from a central stem.

Kohl rabi

Kohl rabi is easy to grow and delicious to eat. The plant forms a swollen stem above the ground, so it is really a turnip-rooted cabbage. It can be sown in all climates from late summer to autumn. In temperate and cold districts, early spring sowings are also successful.

Prepare soil well for direct sowing, adding plenty of organic matter. Scatter mixed fertiliser in a band where seeds will be sown and rake into topsoil. Sow seeds in clumps 10–15 cm apart with 30–40 cm between rows. Cover seeds with compost or vermiculite, spread a light grass-clipping mulch over each clump, and water gently. Thin seedlings at each position to the strongest. Kohl rabi is best when grown quickly with regular watering and side-dressings of nitrogen fertiliser or liquid feeds. Do not mound up soil around plants as this could cause the kohlrabi to rot. Remove weeds by shallow cultivation between the rows. Control caterpillars and aphids as for cabbage. For the average family a 1–2 m row is sufficient for each sowing at four- to five-week intervals from mid-summer to autumn.

Kohl rabi is ready to pick in eight to ten weeks. Start pulling the 'bulbs' early to spread the harvest. For top quality, bulbs should not exceed 5–7 cm in diameter. They store well in the refrigerator for a week or two. For freezing, select young bulbs, peel and dice or slice, blanch for two minutes, package and freeze.

Leeks

Leeks are close relatives of onions but are grown for their long, white (blanched) stems and bulbous bases. They are more adaptable to climate than onions and grow more quickly. In temperate and cold climates you can sow seeds from spring to autumn but in warm or tropical areas the best sowing period is late summer and autumn for plants to grow during the cooler months.

Leeks are best raised as seedlings in pots or punnets. Grow them on to 12 cm tall before transplanting into a bed that's been well prepared with organic matter and added mixed fertiliser. The easiest method of planting is to make holes with a dibble or rake handle, 2–3 cm wide and 10 cm deep. Drop seedlings into the holes so that the roots rest on the bottom. When watered, enough soil will wash into the hole to cover the roots. As plants grow, regular watering will fill the hole with soil. Another method is to set seedlings at the bottom of a trench and fill in with soil as plants grow. With either method, space plants 15–20 cm apart.

Leeks need regular watering and respond well to side-dressings of nitrogen fertiliser or

Growing Microgreens

Microgreens are tiny edible plants that are harvested when they are very young. Unlike sprouts, seeds for microgreens are sown into a medium (usually, but not always, potting mix) where they can develop a root system.

Seed varieties must germinate readily, be fast growing, look attractive and, most importantly, taste good. Rocket, amaranth, cabbage, radish, mizuna and mibuna are popular choices, but there are many others.

Start by putting a layer of fine potting mix into a 5cm to 8cm deep container with some drainage holes in the base. The mix should come near, but not right up to, the top. Firm the mix into place, water and allow to drain. Sprinkle the seed thickly over the top and cover with a thin layer of mix (a kitchen strainer can be helpful for evenly spreading the mix). Water with a mist sprayer or by sitting the container in water and allowing moisture to seep up from below. Keep in a spot that gets good, indirect light.

Harvest microgreens with scissors when they are about 3–5cm tall and add to soups, salads, sandwiches and omelettes, or simply sprinkle as an attractive and nutritious garnish. Then sow some more!

liquid fertiliser feeds every two or three weeks. Generous feeding promotes quick growth and plump, tender stems. Make successive sowings every four to six weeks.

Start harvesting when stems are 2 cm thick, usually twelve to fourteen weeks after transplanting. This way you can harvest each week for several weeks. On heavier soils, dig each plant with a long trowel so that stems are not damaged. Some plants may form small stems around the main one. Separate these carefully and replant to grow on. Leeks store well in the refrigerator crisper for several weeks. 'Welsh Wonder' is the most widely grown variety.

Lettuce

Lettuce is not difficult to grow but must be grown quickly for crisp, tender hearts. The main requirements for lettuce are:

1. Friable, well-prepared soil that absorbs and holds moisture but drains readily.
2. The right lettuce varieties for the time of the year.
3. Regular and thorough watering.
4. Generous, high-nitrogen feeding.

Lettuce, by nature, is a cool-season crop, but plant breeders have evolved sure-hearting varieties that can be grown in summer. You can sow lettuce all year round in most climates. Lettuce is the mainstay of summer salads, so make successive sowings from early spring to January or early February.

Prepare the bed with plenty of organic matter for good soil structure and rake in a pre-planting fertiliser. You can raise seedlings in a good seed-raising mixture for transplanting, but direct sowing in clumps or stations is more reliable, especially in warm weather. Make shallow, saucer-shaped depressions 20 cm apart for small varieties or 30 cm apart for large varieties. Tap out several seeds at each depression, then barely cover with compost or vermiculite and water gently.

Keep the bed moist (a light mulch of grass clippings helps tremendously) until seedlings emerge. Scatter snail baits to protect the seedlings from snails and slugs. Thin each clump to the strongest seedling.

Poor germination of lettuce seeds may be a problem when sown direct in very hot weather. When the soil temperature is 30°C or above, lettuce seeds have trouble germinating. You can overcome this by moistening the seeds, spreading them on a piece of damp paper towel, and keeping them in the refrigerator for a day or two. Then sow them direct as before. Or sow into punnets, refrigerate overnight and keep in a cool, lightly-shaded spot until seedlings emerge. Water with chilled water during warm weather. Nine to twelve plants should be more than adequate for each sowing. Make successive sowings every three to four weeks.

Lettuce plants have shallow roots so they need plenty of water – every day in summer. Mulch plants with grass clippings or compost. Give light side-dressings of nitrogen fertiliser or liquid feeds of Thrive every ten to fourteen days while the plants are growing. Start picking lettuce early when hearts are just forming. The young plants are crisp and tender and this spreads your harvest. Each sowing should then give a two- to three-week harvest. Lettuce keeps well in the refrigerator crisper for about a week but can't be frozen because leaves become soggy when thawed.

Varieties
Iceberg types
Iceberg is the term used for full headed lettuce with a central heart. 'Great Lakes' is a large, sure-hearting variety for growing in summer. It has crisp, solid hearts and will not run to seed when well grown. 'Winter Triumph' is a large, cool-weather variety for winter cutting. Both are classed as iceberg varieties. 'Greenway' and 'Yatesdale' are Australian bred iceberg lettuce varieties that have good flavour and disease resistance. Yatesdale is suitable for growing in warmer weather.
Loose leaf varieties
Small-growing lettuce varieties are often preferred in the home garden. They can be planted more closely but do not form hearts as solid as the large types. 'Red Coral' (Lollo rosso) variety is a loose-leafed, red-pigmented lettuce with unusual frilly leaves. It is a common component of lettuce mixes.

'Red Oak Leaf' has similar colouring to 'Red Coral' but has leaves that are slightly less 'frilly'.

'Mignonette' is an old garden favourite that can be sown all year round in many climates. 'Green Mignonette' has pale-green loose hearts and 'Brown Mignonette' is a brighter green, tinged with reddish-brown. 'Buttercrunch' ('Butterhead' type) is a small variety with leathery, light-green outer leaves and yellowish-green hearts, an excellent variety for tossed salads. 'Cos' or 'Romaine' lettuce has rather upright leaves forming a tall, loose heart. All small varieties are excellent for growing in large pots, tubs or troughs, but must be kept well watered.

Mesclun mixes, which combine many different lettuce varieties with other leafy salad ingredients, are popular nowadays for tossed salads.

Melons
Melons belong to the warm-season group of vine crops, often referred to as 'cucurbits' after the family name. This family includes cucumbers, marrows, melons, pumpkins, zucchinis and squash. Climatic requirements, time of sowing, soil preparation and fertiliser, cultivation and pest control for each of these vegetables is much the same. Check the cucumber section for this information.

Rockmelon or cantaloupe
Rockmelon requires a long, warm period to produce a crop and isn't particularly suitable for cool summer areas. 'Hales Best' is the leading variety of rockmelon. It is powdery mildew-resistant. Fruit weighs about 1 kg with a netted yellow skin and sweet, salmon-coloured flesh. Honeydew melon has oval fruit with smooth white skin and sweet green flesh. 'Greenflesh' is an interesting honeydew melon with cream-coloured skin and green flesh. Rockmelons are ready to harvest when the stem pulls easily from fruit. Ripen indoors for a day or two for full flavour.

Watermelon
'Candy Red' is the leading large-fruited variety. It has large, oblong fruit to 14 kg in weight with grey-green skin and deep-red flesh. It is resistant to fusarium wilt and to a disease called anthracnose. 'Country Sweet' is a big, roundish melon with dark-green, striped skin. The fruit is dense and full-flavoured. Harvest watermelons when the underside (the part in contact with the soil) turns yellow and the fruit gives a dull, hollow

sound when tapped. Melons need plenty of room in the garden. Seed for seedless watermelon is available commercially (and occasionally for home gardeners) but has very specific growing requirements.

Mushrooms

The mushroom is not a vegetable but a fungus that has a fleshy, fruiting body (the mushroom) arising from an underground web of hair-like filaments known as mycelium. The stalk of the mushroom is topped by the cap, beneath which are the gills containing the spores or reproductive cells. Mushrooms are prized for their delicate flavour and are used as vegetables in cooking, either alone or combined with many ingredients.

In their natural habitat, mushrooms and their inedible, and sometimes poisonous, relatives called toadstools occur in open grassland in autumn or spring when favourable conditions of moisture, temperature and humidity are present. Care must be taken when gathering field mushrooms because edible and inedible species are similar in appearance. Never eat any mushrooms unless you are sure they are correctly identified.

Mushrooms can be grown artificially on compost. Those bought in shops are nearly all produced in this way. Commercial mushroom growing is a highly specialised process that involves careful preparation and pasteurisation of the compost, the addition of the mushroom inoculum (called spawn) and a covering of peat or soil (the casing layer). The commercial crop is grown in specially constructed growing houses in which the temperature, humidity and ventilation are controlled. Similar, but less sophisticated, methods were used by home gardeners in the past, but preparing the compost from fresh animal manure, straw, soil and lime is a laborious task and accurate control of moisture and temperature during the composting process is not easy.

However, an offshoot of commercial mushroom growing is the marketing for home growers of 'mushroom farm' compost in plastic bags or boxes. The compost is already inoculated with spawn and a casing layer is also supplied, together with instructions. For best results, the 'farm' should be placed in a well-shaded location with still, fresh air, a high humidity level and a temperature between 15–18°C. A good spot for a mushroom farm is a corner of the garage or garden shed, in a cellar or underneath the house. Complete darkness is not necessary.

After spreading the casing layer of peat, sprinkle the surface with water to keep it damp but not wet. A light sprinkle two or three times each week is usually sufficient. The whitish-grey strands of the mycelium will cover the surface of the peat in ten to fifteen days and a few days later the filaments will clump together to form 'pin heads' which then develop into the first flush of mushrooms. After picking the first crop, sprinkle again regularly to keep the surface damp, and new pin heads will form for the next flush. A well-grown bag of mushrooms should produce a crop about every ten days over a period of two to three months. If, after several crops, no mushrooms appear for two or three weeks, the compost is exhausted and a new bag should be started. Use the spent compost for mulching or digging into the vegetable or flower garden.

Mushrooms can be picked in the button, cup or flat stage, whichever you prefer. Hold the cap of the mushroom in your fingers and gently twist the stalk from the casing layer.

It is a good idea to keep a small amount of peat in reserve for filling in small holes which may occur on the surface when removing the mushrooms.

Success with mushrooms grown in bags or boxes depends largely on their location (which must be free of draughts) and on very careful attention to watering. Growth rate is affected by temperature, so the flushes of mushrooms take longer in cold weather. Mushroom kits usually produce most mushrooms in autumn and spring, when temperatures are close to the optimum of 15–18°C.

Keep the area around the kit clean at all times, especially before starting a new box or bag. Pests such as slugs, slaters, cockroaches and mice may be a problem, so take appropriate control measures.

Mustard

Mustard is now popularly grown as a leafy vegetable, especially for use in Asian-style cooking. Seeds can be sown direct where they are to grow in autumn or spring. Grow in sun or semi shade and mulch well to keep moisture in the soil. Feed regularly with a liquid, high nitrogen fertiliser such as Thrive All Purpose. The red-leafed mustard is especially attractive and adds ornamental touches to the garden. Begin picking outer leaves from the early stages (usually starting at about 8 weeks). Dig spent plants in to improve the soil at the end of the season.

Okra

Okra or gumbo is an annual plant related to hibiscus. It is most suited to tropical/ subtropical climates or warm–temperate climates with a long growing season. Plants grow to 90 cm tall and have large, hibiscus-like, yellow flowers with red centres. Flowers are followed by edible pods that are 7–10 cm long.

Raise seedlings in late spring or early summer in a similar way to capsicum. Transplant seedlings when 10 cm high to a well-prepared bed, spacing plants 50–60 cm apart. For an average family, four or five plants are sufficient. Plants are grown on in the same way as capsicum, with a side-dressing of mixed fertiliser when flowering commences. The tender pods are ready to pick four or five days after the flowers have opened. They become very tough if left on the bush, and plants stop flowering. The pods, fresh or dried, are used for flavouring soups and stews. They can also be served lightly sautéed.

Onions

Onions are a very good winter crop in the home garden. For best results, it is important to choose the right variety for sowing at the right time of the year in different climate zones. Generally, onions are classified as early, mid-season and late-maturing types.

In warm northern areas, early onions are sown from February until May. In temperate climates like Sydney's, sow early onions from March to May and mid-season onions June to July. In cold southern areas sow early, mid-season and late onions in succession from April to August or September. It is important to sow early onions first, mid-season onions next and late onions last. Premature bolting

(running to seed) may occur if maturity groups are sown out of sequence or season.

You can raise onion seedlings in beds, pots or punnets for transplanting when 10–15 cm tall, spacing plants 7–10 cm apart in rows 20–30 cm apart. Do not plant deeply; just cover the roots and the base of the stem. Direct sowing saves double handling and is less trouble. Prepare the bed well, as you would for sowing carrots, scatter a pre-planting fertiliser in a band where seed is to be sown, and rake in. Make a shallow furrow 6 mm deep and tap out seeds thinly onto the 'dark damp' soil. Cover with compost or vermiculite and water gently. Seedlings generally emerge in ten to fourteen days, but may take longer in colder weather. Thin seedlings early to 2–3 cm and later to 7–10 cm. For the average family a 4–6 m row is sufficient. Make successive sowings with varieties of different maturity.

If the bed is well prepared and fertilised, additional fertiliser is seldom necessary. A light side-dressing of mixed fertiliser or liquid feeds when bulbs start to form will boost plants along if they are not growing strongly. Control weeds by hand, weeding between plants and shallow cultivation between rows. Do not hill the plants; bulbs sit on the soil surface, not below it. For control of diseases and pests see Chapter 8.

Onions take six to eight months to picking. Bulbs are ready to pull when tops dry and fall over. After pulling, leave them in the sun for a few days to cure. When outside skin is quite dry, screw off tops and rub off remaining roots. Select sound bulbs without blemishes for storage in a cool, dry place. Wire baskets or plastic mesh bags give good ventilation.

Varieties

Onions not only vary in maturity but come in different shapes, colours and degree of onion flavour (strong or mild). Generally, early-maturing onions do not keep as well as mid-season and late onions. 'Early Barletta' is the earliest onion, with flat, white bulbs. It is a favourite for early sowing. 'Hunter River White' and 'Hunter River Brown' are also early onions. All three have small- to medium-sized, globe-shaped bulbs with fair keeping qualities. They are the main varieties for early sowing in warm and mild–temperate climates.

'Sweet Red' is mid-season in maturity with purple-red, globe-shaped bulbs which keep fairly well.

A late-maturing variety such as 'Brown Spanish' has medium-sized, globe-shaped bulbs and excellent keeping qualities.

Many varieties of onion can be used as green salad or spring onions, but it is best to sow seed that is labelled 'Spring Onion' or 'Shallot Bunching Onion'. You can sow direct at almost any time of the year, from spring through to autumn. Sow seed more thickly with rows 5–10 cm apart. Thinning is seldom necessary. Spring or bunching onions are ready to harvest in eight to twelve weeks. Make successive sowings every four to six weeks as required. A popular variety of spring onion called 'Straight Leaf' has very upright stems that stay well clear of the soil. Spring onions are ideal for growing in pots or troughs. Immature onions with partially formed bulbs are sometimes called spring onions. True shallots develop brown-skinned, underground bulbs. These are harvested after the tops die down in winter.

Potato onion (multiplier onion) is grown from small sets of bulblets planted in autumn. Groups of bulbs are formed below the ground. Tree onion (Egyptian onion) is grown from sets in the same way. Bulbs are formed below ground and at the top of the flowering stem.

Parsnips

Parsnips, like carrots, produce good yields for the space they occupy and can be grown in all climate zones. In warm tropical/subtropical areas, sow seed from February to September in order to avoid the hot, wet season. In temperate districts, sow parsnips from July to March and in cold districts from August to February. Late sowings in autumn and winter may produce small roots and plants may run to seed prematurely.

Parsnips like a friable, open soil and good drainage for best root development. Compost or animal manure should be added well before sowing to avoid the development of forked or misshapen roots. Dig the bed to spade depth and prepare the bed for direct sowing in the same way as for carrots. Add mixed fertiliser and rake into the soil. Sow seed thinly in a furrow 6 mm deep. Rows should be 30–40 cm apart. Cover seed with compost or vermiculite and water gently. Parsnip seeds are slow to germinate (three to four weeks), so keep the bed damp with light watering until seedlings emerge. A light grass-clipping mulch will help to control moisture loss in hot weather. For the average family, a 3–5 m row is sufficient. Late summer and early autumn sowings are the most useful for harvesting the best quality roots.

Thin seedlings to 5–7 cm apart and control weeds. If parsnips are grown on a well-prepared and fertilised bed, extra fertiliser is rarely needed, but liquid feeds when roots start to form will promote faster growth. Do not over-feed, especially with high-nitrogen fertilisers.

Parsnips take eighteen to twenty weeks to grow. Start pulling roots early to spread the harvest. The remainder keep well in the soil, especially in winter when growth is slow. Roots store well for a week or two in an airy cupboard (remove the tops) but for several weeks in the refrigerator crisper.

Peanuts

Peanuts are sometimes called ground nuts, earth nuts or monkey nuts. Commercially, peanuts are grown on a large scale for eating raw or roasted, or to be ground for peanut

HINT

Spray snow peas with two parts full cream milk and eight parts water to manage powdery mildew. By keeping powdery mildew under control, snow peas can continue to produce right through to the end of October in warm regions and longer in the cooler, more temperate zones.

GEOFF MIERS

GEOFF MIERS GARDEN SOLUTIONS,
ALICE SPRINGS, NORTHERN TERRITORY

butter or crushed for peanut oil. They are very nutritious and contain 50–55 per cent oil and 40–45 per cent protein. Peanuts are not commonly found in the home vegetable garden but they are an interesting crop to grow. The plants are semi-erect, annual legumes that add nitrogen to the soil in the same way as beans and peas. They are natives of Brazil and need a long, warm growing season of about five months to mature. For this reason, they are best adapted to tropical, subtropical and warm–temperate climates. The plants are very susceptible to frost damage.

Peanuts are grown in much the same way as dwarf beans, but peanuts are strange plants. After the small, yellow flowers are pollinated, the flower stalks (called 'pegs' by peanut growers) lengthen and push downwards into the soil. The pods, containing one to four kernels, develop underground. The crop is dug when the top growth begins to yellow and die down.

Peanuts prefer a well-drained, sandy soil through which the 'pegs' can penetrate easily. Heavy soils are less suitable but satisfactory if they contain plenty of organic matter to give them a friable structure. When preparing the soil, add a dressing of lime, if necessary, to raise the pH level to 6.5 or 7.0. (See Chapter 5.) Seeds (raw peanuts – roasted ones will not germinate) are usually available from health food stores and are sown direct in the garden when soil temperatures reach about 20°C. Like bean seeds, peanuts are susceptible to fertiliser burn, so put a band of pre-planting fertiliser alongside the line where the seeds are to be sown. Also dust the seeds with fungicide before sowing. (See Chapter 9). Press the seeds into 'dark damp' soil at the bottom of a furrow about 50 mm deep, spacing the seeds 10–15 cm apart. If sowing more than one row, allow 60–75 cm between each. Cover the seeds with soil and tamp down firmly with the back of a rake. Then level the surface and scatter a mulch of dry grass clippings over the whole bed to retain moisture and prevent the soil caking. If seeds are sown in 'dark damp' soil, there is usually no need for extra watering until the seedlings emerge in seven to ten days.

Cultivate between the rows to destroy weeds and water the plants regularly, especially in hot weather. As the plants grow, hill the soil slightly against them for support. Alternatively, apply a mulch of compost or grass clippings between the rows. If a pre-planting fertiliser has been used, additional fertiliser is rarely needed. However, if the plants lack vigour at any stage, give liquid feeds of Thrive or Aquasol. Well-grown peanut plants should reach a height of 30–40 cm at flowering time.

When the foliage turns yellow and starts to die down it is time to dig the plants, usually sixteen to twenty-two weeks after sowing the seed. If dug too early, yields will be reduced and the kernels may be shrivelled. If left too late, the pods may break off the 'pegs' and remain in the soil. Lift each plant with a large fork and turn it upside down to dry in the sun for a few days. After the plants have wilted, shake the roots and pods free of soil and dry them further under cover. When the pods are quite dry, strip them from the plants and store them in bags or boxes. After shelling, the kernels can be eaten raw, or roasted on a shallow tray in an oven.

Obviously check to make sure that no-one who will come into contact with the plants or crop suffers from an allergy to peanuts.

Peas

Peas are one of the best cool-season crops for the home garden. The yield for space occupied is not as high as some of the other vegetables, but peas are easy to grow and space is usually available in winter to sow them. You can grow peas in all climates. In warm northern zones, sow seed from March to July. In temperate climates sow from February to August, and in cold climates sow from June to September or early October.

In any district where frosts are likely, make sowings so that the crop is not in flower during the frost period. Frost will damage both flowers and young pods.

Peas will adapt to heavy or light soils but need good drainage and a friable, well-structured soil. If your soil is acidic, apply lime as described in Chapter 5. Cultivate to prepare the bed and water well the day before sowing. Apply pre-planting fertiliser in furrows alongside where the seed is to be sown to avoid fertiliser burn. (See Chapter 9 for direct-sowing large seeds.)

HINT

As soon as the first female pumpkin flower appears, cut the runner and hand-pollinate the flower. Each runner should ideally receive the same treatment. The result: plenty of pumpkins for winter.

MORRIS HOLMES

HORTICULTURAL CONSULTANT AND
GARDEN DESIGNER

Mark out a furrow 25 mm deep and press the seeds into the soil 3–5 cm apart. For dwarf peas allow 40–50 cm between rows. For climbing peas, space seeds at the same distance against a fence or trellis on which the plants can climb. If making large sowings of climbing peas, allow 1 m between rows. For the average family a 3–5 m row is sufficient for each sowing of dwarf peas. A smaller row of 1–3 m is usually ample for climbing peas because they yield more pods over a longer period.

After sowing pea seeds, fill in the furrow with soil, tamp down and rake the bed. If seeds are pressed into pre-moistened, 'dark damp' soil, no further watering is required until seedlings emerge. Too much moisture, especially in the first couple of days after sowing, may do more harm than good. (See Chapter 9.) Birds can be a problem to emerging seedlings too. If you have bird trouble, cover the rows or the whole bed with bird netting or with black cotton thread stretched between short stakes. Remove these bird deterrents when the seedlings are 10 cm high. The birds have usually lost interest by this stage. Peas nearly always crop well without extra fertiliser while they grow. Yellow, stunted plants are more often the result of wet soil and poor drainage than lack of nutrients. If drainage is adequate and the plants still lack colour and vigour, apply a mixed fertiliser or give liquid feeds.

Climbing peas need some type of support to climb on but dwarf peas, too, yield better if their tendrils can cling to low supports –

twigs, strings or wire netting. This keeps the bushes upright and means the pods are easier to pick. For all pea crops, cultivate regularly (a day or two after watering) to destroy weeds and hill slightly at the same time. This discourages weeds close to the row and gives the stems more support.

Pests and diseases are minimal although powdery mildew can be troublesome (use lime sulfur as directed to control). (See Chapter 8.)

Pick well-filled pods before any etching of veins shows on the surface. Pick peas every few days for high quality and to prolong flowering. Peas in the pod keep well in the refrigerator crisper for a week or two, or you can shell the peas, blanch them for one minute, package and freeze them.

Varieties

'Earlicrop Massey' is an early dwarf variety. It is ready to pick twelve to fourteen weeks from sowing. 'Greenfeast', the main crop variety, is rather taller and bears masses of pods from fourteen to sixteen weeks after sowing. 'Telephone' is the standard climbing variety. Pods are ready about the same time as 'Greenfeast' but plants bear for much longer (three to five weeks). 'Snow Pea' (Chinese pea) is an edible podded variety. You can pick very young pods for cooking without shelling or you can slice them like beans. 'Snow Pea' is a climbing variety with white or purple flowers but there are dwarf varieties too. 'Sugarsnap' is an edible podded pea that has enjoyed wide acceptance. It is available as a vigorously growing, heavy cropping climber and produces delicious pods over a long period.

Popcorn

See Sweet corn.

Potatoes

Potatoes are warm-season plants that are very susceptible to frost. Severe frosts will kill the tops completely. In frost-free tropical/subtropical zones potatoes can be grown all year round, but the most suitable months are January to August (this period avoids the wet season.) In southern Queensland and warm to mild temperate districts, most gardeners prefer to grow a spring crop of potatoes (planted July to September) and an autumn crop (planted January to February). In cold districts the planting season is restricted to warmer months only, from August to December. The time of spring sowings depends on late frosts and soil temperatures.

Potatoes will adapt to light or heavy soils but good drainage is essential. They do best on friable soils with a good crumb structure. Potatoes are grown from tubers and not from true seeds. Tubers (called seed potatoes) are available from nurseries and garden stores in late winter and spring. When buying seed potatoes, look for certified tubers as these are free of virus diseases. If you want to grow an autumn crop too, you can save some seed potatoes from healthy, high-yielding plants in your spring crop.

For planting, tubers should be 30–60 g in weight. Cut large tubers into chunky pieces with at least one eye or sprout on each. Do not rub the cut surface in ashes or similar material, just let it dry out naturally. Spread tubers out in a shady spot for a week or two before planting. This allows the young sprouts to 'green' or harden. As a guide, a 3 kg bag of certified seed potatoes should provide fifty to sixty plants.

Prepare the bed to spade depth well beforehand to have the soil in friable, 'dark damp' condition at planting. Mark out furrows 15 cm deep and 75 cm apart. Scatter fertiliser along the bottom of the furrows at one-quarter of a cup per metre and cover with about 5 cm of soil from the sides. Place tubers 30–40 cm apart, cover with soil and rake the surface level. Sprouts emerge in three to four weeks.

Cultivate between rows to keep down weeds and gradually hill the plants to form a furrow between the rows. Hilling supports the plants, protects new potatoes from exposure to light and prevents them being attacked by caterpillars of potato moth. (See Chapter 8.) On level or slightly sloping beds, the furrows between rows can be used for irrigating. On well-prepared and fertilised soil, no extra fertiliser is needed, but water regularly to promote smooth, well-developed potatoes. It is possible to start digging 'new' potatoes about three to four weeks after plants have flowered and the lower leaves have turned yellow. If potatoes are to be stored, allow the tops to die off completely before digging. Discard any damaged or blemished potatoes and store in a cool, dry place, which must be dark to prevent the skin from 'greening'. Wooden crates or wire baskets are good containers for storage.

Potatoes can be grown in containers but this is usually more of a novelty rather than a serious attempt at producing abundant crops.

Pumpkins

Pumpkins are grown in the same way as cucumbers.

Most pumpkins grow on large running vines and can take up a lot of space. If possible, grow them in a corner of the garden where they can scramble over a fence or garden shed. Some varieties with smaller vines are described as 'bush' pumpkins. These are excellent for small gardens. Generally, all pumpkins are harvested when the vine dies and the fruit stalk is dry and brittle. Fruit is then fully mature with best flavour. Mature pumpkin fruit stores well for many months, although some varieties keep better than others. Store fruits in a cool, airy cupboard or in cardboard cartons. Fruit for storage must be free of blemishes or broken skin through which storage rots can invade. Inspect stored pumpkins periodically for signs of damage by rot, rats and mice.

Varieties

Of the large pumpkins, 'Queensland Blue' is

HINT

Many gardeners worry because their rhubarb stems aren't green, but this is often just the nature of the plant. Green rhubarb stems are quite safe to eat (unlike the leaves, which are poisonous). Add a small amount of red food colouring to improve colour if desired.

JUDY HORTON

GARDEN WRITER, BROADCASTER AND HORTICULTURIST

an old favourite with green, turning grey, creased fruit and deep-orange flesh. It is a good, long-keeping variety. 'Sweet Grey' is a medium-sized pumpkin with very smooth, easily cut and peeled skin. It performs best in areas with cool night temperatures. It has a firm, 'bone'-free flesh that is sweet and nutty. 'Jap' or 'Kent' pumpkin has a sweet flavour with attractively mottled skin. It is best grown in warmer areas as it takes a long time to get to flowering and fruiting stage (hence requires a long growing season).

'Gramma' ('Trombone') is an old-fashioned variety with horseshoe-shaped orange fruit and sweet, yellow, rather dry flesh. It's a favourite for gramma or pumpkin pie.

Of the smaller pumpkins, 'Butternut' has yellow-skinned, pear-shaped fruit 1–2 kg in weight with deep-orange flesh. It grows well on a fence or trellis to save space and keeps well if it's fully mature when picked.

'Golden Nugget' is described as a 'bush' variety of pumpkin. Each plant can be set about 1 m apart or you can grow a single plant in a large tub. It is an ideal home garden pumpkin and can be picked when fully coloured, but for better keeping qualities is best left until the bush dies. In warm and mild–temperate climates, two, or perhaps three, sowings are possible during spring and summer. 'Golden Nugget' bears six to ten small, round, orange fruit with deep-yellow flesh. The fruit is ready for picking about fourteen or fifteen weeks after sowing.

Radicchio

See Chicory.

Radish

Radish can be successfully sown almost the year round in all climate zones. Successive sowings from early spring to late summer will give crisp roots for the salad season. Radish is one of the quickest and easiest crops to grow. Seeds germinate in five to eight days and roots are ready to harvest in six to eight weeks.

Sow seeds direct in a well-prepared bed as for carrots. Spread fertiliser or scatter in a band where seed is to be sown. Space rows 10–15 cm apart and tap out seeds in a furrow 6 mm deep. Cover seeds with compost or vermiculite and water gently. Thin seedlings to 3–5 cm apart when they have grown their second leaf. Water regularly and give liquid feeds (e.g. Thrive Flower & Fruit) every seven to ten days. Mulch between rows to keep soil moist in hot weather. Make sowings every two to three weeks as required. A short row 50–100 cm long is usually sufficient for the average family. Start picking roots early because they get old and tough quickly. Roots keep well in the refrigerator crisper for a week or so. Radish can be grown as a piquant microgreen that can be ready for harvest within a matter of two weeks.

Varieties

Radishes come in different shapes and sizes. 'French Breakfast' (red with white top) is tankard-shaped. 'Salad Crunch' is the best of the globe-shaped varieties. 'Long Scarlet' and 'Long White Icicle' have tapering roots to 15 cm. All varieties are ideal for growing in pots and troughs. 'Gentle Giant' is a hybrid that grows to a large size (up to 6 cm) without becoming stringy.

Rhubarb

Rhubarb, one of the few perennial vegetables, is best grown in a separate bed where it can be left undisturbed for three or four years. It tolerates some shade and stems are usually longer when plants are grown in semi-shade. Rhubarb is adapted to all climate zones and a variety of soils but needs good drainage, regular watering and generous feeding.

You can propagate rhubarb by dividing established plants in late winter or early spring in most areas although, where it's warmer, clumps are often divided in late summer. Division allows the selection of the best-yielding plants. Rhubarb crowns (clumps of roots) or sets are usually available from nurseries during winter months. Rhubarb can also be grown from seeds sown during the warmer part of the year. Allow the plants to establish well (two to three years) before beginning to harvest.

When plants are established, apply a nitrogen fertiliser or liquid feeds every four or five weeks during the main growing season, from early spring to autumn. In winter each year, loosen soil around the plants and fork in compost or animal manure plus another ration of mixed fertiliser to give them a good start for spring growth.

Pick stalks (outside ones first) as required with a downward and sideways action so that they pull away cleanly from the crown. Always leave the youngest stalks in the centre of each plant to promote new growth. If flowering stems appear, cut these off at the base and apply a nitrogen fertiliser or liquid feeds to encourage more stalks and leaves. After picking, cut the leaves from stems. Do not use the leaves, as cases of rhubarb poisoning have been reported. Stalks keep well in the refrigerator crisper for a week or two but it is better to cook them immediately. Cooked rhubarb will keep well in sealed containers in the refrigerator and can be served chilled as required.

Note that rhubarb does not always develop red stems. Green stems are quite safe to eat and the flavour is just as good. Stems tend to develop stronger colouring in cooler climates.

Rockmelon
See Melons.

Rosella
Rosella or Jamaica sorrel is grown for its red fleshy fruits which are used to make sauce or jelly with a cranberry flavour. It is an annual plant closely related to hibiscus and grows to 2 m tall. Rosella is a warm-season plant which needs a growing season of at least six months, so it is only suitable for tropical/subtropical or warm–temperate climates.

Rosella seedlings are raised in the same way as capsicum and transplanted to the garden when 15–20 cm tall. Space plants 150 cm apart.

Grow plants as for other fruit vegetables with a side-dressing of mixed fertiliser when flowering commences. Pick fruit, which consists of red fleshy scales surrounding the green centre, when fully ripe. Two or three plants will provide plenty of fruit.

Salsify
Salsify, often referred to as oyster plant or vegetable oyster, is grown for its cream-coloured roots which are used in the same

way as parsnips. It is not widely grown in Australia but is adapted to all climates. Time of sowing, soil preparation, fertilisation and cultivation are the same as for carrots or parsnips. Salsify roots are long and thin and ready to dig in about twenty weeks from sowing. Wash, boil and scrape roots before baking or frying. For those who like the flavour of this vegetable, a 1–2 m long row is sufficient for one sowing.

Scorzonera
Scorzonera is also referred to as vegetable oyster. It, too, is grown for its roots which have a dark skin with beautiful creamy-white flesh and are used in much the same way as salsify. The long, thin roots are ready to dig in about four months from sowing. The seed should be sown in rows about 5–7 cm apart with row spacings of about 30–40 cm. A 2 m row is enough for one sowing.

Shallots
True shallots or eschalots are a different species from spring onions or bunching onions, which are often referred to as shallots. True shallots are grown from bulblets or cloves like garlic. The 'mother' bulbs are usually planted 5–7 cm deep in autumn or early winter. Space plants 15–25 cm apart. As plants and 'daughter' bulbs develop, push soil around them to blanch the stems. Grow them quickly with generous feeding as for leeks or spring onions.

You can harvest plants as chopped leaves (like chives), as green onions for salads, or as dry bulbs (like garlic) for flavouring. Small bulblets or cloves can, of course, be replanted. If you start with a few plants, you can grow shallots for ever.

Silver beet
Silver beet or Swiss chard is a close relative of beetroot and is, in fact, a variety of the same species. It is not a true spinach but it is often called spinach, especially in New South Wales and Queensland. Silver beet, with its large crinkly leaves and white stalks, is an excellent, cut-and-come-again vegetable that's easy to grow in the home garden. It is adapted to all climate zones. In warm northern areas it is sown almost any month of the year; in temperate and cold districts

A healthy crop of silver beet growing happily with herbs.

from early spring to early autumn. Late autumn and winter sowings may run to seed. (See Sowing Guide for best months to sow.) Silver beet, like other leaf vegetables, needs well-drained soils with plenty of organic matter for good structure, and generous feeding.

Silver beet can be raised as seedlings in boxes or punnets but direct sowing avoids double handling and transplant shock. After scattering pre-planting fertiliser in a band where seed is to be sown, soak seeds for a few hours and sow in clumps 30–40cm apart. Cover seeds to 12 mm deep and water gently. Seedlings emerge in ten to fourteen days and can be thinned to the strongest when 10 cm high. You can have a year-round supply with two to three sowings between spring and autumn.

Grow silver beet quickly, like lettuce, with regular watering and side-dressings of a nitrogen-rich fertiliser or liquid feeds every two to three weeks. Cultivate to control weeds and mulch around plants in hot weather. Diseases and pests are not serious but leaf spot may be troublesome. (See Chapter 8 for control.)

Start picking outside stalks and leaves when large enough. Break them off at the base with a downward and sideways action. Always leave four or five centre stalks for quick regrowth. Cut off any flower stems that appear, but once flowering commences plants become unproductive very quickly. Silver beet keeps well in the refrigerator crisper for up to a week but for the best flavour, cook leaves immediately after picking. Silver beet, like lettuce, does not freeze well.

Varieties

'Fordhook Giant' has been selected over many years for quality and high yield to become the leading variety for home gardens and commercial growing. It has dark-green, blistered leaves and creamy-white stalks. 'Compact ' is a smaller-growing variety that can be sown all year round and resists going to seed. Novelty varieties are 'Rainbow Chard' with leaf stalks in purple, red, pink and yellow, and 'Ruby Chard' or 'Red-Stemmed' with bright-crimson stalks. Silver beet 'Perpetual Green' has smooth, spinach-like leaves on slender stalks. It can be harvested over a long period.

Spinach

Spinach is a cool-season, short-day crop that

tends to run to seed in warm weather with long days. For this reason it is most widely grown in Victoria and Tasmania. Home gardeners in New South Wales and Queensland often prefer to grow the more adaptable silver beet as 'spinach'. In warm northern areas, sow spinach in winter months only. For temperate climates, sow from late summer to early winter. In cold climates, sow from late summer right through to early spring. Seed can benefit from being soaked in water overnight before sowing.

Sow seeds direct into well-prepared beds with plenty of organic matter plus added mixed fertiliser. Plants prefer well-drained fertile soil with good structure, similar to that for lettuce. Sow a few seeds in clumps 30–40 cm apart, cover and water. Thin seedlings in each clump, leaving the strongest. For the average family, twelve to fifteen plants is sufficient. Plants grow quickly so make successive sowings every three to four weeks for a continuous supply. Baby spinach is harvested when leaves are very small and used as a salad ingredient.

Like lettuce, spinach needs regular watering and side-dressings of nitrogen fertiliser or liquid feeds every ten to fourteen days. A grass or straw mulch tucked around each plant will keep the leaves free of dirt. Major pests are leaf miners and mites. (See Chapter 8 for control.) When plants are large enough, pick outside leaves individually, like silver beet. Each plant will keep producing for about four weeks or so. Leaves keep well in the refrigerator crisper for up to a week but are best cooked immediately after picking. Like lettuce and silver beet, spinach leaves tend to collapse when frozen.

Varieties

Improved hybrid varieties have largely replaced open-pollinated varieties. 'Winter Queen' is the most widely grown variety. It has rather upright, plain, medium-green leaves with excellent flavour. 'Winter Queen' and 'Summer Supreme' both have large leaves with a sweet flavour but 'Summer Supreme' is more heat-tolerant. Baby spinach grows quickly and is ready for picking in 6 – 8 weeks. 'Native Spinach' (*Tetragonia tetragonioides*) is a drought-hardy native

vegetable that is long-lived and can be harvested for months. Always cook or blanch before eating.

Squash

Squash is another warm-season vine crop grown in the same way as cucumber. Refer also to the Sowing Guide.

Varieties

There are two types of squash. Summer squash are picked when immature, like cucumbers or marrows. Winter squash are picked when fully mature, like pumpkins, and keep well in storage through the colder months. Both types are grown during the spring–summer–autumn period but these days the small baby summer squash are the most widely grown.

'Early White Bush' is a widely known variety of summer squash. The fruits are round, 15 cm in diameter with scalloped edges. Both skin and flesh are creamy white. Each fruit weighs 1–1.5 kg. 'Green Button' and 'Yellow Button' are popular varieties. They are best picked when 5–10 cm in diameter. Pick regularly to encourage further flowers and fruit. 'Green Button' and 'Yellow Button' can be grown in a large pot or tub about 40 cm in diameter and the same depth.

Of the winter squash, 'Green Warted Hubbard' is a running vine with round, dark-green fruit with pointed edges. The fruit weighs about 5 kg and contains deep-orange flesh. 'Table Queen' (acorn squash) has smaller, grey-green, pear-shaped fruit to 1 kg in weight. These varieties of winter squash are good keepers but are not as widely grown as they used to be.

Swedes and turnips

Swedes and turnips are cool-season root crops that are grouped together because their climatic requirements and cultivation are almost identical. Both vegetables can be grown in all three climate zones. In all climates, sowing takes place in late summer and autumn, but in cold districts both swedes and turnips can be sown in late winter or early spring as well (see Sowing Guide for best months to sow in each zone). Swedes take three to four months to grow and have large roots with yellow or buff-coloured flesh. The roots store well. Turnips take less time (ten to twelve weeks) to grow, have smaller globe-shaped roots with white flesh and do not store as well as swedes.

Prepare the soil well for direct sowing in the same way as for carrots. Both crops respond well to liberal quantities of organic matter and a scattering of pre-planting fertiliser in a band where seed is to be sown. Mark out shallow rows 6 mm deep and 20–30 cm apart. Tap out seeds thinly along the rows, four or five seeds to each 5 cm, cover and water gently. Seedlings emerge in six to ten days, depending on temperature. Thin seedlings to 7–10 cm apart. Make successive sowings every three or four weeks.

Water plants regularly at the base (keeping leaves dry) and, if plants are slow, give side-dressings of nitrogen fertiliser or liquid feeds. Cultivate between rows to keep down weeds but do not hill around the plants. The roots are really swollen stems which sit on the soil surface, not below it. Control caterpillars and aphids as for other cabbage crops. (See Chapter 8.)

Start harvesting early for best quality and to give the remaining roots more space to grow. Dig all roots before they become coarse and stringy. Swedes store better than turnips at normal temperatures but both keep well in the refrigerator crisper for eight to ten weeks.

Varieties

Best variety of swede is 'Champion Purple Top'. 'Purple Top White Globe' is the most popular turnip. Another sweet, tender turnip is the Japanese Turnip, 'Hakurei'.

Sweet corn

Sweet corn is a very popular vegetable that looks good in the garden and is easy to grow. It takes up a fair amount of space for a relatively small harvest but home-grown cobs are so much tastier than the ones you buy that it's worth the extra space. A warm-season crop, sweet corn will grow in all climates. In warm northern areas the best months to sow are July to February, but you can sow in almost any month (providing there are no frosts) in tropical parts of Queensland and the Top End. In temperate climates, sow from August to January and in

cold climates, from October to December. Sweet corn grows well on both light and heavy soils, providing drainage and soil structure are good. Plenty of fertiliser and water are needed for a bumper crop.

Prepare soil well with organic matter added to have the bed in friable damp condition for direct sowing. It is best to grow sweet corn in a block of short rows rather than one long row. This way pollen from the male flowers or tassels at the top of the plants has the best chance of falling on the female flowers or silks halfway up the stems. You can grow three rows spaced 50–60 cm apart in a bed 150 cm wide.

Apply a pre-planting fertiliser in furrows where each row is to be sown so that seed is not in direct contact. It can be helpful to dust seed with fungicide before sowing to protect against 'damping off'. Mark out the seed furrows 25 mm deep and press seeds into 'dark damp' (just moist) soil. Space seeds 15 cm apart. This allows for some misses when seedlings are thinned to 20–30 cm apart. Another method is to sow two seeds close together, with 30 cm between each pair, and thin to one seedling. Cover seeds with soil, tamp down, rake the bed and scatter a light grass mulch on the surface. If seed is sown in 'dark damp' soil, seedlings will emerge without further watering. Scatter snail baits to protect seedlings from slugs and snails. For the average family, a sowing of three rows 2 m long will provide twenty to twenty-four plants after thinning out. Make the next sowing when the previous plants are 15–20 cm tall.

After thinning, scatter a side dressing of fertiliser around each plant. Repeat this treatment when the tassels first appear between the top leaves. Regular watering is needed while the crops grow, especially in hot weather. A good soaking once or twice a week is better than a light sprinkle every day. Cultivate between rows to control weeds and draw soil around the stems to hill the plants at the same time. Corn earworm and aphids are serious pests. (See Chapter 8 for control.) When tassels open out fully they are ready to shed pollen. Overhead watering in the early morning will create a humid atmosphere in the crop to promote good pollination of the silks. Pollen is shed, usually about mid-morning, for several days. Shaking the plants will help release the pollen.

Don't allow the plants to dry out or become stressed from lack of fertiliser. Stressed plants will produce undersized cobs or may not produce any cobs at all.

Cobs must be harvested at the right time. They are ready to pick when the silks have turned brown and cobs stand out from the stem at about a 30-degree angle. Make a further check by pulling open the husk from the top and pressing the grains with the thumbnail. If grain is soft and exudes juice with a creamy consistency, the cob is ready to pick. In over-ripe cobs, sugar quickly turns to starch and the grains are tough and doughy. Pick cobs with a downward and twisting action.

For top quality, remove husks and cook as soon as possible. Water must be boiling before cobs are put in saucepan. Cobs in-the-husk keep well in the refrigerator crisper for three or four days and may be lightly cooked on the barbecue or in a microwave oven. To freeze corn on the cob, remove the husks, blanch the cobs for eight minutes, cool quickly and package each cob separately.

Varieties

Most are now F1 hybrids, the older strains having been replaced by the superior high-yielding varieties such as 'Early Chief' and 'Honeysweet'. 'Honeysweet' has attractive yellow kernels, extremely sweet, and a superb flavour. 'Early Chief' is a strong grower with good-quality, even cobs. 'Sun 'n' Snow' has white and yellow kernels on cobs of exquisite flavour and sweetness. 'Popcorn' is different from sweet corn but it is grown in the same way. The cobs are harvested when the grain is hard and fully mature. The very high starch content in the grains makes them explode or 'pop' when heated.

Sweet potatoes

Sweet potato, which is a close relative of convolvulus, is a warm-season, frost-susceptible vegetable that needs a growing season of at least five months. Sweet potato is suitable for tropical/subtropical or very warm-temperature areas. The plant is a vigorous, rather untidy vine that prefers light soils.

Start plants from cuttings or buy a few sweet potatoes and bury them in a box of

moist sand placed in a warm spot. When tubers shoot, divide them up for planting or remove shoots and place them in water to develop roots. Prepare soil as for potatoes and dig in some fertiliser where the plants are to grow. Planting on a raised ridge makes for better drainage and easier harvesting. Set cuttings 40–50 cm apart and 5–7 cm deep with 100 cm between rows. For an ample supply of tubers, eighteen to twenty-four plants is sufficient.

Lift vines occasionally as they grow to prevent rooting at the nodes along the stems. Do not give additional fertiliser, especially not nitrogen, which promotes top growth at the expense of tuber development. Diseases and pests do not often cause problems. It is best to wait until plants are completely yellow and tubers fully mature before digging. Mature tubers have firm skin and when cut, dry quickly to a creamy-white colour. After digging, leave tubers in the sun for a few days to cure. Discard diseased or damaged ones and store remainder in sacks in a cool, dry, airy place.

Tomatoes

Tomatoes usually top the list for the most popular home-grown vegetable. Tomatoes give a higher yield for space occupied than just about any other vegetable. A good average yield is 3–5 kg per plant but well-grown plants can yield 10 kg of fruit or more.

Tomatoes are warm-season, frost-susceptible plants that need a growing season of about three months, so they'll grow in all climate zones in Australia. In frost-free, warm northern areas, tomatoes are grown throughout the year. In temperate climates the best months to start tomatoes are August to December and in cold districts September to November. In mild districts like Sydney, an early crop (August sowing) and a late crop (November sowing) will supply tomatoes for about five months of the year (mid-December to mid-April). Tomatoes grow well on light and heavy soils but the usual rules for vegetable soils apply: good drainage, organic matter for soil structure, and adequate water and fertiliser. Phosphorus is a most important nutrient for tomatoes, and lack of it, especially in the seedling stage, will reduce yields of fruit. Nitrogen is needed too but not

Top five tomatoes

'GROSSE LISSE'

The name means 'large smooth' and these tomatoes are just that: perfect balls of bright red with a much-loved flavour.

'SWEETIE'

Miniature tomatoes hang like bunches of grapes from the stems of this easily grown variety. 'Sweetie' seems to be pest- and disease-free.

'SUMMERSTAR'

Although it will grow anywhere, this variety of tomato, because of its disease resistance, is a particularly good choice for warmer climates.

'ROMA'

The traditional egg tomato is a favourite for cooking and sauce-making.

'TINY TIM'

Number one choice for pots, 'Tiny Tim' has compact growth that doesn't need staking. The small fruit is yummy and also ornamental.

'SWEETIE'

'ROMA'

in the same quantities as for leaf vegetables.

Seeds can be sown direct (especially for a late crop) but it is more usual to raise seedlings in pots or punnets for transplanting. Seedlings for the early crop can be pricked out into 10 cm plastic pots and grown on for several weeks in a warm sunny spot (especially if conditions are still cold). If the garden bed is not ready, transfer the seedlings to 15–20 cm pots.

For tall, staking tomatoes, set seedlings 50–60 cm apart each way. This relatively close spacing (much closer than commercial crops) gives enough light to each plant, but plenty of watering and fertiliser will be needed. For an average family, twelve to fifteen plants is sufficient for one sowing. Cultivate around plants and between rows to destroy weeds. On flat or sloping beds you can make furrows between the rows for irrigation. This is a useful method of watering, as many leaf spot and leaf blight diseases are spread by overhead watering.

With adequate fertiliser in the bed preparation, extra fertiliser is not needed until plants have set their first truss of fruit. At this stage, scatter a tablespoon of mixed fertiliser around each plant and water in. Repeat treatment every four to five weeks as plants grow. Water regularly to maintain a good level of moisture in the soil, weekly when plants are small, but increase this to twice a week when plants are carrying a heavy crop or when weather is hot and dry.

Most tomatoes are grown on stakes about 2 m in length. Hammer stakes into the soil 5 cm from stem of plants after transplanting. Plants are traditionally pruned to two leaders (main stems), which are tied to the stakes. If desired, break off laterals (shoots that grow from leaf axils) with a sideways twist when small, or cut with a sharp knife when larger. The lateral to select for the second leader (main stem) is the one immediately below the first flower truss. This lateral is more vigorous than others.

Tie the leaders to the stake with a soft tie just above a leaf stalk to stop it from slipping down the stem. Ties should be about 30 cm part. Make a figure-eight tie which allows the leader to increase in size. Take care that flower trusses aren't squeezed between leader and stake. Carefully twist the leader so that each truss faces outwards.

Solving Problems with Tomatoes

PROBLEM	CAUSE	SOLUTION
Split fruit.	Heavy watering or rain after soil has been dry.	Water regularly through dry periods
Blossom drop.	Low temperatures in spring or very high temperatures in summer.	Grow a variety suited to the season, e.g. 'Apollo Hybrid', for early or late crops
Sun scald – papery brown patches on fruit.	Exposure to bright sunlight.	Do not remove too many old leaves at once
Blossom end rot – bottom of fruit sunken, leathery and blackened.	Lack of calcium, together with irregular watering.	Add lime or dolomite to soil when preparing bed; water regularly
Blotchy ripening – parts of fruit remain yellow or orange.	Too much heat, too little potash.	Add potash
Misshapen fruit.	Poor pollination caused by cold weather at flowering or very high temperature. Also virus diseases.	Apply Thrive plant food or a specialist tomato fertiliser
Rolling of older leaves.	Excess deleafing or a wide variation between day and night temperatures.	Maintain leaf cover
Yellowing between veins beginning with lower leaves.	Magnesium deficiency. Can also be nitrogen and potash deficiency.	Apply Aquasol or Thrive as a liquid every two weeks
Insects clustered on young shoots.	Aphids	Natrasoap, Pyrethrum
Tiny white insects on underside of leaves which fly when disturbed.	Whitefly	Pyrethrum, Natrasoap
Small caterpillars tunnel holes in fruit.	Tomato fruit worm	Mavrik, Success Ultra
Unthrifty plants which grow slowly and wilt easily for no apparent reason.	Root knot nematodes	Increase organic matter in the soil or grow in pots
Leaves become yellow (mottled) and dehydrated in hot, dry weather especially in glasshouses. Minute pests under leaves.	Mites	Lime Sulfur, Natrasoap

Solving Problems with Tomatoes (cont'd)

PROBLEM	CAUSE	SOLUTION
Irregular green/brown or black patches on leaves spreading rapidly in wet weather.	Late blight	Yates Tomato Dust, Liquid Copper
Small spots on older leaves increasing to 1 cm. Common in hot, humid weather.	Early blight	Yates Tomato Dust, Liquid Copper
Leaves yellow and wilt, followed by total collapse of the plant.	Verticillium wilt	Do not grow in same area for at least three years.
Leaves pale and stunted, blackening of stems, followed by stunting and death.	Bacterial wilt	Destroy plants. If severe, grow future plants in a new area.
Plants suddenly stop growing and tops become yellow/purplish and bunched.	Spotted wilt virus	Destroy plants. Control thrips with Natrasoap.

Diseases and pests can be a problem with tomatoes. Fruit fly (in warm climates) and tomato caterpillars are the worst pests and must be controlled. (See Chapter 8.)

Tomato dust will control most common problems, although not fruit fly. For top-quality fruit, pick when red-ripe, although slightly coloured fruit ripens well indoors. Fruit keeps well in the refrigerator for one or two weeks (ripe) or four or five weeks (green). Fresh tomatoes cannot be frozen. Preserve them by bottling or cook them and then package for freezing.

There are more varieties of tomatoes than any other vegetable crop. This reflects their worldwide popularity and emphasises the many different types available for selection and breeding.

Varieties – large and medium

'Grosse Lisse', released over seventy years ago, is still the most popular garden variety. It is mid-season in maturity with medium to large, globe-shaped fruits. Grosse Lisse means 'big, smooth'.

Marmande-type tomatoes have soft skins and distinct vertical ribs on the side of the fruit. 'Burke's Backyard Italian Tomato' is a good example.

'Improved Apollo' sets fruit early in the season, is a prolific cropper and an excellent home-garden variety. 'Ox Heart' is a large, fleshy, variable variety with orange–scarlet fruit. Maturing mid-season, the fruit is firm and smooth. 'Summerstar' is resistant to bacterial wilt and has good flavour. It is an excellent choice for the tropics and the subtropics but will grow happily in a wide climate range.

'Roma' is an egg tomato with a slightly 'pear-like' shape. Although it can be used in salads, 'Roma' is most popular for cooking, saucing and soups. 'Big Beef' has a wonderful beefsteak flavour with medium to large, thick-skinned fruit. Heirloom varieties of tomatoes are increasingly popular. Although they usually have good flavour, they don't always have the disease resistance of more modern varieties so may not be the wisest choice, particularly in areas with humid summers.

Varieties – small
'Sweetie' has prolific clusters of cherry-sized fruit. It is best grown on a sunny fence where the plant receives some support. 'Tiny Tim' is a true mini-tomato. Plants grow to 30–40 cm tall and bear masses of bite-sized fruit. This variety is ideal for growing in large pots or tubs, but don't forget to give it lots of water in hot weather.

Turnips
See Swedes and Turnips.

Zucchinis
Zucchinis (also known as courgettes) are immature marrows and have become one of our most widely grown vegetables since the middle of the 20th century.

Zucchinis grow in the same conditions as cucumbers and pumpkins, with good drainage and plenty of sun. Sow seeds direct in spring into a slight depression on top of a raised mound. Pick regularly to encourage further crops. Don't allow zucchini fruit to grow too large. This reduces future cropping and spoils the flavour of the crop. All zucchinis crop quickly and are easy to grow, but need warm conditions. If immature fruit drop off in the early stage, this is due to poor pollination. Pollination may improve as the weather warms. Hand pollination, moving the pollen from the male flower to the centre of the female (the flower with the tiny fruit at its base), may help.

Varieties
'Blackjack' is a prolific bush variety with very dark green fruit. Pick when no more than 15cm long. 'Greyzini' is similar to Blackjack but has a grey-green mottled skin. Lebanese zucchini grows on a more spreading plant and has tear-shaped, light-coloured fruit in great quantities.

Asian vegetables
In addition to the popular Chinese cabbage and Chinese snow peas there is a wide variety of vegetables grown in Asia. Around them much of the specialised regional cooking has developed. Many of these vegetables are not commonly available in Australia so we have selected for description those few varieties whose seed supply is easily accessible.

Varieties
'Chinese Broccoli Kailaan' produces much smaller heads than common broccoli and is used, stem and all, when the flowers start opening. The plants are very heat-tolerant.

Cabbage 'Michili' is upright-growing to about 50 cm, with cylindrical, firm heads weighing about 1.5 kg. The delicate flavour is much favoured in Asian cuisines.

Radish 'Daikon Long White' is widely used in Asian cooking and particularly in Japanese-style dishes. Grows easily from seed, and is ready for picking seven weeks from sowing. Its growing conditions are the same as for as other radishes.

Tatsoi is a versatile vegetable served cooked or in salads. Excellent flavour. The deep-green, spoon-shaped leaves of this vegetable are produced in profusion. For cultivation directions, treat as lettuce: ample water and regular applications of a nitrogenous soluble fertiliser such as Aquasol or Thrive. Pick young for best flavour.

Turnip 'Hakurei' is an economical vegetable, as both the root and leaves may be used. The root is white-skinned with crisp, sweet flesh, excellent for salads, soups or stir-frying. Use the leaves in the same way as you would use Chinese cabbage.

'Mibuna' and 'Mizuna' are Asian mustards that grow easily and quickly from seed. They can be grown for much of the year and are also successfully produced in outdoor pots or indoors as microgreens. Their mild mustard flavour adds a piquancy to salads. Most of the Asian vegetables are best grown from seed sown in summer and autumn in cool or temperate climates, or all year round in the tropics and subtropics.

Sowing Guide for Vegetables

VEGETABLES	TROPICAL/SUBTROPICAL • SUBTROPICAL ONLY ▲ TROPICAL ONLY ■												TEMPERATE											
	J	F	M	A	M	J	J	A	S	O	N	D	J	F	M	A	M	J	J	A	S	O	N	D
Artichokes (suckers)	•	•	•													•	•	•	•	•	•			
Asparagus (2-year crowns)					•	•	•											•	•					
Beans (dwarf)	▲	•	•	•	•	•	•	•	•	•	▲	▲	•	•							•	•	•	•
Beans (climbing)	▲	•	•	•	•	•	•	•	•	•	▲	▲	•								•	•	•	•
Beetroot		•	•	•	•	•	•	•	•	•			•	•	•				•	•	•	•	•	•
Broad beans				•	•	•	▲									•	•	•	•					
Broccoli	▲	▲	•	•	•	•	•	•	▲	▲	▲		•	•	•	•	•							•
Brussels sprouts	Not suitable												•	•	•									•
Cabbages	▲	•	•	•	•	•	•	•	•	•	•	▲	•	•	•	•				•	•	•	•	•
Cape gooseberry	•	•	•	■	■	■	•	•	•	•	•	•								•	•	•	•	•
Capsicums (Peppers)	•	•	•	■	■	■	•	•	•	•	•	•								•	•	•	•	•
Carrots		•	•	•	•	•	•	•	•	•			•	•	•				•	•	•	•	•	•
Cauliflowers	•	•	•	•									•	•	•									•
Celery	•	•	•	•							▲	▲	•	•						•	•	•	•	•
Chicory			•	•	•	•	•	•	•				•	•	•					•	•	•	•	•
Chinese cabbages	•	•	•	•	•	•	•	•	•	•	•	•	•	•	•	•			•	•	•	•	•	•
Choko (see Note 1)					■	■	•	•	•	•										•	•	•		
Cress	•	•	•	•	•	•	•	•	•	•	•	•	•	•	•	•	•	•	•	•	•	•	•	•
Cucumbers (see Note 3)	•	•	•	■	■	■	•	•	•	•	•	•	•								•	•	•	•
Eggplants	•	•	•	■	■	■	■	■	•	•	•	•									•	•	•	•
Endive			•	•	•	•	•	•					•	•	•					•	•	•	•	•
Kale			•	•	•									•	•	•	•							
Kohl rabi	▲	•	•	•	•								•	•	•				•	•	•			

Note 1 – Usually grown on fence or trellis.
Note 2 – Make successive sowings as required.

COLD

J	F	M	A	M	J	J	A	S	O	N	D	SOWING METHOD BED (S) DIRECT (D)	SOWING DEPTH (MM)	SEEDLING EMERGE (DAYS)	SOW AND THIN OR TRANSPLANT TO ... CM APART ROWS	PLANTS	TIME TO PICKING (WEEKS)	QUANTITY FOR FAMILY OF FOUR PLANTS (P) LENGTH (M)
						•	•	•	•			D	150	–	100	100	20–28	3–5p
					•	•						D	150–200	–	100	30–50	16–24	20–25p
•									•	•	•	D	25	7–10	50–60	7–10	8–10	3–5m
									•	•	•	D	25	7–10	100	10–15	10–12	2–3m
•	•						•	•	•	•		S or D	12	10–14	20–30	7–10	10–12	2–3m
		•	•	•			•	•				D	50	10–14	60–75	15–20	18–20	5–6m
•	•								•	•		S or D	6	6–10	45–60	45–60	12–16	9–12p
•	•								•	•	•	S or D	6	6–10	60–75	60–75	16–20	6–9p
•	•	•					•	•	•	•	•	S or D	6	6–10	40–75	40–75	8–16	9–12p
									•	•	•	S	6	14–28	100	100	20–24	2–3p
									•	•	•	S or D	6	10–14	50–60	50–60	10–16	4–6p
•	•					•	•	•	•	•	•	D	6	10–21	20–30	3–5	12–16	4–6m
•									•	•		S or D	6	6–10	50–75	50–75	14–26	9–12p
								•	•	•	•	S or D	6	14–21	30–40	30–40	20–22	16–20p
•	•								•	•	•	S or D	12	10–14	20–30	3–5	16–20	1–2m
•	•	•				•	•	•	•	•	•	S or D	6	6–10	30–40	30–40	8–10	6–9p
		Not suitable										D	50–75	–	–	100	18–20	1–3p
•	•	•	•	•	•	•	•	•	•	•	•	D	3	6–10			4–6	(see Note 2)
									•	•	•	D	12	6–10	100	40–50	8–12	4–6p
									•	•		S or D	6	10–14	60–75	60–75	14–16	4–6p
•	•						•	•	•	•		S or D	6	10–14	20–30	20–30	8–12	6–9p
•	•	•	•									S or D	6	6–7	30	30	7	9–12m
•	•	•					•	•	•			D	6	6–10	30–40	10–15	8–12	1–2m

Note 3 – Early plants can be raised in punnets or pots.
Note 4 – Many herbs are perennials that will grow for several years.

VEGETABLES	TROPICAL/SUBTROPICAL • SUBTROPICAL ONLY ▲ TROPICAL ONLY ■												TEMPERATE											
	J	F	M	A	M	J	J	A	S	O	N	D	J	F	M	A	M	J	J	A	S	O	N	D
Leeks	▲	▲	▲	•	•	•							•	•	•	•					•	•	•	•
Lettuce	•	•	•	•	•	•	•	•	•	•	•	•	•	•	•	•	•	•	•	•	•	•	•	•
Marrows (see Note 3)	•	•	•	■	■	■	•	•	•	•	•	•	•									•	•	•
Melons (see Note 3)	•	•	■	■	■	■	•	•	•	•	•											•	•	•
Mustard			•	•	•	•	•	•					•	•	•						•	•	•	
Okra	•	•	■	■	■	■	■	■	•	•	•	•												
Onions	•	•	•	•	•													•	•	•	•	•	•	
Onions (spring)	•	•	•	•	•	•	•	•	•	•	•	•	•	•	•	•	•			•	•	•	•	•
Parsnips	▲	•	•	•	•	•	•	▲					•	•	•					•	•	•	•	•
Peas (dwarf)			•	•	•	•	•	•					•	•	•					•	•	•	•	
Peas (climbing)			•	•	•	•	•	•					•	•	•					•	•	•	•	
Potatoes (tubers)	▲	•	•	•	•	•	•	•					•	•							•	•	•	
Pumpkins (see Note 3)		•	•	■	■	■	■	•	•	•	•											•	•	•
Radishes	•	•	•	•	•	•	•	•	•	•	•	•	•	•	•					•	•	•	•	•
Rhubarb (seed)	▲	•	•	•	•			▲	▲	▲	▲	▲									•	•	•	•
Rhubarb (crowns)	▲	▲	▲	▲		•	•	•	▲	▲	▲	▲	•	•						•	•	•	•	•
Rosella	■	■	■	■	■	■	■	•	•	•	•											•	•	•
Salsify	▲	•	•	•	•	•	•	▲	▲				•	•	•					•	•	•	•	•
Shallots (bulbs)	■	•	•	•	•	•	•										•	•	•	•	•	•		
Silver beet	•	•	•	•	•	•	•	•	•	•	•	•	•	•	•					•	•	•	•	•
Spinach			•	•	•	•	•						•	•	•						•	•	•	
Squash (see Note 3)	•	•	■	■	■	■	•	•	•	•	•	•										•	•	•
Swedes	•	•	•										•	•	•									
Sweet corn	•	•	■	■	■	■	•	•	•	•	•	•	•							•	•	•	•	•
Sweet potatoes (shoots)	•	•	■				•	•	•	•	•											•	•	•
Tomatoes	•	•	•	•	•	•	•	•	•	•	•	•								•	•	•	•	•
Turnips	•	•	•	•									•	•	•	•								
Zucchinis	•	•	•	■	■	■	•	•	•	•	•	•	•							•	•	•	•	•

Note 2 – Make successive sowings as required.

COLD — J	F	M	A	M	J	J	A	S	O	N	D	SOWING METHOD BED (S) DIRECT (D)	SOWING DEPTH (MM)	SEEDLING EMERGE (DAYS)	SOW AND THIN OR TRANSPLANT TO … CM APART — ROWS	PLANTS	TIME TO PICKING (WEEKS)	QUANTITY FOR FAMILY OF FOUR PLANTS (P) LENGTH (M)
•	•	•							•	•	•	S or D	6	10–14	15–20	15–20	12–20	40–50p
•	•	•	•	•	•	•	•	•	•	•	•	S or D	3	6–7	20–30	20–30	8–12	9–12p
									•	•	•	D	20	6–10	100	100	8–14	3–6p
									•	•	•	D	20	6–10	150	100	14–16	2–3p
	•	•	•						•	•	•	D	6	6–10	Sow seeds in pots or garden		8	(see Note 2)
									•	•	•	S or D	6	10–14	100	50–60	16–20	4–5p
		•	•	•	•	•	•					S or D	6	10–14	20–30	7–10	24–32	4–6m
•	•	•	•			•	•	•	•	•	•	D	6	10–14	5–10	1–2	8–12	0.5–1m
•	•					•	•	•	•	•	•	D	6	21–28	30–40	7–10	18–20	3–5m
			•	•	•	•	•	•				D	25	7–10	40–50	3–5	12–16	3–5m
				•	•	•	•	•				D	25	7–10	100	3–5	14–16	1–3m
						•	•	•	•	•		D	100–150	–	60–75	30–40	16–20	50–60p
							•	•	•	•	•	D	20	6–10	100	100	14–16	3–6p
•	•	•	•			•	•	•	•	•	•	D	6	5–8	10–15	3–5	6–8	0.5–1m
						•	•	•	•	•		S or D	12	10–21	40–50	40–50	16–20	12–15p
•	•					•	•	•	•	•	•	D	80–100	–	40–50	40–50	8–12	12–15p
Not suitable												S	12	10–14	150	150	20–22	2–3p
•	•					•	•	•	•	•	•	D	6	10–14	30–40	5–7	20–22	1–2m
•	•	•	•	•								D	50–75	–	15–25	15–25	12–14	6–9p
•	•					•	•	•	•	•		S or D	12	10–14	30–40	30–40	8–12	9–12p
•	•	•	•	•	•	•	•					D	12	7–21	30–40	30–40	8–10	12–15p
									•	•	•	D	20	6–10	100	100	6–14	4–6p
•	•				•	•						D	6	6–10	20–30	7–10	12–16	3–5m
									•	•	•	D	25	6–10	50–60	20–30	12–16	20–24p
Not suitable												D	50–70	–	100	40–50	18–20	18–24p
									•	•	•	S or D	6	6–14	50–60	50–60	12–20	12–15p
•	•	•					•	•	•	•		D	6	6–10	20–30	7–10	10–12	3–5m
									•	•	•	D	20	6–10	70	70	6–8	3–6p

Note 3 – Early plants can be raised in punnets or pots.

Attracting Bees to the Garden

Bees play an essential role as pollinators in the garden. Without bees many of our vegetables and fruit would never reach harvest stage. The members of the pumpkin family provide classic examples. These all have separate male and female flowers and, unless the pollen gets carried from the male to the female, there's no way that plants such as cucumber, zucchini and pumpkin will develop.

One solution is to plant lots of flowers in the garden to attract pollinators. Mixing flowers among the vegies not only adds colour, it helps to ensure that there are enough bees around to do the job. Of course the bees aren't interested in helping the flowers; they're simply chasing the nectar that the flowers produce. Pollination is incidental.

Here are some easy-to-grow, bee-attracting flowers. Favourite, bee-friendly colours seem to be yellow, purple or blue.

- Forget-me-nots are spring annuals that produce copious quantities of seed, ensuring that the plants re-appear year after year.

- Lavender in all its forms is a wonderful bee attractant and, because of its long flowering period and its range of varieties, it's possible to have lavender in flower for most of the year. Dwarf Lavender Munstead can be grown from seed.

- Nasturtiums, too, grow readily from seed. Both the bee-attracting flowers and the leaves are edible.

- Catmint, with its grey foliage and soft mauve blooms, makes a delightful edging for vegie beds.

Growing herbs like thyme and basil will attract bees to your garden.

- Phacelia is renowned for its appeal to 'good' garden insects, including hoverflies and honeybees.
- Salvia, especially the blue flowering variety, attracts bees.

Some of the herbs are also very bee-friendly. They have a natural affinity with vegetables and many are said to deter insect pests in the garden.

Try these herbs:
- Basil is an annual that grows right through the warmer weather, producing sprays of white, pink or mauve flowers in late summer and autumn. Allowing a few flowers to develop will attract bees.
- Thyme is a perennial mini shrub that, like basil, flowers in late summer.
- Sage, the culinary form of the ornamental salvias, does a good job as a bee attractant.
- Rocket can be classed either as a herb or a salad vegetable. Allowing some rocket to flower and go to seed will encourage friendly insects to visit the garden.
- Also try borage, chives, garlic chives and coriander.

Create bee-friendly havens in your garden. Bee 'hotels' are made out of bunches of hollow sticks tied together. Rocks, logs and bushes will encourage native bees in the warmer months. Interestingly, common vegies in the tomato/potato family can't be pollinated by European honey bees but the attractive native blue-banded bee can do the job.

Don't forget, though, that some people have a life-threatening allergic reaction to bees and bee-stings. Perhaps a cute sign about yours being a 'bee-friendly garden' will provide visitors with an appropriate warning.

KEEPING BEES

Bee-keeping is becoming popular in urban areas, but do check your local council's regulations if you wish to try this. Consider keeping stingless native bees as an alternative to the more traditional European honey bees.

If you don't want to DIY, you can still host a beehive. Some organisations will set up and manage the hive for you in return for a share of the honey harvest.

There are beekeeping associations in every state and territory, and many amateur clubs. A useful list of associations can be found at www.theabk.com.au/service-directory

12
Herbs

Growing herbs is one of the most satisfying ways to produce useful plants in the garden. Herbs may be grown primarily for their fragrance or for their value in cooking, and even for their historical associations. Many herbs are regarded as practical medicinal remedies and a browse through old books will clearly show that a great many of them were once used for these purposes.

Today there are hundreds of herbs that are being cultivated for medicinal or culinary uses in different parts of the world. This chapter will concentrate on the commonly available varieties, so if you want to learn about some of the more unusual herbs you will probably need to consult one of the excellent specialist books.

For thousands of years herbs have been used for medicine throughout the world and today the research into medicinal herbs is on the increase. Before the days of refrigeration and the wide availability of food in many forms, herbs played an essential part in the preservation and flavouring of foods. With the introduction of refrigeration, many of these uses were forgotten.

In recent years, there has been a resurgence of interest in the use of herbs for flavouring food. Arguably the most commonly used kitchen herbs are basil, chives, garlic, parsley, thyme, marjoram, sage and mint, but coriander, dill, horseradish, hyssop, oregano, rosemary and tarragon are also frequently used and are readily available.

CULTIVATION

Most herbs need a friable, well-drained soil and enjoy full sunlight, but a few grow well in partial shade.

Herbs may be grown in a separate, designated garden, but many of the smaller varieties can be grown as rockery plants or as borders to flower gardens. All but the very tall herbs can be grown in pots, tubs or troughs. However, small containers are really not suitable for most herbs for any length of time. Herbs grown in pots will benefit from an application of liquid fertiliser as they grow, but, once established, most herbs (especially the hardy Mediterranean varieties such as oregano and thyme) need only minimal care.

Harvest fresh herbs as required. For drying, cut off stems when the plants are well grown, tie them with string and hang them upside down to dry in a shady place. When completely dry, store the leaves and stems, uncrushed or crushed, in air-tight bottles or jars. Many herbs (such as parsley) can be preserved by lightly washing, shaking off the excess water, and then wrapping in plastic wrap before freezing.

Here are some brief notes on the most popular herbs.

Aloe (*Aloe vera*)

This is a succulent perennial, with fleshy leaves that contain a bitter juice used as a balm for insect bites and sunburn, and extensively in cosmetics. The sap is an ingredient in the manufacture of the drink additive known as bitters and in medications to discourage nail biting in children (bitter aloes). The thick, leathery, strap-like green leaves grow to a length of 20–60 cm and are usually edged with spines. When young, the leaves are dotted with white spots. A succulent plant, aloe is quite low maintenance and can be grown outdoors in frost-free areas, or indoors, or in a pot on a terrace or patio. Propagate by detaching the small, rooted suckers that come up around the base of the plant, planting them into pots of a light, sandy, well-drained mixture.

Angelica
(*Angelica archangelica*)
This herb stands 1.5–2.4 m tall. It is a biennial with bright-green serrated leaves, branching hollow stems, and a celery-like texture. The hollow stems and stalks may be crystallised and used for decorating cakes and pastry, whilst the leaves may be added to salads. A tea can be made from either the leaves, stems, seeds, or the dried roots. Grows well in light shade.

Basil or Sweet basil
(*Ocimum basilicum*)
This is an attractive annual plant (or short-lived perennial in warm climates), up to 40 cm tall, with shiny oval leaves and white flowers. It prefers full sun but tolerates semi-shade. Basil is a useful border plant and grows well in pots or tubs. Leaves have a clove-like flavour and can be used fresh or dried. Sow seeds in spring and space plants 20 cm apart. There are several ornamental cultivars available that are mainly grown for their colourful foliage plus a range of specialty basils such as cinnamon basil, Thai basil and Greek basil. Basil is renowned as a companion plant for tomatoes.

Bay tree (*Laurus nobilis*)
This is a large, evergreen, slow-growing tree to about 12 m. It is the laurel tree of ancient Greece and Rome. Bay trees have glossy, dark-green leaves which are narrow and about 4 cm long. The leaves are used extensively in many different types of cooking. Propagation is by seed or cuttings. Leaves can be scattered in cupboards as an insect repellant.

Borage (*Borago officinalis*)
An annual herb that grows up to 60–90 cm, with bee-attracting, purple-blue flowers, its leaves and flowers are used for flavouring soups and stews. Sow seeds in spring and summer and space plants at 30 cm.

Caraway (*Carum carvi*)
A 60 cm biennial, requiring a sheltered, sunny position, it has finely cut, frond-like foliage with white flowers in summer. Caraway is most often grown for its seeds which contribute a liquorice-like flavour to many dishes. To harvest caraway seeds, cut the seed heads off in late summer as soon as the seeds turn brown. Do not leave them on the plant until they are thoroughly dry. Otherwise, they will scatter.

Catmint (*Nepeta cataria*)
Noted for the way its leaves and blossoms attract cats, the leaves of this lemony, mint-scented herb are used for brewing tea and for flavouring meats and salads. This hardy perennial grows to 60–90 cm and features 5 cm-long, heart-shaped, grey-green leaves with downy grey undersides. The flowers may be pale pink or white. Catmint flower spikes attract bees. Seed may be sown where the plants are to grow, or plants can be started from root divisions in spring. The lower-growing *N. x faasenii*, with smaller grey leaves and mauve flowers, is usually grown as an ornamental.

Chamomile (*Chamaemelum nobile*)
This is an ancient herb and a traditional ground cover for around garden paths and walks. The flowers may be used to flavour dry sherry, and a tea may be brewed from the blossoms. The whole plant has a pleasantly pungent fragrance, and the dried flower heads are quite popular in hot tisanes for the relief of head colds. Chamomile oil is used for cosmetic purposes such as soaps and in body lotions. Grow from seeds or cuttings. Chamomile lawns are used as grass substitutes in light traffic areas. They are best produced from non-flowering chamomile varieties propagated by cuttings.

Chervil (*Anthriscus cerefolium*)
One of the classic *fines herbes* of French cooking, chervil will grow for eighteen months or more under good conditions. Plants grow to 30–60 cm tall and the divided parsley-like leaves have a mild aniseed flavour. Chervil grows well in partial shade and prefers a moist position. It loses its delicate flavour quickly when cooked and should only be added finely chopped to soups and sauces at the very last minute. It is ideal to add piquancy to salads, fresh vegetables and salad dressings. Chervil does not dry

well. Sow seed in spring, summer or early autumn, spacing plants 30 cm apart.

Chives (*Allium schoenoprasum*)

Close relative of onions, shallots and garlic, chives are perennial plants that grow in grass-like clumps about 20–30 cm tall. They grow well in sun or semi-shade and are ideal plants for pot culture, probably in a relatively large pot (say, about 30 cm diameter). Sow seeds in spring, summer or early autumn, spacing the clumps about 30 cm apart, or in rows with plants 10 cm apart. New plants can be started by dividing clumps if they become overcrowded. The chopped leaves are useful in salads, soups and egg dishes. Flat-leafed garlic chives (*A. tuberosum*) have a mild garlic flavour. They are very hardy and will tolerate more neglect than common chives.

Coriander or Chinese parsley (*Coriandrum sativum*)

This is one of the ancient herbs that has been used for many hundreds of years in cooking and in medicine. An annual, it reaches about 40 cm tall and prefers a cool soil or partial shade. Seed is best sown in spring or early autumn. Space the plants about 20 cm apart. The parsley-like leaves are popular in Asian dishes and the mature seeds are used for flavouring salads, bread and confectionery. Heat and long days will cause coriander plants to go to seed, so if you are growing them for their leaves it is best to grow when conditions are milder.

Cress (*Lepidium sativum*)

Garden cress makes a tasty addition to salads and is used for sandwiches and garnishes. It grows in all climate zones and seed can be sown at any time of the year. Seeds are best sown in separate boxes, pots or punnets. Prepare a good seed-raising soil plus a mixed fertiliser as described in Chapter 9. Broadcast the seed freely on the surface to have plants spaced 1–2 cm apart. Cover seed lightly with compost or vermiculite and water gently. Keep damp until the seedlings emerge, usually in six to ten days, but often less in warm weather. Thinning is seldom necessary. Plants are ready to harvest in about four weeks' time

Top five culinary herbs

BAY

Use a whole, fresh bay leaf to flavour cooked dishes, but remember to remove it before serving. Bay trees are hardy ornamentals, especially for containers.

BASIL

Sweet Basil is a summer-growing annual. It's also reputed to function as an effective companion plant for tomatoes, repelling whitefly and other insect pests.

CORIANDER

Use the leaves or seeds of coriander, according to your cooking styles. Coriander is one of the most cosmopolitan of herbs.

MINT

Mint loves a cool, moist spot and can become a pest if conditions are too much to its liking. Use mint in drinks and food for its fresh flavour.

PARSLEY

Legend says that you have to be wicked to be able to grow parsley successfully. The plants have a disconcerting habit of disappearing from the garden just when you think they're established for good. Replace on a regular basis.

but may take longer in the cooler months of the year. When plants are 10–15 cm tall, cut them with scissors just above ground level. Sow successively for a continuous supply.

Watercress, a close relative of nasturtium, grows in running streams. You can grow it in pots standing in water, placed in the shade.

It is a perennial plant and is started from cuttings, root divisions or seed.

American or land cress is another cress. It prefers damp, shady conditions, but plants or seed may be difficult to obtain.

Dill (*Anethum graveolens*)

A hardy, annual herb to 90 cm tall with light-green, feathery leaves and umbrella-shaped flower heads, dill prefers full sun but will accept light shade. Sow seeds direct in spring or early summer in clumps spaced 30 cm apart. The leaves have a pungent, bitter-sweet taste. The seed can also be used for flavouring.

Fennel (*Foeniculum vulgare*)

A perennial herb, and one of the oldest known culinary herbs, fennel is usually grown as an annual. Plants resemble those of dill but are taller and coarser. Sow seeds direct in spring or early summer, spacing plants 50–60 cm apart. Both leaves and seeds have an aniseed flavour. Remove flower heads to self seeding in some climates. Bronze-leafed fennel is grown as a garden ornamental. Florence fennel is a variety that is not so tall. Its bulbous base is eaten as a vegetable (sometimes called finocchio).

Feverfew (*Tanacetum parthenium*)

Feverfew is grown in gardens as a decorative plant for its attractive leaves and for its long blooming season. A related species is used in the manufacture of the insecticide pyrethrum. A perennial, it is rather short-lived and is usually treated as an annual. It reaches a height of about 60 cm. 'Aureum' is a golden-leafed cultivar.

Feverfew has traditionally been used as a herbal remedy and is topped with an abundance of button-shaped flowers with golden centres surrounded by white florets. It grows best in light, well-drained soil and prefers a sunny position. Seed is sown in spring or in autumn in mild districts.

The crunchy, swollen base of Florence fennel with its aniseed flavour can be lightly cooked or used raw in salads.

Break up garlic bulbs into individual cloves before planting in late autumn or winter.

Garlic (*Allium sativum*)

Another close relative of the onion, garlic is a bulbous perennial with a clump of flat leaves growing to about 60–90 cm tall. Plants die back after flowering. Plants are grown from separate bulblets or cloves which make up the compound bulb. Slow growing, garlic requires at least six months growth before harvest. After flowering, dig the bulbs for use as flavouring or for replanting in autumn and winter. Different garlic varieties are becoming more readily available. Elephant garlic is a large growing plant with a single bulb. It is closely related to leeks. Dig the bulbs for use as flavouring or for replanting in autumn and winter.

Ginger (*Zingiber officinale*)

Grown for its flavourful roots, ginger does best in frost free humid climates. Plant from root pieces in early spring and dig roots as required from established plants. Ginger will die back in winter and can be lifted and divided before new growth takes off in spring.

Horseradish (*Cochlearia armoracia*)

Horseradish is a plant with large, spinach-like leaves and a long white taproot. Start plants in late winter or early spring from sections of root 15 cm long. Space them in well-prepared soil about 30 cm apart at an angle and cover the thick end with 2.5 cm of soil. When the shoots appear, reduce them in number to two or three. Although a perennial, horseradish is best grown as an annual. Take care to dig up all the pieces of root as the smallest piece will regrow. Well-grown roots are 5 cm in diameter and can be freshly grated or dried for use in spreads, dressings and horseradish sauce.

Hyssop (*Hyssopus officinalis*)

A strongly flavoured, perennial herb growing to a height of about 50 cm, hyssop was once very popular as a household strewing herb as it is fragrant when walked upon. The leaves

HINT

When planting garlic, use cloves only from organic sources. Non-organic cloves are sprayed with sprout inhibitors to prolong storage, and will rot in the ground before they sprout.

PENNY WOODWARD

GARDEN WRITER AND PHOTOGRAPHER

have a minty taste and are particularly useful for flavouring salads and soups. This herb is reputed to make rich food easily digestible.

Lavender (*Lavandula* spp.)

This traditional herb is a hardy, perennial plant that is widely grown. The English lavender (*L. spica*) is the most widely planted and the French lavender (*L. dentata*) is also well known. Both species are compact bushes growing in excess of 50 cm. They need a warm, sunny location in the garden but must have free-draining soils.

Lemon balm (*Melissa officinalis*)

A bushy, perennial herb in the mint family, lemon balm grows to a height of 50 cm. The crushed leaves have a delightful lemon fragrance. Sow seed from spring to early autumn. A useful herb for adding to poultry, fish and pork. Also used for fruit jellies, tarts and custard.

Lemon grass (*Cymbopogon citratus*)

Grows best in frost free gardens to form a substantial, grass-like clump. Leaf sections can be harvested by pulling as required. Chopped leaves, especially the white bases, are used for flavouring Asian dishes. Plants can be grown from seed or by dividing established clumps.

Lemon verbena (*Aloysia citriodora*)

This is an aromatic, semi-evergreen shrub. Scented leaves are used to flavour sweet dishes, beverages and fruit drinks, and to perfume colognes, soap and body lotions. Also used in potpourri. Lemon verbena grows to about 2 m and can be frost-tender. Propagation is by stem cuttings of new growth taken in spring.

Lovage (*Levisticum officinale*)

Lovage is the giant of the herb garden as, at maturity, it can reach more than 2 m. This size is reached over a period of several years

Herbs bordering a crossed path give a formal look to a garden.

as the plant dies back to the ground each winter. Somewhat resembling celery in appearance, taste and use, the dark-green leaves are used as a salad green or to flavour soups and stews. The seeds add a tasty celery- and lemon-like flavour to many dishes, particularly cheese. The stems are sometimes used like angelica and candied, whilst the roots can be cooked as a vegetable. Usual method of propagation is by seed sown in late summer and autumn but can also be grown by dividing the clump in spring.

Marjoram or Sweet marjoram (*Origanum majorana*)

This is a perennial herb that grows to 30–40 cm tall, but is often grown as an annual. Sow seed in spring or autumn and space plants about 20 cm apart. Plants need full sun and rather moist conditions but will accept light shade in warmer areas. The oval leaves and small white flowers are used fresh or dried for flavouring meat dishes.

Mint (*Mentha* spp.)

A rambling perennial, spreading by means of rhizomes, mint can often spread too well in the garden, so it is a good idea to grow it in a large pot or tub. Seed of some varieties is available or you can start plants from pieces of stem at any time of the year. It is one of the few herbs that prefers shade and very damp conditions. Leaves have a strong aroma and flavour and are used in mint sauce, mint jelly and for garnishing. Peppermint, spearmint and curled mint are the most common varieties but there are also others, including applemint, golden applemint (variegated leaves), eau de cologne mint (orange or bergamot) and pennyroyal. Unrelated, spicy Vietnamese mint grows well in moist soils.

Nasturtium (*Tropaeolum majus*)

This well-known climbing or trailing annual is cultivated mainly for its ornamental qualities, but sometimes used for its spicy, peppery-tasting leaves, seeds and flowers. The leaves are eaten in sandwiches and salads, the flowers are used as a garnish for salads and to flavour vinegar. For cultivation details, see Chapter 15.

Oregano (*Origanum vulgare*)

This herb is also known as wild marjoram or pot marjoram. A perennial herb very similar to sweet marjoram but with a distinctive aroma and flavour. Sowing, spacing and cultivation are the same as for marjoram. Leaves have a sharper flavour than marjoram and are used fresh or dried in Italian, Spanish and Mexican dishes, especially those with pasta and tomato.

Parsley (*Petroselinum crispum*)

One of the best known of all herbs, the most common variety is curled parsley. Another variety with stronger flavour is Italian plainleaf parsley. Parsley is a biennial plant to 30 cm tall, but much taller when it runs to seed. It is best grown as an annual. Sow seeds direct in spring, summer and early autumn, either in clumps spaced 15–20 cm apart in the garden or broadcast in large pots or tubs. Seedlings may take three to four weeks to emerge, so keep the bed or container damp for this length of time after sowing. Some recommend soaking seeds overnight before sowing. Parsley grows well in sun or semi-shade and prefers fertile soil and rather damp conditions. When established, plants respond to regular side-dressings of nitrogen fertiliser or liquid feeds. Parsley leaves are used fresh as a garnish and fresh or dried for flavouring salads, vegetables, meats, stews, soups and egg dishes.

Perilla (*Perilla frutescens*)

Also known as beefsteak plant, perilla is a fast growing annual with thick leaves that can be shredded into salads or Asian dishes. The purple-leafed variety is often grown as an ornamental. Perilla grows readily from seed but the fine seed needs light for germination and seedlings must be transplanted carefully.

Rocket (*Eruca sativa*)

This fast-growing salad herb mixes well with other salad greens. It has a peppery, bitter flavour and should be encouraged to grow quickly with good watering and liquid fertilising. Rocket is ready for picking in just a few weeks from sowing.

Rosemary (*Rosmarinus officinalis*)

This is an attractive perennial shrub that grows to 60–150 cm with dark-green, needle-like leaves and lavender-blue flowers. It grows well in sun or semi-shade but the soil must be well drained. Rosemary is very suitable for growing in large pots or tubs. Sow seeds in boxes or punnets in spring, summer and early autumn, or start the plants from cuttings in late winter. The leaves have a pine-like appearance and flavour and are used, fresh or dried, with chicken or meat dishes and stews. Low-growing forms are available. Rosemary prefers slightly alkaline soil.

Sage (*Salvia officinalis*)

A perennial herb to 60 cm tall with long grey-green leaves and tall spikes of violet-blue flowers, sage is sown direct in spring, summer and early autumn in clumps 30 cm apart or seedlings are raised for transplanting at this distance. Plants need full sunlight and will tolerate quite dry conditions. but tend to struggle in humid summer areas. Leaves, fresh or dried, are traditional for flavouring seasonings for poultry, pork, lamb and beef.

Salad burnet (*Sanguisorba minor*)

It is an old-fashioned herb whose cucumber-flavoured leaves were once popular in

Dark-leaved basil, curled parsley and lettuce growing together in a tub near the door can be harvested as needed.

cooling drinks. The young leaves are also used in salads and as a flavouring for sauces. A hardy perennial, it grows to about 60 cm in height and produces thimble-shaped tufts of greenish flowers with purple-red stamens in early summer. It needs full sun and grows best in well-drained, limey soils. It may be grown as a pot plant indoors but needs plenty of direct sunlight. Sow seeds in spring or early autumn.

Sorrel (*Rumex* spp.)

Sorrel is a perennial plant which grows to 60 cm tall, but flower stalks may reach as high as 120 cm. Sow seeds direct in clumps 20 cm apart in spring or early summer. Sorrel needs full sunlight and prefers rather damp conditions. Leaves have a sharp, acidic taste and are used as an addition to salads or cooked like silver beet or spinach. Also used for flavouring meat dishes, stews and soups. Red sorrel has red veining through the leaves and can be planted as an ornamental.

Stevia (*Stevia rebaudiana*)

Harvested from a perennial soft leafed shrub 60cm to 1m tall, stevia leaves are renowned for their sweetness, Stevia extract is a popular sugar substitute that is said to contain almost no calories. Easy to grow in frost free areas but requires winter protection in cold climates. Pinch off flowering stems to preserve best leaf flavour.

Summer savory (*Satureja hortensis*)

An annual herb to 30 cm tall. Sow seeds direct in clumps 15 cm apart in spring and/or early summer. Summer Savory needs full sunlight and well-drained soil and is suitable for container growing. Leaves have a peppery flavour and are used with meats, fish, eggs, beans, stews and soups.

Tarragon (*Artemisia dracunculus*)

A perennial herb 60–90 cm tall, with dark-green, pointed leaves that have a liquorice flavour. The desirable, herbaceous French tarragon is usually grown from pieces. Annual Russian tarragon grows readily from seed but is thought to have an inferior

HINT

Herbs are a natural pest control and can be used to ward off many common pests in the garden as well as indoors. Plant the following herbs throughout your flower and vegetable garden areas to reduce the number of pests and help to control disease: rue, wormwood, rosemary, southernwood, pennyroyal, santolina, tansy, lavender, costmary, pyrethrum, mint, thyme and garlic.

JUNE TAYLOR
GARDEN WRITER

flavour. Sow seeds direct into clumps 60 cm apart in spring or early summer. Tarragon needs full sunlight. Leaves are used in salads, egg and cheese dishes, with fish, and in sauces. Mexican tarragon (*Tagetes lucida*) is used as a substitute in warm climates.

Thyme (*Thymus vulgaris*)

Thyme is a small, prostrate, perennial herb 20–30 cm tall. Sow seeds in spring, summer and early autumn in clumps spaced 30 cm apart. It is a useful plant for ground cover and for rockeries and garden borders, and is also suitable for container-growing. Plants prefer full sunlight and will tolerate rather dry conditions. There are many different varieties of thyme and all are suitable for flavouring. Use the fresh or dried leaves in soups and stews or in seasoning for poultry, meat and fish dishes.

Turmeric (*Curcuma domestica*)

Valued for the attractive yellow colouring it adds to a range of dishes, turmeric has also developed a reputation as a superfood. It is grown in the same way as ginger and must have a long, warm growing season.

Sowing Guide for Herbs

HERBS	TROPICAL/SUBTROPICAL												TEMPERATE											
	J	F	M	A	M	J	J	A	S	O	N	D	J	F	M	A	M	J	J	A	S	O	N	D
Angelica			•	•	•																	•	•	•
Basil	•	•	•	•	•	T	T	T	•	•	•	•	•	•	•						•	•	•	•
Bay tree			•	•	•									•	•	•								
Borage	•	•	•	•	•	T	T	T	•	•	•	•	•	•	•	•	•				•	•	•	•
Caraway			•	•																	•	•	•	
Catmint						•	•	•	•	•	•	•	•	•	•	•					•	•	•	•
Chamomile	•	•	•	•	•	•	•	•	•	•	•	•	•	•							•	•	•	•
Chervil			•	•																	•	•	•	
Chives	•	•	•	•	•	•	•	•	•	•	•	•	•	•	•						•	•	•	•
Coriander			•	•	•	•	•								•	•	•	•			•	•	•	
Cress	•	•	•	•	•	•	•	•	•	•	•	•	•	•	•	•	•	•	•	•	•	•	•	•
Cumin			•	•	•	•	•	•									•	•			•	•	•	•
Dill	•	•	•	•	•	•	•	•	•	•	•	•	•	•	•	•	•				•	•	•	•
Echinacea			•	•	•		•	•	•						•	•	•				•	•	•	
Fennel	•	•	•	•	•	•	•	•	•	•											•	•	•	•
Feverfew	•	•	•	•	•	•	•	•	•	•	•		•	•							•	•	•	•
Garlic*			•	•	•										•	•	•	•	•					
Ginger*								•	•														•	•
Horseradish*	Not suitable																					•	•	•
Hyssop			•	•	•		•	•	•						•	•	•				•	•	•	
Lavender							•	•	•												•	•	•	
Lemon balm			•	•	•			•	•	•	•		•	•	•						•	•	•	•
Lemon grass	•	•	•	•	•	•	•	•	•	•			•								•	•	•	•

* Best to grow from cuttings or roots, not seed.
T Can only be grown in tropical areas

COLD (F M A M J J A S O N D)	SOWING METHOD POTS (S) DIRECT (D)	SOWING DEPTH (MM)	SEEDLINGS EMERGE (DAYS)	TIME TO PICKING (WEEKS)	
J A S	S	1	21 to 25	40	Grow from root division. Stratify seed in fridge for a few weeks before sowing
F M A · S O N D	D	5	5	8	
M A	S	6	20 to 50	100	Seed should be abraded between sheets of sandpaper before sowing
A M J J A	D	5	5 to 10	12	
J A S	D	5	7 to 14	20	
F M A · J A S	S or D	3	7 to 10	12	
A M J · S O	S or D	5	7 to 10	16	'Treneague' non-flowering variety best for lawns. Propagate from cuttings
A M J	D	5	7 to 14	12	
F M A	D	5	14	8	
F M A M	D	6	10 to 12	6	
F M A M J J A S O N D	S	3	6 to 10	4	Grow indoors in hot weather
A M J	S	5	5 to 10	12 to 20	
F M	D	1	10 to 12	8	
M A M · J A S	S or D	3	10 to 20	16	Stratify seed in fridge for a few weeks before sowing
J A S	S or D	6	10 to 14	12	Remove seed heads to prevent weeds
J A S	S or D	3	10 to 15	16 to 20	
M A M	D	20	21 to 60	20 to 30	Grow from cloves planted pointy end up
Not suitable					Grow from rhizomes in spring
M A M					
M A M · J A S	S	5	14	10	Grow from seed in spring or root divisions in autumn
J A S	S	5	14 to 21	52	
F M A · J A S O	D	5	5 to 10	8	
J A	D	5	10 to 14	12	Clumps can be divided in spring

Sowing Guide for Herbs (cont'd)

HERBS	TROPICAL/SUBTROPICAL												TEMPERATE											
	J	F	M	A	M	J	J	A	S	O	N	D	J	F	M	A	M	J	J	A	S	O	N	D
Lemon verbena*			•	•	•										•	•	•					•	•	
Lovage			•	•	•	•									•	•	•	•			•	•	•	•
Marjoram	•	•	•	•	•	•	•	•	•	•	•	•	•	•						•	•	•	•	•
Mint	•	•	•	•	•	•	•	•	•	•	•	•	•	•						•	•	•	•	•
Nasturtium			•	•	•	•	•	•	•				•	•	•						•	•	•	•
Oregano	•	•	•	•	•	•	•	•	•	•	•	•	•	•						•	•	•	•	•
Parsley				•	•	•			•	•	•		•	•	•	•	•				•	•	•	•
Perilla	•	•	•	•	•	•	•	•	•	•	•	•	•							•	•	•	•	•
Rocket			•	•	•	•			•	•	•				•	•	•				•	•	•	•
Rosemary			•	•	•	•	•	•	•													•	•	•
Sage	•	•	•	•	•	•	•	•	•	•	•										•	•	•	•
Salad burnet			•	•	•	•	•	•	•												•	•	•	
Sorrel	•	•	•	•	•	•	•	•	•	•	•										•	•	•	
Stevia	•							•	•	•	•	•	•							•	•	•	•	•
Summer savory			•	•	•	•	•	•	•												•	•	•	
Tarragon French	Not suitable																						•	•
Tarragon Russian			•	•	•	•	•	•	•						•	•	•	•	•	•	•			
Thyme	•	•	•	•	•	•	•	•	•	•	•	•									•	•	•	•
Turmeric*							•	•															•	•
Watercress	•	•	•	•	•	•	•	•	•	•	•	•	•	•	•	•	•				•	•	•	•

* Best to grow from cuttings or roots, not seed.

COLD (F M A M J J A S O N D)	SOWING METHOD POTS (S) DIRECT (D)	SOWING DEPTH (MM)	SEEDLINGS EMERGE (DAYS)	TIME TO PICKING (WEEKS)	
					Propagate from tip cuttings
	S or D	3	14	24	Sow direct in autumn
	D	5	8 to 10	8	
	S	2	10 to 20	12	
	D	12	14 to 21	10 to 12	
	D	5	8 to 10	8	
	S or D	3	21 to 28	16	
	S or D	1	15 to 20	12	Transplant carefully
	D	3	7 to 10	7 to 8	
	S or D	5	7 to 14	50	Easier to grow from cuttings
	3	14 to 21	8 to 12		
	S or D	5	14 to 28	12 to 20	
	S or D	5	5 to 10	12 to 20	
	S	3	7 to 14	12	Best grown from spring cuttings
	S	3	7 to 14	12 to 20	
					Grow from cuttings or root division
	S	1	10 to 20	12 to 20	Seeds need light for germination
	D	5	12 to 14	8 to 10	
Not suitable					Grow from rhizomes in spring
	D	5	5 to 7	8	

13
Fruit

Wherever you live in Australia – whether in sunny Queensland, the Apple Isle or any place in between – you can grow garden-fresh fruit. Very often, a suitable microclimate exists or can be created in your garden. This means that the most unlikely fruits can be grown outside their natural climate – a passionfruit or grapevine against a wall in the cool highlands, a pineapple on a sunny patio in Sydney, or an avocado in a sheltered site in Melbourne. Once upon a time, fruit trees and fruit plants grew in nearly every Australian garden. Nowadays, gardens are smaller so it is difficult to find space for this very rewarding activity. But most home owners can grow two or three trees, especially citrus, which take up little room. Many fruit plants – passionfruit, grapes and trailing berries – are great space-savers because you can train them on a fence or trellis. And many fruit trees are now available as dwarf varieties. The aim of this chapter is to give background information on some of the basic varieties of fruit, together with recommendations for planting and management. Pests and diseases of fruit trees and fruit plants are dealt with in Chapter 8.

CITRUS TREES

Citrus (lemons, oranges, grapefruit, mandarins, limes and cumquats) have never lost their popularity. The vitamin-rich fruit can be picked progressively over a long time, which makes them ideal for home growing. But they are ornamental as well as useful, and grow into attractive trees with dark-green, glossy foliage and fragrant blossoms in spring.

Citrus trees do well in all warm and mild climate zones. Providing frosts are not severe, citrus trees will tolerate cool conditions. With irrigation, they also thrive in hot, dry, inland districts. Citrus require a sunny position, preferably facing north, and protected from strong winds. They are most successful on sandy or loam soils and dislike clay soils or those with a heavy subsoil. Heavy soils become over-wet and drain poorly, leading to root-rot problems. If drainage is poor, build the bed up 25–30 cm above the surrounding soil. Improve the texture of clay soils by adding generous amounts of sand and organic matter. (See Chapter 4.)

Advanced citrus plants are available from nurseries and garden stores. They usually come in large plastic pots or flexible plastic bags. Make sure the trees have not been in the container too long, as they may have become root-bound and affected plants often fail to make satisfactory growth. The ideal tree is one or two years old from budding. It is best to plant trees in early autumn or early spring. This way, young trees avoid the extreme effects of both winter cold and summer heat. Citrus grafted onto 'Flying Dragon' rootstock are smaller and slower growing, making them better suited to pots and small gardens.

Make the planting hole shallow, but 30–50 cm wider than the container. Tip the tree from the pot or cut away the plastic bag. Gently tease out any roots which are pot-bound. For planting depth, keep the bud union (the knee-like joint where the tree has been grafted) above the soil level of the planting spot. Gently pack damp, crumbly soil, to which some compost has been added, around the tree and water well. Mulch the soil with dry grass clippings, compost or leaf mould, but keep it 5–7 cm away from the stem. An acceptable and simple method of applying fertiliser at planting is to use Dynamic Lifter pellets. Mix these well with the soil. Do not use powdered fertilisers at planting time as root damage may occur. A few months after planting, spread a powdered citrus food or Dynamic Lifter (this should only be done in the spring–summer–early autumn period. Do not over-water newly planted trees – a good drink every week is usually sufficient when the weather is dry.

Citrus trees tend to be self-shaping and so need little pruning. If growth is overcrowded, thin out the stems after fruiting because flowers and fruit are carried at the ends of the branches.

Top five citrus varieties

'VALENCIA' ORANGE

Easily grown with sweet-tasting fruit (if you let it ripen on the tree), 'Valencia' is probably the best variety for making orange juice.

'EMPEROR' MANDARIN

A loose-skinned mandarin that's beloved by children because it's so easy to peel, 'Emperor' has a typically sweet mandarin flavour.

'MARSH' GRAPEFRUIT

Almost seedless, this grapefruit has pale-yellow skin and a typical tart flavour.

'EUREKA' LEMON

An almost thornless variety that produces fruit just about year round, 'Eureka' is an ideal home-garden lemon but must have good drainage.

'TAHITIAN' LIME

The small green fruit of the lime tree is used for drinks and, to a lesser extent, in cooked dishes. It needs warmer conditions than other citrus.

'TAHITIAN' LIME

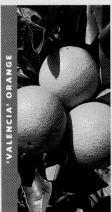

'VALENCIA' ORANGE

'MARSH' GRAPEFRUIT

Don't thin oranges and grapefruit severely, but mandarins can be cut back to the second or third shoot down the branch. Lemon trees are taller and less compact so prune them back well to keep them at a manageable height. Sappy water shoots of lemon and grapefruit should be cut away unless they can improve the tree shape.

Any shoots below the bud union must be removed too. Old citrus trees can be 'skeletonised' in early spring by cutting back to the main branches. They will take a year or two to recover and begin bearing again.

HINT

Leave any fruit that may fall from your lemon tree, and be sure to return all the peel and pulp from any fruit used as fertiliser for your tree. Providing the drainage is good, this will result in a very healthy and robust tree.

MORRIS HOLMES
HORTICULTURAL CONSULTANT
AND GARDEN DESIGNER

Feeding roots of citrus are located at the drip line underneath the outer foliage, so do not cultivate deeply in this area but try to keep it mulched and free of grass. When applying fertiliser, scatter it around the drip line and not close to the trunk. Use a complete fertiliser containing about 10 per cent nitrogen. There are several brands of citrus fertiliser including Dynamic Lifter PLUS Fruit Food. A well-grown, mature citrus tree should be given fertiliser three times a year – in late-winter/early spring, early summer, and early autumn. Water trees well both before and after fertilising. Fruit drop is a common citrus problem, associated with irregular or uneven watering, especially when young fruits are forming. Lack of fertiliser (or too much of it) can aggravate this condition. Apply a fertiliser with trace elements and water trees regularly through spring and summer.

Lemon

'Lisbon' and 'Eureka' are the most popular tall varieties. 'Meyer' is rather sweeter in flavour and the trees are more tolerant of cool conditions. 'Villa Franca' does well in warm areas. Most lemons bear overlapping crops for picking throughout most of the year.

Orange

The 'Valencia' orange is the most widely grown. It is a reliable cropper with fruit for picking from spring right through to the following autumn. A seedless form is now available. 'Washington Navel' is an excellent-quality orange and usually seedless. It bears from late autumn to spring. It is not as consistent a bearer as 'Valencia' and is more liable to fruit drop. 'Seville' is a sour variety that is used for jams and marmalade. Blood oranges have much-desired red flesh and juice but have very specific climatic requirements (generally cool nights and hot, dry days).

Grapefruit

'Marsh Seedless' is the most popular variety; a good cropper which ripens from early winter for picking over some months. The 'Wheeny' variety also bears well but fruits have an acidic, lemon-like flavour and many seeds. 'Thompson' is a good variety for dry inland districts. Red- and pink-fleshed grapefruit are growing in popularity but only develop good colour in certain climates. Unfortunately, grapefruit are very attractive to fruit fly in warmer areas. (See Chapter 8 for methods of control.)

Mandarin (Tangerine)

Best early varieties are 'Imperial' and 'Unshiu Satsuma)'. Both are ready to pick in late autumn. A good late variety is 'Emperor'. 'Ellendale', another late variety sold as a mandarin, is more correctly a 'tangor': a mandarin-orange hybrid. 'Honey Murcott' is a mandarin-orange hybrid with many seeds and tight skin. The tangelo (a mandarin-grapefruit hybrid) has large, juicy, mandarin-like fruits with a slight tang. Many mandarin varieties benefit from pruning after cropping.

Cumquat

These small, attractive trees are suitable for the open garden or for tub specimens. The small, bitter fruit make excellent jams, jellies and liqueurs. 'Marumi' (round fruit) and 'Nagami' (oval fruit) are the best varieties.

Lime

The lime or sweet lime is a small, many-branched tree with green, thin-skinned fruit about 5 cm in diameter. 'Tahitian' is the most popular variety and best for Australian conditions. Limes are often grown as pot specimens. A range of selected Australian native limes is now available, including the long, narrow 'finger' lime.

DECIDUOUS FRUIT TREES

These summer-fruiting trees lose their leaves in winter, so can be used where summer shade or winter sun is needed in any part of the garden. Most trees have a magnificent display of spring blossom and some, especially pear trees and persimmons, have attractive autumn foliage. Because they are dormant in winter, deciduous fruit trees can be grown in districts with cold winters and severe frosts, although late frosts in spring can damage flower and leaf buds. Fruit fly is also a problem, especially in warm coastal areas. Fruit ripens in summer when these pests are most active. Apples and pears are also attacked by codling moth, which can be even harder to control than fruit fly.

Deciduous fruit trees prefer an open, sunny position but will grow on a variety of soils. Like citrus trees, they need good drainage and will not tolerate heavy or waterlogged soil.

Most deciduous fruit trees are planted in winter – June or July are the best months in most districts. Unlike citrus, they are usually sold as 'bare-root' trees, rather like rose bushes. Sometimes these bare-rooted trees are newly potted into fresh potting mix, which will fall away from the roots at planting time. Although the trees are dormant, roots must not dry out. Dig shallow holes for planting but break up further soil at the bottom. Very wide holes are not necessary – for most trees a diameter of 60 cm is ample. Plant trees rather deeper than they were in the nursery but keep the bud union well above soil level. Spread roots carefully on a mound of soil, placing the longest and strongest in the direction from which prevailing winds will blow. Fill the hole with crumbly topsoil and firm it gently

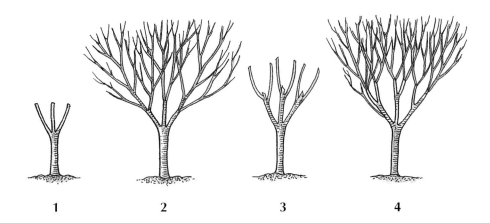

1   **2**   **3**   **4**

Deciduous fruit trees are pruned to an open-centred vase shape. This shape forms a sturdy framework. Diagrams show: (1) tree pruned after first-year growth; (2) second-year growth; (3) tree pruned after second-year growth; (4) third-year growth.

into place. Now add a bucket of water to settle soil around the roots and fill the hole with dry soil to ground level. Trees cannot use fertiliser when they are dormant but they do require it when growth starts in spring. A slow-release fertiliser can be mixed into the soil in the perimeter of the planting hole at planting, or a mixed fertiliser such as Dynamic Lifter PLUS Fruit Food can be scattered around the tree. Chip or rake fertiliser into the topsoil and water well.

Pruning aims to regulate growth of branches, allow light to enter the framework and encourage flowers and fruit. Most deciduous fruit trees are pruned to a 'vase' shape but many can be trained as an espalier, which requires a frame support. The traditional practice has been to prune in winter but recent recommendations are to prune after harvest. Generally, trees are pruned hard for the first few years to make a sturdy framework and to shape the tree. Later, the main concern of pruning is to remove dead and diseased wood, in-growing branches, thin overcrowded growth and to cut back leaders or main limbs.

Each type of fruit tree has its own habit of growth. Fruit may set on current spring growth, on wood formed the previous year or on fruiting spurs which may bear for several years, so it is important to know the bearing wood for each kind before pruning. Brief notes are given in this chapter but detailed information on pruning each kind of tree is available from specialist books or websites.

Fruit trees, like other plants, require feeding. On deep fertile soils it may be some years before fertilisers are needed, but in most gardens, yearly applications of fertiliser will improve growth and fruit yield. A mixed fertiliser that contains about 10 per cent nitrogen is recommended. Apply fertiliser in late winter or early spring when growth starts and supplement this by a further application in mid-summer (December–January). Slow-release fertilisers used in late winter are also suitable. Animal manures, if available, are a useful way of supplying some plant nutrients and can be applied as an organic mulch layer to retain moisture in the roots and add humus to the soil.

Apples

Apples grow best in cool to cold climates with a mild summer and cold winter. Most varieties are self-sterile so two varieties are needed for pollination. Some nurseries can supply two or three varieties budded on to one root stock to solve this problem or two trees can be planted into the one hole. Apple trees bear fruit on spurs and two-year-old or older laterals. Fruiting wood is encouraged by allowing laterals to develop on terminal branches to remain uncut until buds form. Then shorten them if necessary. Three popular early varieties are 'Gala', 'Early McIntosh' and 'Red Gravenstein', any two of which will cross-pollinate. Late-maturing varieties, however, have better quality fruit. The best of the reds are 'Delicious', an excellent eating apple with a characteristic flavour, and 'Pink Lady' and 'Jonathan', good for eating. 'Granny Smith' is the most popular green apple, excellent for cooking and pleasant eating when fully ripe. Any two late varieties will cross-pollinate. Dwarf and upright varieties of apple and pear trees are now available. They are becoming increasingly popular for the small home garden and for container growing.

Apricots

Apricots grow particularly well in the cool highlands and in hot inland areas. All varieties are self-fertile. Apricots bear fruit on laterals produced the previous year and on spurs which often bear for several years. Strong water shoots develop on some varieties. Cut these back in mid-summer to produce fruiting laterals and spurs.

'Glengarry' is a popular variety in coastal districts. It is a good cropper, maturing fruit in mid to late spring. 'Trevatt', the leading apricot variety for canning, is recommended for cool highlands and inland districts. Australian bred 'Moorpark' is the most popular home-garden apricot.

Cherries

A highland climate with mild summers and cold winters is best for cherries. Soils must be deep and well drained. Trees grow to a large size, so are not well suited to small gardens. Almost all varieties are self-sterile so two varieties are needed for pollination. Cherries bear fruit on spurs growing on two-year-old or older wood. After initial tree shaping, little pruning is needed. Pruning, when necessary, should be done in autumn as trees are subject to 'gumming'. Cuts heal quicker during this time than when trees are fully dormant. Early varieties are 'Burgsdorf' and 'Early Lyons'. Both have dark fruit and will cross-pollinate. 'Ron's Seedling' is a dark-red, mid-season variety. 'Napoleon' is a mid-season, white-flesh variety. 'St Margaret' is the leading late variety with red flesh. Use 'Florence' or 'Black Boy', another very dark-skinned, late variety, as pollinators. 'Stella' is self-fertile and will pollinate most varieties.

Figs

Figs are very adaptable to a wide climate range – cool, warm or hot. Trees flourish on the more humid coast but fruit may rot on the tree in wet seasons. Figs are self-fertile and fruit ripens over a long period. Birds can be a problem – nylon netting over the tree is probably the best answer to this problem. Figs bear fruit on current season's growth. Trees usually form a well-balanced framework so little pruning is needed. 'Purple (Black) Genoa' has dark skin and red flesh. 'White Genoa', with pale-green skin and creamy flesh, and 'Brown Turkey', a prolific cropper with dark-skinned fruit, are popular dessert varieties. 'White Adriatic', with green-brown skin and yellow flesh, is a smaller fig but excellent for making jam. Prune in winter and use cuttings to grow new plants.

Mulberry

Mulberry trees grow to about 6 m with large leaves and small fruit – about blackberry-sized but rather longer. They grow well in subtropical, temperate and cool climates and are often grown as ornamentals for summer shade. Mulberries grow easily from cuttings

HINT

Australian parents have traditionally dealt with the problem of mulberry stains on hands and clothing by using green mulberries. Simply crush some green mulberries and place them in the water with the item being washed. Alternatively, grow a white mulberry or the very sweet 'Shatoot' variety and staining will never be a problem.

ANNETTE McFARLANE
ABC RADIO, BRISBANE GARDENING
TALKBACK HOST

and usually bear fruit in the second year. Apart from initial shaping, little pruning is needed. Top growth and long leaders on older trees can be cut back for easier picking. 'Black English' is the best variety for cool districts. 'Hicks', a variety of white or Chinese mulberry, is more suitable for warm climates. The fruits of both varieties make a pleasant, fresh dessert and are excellent for jam or jelly. Leaves of Chinese mulberry are a favourite diet for silkworms if the younger members of your family keep them.

Olive

Olive trees are ornamental as well as supplying fruit for storage and pickling. Trees are evergreen and grow quickly to about 6 m tall. They are suited to temperate climates and withstand hot, dry summers and cool winters with some frosts. The leaves are dark-grey (silver underneath) and the white flowers in spring are followed by green to black fruit in summer. Some varieties are 'Sevillano', 'Manzanillo', 'UC13A6' and 'Verdale'. Named plants from nurseries should be planted in well-drained, sunny situations in autumn or spring. Pruning is rarely needed unless the trees become too large. Add lime or dolomite in acid-soil areas.

Peaches and nectarines

Some varieties of peaches and nectarines (which are really a smooth-skinned peach) grow in subtropical and temperate climates

with a mild winter, while others have a high 'chilling requirement' and need a cold winter.

Selecting varieties suited to your area is important. All peaches and nectarines are self-fertile, with the exception of 'J.H. Hale', which requires a pollinator flowering at the same time. There are many peach varieties – white or yellow flesh, both clingstone and freestone with a range of in-betweens. Peaches and nectarines bear fruit on laterals produced the previous summer. Laterals fruit for one season only so there must be plenty of new ones coming on each year for continuity of cropping. Prune back trees after fruiting to encourage new growth. In warm coastal climates, early varieties that mature before Christmas should escape damage by fruit fly. 'Sherman's Red' (yellow freestone), 'Anzac' (white freestone) and 'Coronet' are recommended. For cool, highland and cold inland regions, varieties must flower late to avoid frost damage. The best varieties (in order of maturity) are 'Early Becky' (white freestone), 'Starking Delicious' (yellow freestone), 'Redhaven' (yellow semi-freestone), 'Halehaven', 'J.H. Hale' and 'Blackburn'. 'J.H. Hale' needs 'Blackburn' as a pollinator. An old-favourite nectarine is 'Goldmine' (white freestone). It matures in mid-season and does well in all districts. 'May Grand' is a variety with excellent flavour.

Pears

Like apples, good-quality pears require a mild summer and cool to cold winter. Old-fashioned China pears do well in warm coastal districts and are used mainly for cooking. The trees are attractive with spring blossoms and coloured autumn leaves. Pruning pear trees is the same as for apple trees. Trees take five years or more to bear but they are very long-lived. 'Williams' ('Bartlett') is the most popular variety for eating and cooking. Pick fruit when firm and ripen indoors. 'Williams' is self-fertile but usually crops better with another variety as a pollinator. 'Beurre Bosc' and 'Packham's Triumph' bear high-quality fruit which keep well. Fruit is left to ripen on the tree. 'Williams' is the best pollinator for both varieties. Asian 'Nashi' pears bear round, juice-filled fruit. Allow to ripen on the tree.

HINT

Forget box and grow an edible hedge. *Acca sellowiana* produces bright flowers and fragrant autumn fruit which can be eaten fresh or made into jam. Also try planting rhubarb crowns to allow for spectacular seasonal growth with red or green stems which can be stewed or turned into a crumble.

SUSAN PARSONS

KITCHEN GARDEN WRITER

Persimmon

Persimmons, like apricots and figs, are adaptable to a wide climate range. Unlike most deciduous fruit trees, they tolerate moist conditions and heavy clay soils. These attractive, spreading trees grow to about 5 m in height. They are ornamental, too, with brilliant autumn foliage. The salmon-pink fruit is picked when coloured but still firm.

Fruit of astringent varieties should be ripened indoors until quite soft, before eating. The newer non-astringent varieties can be eaten while still firm. Persimmons have a unique texture and flavour. After the tree has been shaped, little pruning is needed. Fruit is produced on the current season's wood. Fruit on the topmost branches can be picked with a long-handled picker or rake. As most persimmon varieties are harvested in autumn or early winter, they escape fruit fly attack. The variety 'Yemon' ('Nightingale') is a compact tree suitable for small gardens. Larger varieties are 'Dai Dai Maru', 'Hachiya' and 'Tanenashi', all astringent. 'Fuyu' is the main non-astringent cultivar.

Plums

There are two types of plums: the European plum, which has a high chilling requirement suited to cool climates, and the Japanese plum, which has a lower chilling requirement and grows best in warmer areas. The cherry plum is small fruited and does best in cool areas. While good drainage is recommended, plum trees usually tolerate heavy soil and moist conditions better than other stone fruits. Neither European nor Japanese plums (with the exception of 'Santa Rosa') are self-fertile and require a pollinator belonging to the same group. Cherry plums are usually self-pollinating. After the plum tree is shaped it needs little pruning. Fruit is carried on two-year-old laterals (European type) or on one-year-old laterals (Japanese and cherry type) and on spurs which crop for a few years. 'Angelina', 'President' and 'Grand Duke' are popular European varieties. Any two will cross-pollinate. Early varieties of Japanese plums are 'Wilson' (yellow flesh), which is pollinated by 'Santa Rosa' (red flesh). 'Santa Rosa' is self-fertile – if you only want one plum tree, this is it. Mid-season Japanese varieties are 'Narrabeen' (yellow flesh) and 'Mariposa' (dark red, blood plum). These two will cross-pollinate but 'Santa Rosa' can be used as pollinator for both.

VINE FRUITS
Grapes

Grapes have been traditionally grown on a two-wire trellis but they can be trained over pergolas, arbours and screens. Grape vines are best suited to inland climates with a dry summer and cool to cold winter, and to the winter-wet, summer-dry coastal districts of Victoria, South Australia and Western Australia. Fruit splitting and disease are often problems in coastal districts of New South Wales and southern Queensland.

Grapevines are planted in winter about 3 m apart. They grow readily from winter cuttings. The basic principle of pruning is that fruit buds are borne on one-year-old wood which arises from two-year-old wood. Water shoots grow from wood older than two years and are not fruit-bearing. Cut the strongest cane on the plant to two buds.

Grapes grow best in a relatively dry climate.

Train growth from these in both directions along the bottom wire of the trellis or lateral support. Next winter, prune these main arms back to sturdy wood leaving three buds on each. The following winter, prune back at the base. Continue this process each year. 'Carolina Black Rose' and 'Isabella' are the most suitable varieties for humid, coastal districts. European types are best for inland regions and southern states where summer is dry. The muscats, good mid-season varieties, are only suited to areas with low humidity. Late varieties are 'Crimson Seedless', 'Waltham Cross' and 'Purple Cornichon' ('Black Lady's Finger'). All grape varieties are self-fertile and seedless cultivars are increasingly popular.

Passionfruit

This evergreen, perennial vine is very prolific. The dark-green leaves and white and purple flowers are also attractive. Passionfruit do well in subtropical and temperate climates which are free of frost. They need a sunny aspect and prefer light soils with good drainage. Black passionfruit are self-fertile and you can start by sowing seed from a good cropping vine. Seedlings and grafted plants are also available from nurseries and garden stores. With grafted plants, check and remove any rootstocks with different leaves growing from below the graft. For trellis growing, wires at 1.2 m and 2 m should run north–south for maximum sun. Vines can be trained on fences, the railings of balconies or terraces and on pergolas. Provide wires or wire netting for the tendrils to cling to. One well-grown vine will give sufficient fruit for the average family but if more than one is required, plant vines 2.5 m apart.

Passionfruit respond to generous feeding. Apply a complete fruit tree fertiliser when growth starts in spring. Continue feeding through spring and summer. Regular watering is needed because roots are quite shallow. Mulching is useful too, but keep mulch away from stems as this may encourage collar rot.

Vines planted in spring sometimes give a light crop in autumn but usually won't bear until the following summer. After fruiting, cut the vines back or thin them out if the growth is dense. This allows better air movement and encourages new laterals on which fruit is formed. Vines may become weak, spindly and disease prone after four or five years so it pays to have new ones coming on as replacements. Fruit colour changes from green to purple when ripe and fruit usually falls. Gather fallen fruit every day in summer. The banana passionfruit is a close relative grown in the same way. It has pink flowers and banana-like fruit with a soft yellow skin. It can become weedy in some climates.

Kiwi fruit

Chinese gooseberries or Kiwi fruit, as they are often known, are becoming more popular with home gardeners. The fruit is 5–7 cm long and covered with short, brown bristles. The flesh, which is light green with dark, soft edible seeds, can be used fresh or frozen or in jam, pickles or chutney.

The Chinese gooseberry is a vigorous, deciduous vine suited to mild or temperate climates with warm summer months and freedom from late frost. The fibrous roots are shallow so regular watering is needed from spring to early winter when fruit ripens (usually May or June). Chinese gooseberries have male and female flowers on separate vines so you must buy at least one of each. Nurseries sell them in pairs although one male plant will provide enough pollen for several females. Female vines take four to five years to bear and keep on bearing for at least twenty years.

Vines, which are planted in winter, can be trained on trellises 2 m high with two or three strands of wire. Space vines 3 m apart. Many home gardeners train the vines over a strong pergola about 2.5 m high and 3 m square. Wires spaced 60–75 cm apart on the sides and top provide support for the twining laterals. Fruit is formed on the first three to five buds of current season's growth. Each winter, prune laterals back to two or three buds beyond the previous season's crop. If overcrowded, cut some laterals out completely. In summer, shorten back growth if it is too vigorous. Many varieties, which vary in shape and size, have been selected. 'Hayward', with large fruit of good keeping quality, is popular.

TROPICAL FRUITS
Avocado

This handsome, evergreen tree grows to a height of 9 m. The pear-shaped fruit – green or green turning black – contains cream-coloured, butter-textured flesh surrounding a large, oval seed. Although of tropical origin, avocado trees can be grown in sheltered positions in temperate climates. The trees prefer deep, well-drained soil and need regular watering in summer. Seedling trees are unreliable and may never bear fruit, so it's best to buy grafted plants from nurseries. The trees are self-shaping, so no pruning is necessary. Scatter a complete fertiliser beneath the drip line of the tree in spring and repeat the treatment two or three times during summer and early autumn. Avocados are prone to root rot so treat annually with Yates Anti Rot Fungicide.

Avocados have a peculiar sex life. Flowers function as female for a few hours, close and then reopen as male flowers next afternoon or the following day, or vice versa. Fortunately, pollination of the variety 'Fuerte' is not so critical because these sex changes overlap in different flowers on the one tree. The variety 'Sharwill' is mid-season

and flowers later, but can be pollinated by 'Fuerte' or 'Hass', a late variety. 'Hass', in turn, is pollinated by 'Sharwill' but not by 'Fuerte', which has finished flowering. In the Sydney area, 'Fuerte' fruit ripens from April onwards for several months. Fruit does not ripen well on the tree, so pick when the fruit is fully formed and the gloss on the skin fades, then ripen indoors.

Bananas

Bananas are ornamental as well as useful. They will grow very well outside their tropical environment if they are planted in a sunny spot in a sheltered garden. Older plants will tolerate light frosts. Bananas are shallow-rooted and need fertile, well-drained soil with regular watering in summer. Start your banana tree from a vigorous sucker with a large, round base. Trim off roots (these will not grow again) and reduce the 'top' by one-quarter. Plant the sucker in spring with its base 20–25 cm deep. It will produce fruit in fifteen to eighteen months but may take longer under cooler conditions. Many new suckers will develop, so gouge these out but keep the strongest to replace the parent plant. Strip off any dead or wind-shredded leaves. A banana bunch is right

The Hass avocado is grown in warm to tropical climates.

for cutting when fruits have lost their angular shape. Still green, you can ripen them by hanging the bunch upside down in a warm place indoors. Protect bunches which form in cool weather with a blue plastic 'bunch cover'.

Most banana varieties grow to 6 m tall but 'Cavendish' is shorter at 3 m. Some popular varieties are 'Cavendish', 'Williams' (which are more tolerant to cool weather), 'Lady-finger', 'Sugar' and 'Grand Michel'. Friends and neighbours are a good source of planting material. In districts where bananas are grown commercially, home gardeners must apply to the local regulatory authorities for for permission to plant.

Mango

The mango is an attractive evergreen tree with slender, dark-green, leathery leaves. Trees may grow to 9 m (or more) under favourable conditions. Mangoes grow best in tropical and subtropical regions but can be successful in coastal districts of New South Wales and warm inland districts such as the Murray River Valley. A sunny, sheltered, frost-free aspect is best. They grow on a wide range of soils but need good drainage in the topsoil. The trees flower in spring and the large oval fruit are ready for picking in late summer and autumn.

You can often start a mango tree by germinating a fresh seed from a fully ripe fruit. The popular 'Kensington Pride' or 'Bowen' variety can be grown this way as it will reproduce true to type. Place the cleaned seed in a large pot filled with sand and peat moss. One seed may produce several shoots. Retain one shot only and transplant the seedling when 20–30 cm tall. Grafted plants are also available from nurseries. Apart from training the tree to four or five main limbs, pruning is rarely needed. Thin inside branches if too crowded. Mangoes respond to fertiliser in small doses. Use a complete fruit tree fertiliser (e.g. Dynamic Lifter PLUS Fruit Foods) in four applications – in October, December, February and April. Trees start bearing in three or four years. Fruit is ready to pick when the skin turns from green to yellow or orange. 'Kensington Pride' ('Bowen') has a bright-yellow skin with a pinkish blush. R2E2 has very large fruit.

Pawpaw

Pawpaw or papaya, like other tropical fruit, does best in warm, humid climates with good summer rainfall, but if you choose a sunny, sheltered site, this attractive tree will succeed in frost-free temperate climates. A well-drained loam or light soil is preferred.

Most pawpaws have male and female flowers on separate trees but there are some bisexual trees. The fruit from bisexual trees is long rather than oval and the trees are not as tolerant of cool-climate conditions. Hybrid bisexual trees are available from nurseries. Seeds from fruit of female trees germinate easily in punnets or pots. Transplant seedlings when 20 cm tall. You cannot tell whether seedlings are male or female, so it is wise to set four or five plants in a group spaced about 1.5 m apart. Odds are you will have at least one male tree for pollination. Unwanted male trees can be removed, unless you want to keep them as ornamentals. Identify males at flowering stage by the thinner flowers that lack embryo fruit.

In favourable conditions, female or bisexual trees will bear fruit within fifteen months but take longer where it is cooler. Trees bear well for about five years, so it is best to have younger ones coming on as replacements. Harvesting fruit from older trees is difficult too – even with an extension ladder. Trees that develop three or four lateral stems can be kept at a lower height by cutting out the main stem.

Pick the fruit when fully coloured, but if the weather is cool, pick when the fruit is showing a tinge of yellow and ripen indoors. Flowering takes place over several weeks so fruit at different stages of development will appear on the tree at the one time. Most pawpaws have bright-yellow or orange flesh, but there are some with red flesh.

Pineapple

Pineapples belong to the bromeliad family and are easy to grow in a warm tropical climate. They are one of the few fruit plants which grow in a small space. They are successful in a large pot or tub on a sunny terrace or patio too. Soil must be well drained with plenty of organic matter. Acidic soils with a pH 5.0–6.0 are best and you may need to add sulfur to achieve this level. (See

Like most other bromeliads, pineapples reproduce by means of suckers (sometimes called 'pups').

Chapter 5.) Starting a plant from a 'top' (the usually discarded leafy part of a fruit) is an easy way to grow a new pineapple. Allow the top to dry for a day or two and plant about 5 cm deep in spring. It may take two years to produce a new fruit.

After fruiting, prune the plant back to the strongest sucker for the next crop. Surplus suckers can be used for new plants. Feed plants with a mixed fruit tree fertiliser in spring each year. Slow- or controlled-release fertilisers are the most suitable for pot culture.

Litchi

Litchi, also known as lychee nut or Chinese nut, is a compact, evergreen tree growing to 12 m. Trees are slow-growing but they are very long-lived. They start bearing at four to five years old but cropping can be very variable from year to year. The fruit is round or oval with a red, leathery and rather bumpy skin. The white, juicy flesh is very sweet and surrounds a single dark-brown seed. Like other subtropical trees, the litchi needs warm, moist conditions, especially at flowering and for several weeks afterwards, to ensure fruit setting, but trees can be damaged by very strong sunlight.

Trees from seed are variable so it is best to buy plants grown from layers. Spring or late-summer planting is best. Prune young trees to a strong framework and later remove branches to shape the tree. Fertilise trees in the same way as described for mangoes. Fruit ripens over a four- or five-week period in December or January. Cut off the small branches with fruit clusters attached every few days. This ensures that new growth for the next crop is on the outside of the tree. 'Tai so' (Kwai Mi) is the best known variety.

Custard Apple

Custard apple or sugar apple is a small, semi-deciduous tree growing to 6 m. It is suited to warm, humid districts in coastal Queensland and northern New South Wales. The fruit is heart-shaped and very knobby with a diameter of 5–8 cm. Flesh is custard-like with many dark, smooth seeds. It is best to buy grafted plants of the 'Cherimoya' or 'Peruvian' custard apple because plants from seeds are unreliable. Plant in early spring or summer. Prune young trees to a vase shape over the first three to four years. Apply fertiliser each year in small doses as for mangoes. Flowering starts in October or November and may continue until January or February, so the fruit ripens over a long period. Pick the fruit when skin turns a greenish-cream colour. They may take a few days to soften up for eating. 'African Pride' is the most widely grown variety. It is a compact tree, bearing fruit (March–June harvest) after three to four years. 'Pink's Mammoth' is a larger custard apple tree with better quality fruit (April–July harvest) but takes six to seven years to bear.

Guava

Guavas are not really tropical fruits and can be grown in warm–temperate, frost-free climates. Yellow guava, an evergreen tree, is hardier than citrus and grows to 5 m tall. The yellow, oval or pear-shaped fruits are about 5 cm in diameter. Strawberry guava is a taller tree but fruits are smaller, purplish-red in colour with a tart flavour. Pineapple guava or feijoa is rather more adaptable to cool conditions and will tolerate light frosts. Fruit is oval, about 8 cm long with a greenish-yellow, waxy skin and pineapple-like aroma and flavour. Guavas can be eaten fresh but are more popular as jam or jelly. Fruits of the yellow guava trees ripen in late summer and are susceptible to fruit fly attack.

Tree Tomato (Tamarillo)

This is a small, umbrella-shaped tree growing to 3 m tall. The stem is quite brittle so it is best to support it with loose ties and a strong stake. Tree tomato is not strictly a tropical fruit and grows well in temperate, frost-free districts. It prefers a sunny, sheltered aspect. You can raise tree tomatoes from seed but cuttings are easy too. Prune the main stem at a height of 1 m to encourage growth of three or four branches. The egg-shaped, purplish-red fruits are 5 cm long with many seeds. The fruits slightly resemble tomatoes in appearance but have an acid-sweet flavour. They are used fresh or cooked.

BERRY FRUITS
Strawberries

Strawberries are very adaptable to climate and soil, so it is not surprising they are grown from tropical Queensland to Victoria and Tasmania. The plants need a sunny position, a well-drained soil with good structure, regular feeding and watering.

Most home gardeners grow strawberries in a raised bed in the vegetable garden with plants spaced at 30 cm but they also do well in pots. Surface mulching between plants will prevent weeds, maintain an even soil temperature and reduce moisture loss in summer. A mulch helps to keep fruit clean, too. Grass clippings, compost, leaves, straw, sawdust, wood shavings or pine bark are all suitable for mulching. Black, woven weed mat sheeting makes an excellent mulch for raised beds, and fruiting is earlier because of the warmer soil. Spread the weed mat and cut a small slit for each plant, making a depression in the soil below to direct water to roots. Strawberries do well in large pots, tubs or barrels with holes cut in the sides. There are a few non-running varieties that are specially suited to this kind of growing.

Prepare soil with poultry manure, Dynamic Lifter pellets or compost plus a well-incorporated mixed fertiliser. You can start plants any time between April and August, but early plantings will give fruit in October and November. Remove old, dead leaves and trim any straggly roots before planting. After flowering commences, give plants liquid feeds of Thrive or Aquasol every few weeks. Many runners will develop, so pick these off progressively. Plants will bear well for about three seasons. Use runners to start a new bed in autumn of the third year. Packaged strawberry crowns that are certified to be virus-free are available in

Most soft berry fruits, like these raspberries, grow best in an area with cold winters.

winter. Seed of a European wild (alpine) strawberry is readily available. The plants produce fruit in the first season after sowing and heavy crops of small to medium-sized, flavourful fruit are borne on neat, bushy plants. These non-running plants can be grown in pots and are ideal for courtyards and balconies. Sow autumn and spring.

Raspberries

Raspberries grow best in cool temperate or cold climates. Districts where apples or cherries do well are ideal. Raspberry bushes need deep, well-drained soil with lots of organic matter. Prepare and fertilise the soil as for strawberries and set out the dormant canes 60 cm apart in rows 2 m apart. Most raspberry bushes bear fruit on one-year-old wood. Cut back canes that have fruited in winter. Some 'ever-bearing' varieties (e.g. 'Heritage') have an autumn crop on the current season's wood. Cut Heritage canes to just above ground level as soon as leaves fall. Thin the strongest of the new canes to 15 cm apart to prevent overcrowding and top them slightly for a manageable height. The canes can be tied together loosely with twine. Raspberries continue to bear for many years. Pick fruit when ripe and well coloured. Fruit is delicious as a fresh dessert, freezes well and makes excellent jam or jelly.

Trailing berries or brambles

Loganberry, boysenberry and youngberry are the main trailing berries. They are hybrids derived from the dewberry or trailing blackberry.

Loganberries prefer a cool to cold climate similar to that for raspberries, but boysenberries and youngberries are more adaptable to warm climates, providing that winter months are cool. They grow on a variety of soils, but drainage must be good. Propagate these berries by cuttings or rooted tip-layers. Plant these 2 m apart underneath a two-wire trellis. Like raspberries, they bear fruit on one-year-old wood. Canes produced the previous summer are tied to the top wire and then cut back to ground level after fruiting. New canes are tied to the bottom wire as they grow to keep them tidy, and transferred to the top wire when the old canes are cut away. Prepare the ground well

by adding animal manure or compost plus a mixed fertiliser, as for strawberries. Each year, apply fertiliser such as Dynamic Lifter PLUS Fruit Food when growth starts in spring. Slow-release fertilisers are also suitable. Pick fruit when well-coloured (red for loganberries, and purplish-black for boysenberries and youngberries).

Well-grown trailing berries will bear for up to fifteen years. A single vine may yield 5 kg of fruit each year.

Blueberries

Blueberries are ornamental shrubs, with attractive white, bell-shaped flowers followed by the classic blue-coloured fruit. Soil must be light, friable, well-drained and acidic. Deciduous 'Highbush' blueberries need cold winters, while the rabbiteyes and hybrids do well in temperate areas. It's best to plant at least two different varieties for good fruit set. 'Sharpeblue' will usually produce fruit off one bush and is considered the best all-round variety by many but new cultivars are being continually introduced. Birds are the most common pests and bushes will often require netting to protect ripening fruit from attack.

Gooseberries and currants

Both fruits grow on small bushes that are suited to cool to cold climates. The English or European gooseberry is started from cuttings in winter and planted 1.5 m apart each way. Gooseberry bushes bear fruit on one-year-old wood which is cut out after fruiting. The bush is trained as a vase-shaped, small tree which means that some pruning is needed. Prepare soil as for raspberries, adding manure or compost plus a mixed fertiliser. 'Roaring Lion' is the most widely grown variety.

Black currants and red currants need a similar climate and soil. Propagate them from cuttings and plant 1.5 m apart. Generally, black currants and red currants are grown as a many-stemmed bush, which may need thinning when crowded. They bear fruit on one-year-old wood and red currants have fruiting spurs as well. There are varieties of black currants, red currants and white currants. All are worth growing but only in cold-winter areas.

NUT TREES

Nut trees are quite ornamental as well as useful. This short summary is given as a guide to the most popular varieties.

Almond

A deciduous tree, to 6 m tall, suited to winter-wet, summer-dry climates. Dry inland districts with cool winters such as the irrigation areas of southern New South Wales, Victoria and South Australia are ideal.

Almonds have similar soil and management requirements to peaches, which are close relatives. Nuts are enclosed in a fleshy husk. The husk dries at maturity and splits open or is easily separated. Two varieties are usually needed for cross-pollination but 'All In One' is self-fertile.

Hazelnut

Hazelnuts or filberts grow on small, much-branched deciduous trees to 5 m tall. They are suited to cool climates. The shell is hard and woody but the smooth, brown kernel separates easily when cracked. Trees may take several years to bear and two or more are required for cross-pollination.

Macadamia

This handsome native tree, also known as Queensland nut, grows to 9 m tall. It is suited to warm, humid climate zones but grows quite well in temperate coastal districts such as the Sydney area. The round white kernels are enclosed in a very hard, woody shell. Nuts mature during late autumn and winter and fall when ripe. Seedling trees are extremely variable so it is best to buy grafted trees from nurseries.

Pecan

Pecans grow on handsome deciduous trees that can be used as summer shade trees. Fruit production on a single tree can be unreliable but most develop at least a light crop. Deep, well-drained soil is required and generous fertilising, especially in the early stages of growth. The trees will tolerate very cold winters and hot summers so will grow in a wide range of climates. Nuts are smooth-shelled with sweet, walnut-like flesh. They are easy to crack and very popular with marauding parrots.

Macadamia flowers.

Pistachio

The pistachio nut is a small deciduous tree to 6 m tall with compound leaves composed of three to five leaflets. It will only grow in a narrow climate range with hot, dry summers and cool to cold winters. The fruit is oval-shaped, about 2 cm long, containing the nut within a thin, woody shell which splits open when ripe. The kernel is smooth, light green and richly flavoured.

Walnut

The common walnut is a shapely, deciduous tree growing to over 15 m unless restricted by pruning. It thrives in cool to cold climates but is susceptible to late spring frosts. Nuts split open or are separated easily when mature. Many varieties are available. Two varieties are desirable for effective cross-pollination.

Fruit

WHAT TO LOOK FOR	NUTRITION	STORAGE	PREPARATION	METHOD OF COOKING
APPLES Fruit should be the true variety colour, with skin free of bruises. Large apples do not keep as well as smaller fruit.	Fair source of vitamin C and dietary fibre. 222 kilojoules per 100 grams.	Keep in vented plastic bag in refrigerator.	Tart and sharp-tasting apples are best for cooking. Remove stalk, wash and dry well. Peel only if necessary.	As fresh juice or cider. Superb raw, pureed, in a tart or strudel, preserved as apple jelly. Use for fritters or bake.
APRICOT Firm, plump, fully developed fruit with a bright apricot colour. Avoid soft or shrivelled fruit.	Fair source of vitamin C, vitamin A and dietary fibre. Some iron. 188 kilojoules per 100 grams.	Keep in unsealed plastic bag in refrigerator for 2–3 days. Will deteriorate quickly at room temperature.	Wipe over, cut and remove stone.	As a snack. Use in fruit salad and jam. Cooking draws out the flavour. Serve with ham, lamb and duck.
AVOCADO Generally glossy and hard when unripe. When ripe, skin colour is dull, and a toothpick easily pierces flesh at stem. 'Hass' variety has rough, dark skin.	Fair source of vitamin C, riboflavin and dietary fibre. Some iron, thiamin and niacin. Fair source of poly-unsaturated fat. 674 kilojoules per 100 grams.	Ripen at room temperature, then store in refrigerator.	Remove stone, discard skin. Slice flesh as required. Lemon juice will stop discolouration.	Use mashed on bread and sprinkle with lemon juice. Fill with seafood and dressing. Ideal accompaniment to smoked fish and as a soup. A great ice cream.
BANANAS Best eating quality will be bright, medium-sized fruit, yellow to gold in colour, well rounded and free of bruises.	Fair source of vitamin A, vitamin C and dietary fibre. Some iron and thiamin. 364 kilojoules per 100 grams.	Store at room temperature to continue ripening process. Skin will blacken if refrigerated.	Simply peel, or if baking on the barbecue, slightly slit the skin. Lemon juice will prevent discolouration.	Sliced with cinnamon and cream. Ingredient in cakes, biscuits, desserts. Blend with milk for a nourishing drink. Bake on barbecue. Use for fritters.
CHERRIES Firm, fresh, bright, uniformly coloured fruit, with green stems. Use the taste test.	Fair source of vitamin C and dietary fibre. Some vitamin A. 265 kilojoules per 100 grams.	Keep in unsealed plastic bag in refrigerator to stop from drying out. Highly perishable. Eat soon after harvest.	Wash and remove stem. May be stoned before serving.	Use fresh, or as a tart filling. Blend stoned cherries for fruit sauce. Combine with walnuts and chicken in salad. As a soup.
GRAPEFRUIT Firm and heavy fruit. Skin should be smooth and bright yellow in colour.	Excellent source of vitamin C. 155 kilojoules per 100 grams.	Can be kept outside refrigerator in cool place. Keep in refrigerator crisper for longer storage.	Wipe over and peel. Use grapefruit knife to segment.	Popular as juice or served in halves for breakfast. Serve spiced and grilled as entree. In salads, mix with prawns and mayonnaise.

WHAT TO LOOK FOR	NUTRITION	STORAGE	PREPARATION	METHOD OF COOKING
GRAPES Select bunches of uniformly shaped berries, smooth and plump with natural bloom not rubbed off. Stems should be green with fruit firmly attached.	Some vitamin C, iron and thiamin. 276 kilojoules per 100 grams.	In vented plastic bag in refrigerator. Use as quickly as possible.	Wash, dry and remove stems. Pips may also be removed.	Great as a snack. Serve with cheese or pâté, and in fruit salad. Combines well with duck, quail and sole.
LEMONS Firm and heavy fruit. Skin should be clean with fine texture. Choose lemons tinged with green for jam-making.	Good source of vitamin C. Some calcium and iron. 134 kilojoules per 100 grams.	Keep in cool place, can be home-cured for longer storage. Juice can be frozen for use at later date.	Wipe over. Juice, slice for decoration. Cut into wedges and dip in parsley to serve with fish.	Use as a meat tenderiser (mix with mustard to coat meat before baking) and in sorbets. Helps stop apples and bananas from discolouring.
MANDARINS Firm and heavy fruit. Skin should be glossy with a strong orange colour. Heavy fruit gives high juice yield.	Excellent source of vitamin C. Some vitamin A, thiamin and calcium. 193 kilojoules per 100 grams.	Can be kept outside refrigerator in cool place for short time. Keep in crisper for longer storage.	Wipe over and peel. Best eaten raw.	Ideal for lunch box. Use in the same way as an orange, as a crystallised fruit, or in sorbets.
NECTARINES Smooth, plump and highly coloured fruit with no skin blemishes. Avoid hard, dull and immature fruit.	Good source of vitamin C. Fair source of vitamin A and dietary fibre. Some iron and thiamin. 260 kilojoules per 100 grams.	Bruise easily. Handle with care. Refrigerate fruit that is riper. Use as quickly as possible.	Wash, cut and discard stone.	Delightful as a snack. Combine with roast beef, cheese and wholemeal bread as a sandwich. Enjoy with cereal or ice cream.
ORANGES Firm and heavy fruit. Skin should be glossy with a fine texture. Colour does not indicate maturity.	Excellent source of vitamin C. Fair source of dietary fibre. Some vitamin A, thiamin and calcium. 188 kilojoules per 100 grams.	Can be kept outside refrigerator in cool place for short time. Keep in crisper for longer storage.	Peel before eating, slice whole for salads, halve for juicing, quarter and freeze as a snack.	Serve with meat, rice. Use to flavour puddings, breads, biscuits, desserts and in fruit salad, marmalade. Ideal as juice.
PAWPAWS Select well-coloured fruit. Skin should not be shrivelled or dull, and have no ripe rots or bruising. Aroma is good indicator of ripeness.	Excellent source of dietary fibre. Good source of vitamin C. Fair source of iron. Some riboflavin and niacin. 381 kilojoules per 100 grams.	Ripen at room temperature. Keep ripe fruit in refrigerator. Use as soon as possible.	Wipe over. Slice as required and remove seeds.	Use as meat tenderiser. Serve as accompaniment to smoked beef. Use in fruit salad, or with yoghurt and honey as dessert. Lovely water ice.

WHAT TO LOOK FOR	NUTRITION	STORAGE	PREPARATION	METHOD OF COOKING
PASSIONFRUIT Select full, heavy fruit with smooth dark-purple skin. Avoid withered fruit.	Excellent source of vitamin C. Fair source of vitamin A. 172 kilojoules per 100 grams.	Keep in plastic bag in crisper of refrigerator. Pulp may be frozen for later use.	Wipe over. Cut in half. Remove pulp and use as required. Discard skin.	Use in fruit salad and fruit punch. Serve as topping over ice cream, pavlovas and flummery or as a fruit sauce. Include in icings.
PEACHES Firm fruit which is just beginning to soften, with a 'peachy' smell. Avoid bruised or under-developed fruit.	Fair source of vitamin C and dietary fibre. Some vitamin A, iron, niacin. 172 kilojoules per 100 grams.	Keep in unsealed plastic bag in refrigerator. Will deteriorate quickly at room temperature.	Wash and discard stone. If peeled, use lemon juice to prevent discolouration.	Pies. Top with cinnamon and butter and lightly grill. Eat fresh with cereal, ice cream, cream or yoghurt. Use in compotes and mousses.
PEARS Pears ripen from the inside out after harvesting. Test for ripeness by applying gentle pressure at the stem area. Avoid immature fruit.	Fair source of vitamin C and dietary fibre. 234 kilojoules per 100 grams.	Store firm pears in vented plastic bag in refrigerator. Ripen at room temperature.	Wash and dry. Remove stalk for cooking. Peel only if recipe calls for it.	Eat raw with cheese and walnuts. Preserve. Serve with roast lamb, smoked fish or ham. Poach in vanilla syrup and coat with chocolate. Bake in wine.
PINEAPPLES Skin colour not a reliable guide, but in winter select fruit with quarter yellow colour and no soft spots. Look for fresh deep-green leaves and pleasant aroma.	Good source of vitamin C. Fair source of dietary fibre. Some vitamin A, thiamin. 218 kilojoules per 100 grams.	Keep in cool place or in refrigerator. Refrigerate before serving, if desired.	Remove leaves. Make slanting cuts downwards between eyes, and slice as required, using a stainless steel knife.	Fruit salads, upside-down cakes, with ham in salads or sandwiches. Serve with bacon as hors d'oeuvres, or with cheese or sausages. Use in Chinese cookery.
PLUMS Firm, bright and fully developed fruit, with no sign of wrinkling.	Fair source of dietary fibre. Some vitamin A, vitamin C and thiamin. 247 kilojoules per 100 grams.	Ripen at room temperature. Then refrigerate and use as soon as possible.	Wash, cut and discard stone.	Jam, compotes. Serve chilled with camembert or blue cheese. With ice cream. Bake with roast lamb for added flavour. Use as a snack.
STRAWBERRIES Fruit should be clean and brightly coloured with no sign of soft spots or mould. Look for green stem cap and avoid fruit with white or green areas.	Excellent source of vitamin C. Fair source of dietary fibre. Some iron. 155 kilojoules per 100 grams.	Keep in refrigerator. Very perishable. Use as soon as possible.	Hull and wipe over.	Preserves, jams, tarts. Puree for fruit sauce. Combine with pineapple. Add to fruit salad. With cream or yoghurt. In fruit punch.

Just as your lettuce plants begin to form hearts, dress the rows with magnesium sulphate (Epsom salts) for lovely sweet and crisper lettuce.

MORRIS HOLMES
HORTICULTURAL CONSULTANT AND
GARDEN DESIGNER

Fine bamboo canes, which are great for staking tomatoes or any new plantings, should be placed in the ground upside down to prevent reshooting.

ROS ANDREWS
WWW.GUTMATTERS.COM

Hang an 'S' butcher's hook (or a few of them at intervals) on the fence to support and train new canes for bramble-type berries at shoulder height. This will enable easier access for picking in the fruiting season.

GAIL THOMAS
WRITER AND PHOTOGRAPHER

Tie a small, green plastic tie around the base of current fruiting canes of berries such as loganberries or blackberries. In winter when it's time to prune the canes that have fruited, it is easy to identify them from new growth canes, which won't have any ties.

GAIL THOMAS
WRITER AND PHOTOGRAPHER

Plant some lavender or *Nepeta* (catmint) in your vegie patch. These plants not only look great, they do a fantastic job of attracting bees to the garden. They'll do all your pollination work and you'll have bumper vegie crops.

CAROLYN BLACKMAN
HORTICULTURIST – VIVID DESIGN

Grow vegies in a small compound where you keep a dog. This deters possums. The compound must be small enough to concentrate the dog's scent.

JOHN MASON
GARDENING AUTHOR, PRINCIPAL –
ACS DISTANCE EDUCATION

Create a link between the vegetable garden and ornamental garden by planting fragrant herbs (which will also keep insects at bay) or coloured silver beet, coloured kale or purple basil as a low-growing divider. Erect a permanent screen to support runner beans, sweet peas, asparagus or small-fruited pumpkins.

HELEN MOODY
HORTICULTURAL JOURNALIST AND PUBLIC
RELATIONS CONSULTANT

When harvesting fruit and vegetables that have been sprayed with pesticides, ensure that you adhere to the withholding period of the chemical. This information can be found on the label of the pesticide.

JOHN GABRIELE
GARDEN WRITER *ILLAWARRA MERCURY*
WEEKENDER MAGAZINE, GARDENING PRESENTER
ABC ILLAWARRA 97.3FM

If a plant looks sick take a closer look. Nine times out of ten it will be scale, mites or other sap suckers.

JACKIE FRENCH

GARDEN WRITER, BROADCASTER, COLUMNIST, AUSTRALIAN CHILDREN'S LAUREATE 2014 2015 AND SENIOR AUSTRALIAN OF THE YEAR

Turn friends gourmet-green by sowing Yates Lettuce Salad Mix into polystyrene boxes of good-quality potting mix. Sow a fresh box every few weeks. The crops can be moved easily to maximise sunshine, or elevated to keep leaves away from slugs and snails. Take a box to a picnic.

SUSAN PARSONS

KITCHEN GARDEN WRITER

Salad vegetables don't take up a lot of space. A large bowl-shaped container placed on a sunny patio will provide space for Tiny Tim tomatoes (in the centre), a punnet of mixed lettuce, some radish and parsley, chives or basil.

SHIRLEY STACKHOUSE

GARDEN WRITER

When growing vegetables, don't over-plant any one crop. Stagger your plantings so you get different maturity times. For example, plant six lettuce or sow a row of carrots one day, repeat the process two weeks later and again three weeks later.

GRAHAM ROSS

THE GARDEN CLINIC, *BETTER HOMES AND GARDENS* TV

Root crops and tubers such as potatoes and sweet potatoes are subject to damage by a range of leaf-eating insects. Spraying for these pests is rarely warranted, as a significant amount of leaf damage can occur without any effect on the root or tuber harvest.

ANNETTE McFARLANE

ABC RADIO BRISBANE GARDENING TALKBACK HOST

When pruning your tomato bush, don't throw the pieces into the compost pile. Poke the shoots into the soil or put them in pots to grow into other plants. This provides a succession of ripening tomatoes on the bushes that develop, and plants grown from shoots seem to fruit better than the original plants.

ALLEN GILBERT

HORTICULTURAL CONSULTANT AND AUTHOR

Plant a low herb garden under the clothes hoist. When the leaves brush against the clothes, they will scent them.

FRANCES HUTCHISON

GARDENING AUTHOR AND EDITOR

Thyme makes a wonderful and useful ground cover but it does not like to lie on cold, wet soil. It will often rot when it is grown in these conditions. The best way to prevent this is to spread a layer of crushed rock or gravel over the surface of the soil where the thyme is planted.

PENNY WOODWARD

GARDEN WRITER AND PHOTOGRAPHER

For those troubled by fruit flies or birds ruining the fruit crop, old pantyhose can be used to enclose individual fruits as they mature. They may look peculiar, but they work!

JOHN 'GREENFINGERS' COLWILL
GARDEN WRITER AND BROADCASTER

Birds getting to your fruit? Then use onion or orange net bags available from greengrocers. Place the bags over the fruit and tie firmly to the branches. The birds will keep away from your trees and visit your neighbours' instead!

PETER DE WAART
HORTICULTURIST

If gardeners have a seedling tree that is unproductive or producing inedible fruit, they should not remove it but rather utilise the framework of the tree. Cut it off to about hip level during mid-winter and graft scions of other fruits onto it. This could result, for example, in an apple tree with up to eighty or more cultivars producing different tree-ripened fruit from Christmas until July. Or an old seedling plum tree could be grafted over to produce plums, prunes, peaches, apricots, almonds and nectarines.

ALLEN GILBERT
HORTICULTURAL CONSULTANT AND AUTHOR

A space-saving method to grow a large variety of vegetables, herbs or flowers is a small hydroponic set-up. It allows you to control plant growth and the results can be much better than plants produced in the ground. An added advantage is that it requires no weeding!

JOHN MASON
GARDENING AUTHOR, PRINCIPAL –
ACS DISTANCE EDUCATION

For a quick and easy vegetable garden that won't bust your back, lay down some newspaper on the ground, eight sheets thick, and place some straw bales on top with the string ties left on. Give them a thorough soaking with water, then sprinkle a few good handfuls of blood and bone and chook pellets over the top and water that in. Cover the lot with a sheet of plastic and leave it for a few weeks. Then make depressions in the top of the bales, tip in some compost or potting mix and plant into that. Keep them moist and use a liquid fertiliser every week or two.

PHIL DUDMAN
RADIO AND TV PRESENTER, AUTHOR
AND GARDENING JOURNALIST

Plant a perennial vegetable garden separate to your annual vegetables to give you years of produce. Perennial vegetables do best in garden beds just for them because their extensive root systems can grow undisturbed. Try rhubarb, horseradish, asparagus, sorrel, chicory, and perennial basil.

MARIANNE CANNON
PRESENTER, REAL WORLD GARDENER ON 2RRR
AND ACROSS AUSTRALIA ON THE COMMUNITY
RADIO NETWORK

Locate your compost bin in the vegie garden for surprising benefits. I planted a couple of 'Tommy Toe' and 'Sweet Bite' tomato vines alongside my bin and they set more fruit than ever. Lemon grass and basil nearby have never looked better. It must be a combination of heat and low-level nutrients.

MALCOLM CAMPBELL
ABC RADIO 891 PRESENTER AND WEEKLY
COLUMNIST FOR NEWS LIMITED IN ADELAIDE

When passionfruit vines are growing strong but are unfruitful, take a knife or razor and cincture the main limbs. Cut a ring around the branch to the depth of the bark (about 2 mm). Do not remove any bark layers. The cincturing allows the plant to utilise food processed by plant leaves. This produces flowers, and fruiting begins soon afterwards.

ALLEN GILBERT
HORTICULTURAL CONSULTANT AND AUTHOR

Fruit fly-infected fruit should be gathered or stripped from trees and placed in a container of water that can be sealed, or placed in a large plastic bag and allowed to cook in the sun. Once all larvae have died the residue can be placed into the compost heap.

GEOFF MIERS
GEOFF MIERS GARDEN SOLUTIONS,
ALICE SPRINGS, NORTHERN TERRITORY

If you have no space for a vegetable garden, buy half a dozen very large woven baskets and line each basket with a plastic garbage bag with a few holes punched in the bottom. Use a lightweight soilless potting mix and water in fertiliser regularly. The baskets won't last forever but will be light to move and good to look at.

FRANCES HUTCHISON
GARDENING AUTHOR AND EDITOR

Plant calendulas in the vegetable garden as an alternative to marigolds. They will attract pollinators, add colour to the garden, the petals can be used to decorate food dishes and they are said to deter nematodes.

GEOFF MIERS
GEOFF MIERS GARDEN SOLUTIONS, ALICE SPRINGS,
NORTHERN TERRITORY

When planting advanced tomato seedlings, don't be shy to plant them a little deeper than usual. Burying the lower portion of the stem encourages the development of aerial roots, resulting in an expanded root network to assist the plant with more effective water and nutrient up take.

JOSH BYRNE
ABC GARDENING AUSTRALIA

One of the biggest challenges of city gardening must be how to grow tasty fruits and vegetables in tiny spaces. Make the most of small areas with climbing crops and bush or compact fruiting varieties.

MELISSA KING
HORTICULTURALIST, TV PRESENTER AND AUTHOR

Let a lettuce go to seed and you'll never have to buy lettuce seedlings again! The same can be said for rocket, parsley and coriander.

MELANIE KINSEY
HORTICULTURAL JOURNALIST

PART FIVE

Growing your Garden

14
The Perfect Lawn

Lawns have been a feature of home gardens for centuries. Australian gardeners have followed this tradition, but there are many other reasons why we grow lawns. A lawn is the best way to cover and maintain large sections of garden easily and quickly. The initial cost of establishment is relatively low and a lawn will last indefinitely. A lawn blends the house with the garden, softens harsh outlines, and complements trees, shrubs and colourful annuals. Even in the smallest garden an attractive lawn adds a touch of spaciousness. On hot summer days a lawn reduces temperature and glare to give a feeling of coolness. Last, but not least, a lawn is a place for relaxation, pleasant to look at, delightful to walk or lie on, and the ideal surface for children to romp and play.

LAWN PLANNING

In many respects, a lawn is an unnatural way to grow millions of grass plants which are all competing for light, water and nutrients. We cut them constantly, which makes their task of growing more difficult. We remove grass clippings for mulching garden beds or composting. This is an added drain on soil nutrients. Fortunately, lawn grasses are well adapted to this harsh treatment and will thrive if we understand their needs and go about providing for them in the right way. Because a lawn is permanent, it pays to spend some time planning it. This will help with maintenance and often makes the difference between a good lawn and a poor lawn.

It's best to shape the lawn area with flowing curves. Curves are easier to water and mow than square or sharp corners. Small beds and specimen trees or shrubs can detract from the space of the lawn and make mowing more difficult. Very steep slopes are also hard to mow. Concrete mower strips adjacent to gravel paths, driveways, gardens, rockeries or other features will reduce edge maintenance enormously. It is best to construct mower strips or paving after the lawn is well established and there is no longer any risk of lawn subsidence.

Avoid growing grass to the building line. Pathways or paving adjacent to walls are better, because they eliminate wetting and drying effects in the foundation area if it's necessary to water the lawn. And grass that is grown under overhanging eaves misses out on rain and will need extra watering.

Avoid heavily shaded areas for lawns – especially the southern side of buildings, beside fences or underneath dense shrubs or trees. Grasses are essentially sun-loving plants, and even varieties described as 'shade tolerant' will struggle in heavy shade. Trying to grow grass under trees has limited success – there is competition for moisture and nutrients as well as for light. These areas are best paved or separated from the lawn by a mower strip and covered with gravel, pebbles or pine bark. Shade-loving ground covers are an attractive alternative and are discussed later in this chapter.

Avoid growing grass in situations liable to excessive wear – at the corners of buildings, outside doorways and so on. Paths or paving are the best solution here, although a few stepping stones may be enough to solve the traffic problem.

PREPARING THE SITE
Soils and drainage

Whether you sow lawn seed, plant sprigs of running grasses or lay turf, soil must be well prepared. The success of the lawn largely depends on the effort you put into soil preparation and you have an opportunity before establishment that you will never get again during the life of the lawn. Most grasses prefer well-drained loam or sandy loam soils rather than heavier, wetter soils. Good drainage means better penetration of water, air and grass roots. On very heavy soils it is

A lush green lawn is dependent on good soil preparation and drainage.

wise to import some sandy loam soil, spread it over the area to a depth of 8–10 cm and incorporate it into the topsoil. In extremely wet situations, artificial drainage may be needed. (See Chapter 4.) Very sandy soils may drain too easily, so improve them by

HINT

Hire a vertimower to put a spring into your step and not your lawn. September and October are ideal months to remove 'thatch' – the build up of decaying organic matter from the leaves, stems and roots that stops water and fertiliser from reaching the lawn roots. After vertimowing apply a wetting agent like Yates 'Waterwise' and then fertilise a fortnight later to have your lawn in tip-top condition and ready for summer.

COLIN BARLOW

GARDEN WRITER, DESIGNER AND HORTICULTURALIST, TV PRESENTER – HOME IN WA MAGAZINE, GARDENING PRESENTER ABC ILLAWARRA 97.3FM

adding animal manure, spent mushroom compost, or other organic matter to increase their water-holding capacity.

Start preparing the soil well before the time for sowing or planting. This allows you to form the correct levels and contours, to prepare a crumbly soil structure and to get rid of weeds. Start by spraying existing ground cover with a herbicide like Zero Glyphosate. Leave for at least a week to ensure the herbicide can kill the roots of perennial weeds. You can dig small areas with a fork or spade, but it is worthwhile in the long run to hire a mechanical cultivator to save time and labour for large areas. There is no need to dig the soil deeply. On most sites, a depth of 15 cm is ample. Always dig the soil, especially heavy soil, when it is damp, but keep in mind that cultivating heavy soil when it is either too wet or too dry will spoil its structure. After the initial cultivation remove large stones, gravel and other rubbish.

Allow the soil to remain in a loose or fallow condition for several weeks. Exposure to weather will often help to break down large clods and form a crumbly structure, but further cultivation may be necessary. Watering (or rain) will germinate many weed seeds. Destroy them by hoeing, raking or spraying again with Zero Glyphosate. (See Chapter 8.)

Soil pH and use of lime

Grasses grow happily in medium acid or slightly acid soils (pH 5.5–6.5). In high rainfall districts, soils may be strongly acid (less than pH 5.5). To these, apply lime, on a still day, at the rate of 25 kg per 100 square metres. This is equivalent to one cup per square metre. Lime also helps to improve the structure of heavy soils, so a good time to apply it is soon after initial cultivation. After spreading the lime, rake it into the topsoil.

Levelling and grading

Levelling with pegs and lines is rarely necessary unless the lawn is to be used for tennis or bowls. Lawns need not be flat. Those which follow the natural slope of the ground are usually more attractive. For drainage reasons the lawn should slope away from the house. Grading the soil is necessary to fill in noticeable hollows and to scrape off high spots. You can make an improvised grader from an old window frame or wooden gate, or you can nail together some pieces of 75 mm x 50 mm hardwood to make a frame for the same purpose. These do a good, if somewhat rough, grading job when dragged across the surface. The amount of bite taken into the soil by the leading edge depends on where you attach the rope. If it is too far forward the grader skims over the high spots rather than levelling them. A rake is useful for final grading and for spreading soil evenly. Grading must be done when the soil is loose and fairly dry. When you are satisfied with the lawn's levels and contours, water the area well and leave it for approximately a week. Then rake and cross-rake again and adjust any spots by further grading.

Consolidating

During the fallow period, natural settling or consolidation of soil below the crumbly surface will occur. Walking over the area for grading, raking or destroying weeds (plus occasional watering or rain) does this for you. If soil is still soft and spongy all over, rolling may be necessary. To avoid compaction, only roll or tread when soil is damp, but not wet. Sandy soils will settle and become firm when watered. Rake the area again after rolling.

HINT

New rolls of lawn must be butted very closely together and laid on a freshly installed sandy soil mix to help the new roots to establish. Never let them dry out during the first two to three weeks after laying.

DON BURKE

BURKE'S BACKYARD

Pre-planting fertiliser

If you now have a 12–20 mm layer of loose, crumbly surface soil and firmer soil below, it is ready for sowing seed, planting sprigs or laying turf. Apply a base fertiliser or pre-planting fertiliser. All soils for lawns need fertiliser. Having a dark, rich-looking loam is no guarantee of its fertility. Some soils in high rainfall districts and most previously uncultivated soils are deficient in phosphorus, which is the nutrient most needed by developing seedlings. Phosphorus is important for new root growth of sprigs and turf too. Use either a specific lawn starter fertiliser (typically these have more than 5 per cent phosphorus) or a composted organic fertiliser like Dynamic Lifter that stimulates microbial activity in the soil. Do not use standard lawn fertilisers at sowing or pre-planting time. These are low in phosphorus and high in nitrogen, and are intended for regular feeding of established lawns only.

Establishing turf or seedlings may also benefit from weekly or fortnightly applications of liquid biostimulants such as plant starters or seaweed solutions that will encourage root growth and speed up grass establishment.

Spreading fertiliser

It is essential to spread fertiliser evenly. Mechanical spreaders are available but fertiliser can be broadcast very effectively by hand. Probably the best method is to divide the total quantity of fertiliser into halves. Then spread the first half in one direction (say, north/south) and the other half at right angles to it (east/west). This way you cover

HINT

Laws for lawns are simple – feed, don't mow too low, choose the correct type for your area, allow adequate drainage, attend to pests and diseases and root out the weeds.

ANNE THOMSON

GARDEN DESIGNER – THE GARDEN DESIGN STUDIO

the area twice. You can be even more accurate if you divide the area into strips with garden twine stretched between pegs at 2 m intervals. This is a convenient width for scattering fertiliser by hand. Calculate the quantity of fertiliser for each strip. After spreading the first half of the fertiliser, move the twine and pegs to make strips at right angles for spreading the second lot. After spreading, water well.

SOWING SEED

Lawn grass seed is small and light, so choose a calm day for sowing. A good time of the day is early morning when there is generally little or no wind. Only sow an area which you can effectively water. It is better to sow small sections over a few weeks than to have patchy germination of the whole lawn because of inadequate watering. For even sowing, use the same method as suggested for spreading fertiliser. That is, sow the seed in two directions. Best sowing rates and sowing times are given in the section 'Selecting your Grass' (see page opposite).

After sowing, lightly rake the crumbly surface. On sandy soils, a very light covering of dry, sieved mushroom compost retains moisture and helps to prevent soil washing away during rain or watering. On sloping sites, hessian or light cloth can be stretched over the surface and anchored with pieces of light timber to prevent soil wash, but remove it as soon as seeds start to germinate. Avoid any kind of traffic over the newly sown lawn until it has reached full germination. Keep the surface soil moist with light watering until seeds germinate and seedlings are well

established. As they grow stronger, water the lawn more heavily but less frequently. This will encourage roots to go deeper.

PLANTING SPRIGS OR RUNNERS

This method is often used to establish creeping grasses such as couch, Queensland blue couch, buffalo grass and kikuyu. A sprig or runner is a small piece 7–15 cm long, with one or more nodes (joints) from which leaves and roots grow. Planting runners does not require as much attention as sowing seed. It is a fairly inexpensive method, but time-consuming.

Prepare the soil in the same way as for sowing seed. Plant runners into damp soil about 30 cm apart, by hand or with a trowel. Alternatively, make a furrow 5–7 cm deep, lay runners in the furrow and firm the soil around the roots. Make sure some of the leaves are above ground. On very large areas, runners can be 'chaffed' (chopped into small pieces), broadcast and covered with a light sandy soil. Some landscape contractors will quote for the complete operation.

Only plant sections you can handle and water. Cover unplanted runners with a wet bag or hessian to prevent drying out. Keep soil moist for a few weeks, especially in hot, dry weather. The best time to plant runners is spring and early summer, but early autumn is acceptable in subtropical and tropical areas.

LAYING TURF

Laying turf is a more expensive method of growing a new lawn but provides an instant lawn with little chance of erosion or loss of planting material. It is a good method for sloping sites. Soil preparation need not be as thorough as for sowing seeds or planting runners, but the surface should be crumbly and well graded. Early maintenance, especially watering, is less critical. Turfing is usually confined to the creeping grasses – couch, Queensland blue couch, buffalo, Durban grass and kikuyu – although cool-season turf grass rolls containing tall fescue, Kentucky bluegrass and perennial ryegrass are available from turf farms servicing cooler regions such as Canberra and Melbourne. Turf supplies are available from turf farms, contractors and nurseries. Obtain your turf from a reliable supplier of weed-free turf. The turf must be free of weeds such as nut grass and onion weed and also of the 'grassy' weeds (paspalum, water couch, Mullumbimby couch and winter grass).

Cultivated turf is machine-harvested and cut to an even thickness. It comes sometimes in 30 cm squares, more often in rolls 30 cm (or more) wide, which are laid in place like a chequerboard. Place individual squares or edges of rolls to fit snugly against each other, and fill cracks between them with dry, sandy soil. Tramp or roll the turf after laying, and water well. Turfing can be done at almost any time of the year, but late winter or early spring is probably best. It is important to lay turf as soon as possible after delivery. The turf tends to deteriorate, especially in warm weather, if stored for more than a couple of days.

SELECTING YOUR GRASS

Lawn grasses can be divided into two groups depending on their growth pattern. Warm-season grasses grow well from spring to autumn with peak growth in summer. They grow slowly or become dormant in winter. They tend to discolour if subjected to sustained or heavy frosts but usually recover in spring. Generally, grasses in this group are best suited to humid coastal and hot inland districts.

Cool-season grasses are cold-tolerant, frost-resistant, somewhat more shade tolerant and stay green all year round. Peak growth is in spring with a smaller flush of growth in autumn. They are best suited to cool and cold climates but play a worthwhile role in repairing shade-damaged areas within warm-season grass lawns or providing a quick fix where required. Cool season grass lawns are best started in early spring or autumn.

The growth pattern of these two groups of lawn grasses is shown in the diagram to the right, which tells us how they grow each month in a temperate climate like Sydney, Adelaide or Perth. This is important because it determines the time of the year when each group needs water and fertiliser.

Warm-season grasses
Couch grass

Couch grass (known as Bermuda grass in the United States) is the finest and most drought tolerant of the warm-season grasses available

in Australia. It isn't successful in cold climates such as the eastern highlands of New South Wales and colder parts of Victoria and Tasmania. It is an aggressive 'running' grass with strong stolons which form a dense mat of hard-wearing turf. It is heat-resistant and tolerates dry weather better than most grasses. Couch grows on a wide range of soils but responds dramatically to nitrogen fertilisers applied during the growing season. It needs full sunlight and will not grow in shade. In cool or cold areas it will become dormant and brown off in winter. A couch lawn can be grown from seed, runners or turf. Sow seed in late spring or early summer (seed won't germinate in cool temperatures) at 1 kg per 100 square metres. Seedlings emerge in seven to twelve days in warm weather. Sprigs or runners of couch are planted at the same time, but couch turf can be laid in late winter or early spring. Popular couch cultivars (such as Santa Ana, Wintergreen and Conquest) are only available from turf suppliers and must be reproduced vegetatively. They are not grown from seed.

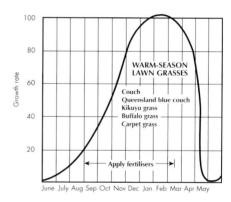

Growth pattern of warm-season grasses.

Couch seed can be hulled (outer husk removed) or unhulled (with outer husk intact). Hulled seed germinates more quickly.

Zoysia japonica

Zoysia japonica is a promising, relatively new lawn grass. It's said to grow an easy-care lawn that's soft to touch. It copes with wear and needs little mowing. It is also cold- and drought-tolerant. It can be grown from either runners or turf.

Queensland blue couch

This lawn grass is very similar in appearance to couch grass but the stolons and leaves are softer and finer and blue-green in colour. It is slightly more shade-tolerant than couch but is not as resistant to wear, close cutting and dry weather. Blue couch makes a beautiful lawn and is best suited to southern coastal Queensland, the north coast of New South Wales and southern parts of Western Australia. Seed is scarce but available, providing a quicker method of establishment than sprigs; turf is also available. The best time to lay it down is spring or early summer.

Buffalo grass

Buffalo grass has broad, light-green leaves and forms a dense, coarse-textured lawn which resists wear and weeds. It does not set fertile seed and must be established from turf or runners. Buffalo prefers full sunlight but tolerates shade better than most warm-season grasses. It tends to become dense and spongy after a few years and requires frequent cutting and renovation to preserve its well-kept appearance. Generally suited to warm coastal climates, it tolerates heat and dry weather well. Plant runners or lay turf in spring or early summer.

New buffalo cultivars with softer leaves and better shade tolerance are now available. Buffalo is less tolerant than many other grasses to broadleaf weedkillers. The active constituent Dicamba can have a detrimental effect under certain conditions so it is important to only apply a weedkiller that is specifically labelled as safe for buffalo lawns. These are becoming more widely available.

Kikuyu grass

Kikuyu, a native of the highlands of East Africa, is now naturalised in many coastal and inland regions of Australia. It is the most vigorous of all lawn grasses, with stout stolons and rhizomes. For this reason it has often been regarded as undesirable in home gardens. But when kept within bounds, by mower strips and the use of weedkillers, kikuyu makes an attractive, hard-wearing lawn. It stays greener in winter than other warm-season grasses and tolerates partial shade, growing well to the base of trees. It revels in warm weather, tolerates dry spells but needs watering in very hot conditions. Kikuyu responds dramatically to nitrogen fertilisers and the dense turf resists weeds, insects and disease.

Although, at one time, kikuyu seed could

Couch cultivars like Greenlees Park are available from turf suppliers.

Once established, buffalo tolerates heat, dryness and a little bit of shade.

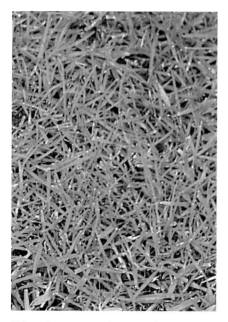

Kikuyu is a very rapid-growing lawn grass.

Durban grass is a shade-tolerant grass for warm climates.

not be purchased in Australia, it is now occasionally available. In late spring or early summer sow 100 per cent kikuyu seed at 125 g per 100 square metres, or blends containing kikuyu and a nursery grass (such as annual rye) at 1 kg per 100 square metres or as directed on the product label. Kikuyu germinates best when soil temperatures are above 21°C. The vigorous seedlings emerge in seven to twenty-one days. Runners can be planted in spring or summer, and kikuyu turf can be laid at almost any time of the year.

Carpet grass

Carpet grass has become naturalised in southern Queensland (where it is often called mat grass) and coastal New South Wales. It is a vigorous grass, spreading by stolons to form a hard-wearing, weed-resistant but rather coarse-textured lawn. Like other warm-season grasses it is dormant in winter. It tolerates shade fairly well and does not become as spongy as buffalo or kikuyu. Generally, carpet grass is suited to warm coastal and subtropical climates. Carpet grass seed is sometimes available but it is usually established from runners. Carpet grass comes in two forms: narrowleaf carpet grass, which is found in subtropical and temperate climates; and broadleaf carpet grass, which is a related species widely used for lawns in tropical regions, including northern Queensland and Darwin.

Durban grass

Durban grass (sweet smother grass) is a broadleafed warm-season grass that is more shade-tolerant than other warm-season grasses. It is used as a ground cover under trees in warmer climates. Durban grass leaves are light to mid-green, very soft, and fairly slow growing but, because it tolerates shade, this grass is gaining in popularity. It will not take close mowing.

Durban grass's broad leaves can be easily damaged by selective herbicides, so test on a small portion before applying to your lawn.

Native lawn grasses

Some Australian native grasses are being used as lawn grasses, with their major advantages being that they require less watering and fertilising than traditional lawn varieties once established. Two of the most popular are wallaby grass and weeping meadow grass

(*Microlaena stipoides*). 'Nara', a commercially developed form of the native *Zoysia macrantha*, is now available as ready-to-lay turf.

Cool-season grasses

Bent grass

Bent grass (also known as New Zealand Bent, Browntop or Highland Bent) was at one time the most widely grown cool-season grass, either by itself or in grass seed mixtures. While it makes a beautiful, evergreen, fine-textured lawn, and is preferred for top-class bowling and golf greens, it is less favoured by home gardeners these days as it requires a continual high level of maintenance.

Bent grass is best suited to cool–temperate or cold climates, but will grow in warmer areas provided plenty of water is applied throughout summer. It prefers full sunlight but will tolerate partial shade and is resistant to wear when very well established.

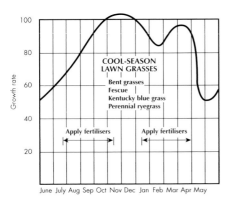

Growth pattern of cool-season grasses.

Sow seed in early spring or autumn. Seedlings emerge in seven to ten days, sometimes sooner in favourable weather.

Kentucky bluegrass

Kentucky bluegrass is hardier than bent grass and makes an attractive lawn. It withstands extreme cold and frosts in climates like Canberra's, where it is often mixed with other cool-season grasses. It also does well in warmer districts of southwestern New South Wales, northern Victoria and South Australia, where it is used in mixtures with rye grass and tall fescue. Kentucky bluegrass

lawns are more resistant to wear than most cool-season grasses, but thin out when poorly grown or too closely cut. Apply fertiliser in both spring and early autumn (but not in summer when it is dormant). Lenient mowing at a cutting height of 3–5 cm is strongly recommended. Sow seed in spring or autumn at 2 kg per 100 square metres. Seedlings emerge in three to four weeks. Kentucky bluegrass has underground rhizomes that rapidly fill worn areas.

Fine fescue

Fine fescue is a name that covers several species with similar features. They include creeping red, Chewings, hard and sheep fescue species. Seeds germinate in seven to fourteen days and seedlings grow quickly. This gives good protection to slower seedlings in the mixture. Fine fescue prefers full sunlight but will tolerate partial shade. It needs lenient mowing and is often used in mixtures with other grasses. Lawn seed mixes recommended for use in shady areas usually contain high percentages of fine fescues (such as Chewings fescue and creeping red fescues).

Perennial ryegrass

Ryegrass mixtures are less expensive than those containing 'fine' turf grasses only. They are popular for play areas, swimming pool surrounds and nature strips. They are widely used to give quick cover for large-scale planting on playing fields and parks. Perennial ryegrass has deep roots and withstands heat and dry weather better than bent grass and Chewings fescue, but requires lenient mowing – a 4 cm cut – for best results. Ryegrass mixtures are sown at heavier rates (typically 3 to 4 kg per 100 square metres) than most other grasses to form an attractive, hard-wearing lawn.

Tall fescue

A great deal of recent research and development has gone into modern, turf-type fescue grasses.

They no longer deserve the title 'tall' as the newer varieties are much more compact in growth and have greater tolerance to low mowing heights. They have a delightful deep-green leaf colour. Tall fescues are non-running grasses that perform best in mixes with other grasses. They are best planted in autumn, as their drought tolerance depends on the establishment of a deep root system, and they perform best if they have time to establish their root system before the onset of very hot and dry weather. Tall fescue is hard-wearing, prefers full sun but tolerates partial shade. Being a drought- and frost-resistant grass, it is suitable for areas that experience cool winters and hot, dry summers. Tall fescues should never be cut lower than 4 cm.

Sow seed in spring and autumn at the rate of 3 to 4 kg per 100 square metres. Seedlings emerge in fourteen to twenty-one days.

Lawn grass mixtures

A wide range of lawn seed mixtures are available in home-garden packs or in bulk for larger areas.

Mixtures containing common perennial ryegrass are economical and give a quick cover for less formal lawns.

All Season is a tall fescue-dominated blend that is ideally suited as a permanent lawn for cooler regions such as Canberra and the tablelands. It can also be used as an oversow blend to repair shade-damaged areas in warm-season lawns. Tall fescue's wide leaf blade makes it the most compatible cool-season grass for blending with popular warm-season grasses such as buffalo or kikuyu.

CARE OF NEW LAWNS
Watering

Lawns sown from seed need frequent watering until the grass is growing strongly. When the grass is about 2 cm high, allow the soil to dry out for a few days to encourage roots to go deeper. Then give a good watering and repeat the process. Unless the weather is very hot, you will find that watering may now be reduced to one good soaking each week. Always aim to wet the soil thoroughly to a depth of 15–20 cm with each watering. Lawns from planted runners need care in watering, too, because there can be a lot of bare soil between individual plants. Again, encourage deep rooting by a few days' spell between waterings. Unless the weather is very hot, lawns from turf will get by with a good soaking each week after laying.

Mowing

Don't allow grass to grow too high before you cut it. When warm-season grasses are 4–5 cm tall, mow with the blades set at 2.5 cm above the soil. This will encourage new shoots at the base of each plant. The next three or four cuts should be repeated at the same height – a light 'topping' only. Most cool-season grasses – ryegrass, fescues and Kentucky bluegrass – should be treated more leniently. The first cut should be made when the grass is 5–6 cm tall with the blades set at least 4 cm above the soil. The ideal practice is to avoid cutting more than one-third of the total height at each cut.

Fertiliser

A pre-sowing or pre-planting fertiliser will keep the new lawn green and vigorous for eight to ten weeks after sowing or planting. At this stage, the need for nitrogen will be increasing. Lack of this nutrient will cause yellowing of leaves and a generally unpromising appearance. Nitrogen fertilisers, such as sulfate of ammonia, can be used occasionally, but a slow release lawn food such as Lawn Master is recommended for regular application. These fertilisers typically contain more than 20 per cent nitrogen in fast and slow release forms that continue feeding for up to three months. Should young grass seedlings be stunted and show a reddish-brown or purple pigment in the leaves, this points to a phosphorus deficiency. It may only occur in patches due to uneven spreading of the base fertiliser. Correct it by watering each discoloured patch with a water-soluble or liquid fertiliser like Thrive All Purpose or Aquasol.

HINT

Before mowing long grass check carefully for toys, hoses and fittings, tools and other bits and pieces which could be damaged by the blades as well as being thrown out as potentially dangerous missiles.

PETER DE WAART
HORTICULTURIST

HINT

If you are doing any maintenance on mowers, don't forget to remove the spark plug or, if electric, make sure the plug is removed from the power point.

PETER DE WAART

HORTICULTURIST

LAWN MAINTENANCE

For good lawn maintenance you must consider the kind of grass and its growing season. Refer to the charts of warm-season grasses on page 273 and cool-season grasses on page 276.

Watering

There are no set rules on when to water or how much water to use. This will depend on the kind of grass, the soil type and the weather conditions. Bent grass and other cool-season grasses need more water than tougher summer growers like couch, especially in hot weather. Heavy soils hold moisture well and may only need a good soaking once or twice a week in summer, but sandy soils may need watering every day or two under the same conditions.

Encourage deep rooting by thorough watering. Frequent surface watering makes for soft, sappy growth which is more prone to disease. Generally, it is best to have a fairly dry surface soil and damp soil below. Check this by removing a square or plug of lawn to see how far water has penetrated. The plug can be replaced without damage to the lawn.

Early morning is the best time to water lawns because the sun will dry out the surface during the day. Watering in the evening or at night creates a high humidity layer in the lawn. This also favours the spread of disease. A very common mistake is to apply too much water, especially on couch and other summer growers which are dormant in winter. Watering at this time of the year does nothing for the lawn and very often encourages annual weeds like winter grass to germinate and grow.

Fertilisers and lime

Only fertilise lawns when they are growing or starting to grow actively. This is when they make best use of it. Use lawn foods which are high in nitrogen, because this is the nutrient removed in greatest amounts in grass clippings. Apply high nitrogen, slow release lawn fertilisers at a rate of 2 kg per 100 square metres every three months while the lawn is actively growing (check product labels for detailed directions) or, alternatively, apply non-slow-release lawn fertilisers (that usually contain about 10 per cent nitrogen) at a rate of about 3 kg per 100 square metres every five or six weeks during the growing season: for summer growers, from spring through to autumn; for cool-season grasses, from late winter to early summer and again from late summer to autumn. Except in tropical and subtropical climates with very mild winters, fertilising lawns in the colder months is unnecessary and wasteful.

When applying fertilisers, make sure to spread them evenly. Some advanced slow-release fertilisers have very low burn potential so don't have to be watered in immediately. However, it's always best to water immediately after application to activate the fertiliser and ensure rapid lawn greening. Most other lawn fertilisers must be watered in well immediately to avoid damage caused by fertiliser burn. Some lawn foods are soluble and may be applied with a watering-can or through a hose-end sprayer. Continuous use of sulfate of ammonia, or of lawn foods containing it, increases soil acidity. Couch and Queensland blue couch lawns do not thrive on acid soils, although bent grass is less particular. The degree of acidity can only be determined accurately by a soil test. In high rainfall districts a general recommendation is to apply lime at 25 kg per 100 square metres every second or third year.

Mowing

Always mow lawns regularly at a constant cutting height. This develops a balance between the shoot and root system. Mowing too closely results in shallow roots and weakens the turf, which in turn encourages weeds. Close mowing of couch in autumn causes premature browning and interferes with food storage in the stolons (sideways growth), on which spring growth depends.

For home lawns made up of warm-season grasses or bent grass, a cutting height of at least 2 cm is suitable. A slightly higher cut of 2.5 cm helps to lower soil temperatures in summer. Kentucky bluegrass, ryegrass and fescues need a higher cut at all times (at least 4 cm). In the growing season, mow once each week, but during winter mowing every four or five weeks will probably be sufficient. Remove the clippings to improve the appearance of the lawn and provide material for compost, or use a mulching mower. Removing clippings also helps to prevent a spongy surface developing, especially in running grasses. Clippings left on the lawn surface can form matted clumps that damage the lawn. But removing clippings takes away some nutrients from the soil. This is one reason for a good fertilising regime.

Renovation

Renovation is any mechanical measure to improve the surface of lawns and to allow free entry of air, water and nutrients. Always renovate lawns when they will recover quickly – in spring for summer growers, in late winter or early autumn for the cool-season grasses.

'Mat' or 'thatch' is an undecomposed layer of old roots and runners which builds up between the grass leaves and the soil. Thatch prevents the entry of air, water and fertilisers into the soil. To get rid of it, cut the lawn closely and rake severely. Then cut again and repeat the raking until there is a bare cover of grass over the soil. Follow with fertiliser and water well. The use of organic lawn fertilisers (like Dynamic Lifter) can help reduce thatch as they will encourage breakdown of lawn clippings.

Bare patches may occur in compacted heavy soil, or perhaps as a result of severe traffic. Compacted soil, like thatch, prevents the entry of air, water and nutrients to the roots of the grass. Give the soil a thorough soaking and use a garden fork to penetrate the soil 10–15 cm deep and the same distance apart. Work the fork back and forth to enlarge the holes. Special hollow-tined forks can be bought for this coring treatment, and mechanical corers can be hired for very large areas.

Topdressing

Fortunately for most gardeners, topdressing is no longer the annual ritual advocated in the past. The main purpose of topdressing is to correct any unevenness in the lawn surface, so it is still very important in turf used for cricket, tennis, bowls and golf putting greens. It has little place in home lawns once the correct levels and grades are made. Topdressing is useful as a light soil covering after de-thatching or coring, and also for oversowing cool-season grasses on couch lawns in autumn.

Soils for topdressing are usually light, sandy loams and provide little in the way of nutrients; that is, they are no substitute for fertilisers. If topdressing is used for any reason, spread it thinly with the back of a rake or a dummy rake. Do not bury the grass completely, as deep covering will retard it. After rubbing in the topdressing, at least half of the grass leaf blades should show through the soil. Usually, a bucket of topdressing soil per square metre is sufficient. Apply a mixed fertiliser at the recommended rate.

Weed control

A healthy, vigorous turf which is difficult for weeds to invade is the first line of defence in the battle for weed control. Adequate and regular fertilising is essential to achieving this. Low nutrient supply means poor, open turf which invites weed invasion. Nitrogen and potassium are the key nutrient elements necessary in achieving excellent turf growth. Phosphorus needs to be supplied during establishment, but once the turf is growing well, special lawn fertilisers that have a low phosphorus content will give best grass growth and will discourage the growth of clovers and some grass weeds. Deep but infrequent watering and regular mowing are important factors in having a weed-free lawn. A wide range of herbicides (or weedicides) can be applied to lawns as selective sprays. These chemicals, together with those to control insects and diseases in lawns, are discussed in Chapter 8.

GROUND COVERS

A grass lawn is the most popular ground cover but there are some situations where grass will not grow, is difficult to maintain or

Lawn Pests

PEST	SYMPTOMS	MOST OBVIOUS	CONTROL
Army worm/ lawn grub	Feed on grasses, chewing them off at ground level. They do not eat roots. Leave tunnels (of about 1–2 mm diameter) and soil casts with silken threads. Grub is a grey colour with dark head; grows up to 6 cm.	December– March	Nature's Way Dipel or Complete Lawn Insect Control applied as soon as pests occur. Both are most effective if applied late in the day.
Lawn beetle	Grubs (Curl grubs or cockchafers) feed on roots, causing yellow patches and stunted lawn growth. Adult beetles feed on foliage taking notch-shaped bites and can cause considerable damage on ornamentals in November.	Spring–summer	Apply Baythroid Lawn & Garden Grub Insecticide as the adults emerge. Apply Complete Lawn Insect Control in spring to give season-long control.

ought not to be grown. Such situations include shady areas under trees, steep banks which are difficult to mow, rocky outcrops, and damp, soggy spots with poor drainage. The answer to these problem areas is ground cover. Even gravel, pebbles, quartz chips and pine bark can be considered as ground covers. The materials can be used alone or can be combined with plants. Very often the best solution to a damp, shaded area is a mulch of one or other of these materials softened by shade-loving plants such as plantain lily (*Hosta*), saxifraga (*Bergenia*), bugle flower (*Ajuga*) or native violet (*Viola hederacea*).

Most ground-cover plants are prostrate perennials that spread rapidly by above-ground stolons or underground rhizomes. When established, ground covers need little attention and maintenance. An annual dressing of fertiliser – slow-release fertilisers are the most suitable – and occasional pruning to keep the plants from getting out of hand is about all that is necessary.

It does pay dividends to prepare the site thoroughly before you establish your ground cover. If possible, start preparations in winter and keep the soil cultivated through the spring months to destroy weeds, especially perennial weeds with persistent underground parts. The weedicide glyphosate, known as Zero, is very useful because it does not have a long term effect on the soil. Early summer is a good time for planting. Close planting will give a quick cover (assisted by a scattering a mixed fertiliser, such as Dynamic Lifter pellets, before planting). You may need to continue with some weeding until the ground cover is well established and forms a dense mat.

On a bank or sloping site, prostrate shrubs can be used to bind the soil and form a weed-resistant cover. One of the best native shrubs is *Grevillea* 'Poorinda Royal Mantle'. It has 10 cm-long, lobed, green leaves and red toothbrush-shaped flowers. Another attractive, shrubby ground cover is shore juniper (*Juniperus conferta*), which has tiny, grey-green leaves and grows to 60 cm in height. Creeping juniper (*J. horizontalis*) is not quite so tall (30 cm), but spreads over the ground covering 2–3 m. Bulbous plants like agapanthus, clivia and hemerocallis are also good, low-maintenance soil binders for steep banks.

Climbing plants are very suitable for ground covers on sloping or flat sites. Star jasmine (*Trachelospermum jasminoides*) is one of the most popular. There is a pretty, variegated variety of this adaptable plant. Creeping boobialla (*Myoporum parvifolium*) is another attractive ground-cover plant. It forms a dense, green mat with white, tubular flowers followed by purple berries. Other climbing plants which are useful for soil binding or covering rock faces are Australian sarsparilla (*Hardenbergia*), creeping fig (*Ficus pumila*), Virginia creeper (*Parthenocissus*) and ivy geranium (*Pelargonium*).

Many perennials make suitable ground covers, among them bugle flower (*Ajuga*), chamomile (*Anthemis*), ground morning glory (*Convolvulus*), pig face (*Mesembryanthemum* or *Carpobrotus*), lamb's ear (*Stachys byzantina*), snow-in-summer (*Cerastium*) and violets (*Viola odorata*).

Other widely grown ground covers are Japanese spurge (*Pachysandra*), with glossy foliage and greenish-white flowers; London pride (*Crassula*), a shrubby succulent with oval leaves and small, pink flowers; Spanish shawl (*Schizocentron*), with a dense mat of short foliage and small carmine flowers; periwinkle (*Vinca*), with glossy green or variegated leaves and blue or mauve flowers; and thyme (*Thymus*), of which there are many forms, all with aromatic leaves. Lemon-scented thyme (*T. citriodorus*) and wild thyme (*T. serpyllum*) are both prostrate, creeping species. Creeping mint (*Mentha requienii*) is also a good carpeting plant with aromatic leaves. Lippia (*Lippia nodiflora*), which forms a loose mat of small leaves with clusters of tiny white flowers, is a very popular ground cover in South Australia but may become weedy in some areas. Most of these ground covers will tolerate some shade but not heavy traffic. You will need to lay stepping stones or paving blocks or make a pathway in areas where people are likely to walk.

Top five exotic ground covers

SPANISH SHAWL

When this mat-growing plant produces its mass of rosy purple flowers, you can see why it's called 'Spanish Shawl'. Protect from frost.

IVY GERANIUM

Smooth, shiny, slightly ivy-shaped leaves make a perfect foil for clusters of brightly coloured flowers on these easily grown plants. Plenty of sun is essential.

SHORE JUNIPER

This low-growing conifer is remarkably hardy and is especially useful in exposed coastal locations.

CREEPING THYME

Good for carpeting small areas, creeping thyme will release its attractive perfume when walked on or brushed against. It won't, however, take heavy traffic.

CONVOLVULUS SABATIUS

This sweet little plant develops a dense carpet of grey-green leaves that are studded with lavender-blue blooms throughout the warm season.

JUNIPER

THYME

15
The Flower Garden

There are many hundreds of flowering plants available around the world, but in this chapter we are concentrating on those of most interest to Australian home gardeners. Space dictates that full growing details for a particular variety – soil preparation and cultivation – are only given where there is a special requirement. New gardeners would probably find it helpful to read the general information on soil and fertilisers in Chapters 4 and 5, and the methods for sowing seed and raising seedlings in Chapter 9.

TYPES OF FLOWERING PLANTS

Annuals

These plants complete their life span in one year, and most of them flower in three to four months from the time of sowing. Flowering finishes as the seeds ripen and the plants die. Annuals are divided into two groups: summer-flowering and winter/spring-flowering. The former are sown in spring; the latter in summer and autumn. Some flowers have both annual and perennial varieties – gypsophila and statice are good examples. Many so-called annuals are really short-lived perennials. In cool climates they may last for three or four years, but in warmer districts their effective life is much shorter as they have difficulty surviving hot summers.

Annual flowers are always favourites for the home garden; no other plants give such a colourful display in such a short time and for so little trouble. They can be changed seasonally to create varied effects and colour combinations. The brilliant colours look wonderful in large masses, clumps or drifts, but they can be used effectively in containers or narrow borders too. Annuals complement other garden plantings and can be arranged so that flowers are in bloom (except in the very coldest districts) at almost any time of the year.

Biennials

These plants usually live for two years and, in cool climates, they may not flower until the second year. In warmer areas, however, they often flower in the first year. Then, at the end of this first flowering, the leaves die back or the plant becomes dormant. As the flowering period comes around again, the plants break into fresh growth and another flowering follows. After this second flowering the plants die.

Cool and temperate climates suit most biennials, but there are a few exceptions that only do well in areas with very cold winters. Many others will grow successfully in warm climates if treated as annuals. It is the cooler conditions between flowerings which encourage the dormant period. Without a cold period, the plant is less likely to make a good flush of growth in the second year. In cold climates, biennials are usually sown in spring.

Perennials

This term applies to plants which have an effective life of three years or more. Some, under favourable conditions – especially in cool climates – may remain in the garden permanently. But in this chapter we will concentrate on those perennials which flower the first season from seed. Most perennials bloom at the same time each year, but a few, such as carnations, have been bred and selected to bloom over a longer time. As a rule, perennials which flower quickly from sowing seed (say, within six months) should be freshly sown each year, especially in warm climates. This does not mean that some, for example snapdragons, will not stand cutting back at least once to give a good display at their second flowering. The term 'herbaceous perennial' refers to soft leafed flowering plants that die back completely each winter. Herbaceous borders are great features of many English gardens. They are used less here but Australia has some good examples, especially in cooler areas.

Flowering bulbs, like anemones and ranunculus, are perennials because under good conditions they continue to flower each season without special attention. Dahlias, which are grown from tubers, are included in the same category because the tubers carry over from year to year. However, bulbous-type plants like these are not usually classified as perennials in the same way as carnations and hollyhocks, where it is the plant itself which persists.

Carnations, chrysanthemums, dahlias and some other perennials may be propagated from seed or by vegetative methods: plant division, cuttings or layers. (See Chapter 10.) They are not always grown from seed because most named varieties do not breed true to type. Plants grown from seed will vary in type and colour.

DWARF, MEDIUM AND TALL FLOWERS

Dwarf flowers — 30 cm or less

Ageratum, alyssum, aster (dwarf), begonia (bedding), bellis (English daisy), calendula, candytuft, carnation, celosia (dwarf), chrysanthemum (dwarf), cineraria (dwarf), cockscomb, dianthus, Californian poppy, forget-me-not, fairy pinks, gazania, globe amaranth, godetia (dwarf), impatiens, linaria, livingstone daisy, lobelia, marigold (dwarf), mignonette, nasturtium (dwarf), nemesia (dwarf), nemophila, nigella, ornamental basil, ornamental chilli, pansy, phlox (dwarf), polyanthus, portulaca, primula, salvia (dwarf), stock (dwarf), sweet pea (dwarf), torenia, verbena, viola, Virginian stock, zinnia (dwarf).

Medium-height flowers — 30–60 cm

Acroclinium (everlasting daisy), antirrhinum (snapdragon), aquilegia (columbine), aster, aurora daisy, balsam, boronia, brachyscome (Swan River daisy), calendula, candytuft, Canterbury bells, carnation, celosia,

centaurea (cornflower), chrysanthemum, cineraria, coleus, dahlia (dwarf), dianthus, gaillardia, geranium, gerbera, godetia, gomphrena (globe amaranth), gypsophila, helichrysum (strawflower), honesty, linaria, lupin, French marigold, molucella (Irish green bell), nasturtium, ornamental chilli, petunia, phlox, poppy (Iceland), rudbeckia (gloriosa daisy), salpiglossis, salvia, saponaria (big gyp), schizanthus, statice, stock, sweet William, viscaria, wallflower, zinnia.

Tall flowers — 60 cm or over

Amaranthus, aster, cleome, cosmos, chrysanthemum, dahlia, delphinium, hollyhock, larkspur, lupin (tall), marigold (tall), salvia (tall), scabiosa, sunflower, sweet pea, zinnia (tall).

FLOWERS FOR SHADE OR SEMI-SHADE

Ageratum, alyssum, aquilegia, begonia (bedding), calendula, cineraria, coleus, cyclamen, Canterbury bells, forget-me-not, foxglove, impatiens, linaria, lobelia, mimulus, nasturtium, nigella, pansy, polyanthus, primula, schizanthus, viola, Virginian stock, wallflower. (Viola and pansy require at least half sunlight.)

SPRING FLOWERS

Acroclinium, ageratum, alyssum, antirrhinum, aquilegia, candytuft, Canterbury bells, centaurea, annual chrysanthemum, cineraria, delphinium, dianthus, forget-me-not, gaillardia, godetia, gypsophila, helichrysum, larkspur, linaria, lobelia, French marigold, mignonette, nasturtium, nemesia, pansy, polyanthus, poppy, primula, saponaria, scabiosa, schizanthus, statice, stock, sweet pea, sweet William, viola, wallflower.

SUMMER AND AUTUMN FLOWERS

Amaranthus, antirrhinum, aster, balsam, begonia (bedding), carnation, celosia, chrysanthemum (perennial), cockscomb, dahlia, dianthus, Californian poppy, gaillardia, gerbera, gomphrena, gypsophila, African marigold, petunia, phlox, portulaca, salpiglossis, salvia, sunflower, torenia, verbena, viscaria, zinnia.

Garden flowers of varying heights can add interest to a landscape.

Sowing Guide for Flowers

FLOWER	TROPICAL/SUBTROPICAL • / SUBTROPICAL ONLY ▲ / TROPICAL ONLY ■												TEMPERATE											
	J	F	M	A	M	J	J	A	S	O	N	D	J	F	M	A	M	J	J	A	S	O	N	D
Acroclinium (see Everlasting daisy)																								
Ageratum	•	•	•	•	•	•	•	•	•	•	•		•	•	•	•	•			•	•	•	•	•
Alyssum	▲	•	•	•	•	•	▲						•	•	•	•	•			•	•	•	•	•
Amaranthus				•	•	•	•	•												•	•	•	•	•
Antirrhinum (see Snapdragon)																								
Aquilegia (Columbine)		•	•	•										•	•	•	•							
Arctotis (Aurora daisy)		•	•	•	•	•	•	•						•	•	•	•							
Aster	•			■	■	•	•	•	•	•	•	•							•	•	•	•	•	•
Aurora daisy (see Arctotis)																								
Baby blue eyes (see Nemophila)																								
Balsam	•	•		■	■	•	•	•	•	•											•	•	•	•
Begonia, bedding				•	•	•	•	•	•												•	•	•	•
Begonia, tuberous				•	•	•	•														•	•	•	•
Bellis (English daisy)		•	•	•	•									•	•	•	•							
Big gyp (Saponaria)		•	•	•	•	•	•	•	•					•	•	•	•							
Boronia				•	•	•	•						•	•	•	•	•			•	•	•	•	•
Brachyscome (see Swan River daisy)																								
Calceolaria		•	•	•	•								•	•	•	•								
Calendula (English marigold)		•	•	•	•			•	•	•			•	•	•	•	•							
Californian poppy (Eschscholtzia)				•	•	•	•	•	•											•	•	•	•	•
Candytuft		•	•	•	•	▲							•	•	•	•	•	•						
Canterbury bells														•	•	•	•	•	•					
Carnation		•	•	•	•	•	•	•						•	•	•					•	•	•	
Celosia	•	•			■	•	•	•	•	•	•	•								•	•	•	•	•

COLD (sowing months, J–D)	HOW TO SOW: SEED TRAYS (S) DIRECT (D)	SOWING DEPTH (MM)	SEEDLINGS EMERGE (DAYS)	TRANSPLANT OR SOW DIRECT AND THIN TO ... CM APART	APPROX. TIME TO FLOWERING (WEEKS)
J F · · · · · · S O N D	S or D	6	14–21	15–20	12
J F M A · · · · S O N D	S or D	2	10–14	7-10	8
· · · A · J · A · · · ·	D	6	14–21	40	14
· F M A · · · A · · · ·	S	3	21–28	30–40	28
· F M A · J · A · · · ·	S or D	6	18–21	30–40	16
· · · A · J · A S · · ·	S	2	10–14	20–30	14
· · · · · · · A S O N ·	S or D	2	10–14	30	8–12
· · · · · J · A · O · ·	S	1	14–21	20	16
· · · · · J · A · O · ·	S	1	14–21	pots	28
· F M A · · · A · O · ·	S	3	10–14	10–15	12
J F M A · J · A S O N D	D	6	14–21	20–30	8
· · · · · · · A S O · ·	S or D	3	45–70	40	56
J · · · · · · A S O N ·	S	12	14–21	pots	20
· F M A · · · A · O · ·	S or D	12	10–14	40	10
· · · · · · · A S O N ·	S or D	3	10–14	30	8
· F M A · · · A · O · ·	D	6	14–21	20–30	12
· F M A · · · · · · · ·	S	1	14–21	30	14–24
J F M A · · · A S O · ·	S	6	10–14	30–40	28
· · · · · · · · S O N ·	S or D	6	10–14	20–30	12

Legend for the months columns: the first group of months (J–D) is **TROPICAL/SUBTROPICAL ●**, **SUBTROPICAL ONLY ▲**, **TROPICAL ONLY ■**; the second group of months (J–D) is **TEMPERATE**.

FLOWER	J	F	M	A	M	J	J	A	S	O	N	D	J	F	M	A	M	J	J	A	S	O	N	D
Centaurea (see Cornflower)																								
Chrysanthemum (Painted daisy and Star daisy)			•	•	•	•	•												•	•	•	•		
Cineraria			•	•	•	•								•	•	•	•							
Cleome (see Spider flower)																								
Cockscomb	•	•			■	•	•	•	•	•	■	■							•	•	•	•	•	•
Coleus	•	•	•	•	•	•	•	•	•	•	•								•	•	•	•	•	•
Columbine (see Aquilegia)																								
Coreopsis			•	•	•	•	•	•	•	•					•	•	•				•	•	•	
Cornflower (Centaurea)			•	•	•	•	•							•	•	•	•							
Cosmos					•	•	•	•	•	•										•	•	•	•	•
Cyclamen	•	•	•	•	•	•							•	•	•	•	•	•						•
Dahlia (seed)					•	•	•	•	•	•											•	•	•	•
Delphinium			•	•	•								•	•	•	•	•	•	•	•				
Dianthus			•	•	•	•	•	•	•	•				•	•	•	•	•	•	•	•			
English daisy (see Bellis)																								
English marigold (see Calendula)																								
Eschscholtzia (see Californian poppy)																								
Everlasting daisy (Acroclinium)			•	•	•	•	•	•	•				•	•	•	•					•	•	•	
Forget-me-not			•	•	•								•	•	•	•	•	•						
Foxglove			•	•	•								•	•	•	•								
Gaillardia	■		•	•	•	•	•	•	•	•				•	•	•	•				•	•	•	
Gazania					•	•	•	•	•											•	•	•	•	•
Geranium (seed)					•	•	•	•	•										•	•	•	•	•	
Gerbera	■	■	■	■	•	•	•	•	•										•	•	•	•	•	•

J	F	M	A	M	J	J	A	S	O	N	D	HOW TO SOW: SEED TRAYS (S) DIRECT (D)	SOWING DEPTH (MM)	SEEDLINGS EMERGE (DAYS)	TRANSPLANT OR SOW DIRECT AND THIN TO ... CM APART	APPROX. TIME TO FLOWERING (WEEKS)
								•	•	•	•	S	3	14–21	30	18–20
•	•	•	•									S	1	10–14	30–40	20
								•	•	•		S or D	6	10–14	30	12
							•	•	•	•		S	1	14–21	30 or pots	10
							•	•	•	•		S	6	7–21	30	12
•	•	•				•	•					S or D	3	14–21	40–50	14
							•	•	•	•		S or D	6	14–21	40–50	12
•	•	•	•						•			S	3	28–42	Pots	64
							•	•	•	•		S or D	12	14–28	50–100	16
•	•	•				•	•					S	3	21–28	50	20
•	•	•				•	•					S orD	3	10–14	15–30	20
•	•	•				•	•					S or D	12	21–28	20–30	14
•	•	•	•							•		D	3	21–28	20–30	12
•	•	•										S or D	3	14–21	50	20
•	•	•				•	•					S or D	6	14–21	30	16
							•	•	•	•		S or D	6	14–21	20	12
							•	•	•	•		S	3	14–28	40–50	16
							•	•	•	•		S	1	14–21	40–50	30–50

COLD

Flower	Tropical/Subtropical ● Subtropical only ▲ Tropical only ■												Temperate											
	J	F	M	A	M	J	J	A	S	O	N	D	J	F	M	A	M	J	J	A	S	O	N	D
Gloxinia					●	●	●	●	●												●	●	●	●
Godetia		●	●	●	●								●	●	●	●	●	●						
Gomphrena (Globe amaranth)	●	●	●	●	●	■	■	●	●	●	●	●								●	●	●	●	●
Gypsophila		●	●	●	●								●	●	●	●	●	●	●	●				
Helianthus (see Sunflower)																								
Hollyhock		●	●	●	●								●	●	●	●								
Honesty (Lunaria)		●	●	●	●	●	●	●					●	●	●	●					●	●	●	●
Impatiens	●	●	●	●	●	●	●	●	●	●	●		●	●	●	●					●	●	●	●
Irish green bellflower (Molucella)				●	●	●	●	●	●							●	●	●	●		●	●	●	
Kangaroo paw						●	●	●													●	●	●	
Larkspur				●	●	●							●	●	●	●	●							
Linaria		●	●	●	●	●	●						●	●	●	●	●	●						
Livingstone daisy (Dorotheanthus)		●	●	●	●								●	●	●	●								
Lobelia		●	●	●	●								●	●	●	●								
Lunaria (see Honesty)																								
Malope		●	●	●	●	●	●	●					●	●	●	●	●	●	●					
Marigold, African	●	●	●	●	●	●	●	●	●	●	●							●	●	●	●	●	●	●
Marigold, French	●	●	●	●	■	■	■	●	●	●	●	●	●	●	●									
Marmalade daisy (see Rudbeckia)																								
Mexican sunflower (Tithonia)						●	●	●	●	●	●	●									●	●	●	●

COLD (J F M A M J J A S O N D)	HOW TO SOW: SEED TRAYS (S) DIRECT (D)	SOWING DEPTH (MM)	SEEDLINGS EMERGE (DAYS)	TRANSPLANT OR SOW DIRECT AND THIN TO ... CM APART	APPROX. TIME TO FLOWERING (WEEKS)
• • •	S	3	21–28	pots	30
• • • • •	S or D	6	10–14	30	12
• • • •	S or D	6	14–21	30	12
• • • • • • • • • •	D	6	10–14	20–30	10
• • • •	S	6	14–21	30–40	28
• • • • •	S	3	14–21	40–50	12
• • • • •	S	1	14–21	30–40	12
• • • • • •	D	6	14–21	20–30	12
• • •	S	6	30–90	40–60	16
• •	D	3	14–21	20–30	20
• • • • •	D	3	10–14	10–15	10
• • • • •	S or D	3	14–21	10–15	20
• • • • •	S	1	10–14	10	14
• •	S or D	5	14–21	25–30	12–14
• • • •	S or D	6	10–14	20–40	12
• • • • •	S or D	6	10–14	20–40	12
• • • •	D	5	7–21	60	12

FLOWER	TROPICAL/SUBTROPICAL ● SUBTROPICAL ONLY ▲ TROPICAL ONLY ■												TEMPERATE											
	J	F	M	A	M	J	J	A	S	O	N	D	J	F	M	A	M	J	J	A	S	O	N	D
Mignonette	•	•	•	•	•								•	•	•	•	•	•	•	•	•	•		
Molucella (see Irish green bellflower)																								
Nasturtium	•	•	•	•	•	•	•	•	•				•	•						•	•	•	•	•
Nemesia	•	•	•	•	•								•	•	•	•								
Nemophila (Baby blue eyes)	•	•	•										•	•	•	•								
Nigella	•	•	•	•	•								•	•	•	•								
Ornamental basil		■	■	•					•	•	•		•	•	•						•	•	•	•
Ornamental chilli		■	■	•	•	•	•	•												•	•	•	•	•
Painted daisy (Chrysanthemum carinatum)	•	•	•	•									•	•	•	•	•	•						
Pansy	•	•	•	•									•	•	•	•	•							
Petunia		■	■	•	•	•	•	•											•	•	•	•	•	•
Phlox		■	■	■	•	•	•	•											•	•	•	•	•	•
Pin-cushion flower (see Scabiosa)																								
Pinks (see Dianthus)																								
Polyanthus	•	•	•	•									•	•	•	•								
Poor man's orchid (Schizanthus)	•	•	•	•	•								•	•	•	•								
Poppy, Iceland	•	•	•	•	•								•	•	•	•	•							
Portulaca			•	•	•	•	•													•	•	•	•	•
Primula	•	•	•	•									•	•	•	•								
Rudbeckia (Marmalade daisy)			•	•	•	•	•	•												•	•	•	•	•
Salpiglossis	■	■	■	■	■	■	■	•	•	•	•									•	•	•	•	•
Salvia	•	•	•	•	•	•	•	•	•	•	•									•	•	•	•	•
Saponaria (see Big gyp)																								

				COLD								HOW TO SOW: SEED TRAYS (S) DIRECT (D)	SOWING DEPTH (MM)	SEEDLINGS EMERGE (DAYS)	TRANSPLANT OR SOW DIRECT AND THIN TO ... CM APART	APPROX. TIME TO FLOWERING (WEEKS)
J	F	M	A	M	J	J	A	S	O	N	D					
•	•							•	•	•		D	3	15–20	15–20	12
								•	•	•	•	D	12	14–21	20–30	10–12
								•	•			S or D	6	10–14	15–20	14
•	•	•						•	•			D	3	10–14	15	12–14
•	•	•										S	3	21–28	20	14
								•	•	•	•	S or D	6	10–14	20–30	–
								•	•	•	•	S or D	6	10–14	60	20
•	•	•						•	•			S	6	14–21	40–50	12–14
•	•	•	•					•	•			S	6	21–28	20–30	16
								•	•	•	•	S	1	10–14	25–40	12
								•	•	•	•	S or D	3	14–21	10–15	10
•	•	•	•									S	3	21–28	15–20	24
•	•	•	•									S	3	14–21	30	14
•	•	•	•									S	3	10–14	20-30	24
								•	•	•	•	S or D	6	10–14	10	6
•	•	•	•									S	3	21–28	15–20	24
								•	•	•		S or D	1	10–20	30	12–16
								•	•	•		D	3	14–21	15	12–14
								•	•	•	•	S or D	3	14–21	20–40	12

FLOWER	TROPICAL/SUBTROPICAL ● SUBTROPICAL ONLY ▲ TROPICAL ONLY ■												TEMPERATE											
	J	F	M	A	M	J	J	A	S	O	N	D	J	F	M	A	M	J	J	A	S	O	N	D
Scabiosa (Pin-cushion flower)	•	•	•	•	•								•	•	•	•								
Schizanthus (see Poor man's orchid)																								
Snapdragon (Antirrhinum)			•	•	•	•	•	•	•	•	•			•	•	•			•	•	•	•	•	•
Spider flower (Cleome)	•	•	•	•	•	•	•	•					•							•	•	•	•	•
Star daisy (see Chrysanthemum)																								
Statice			•	•	•	•	•	•					•	•	•	•	•	•	•	•	•			
Stock			•	•	•	•							•	•	•	•	•	•						
Sturt's desert pea (Swainsona)				•	•	•	•												•	•	•	•	•	•
Sunflower (Helianthus)	•	•	•	•	•	■	■	•	•	•	•	•							•	•	•	•	•	•
Swan River daisy (Brachyscome)				•	•	•	•												•	•	•	•	•	•
Sweet pea	■	•	•	•										•	•	•								
Sweet William (see Dianthus)																								
Torenia	•	•	•	■	■	■	■	•	•	•	•								•	•	•	•	•	•
Verbena			•	•	•	•	•	•	•	•	•		•	•					•	•	•	•	•	•
Vinca	•	•	•	•				•	•	•	•	•									•	•	•	•
Viola			•	•	•	•							•	•	•	•	•	•						
Virginian stock			•	•	•										•	•	•	•						
Viscaria				•	•	•	•												•	•	•	•	•	•
Wallflower			•	•	•	•							•	•	•	•	•	•						
Waratah				•	•	•	•												•	•	•	•	•	•
Zinnia	•	•	■	■	■	■	•	•	•	•	•								•	•	•	•	•	•

COLD												HOW TO SOW: SEED TRAYS (S) DIRECT (D)	SOWING DEPTH (MM)	SEEDLINGS EMERGE (DAYS)	TRANSPLANT OR SOW DIRECT AND THIN TO ...CM APART	APPROX. TIME TO FLOWERING (WEEKS)
J	F	M	A	M	J	J	A	S	O	N	D					
	•	•	•						•	•		S or D	6	14–21	40	14
								•	•	•	•	S	1	10–14	25–40	16
								•	•	•	•	S or D	3	14–21	50–60	12
	•	•	•						•	•		D	6	14–28	30–40	20
•	•	•	•									S or D	3	10–14	20–40	20
								•	•	•	•	D	6	14–28	40	24
								•	•	•	•	S or D	12	10–14	50–60	12
								•	•	•	•	S or D	3	14–21	20	16
	•	•	•						•	•		D	25	10–14	5–7	14
								•	•	•	•	S or D	2	10–14	15–20	16
•								•	•	•	•	S or D	6	21-28	25–30	10
								•	•	•	•	S or D	2	7–10	20–30	11–12
•	•	•						•				S	6	21–28	20	16
	•	•	•						•	•		D	3	10	15	14
								•	•	•	•	D	6	14–21	15	12
•	•	•	•									S	6	10–14	20–30	24
								•	•	•	•	S	12	21–28	120	50–100
								•	•	•	•	S or D	6	7–10	20-40	12

HOW TO GROW INDIVIDUAL FLOWERS

Acroclinium
See Everlasting daisy.

Ageratum
Sometimes known as floss flower, ageratum, an attractive blue annual, is usually grown for spring, summer and autumn display.

All ageratum varieties make splendid border plants, and their soft blue flowers are excellent for garden display and indoor decoration. They will succeed in a variety of soils but respond to good conditions and added fertiliser. They are fairly drought-resistant but need regular watering in dry weather. They are at their best when grown in full sunlight, but will give reasonable results in semi-shade.

HINT
Plunging cut flowers into cold water will extend their life in a vase. Just before arranging, re-cut the stems by 2 cm and quickly plunge them into the water; this helps them to draw up as much water as possible.

MARK HAY

GARDEN CENTRE PROPRIETOR, FORMER TV AND RADIO TALKBACK HORTICULTURAL HOST, GARDEN ADVISER

In warm climates you can sow seed in almost all seasons, but in cold districts spring and summer sowings are best. Seed can either be sown in seed beds, and the seedlings transplanted, or sown direct in the garden bed. The seeds need light for germination so press them into the top of the seed-raising mix or soil and keep moist until seedlings emerge. Seedlings are transplanted or thinned to a distance of 15–20 cm apart. Plants need very little care apart from normal cultivation and watering. Liquid feeds of Thrive or Aquasol at regular intervals will promote flowering. Cut back all spent blooms to prevent self-seeding (they can be weedy in warm climates). 'Blue Mink' is a popular dwarf variety.

Alyssum
Sweet Alice, as this plant is often called, is popular for edging and borders. Alyssum is renowned as a bee attractant so can be planted to attract pollinators to the garden. It is ideal for rockeries and wall gardens, as it flowers all the year in most climates. It does quite well in semi-shade but flowering is more prolific in open sunlight. It grows well in all types of soils, but thrives in good, friable soil with added fertiliser. Good drainage is essential as it resents damp conditions.

In temperate climates you can sow seed at almost any time of the year but in cold districts it is best to sow during spring and autumn. Seedlings can be raised in pots or punnets for transplanting, or seed can be sown direct in the garden in clumps 7–10 cm apart and thinned as necessary. Cover seeds lightly with vermiculite or seed-raising mix and keep damp until seedlings emerge. Water plants regularly in dry weather, giving a good soaking once or twice a week rather than frequent sprinkling. Control weeds while they are small, otherwise the fine roots of the plants will be damaged when large weeds are pulled out. Give regular liquid feeds of soluble fertiliser as plants grow. This will promote flowering over a longer period. Cut back plants after flushes of flowering.

Varieties
'Carpet of Snow' has masses of pure white flowers on dwarf bushes 10 cm tall. It is excellent for borders and edging, in rockeries and between bricks or stones in paths or paving. 'Royal Carpet' has deep-violet flowers on bushes the same height as 'Carpet of Snow', with which it combines for a beautiful colour combination. 'Cameo Mixture' is a delightful blend of mixed colours and is ideal for mass planting. *A. saxatile* (now known as *Aurinia saxatile*) grows to about 15 cm with clusters of deep-yellow flowers. It is spring-blooming but plants last two to three years. Alyssum is ideal for borders, mass planting and for adding colour to rockeries.

Amaranthus
This summer annual has made a return to popularity. It is grown for its brilliant foliage

and its ability to stand very hot weather.

Plants grow to 1–2 m tall. Amaranthus revels in hot, sunny situations, but requires ample water during dry times. Prepare soil well a week or two before planting by blending in aged manure or compost, plus a mixed fertiliser such as Dynamic Lifter.

Sowings can be made in spring when the danger of frost is over and can be continued until early summer. It is best to sow a few seeds direct in the garden in clumps 40 cm apart and thin out to one or two seedlings. You can also raise seedlings and transplant to the same distance apart. Cover seed with vermiculite or seed-raising mix and keep damp until seedlings emerge. If transplanting seedlings, discard any paler plants that aren't well coloured. Water regularly while plants are growing and keep weeds under control. As hot weather approaches, a mulch of compost or grass clippings will protect shallow roots and conserve moisture. When the plants are about 30 cm tall, begin giving liquid feeds of soluble fertilisers and repeat this treatment every ten to fourteen days.

Varieties: 'Flying Colours' has long central leaves in various colour shades of red, yellow and green. 'Love Lies Bleeding' is a tall grower (to 1.5 m) with long green leaves and drooping red or pink, millet-like flower spikes that dangle attractively from the plant (hence the common name).

Anchusa

Sometimes known as summer forget-me-not because it is similar to, but later flowering than, the common forget-me-not, anchusa has vibrantly blue flowers with small, creamy-white centres. It can be sown either direct in the garden or in seed punnets filled with seed-raising mix. The compact bushy plants grow to 25 cm. After the first flush of blooms is finished, the plants can be cut back and fed with Thrive Flower & Fruit to promote further flowering. These plants need good drainage and dislike humid conditions.

Antigonon
See Chapter 18.

Antirrhinum
See Snapdragon.

Aquilegia (Columbine)

This unusual and attractive flower has been improved by selection and the present-day strains have larger flowers that have retained their initial charm. Aquilegia is a perennial that's best suited to cool climates. Plants prefer a sunny position, but they can be grown in semi-shade. Sow seed in autumn, but in cool climates you can sow in early spring too.

Sow seed in seed beds or punnets and transplant seedlings when 5–7 cm tall, spacing 30–40 cm apart. Water regularly, especially in dry weather, and scatter a light mulch of grass clippings or compost around each plant. Apply liquid feeds of Thrive or other soluble fertilisers as buds start to form. In cold districts, flowering in the first year is not as prolific as it is in subsequent years. In cool climates, plants will last for many years but in warmer climates it is best to start new seedlings at least every second year.

Aster

Rich, bright flower colours have made asters summer favourites. Although subject to a disease called aster wilt, strains such as 'Giant Crego' will give good results if planted in a different spot each year. Good drainage and a well-structured soil also help plants to resist wilt problems.

Asters grow best in an open, sunny position, and careful soil preparation, well before the seedlings are transplanted, will pay dividends. Asters prefer a light sandy soil that isn't heavily manured. Improve structure of heavy clay soils by mixing in compost and gypsum. When preparing the bed, add a mixed fertiliser to the soil.

You can sow seed from spring (but wait until frosts are over) through until mid-summer. There is little advantage to be gained from sowing seed too early in spring. Later sowings will bloom at the same time – about mid-summer. In mild districts, sowing can continue until late summer. Raise seedlings in seed beds, boxes or punnets as described in Chapter 9. After sowing, cover the seeds lightly with vermiculite, compost, a light, sandy soil or seed-raising mixture.

When the seedlings are large enough, transplant them into the prepared bed, spacing them 20–30 cm apart each way.

On heavy soils seedlings may have difficulty in establishing their root systems. You can assist root development by mixing some seed-raising mix or a handful of sand into the holes where the seedlings are planted.

In hot weather, spread mulch over the surface of the bed to conserve moisture and keep the roots cool. Plants usually flower in four or five months from sowing the seed but later sowings will bloom a little more quickly. It is important to remember that asters are very susceptible to frost, so don't sow too late in summer because the plants won't have time to get to flowering stage.

Varieties

'Dwarf Colour Carpet' is a colourful dwarf aster growing to 20 cm high. It is ideal for borders and rock gardens.

There are many other strains and cultivars. Some of the better known are 'Giant Crego', which has large double flowers in an excellent colour range and made up of long, curled and twisted petals, and 'King Aster', a free-flowering variety with large, fully double blooms made up of attractive quilled petals.

Arctotis (Aurora daisy)

Arctotis can be an annual or perennial (depending on climate) that flowers during winter, spring and summer. The large daisy-like flowers are produced freely on strong stems about 40 cm tall and come in a wide range of brilliant colours, including tangerine, rose, pink, red, claret, lemon, orange and white. Some flowers show attractive two-tone effects.

Plants will grow on a wide range of soils and do very well in light, sandy soils. Sow seed in autumn (for winter flowering) and also in spring. Seed may be sown direct in the garden bed or seedlings may be raised in boxes or punnets and transplanted when 5–7 cm tall. Space plants 30–40 cm apart. Water well during hot, dry weather, keeping leaves dry, and give liquid feeds of soluble fertilisers as flowering commences. A sunny, well-drained position is best.

Baby blue eyes

See Nemophila.

Balsam

This colourful flower is an excellent plant for borders or massed display. It can also be grown in window boxes, pots and troughs. Balsam likes a reasonably sunny position but will do well in semi-shade, too. Prepare soil well and add organic matter and a pre-planting fertiliser. Balsam is sometimes also called impatiens but the rose-shaped flowers are clearly quite different.

Sow seeds close to the surface and raise seedlings in boxes or punnets in early spring. Direct sowing is best delayed until all danger of frosts is past. Transplant or sow in clumps 30 cm apart each way. Plants eventually grow to a height of 50 cm and flower in about three months from sowing.

Begonia

Bedding begonias

Few other flowers grow so well in heavily shaded places as the bedding or fibrous-rooted begonia. Begonias are well suited to southerly and westerly aspects which receive little direct sunlight. While these plants thrive in shade, they do quite well in a sunny position also, but need regular watering in dry weather. Prepare soil well with added compost plus a general mixed fertiliser. Spring and early summer are the best times to sow seed in most climates, but in warm climates with mild winters you can sow in autumn too.

Begonia seed is almost as fine as flour, so seedlings need to be raised in seed boxes or

HINT

One of the best ways to keep your garden beds looking attractive is to deadhead regularly. Try to go out every two or three weeks to cut off tired old flower heads, and shoots that have died back. This will keep plants in shape and the garden looking so much better. And as an added bonus, it promotes new growth.

ANNE LATREILLE

GARDEN WRITER

punnets. Mark out rows 3–5 cm apart with the point of a nail, or lay the edge of a ruler on the surface and press down gently. Sprinkle seed thinly along the rows and press it in. Do not cover, as the seeds need light for germination.

Water gently with a very fine spray so as not to disturb the surface. Alternatively, stand containers in shallow water until moisture seeps to the surface. Keep damp until seedlings emerge (in two to three weeks). Transplant small seedlings into a seed tray and grow them on until 5–7 cm high before moving to the garden bed. Space dwarf begonia seedlings 20 cm apart. Water regularly until well established. Liquid feeds of soluble fertiliser at intervals of ten to fourteen days will promote more rapid growth, especially towards flowering time. When watering, keep leaves as dry as possible because begonias are very susceptible to powdery mildew fungus. Spray with a rose gun to control this disease. 'Thousand Wonders' is a delightful dwarf bedding begonia with dense compact growth. It is covered in flowers in all but the frosty months of the year.

Flower colours include dark and light reds, pinks of various shades, and white.

Tuberous begonias

Showy tuberous begonias often have double flowers in a very wide range of colours. They're usually grown in pots under shade or in glasshouses. They make beautiful pot plants and can be raised from seed, but are mostly grown from tubers that are planted during winter and spring.

Bellis (English daisy)

Although they're short-lived perennials in their native habitat, these hardy daisies are best treated as annuals and should be sown from fresh seed each autumn. They are very attractive and, with their fully double blooms carried on stems up to 15 cm high, they make excellent edging plants.

English daisies prefer full sun, but grow quite well in semi-shade. The plants are adapted to a wide range of soils but appreciate good soil structure so it's worthwhile adding organic matter and a pre-planting fertiliser when preparing the bed. In warm climates the seeds should be sown in autumn but, in very cold districts, you can sow seed in spring too.

Raise seedlings in seed beds, trays or boxes as described in Chapter 9, covering the seed with vermiculite, compost or seed-raising mixture. Transplant seedlings, spacing them 10–15 cm apart each way. Give them ample water during dry weather and keep down weeds by shallow cultivation. This is important, as the plants are small and could easily be choked by weeds. When the first flower buds appear, begin giving the plants liquid feeds of a soluble fertiliser. This will promote flowering over a long period. Cut off faded flowers regularly to prevent free seeding, especially in cooler climates.

Big gyp (Saponaria)

This old-fashioned plant is not related to gypsophila, but the rose-coloured flowers are similar and are used for cut flowers with other blooms like gerberas and carnations. The flowers last well after cutting.

Big gyp is adaptable to most soils but does best in soil that has been improved with organic matter and an application of complete fertiliser. In warm weather the

HINT

The sowing depth of seeds roughly correlates to seed size. As a general rule, the larger the seed the more deeply it's sown. Some tiny seeds have to be sown on the soil surface so they can remain in contact with light (e.g. begonia, impatiens, primula and aquilegia). Conversely, pansies, nasturtiums, sweet peas, phlox and violas need darkness to germinate well. Cover their seed trays with newspaper. Check regularly and remove the paper after the seedlings emerge.

JUDY HORTON

GARDEN WRITER, BROADCASTER AND HORTICULTURIST

plants will produce flowers about two months after sowing. Seed can be sown almost year round, except in very cold or very hot weather. Many gardeners make small successive sowings, which provide a continuous supply of cut flowers. The seed germinates freely in the open garden where the plants are to flower. Sow thickly in rows about 12 mm deep, spaced 20–30 cm apart, and cover with vermiculite, compost or seed-raising mixture. There is seldom any need to thin the seedlings and the plants will produce good blooms even when grown closely together.

HINT

Keep a few flowering potted plants handy to put in a border if something has keeled over, leaving a gap. This is especially useful if you have been getting a part of the garden ready for a special occasion, or are selling your house.

LORNA ROSE M.A.I.H.

HORTICULTURAL PHOTOGRAPHER

Brachyscome

See Swan River daisy.

Calceolaria

Calceolarias are sometimes called 'ladies' slippers' because of the shape of their blooms. They make attractive pot plants for spring flowering or short-term indoor use. The plants are excellent for shade-houses and glasshouses (in cold climates), but aren't really suitable for outdoors. In mild climates they can be grown in a shade-house with moderate warmth during the flowering period.

In temperate climates, sow the seed from mid-summer to early autumn, but in cold districts seed can be sown in both spring and summer. Raise seedlings in seed boxes, trays or punnets of seed-raising mix. Sow the seed on the surface, barely covering it with a sprinkling of sand, vermiculite or sifted

compost, then firm the soil down. Water gently with a very fine spray or by standing the box or punnet in a dish of water until moisture seeps to the surface.

Transfer young seedlings from the box or punnet into 7–10 cm pots and, as they grow larger, move them into bigger pots, with a final planting into pots about 20 cm in diameter. When the plants are growing strongly, give them weak liquid feeds of soluble fertiliser. Calceolarias resent excessive heat and need only moderate warmth during their flowering period.

Calendula (English marigold)

Calendulas are the traditional marigolds that appear in old European herbals. They're popular because they're hardy and easy to grow and, in all but the coldest areas, early sowings will provide warm colour during the winter months. Calendulas do best in fertile, well-drained soil but succeed on a variety of soil types. They prefer an open, sunny position but must be watered regularly during dry weather. In cooler climates, seed can be sown in autumn and also in spring.

Sow seed either directly in rows, or in clumps in garden beds, or the seedlings can be raised in seed beds or boxes for transplanting. Whichever method you use, cover the seed to a depth of 12 mm with vermiculite or seed-raising mixture. Transplant when seedlings are large enough to handle easily. It is better to have them on the large side rather than too small. Always apply a pre-planting fertiliser to the bed when preparing the soil. This will improve the vigour of the plants and increase the size of the flowers. Remove spent blooms to prolong flowering, and keep down weeds by shallow cultivation.

Rust is the most serious disease of calendulas and can be prevented by regular spraying with a fungicide. (See Chapter 8.) Badly affected plants should be removed.

Varieties

'Pacific Beauty' is a delightful tall strain. It reaches 60 cm and the colour range includes some lovely pastel shades. 'Bronze Babe' grows to about 40 cm and is a free-flowering compact plant with a strong main colour of yellow or orange with a bronze highlight on the underside of the petals.

Californian poppy (*Eschscholtzia*)

These sun-loving plants with brightly coloured flowers thrive in warm summer months. Seed can be sown in spring and summer in both temperate and cool climates. You can sow seed direct in the garden or raise seedlings for transplanting. With either method, cover seed lightly with vermiculite or seed-raising mix and keep damp until seedlings emerge. Thin seedlings or transplant to 30 cm apart. Keep down weeds by shallow cultivation and give liquid feeds of soluble fertilisers to encourage healthy growth.

Candytuft

There are two distinct types of annual candytuft. The most popular, *Iberis umbellata*, carries its flowers at the top of the stem. The second is called hyacinth-flowered candytuft. It produces a mass of pure white florets that resemble hyacinth blooms. Candytuft grows well in most soils, but it must have good drainage. The plants do best in a sunny situation, sheltered from strong winds. Plants must not be crowded because they become too spindly and flowers are poor. In temperate climates, sow seeds from autumn to early winter. In cold districts, seed can be sown in spring too.

Prepare the bed well with organic matter plus a pre-planting fertiliser at one-third of a cup per square metre. Seed can be sown direct in the garden in clumps 20–30 cm apart, or seedlings can be raised in seed boxes or punnets for transplanting at the same distance. Hyacinth-flowered varieties can be spaced more closely at about 20 cm.

Candytuft is an easy plant to grow. Keep down weeds by mulching or shallow cultivation and give liquid feeds of soluble fertiliser when plants are establishing.

Canterbury bells

Canterbury bells form a spire of large 'cup and saucer' flowers with the texture of fine porcelain. They look at their best when planted in clumps or drifts and make attractive cut flowers. Colours range from dark blue to mauve, rose, soft pink and white. Sow seed in autumn in seed boxes or punnets, just covering with vermiculite or seed-raising mix; firm down gently. Keep soil moist until seedlings emerge – usually in two to three weeks. Transplant seedlings when 5–7 cm tall into the garden bed, spaced 30 cm apart. These plants are technically biennials and, in cooler climates, the plants often won't flower until the second year.

Carnation

Like most garden flowers, this fragrant favourite had humble beginnings. It was introduced to England in a wild form in about the sixteenth century, but it was not until about 1900 that the Perpetual (long) Flowering types were developed.

In Australia we are mainly interested in two types (either of which can be grown from seed): the Chabaud (bedding carnation) and the Perpetual Flowering. Chabaud is the most widely known and is easily recognised by its deeply serrated or fringed petals and a strong, clove-like scent. Perpetual Flowering types are the source from which most named varieties are obtained. It should be understood, however, that named varieties of carnation will not breed true to type from seed. Named varieties must be started from cuttings or purchased as small plants.

When starting carnations from seed it is best to raise seedlings in beds, boxes or punnets using seed-raising mix. Germination may be slow and rather erratic. For this reason the seed bed or containers need close attention for ten to fourteen days – perhaps longer – until seedlings emerge. Carnation seed can be sown direct into garden beds but it is difficult to give the germinating seeds the same attention. Seed can be sown at almost any time of the year, but spring or autumn are regarded as the best periods.

Whether carnations are started from seed, cuttings or as nursery plants, the requirements for soil, cultivation and general care are the same. Carnations prefer an open position exposed to full sunlight and resent being crowded by other plants or shrubs. It is best if they are protected from westerly and southerly winds too. They will grow in a wide range of soils from heavy (but well structured) to light, sandy soils. On heavy soils add organic matter and sand to improve both structure and texture. On sandy soils add organic matter in the form of animal manure, garden compost, peat moss or vermiculite to improve structure and increase water-holding capacity. Manure, compost, peat moss, vermiculite and other materials for soil improvement should be dug into the soil some weeks beforehand. At the same time add some lime or dolomite (in acidic soils) and a pre-planting fertiliser. As a general guide, use one handful of lime per square metre on sandy soils but double this amount on heavier soils.

HINT

Keep a notebook or diary solely for your garden. List planting times, flowering times, fruiting seasons, as well as a list of all the things that did well, and those that did not. This book is more than a journal; it will become one of the best garden reference books in your library.

MARCELLE NANKERVIS

HORTICULTURIST AND
FREELANCE WRITER

Dig the bed to a depth of 10 cm to thoroughly mix the soil, moisture-holding materials, lime and fertiliser. Leave for a few weeks and then gently break the surface soil a few days before planting, to destroy any weeds. The bed should contain sufficient nutrients to feed the plants through the main growing period.

Just before flowering, scatter another ration of mixed fertiliser around the plants or begin feeding with Thrive Flower & Fruit Soluble plant food every two weeks. Bad drainage is probably the greatest enemy of carnations and the plants are likely to be attacked by root rot and collar rot diseases. Beds should be raised above the surface – about 10 cm for light soil and 15 cm for heavy soil.

Space plants 30–40 cm apart. When planting out, keep the lower leaves well out of the ground so that no more than 12 mm of soil covers the top of the roots.

Compact, sturdy plants will produce the greatest number of good blooms. Encourage sturdiness by regularly nipping back the early-flowering stems. When the plants are about 15 cm tall, pinch them back to induce side shoots, which in turn are pinched back when they reach the same height. When plants have developed eight to twelve shoots (depending on the growth habit of the variety), allow these to send up flower stems. When picking flowers, always break them off near the base of the plant. If first-class blooms are desired, each main stem should bear only one flower. This means the removal of all side buds growing from the leaf axils, leaving only the main bud at the top of the stem. In some varieties, buds will have a tendency to burst at the calyx (the green collar beneath the flower). Commercial growers prevent this by fitting small rubber bands around them.

After about twelve months of flowering, plants may begin to look straggly. But if they still appear healthy and vigorous, cut them back hard to within 5 cm of the centre stem. With normal attention, these plants should produce a further flush of blooms as good as the previous flowering. In some soils, especially light ones, plants which have flowered abundantly may not be worth this treatment so it is best to renew them – either from seedlings or cuttings taken in autumn.

Pests and diseases are not a serious problem for carnations. Aphids and thrips, the most common pests, can be controlled by spraying with insecticides. Rust and collar rot are the most serious fungus diseases. For control of both pests and diseases see Chapter 8.

Celosia

This brightly-coloured annual bedding plant, with its plume-like, feathery flowers, revels in a hot, sunny situation. Plants are susceptible to frost and seed must be sown into warm soil in spring and early summer. Plants grow well in almost any garden soil but will do better if some organic matter and mixed fertiliser have been added before planting.

Seed can be sown direct in the garden in rows or clumps, or seedlings can be raised in seed beds, boxes or punnets for transplanting. Thin seedlings or transplant to 20–30 cm apart.

Celosia is an easy plant to grow. Water plants regularly, especially in hot weather, and give regular liquid feeds of soluble fertilisers. Cultivate shallowly to destroy any weeds but avoid damaging surface roots. A mulch of grass clippings around the plants discourages weeds and conserves moisture. The showy, dwarf varieties are the most widely grown nowadays. Flamingo Feather is an unusual variety of Celosia, with spikes of soft-pink flowers that fade as they age.

Centaurea

See Cornflower.

Chrysanthemum

Traditional Mother's Day chrysanthemums (*Chrysanthemum* hybrids) include a very wide range of flower types: single, semi-double and fully double. They are the source of all modern named and exhibition varieties. Named varieties must be propagated

HINT

Plant white or pale-coloured flowering plants to create a lovely atmosphere in which to enjoy the garden on summer evenings – white petunias, white or lime-green nicotianas, alyssum, gardenias, Achillea 'Moonlight' and frangipani will work. Plus, if you have planted mixed colours of bulbous plants like ixias but want to select specific colours for the following season, tie coloured wool around the base of plants while they are in flower, or insert plastic markers beside the plants so you can sort them out after lifting.

MARGARET HANKS

HORTICULTURIST

vegetatively from root divisions or cuttings. Plants are often available from nurseries in October or November or in flower for Mother's Day. Seed of perennial chrysanthemums will produce plants with a variety of flower forms and colours – an interesting (and economical) way of growing them.

The Shasta daisy (*Leucanthemum x superbum*) is another popular perennial type of chrysanthemum. There are also annual chrysanthemums, of which the small, white-flowered, yellow-centred star daisy (*Mauranthemum paludosum*) is one of the most popular. The colourful painted daisy (*C. carinatum*) is another widely grown annual.

Chrysanthemums grow well in a variety of soils, but all types of soils are improved by adding garden compost plus some mixed fertiliser before planting. It is a good idea to dig the soil over two or three times before planting, to bring it to an open, friable condition.

Chrysanthemums dislike poorly drained soil. Raising the beds above the surrounding level is probably the easiest method of ensuring they have good drainage. Plant chrysanthemums in a warm, sunny position, avoiding shady sites and those exposed to wind.

Spring is the best time for sowing seed. Raise the seedlings in seed beds, boxes or punnets as described in Chapter 9. Sow the seed and cover with a sprinkling of vermiculite or seed-raising mix about 6 mm deep. Keep damp until seedlings emerge in ten to fourteen days. Seedlings are ready to transplant when 7–10 cm high.

If growing show chrysanthemums, space plants 100 cm apart, but for general garden display or cut flowers this distance can be reduced to 75 cm. Firm the soil well around the roots of each plant and water well. Continue regular watering until plants are established. Keep the plants growing strongly by giving liquid feeds of soluble fertiliser and cultivate the soil surface regularly to control weeds. Liquid feeds can be discontinued when the flower buds show colour.

When setting out to grow chrysanthemums, management practices will largely determine the habit of growth, the number of flower stems and the size and quality of the flowers. 'Stopping' consists of breaking out the growing tip of the plant to promote three or four lateral stems to develop. This is done when the plants are about 20 cm tall. Lateral stems can also be stopped when 5–10 cm tall to induce further laterals and a bushy plant. 'Disbudding' (the removal of surplus buds) influences the size and quality of the flowers. If you wish to have very large blooms, leave the centre or top bud only. Small-flowered types of chrysanthemums are not usually disbudded.

HINT

The art of successful gardening is, quite simply, putting things in the right place. When in doubt, throw it out!

JACKIE FRENCH

GARDEN WRITER, BROADCASTER, COLUMNIST, AUSTRALIAN CHILDREN'S LAUREATE 2014 2015 AND SENIOR AUSTRALIAN OF THE YEAR

The eight main varieties of perennial chrysanthemums are: Large Flowered Exhibition, which has giant, waratah-shaped blooms to 15 cm diameter with broad, in-curving petals; Decorative, which has similar flowers to the Exhibition type but rather smaller; Spider or Quilled, on which the petals are loose and finely rolled or quilled; Anemone-centred, which has a tightly packed centre and is surrounded by a row of outer petals, often in contrasting colours; Singles, having daisy-like flowers with a distinct centre and three to five rows of petals; Pompon or Button, which displays clusters of small, double, anemone-like flowers 3–5 cm in diameter; Cascade, which has small, single blooms on trailing stems giving a cascade effect (suitable for pots, troughs and window boxes); and Charm, consisting of compact plants to 60 cm tall with masses of small daisy-like flowers for massed display.

Exhibition, Decorative and all but the low-growing types of chrysanthemums (Anemone-centred, Pompon, Cascade and Charm) need staking by the time buds form. It is best to surround the plants with two or three light stakes and tie garden twine around them at intervals of about 30 cm.

White rust, a debilitating fungal disease, has affected chrysanthemums quite severely in recent years and has contributed to a decline in their popularity. The relatively new Zaleton fungicide will give effective control of this disease.

Cineraria

Cinerarias, with their mounds of bright, jewel-coloured daisy blooms, are among the few garden flowers that prefer semi-shade.

In very warm climates, a protected area is essential to grow cinerarias successfully. Modern varieties have a much wider colour range, and both large-flowered tall and compact dwarf types are available.

Generally seed is sown during the late summer and autumn for flowering in late winter and early spring. But remember, cinerarias are frost-sensitive and in cool climates should be protected from cold.

Cineraria seeds are quite small and should be sown in seed boxes or punnets, lightly covered with vermiculite or seed-raising mixture and watered gently.

To grow strong seedlings it is a good idea to prick them out as soon as they are large enough to handle into 5–7 cm pots, or into larger boxes or trays, spacing them about 10 cm apart. If you wish to grow the plants on in pots, transfer them to 15 cm pots and finally to 20 cm pots for flowering. The potting mix should be open and friable so that it drains easily. Add a ration of mixed fertiliser to each batch of soil. As the plants grow, give regular liquid feeds of a soluble fertiliser, especially towards flowering time. The main insect pests of cinerarias are aphids and leafminer. Spray regularly with insecticide to control them. (See Chapter 8.)

Varieties

'Star Ships' is a dwarf strain that has medium-sized flowers on compact plants. It is excellent for growing in pots. 'Exhibition Strain' is a taller variety with a mass of larger flowers held above a compact, robust bush.

Cleome

See Spider flower.

Cockscomb

Cockscomb is an annual bedding plant that is a form of celosia but instead of feathery plumes it has velvet-coated, twisted crests (which look somewhat like a rooster's comb). See Celosia for cultivation notes.

Coleus

Coleus is grown not so much for its flowers as for its brilliantly coloured leaves. It's an ideal plant for adding colour to lightly shaded parts of the garden. Although coleus plants prefer semi-shade, they need a warm, sheltered position and are very susceptible to frost.

Sow coleus seed in boxes or punnets in spring or early summer. The seeds are quite small, so cover lightly with vermiculite, compost or seed-raising mix. Transplant seedlings when 5 cm high and space them 30 cm apart in the garden. If growing the plants in pots, select seedlings with the best colouring – this can be determined when the plants are quite small. The seedling stems are soft and tender so handle them carefully to prevent damage. When the plants are established, water regularly so that the soil is always damp but not wet. Pinch back main shoots to encourage branching and bushiness. Give liquid feeds of soluble fertiliser every seven to ten days to promote large leaves and to intensify the colours. Pinch out any flower buds to prolong leaf growth.

Columbine

See Aquilegia.

Coreopsis

This is a very hardy (sometimes weedy) daisy that flowers during the warm weather. It comes in both annual and perennial forms. Plants need full sun, good drainage and should be watered sparingly. Flowers are excellent for picking. Remove faded blooms to promote further flowering and prevent seeding.

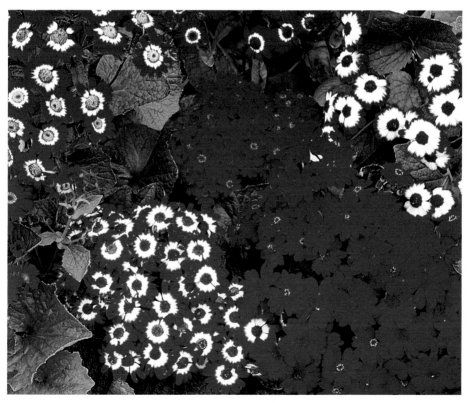

Cinerarias thrive in semi-shade conditions.

Cornflower (*Centaurea*)

C. cyanus is the well-known blue cornflower but seed mixtures also contain other colours such as rose, maroon, lavender and white. Cornflowers grow well in temperate climates if they have good drainage and a well-structured and fertilised soil. Ideally, plant them in a position that receives morning sun.

Sow seed from early autumn until early winter in prepared seed boxes or punnets. Cover the seed with vermiculite, compost or seed-raising mix and water gently. Transplant seedlings to the garden and space them 40–50 cm apart. Cultivate regularly to control weeds and give soluble fertilisers every ten to fourteen days after plants show flower buds. Cornflowers make excellent cut blooms.

Cosmos

These tall, colourful, warm season plants make an attractive and useful background for low-growing annuals and supply plenty of cut flowers for indoor decoration. Cosmos are easy plants to grow and need little attention. Newer varieties are much improved in both flower form and colour range. The flowers, with their fine colours and lasting qualities, make cosmos well worth growing in any garden.

Cosmos will grow in a wide range of soils but responds best to well-drained, friable soil with added mixed fertiliser. The plants need a sunny position and, because of their height, should be sheltered from strong winds. You can start sowing seed in spring and continue through to summer. Seed sown as late as January in most districts will produce plants that flower before cold weather or frost arrives.

It is best to raise seedlings in seed beds, boxes or punnets for transplanting into the garden but, as the seeds are quite large, you can sow a few seeds direct in clumps spaced 40–50 cm apart in the garden and thin to the strongest one or two seedlings. Transplanted seedlings should also be spaced at about the same distance apart. Keep the soil between the plants free of weeds and in hot weather spread a mulch over it to keep the roots cool and moist. Staking plants is rarely needed because they support each other when grown closely together.

Varieties

'Sensation' has large rose and crimson flowers with a sprinkling of white. Plants grow to a height of about 90 cm and are highly recommended. The flowers of 'Seashells' have unusual recurved edges on the petals, creating a fluted effect. Cosmos 'Bright Eyes' (*C. sulphureus*) has yellow and orange flowers and coarser foliage.

Cyclamen

Delicate flowers in white, pinks, mauves and reds make cyclamen one of the most popular plants for winter and early spring flowering. They can be grown in an open, friable soil in a semi-shaded position in the garden but are more often grown in pots. They do well indoors but need a well-lit, well-ventilated, cool but draught-free spot – preferably with an hour or two of sunlight each morning.

The plants form a corm or bulb that can be carried on from year to year. Corms more than two or three years old, however, are best replaced by new plants. Sow seed from late summer to early autumn in a seed box or punnets using a soil mixture made up of garden loam, vermiculite or peat moss and coarse sand. (See Chapter 9.) Stand containers in water until moisture seeps to the surface, allow to drain for at least a day and press the seeds into the damp soil mixture to a depth of 3 mm, spacing them 2–3 cm apart. Seedlings emerge over a period of four to six weeks. Prick them out when small into individual 5–7 cm pots using a similar soil mix, and transfer them to larger pots as they grow. Give liquid feeds of half-strength, soluble Thrive or Aquasol every three or four weeks. Water regularly by standing the pots in water until soil is wetted and then allow to drain. Do not over-water – plants will benefit from short spells of dryness.

Buds form in autumn and respond to regular liquid feeds until flowering ceases in late spring. Then, as leaves turn yellow, reduce the water supply. Some people tip pots on their side for final drying. The corm or bulb which has formed during the flowering period can remain in the pot or can be taken out and stored in damp sand or peat moss before re-potting in late summer. Water sparingly until new growth starts.

Dahlia

Named in honour of a Swedish botanist, Dr Andreas Dahl, this popular flower is a native of Mexico that found its way to the Botanic Gardens, Madrid, in 1789. At that time, only three kinds of flowers were known: a double purple, a single rose colour and a single red. Tubers from each of these were sent to Kew Gardens, London, but they did not survive. Some years later, another lot of tubers brought from France were grown successfully. Today there is a tremendous array of dahlias, both in colour range and flower form. They are easy to grow and, given reasonable care, will produce a mass of blooms for many weeks in late summer and autumn.

You can grow dahlias from seed or from packaged tubers of named varieties that are usually available in late winter and spring.

When growing dahlias from seed there is always the possibility of obtaining an unusual variation in colour or flower from the plants you grow. Plants will flower within three or four months after seedlings are planted out and will continue flowering for many weeks. During this time, the plants are forming small tubers. Save tubers of the best plants for replanting next season. Named dahlia varieties will not grow true to type from seed.

Dahlias prefer a sunny position that's sheltered on the southern and western sides. They need a well-drained soil with an open, friable structure. In sandy soils add organic matter in the form of compost, leaf mould or peat moss. Animal manure is also suitable but too much will produce excessive leaf growth at the expense of flowers. Dig over the bed before planting and add well-rotted organic matter at the same time. Very deep digging is not necessary – spade depth is ample in most soils. A ration of lime is recommended if the soil is acidic but apply no more than two-thirds of a cup per square metre on heavy soils. A light scattering of a mixed fertiliser before planting is also beneficial.

Sow seeds in spring or early summer – plants from early sowings will flower in January and those from late sowings in autumn; autumn blooms often appear fresher as they aren't bleached by the hot sun. Use seed boxes, trays or punnets, covering the seeds with about 12 mm of vermiculite, compost or seed-raising mixture. Seedlings may take two to four weeks to emerge so keep the containers damp for this length of time. Transplant seedlings when 5–7 cm tall.

Tall-growing dahlia plants should be supported by a stake to protect them from wind damage. After planting out, water regularly to make sure that the soil does not dry out. Slugs and snails should be controlled as soon as young shoots appear. When the plants are well established, apply a ration of mixed fertiliser to each plant. Spread the fertiliser in a circle around the plant, rake it in and water thoroughly. When the buds appear, give liquid feeds of soluble fertilisers every ten to fourteen days to promote large blooms and to prolong the flowering period. It is important to remove all spent flowers regularly to encourage further bud formation.

Flowers for indoor decoration should be picked in the cool of the evening and the stem ends dipped in boiling water for about thirty seconds. Take care that the rising steam does not scald the blooms. Do this by tilting the container slightly or covering them with a double thickness of newspaper wrapped around the stems.

If you wish to propagate dahlias from tubers, these should not be lifted until the plants have completely died down – usually

HINT

After dahlia foliage has died down the tubers can either be left in the ground (if the soil is well drained and you can spare the garden space) or they can be lifted for storage. Label the tubers before lifting them if you want to keep the colours separate. Try fastening a plastic clothes peg the colour of the flower to each clump.

SHIRLEY STACKHOUSE
GARDEN WRITER

early winter. Dig them with a garden fork, taking care not to damage the crown and tubers attached to it. The lifted crowns can be stored in the shade under trees or in a corner of the garden shed during winter. In colder areas, they can be stored in boxes filled with sand. As warm weather starts in spring, tubers will form 'eyes' or shoots. Cut between the shoots to leave some stem tissue surrounding the shoot and one or two tubers still attached. Set the tubers so that the root end is covered by about 10 cm of soil but the shoot is at soil level. It's best to put stakes in at planting time to avoid damaging the growing tubers later in the season.

Varieties

Like chrysanthemums, there is a wide range of dahlias, summarised as:

Decorative: Large, heavy, double flowers 15–25 cm in diameter produced on long stems; mature plants are 2 m or more tall.

Hybrid Cactus: Flowers with narrow, curled petals but smaller than Decorative types; plants grow to 1.5 m tall.

Charm: Rather smaller flowers than Cactus dahlias, usually in pastel colours, free-flowering; plants grow to 1.2 m.

Collerette: Flowers have a distinct centre with space between petals; 60–75 cm tall.

Nymphaea or Water Lily: Daisy-like flowers with space between petals, pastel shades with one colour fading into another; plants 60–75 cm tall.

Paeony-flowered: Small, semi-double flowers in soft colours.

Pompon Small: Tightly packed flowers in a wide colour range.

All tall-growing dahlias need some support. Place three stakes about 15 cm apart around the base of the plant. Incline these outward so that they are about 30 cm apart at the top. Encircle with twine at 40 cm height and again at 80 cm. Then join the centre of each tie to form a second triangle and encourage the branches to grow naturally through the crossing sections. As with chrysanthemums, stopping (that is, pinching out the growing point) and disbudding are often practised in the tall-growing dahlias, but this is rarely necessary with dwarf bedding types.

Dwarf dahlias are ideal for planting in containers or for massed displays in garden beds.

Much breeding work in recent years has produced a range of single-flowered dahlias with dark coloured foliage. These provide wonderful colour contrast in the garden.

Delphinium

Delphiniums have few equals for producing tall, stately spikes of flowers in rich shades of blue, white and purple. In warm-temperate climates delphiniums are best treated as annuals but in cold districts the plants will last for several years, providing summer temperatures are mild. Delphiniums prefer a well-drained, fertile soil with plenty of organic matter and some mixed fertiliser. Prepare the bed well so that the soil is in friable condition for transplanting the seedlings. In temperate climates you can sow seed in autumn, winter and early spring, but in cold districts restrict sowing to autumn and spring only. Once established, delphiniums are very hardy and tolerate frost well, but in very cold districts seedlings from autumn sowings should be protected during the first winter.

Sow seed in a good soil mixture in seed boxes, trays or punnets. Cover them well because seeds germinate most successfully in the dark. Germination is often slow and seedlings may take three to four weeks to emerge. Transplant seedlings, spacing them about 50 cm apart each way. As the plants grow, keep the soil well cultivated to control weeds. During summer months a mulch of compost or grass clippings will prevent evaporation and keep the roots cool. Delphiniums are gross feeders and will respond dramatically to dressings of liquid fertiliser at regular two- to three-weekly intervals.

Varieties

'Pacific Giants' is a magnificent, tall hybrid variety. The giant flower spikes are closely packed, with satin-textured blooms in glorious colours which range from white through shades of pink and lavender to pale-blue, mid-blue, royal blue and purple. 'Belladonna' has mixed single flowers with a slightly looser arrangement on the stems. Dwarf delphiniums, like 'Blue Pygmy', are small growers (to about 25 cm) that produce intensely blue flowers.

Dianthus (Pinks)

Dianthus is a close relative of carnation and its sowing times and cultivation requirements are the same (see Carnation in this chapter). The plants are possibly more adaptable to a wider variety of soils and they tolerate very dry conditions. They make excellent rockery and edging plants and produce large quantities of fragrant flowers in reds, mauves, pinks and white. Dianthus is usually treated as an annual but, if the plants are cut back after the first flowering and given liquid feeds of soluble fertiliser, they will flower again in the second year. Dwarf varieties are excellent for rockeries and low borders. Sweet William (*D. barbatus*) is a close relative. Like carnations, dianthus prefer a sweet soil so add lime or dolomite to acidic soils before planting.

English daisy

See Bellis.

English marigold

See Calendula.

Eschscholtzia

See Californian poppy.

Everlasting daisy

Everlastings are always handy for indoor decoration because they can be dried and kept without water for many weeks. Everlasting daisies will grow on a wide range of soils but need good drainage and an open, sunny position. Applications of fertiliser will promote vigorous growth and increase the size of flowers.

Everlasting daisies can be sown in both autumn and spring. It is best to sow seeds direct into the garden where the plants are to flower. Mark out shallow rows 12 mm deep, sprinkle seed sparsely along them and cover with seed-raising mix or vermiculite. Thin seedlings to 20–30 cm apart.

Alternatively, sow a few seeds in clumps at this distance and cover as before. Keep the soil moist until the seedlings are well established. The plants usually need very little attention apart from regular watering and shallow cultivation to destroy weeds. Take care not to cultivate too close to the plants. When buds start to form, apply a side dressing of mixed fertiliser and water in. Alternatively, give liquid feeds of soluble fertiliser every ten to fourteen days. If flowers are required for drying, cut them in full bloom, tie in bunches and hang head downwards for a few weeks until the stems are dry.

The stately spires of delphiniums.

Forget-me-not

Forget-me-not is a very popular flower for edging, borders and rockeries. Although the flowers are traditionally blue with small yellow centres, there are also pink and white varieties. The plants thrive in moist, semi-shaded situations with morning sun for a few hours each day. An open, friable soil is needed to grow them to perfection. Sow seed in late summer or early autumn in seed boxes, trays or punnets. Cover the seed very lightly with seed-raising mix or vermiculite as described in Chapter 9. Seed may be slow to germinate and seedlings may take three to four weeks to emerge. Keep the containers damp but not wet for this period. Transplant seedlings when large enough to handle and space them 20–30 cm apart. Although best treated as annuals, forget-me-nots will very often seed naturally and new seedlings will appear each year. Trim after flowering to prevent self-seeding.

Foxglove

Although foxgloves are really biennials, some of the newer varieties will flower the first year and can be treated as annuals. They have exquisite, bell-shaped blooms in cream, salmon, purple and rose colours. The flattened tubular flowers open gradually from the bottom to the top of the spike (which usually reaches about 1 m). After the main spike has finished flowering, it can be cut off and smaller spikes will develop from the base. Foxgloves prefer moist soil and a semi-shaded garden situation. Sow the fine seed direct into the garden position, in soil that has been well prepared with some complete fertiliser and old compost. Cover very lightly with vermiculite or seed-raising mix. 'Foxy' is the most widely grown variety.

Gaillardia

There are both annual and perennial species of this plant and each has its own special merits. The annual types flower quickly from seed but the perennials have a longer flowering period and can be cut back several times. You can sow seed of the annual types either in autumn or spring in most districts; perennials are best sown in autumn. Seed can be sown in seed boxes or punnets and the seedlings transplanted, spacing them 30 cm apart each way. Alternatively, sow a few seeds direct in clumps at the same distance apart and thin to the strongest two or three seedlings. Plants grow quickly from seed to a height of 40 cm and flower throughout the summer. Perennial gaillardia (*G. grandiflora*) has large single flowers in shades of gold, orange and scarlet, many with contrasting colours in the centre.

Gazania

This dwarf perennial plant with slender, leathery leaves and daisy-like flowers in shades of cream, yellow, pink and mahogany is a native of South Africa. It revels in full sunlight and does well in dry situations. It's excellent for banks, rockeries and sunny borders. Established plants can be divided after flowering in spring and summer. Sow seeds in boxes or punnets in spring or summer and transplant seedlings when 5 cm tall, spacing them 20 cm apart. Remove flowering heads to prevent self-seeding. Gazania is a declared weed in some areas so check with local authorities before planting.

Geranium

Geraniums are ideal perennial plants for pots, window boxes, or massed flower displays in beds and borders, especially in sunny situations. Plants of named varieties can be purchased from nurseries or started from cuttings, but geraniums can also be grown from seed. Sow seeds in boxes or punnets in spring or early summer. Conditions must be reasonably warm as the seeds need a temperature of 25°C to germinate.

Fill the containers with seed-raising mix. Scatter seeds on the surface, cover lightly and press down firmly. Water gently or stand the container in water until moisture seeps to the surface. Ensure the soil is kept moist until seedlings emerge.

Transplant seedlings when large enough to handle into pots filled with a similar mix and grow on until well established for transplanting into tubs or the open garden. When planting for massed colour in the garden, space plants 40–50 cm apart. Geraniums, or more correctly pelargoniums, are very adaptable perennials. Provided the plants are in full sunlight they will thrive in both warm and cool climates. They withstand light frosts. The soil in which they grow must be well drained but not overly rich. Too much nitrogen or animal manure tends to promote excessive leaf growth at the expense of flowers.

Geraniums may become straggly as they grow, so regular pruning is needed to keep the plants compact and to encourage more flowers. Light pruning can be carried out after each flush of flowers during the warmer months, followed by a general pruning and 'clean up' in autumn when flowering is over (leave this until early spring in cooler climates). Vigorous stems should be cut back by one- or two-thirds, making the cut just above a node or joint with a bud facing outwards. At the same time, remove dead or diseased wood and any inward-growing or crossing stems. When new growth starts, 'tip pruning' or 'pinching out' may be necessary to encourage further branching.

Geraniums are very easily propagated by cuttings, which are best taken in autumn. Both tip cuttings and stem cuttings develop roots easily. Take the cuttings with two to four nodes or joints and make the cut just below the lowest one. With tip cuttings, remove all but the top leaves. With stem cuttings, remove lower leaves and retain the top leaf only, which may be cut in half to reduce loss of moisture by transpiration. Cuttings may be planted directly in the garden if the soil is crumbly, but it is more reliable to place them 4–5 cm deep in pots filled with coarse sand or a mixture of coarse sand (three parts) and peat moss or vermiculite (one part). Most of these cuttings will develop roots within three or four weeks of planting.

Gerbera

Gerberas, which are naturally adapted to hot, sunny conditions, have become one of the most popular flowers in warm parts of Australia. They do well in temperate climates too, providing they are grown in a sunny position sheltered from strong winds. The daisy-like flowers come in a wide range of colours and make excellent cut flowers for indoors. Gerberas prefer light soils but will grow well in heavier soils that have been improved by the addition of organic matter and sand. The soil must be open and well drained and, because they are susceptible to a condition known as 'crown rot', it is best to grow them in beds raised at least 20 cm above the surrounding level. Mixed fertiliser can be added when the bed is being prepared

Lavender, delphiniums and penstemon feature in this summer garden bed.

HINT

If you want quick colour in your garden, try growing daisies, foxgloves, South African daisy (*Osteospermum*), banksia rose and *Clematis montana*. You won't be disappointed.

PETER DE WAART

HORTICULTURIST

and, where soil is acidic, gerberas appreciate an application of lime every year or so (but not at the same time as fertilising).

Sow seed in spring or early summer when the weather is warm. Prepare an open, friable soil mixture to use in seed boxes, trays or punnets as described in Chapter 9. A mixture with added sand (say, one part sand and one part potting mix) is recommended. Press the pointed end of the seed into the surface of the seed-raising mix, and press firmly so the seeds make contact with the dark, damp soil. Seed containers must be kept in a warm spot until seedlings emerge – usually about two or three weeks. The soil in the containers can be kept warm if they are kept indoors and covered with glass or a clear plastic bag. The cover should be removed when seedlings appear and the container transferred to a warm, sheltered, but shady spot in the garden.

It is best to prick out the seedlings when they are quite small. Transfer them into a larger container spaced 5 cm apart or into individual 5–7 cm pots. They can then be grown to a good size before planting in the open garden, spaced 40–50 cm apart. When planting it is important to keep the crowns well above the surface, especially on heavy soils. Soil washing into the centre of the crowns often promotes rotting. Gerberas can be grown in the same position for two or three years. Old plants can be lifted, divided and replanted. This is best done in late summer or early autumn in temperate areas before cold weather sets in. In tropical climates you can divide the plants at almost any time of the year.

Globe amaranth

This attractive summer-flowering annual grows to a height of 30 cm (less for some dwarf varieties) and has round, clover-like, 'everlasting' flowers in rich purple. It is an adaptable plant in regards to soil but responds well to improved soil with added fertiliser. It is excellent for bedding, low borders or edging in a sunny position. Sow seeds in spring or early summer in seed boxes or punnets and transplant seedlings to the garden, spaced 30 cm apart. Alternatively, sow a few seeds direct in clumps at the same distance and thin to two or three seedlings at each position. Keep the plants well watered in dry times and mulch with compost or grass clippings to conserve moisture and deter weeds. Give liquid feeds of soluble fertiliser when buds appear. 'Little Buddy', with masses of purple, globe-shaped blooms, grows to 20–30 cm tall and is popular. Flowers may be used fresh for indoor decoration or may be bunched and hung, head downwards, in a cool place to dry for 'everlastings'.

Gloxinia

These exquisite pot plants are ideal for growing in a glasshouse, shadehouse or fernery and flower well indoors in a well-lit position. The velvety, bell-shaped flowers have rich colours with mottled or spotted effects. Deep red, rose, violet or purple are the predominant colours, overlaid with white, pink, mauve or lavender-blue markings.

Sow seed in winter or early spring. Under glasshouse conditions, autumn sowing is also possible. Seed is extremely small and rather slow to germinate, so extra care is needed. Sow seed in seed trays, punnets or pots using an open, friable, rather sandy soil mixture as outlined in Chapter 9. Enclose containers in a plastic bag until seedlings emerge.

When seedlings are large enough to handle, prick them out into small individual pots and transfer to larger pots as they grow. They reach a height of 30 cm and flower in mid to late summer. Give liquid feeds of soluble fertiliser when buds appear. The plants die back to a dormant tuber in winter. The small tubers that form during the flowering period can be replanted the next spring.

Godetia

Godetias are attractive annuals which have been aptly called 'farewell to spring' because they flower late in spring, helping to bridge the gap between spring and summer flowers. The dwarf type, to 60 cm tall, has masses of single blooms on top of the plant and is more widely grown than the tall, azalea-flowered type with double flowers.

Godetia plants prefer a sunny aspect sheltered from strong winds. They will grow on a wide range of soils but tend to make too much foliage in over-fertile soils. Prepare the bed with a mixed fertiliser that doesn't have too high a proportion of nitrogen (blood and bone would be ideal). In most climates, sow seeds in autumn to early winter. Spring sowings can be made in cold districts. You can raise seedlings in boxes or punnets for transplanting when 5–7 cm high. When transplanting, space seedlings 30 cm apart. Alternatively, sow a few seeds direct in clumps spaced at the same distance and thin to two or three seedlings at each position.

The plants tolerate dry conditions well but respond to occasional watering as they grow. Cultivate or hand-weed around the plants but take care not to disturb the rather shallow root system.

Gourds

Ornamental – see Chapter 18.

Gypsophila

Gypsophila is an extremely useful plant for flower arrangements. It is also attractive grown in odd clumps in the garden. The plants need a well-prepared soil with organic matter and mixed fertiliser added. If soil is acidic an application of lime is recommended, as these plants prefer a near-neutral pH. Select a sunny but sheltered position. Seeds can be sown at almost any time of the year except in the very coldest or hottest months. By making small successive sowings you can have a continuous supply of flowers for indoor decoration. Sow seeds direct in the open garden, either in rows 20–30 cm apart or in clumps at the same distance. Cover with vermiculite or compost and keep damp until seedlings emerge. Thinning the seedlings is rarely needed as plants flower well when closely spaced. This way plants support each other too.

Varieties

'Baby's Breath', with tiny, double white flowers, is the most popular for picking. Other varieties with single or double flowers in shades of pink, white or red are also available.

Helianthus

See Sunflower.

Hollyhock

Among the tallest flowers in the garden, hollyhocks are old English cottage garden favourites. Related to hibiscus, the plants grow to 2–3 m or more with magnificent spikes of large, closely packed flowers. They prefer full sunlight and a well-sheltered position. In exposed situations, plants need staking or a support such as a trellis to which they can be tied. Hollyhocks are adapted to both light and heavy soils but respond best to fertile soil with added organic matter and pre-planting fertiliser.

The best time to sow is late summer and autumn. In most temperate climates, when frosts are not severe, annual hollyhocks will flower in spring. Perennial hollyhocks often do not flower well until the second year. Sow seed in boxes or punnets and cover with vermiculite or compost to a depth of 6 mm. Seedlings emerge in two to three weeks and are ready for transplanting in six to eight weeks. Space the seedlings 30–40 cm apart. Do not crowd hollyhocks with other plants and leave space around them for cultivation. Small bedding plants that grow no more than 30–40 cm are suitable companions. When hollyhocks are 30 cm tall, give them a side dressing of mixed fertiliser and another application when buds appear. Hollyhocks are very attractive to snails and slugs, so protect the plants with a regular scattering of Baysol or Blitzem Snail and Slug Pellets. Plants are very susceptible to rust fungus, especially in humid weather, so spray regularly with fungicide (e.g. Rose Gun Advanced) to control. (See Chapter 8.)

Varieties

'Double Elegance' is an early-flowering annual hollyhock growing to 2 m in height with magnificent spikes of double flowers in a wonderful colour range.

Honesty (Lunaria)

Honesty is a biennial plant that is usually grown as an annual. Plants grow to 60 cm with attractive but rather insignificant lavender or purple spring flowers. The decorative seed pods, which are prized for dried flower arrangements, mature in mid-summer. Plants do best in a cool, partly shaded position in the garden.

Sow seed in autumn in most districts; spring sowings can be made in cold climates. Raise seedlings in boxes or punnets using an open, friable soil mixture as described in Chapter 9. Transplant seedlings when large enough to handle, spacing them 40–50 cm apart. Give liquid feeds of soluble fertilisers towards flowering time. To preserve the pods for indoor decoration, cut the stems when pods are ripe and allow them to dry. When completely dry, peel the outside of the pod by flicking between forefinger and thumb to reveal the silvery, transparent lining.

Impatiens

Sometimes known as Sultan's balsam or busy Lizzie, impatiens is a close relative of balsam with flowers in shades of white, pink, purple, salmon and deep rose. Impatiens is an excellent plant for moist, shady areas but also does well in full sun if temperatures are not too high and water supplies are adequate. It grows well in pots, troughs, window boxes and hanging baskets. Seeds can be sown in autumn (in warm areas only) or spring and is best raised in seed boxes, trays or punnets. Press the seeds lightly into the top of the mix and avoid covering, as the seeds need light for germination. When seedlings have grown their second leaf, prick them out into small individual pots. At a height of 5–7 cm, transfer the seedlings to larger pots or plant in the open garden, spacing them 30–40 cm apart. Water regularly in dry weather and give liquid feeds of soluble fertiliser as flowering commences.

Old-style 'busy Lizzie' impatiens are susceptible to a recently-introduced downy mildew disease that has seen these plants almost disappear from Australian gardens. However, the 'New Guinea' or 'Butterfly' impatiens, with their large, showy flowers, seem to have resistance to the disease. New Guinea impatiens grow well in pots or garden beds. They flower for months during the warmer weather. They cope well with sun but don't like cold and will die in cold winters.

Irish green bellflower (*Molucella*)

Irish green bellflower is also known as molucella or molucca balm. It is an attractive plant with closely packed, pale-green, bell-shaped flowers (bracts) borne on stems 60 cm long. The stems are much in demand for flower arrangements. Sow seed in autumn or spring, direct in the garden, because seedlings do not transplant easily. Sow a few seeds in clumps spaced 20–30 cm apart and cover with vermiculite or seed-raising mix. Thin each clump to the strongest one or two seedlings. The plants are very adaptable to different soil types and need little attention apart from regular watering.

Kale

Ornamental cabbage or kale is a popular, cool season bedding or pot plant with colourful leaves that emerge from the centre of the plant. Leaves can be frilly or crinkled, and usually come in shades of pink, purple, yellow, cream and green. Colour is more intense in cold climates. Seed can be sown direct into garden beds or into pots of seed raising mix in late summer and early autumn or in early spring in cold areas. Pinch off any flowering shoots and treat pests with Rose Gun Advanced.

Kangaroo paw

There are several species of these attractive and unusual native plants. The red and green kangaroo paw (*Anigozanthos manglesii*), the floral emblem of Western Australia, is a clumping plant growing to over 1 m tall with velvety, claw-shaped blooms in red, green and black. There are many other varieties and much breeding work has been done to develop improved strains. Like many Australian native plants, kangaroo paw prefers light, sandy soils with good drainage. Add washed sand if the soil is heavy. Plants do best in full sunlight. Sow seed in boxes, punnets or pots using an open, rather sandy soil mixture. Seed germination is slow and erratic, so keep the containers moist, but not wet, until seedlings emerge. Transplant them to their permanent position when 10 cm tall, spacing them 40–60 cm apart.

Kochia

Kochia is also known as mock cypress or summer cypress because of its symmetrical shape and dense, soft-green summer foliage turning to shades of russet and gold. Because it is an environmental weed in certain climates, this plant is no longer grown in Australia.

Larkspur

Larkspurs are tall, spring-flowering annuals which are ideal for accent planting or as background planting for other low-growing bedding or border plants. They are closely related to delphiniums but have a wider colour range and looser flower heads. Larkspur grows to 60–75 cm and the flower spikes, in pink, rosy-red, light blue and dark blue, make excellent cut flowers. Larkspurs are adaptable to a wide range of soils but perform best in well-drained fertile soils with added organic matter plus a mixed fertiliser. Application of lime is recommended for acidic soils. Soil should be prepared well beforehand and in 'dark damp' condition for sowing the seeds direct in position. Plants prefer full sunlight and protection from strong winds. In exposed situations they may need staking.

In most temperate climates sow seed in autumn and early winter, but in cold districts spring sowing is successful. Seeds germinate best at a temperature of about 15°C, so sowing in late summer or early autumn may not be as successful as later sowing when soil is cooler. Sow a few seeds direct in clumps or stations spaced 20–30 cm apart. Cover seeds with vermiculite or seed-raising mix about 3 mm deep and keep moist until seedlings emerge in two or three weeks. Thin seedlings to two or three in each position. This close spacing gives a good mass of colour and helps the tall plants to support each other. Control weeds by regular, shallow cultivation and give liquid feeds of soluble fertiliser when buds appear. 'Rainbow Mixed', the most widely grown variety, has an excellent range of colour from pale pink to deep blue.

Linaria

Linaria is an adaptable and colourful little annual for flowering in winter and spring. Plants grow 30–40 cm tall with spikes of flowers like tiny snapdragons in delicate pastel shades. Linarias are adaptable to a wide range of soils but respond to good soil structure, added fertiliser and an application of lime to acidic soil.

HINT

The brightly coloured, furry flowers of kangaroo paw are highly attractive to birds and make great cut flowers as well. Ever-blooming varieties will keep flowering indefinitely, provided they are not subjected to frost.

ANGUS STEWART
PRESENTER – *GARDENING AUSTRALIA*, RADIO TALKBACK PRESENTER ABC702; WRITER – *GARDENING AUSTRALIA* MAGAZINE

Prepare the bed well beforehand to have it in friable, 'dark damp' condition for direct sowing. Seed can be sown from early autumn to early winter in temperate climates but spring sowings are successful in cold districts too. Like larkspur, seeds germinate well in cool soil. Sow seeds direct in shallow rows quite thickly. Thinning is only needed if the seedlings are overcrowded. Alternatively, sow a few seeds in clumps about 10–15 cm apart – usually all seedlings can be retained to give a dense mass of colour. Watch out for weeds. Shallow cultivation or hand-weeding is needed from the seedling stage onwards to avoid weeds becoming too competitive. Water plants regularly, especially in dry weather, and give liquid feeds of soluble fertilisers every ten to fourteen days when the plants are well established. After the first flowering, cut back plants to promote a further flush of blooms. 'Fairy Bouquet' is a popular dwarf variety with flowers in shades of cream, yellow, gold, apricot, pink and mauve. It is excellent as a low border or for growing in clumps in rockeries, and flowers very quickly from sowing.

Linum (Scarlet flax)

This flower is an ornamental version of the flax plant from which linen is derived. It has glowing red flowers with a satiny sheen that sit on top of low mounds of mid-green foliage. Each individual flower lasts for a short time, but the overall display goes on for weeks through spring and early summer. Sow linum seeds direct where they are to grow – try to minimise disturbance. Choose a sunny position as these plants must have full sunlight to produce their best flower display.

Livingstone daisy

Livingstone daisies are among the brightest of flowers for late winter and spring. The dwarf plants with succulent leaves only reach about 15 cm tall and cover themselves with tightly packed daisy flowers in yellow, pink, cerise and purple. They are ideal plants for carpeting, edging and rockeries. The plants are very adaptable to light or heavy soil, withstand dry conditions well but need good drainage. They must be grown in full sunlight, as the flowers will close up in shade or on cloudy days. In temperate climates, seed can be sown from early autumn to early winter and again in early spring in cold districts. Sow into pots or punnets for transplanting 10–15 cm apart or sow a few seeds direct in clumps spaced at the same distance. Cover lightly with seed-raising mixture or vermiculite. Seeds may take two or three weeks to germinate so keep moist until seedlings emerge. Thin each clump to two or three seedlings. Water regularly until the plants are established and then only if the weather is dry. If a pre-planting fertiliser has been added to the garden bed before sowing or transplanting, additional fertiliser is rarely necessary.

Lobelia

Lobelia, another dwarf, spring-flowering plant, is excellent for producing massed colour for edging garden beds, rockeries and window boxes. Few plants flower in as deep and rich a blue as lobelia, although modern varieties come in mixed shades of deep blue, light blue, pink, mauve and white. Plants do best in a friable, fertile soil to which mixed fertiliser has been added. A sunny aspect, especially morning sun with protection from strong winds, is preferred although plants will grow in dappled shade. Sow seed in autumn in pots or punnets. Seed is small and needs light for germination, so use a good quality seed-raising mix which holds moisture well. Sow seed on surface and press carefully into the mix.

Water gently or stand the container in water until moisture seeps to the surface. Or mist-spray to avoid dislodging the tiny seeds. Transplant seedlings when small (2–3 cm), spacing them 10 cm apart. Water regularly and give liquid feeds of soluble fertiliser when buds appear.

HINT

Get the best out of Brachyscome ground covers and Chrysocephalum 'Golden Buttons' by cutting them back hard in late winter to early spring each year. This will rejuvenate the plants and provide plenty of flowers over the following months.

RODGER ELLIOT AM

CO-AUTHOR OF *ENCYCLOPAEDIA OF AUSTRALIAN PLANTS*

Varieties

'Crystal Palace' grows to 15 cm tall with bronze-green foliage and dark-blue flowers. 'String of Pearls' grows to a similar height but has flowers in shades of pink, mauve and rose-purple as well as crisp white and clear sky blue. 'Sapphire Streamers' is an interesting variety with trailing stems up to 30 cm in length. The leaves are bright green and the flowers, rich blue with a white eye, are borne in great profusion. Ideal for hanging pots. Use four seedlings per 30 cm container. 'Cascade Mixture' provides a wide colour range and flowers over a long period.

Lupin

Lupins belong to the legume group of plants and are able to add nitrogen to the soil because of the nitrogen-fixing bacteria contained in their root nodules. (See Chapter

5.) For this reason lupins are often used as a green manure crop to improve the soil. Most garden varieties of lupins are winter-growing annuals that flower in spring and early summer. They are very adaptable to climate and soil and grow well in warm and temperate districts.

The Russell lupin is a perennial type which is best suited to cold climates such as the eastern highlands of New South Wales, southern Victoria and Tasmania.

Very few annual lupins are grown in Australian gardens, because a few years ago a fungal disease was detected in field lupins. Although the disease is now controlled, seed supply of lupins is severely limited.

Malope

Malope, a member of the mallow family, is related to hibiscus. The soft plants reach about 1 m in height and should be grown in a sunny, sheltered position. *M. trifida* is a warm season annual that produces large, rosy-pink single flowers with darker veining. Plants are grown from seed sown in early spring.

Marigold

Marigolds are summer-flowering annuals that are best sown in spring or early summer because they prefer the warm weather and are susceptible to frost. African marigolds are tall with large flowers while French marigolds are shorter, more compact – some are dwarf types – and have smaller flowers. Some French marigolds can also be sown in autumn, providing they're to grow in a frost-free area. Marigolds prefer friable, fertile soils with added organic matter and fertiliser but they'll tolerate poor soils. They need a warm, sunny aspect, well sheltered from wind.

Commence sowing seed in spring after all danger of frost is over; sowing can be continued until mid-summer for late-summer and autumn flowering. Generally speaking, a frost-free period of five months is needed from sowing. Sow seed in pots or punnets for pricking out into larger containers when the seedlings are about 1 cm tall. Transplant into garden beds or larger containers when 7–10 cm high. Or, because the seeds germinate quickly and seedlings are quite vigorous, you can sow seeds direct in rows or in clumps. The distance apart for transplanting or sowing direct depends on the height and spread of the plants. Generally, allow a distance of 40 cm apart for tall varieties, 30 cm apart for shorter varieties and 20 cm apart for dwarf types. Marigolds are shallow-rooted plants, so they need regular watering in dry weather. A mulch of grass clippings, compost or leaf mould will prevent moisture loss, keep the roots cool and discourage weeds. Give liquid feeds of soluble fertiliser as buds appear and remove spent blooms regularly to prolong flowering.

Varieties
African marigolds
'African Queen' is a robust-growing variety with very large, double, golden blooms on bushes reaching about 50 cm in height. The blooms have very good wet-weather tolerance and are highly recommended for home gardens. 'Jubilee' has vigorous, sturdy bushes to 75 cm tall with huge, tightly ruffled flowers in lemon, gold and orange. 'Crackerjack' is even taller and has a wide colour range of double blooms. These varieties are extremely showy and produce masses of flowers suitable for cutting. 'Cupid Mixed' is lower-growing – to 40 cm – with softly curled flowers in orange, yellow and gold.
French marigolds
'Honeycomb' grows to about 30 cm and is covered in flowers in shades of rich brown and yellow. An excellent bedding variety. 'Petite Yellow' is a dwarf type, growing to

HINT
Preserve everlasting daisies for use indoors by picking as soon as the first buds open. Cut the stem off just below the flower and replace with thin florist's wire, pushed up into the base of the flower. Flowers treated this way can be kept for several years.

GWEN ELLIOT AM
GARDEN WRITER AND BROADCASTER

15–20 cm high. It is free-flowering with double, clear yellow blooms prominently displayed for many months. It is excellent for mass bedding, low borders or as a rockery plant. 'Safari Mixture' is a mixture of semi-dwarf marigolds to 40 cm high. Plants have attractive, fern-like foliage and double flowers in shades of yellow, gold, orange and red. There are many other low-growing varieties with small blooms.

Marmalade daisy

See Rudbeckia.

Mexican sunflower

Also known as tithonia, this daisy bears orange or scarlet flowers which bloom continuously from mid-summer to mid-winter. One of the largest plants grown as an annual, with stems which may reach over 2 m (although 1 m is normal). The rich, intense colours of the flowers create strong effects. Plants will require staking in strong winds. Use as a background screen, at the rear of a border or for cut flowers. Sow seed outside in spring or indoors six to eight weeks prior to transplanting. Cover seeds sparsely, as light may assist germination. Tithonia prefers average, well-drained soil and tolerates heat and drought. Do not over-water. It is excellent for warm climates but may spread by seed. Mexican sunflower may become weedy, so remove spent flowers regularly.

Mignonette

This dwarf, spring-flowering annual is an 'olde-worlde' favourite, loved more for its spicy aroma than for its relatively insignificant, orange-yellow flower spikes. It is most often seen as a cut flower but is a good subject for low borders, edgings and rockeries and for growing in containers. The plants respond to friable, fertile soils to which organic matter and mixed fertiliser have been added. On acidic soils, an application of lime is recommended.

Seedlings of mignonette do not transplant well so it is best to sow seed direct in the garden bed. Sow seed in autumn, winter and spring in warm–temperate climates but in cold districts autumn and spring only. It is better to scatter seed either thinly in shallow rows or in clumps where the plants are to flower. Cover the seeds with vermiculite or seed-raising mixture. Seed germination is often erratic so keep the soil moist but not wet for about two weeks. When seedlings emerge, thin them if overcrowded. Established plants need little attention apart from occasional watering. Give liquid feeds of soluble fertiliser every ten to fourteen days, especially when plants are growing well. Remove spent flower spikes to prolong flowering.

Mimulus

These low-growing plants are spring bloomers that do well in light shade but must have moist soil at all times. The unusually marked blooms come in shades of red, orange, yellow, cream and white. They have a tubular shape that flares out into a 'grinning face', hence are often given the name 'monkey flower'. The seeds germinate in moderate temperatures and, in most climates, are sown in autumn for spring blooming. Sow seeds in trays of seed-raising mixture and water from below so as not to disturb the small seeds. The seedlings are tiny and very delicate when they first emerge and need gentle handling. The attractive plants are good in shaded borders or can be used in pots and hanging baskets, as long as the potting mix is kept moist.

Mina

See Chapter 18.

Molucella

See Irish green bellflower.

HINT

Plant marguerite daisies en masse for an easy-care and long-lasting display of colour in the garden. Marguerite daisies also look attractive in pots.

JOHN GABRIELE

GARDEN WRITER *ILLAWARRA MERCURY WEEKENDER* MAGAZINE, GARDENING PRESENTER ABC ILLAWARRA 97.3FM

Nasturtium

Nasturtiums are very adaptable, colourful annuals. Old varieties were rather straggly plants, but plant breeders have made great improvements and the modern varieties are more compact than the old types and their flowers are produced well above the foliage to give a brighter display. Nasturtiums will grow on a wide range of soils, but they do best on moderately fertile soils on which the plants produce less foliage and flower more prolifically. Nasturtiums prefer open sunlight and rather dry conditions but will produce quite a good show in partial shade.

Nasturtiums make excellent bedding plants and are also good for growing in rockeries, troughs, tubs or large hanging baskets. Plants flower in ten to twelve weeks from sowing. In warm–temperate climates, sow seed from spring to early autumn; in cold districts make sowings in spring only. Seed germinates best if soil temperatures are not too high. Prepare the bed for direct sowing to have the soil in 'dark damp' condition, but avoid using compost or animal manure, both of which provide conditions favouring excessive leaf growth. A mixed fertiliser can be thoroughly blended into the soil before sowing.

Seeds are large, easy to handle and germinate in two to three weeks. Sow a few seeds in clumps spaced 20–30 cm apart. Thinning is rarely needed. Water moderately until plants are well established, then keep them on the dry side to encourage flowering. Do not give liquid feeds of soluble fertilisers as these will encourage leaf growth. Flowers and leaves are edible if picked from unsprayed plants.

Varieties

'Jewel Mixed' has compact plants and contains a mixture of the choicest colours available – primrose, gold, orange, red and mahogany. 'Cherry Rose' is one of the brightest varieties with semi-double, cherry-rose flowers which contrast dramatically with the foliage. 'Alaska' has splashes of lighter colour on its leaves.

Nemesia

Nemesia is one of the brightest and most colourful bedding and border plants for late-winter and spring flowering. Prepare the soil well before sowing. Nemesias will cope with light or heavy conditions but prefer friable, fertile soil to which organic matter and mixed fertiliser have been added. Direct sowing is the best method, although seedlings can be raised and transplanted if preferred. The plants need a warm, sunny aspect with good drainage. In warm climates, sow seed in autumn or early winter but, in cold districts, sowings are best made in spring to avoid frosty periods. Sow seed direct in rows or, better still, sow a few seeds in clumps spaced 15–20 cm apart. Cover with a light sprinkling of vermiculite, compost or seed-raising mixture. Seedlings usually emerge within ten to fourteen days and thinning is rarely needed.

Alternatively, seedlings can be raised in boxes or punnets, pricked out into larger containers if crowded and transplanted when 5–7 cm high. If transplanting seedlings, harden them off by withholding water for a few days and then give a good watering the night before you transplant. Space seedlings 15 cm apart each way. When the plants are established they need little attention. For bushier plants you can pinch out the leading stems. Water regularly and give liquid feeds of soluble fertilisers every two or three weeks, especially towards flowering time. Plants will flower in fourteen to sixteen weeks from seed sowing.

Varieties

'Carnival Mixture' is the leading dwarf variety. It has large flowers in cream, yellow, gold, orange, scarlet and red on strong, bushy plants 20–30 cm tall.

Nemophila (Baby blue eyes)

Nemophila is another charming dwarf annual for late winter and spring flowering. Plants grow to 20–30 cm with fern-like foliage and small, sky-blue, saucer-shaped flowers. It is an excellent fill-in plant for clump plantings in garden beds or in rockeries. Like nemesia, the plants prefer a friable, fertile, well-drained soil in a warm, sunny position. Seedlings do not transplant well and it is best to sow seeds direct in the garden. In most districts, autumn sowings are best, but in cold districts spring sowings can be made too. Sow seeds thinly in rows, or in

Top five
summer annuals

PETUNIAS

Favourites because of their long-flowering habit and their profusion of blooms, petunias are often regarded as symbols of summer.

SUNFLOWERS

Sunflowers are easily grown from seed and are beloved by children. Almost every part of the plant can be eaten, so they're useful as well as good-looking!

RUDBECKIA

Also called marmalade daisies, rudbeckias are native to North America. Masses of bright orange-yellow blooms reflect the warm colours of summer (see picture on page 329).

PHLOX

Phlox will grow rapidly to blooming stage. If sown direct where it is to grow, it will produce a mass of (inexpensive) summer colour (see picture on page 324).

CALIFORNIAN POPPY

Sun loving Californian poppies have satiny-sheened petals in shades of white, cream, pink, yellow, orange and scarlet. These warm colours contrast with the blue-grey, ferny foliage. Sow seed direct into prepared garden beds.

CALIFORNIAN POPPY

clumps spaced 15 cm apart, and cover lightly with vermiculite or compost. Thin out seedlings if overcrowded. Water regularly and give liquid feeds of soluble, flower-promoting fertiliser when buds appear.

Nicotiana

Once banned from import into Australia, seeds of annual nicotiana plants are now occasionally available (but not necessarily in all states). They cover themselves with star-shaped flowers right throughout the warm weather. Nicotianas are heat-tolerant and bloom in shades of red, white, pink and an unusual lime-green. Taller white or green-flowered varieties are often featured in flower borders.

Nigella

Nigella is also called love-in-a-mist because its attractive flowers are partially hidden in the fern-like foliage. Seed is best sown direct into prepared garden beds in late summer and autumn and seedlings thinned to about 20 cm apart when large enough to handle. Best results are obtained in a moderately rich loam and a position sheltered from winds and the hot sun. Plants grow to about 40 cm in height and are excellent for indoor decoration. The dried seed heads are popular for long-lasting arrangements.

Nolana

A low-growing plant that can be used as a ground cover, nolana has bluebell flowers on a mat of creeping foliage. Its prostrate habit looks especially effective in a hanging basket. Sow seed (after soil has lost its winter chill) directly where the plant is to grow. Although nolana must have plenty of sun the flowers can look a little tired in very hot sunlight. 'Bluebird' is the most popular variety.

Ornamental basil

This attractive annual is also known as 'Dark Opal' basil because of its purple-bronze foliage. Plants grow to 30–40 cm tall and leaves have the same spicy aroma as the herb sweet basil. The spikes of small, lavender-white flowers are not spectacular but the plants are recommended for their foliage and aroma. They are ideal for troughs and pots or dotted here and there among summer bedding plants to add contrasting colour. Leaves can be used to add flavour in a similar manner to green basil although they are slightly spicier. Sow seeds in spring or early summer in pots or punnets for transplanting seedlings 20–30 cm apart, or sow direct in the garden in clumps at the same distance. Plants grow well in sun or semi-shade and need little attention apart from regular watering and weeding. To keep a neat and tidy appearance remove flower spikes as they appear.

Ornamental chilli

Ornamental chilli is a variety of chilli (capsicum) that has been developed for its appearance rather than the hot-flavoured fruit. The fruits are small but very attractive and change colour with maturity from green or purple to yellow, orange and scarlet. In mild climates, plants will overwinter to grow again the following spring but they are usually grown as annuals. They are warm-season plants and frost-susceptible, so the best sowing time is spring to early summer. Chillies need a warm, sunny position with shelter from strong winds. They prefer a fertile soil to which organic matter and a mixed fertiliser have been added during preparation. Ornamental chillies make excellent individual specimens in the garden or in tubs or large pots. Regular watering, together with mulching, is needed in dry weather. Do not give extra fertiliser until the small, white flowers appear. Then give liquid feeds of soluble fertiliser every two or three weeks to encourage and prolong flowering and fruiting. The fruits, or berries as they are often called, are extremely hot, so take care to keep young children away from them.

Painted daisy (see also Chrysanthemum)

This annual chrysanthemum is a good subject for clump planting here and there in the garden or as a background plant. The plants grow to 60–75 cm with large, white flowers zoned with yellow, red and purple. They flower in spring and early summer from seed sown in autumn. In cold districts, seed can be sown in spring too. They do best on well-drained, fertile soils with added organic matter and fertiliser. They need a warm,

sunny position sheltered from strong winds. Sow seeds in pots or punnets, covering the seed with vermiculite or compost to a depth of 6 mm. Transplant seedlings when 7–10 cm high, spacing them 40–50 cm apart. Water frequently and give regular liquid feeds of a soluble fertiliser, such as Aquasol or Thrive. Plants flower within twelve to fourteen weeks from transplanting. Remove any spent blooms to prolong flowering.

Pansy

The pansy was originally known as hearts-ease or wild pansy and is closely related to violas and violets, all of which belong to the genus *Viola*. Pansies come in a wide colour range and used to be distinguished from violas by velvety black or dark-coloured blotches ('faces') but not all of the newer varieties carry these markings. These spring-flowering, biennial plants are treated as annuals and are excellent for mass displays or low borders. They need a well-drained, friable, fertile soil but the tender roots should not be in contact with any concentrated fertiliser. It is best to prepare the bed well beforehand by adding aged compost or animal manure together with a mixed fertiliser.

Thoroughly incorporate these into the top 10–15 cm of soil. Pansies prefer sunlight for most of the day, but shade from hot afternoon sun can be an advantage in warm areas. Modern breeding has developed pansies that can handle more heat and, if spent flowers are removed, can continue blooming well into spring.

Seed can be sown from mid-summer to early winter in most districts. In cold areas autumn and early spring are recommended sowing times. Sow seed in pots or punnets using an open, friable soil mixture as described in Chapter 9. Sow the seed thinly in shallow rows, covering lightly with vermiculite or seed-raising mix. Germination may be slow (three to four weeks) so containers must be kept moist, but not wet, for this length of time. Prick out the seedlings when quite small, spacing them 5 cm apart in seedling trays filled with a similar soil mixture. Grow them on for a few weeks in partial shade until the seedlings are sturdy enough for planting out. Transplant the seedlings into the well-prepared 'dark damp' soil of the garden bed, spacing them at least 20 cm apart. Water plants regularly but do not over-water. Keep weeds under control by careful shallow cultivation, or by tucking a mulch of grass clippings or compost around the plants. This will help to conserve moisture, keep the soil crumbly and encourage a thick mat of surface roots. Once the plants are well established, give weak liquid feeds of soluble fertiliser every two to three weeks. If the first flowers are small, remove some of the buds to increase the size of those which remain. Always pick spent blooms regularly to encourage new buds and prolong flowering. The main pests are aphids, which cluster under the foliage. (See Chapter 8 for control.)

Varieties

'Antiquity' is a variety noted for its profusion of flowers in bronze and pink pastel colours with complementary veining. 'Giant Supreme' is a popular strain with glorious flowers in various shapes and colours. 'Jolly Joker' mix has mid-sized blooms that continue over a long period. One very unusual pansy is 'Black Knight', which produces striking black flowers.

Paper daisies

The Australian paper daisies, or everlastings, are grown for their general hardiness and their long life as dried flowers. Yellow paper daisy (*Schoenia filifolia*) is an Australian native with yellow flowers borne on top of stems that are 30–40 cm tall. Pink paper daisy (*Rhodanthe chlorocephala*), which used to be known as acroclinium, flowers at its best in spring but may also produce a good show from spring plantings. Both of these should be sown where they are to grow. They are suitable for planting here and there in the garden or ideal for open meadow plantings. The plants do well on most garden soils but need a warm, sunny position. They also tolerate hard conditions better than most garden annuals but appreciate extra watering in dry weather. Sow seeds either in autumn or spring, covering the seed lightly.

Cut flowers when half open, tie in bunches and hang head downwards in a cool place to dry. Dried flowers will last for months if they are kept free of dust.

Petunia

Petunias are some of the most colourful annuals for the summer garden. Like many other flowering plants, petunias have been

Pansies are excellent for carpet bedding and provide a colourful display.

improved tremendously by plant breeders in recent years. The multiflora (bedding) type of petunias are sturdy and compact with flowers in strong, clear colours. The grandiflora (large-flowered) types have magnificent single, double or frilled blooms and the plants are stronger and sturdier than old varieties. Spreading and/or landscape petunias (some are short-lived perennials) can cover an area up to 1.5 m across. All petunias are sun-loving plants and will tolerate dry conditions once they are established. Plants should be sheltered from strong winds, especially the taller, large-flowered types. They grow well on a wide range of soil textures, from light to heavy, but grow well with some added fertiliser applied as the bed is prepared. Too much fertiliser and water, however, produces sappy plants which flower poorly.

Petunias are excellent for mass bedding and borders but can also be grown (especially the spreading types) in tubs, troughs and large pots on a sunny terrace or patio. There are semi-trailing varieties, too, for a cascade effect in window boxes and hanging baskets. Seed can be sown in spring, after all danger of frost is over, and continued through to mid-summer in most districts. In cold areas with a shorter growing season, sow seed up to early summer. In warm climates, such as Brisbane and further north, sowings can continue to late summer or autumn. Petunia seed is very small and extra care should be taken in raising the seedlings in pots or punnets. Like many small seeds, petunia seed need light for germination. Prepare an open, friable seed-raising mix. Scatter the seed on the surface and cover very lightly with vermiculite or seed-raising mixture. Press firmly and water very gently. Alternatively, stand the container in water until moisture seeps to the surface. Petunia seed needs fairly warm (25°C) conditions to germinate so it is best to keep the containers indoors until the seedlings emerge – then move them outside immediately, but to a sheltered position. Small containers can be covered with glass or plastic wrap. This helps to maintain an even temperature and prevents drying out. Prick out the small seedlings into seedling trays, spacing them 3–5 cm apart, and grow them on until 5 cm high for transplanting into the garden.

Transplant the small-flowered bedding types at a spacing of 25–30 cm, but allow 30–40 cm for the large-flowered varieties. Always scatter snail baits around the newly planted seedlings to protect them from slugs and snails. When established, petunias need little attention apart from the occasional watering if the soil becomes dry. Plants in tubs, pots or hanging baskets dry out very quickly and need more regular watering. Give weak liquid feeds of soluble fertiliser as the plants are developing.

After the first flush of flowers, plants can be cut back and given a liquid feed for a second flush of flowers in late summer or early autumn. If left until the end of their flowering season, petunias will often seed themselves around the garden. Because most of the modern petunias are hybrids, these second-generation plants will rarely be the same as the parents and are often of inferior quality. It's better to start with fresh seed or plants each year.

There have been some interesting developments with perennial petunias in recent years. They only come in a limited range of colours at this stage, and are best in areas with a warm winter but are of good value for hanging baskets or containers.

Varieties

Small-flowered multiflora (30–40 cm)
'Dazzler' is a hybrid, small-flowered type with compact vigorous plants which are very resistant to wet weather.

Large-flowered grandiflora (40–60 cm)
'Colour Parade' was one of the first Japanese F1 hybrids and is still the most popular strain. Single flowers are a cheerful mixture of colours including carmine, salmon, bright red, dark blue, clear white and several different shades of pink.

Phlox

Phlox is one of the brightest summer flowers for mass bedding or borders. The widely grown dwarf varieties reach about 20 cm in height, but tall varieties can get up to 40 cm or more. The range of flower colours is magnificent, many with contrasting white centres. Others are star-shaped with pointed petals. The plants prefer full sunlight but perform well in any situation which has sun for part of the day. They appreciate a friable, well-drained soil with added organic matter plus a mixed, pre-planting fertiliser. Prepare the soil well for direct sowing in spring or early summer. In warm frost-free northern areas, sow in late summer and autumn too. Seeds can be sown in pots or punnets if preferred but direct sowing is best because seeds germinate easily. Phlox seeds are ideal for sowing in clumps spaced 10–15 cm apart. Scatter a few seeds in each clump and cover with vermiculite, compost or seed-raising mix to a depth of 3 mm. Alternatively, seeds can be sown thinly in rows at the same distance apart. With both methods, thinning is rarely needed and this close spacing of plants gives a denser mass of colour. When seedlings have emerged (two to three weeks) keep them well watered until plants are established. Then water regularly but do not over-water; phlox will tolerate fairly dry conditions. Give the plants liquid feeds of soluble fertilisers. When flowering commences, avoid overhead watering as flowers last better when dry. Watering around the base of the plants and adding a mulch of grass clippings or compost will help to keep soil moist and protect the shallow roots. Remove spent flowers to promote new buds.

Varieties

'Drummondii Dwarf' is the most widely grown variety and is ideal for carpeting, low borders and in rockeries. The plants are compact and grow to 20 cm with a very wide colour range which includes pink, lavender, salmon, scarlet, crimson, blue and white, with some flowers having light-coloured centres.

Phacelia

Phacelia is also known as Californian bluebell. Apart from its pretty, bell-shaped flowers, it is grown for its wonderful ability to attract hoverflies, bees and other useful insects into the garden. Phacelia produces copious quantities of pollen, which is an important food source for the larvae of hoverflies. Successive sowings throughout the warm part of the year will maintain a good population of friendly insects in the garden. As the plants finish blooming, dig them into the soil as these plants make useful green manure. They prefer

Phlox seeds can be sown direct where they are to grow.

Mediterranean conditions with long, dry summers and low humidity.

Pinks
See Dianthus.

Pin-cushion flower
See Scabiosa.

Polyanthus
These winter and spring-flowering, primrose-like plants are herbaceous perennials that are often grown as annuals. The modern strain 'Pacific Giants', has clusters of large florets on strong stems in a range of colours which include apricot, gold, pink, scarlet, red, blue and white. Polyanthus grows well in a cool, sheltered, partially shaded position or in a shadehouse. When grown in shaded situations, the plants may last for two or three years and can be divided when they are dormant. The plants can also be grown in open beds in full sun and make ideal pot plants. If grown in the open, move the plants to shade after flowering and take plenty of soil with the roots. Polyanthus prefer friable soil and respond to liquid feeds of a soluble fertiliser such as Aquasol or Thrive.

Sow seeds in late summer and early autumn in boxes, punnets or pots. Seeds are small and germination may be slow and erratic. Use a good seed-raising mix as outlined in Chapter 9. Scatter the seed along shallow rows in the boxes or on the surface of the soil mix in punnets or pots. Cover to a depth of 3 mm with a moisture-holding material such as vermiculite, compost or seed-raising mixture. Press down carefully with a board and keep the surface moist until seedlings begin to emerge in three or four weeks. Transplant seedlings when large enough to handle. Because of the erratic germination, the seedlings may not all be ready for transplanting at the one time. If growing the plants in pots, use the same mixture as for raising seed. Do not let the pots dry out, and give liquid feeds, especially near flowering time.

Poor man's orchid (*Schizanthus*)
These spring-flowering annuals with orchid-like flowers in shades of pink to violet are very adaptable and should be more widely grown. They thrive in semi-shaded positions but can be grown in the open garden provided they are shaded during the hottest part of the day. They are ideal for growing in pots or hanging baskets under trees. When grown in pots or baskets, the potting mix should have some added moisture-holding material such as vermiculite, compost or peat moss. Add a mixed fertiliser before planting.

In temperate climates, sow seed from late summer to early winter, but in cold districts, late summer and autumn only. Seed is quite small and is best sown in pots or punnets. Germination may take two to three weeks. Cover the seed very lightly, firm down with a piece of flat board or the bottom of a punnet and keep the surface damp until seedlings emerge. Transplant seedlings to the open garden when 5 cm tall, spacing them 30 cm apart, or transfer to small pots for growing on to larger pots or hanging baskets. To promote bushy growth of the fern-like foliage, pinch back the leading stems regularly. Keep the plants well watered and, when established, give liquid feeds of soluble fertiliser every ten or fourteen days to promote flowering.

Poppy
Iceland poppies are among the most popular flowers for late winter and spring. They are magnificent bedding plants, growing to 60 cm, and the cut flowers are unsurpassed for indoor decoration. Modern strains of Iceland poppies are a vast improvement on old varieties, both in flower size and colour range. Colours include lemon, yellow, gold, orange, pink, salmon, red shades and white. If spent blooms are picked regularly, the plants will flower for many months. Iceland poppies need plenty of sunshine, good drainage and a friable, fertile soil. They revel in 'good going', so it pays to prepare the bed well beforehand with plenty of compost or animal manure, together with a pre-planting ration of mixed fertiliser. Sunlight, especially morning sun, is needed to 'pop' the buds, so select a warm, sunny (but wind-sheltered) bed to grow them.

In most temperate climates, you can start sowing in late summer and continue through to autumn. Early sowings will produce plants to flower in winter. In cold districts summer to early autumn sowings are recommended. In warm northern areas sowings can be made later, from early autumn to winter. Iceland poppy seed is small and the seedlings are delicate. It is best to sow seed thinly in pots or punnets as described in Chapter 9 and cover with a very light scattering of vermiculite or seed-raising mix. Keep the surface moist until seedlings emerge in ten to fourteen days. Prick out the seedlings when quite small, spacing them 3–5 cm apart in other boxes or seedling trays. Grow them on to a good size, hardening them off to more sunlight as they grow.

Transplant seedlings 20–30 cm apart each way into the garden bed. Plant out on a cool day and keep the crown of the plants slightly above the surface. Planting seedlings too deeply may cause the crown to rot. Keep the seedlings well watered with a gentle spray until established. With a spacing of 20–30 cm between plants the foliage will eventually cover the soil, but mulching with grass clippings or compost will conserve moisture, keep down weeds and avoid possible damage to surface roots when cultivating. Root damage weakens the plants and may result in twisting of flower stems.

Give liquid feeds when buds appear and then at two-week intervals. Pinch out early buds until the plants have formed good clumps. Remove spent blooms to prolong flowering. For indoor decoration, pick flowers early in the morning in full bud or bud-opening stage. Dip the stems into boiling water for thirty seconds before arranging the blooms.

Other types of poppies are best sown directly where they are to grow.

Varieties

'Artist's Glory' is the most popular Iceland poppy for general garden display. It is a specially formulated mixture containing strong-stemmed flowers in shades of lemon, yellow, gold, apricot, rose pink, salmon and white, and many with distinctive picotee edges. This strain flowers over a long period. 'Matilda' is an Australian-bred variety with short, sturdy, wind-resistant stems, large flowers in a range of colours (many with two colours on the one bloom). 'Flanders Poppy' is a form of the wild European field poppy. It

is traditionally associated with the battlefields of World War I. It has a strong red, single flower, often with a black centre, although plain red blooms are also common. 'Shirley' poppies were bred from the wild European poppy by the Reverend Wilks who lived in the English town of Shirley in the late nineteenth century. They have large, single and semi-double blooms in a mixture of salmon, rose pink and red. Oriental poppy is a tall-growing, showy perennial that does best in cool climates.

Portulaca

Also known as pig face or sun plant, this summer-flowering annual is excellent for low borders, edging, banks and rockeries. The plants only get to 15–20 cm tall and are covered in bright open flowers in lemon, mauve, pink, salmon, crimson and white. Portulacas will grow on a variety of soils but respond well to added fertiliser incorporated into the soil when the bed is prepared. The plants do best in full sunlight (flowers will close up in the shade), need good drainage and will tolerate dry conditions. Sow seed in spring (after soil has become warm) or early summer.

Seeds can be raised in boxes or punnets if preferred. Seedlings transplant easily, but it is best to sow seeds direct in the garden, either in rows, patterns or in clumps spaced 10 cm apart. Cover the seed with a very light sprinkling of vermiculite or seed-raising mix (the seeds need light to germinate) and keep damp until seedlings emerge in ten to fourteen days. With direct sowing there is usually no need to thin the seedlings unless they are very crowded. If thinning is necessary, seedlings – if lifted carefully – can be replanted. The plants are prostrate and creep over the ground, protecting their roots and smothering weeds. A light mulch of grass clippings or compost will assist them to become established. Water the plants in dry weather but do not over-water as they prefer rather dry conditions.

Give liquid feeds of soluble fertilisers regularly. Switch to Thrive Flower & Fruit when plants are mature. A popular strain, 'Sundancer', has a wide range of colours and the large blooms will open more freely under lower light conditions than older types.

Primula

P. malacoides is really a perennial but is always grown as a spring-flowering annual. It has come a long way from the old-type primula with small, mauve flowers on long stems. The modern primula is more compact and the flowers are much larger, with a range of colours that includes mauve, carmine, pink, purple, ruby red and white. Primulas have traditionally been regarded as shade-loving plants, but most varieties available in this country grow equally well in full sunlight. They are ideal plants for bedding or borders but are also attractive when grown in troughs, pots and window boxes. They prefer friable, fertile soil with organic matter and fertiliser added before planting. On acidic soils they benefit from an application of lime (one to two cups per square metre, according to soil type – see Chapter 5) during preparation of the garden bed.

In most climates seed should be sown from mid-summer to early autumn, but in warm areas like Queensland sowings can be made later. Like Iceland poppy, the seed of primula is small and the seedlings delicate. Use specific seed-raising mix for filling seed pots or punnets. Sow seed in very shallow rows or scatter on the soil surface and press firmly with a board. Seeds need light for germination so should be barely covered with vermiculite or seed-raising mix. Seedlings may take three to four weeks to emerge, so keep surface moist for that period. Covering the pot with plastic wrap may help retain moisture around the seeds. When small, prick out seedlings into other boxes or seedling trays, spacing them 3–5 cm apart. Grow them on until large enough to transplant. Space seedlings 15–20 cm apart in the garden. Choose a cool, cloudy day for transplanting and keep the new plants well watered until they are established. Give regular liquid feeds of soluble fertiliser when buds appear. Primulas do well in pots but should always be given plenty of water.

Varieties

P. malacoides

'Carmine Glow' is a vigorous variety with compact, sturdy plants 20–25 cm in height. It has been selected over many years for its large, carmine-rose flowers which hold well in open sunlight. 'Gilham's White' is very

Top five spring annuals

PANSIES

Newer varieties of pansies flower over a long period and are much more heat-tolerant than the old varieties, which means that they are able to continue blooming from spring into early summer (see picture on page 322).

POPPIES

Poppies create new magic each year when their hairy buds open to release the brightly coloured 'crepe paper' petals.

PRIMULAS

Each stem of *P. malacoides* supports its own self-contained bunch of dainty flowers. As long as they have plenty of water, primulas will do well in full sun or light shade.

LOBELIAS

The bluest of blues makes low-growing lobelia an unforgettable sight in the garden. It can also be planted as a ground cover, in large tubs, or made to trail from hanging baskets.

CINERARIAS

A mix of brilliant, jewel-like colours makes cinerarias a popular choice. They grow happily in the shade but won't handle frost.

PANSIES AND POPPIES

similar in growth form but the flowers are pure white. It does well in open sunlight or shade. 'Royalty' has flowers in an attractive shade of pink and prefers semi-shade. 'Lollipops' is a specially formulated mixture of the dwarf annual primulas. Colours include carmine-rose, lavender-pink, ruby red and white. An excellent mixture for bedding or borders in open sun or shade.

Queen Anne's lace
(*Ammi majus*)

This tall-growing plant (to 1 m) is popular as a 'filler' in flower arrangements. The delicate-looking white flower heads are made up of dozens of minute white flowers. The lace-like flower clusters look wonderful in cottage gardens, especially when placed behind lower, more colourful plantings. *Daucus carota*, a flowering form of carrot, is also known as Queen Anne's lace. It has similar white flowers and finely dissected foliage.

Rudbeckia
(Marmalade daisy)

Rudbeckia is an attractive bedding or border plant growing to 40 cm high with masses of flowers in summer and autumn. The blooms are gold-yellow with a purple-black centre cone. The plants are best treated as annuals but in cold districts they can be grown as herbaceous perennials. They are adapted to a wide range of soils and climates but prefer a fertile, friable soil and full sunlight. Sow seed in spring or early summer in seed boxes or punnets for transplanting, or direct in the garden in clumps spaced about 30 cm apart. Give liquid feeds when flower buds appear.

Salpiglossis

Salpiglossis is a tall bedding or background annual for summer flowering. The trumpet-shaped flowers are 5 cm long in shades of gold, bronze, red and violet. The plants require a friable, fertile soil with organic matter and mixed fertiliser added. Prepare the soil well beforehand for direct sowing in spring or early summer. Plants need a warm, sunny aspect.

As seedlings do not transplant well, it is best to sow seeds direct in rows spaced 15 cm apart and thin seedlings to the same distance. Alternatively, sow a few seeds in clumps and thin each position to one or two seedlings. Cover seeds to a depth of 6 mm with vermiculite or compost and keep damp until seedlings emerge in two to three weeks. Once plants are established, water regularly, especially in dry weather, and give liquid feeds of soluble fertiliser every two or three weeks. Plants will flower twelve to fourteen weeks after sowing.

Saponaria

See Big gyp.

Salvia

While there are many hundreds of species of salvia available from specialist nurseries, here we will confine ourselves to the summer-flowering bedding salvias that are usually treated as annuals.

In warm–temperate climates, plants will continue flowering in autumn or winter and may be worth growing on into the second year. Plants grow 30–60 cm in height and are excellent for mass bedding or borders. Modern varieties, in traditional scarlet and a number of other colours, are more compact and bushier than older strains.

Salvias prefer a well-drained, friable soil to which organic matter and mixed fertiliser have been added during soil preparation. Plants do best in full sunlight and need protection from strong winds.

Sow seeds in spring or early summer when the weather is warm, because the seed is difficult to germinate in cold soil. You can raise seedlings in pots or punnets for transplanting, or sow seeds direct in the garden. Space seedlings or sow a few seeds in clumps 30–40 cm apart for tall varieties, but 20–30 cm apart for dwarf, compact plants. When plants are established, they can be pinched back when 10 cm tall to encourage lateral shoots for bushy plants. Plants prefer moist but not soggy conditions so do not over-water. Occasional liquid feeds of soluble fertiliser will keep them growing strongly.

Varieties

S. splendens 'Bonfire' is the traditional bedding salvia with scarlet blooms on long spikes. Modern strains of this variety are more compact than older strains and rarely grow higher than 60 cm. 'Dwarf Scarlet' has

Rudbeckias are also known as black-eyed Susan because of their dark centres.

compact, semi-dwarf plants to 30 cm tall. Flowers are equal in size and colour to 'Bonfire'.

'Touch of Blue' (*S. farinacea*) grows to a height of 45 cm and is excellent for colour effect when grown in clumps in the garden. The deep Wedgwood-blue flowers are borne on long, slender spikes. This variety can be cut back in warm weather for further flowering, and in warm districts the clumps can overwinter for another flowering in late spring. There is a similar strain with white flowers.

Scabiosa (Pin-cushion flower)

Scabiosa or pin-cushion flower is a spring-flowering annual or perennial that blooms in a range of purple, pink and mauve shades. Suitable for bedding or background planting, plants grow to about 60 cm. They require a sunny aspect sheltered from strong winds. Prepare the bed well beforehand, adding a mixed fertiliser at one-third of a cup per square metre, and a ration of lime at one to

two cups per square metre, depending on soil texture. The soil must be well drained but plants need ample water in dry weather.

Sow seed in autumn to early winter in temperate districts, but in autumn and spring where colder. Seed is best sown in boxes or punnets. Cover with 6 mm of vermiculite or seed-raising mix and keep soil moist until seedlings emerge in two or three weeks. Transplant seedlings when 5–7 cm high, spacing them about 40 cm apart. Give liquid feeds of soluble fertiliser when flower buds appear about twelve weeks from transplanting.

Schizanthus

See Poor man's orchid.

Snapdragon (*Antirrhinum*)

A severe rust fungus led to a decline in the popularity of snapdragons for the home garden for some years. However, many of the new varieties are more resistant to this disease, and more effective fungicide sprays have encouraged gardeners to grow these magnificent flowers. Snapdragons are perennial plants but are best treated as annuals and sown from seed each year, although they can be cut back after the first flowering to produce a second flush of blooms.

The plants need well-drained friable soils with plenty of added organic matter. Also apply a pre-planting fertiliser and, in acidic-soil areas, some garden lime. Keep the soil in good condition by cultivating when it is 'dark damp' until ready for transplanting. Snapdragons prefer full sunlight but do quite well if they are in sun for only part of the day.

Seed can be sown at almost any time of the year in temperate climates, but autumn is the best period for a spring display. In cold districts you can sow seeds in spring or early summer. As seeds are small, they should be sown in pots or punnets using a good moisture-holding seed–raising mix as described in Chapter 9. Scatter the seed in shallow rows or broadcast on the surface and press firmly with a piece of board. Cover the seed very lightly with compost or seed-raising mixture and keep damp until seedlings emerge – usually in ten to fourteen days. Seedlings are ready for transplanting in about six weeks from sowing when they are 3–5 cm high. Seedlings of tall varieties should be spaced about 40 cm apart, but dwarf varieties can be planted at 30 cm or even closer. If plants tend to produce buds too soon, nip them back to encourage lateral growth and leave eight to ten flower spikes. Give liquid feeds of soluble fertiliser at this stage. When cutting flowers for indoor decoration, or removing spent blooms, cut the stalks back to 5–7 cm from the crown to encourage a second crop of flowers on long stems. Continue to give liquid feeds while flowering continues.

Varieties

'Tetra Mixed' grows to 60 cm with large, ruffled flowers in shades of yellow, gold, rose, lilac, tango, deep red and white. It has shown some resistance to rust fungus and is an excellent variety for cut flowers. 'Excalibur' grows to 40–50 cm and is best suited for bedding and borders. The large flowers on strong, straight stems are excellent for cutting and come in lovely mixed shades.

'Tom Thumb' is a compact-growing, mound-shaped bush with attractive blooms in a beautiful range of clear colours. The bush grows to about 20 cm and has a beautiful flower display.

Spider flower (*Cleome*)

Spider flower is an unusual, warm season, shrubby annual that usually grows to a height of 1–2 m, although some dwarf varieties are available. It is excellent as a background plant or for planting here and there in the garden. The pink, lilac, mauve or white flowers, with their long, spidery stamens, are followed by decorative seed pods. The plants are adaptable and flower abundantly providing they get plenty of sun. They grow on light or heavy soils that are well drained and have had some fertiliser added during soil preparation. Sow seeds in spring or early summer or again in early autumn. It is best to sow a few seeds direct in the garden in clumps spaced 50–60 cm apart, and thin to the strongest seedlings. Water regularly.

Star daisy

See Chrysanthemum.

Statice

Statice or sea lavender has attractive 'everlasting' flowers for garden display or for cutting and drying. The plants reach 60 cm and are suitable for creating accents in the garden bed. They need a moderately fertile soil and a well-drained, warm, sunny aspect. Statice is a perennial plant that is usually grown as a spring-flowering annual. Cut back for a second flowering.

In temperate climates, sow seed from autumn to early spring, but in cold districts avoid sowing during the colder months. It is best to sow seed direct into a well-prepared and well-fertilised bed. Sow a few seeds in clumps or stations spaced 30–40 cm apart and thin to the strongest seedling. The seeds are large and may have some pieces of the dried petals attached. It doesn't matter if these show above the soil.

Cover the seeds with up to 12 mm of compost or vermiculite. Seedlings often germinate slowly and erratically and may take twenty-eight days or more to emerge, so keep the soil damp for this length of time. When the plants are established they need little attention. Providing a pre-planting fertiliser has been added before sowing, the plants usually flower well, but give them a side-dressing of fertiliser towards flowering time if they need more encouragement. The flowers are borne on long stems in clusters and range in colour from white through yellow to rose and blue. To dry the flowers, cut them when mature, tie in bunches and hang head downwards in a cool, dry place. Well-dried flowers will last for a long time without losing colour.

Stocks

Stocks are one of the most popular spring-flowering annuals. They produce a magnificent garden display, make good cut flowers and are worth growing for their fragrance alone.

Stocks have come a long way from the sixteenth century when Peter Matthioli, an Italian botanist, first classified them in a group of plants which included his own name (*Matthiola incana*). At that time, flower colour was limited to purple only, but today, as a result of plant breeding and selection, there is a tremendous colour range: white, cream, yellow, pink, lilac, mauve, red, port wine and purple. Dwarf and tall stock varieties are now available, but possibly the greatest advance has been the development of strains with a very high percentage of double flowers.

Oddly enough, stocks belong to the same botanical family (*Brassicaceae*) as a number of our important cool-season vegetables – broccoli, cabbage, cauliflower and turnips – so many of their requirements for climate, soil and fertiliser are very similar. They are also susceptible to the same pests, especially

The unusual spidery flowers of cleome look good in mass plantings.

caterpillars. Stocks, like the cabbage group, are really biennials but are grown as annuals. The plants prefer friable, fertile soils with plenty of added organic matter (compost, animal manure or leaf mould). Also apply a mixed fertiliser and a liberal ration of lime, except on alkaline soils. These should all be added to the soil beforehand and dug in to a depth of 15–20 cm so that the soil is in first-class condition for either transplanting seedlings or direct sowing. Drainage is also important because stocks will not tolerate wet feet. Raising the beds 15–20 cm above the surrounding surface will usually give adequate drainage. Generally, the plants prefer rather dry conditions but should be given sufficient water to keep them growing steadily during the season. Stocks prefer a sunny position; tall varieties should be sheltered from strong winds.

In temperate and cold climates, seeds can be sown from mid-summer to autumn, but in warm northern districts autumn sowings are best. Seeds can be sown in pots or punnets for transplanting and this method may be preferable for early sowings. Good results are possible by sowing direct, especially when moisture-holding materials, such as vermiculite or seed-raising mix, are used to cover the seeds. Stock seeds germinate quickly (ten to fourteen days) and seedlings grow rapidly, so direct sowing avoids transplanting shock. When sowing direct, scatter a few seeds in clumps and keep moist until seedlings emerge. Thinning the seedlings in each clump is only necessary if they are too crowded. It doesn't matter if a few seedlings are close together, providing there is sufficient space between each clump. Whether you transplant seedlings or sow direct, the planting distance will depend on the variety (dwarf or tall). As a guide, dwarf and column varieties are spaced 20–30 cm apart, but you should allow 30–40 cm for taller branching types.

When the plants are well established, cultivate regularly between individual plants or clumps to control weeds. Water when necessary, but don't overdo it. Give liquid feeds of soluble fertiliser as the plants grow, especially towards flowering time. An exception is the column type, which may develop lateral branches and new buds from

the centre of the florets if it is fed too generously. Another point of interest is that plants which produce single flowers can often be discarded in the seedling stage. Seedlings which are tall, thin-leafed, dark green and vigorous usually produce single flowers, so many gardeners discard them when transplanting or thinning out. The method is not infallible, but has been used with some success. Most double strains available today will produce from 60 to 85 per cent double-flowered plants, giving good results. When plants are flowering well, remove all spent blooms to promote new buds to form and prolong the display.

Varieties

'Austral' is a beautiful strain bred and selected by Yates in Australia. Plants are vigorous, growing to 50 cm with a brilliant colour range including white, cream, apricot, various shades of pink and lavender, red and purple with other attractive bicolours. A short, closely packed central spike is soon followed by many lateral spikes. This is an excellent garden variety. 'Giant Perfection' ('Giant Imperial') is a popular, semi-bush stock. The central flower spike is followed by lateral spikes. Individual flowers are large, with a high percentage of double flowers. Colours include white, cream, buff, many shades of pink, lavender, lilac, purple and brilliant red. Because they are non-branching, space between plants can be reduced to 20–30 cm. Dwarf stocks are available that grow to 25 cm tall with tightly packed flower spikes of double florets. They have the perfume and full colour range of the taller, branching types. They are excellent for borders and combine well with low bedding plants like alyssum, nemesia, pansy and viola. They are also suitable in exposed situations where taller strains may be damaged by wind.

Sturt's desert pea (Swainsona)

Sturt's desert pea, or glory pea, is a prostrate, trailing plant that is found growing naturally in the dry inland areas of Australia. The large pea-like flowers are borne in clusters. The standard petal and keel are usually a brilliant red with a large black-purple blotch at the base of the standard, but occasionally colour variations can occur. In their natural state, these plants thrive on quite poor, rather sandy soils which are alkaline. Once established, Sturt's desert pea tolerates extremely hot and dry conditions but resents any disturbance to the root system. The plants need a well-drained soil in a warm, sunny position. The soil must not be fertilised heavily, but many growers report success when feeding with half-strength Aquasol every two weeks. The plants do quite well in a window box or in troughs or pots.

Although the plants are biennials, they are best treated as annuals from seed sown in late spring or early summer. Sow seeds in punnets or pots for transplanting later, but take care to lift as much soil as possible with the roots. Seeds can also be sown direct, spacing the clumps about 40 cm apart. The seed coat is very hard and only takes up water slowly. You can assist germination by nicking the seed coat with a sharp knife, but take care not to damage the eye (hilum) of the seed. Seed can then be placed in a small amount of boiling water and left until cool. If the seed is sown in punnets or pots, cover with glass or clear plastic to give extra warmth until seedlings emerge. Keep seedlings watered until well established. After that, little attention is needed apart from careful hand-weeding so that the roots are not disturbed.

Sunflower (*Helianthus*)

Although sunflowers are the 'giants' of the summer flowering annuals, some shorter-growing and dwarf varieties are now available. Plants must be grown in full sunlight and in a sheltered position to avoid wind damage. They are adaptable to both light and heavy soils but do best on well-drained soil that has been improved by adding organic matter and mixed fertiliser before sowing. Sow seed in spring or early summer when weather and soil are warm. Although seed can be sown in boxes or punnets and transplanted when small, it is best to sow seeds direct in the garden by scattering a few seeds in clumps 50–60 cm apart and thinning to one or two seedlings. The plants need little attention when established, apart from watering in dry weather and cultivation to control weeds.

Flowers for indoor decoration should not be too old before cutting. Remove spent blooms to prolong flowering.

Varieties

'Yellow Empress' is a tall strain with extra-large blooms. 'Bronze Shades' is a medium grower (150 cm) with single flowers which are excellent for picking. Flowers are in shades of bronze and terracotta, and many are tipped with yellow and pink.

Swan River daisy (*Brachyscome*)

A native of Western Australia, this delightful little annual grows to 20–30 cm tall with dainty single flowers in blue, mauve or white. It is useful for low borders or as an accent plant. Its rather spreading growth makes it ideal for container growing. Brachyscome will grow on quite poor soil and prefers light, well-drained soil in a sunny position.

Sow seed in spring or early summer, either in seed boxes or punnets for transplanting seedlings 20 cm apart, or sow a few seeds direct in clumps at the same distance. The seed is quite small so cover very lightly with vermiculite or seed-raising mix. When the plants are established they need little attention, as they withstand hot, dry conditions. Do not over-water.

Sweet pea

Sweet peas are one of the most popular spring-flowering annuals for garden display and for cut flowers. Most varieties grow 2–3 m tall, so need support in the form of a trellis, tripod or wire mesh fence. There are also dwarf strains. The dwarf plants grow between 25–60 cm tall and are ideal for borders and pots.

Sweet peas have been improved tremendously in flower form, size and colour range since they were first introduced to England from Sicily in the seventeenth century. The most popular sweet peas grown in Australia are the early bloomers that flower during winter (flowers last longer in cooler conditions). In today's modern sweet pea strains, colours range from pure white and cream through numerous shades of pink, lavender and mauve to light and dark reds, blue and purple. Bicolours and 'flakes' with veined markings on the petals are also available.

Sweet peas need ample sunlight and do poorly when shaded. If growing on a trellis the rows should run north–south so that the vines receive as much sun as possible. Good drainage is essential and it is best to raise the bed 15–20 cm above the surrounding surface so that water is shed quickly after heavy rain. Soil preparation is most important, too. Except on naturally alkaline soils, lime should be added to the soil at about one cup per square metre on light soils and two cups per square metre on heavier soils. Spread a generous layer of compost, animal manure or well-rotted grass clippings on top of the soil and sprinkle mixed fertiliser along the row where seed is to be sown. The organic matter will improve the structure of both light and heavy soils but, as these materials are often low in phosphorus and potassium, the addition of fertiliser will make up for any deficiency. On the other hand, avoid using fertilisers that are high in nitrogen. Dig the lime, organic matter and fertiliser into the surface soil to a depth of 10–15 cm so that the materials are mixed well. Then dig the bed over to spade depth, loosening rather than turning the soil so the topsoil stays on the surface. Always remember to dig or cultivate the soil when 'dark damp' – especially on heavy soil – to preserve a good crumb structure. Give the bed a gentle but thorough watering and leave it to settle for a week or two. Then rake the surface to destroy any weed seedlings and to bring the soil to a crumbly condition for sowing the seeds direct.

In most temperate climates, seed can be sown from mid-summer to late autumn, but March or April (April is better if conditions are warm) are usually the best months. In cold districts, spring sowings can be made as well. As the germinating seeds are susceptible to damping off (especially in cold soil) it is advisable to dust the seed with fungicide before sowing. (See Chapter 9.) It is often a good idea to erect the support before sowing. This will avoid disturbing or treading on the bed after the seeds are sown. Mark out shallow drills 2–3 cm deep and press the seeds into the soil, spacing them 5–7 cm apart. If the soil is loose and crumbly, cover the seed and lightly tamp down. On very heavy soils, cover the rows with vermiculite or seed-raising mix. If the soil is 'dark damp' at sowing, additional watering is usually unnecessary until the seedlings emerge in ten to fourteen days. In very dry weather, or on very sandy soil, give extra water.

Over-watering is one of the main causes of poor germination. For the same reason, soaking seeds in water before sowing may do more harm than good. (See Chapter 9.) If you wish to pre-germinate seeds, spread them out on wet blotting paper or towelling, or mix them with moist vermiculite or seed-raising mixture in a saucer or dish. This way they absorb water quickly but also get plenty of air, which is essential for germination. You can plant out the swollen seeds in a few days but handle them very carefully if they have started to germinate. Another point to remember is that some seeds may be smaller than others and may look pinched or shrivelled. These seeds are often the darker colours – red, mauves and blues – and if you discard them you may not have a full colour range.

Always sow all seeds in the packet or, if you have too many seeds, sow an average sample.

When the plants are 15–20 cm tall, place some twigs along the length of the row to help the tendrils to reach the netting. If the plants are spindly it may be necessary to cut them back slightly to promote sturdier growth. Laterals will appear when the plants are 20–30 cm tall. For general garden display allow these to grow on, but for exhibition blooms cut some out. Water the plants regularly, especially in dry weather, and every ten to fourteen days when buds appear. Remove spent blooms to prolong flowering. Sweet peas are usually not unduly troubled by pests and diseases although powdery mildew can attack leaves. Control with a systemic rose spray (e.g. Rose Gun Advanced). For control measures for other problems, see Chapter 8.

Varieties

'Colourcade' is the most widely grown and popular of all the strains of sweet peas. This mixture of early-flowering blooms contains a complete range of all sweet pea colours and shades.

'Old Fashioned' is a rather later-flowering strain. The plants are extremely vigorous and bear large, ruffled blooms on long, sturdy stems. The flowers are heavily perfumed and very suitable for exhibition purposes.

'Tiffany' is an early-flowering, tall, vigorous sweet pea featuring very large flowers on strong stems. Many blooms are true doubles, deeply frilled and bicoloured.

'Bijou' is an outstanding dwarf sweet pea. Plants grow to 60 cm tall and flowers are beautifully perfumed in a full colour range. The flowers are as large as those of tall varieties and are borne on stems 20 cm long. An excellent variety for borders, rockeries, window boxes and pots, but remember that plants need full sunlight.

'Pixie Princess' is excellent for borders, rockeries, window boxes and pots. It grows to about half the height of 'Bijou', flowers a little later than 'Bijou' and is available in a wide range of colours.

Sweet William

Sweet William (*Dianthus barbatus*) is a biennial or short-lived perennial with clusters of frilly-edged, white, pink or red flowers growing to about 40 cm. It is usually treated as an annual; seeds can be sown from mid-summer to autumn in most climates, but in both autumn and spring where colder. The cultivation of this free-flowering, attractive plant for beds, borders or rockeries is very similar to dianthus (pinks) and carnation, to which it is closely related.

Torenia

Torenia is a warmth-loving, flowering annual with predominantly blue flowers similar to small snapdragons. The plants grow to 20–30 cm and are suitable for low borders, edging, rockeries and window boxes. For borders or edging, the blue flowers combine beautifully with a background of taller annuals in yellow, pink or red. Torenia is very adaptable to soil type. It prefers a well-drained, sunny situation, but will accept light, broken shade.

Verbena

Verbena is a trailing perennial that may persist for two or three years, but is often grown as an annual. The plants grow to 30

Smaller-growing sweet pea varieties make excellent pot subjects.

cm tall and continue to flower for many months. Flower colours include pink, mauve, red and purple, many with a white eye. Verbena is very adaptable and grows well in most garden soils, but it does require good drainage. It prefers full sunlight but will tolerate some shade. Seed can be sown in all the warm months, from spring to autumn. You can raise seedlings in pots or punnets for transplanting, or sow a few seeds direct in clumps spaced 25–30 cm apart. Thin each clump to two or three seedlings. Seed is slow to germinate, seedlings taking 21–28 days to emerge, so take care that the soil is kept damp but not too wet for this length of time. Once established, the plants need very little attention. They tolerate quite dry conditions and grow well without extra fertiliser. Cultivate between plants to destroy weeds in

HINT

If soil is too moist, sweet pea seeds rot away before they germinate. If in doubt, build a raised-up 'mini planting bed' using see-through plastic cups. Remove the bottom from each cup and sit upright on top of the soil. Fill with good-quality seed-raising mix and sow the sweet pea seeds inside. After the seeds germinate in the well-drained mix, the roots can move down into the soil and the plants will start to grow happily.

JUDY HORTON

GARDEN WRITER, BROADCASTER
AND HORTICULTURIST

the early stages but the bushy plants will soon cover the ground to form a dense mat. Cut back plants after flowering to promote a second flush of blooms. New, perennial varieties, free-flowering with a brilliant range of colours, are excellent for planting in odd corners of the garden and in rockeries. They make ideal ground covers.

Viola

Violas are close relatives of pansies and are grown in exactly the same way, although violas can be planted rather more closely together than pansies. The plants will continue flowering for a very long period, especially if the spent blooms are picked regularly. For general notes on soil, sowing and cultivation, refer to Pansy in this chapter.

Varieties

'Toyland' and 'Space Crystals' have large, velvety flowers and are excellent for beds or borders. They are self-coloured and without markings. 'Johnny Jump Up' is the original *Viola tricolour*, a delightful, small-flowered purple viola with streaked yellow centres. It is excellent for borders and containers and it flowers prolifically from early spring to summer.

Virginian stock

Virginian stock is a dainty little spring-flowering annual with tiny flowers in white, cream, lavender and pink. The plants grow to 20 cm tall and are excellent for low borders, edging and odd corners. Virginian stock is often sown over bulbs to disguise the bulb leaves as they die down after flowering. Virginian stock plants prefer a warm, sunny aspect but will tolerate part-shade. They are very adaptable little plants that grow well on most soils, but perform better if mixed fertiliser is added when preparing the bed. In temperate climates, sow seed in autumn; in cold districts, seed can be sown in both autumn and spring.

Although seedlings can be raised in pots or punnets for transplanting, it is best to sow direct – either thinly in rows, or a few seeds in clumps spaced 15 cm apart. Thinning is rarely necessary. Plants flower very quickly from seed. Give liquid feeds regularly while plants are growing.

Viscaria

Viscaria gives masses of dainty summer flowers in shades of pink, mauve, lavender and blue. The plants have thin, branching stems and grow to 30–40 cm. They need a warm, sunny position but are adaptable to both light and heavy soils to which a mixed fertiliser has been added during preparation. Sow seed in spring or early summer direct in the garden, scattering a few seeds in clumps spaced 15 cm apart. Cover with vermiculite or seed-raising mix.

Seedlings rarely need thinning, providing there is sufficient space around each clump. Water regularly in dry weather and mulch around plants to conserve moisture and discourage weeds.

Wallflower

Wallflower is another 'olde-worlde', winter/spring-flowering annual that has been improved in flower form and colour range but has retained its traditional fragrance. The plants grow to 60 cm and are excellent for bedding or borders or for planting here and there in clumps or drifts in the garden. They prefer a warm, sunny aspect sheltered from strong winds. Like stocks (wallflowers belong to the same family) the plants do best in friable, fertile, well-drained soil. Prepare the bed well beforehand, adding liberal quantities of compost or animal manure. On most soils, except those that are alkaline, add a ration of lime at one to two cups per square metre, depending on soil type. Then apply a mixed fertiliser. Mix these additives into the soil to a depth of 15–20 cm and, if possible, leave in this rough state for four to six weeks. Cultivate again about a week before transplanting so that the soil is in a crumbly condition.

In most districts, seed can be sown from mid-summer to autumn. Seed sown before April will produce plants that flower in late winter and early spring. Fill pots or punnets with a seed-raising mixture as described in Chapter 9. Sow the seeds in shallow rows and cover lightly with vermiculite or seed-raising mix. Water gently and keep damp until seedlings emerge in ten to fourteen days. Prick out seedlings when small into other containers (filled with the same soil mix) spacing them 3–5 cm apart. Grow them on until 5–7 cm high and then transplant them to the garden bed, spacing 20–30 cm apart. Water regularly to keep the plants growing strongly. Cultivate lightly to destroy weeds, taking care not to damage the shallow roots. Feed regularly with soluble fertiliser every ten to fourteen days. The double-flowered 'Winter Delight' is very fragrant and has double blooms in many colours. It blooms early and is ideal for cutting.

Zinnia

Zinnias are one of the most colourful summer-flowering annuals. They come in a range of sizes, ranging from tall background plants to dwarf border varieties.

For best results zinnias must be grown in full sun and the tall growers need shelter from strong winds. Soil should be well drained and improved with compost or animal manure, plus some mixed fertiliser and lime if the soil is acidic.

Prepare the bed well in advance so that the soil is in a crumbly condition for transplanting or direct sowing.

In temperate districts seed can be sown in early spring to late summer; in cold districts late spring or early summer sowing is best. Seed germination is often disappointing if seeds are sown in cold soil too early in the season, especially when sown direct in the garden. Germination will be much better if sowing is delayed until the soil warms up to 20°C or more. The seeds are quite large and can be handled easily, but it is advisable to dust them with fungicide to protect against damping off.

Early sowings can be made in pots or punnets using an open, friable seed-raising mix. Extra warmth can be provided by placing the pots in a warm spot (indoors if necessary) or covering the containers with glass or clear plastic until the seedlings emerge (usually in seven to ten days). Grow seedlings on until 5–7 cm high before transplanting. When sowing direct, scatter a few seeds in clumps or stations and cover lightly with vermiculite or seed-raising mix. Thinning each clump is rarely needed unless the seedlings are overcrowded.

Whether transplanting seedlings or sowing direct, the distance between plants or clumps

HINT

These simple tips will help you grow camellias successfully:

- It's best to prune camellias at the end of winter, just as flowering is finishing; don't wait for the last blooms to flower otherwise the new growth will have started.
- When camellias are grown in pots, many fail because they are potted into containers that are too large. Increase the pot size in stages.
- Next year's camellia blooms are generated on the new growth made the spring before. It's what you do in spring that governs the quality and number of next year's blooms.

DIANNE AND JON HALL
NEWMAN'S NURSERY CAMELLIA
SPECIALISTS

will depend on the variety and the size to which it will grow. As a general guide, space tall types 40 cm apart and semi-dwarf types 20 cm apart. Always pinch back the centre shoot of zinnias to promote the growth of laterals and produce bushy plants.

Once established, the plants need little attention apart from regular watering (especially in dry periods) and cultivation to destroy weeds. In very hot weather, a good mulch of grass clippings or compost will conserve moisture and keep the roots cool. Give liquid feeds of soluble fertiliser when the plants are half-grown.

To control mildew, a fungus which attacks the plants in later summer and autumn, use a Rose Gun Advanced or see Chapter 8.

Varieties

'Gold Medal' (dahlia-flowered) is a blend of the best colours in this strain and has large double blooms on strong stems. Plants grow up to 1.2 m in height.

'Palette d'Artiste' grows to 60 cm and is the most suitable variety for cut flowers. It produces a profusion of double blooms.

Z. linearis has masses of small, star-shaped

HINT

If cut flowers are drooping, you can often revive them by cutting about a centimetre or so off the stems under water (so air bubbles don't block the sap vessels) and standing them in two or three centimetres of boiling water. When the water has cooled down, take them out, trim off the boiled parts of the stems (again under water) and stand them in deep water for an hour or two before arranging them.

ROGER MANN

LANDSCAPE ARCHITECT AND AUTHOR
OF *YATES ROSES* AND *NAMING THE ROSE*

yellow flowers over a long period. Plants are dwarf (to 30 cm tall) and are excellent for borders or rockeries. They do particularly well in warm climates.

Zinnias, with their bright, paintbox-coloured blooms, do well in warm conditions.

Pest and Disease Control for Flowers and Ornamentals

PLANT	PEST OR DISEASE	SYMPTOMS	CONTROL
Aster	Aphids	Small insects under foliage and on lower buds.	Bug Gun, Confidor, Pyrethrum, Mavrik, Natrasoap
	Jassids & leaf hoppers	Small leaf-hopping insects which spread virus.	Pyrethrum
	Caterpillars	Caterpillar in leaves which come together.	Bug Gun, Success Ultra, Pyrethrum, Mavrik
	Two-spotted mite	Foliage turns bronze and is unthrifty.	Mavrik, Natrasoap
	Virus	Flowers become green.	Control sap suckers
Azaleas and rhododendrons	Lace bug	Foliage becomes silver-bronze.	Confidor, Rose Gun Advanced
	Leaf miner	See Cineraria	
	Two-spotted mite	See Aster	
	Petal blight	Flecking and collapse of flowers.	Zaleton
Begonia	Powdery mildew	Powdery growths on leaves.	Rose Gun Advanced
Bellis (English daisy)	Rust	Bronze blisters on foliage.	Rose Gun Advanced
	Two-spotted mite	See Aster	
Calendula	Rust	See Bellis	
	Two-spotted mite	See Bellis	
	Powdery mildew	See Begonia	
Camellias	Dieback	Large, dark, dead areas on branches.	Remove and destroy infected twigs
	Balling	Flower buds do not open and bud scales are damaged due to bud mite.	Spray with Natrasoap, Mavrik
Carnation	Thrips	White flecks on petals.	Bug Gun, Confidor, Natrasoap
	Rust	See Bellis	
Chrysanthemum	Black aphids	Small, black insects underneath leaves and on flower buds.	See Aster
	Leaf spot and rust	Various spots on leaves.	Mancozeb Plus, Zaleton, Rose Gun
	Leaf eelworm	Triangular black areas on leaves.	Remove affected leaves

PLANT	PEST OR DISEASE	SYMPTOMS	CONTROL
Cineraria	Leaf miner	Yellow tracks on leaves.	Remove affected leaves
	Two-spotted mite	Discoloured leaves.	Natrasoap
	Leaf spot	Brown target spots on leaves.	Mancozeb Plus
Cornflower	Aphids	See Aster	
	Powdery mildew	See Begonia	
	Collar rot	Plant rots at ground level.	Remove and destroy
Dahlia	Jassids & leaf hoppers	See Aster	
	Two-spotted mite	See Aster	
	Powdery mildew	Powdery film over foliage.	Rose Gun Advanced
Delphinium	Powdery mildew	See Begonia	
Ferns	Mealybug	White insects with filaments under fronds.	Confidor, Natrasoap
	Scale insects	Swellings along stem.	PestOil, White Oil
	Aphids	Soft insects attack young growth.	See Aster
	Two-spotted mite	See Aster	
	Staghorn beetle	Holes in fronds and tips die.	Remove by hand at night
	Leaf eelworm	Dark streaks on foliage.	Remove affected leaves
Foxglove	Aphids	Insects on flower spikes and leaves.	Confidor, Pyrethrum, Natrasoap
Geranium	Rust	See Bellis	
Gerbera	Thrips	Flowers deformed and flecked.	See Aster
	Powdery mildew	See Begonia	
Gladioli	Thrips	Flecks on leaves and flowers.	See Carnation
Hibiscus	Caterpillars	Leaves stick together, holes in leaves.	See Carnation
	Aphids	Young foliage distorted.	See Aster
	Beetles	Holes in flowers.	Confidor
	Thrips	Flowers damaged.	See Carnation
Hollyhock	Two-spotted mite	Flowers become bronzed and dry.	See Aster
	Rust	See Bellis	
Larkspur	Powdery mildew	See Begonia	
Marigold	Jassids & leaf hoppers	See Aster	
	Two-spotted mite	Foliage becomes red-brown and unthrifty.	See Aster
Pansy	See Violas		
Penstemon	Two-spotted mite	See Aster	

PLANT	PEST OR DISEASE	SYMPTOMS	CONTROL
Polyanthus	Two-spotted mite	See Aster	
	Mealybug	White fluffy insects under leaves and on roots.	Confidor, Natrasoap
	Caterpillars	Holes in leaves.	Pyrethrum, Mavrik, Bug Gun
Roses	Aphids	Young foliage distorted.	Rose Gun Advanced, Rose Shield, Confidor
	Thrips	Flowers damaged by flecking.	Rose Gun Advanced, Rose Shield, Confidor
	Caterpillars	Leaf roll and holes in leaves.	Rose Gun Advanced, Rose Shield, Mavrik
	Two-spotted mite	See Aster	
	Black spot	Large black spots on leaves.	Rose Gun Advanced, Rose Shield, Triforine
	Powdery mildew	Powdery growth on leaves.	Rose Gun Advanced, Rose Shield, Triforine
	Downy mildew	Downy growths	Liquid Copper
	Rust	See Bellis	
	Rose wilt virus	Leaves droop and bush is unthrifty.	Control aphids and remove and destroy infected bushes
Snapdragon	Rust	See Bellis	
	Caterpillars	Green caterpillars on young flower buds.	See Aster
Stock	Aphids	Young plants deformed.	See Aster
	Caterpillars	On leaves and buds.	See Aster
	Downy mildew	Seedlings very unthrifty and white downy growths under leaves.	Liquid Copper
Sweet pea	Wilt virus	Plants wither and die, foliage becomes puckered.	Control aphids and plant later in season to avoid attack
	Thrips	See Carnation	
Violas	Aphids	Distorted foliage and shoots.	See Aster
Zinnia	Caterpillars	Holes in leaves and flower buds.	See Aster
	Powdery mildew	White powdery growth on older leaves.	See Begonia
	Leaf spot	Brown target spots on leaves and stems.	Mancozeb Plus, Liquid Copper

Flowers from the Garden

Picking flowers from the garden for the vase can be an intensely satisfying pastime. Each season will provide rich pickings for those who have established a cutting garden or are gathering from a mixed garden. Following a few basic rules will ensure your personal harvest stays fresher for longer.

CUTTING CLUES

- Invest in good-quality equipment. Maintain secateurs and scissors by regular sharpening with a whetstone. Blunt tools will crush stems, damage the parent plant and inhibit the cut flower from absorbing water.
- Cut in the cool of the day when transpiration is at its lowest. When picked early in the morning or in the evening, cut flowers are less likely to droop.
- Carry a bucket one-third filled with water when picking; plunge flowers straight in, rather than laying them in baskets. Collect a range of bucket sizes and use accordingly. Use a deep bucket for long stems and a shallow one for short stems. Separating sizes safeguards the flowers of the shorter, delicate plants from being crushed by the taller, heavier ones.
- Generally, flowers are best cut before they are fully open. The buds should be loose and showing a little colour. Dahlia, zinnia and rose flowers will not develop fully when picked at a tight bud stage.
- Where possible, cut long stems – the longer the stems, the easier the flowers will be to arrange. Strip off the bottom leaves as you go.
- When cutting flowers of bulbs leave the plant with some of its foliage. Without some remnant foliage to draw up new energy stores for the next season they will not survive.

STRAIGHT STEMS

To straighten long-stemmed flowers such as tulips, bind with string, wrap in stiff paper and leave overnight in water.

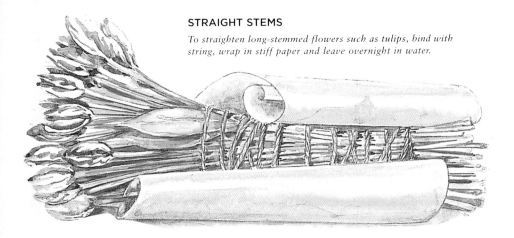

CONDITIONING FLOWERS

Directly after harvesting, bring flowers indoors. Place in a cool place out of direct sunlight and close to a bench and sink. Remove any leaves which will be below the vase water line.

Recut stems under water. Cut at an angle – a slight angle for soft stems, to prevent them from standing flat on the bottom of the bucket; at a 45-degree angle for woody stems to expose more of the fibrous centre which imbibes water.

Sappy and soft stems should be seared in boiling water. Acanthus, delphinium, euphorbia, helleborus, hollyhocks, poppies, sunflowers and sweet peas benefit from this treatment. Keeping the flower heads away

from the steam, dip the stems into 2.5 cm of boiling water for thirty seconds. Bubbles will emerge as the stem seals off. Immediately place the flowers in tepid water. Droopy roses will also revive with this approach.

Strip the leaves off woody-stemmed flowers – hydrangea, lilac, camellia, viburnum, philadelphus, rhododendron – and leave the flowers to soak overnight before arranging them.

The long, thin stems of tulips, roses and gerberas may bend after picking and will remain that way if not treated. To straighten them out, bunch stems together and wind string or florist's tape around the complete stem length. Wrap in stiff paper and

soak overnight (see illustration opposite). After treatment, leave all material to soak in deep, tepid water for several hours – overnight if possible.

IN THE VASE

Keep vases in pristine condition by cleaning them with bleach rather than detergent. To prolong flower life check the water level every day and top up as required. In extremely hot weather change the water every second day. Avoid positioning arrangements in direct sunlight, close to ripe fruit (which emits ethylene) or near a heater during winter.

FLOWER FOOD

Add a commercial flower preserver to the water to prolong the freshness of cut flowers.

As an alternative, add a teaspoon of sugar and a drop each of bleach and vinegar to the vase water.

16
Flowering Bulbs

There are many kinds of flowering bulbs or bulbous plants which are easy to grow in the home garden. In this chapter we include the true bulbs and also those plants which are started from corms, rhizomes and tubers. To a botanist the differences are important, but for the average home gardener they are all sufficiently similar to be regarded as bulbs. However, it may be useful to describe briefly the characteristics of each kind of bulb.

True bulbs

True bulbs have an onion-like structure consisting of layers of fleshy 'scale leaves' which are closely folded on each other. The fleshy scales enclosing the flower shoot are storage tissues filled with plant foods such as protein, starch and sugar, all of which are formed during the previous season's growth. For this reason, it is important to leave plants of true bulbs to die down naturally each year to provide as much nourishment as possible for the next season. It also explains why true bulbs can be grown successfully in fibre or water which contain very little in the way of nutrients. When grown in soil, true bulbs will produce daughter-bulbs or bulbils which in time will become large enough to flower. Good examples of true bulbs are daffodil, jonquil, hyacinth, tulip and lilium.

Corms

Corms do not have fleshy scales but consist of a shortened, swollen stem of solid storage tissue. The leaves arise in the axils of the scale-like remains of leaves of the previous season's growth. A new corm is formed on top of the old corm, which shrivels and dies. Small daughter-corms called 'cormels' may also develop. Examples of corms include anemone, crocus, freesia, ixia, gladiolus and ranunculus.

Rhizomes

Rhizomes are underground stems, usually thick and swollen, containing storage tissue. They develop roots, leaves and flowering stems from the nodes or joints. Good examples are flag or bearded iris, lily-of-the-valley and Solomon's seal.

Tubers

Tubers can be either swollen stems or swollen roots for storage. New shoots arise from axillary buds on stem tubers, or from buds on the short piece of stem on root tubers. Good examples of bulbs of this kind are cyclamen, arum lily and tuberous begonia.

BULBS IN THE GARDEN

Flowering bulbs are very adaptable and can be planted to give attractive garden effects. Some bulbs, especially anemone and ranunculus, are suitable for massed beds or borders. Lachenalias are good for low borders too. But most bulbs are best planted in bold clumps in the garden. Because of their different flowering times, many bulb varieties can be planted together to give a continuous and varied colour display. By choosing bulb varieties that are suited to your climate, you can have colour from late winter to summer or early autumn – jonquils and lachenalias in late winter or early spring, followed by daffodils, anemones and ranunculi. Spring brings hyacinths, freesias, sparaxis and tritonias. Following on in summer are calla lilies, hippeastrums and gladioli.

Terracotta pots filled with tulips create a stunning entrance. They can be easily moved when they are past their best.

Some spring-flowering bulbs can be planted under trees and on lawns or grassy slopes to become a permanent feature of the garden scene. In cold climates, bulbs such as bluebell, crocus, daffodil, grape hyacinth, jonquil, lily-of-the-valley, snowflakes, sternbergia and tulip become naturalised in these situations. In temperate districts, bluebells, jonquils, freesias, grape hyacinths and snowflakes are best for naturalising.

GENERAL BULB CULTURE

In the garden, a well-drained, sandy loam which is not overly rich is the best for bulbs and bulbous plants. Improve heavy soils by adding coarse sand and well-rotted organic matter to make them more friable. (See Chapter 4.) A light dressing of all-purpose mixed fertiliser or a specific bulb food should be incorporated into the soil during preparation and prior to planting. Avoid direct contact between fertiliser (or fresh manure) and the bulbs. Most bulbous plants will respond to feeds of liquid fertilisers when flower buds appear, and again after flowers have finished.

Some bulbs grow in full sunlight, others tolerate semi-shade. The best situation is given

in the notes for each kind of bulb. Depth of planting varies with the size of the bulb, but a good general rule is to plant at a depth equal to twice the width of the bulb. Planting time, together with approximate planting depth and plant spacing, is given in the notes and also summarised in the 'Planting Guide for Flowering Bulbs' (on pages 359–361).

BULBS IN OUTDOOR CONTAINERS

Many bulbs grow to perfection in tubs, pots or troughs which can be moved about in the garden or on the terrace or balcony. Smaller containers can be brought indoors when the plants flower. Daffodils, jonquils, hyacinths (including grape hyacinths), bluebells, lachenalias, freesias and tulips can be grown this way. The containers, which must have drainage holes, should be at least 15 cm deep to allow for good root growth. Use a proprietary bulb potting mixture, or a friable, free-draining potting mix to which a little mixed fertiliser has been added, and fill the pots to the depth required. Set the bulbs in place – about half the distance apart for normal planting in the garden – and fill in the remainder of the mix to within 2–3 cm of the top to leave room for watering. Keep the containers in a cool, shady place until leaves emerge and then move into a sunny but sheltered position. Keep the soil moist at all times but do not over-water. Give liquid feeds of soluble fertiliser if plants appear backward, and especially when buds appear.

HINT

At bulb-planting time try not to plant the bulbs too deep in the soil. There's only so much energy stored in those little starch bombs and if they don't have enough oomph to reach the surface, they may only produce leaves and not flowers.

MICHÈLE ADLER

LECTURER, AUTHOR, TOUR LEADER – ADLAND HORTICULTURAL

BULBS FOR INDOORS

Hyacinths, crocuses, daffodils and tulips are favourites for bringing indoors. If you want all the plants in the pot to flower together, it is best to plant only one variety of daffodil or one colour of hyacinth in each bowl. Make sure the bulbs you buy are firm and free from mould. If you are not quite ready for planting, store the bulbs in a cool, dry cupboard. To promote earlier flowering on tall, strong stems, place bulbs of hyacinths and tulips in the crisper tray of the refrigerator (7–10°C) for three or four weeks before planting. Plant the bulbs in the moistened potting mix so that their tips are just below the surface. Space potted bulbs closely together, allowing 2–3 cm between bulbs. Water the pot well, drain, and keep in a cool, dark spot, or cover with another pot. Shoots emerge in six to eight weeks, although if bulbs have been chilled they may start a week or two earlier. When shoots are clearly visible, move the pots to a well-lit, airy room. When grown near a window, pots need to be turned occasionally to keep the plants erect. Keep the mix damp, but not wet, while the plants are growing. If over-watered, tip the pot on its side to drain. Bulbs grown in pots are probably not suitable for reusing next season.

Top five bulbs for naturalising

FREESIAS

Because of their hardiness and their warm-climate origins (freesias come from South Africa), these plants will grow readily in most parts of Australia and can be left in place for many years (see picture on page 350).

SPANISH BLUEBELLS

Planted under trees, these heat-tolerant bulbs will let you create your very own bluebell wood.

TRITELEIA

Also known as star flower, this dainty little bulb has narrow, grass-like leaves. The flowers are blue or white and look good planted in drifts in well-drained garden beds.

SNOWFLAKES

Snowflakes can be aptly described by that often used phrase, 'harbingers of spring'. They are ideal for planting under trees and will multiply steadily over a number of years (see picture on page 353).

JONQUILS

The test of success in naturalising any bulb is to see it flourishing in old, abandoned gardens. Perfumed jonquils have proved themselves to be hardy survivors. Once established, they'll be with you forever.

TRITELEIA

SPRING-FLOWERING BULBS

Alstroemeria (Peruvian lily)

This lily is a tuberous plant adaptable to many soils and situations. Large flowers in red, pink and yellow (some spotted or streaked in contrasting colours) are borne in clusters over a long period from spring through summer. Clumps are best left undisturbed for a few years. Plant in autumn to early winter, 15 cm deep and 30 cm apart.

Anemone (Windflower)

Anemones produce excellent spring flowers in reds, pinks and blues for mass bedding and borders. They contrast well with ranunculus, which flower about the same time. Flowers of the St Brigid strain are semi-double or double, while the poppy-like flowers of Coronaria are single. Both are ideal for cutting. Anemones prefer full sunlight and a well-prepared, friable soil with a ration of mixed fertiliser added. The plants will carry over for several seasons but the best display is from new corms each year. Plant the corms in autumn, 3 cm deep and 15 cm apart, making sure the flat part of the corm is uppermost. In warmer climates delay planting until late autumn. Some gardeners prefer to start the corms in seedling trays and later transplant.

Babiana

Babiana has violet-blue or mauve flowers, rather similar to those of freesias, which are produced on 20 cm spikes. The plants need full sunlight and, like other bulbs native to South Africa (freesia, ixia, sparaxis and tritonia), will tolerate rather dry conditions. Plant from late summer to autumn 5 cm deep and 7 cm apart. After the plants have died down the bulbs can be lifted and stored for replanting next season, but the plants can be left for several years if preferred.

Bluebells

Also known as bells of the forest, these dainty, lavender-blue, bell-shaped flowers are ideal for clump planting in the garden or in a rockery. The plants are also useful for grassy banks and under trees where they become naturalised. They grow well in full sun or semi-shade. The Spanish bluebell is rather larger and taller (30 cm) than the true English bluebell (which does best in cool climates). Plants can be left undisturbed for a number of years. Plant bulbs in early to mid-autumn, 7 cm deep and 10 cm apart.

Brodiaea (Queen Fabiola)

Small, tubular blue flowers are borne on stems 30–40 cm tall. Plants prefer semi-shade and a well-drained soil and are suitable for borders, clump planting or in rockeries. Plant bulbs in autumn, 7 cm deep and 15 cm apart. They flower in late spring.

Chionodoxa (Glory of the snow)

This charming little plant from the mountains of Crete is only suitable for cold climates. Clumps grow 15 cm tall with blue and white star-shaped flowers in early spring. They need full sun and good drainage and should be left undisturbed once established. Plant bulbs in autumn, 7 cm deep and 10 cm apart.

Clivia (Kaffir lily)

An evergreen, bulbous plant growing to 60 cm tall with clusters of large, trumpet-shaped orange, cream and, rarely, pink flowers followed by attractive berries. It does best in warm–temperate climates and prefers semi-shade. It is excellent for growing under trees and makes a good specimen for large pots or tubs. Newly available, highly desired varieties have bicoloured cream or yellow flowers.

Crocus

One of the earliest spring-flowering bulbs, with small, cup-shaped flowers in purple, lavender and white on short stems, crocuses do best in a cool climate. Excellent for semi-shaded spots and rockery pockets with good drainage. Plants can be left undisturbed for many years. Plant in autumn, 5 cm deep and 10 cm apart. Autumn crocus varieties such as Colchicum flower later in the year.

Cyclamen

These attractive tuberous plants can be started from seed sown in summer and early autumn and grown as winter/spring-flowering pot plants. (See Chapter 23.) If kept dry during summer, the tubers will carry over until the next year but must be repotted

Beautiful striped flowers are features of some crocus varieties.

5 cm deep during late summer or early autumn. The small rock cyclamens are grown in the open garden and do best beneath trees in cool climates.

Cyrtanthus (Ifafa lily)

This is a rather uncommon bulb with small tubular flowers in cream and salmon on stems 20–30 cm tall. Plants prefer full sunlight and a friable, well-drained soil, either in the open garden or as pot plants. Plant in autumn, 7 cm deep and 15 cm apart.

Daffodil (*Narcissus*)

Daffodils are the best-known and most adaptable of all spring-flowering bulbs. They thrive in all climates except very warm northern districts. They grow well in full sun or semi-shade and prefer a friable, well-drained soil to which a bulb fertiliser has been added. The plants respond to liquid feeds when buds appear. Daffodils can be grown in almost every garden situation. On grassy banks they can become a permanent feature, but are very popular for clump planting to combine with other spring annual

HINT

Most South African bulbs, including freesias, lapeirousias, babiana, gladiolus, agapanthus and many others, are so well suited to Australian conditions they can easily become weeds in the garden from their own seeds. Stop this happening by always removing the seed capsules that form straight after flowers finish.

GEOFFREY BURNIE
GARDENING JOURNALIST

flowers such as alyssum, nemesia, pansy, viola, linaria and Virginian stock. They are excellent for growing in tubs, pots or troughs outdoors or for bowls indoors.

Daffodils come in a wide range of gold or cream shades and a variety of flower forms. Of the trumpet types, 'King Alfred' is still the best known, but 'Golden Lion' is another traditional yellow trumpet variety that does better in warmer climates than 'King Alfred'. 'Fortune', 'Ptolemy' and 'Salome' are also popular. Smaller-growing or 'rockery' daffodils are useful for pots and small gardens. Plant bulbs in autumn (preferably before the middle of May in most districts), 12 cm deep and 10–15 cm apart. Bulbs in pots, troughs and bowls can be planted closer together than in a garden situation but will not be suitable to use again next season. Daffodil bulbs will naturalise in suitable climates. Failure to flower may be due to over-crowded bulbs or warm winter temperatures.

Freesia

Freesias have been popular spring-flowering bulbs for a long time and are highly prized for their delightful perfume. The traditional *Freesia refracta* 'Alba' has small, creamy-white flowers with an exquisite perfume. The Bergunden strain has large, perfumed flowers and a wide colour range in shades of yellow, orange, rosy red, ruby and blue. They are excellent for cut flowers too.

Freesias do best in a fairly sunny position but will grow well under shrubs and trees if not too shaded. They need a friable, well-drained soil which is not overly rich but with a scattering of mixed fertiliser worked into the soil during preparation. Usually this pre-planting fertiliser is all that is necessary. The plants are suitable for massing in beds or on grassy banks but are particularly attractive in clumps or in rockery pockets.

Freesias can be left in their permanent position for several years, or the corms can be lifted after the plants die down for storing and replanting. Plant the corms in autumn at a depth of 7 cm at the same distance apart. Packs of red, blue, white, yellow and mixed colours are available. They can become weedy in some conditions.

Fritillaria

These attractive members of the lily family grow most successfully in cool climates. *F. imperialis* ('Crown Imperial') is the best known. The plants are 60 cm tall with drooping bell-shaped flowers in yellow, orange

Freesias are some of the best bulbs for a warm climate.

and bronze. They are best planted in clumps and should be left undisturbed unless they become overcrowded. Plant in autumn, 10 cm deep and 30 cm apart.

Grape hyacinth (*Muscari*)

Grape hyacinths are one of the most attractive dwarf bulbs for spring, with spikes of bead-like, deep-blue flowers on stems 10–15 cm tall. The plants are very adaptable to soil and will grow in full sun or semi-shade. They are good for naturalising and ideal for clump planting in the garden or in rock pockets. Plant bulbs in autumn, 7 cm deep and 10 cm apart.

Hippeastrum

These plants produce magnificent trumpet-like flowers in salmon, red, rose and variegated white and red on strong stems 60 cm tall. The plants prefer friable, well-drained soil in a sunny position but will tolerate some shade during the day. They need plenty of water in spring when flower buds appear. Plant the bulbs in winter, keeping the neck of the bulb at the soil surface. Space bulbs 30–40 cm apart. The butterfly hippeastrum (*Hippeastrum papilio*) is an unusual species with wing-like petals.

Hyacinth

New, improved varieties of hyacinth are very adaptable and will do well in all but very warm climates. They produce spikes crowded with large flowers in white, yellow, pink, red, light blue or dark blue. The plants prefer a sunny position and fertile, well-drained soil for best results. They are excellent for clump planting among spring annuals and are ideal for container growing, both outdoors and indoors. For container growing, select large, plump bulbs of good shape and free of blemishes. Store bulbs in a cool spot in the house and pop them in the refrigerator crisper tray for up to six weeks before planting. Plant the bulbs in autumn (April or early May is a good time in most districts), 15 cm deep and 15 cm apart. Container-grown bulbs can be planted with the neck at soil level and the spacing reduced to 7 cm. Bulbs are available in separate colours or as assortments. Separate colours are best for pots as they will all flower at the same time.

Iris

Bearded, flag or German iris

These plants grow from rhizomes into large clumps of attractive, grey-green leaves to 60 cm or more tall. The silky textured, flag-like flowers come in a wide range of colours including yellow, gold, lavender, mauve, purple, brown and white. Many have combinations of more than one colour. Bearded iris does well in almost any garden situation but prefers a sunny aspect and well-drained soil. Add a ration of all-purpose fertiliser when preparing the soil; an application of lime is recommended on acid soils. Plant in autumn through to winter, keeping the top of the rhizome at soil surface level. Space rhizomes about 30 cm apart.

Dutch and Spanish iris

Unlike Flag iris, the Dutch and Spanish types grow from bulbs and not from rhizomes. The plants form clumps and have flowers in a range of colours including blue, bronze, yellow and white on stems about 60 cm tall. The flowers of the Dutch iris are larger and rather earlier than the Spanish types. Plant bulbs in autumn, 10 cm deep and 15 cm apart.

Ixia (Corn lily)

These attractive South African bulbs have grassy clumps and clusters of bell-shaped flowers in shades of yellow, gold, pink, orange and port wine on stems 60 cm tall. Excellent for cut flowers. The plants need a sunny position and are best grown in clumps among annuals or between shrubs. Plant bulbs in autumn 7 cm deep and 10 cm apart.

Jonquil (Bunch-flowered narcissus)

A close relative of daffodils, jonquils are even more adaptable to climate and soil. They are one of the first bulbs to flower in late winter or spring, with small clusters of fragrant, daffodil-like blooms. They are useful for naturalising on lawns or grassy slopes and are attractive in clumps around shrubs. The plants can remain undisturbed for many years. The most popular variety is 'Soleil d'Or' with its orange-red cups surrounded by gold petals; many other varieties have cream or white blooms. Plant in autumn, 10 cm deep and 10 cm apart.

Lachenalia (Cape cowslip)

These are attractive dwarf plants from South Africa with 15 cm spikes of tubular, waxy flowers in shades of yellow, orange-red, red or green, according to variety. The plants prefer full sunlight and a well-drained, friable soil. They are excellent for borders, clump planting, rockery pockets, outdoor pots and troughs, and indoor bowls as well. The variety 'Tricolor' is yellow, red and green; 'Quadricolor' is a combination of red, yellow, green and purple; 'Pendula' has large, red flowers. Other varieties are 'Aurea' (golden yellow) and 'Pallida' (lime-green). Plants may remain in the ground for several years, or bulbs can be lifted when foliage dies for replanting the following season. Plant in autumn, 7 cm deep and 10 cm apart.

Lily-of-the-valley (Convallaria)

These dwarf plants grow from rhizomes and have tiny, fragrant, bell-shaped white or cream flowers in late spring. The plants need cool climates with a shady, moist but well-drained position and plenty of organic matter

Ranunculus grows from a claw-like corm. Always plant with the 'claws' down.

in the soil. Plants can remain undisturbed for several years. Plant rhizomes in winter 3 cm deep and 10 cm apart. Plants can also be grown in pots for indoor decoration, especially in warmer climates where they do poorly in the garden.

Ornithogalum

There are three widely grown species of this spring-flowering bulb. All three need well-drained soil and prefer sunlight for at least half the day. They are best left for several years to form clumps but can be lifted after foliage dies and replanted next season if preferred. The plants prefer warm climates. *Ornithogalum thyrsoides* (Chincherinchee) grows to 30 cm with clusters of papery, white flowers which open from the base upwards. It is good for cut flowers, which are capable of changing colour when the stems are dipped in dye or coloured ink. *O. arabicum* (Arab's Eye) has papery, white petals surrounding a black centre and the blooms have an aromatic fragrance. *O. umbellatum* (Star of Bethlehem) has waxy, white flowers striped with green on the underside of the petals. Plant bulbs in autumn, 7 cm deep and 15 cm apart.

Ranunculus

Ranunculus, like anemone, is excellent for mass bedding, borders or for planting in clumps or drifts with other spring-flowering annuals. Plants grow to 60 cm and the semi-double and double flowers come in remarkable shades of red, crimson, scarlet, pink, orange, yellow, lemon, cream and white. Bulb packs are available as separate colours (red, pink, orange, gold, white) or as mixtures. Lower-growing strains are proving very popular, as they are less affected by winds. Ranunculus need full sunlight and a friable, fertile, well-drained soil to which organic matter and mixed fertiliser has been added during preparation. They respond to liquid feeds when buds form. You can dig and store the corms after the foliage dies down but results are usually better from fresh corms each year. Plant corms in autumn 3 cm deep and 15 cm apart. Make sure the corms are planted with the 'claws' downwards. The corms can be started in a shallow seedling tray for transplanting later.

HINT

To avoid digging up, and potentially damaging, bulbs when dormant, cut the top rim from a 30 cm plastic pot to remind you where you planted them. Try planting seven to nine bulbs in a group and place the rim just below the mulched surface.

KATE MAIN

WA HORTICULTURIST

Snowdrops (*Galanthus*); Snowflakes (*Leucojum*)

Both these small, spring-flowering bulbs have dainty, white bell-shaped flowers with a green spot on the outside of each petal. The plants are excellent for clump planting and need a semi-shaded or shaded aspect for best results. They are excellent for planting under deciduous trees where winter sun can reach them, or on grassy banks. Plant bulbs in autumn. Snowdrops are usually only grown in cooler climates. Snowflakes are adaptable to a wide range of climates. Plant 7 cm deep and 10 cm apart.

Sparaxis (Harlequin flower or Wand flower)

These bulbs from South Africa need much the same conditions as freesias, including a sunny, well-drained position. They are excellent for naturalising on lawns or grassy slopes and suitable for rock gardens and outdoor container growing. The bell-shaped flowers are quite large and come in shades of red, orange and cream with black geometrical markings. Plant in autumn, 7 cm deep and 10 cm apart.

Triteleia (Spring star or Star violet)

Dwarf plants with soft, green foliage and star-shaped, lavender-blue, mid-blue and white flowers on 15 cm stems. The plants become naturalised when grown under trees or shrubs and are attractive in borders, rockery pockets and containers. Plant in autumn 5 cm deep and 7 cm apart.

Snowflakes are ideal for naturalising in lawns or under deciduous trees.

Tritonia (*Montbretia*)

This is another bulb from South Africa. The plants are very similar in height and flower form to sparaxis. Flower stems are rather longer, however, and flowers are in shades of orange, pink and red. Tritonias are grown in the same way as sparaxis or freesias. Plant bulbs in autumn, 7 cm deep and 10 cm apart.

Tulip

In the sixteenth century, single tulip bulbs fetched fantastic prices in Holland and other European countries. Tulips have large, beautifully formed, bell-shaped flowers in dazzling shades of cream, yellow, orange, pink, scarlet, red and deep maroon. The plants do best in cool climates but are very adaptable and should be grown more widely in temperate climates. The newer Monet series is adaptable to a wider climatic range and features large blooms on strong stems, some reaching 60 cm. These plants prefer full sunlight but will tolerate semi-shade. Tulips need friable, well-drained soil which has been prepared before planting with compost and a mixed fertiliser. Tulips do not like acid soils so it is best to add a ration of lime in most coastal and highland districts. (See Chapter 5.) When flower buds appear, give liquid feeds of soluble fertiliser to promote long, strong stems and large blooms.

Tulips are best grown in clumps in the garden surrounded by dwarf annuals like alyssum, bellis or violas. They are ideal for container growing too. It can be helpful to chill the bulbs in the refrigerator crisper before planting. Plant in autumn (late April or May are best in most districts), 12 cm deep and 12 cm apart. After flowers and foliage die, lift the bulbs for storing in a cool place and replanting next season. In warmer climates it may be best to buy new bulbs each year for a good display.

HINT

Keep tulip bulbs in the crisper section of your refrigerator from February until April. Chilling the bulb holds the flower spike initiation until early spring. Store them in paper bags, or loose, but make sure you label them. Tulips aren't so tasty in stews.

MARK HAY

GARDEN CENTRE PROPRIETOR,

FORMER TV AND RADIO TALKBACK

HORTICULTURAL HOST, GARDEN ADVISER

Watsonia (Bugle lily)

Watsonias develop into large clumps of strap-like foliage 90–120 cm tall. The flower spikes are even taller, with dainty, tubular flowers in pink, salmon, red and white. Flowers are excellent for cutting in late spring when other flowers may be scarce. The plants are useful for background work and can be divided after the foliage dies in late summer or early autumn. Watsonias have become environmental weeds in some parts of Australia. Check local conditions before planting. Plant in autumn, 7 cm deep and 30 cm apart.

SUMMER-FLOWERING BULBS

Agapanthus (African lily)

These vigorous, bulbous plants are evergreen and grow into large clumps 60–90 cm tall,

although there are some lower-growing dwarf varieties. The large clusters of tubular flowers are blue or white. Agapanthus are good background plants but will grow almost anywhere – even on dry banks in full sun, or in shade under trees. Because of their vigorous roots and spreading habit, they crowd out weaker plants and can tend to take over the garden. Clumps can, of course, be thinned and replanted if necessary. Plant from late autumn to early winter. Agapanthus can be weedy in certain climates so remove flower heads to prevent self-seeding or look for new, non-seeding cultivars.

Amaryllis (Belladonna lily)

These plants are also known as Naked Ladies. Large, fragrant, trumpet-shaped flowers are usually pink but also creamy white. Plants grow in full sun or under deciduous trees in semi-shade.

They are best left undisturbed for a few years but can be lifted when dormant after flowering. Plant bulbs in late autumn or early winter, with the neck of the bulb protruding from the soil, and space them 30 cm apart. Brunsvigia is a close relative and is grown in the same way.

Begonia (Tuberous)

Usually grown in pots in a sheltered area, shadehouse or glasshouse, the magnificent semi-double or double blooms of tuberous begonia come in shades of red, pink, orange, yellow and white. The plants need a rich, friable, well-drained soil. Tubers can be carried over for repotting the following year. Plant or repot tubers in spring with the top or crown level with the soil surface.

Calla

Callas prefer a sunny but damp position with fairly rich soil. Too much moisture when the bulbs are dormant in winter may cause them to rot, so lift them after foliage dies for replanting in late winter. *Zantedeschia elliotiana* grows to 60 cm with bright-yellow lilies and white-spotted leaves. *Z. rehmannii* is smaller (30 cm) with dainty, mauve-pink blooms. *Z. aethiopica* is the Lily of the Nile or arum lily. It is tolerant of poor drainage and, in warmer climates, the leaves are evergreen. Plant in late autumn or early winter, 10 cm deep and 20 cm apart.

Canna

Canna is a vigorous plant 90–150 cm tall and forming dense clumps of brilliant green or bronze leaves from its tuberous roots. The large flower clusters, with lily-like blooms, come in shades of cream, yellow, orange, pink and red. Some flowers are attractively spotted. Cannas prefer full sun but need damp or even wet conditions. After flowering, the stems can be cut down to ground level for regrowth in spring, or divided for replanting. Some varieties, however, tend to remain green all year round. Plant rhizomes in winter or early spring, 5 cm deep and 50 cm apart.

Crinum (Veldt lily)

The white or pinkish, fragrant flowers of crinum resemble lilies and are borne on stems 60–90 cm tall. Some species are evergreen while others die down after flowering. The plants prefer an open, sunny aspect and do best in warm coastal areas. The unusually large bulbs may be planted with a light soil covering at almost any time of the year, spacing them 30 cm apart.

Dicentra (Bleeding heart)

Dicentra grows to 25 cm tall with sprays of red, heart-shaped flowers. The plants do best in cool–temperate or cold climates and prefer deep, well-drained soils, but need plenty of water in spring to mid-summer when flowers appear. The plants are dormant from late summer to spring. Plant the tuberous roots in autumn or early winter, 10 cm deep and 60 cm apart.

Eucharis lily

This is an evergreen, bulbous plant best suited to subtropical and tropical climates. The plants may be grown in clumps in the garden, or in large tubs, and need a sunny, sheltered position. The white, trumpet-shaped flowers have a sweet fragrance. Plant bulbs in winter to spring, just covering with soil and spacing them 20 cm apart. Flowering is improved if clumps are left undisturbed for a few years. Plants bloom in response to a dry period.

Agapanthus will grow almost anywhere.

Eucomis (Pineapple flower)

This unusual bulbous plant grows in clumps to 60 cm tall. Its large, cylindrical flower spikes are made up of masses of greenish-white to red petals tipped with lilac. The flowers are excellent for cutting and last for weeks in water. The plants prefer open sunlight and are best left undisturbed for several years. Give liquid feeds during late spring and summer and water well in hot weather. Plant bulbs in winter or early spring, 12 cm deep and 30 cm apart.

Galtonia (Summer hyacinth)

A tall (120 cm) bulbous plant from South Africa with clusters of white, drooping, bell-shaped flowers, galtonia is a good background plant but needs a sunny position. It is best in warmer districts, as the plants are sensitive to frost. Plant bulbs in spring, 10 cm deep and 20 cm apart.

Gladiolus (Sword lily)

Gladiolus is one of the most spectacular of summer-flowering plants, both for garden display and cut flowers. The orchid-like blooms come in a wide range of clear colours and pastel shades. Packs of separate or assorted colours are available from garden stores and nurseries. The plants prefer full sunlight and are best planted in clumps alongside dwarf summer-flowering annuals. The plants, when well grown, may reach 150 cm in height, so it is best if they are sheltered from strong winds. To prevent wind damage, tie three or four plants in a clump to a garden stake just before the flower buds appear.

Gladioli adapt easily to a variety of climates and can be grown in hot, mild and cold districts. Flowering takes about 90 to 100 days from planting and it is best to plant so that flowers appear before or after the extreme heat of summer. They need a well-drained, friable soil which should be prepared in advance by adding compost and some mixed fertiliser. In warm districts, planting can be made from May to September so that the plants flower before the hottest months. In cold districts it is best to delay planting until August or later. It is good insurance to dust the corms with a fungicide before planting. Plant the corms 10 cm deep, spacing them 20 cm apart. Thrips are a serious insect pest of gladioli so it is necessary to spray with insecticide every two weeks after the plants reach the four-leaf stage. (See Chapter 8.) In warm weather, always cut flower spikes when the first flowers open. The remaining buds will open indoors if the stems are in water. Corms can be lifted after the leaves turn yellow and start to die – generally about four to six weeks after flowering. Allow the leaves to dry out, then cut them off close to the corm. Dust the corms with fungicide and store in a dry, cool place until the next planting season.

Gloriosa (Climbing lily)

Gloriosa is a climbing lily that uses its leaf tips to cling onto a support. It grows 2–3 m tall with orange or red, flared trumpet-shaped flowers in summer. The plants prefer a sunny position but tolerate semi-shade. The offsets must be carefully removed from the corm as the roots are brittle and easily damaged. Plant corms horizontally in early spring, 3 cm deep and 30 cm apart.

Gloxinia

These spectacular tuberous plants are best grown in pots in shadehouses or glasshouses where they are protected from wind and rain. They can also be grown indoors in a well-lit spot, but not in direct sunlight. They need ample moisture and a fairly even temperature (about 20°C). The bell-shaped flowers have a velvety texture and come in many shades of cream, pink, red, blue and purple, many of which are spotted or have contrasting edges and throats. Tubers can be dried off like cyclamen at the end of the flowering season for replanting. (See Chapter 15.) Plant tubers in winter or spring with the top of the tuber at soil level. Gloxinias can be raised from seed.

Hemerocallis (Day lily)

These evergreen or deciduous bulbous plants produce clumps of pale-green foliage 60–75 cm tall with flowers in cream, orange and red. Flowers last one day, but new flowers open over a long period. They prefer a sunny position. Plant bulbous roots in autumn to winter, 10 cm deep and 30 cm apart or plants in leaf at any time.

Kniphofia (Torch lily or Red hot poker)

These attractive plants form large, dense clumps with long, poker-like stems bearing masses of small, tubular flowers which open from the base. Colours range from yellow through to orange and red. Plants prefer a sunny position and are useful as background plants. They are best left undisturbed for several years. Plant bulbs in autumn or winter, 10 cm deep and 60 cm apart.

Lilium

These are the true lilies. There are many species and varieties and hundreds of hybrids with an endless array of attractive flower forms and colours. The most widely grown are the November Lily or Christmas Lily (*L. longiflorum*) with white, trumpet-shaped flowers; Tiger Lilies, *L. tigrinum* (orange), *L. speciosum* (pink), *L. speciosum album* (white); *L. regale* (large creamy-white, purple-backed flowers); and Golden Rayed Lily of Japan (*L. auratum*) with large, white flowers spotted purple and striped yellow. Most of the liliums form large clumps which should ideally be left undisturbed. They need half-sun and a friable, well-drained soil, but respond well to generous watering in summer and mulching to keep the soil cool and moist. Plant the scaly bulbs in late autumn to winter, 10–20 cm deep (according to bulb size) and 30–40 cm apart. They flower in late spring to late summer, according to variety.

Lycoris

See Spider lily.

HINT

Put a pot of flowering plants on top of an area where bulbs or perennials have died down. This is also useful to prevent any 'non-gardener' from mistakenly digging in that area!

LORNA ROSE M.A.I.H.

HORTICULTURAL PHOTOGRAPHER

Nerine

See Spider lily.

Solomon's seal (*Polygonatum*)

Solomon's seal is a good bulbous plant for cool, shady situations or dappled sunlight. The slender, oval leaves grow in clumps (60 cm tall) from shallow rhizomes and the curving stems bear white, bell-shaped flowers tipped with green. Plant rhizomes in late autumn to winter, 3 cm deep and 25 cm apart.

Spider lily (*Lycoris, Nerine*)

These two plants have similar flowers and are usually grown in clumps which are best left undisturbed. They prefer a well-drained soil and sunny position. Lycoris flowers are yellow (*L. aurea*) or red (*L. radiata*). Nerines flower before the foliage appears, in the same way as Belladonna lilies. Flowers are pink (*N. bowdenii*) or scarlet (*N. sarniensis*).

All the spider lilies are excellent for cut flowers. Plant bulbs in winter or early spring, keeping the neck of the bulb above the soil surface. Space the bulbs 15 cm apart.

Liliums, the true lilies, are garden aristocrats.

Lycoris, one of the spider lilies, blooms in late summer and autumn.

Sprekelia (Jacobean lily)

Sprekelia have large, crimson, orchid-like blooms 10 cm in diameter and borne on naked stems 15–30 cm tall. The plants prefer sandy, well-drained soil in a situation with half-sun. Plant bulbs in late winter and early spring with the necks of the bulbs just above the surface. Space them 12 cm apart.

Sternbergia (Autumn daffodil)

A dwarf, bulbous plant to 20 cm high, sternbergia needs full sunlight and rather dry conditions. The golden, crocus-like flowers appear with the leaves in autumn. Plant in early summer, 10 cm deep and 15 cm apart.

Tigridia (Tiger flower or Jockey's cap)

These unusual, colourful flowers with broad pink or red petals surrounding smaller, spotted petals are borne on 30–40 cm stems in early summer. Individual flowers last for only one day but there is a succession of blooms. The plants need a well-drained, sunny position and are best planted in clumps to remain undisturbed for a few years. Plant late autumn and early winter, 7 cm deep and 7 cm apart. Plants can also be raised from seed.

Tuberose (*Polianthes*)

The fragrant, white flowers of tuberose are favourites for bridal bouquets. In warm and mild climates the plants will flower at any time of the year, but summer is the best flowering period. The plants prefer a warm, sheltered position with plenty of moisture in summer. Once an individual bulb has bloomed, it will not flower again but will develop a number of bulblets. These should be separated from the clump in spring. Plant in winter or early spring, just covering with soil and spacing them 20 cm apart.

Vallota (Scarborough lily)

These evergreen bulbous plants grow to 40 cm tall with clusters of large, orange-scarlet, trumpet-shaped flowers on strong stems. The plants prefer a sunny position but are very adaptable to soil. The clumps are best left undisturbed. Plant bulbs in winter or early spring with the neck of the bulb level with the soil surface. Space bulbs 20 cm apart.

Zephyranthes (Autumn crocus or Storm lily)

Zephyranthes is an excellent bulbous plant to grow for late summer and autumn flowering. The clumps grow to 20–30 cm tall with white (*Z. candida*), pink (*Z. rosea*) or yellow (*Z. citrina*) crocus-like flowers. The plants are evergreen in most climates. Plant bulbs in late autumn, winter or early spring, 7 cm deep and 30 cm apart. They are called storm lilies because of their habit of bursting into flower after summer rains or storms.

Planting Guide for Flowering Bulbs

NAME AND COMMON NAME OF BULB	PLANTING SEASON	PLANTING DEPTH (CM)	DISTANCE APART (CM)	SEASON
Agapanthus (African lily)	Spring	Note A	50	Summer
Alstroemeria (Peruvian lily)	Autumn–winter	15	30	Spring–summer
Amaryllis (Belladonna lily)	Late autumn–winter	Note A	30	Summer
Anemone (Windflower)	Autumn	3	15	Spring
Babiana	Late summer–autumn	5	7	Spring
Begonia (tuberous)	Spring	Note B	In pots	Summer
Bluebells (Scilla)	Autumn	7	10	Spring
Brodiaea (Queen Fabiola)	Autumn	7	15	Late spring
Calla	Late autumn–winter	10	20	Summer
Canna	Winter–early spring	5	50	Summer
Chionodoxa (Glory of the Snow)	Autumn	7	10	Early spring
Clivia (Kaffir lily)	Autumn	Note A	30	Late spring
Crinum (Veldt lily)	Autumn–spring	Note A	30	Summer
Crocus	Autumn	5	10	Late winter–early spring
Cyclamen	Late summer–autumn	6	In pots	Late winter–early spring
Cyrtanthus (Ifafa lily)	Autumn	7	15	Late spring
Daffodil (Narcissus)	Autumn	12	10–15	Spring
Dicentra (Bleeding Heart)	Autumn	10	60	Early summer

Note A. Just cover root system or bulb with soil.
Note B. Plant with top of bulb at soil surface.

NAME AND COMMON NAME OF BULB	PLANTING SEASON	PLANTING DEPTH (CM)	DISTANCE APART (CM)	FLOWERING SEASON
Eucharis lily	Winter–early spring	Note A	20	Summer
Eucomis (Pineapple flower)	Spring–early summer	12	30	Summer
Freesia	Autumn	7	7	Spring
Fritillaria	Autumn	10	30	Spring
Galtonia (Summer hyacinth)	Spring	10	20	Late summer
Gladiolus (Sword lily)	Late winter–spring	10	20	Summer
Gloriosa (Climbing lily)	Winter–spring	3	30	Summer
Gloxinia	Winter–spring	Note B	In pots	Summer
Grape hyacinth (Muscari)	Autumn	7	10	Spring
Hemerocallis (Day lily)	Autumn–winter	10	30	Summer
Hippeastrum (Amaryllis)	Winter	Note B	30–40	Late spring–summer
Hyacinth	Autumn	15	15	Spring
Iris—bearded, flag or German	Autumn–winter	Note B	30	Late spring
Iris—Dutch and Spanish	Autumn	10	15	Spring
Ixia (Corn lily)	Autumn	7	10	Spring
Jonquil (Bunch-flowered narcissus)	Autumn	10	10	Later winter–early spring
Kniphofia (Torch lily, red hot poker)	Autumn–winter	10	60	Summer
Lachenalia (Cape cowslip)	Autumn	7	10	Spring
Lilium	Late autumn–winter	10–20	30–40	Summer
Lily-of-the-valley (Convallaria)	Winter	3	10	Late spring

Note A. Just cover root system or bulb with soil.
Note B. Plant with top of bulb at soil surface.

NAME AND COMMON NAME OF BULB	PLANTING SEASON	PLANTING DEPTH (CM)	DISTANCE APART (CM)	FLOWERING SEASON
Lycoris (see Spider lily)				
Nerine (see Spider lily)				
Ornithogalum	Autumn	7	15	Spring
Peacock Iris (Moraea)	Autumn	5	5	Spring
Ranunculus	Autumn	3–5	15	Spring
Snowdrop (Galanthus)	Autumn	7	10	Spring
Snowflake (Leucojum)	Autumn	7	10	Spring
Solomon's seal (Polygonatum)	Late autumn–winter	3	25	Summer
Sparaxis (Harlequin flower, Wand flower)	Autumn	7	10	Spring
Spider lily (Lycoris, Nerine)	Winter–early spring	Note B	15	Late summer
Sprekelia (Jacobean lily)	Late winter–early spring	Note B	12	Summer
Sternbergia (Autumn daffodil)	Early summer	10	15	Autumn
Tigridia (Tiger flower, Jockey's cap)	Autumn–winter	7	7	Early summer
Triteleia (Spring star, star violet)	Autumn	5	7	Spring
Tritonia (Montbretia)	Autumn	7	10	Spring
Tuberose (Polianthes)	Winter–early spring	Note A	20	Summer
Tulip	Autumn	12	12	Spring
Vallota (Scarborough lily)	Winter–early spring	Note B	20	Late summer
Watsonia (Bugle lily)	Autumn	7	30	Spring
Zephyranthes (sp.) (Autumn crocus)	Winter–early spring	7	30	Autumn

Note A. Just cover root system or bulb with soil.
Note B. Plant with top of bulb at soil surface.

17
Roses

Roses have always been a favourite flower in the garden. They were cultivated by the ancient Babylonians, Greeks and Romans, and no other flower has received more attention from gardeners through the ages. Modern rose varieties, with their superb colour range, flower form and fragrance, make them irresistible for garden display or for cut flowers.

Roses are extremely adaptable to both climate and soil. In cool, temperate and cold climates, roses have successive flushes of bloom during warm weather, but in warm subtropical or tropical climates they flower all year round. Many of the rose blooms sold by florists during winter are grown under glasshouse conditions.

There are so many different types of rose that there is one to suit any situation in the garden, always providing there is sufficient sunlight and good drainage. Bush roses can be used in garden beds, generally with low-growing winter or spring-flowering annuals, perennials or bulbs to give colour to the garden during their dormant period. Floribunda roses make good borders or low hedges, while climbing roses can be trained on walls, fences and pergolas. Standard roses or weeping standards, which are grafted on to tall root-stocks, are excellent for borders or accents (e.g. along driveways). They provide lots of cut flowers and allow other annual flowers (and even vegetables) to grow beneath them. In recent times there has been a strong interest in growing and understanding 'old-fashioned' roses with breeders turning to old roses for inspiration. 'David Austin' or 'English' roses combine old rose flower characteristics with modern disease resistance and free-flowering attributes. There seems to be renewed interest in growing perfumed roses, and bushes that produce a good garden display rather than the stiff, upright-growing, cut flower varieties that were popular last century.

Other breeders are concentrating on ground-cover roses, thornless roses and the quest for the elusive blue rose. Delbard roses specialise in multi-coloured flowers.

One spectacularly successful new-generation rose has been the 'Flower Carpet' series.

SITUATION AND SOIL

Roses need a sunny position to grow and flower well. They should not be grown too close to other shrubs or trees that will compete with them for light, moisture and nutrients. Good drainage is necessary too. In heavy soils raising the bed 15–20 cm above the surrounding level will usually provide sufficient drainage.

Roses are very adaptable plants that can be grown on both sandy and clay soils. While they tolerate clay soil better than most plants, they do not prefer or need a clay soil to grow well. The ideal soil is a loamy topsoil with good structure, and a clay subsoil that will provide an even supply of moisture – as long as the clay is well drained and allows excess water to move away from the root zone. Sandy soils, which hold moisture badly, should be improved by adding plenty of organic matter as described in Chapter 4.

Because roses are long-lived plants, it is worthwhile spending some time and energy in preparing the soil well before planting. It is best to add organic matter (animal manure, compost or spent mushroom compost) and dig it into the topsoil about four to six weeks before planting. If the soil is naturally acid, lime can be added at the same time. Use about two-thirds of a cup per square metre on sandy soils and double this quantity on heavy soils. As roses cannot make use of fertilisers until growth commences there is no need to apply them during the soil preparation stage.

Ensure the soil is in a good crumbly condition for planting by digging it over again about two weeks before planting to break up any clods and mix the organic matter through the soil

Top five roses for pots

'BONICA'

Arching canes smothered with pastel-pink, double blooms on a small-growing bush make this a good choice for a wide pot.

'CHINA DOLL'

Endless blooming from spring to autumn is a feature of this tiny bush. The small roses have an old-fashioned appearance.

'ICEBERG'

This popular rose grows to more than 1 m so needs a good-sized tub, but its generous blooming qualities make it worth any extra effort.

'FRIESIA'

The most yellow of yellows on a neat, mid-sized bush – what more could you want!

'SATCHMO'

An old favourite with clusters of vibrant red blooms.

FRIESIA

more evenly. Always cultivate heavy soils when damp (but not wet) so that they crumble easily.

PLANTING

These days many roses are sold in containers and can be planted out at any time of the year. Bare-rooted roses are planted during their dormant season and are usually available at garden stores and nurseries from May to August. In mild climates, June is a good month for planting because the plants are then completely dormant. In colder areas – Victoria, Tasmania and the eastern highlands – planting can be delayed until July or even August.

HINT

To avoid the area beneath rose bushes looking bare, sprinkle the area with alyssum or dwarf Virginian stock seeds and the ground will be decorated with a froth of dainty flowers for most of the year. It's a 'do-it-once' solution as these annual plants will self-seed.

DERYN THORPE
GARDEN WRITER – *THE WEST AUSTRALIAN* NEWSPAPER AND *GARDENING AUSTRALIA* MAGAZINE

Bare-rooted roses dry out quickly and when the roots have dried the plants will very often die. When buying plants, check that the stems, which may be bright green or reddish-brown in colour, are smooth and free of any wrinkling, especially at the top of the stem. Such wrinkling often indicates that the plants have been allowed to dry out at some stage. Don't buy rose plants until you are ready for planting. The bed should be finally prepared and well settled so you can start planting when you bring the plants home. If you are unable to plant that day, unwrap the roses, 'plant' them into a shady spot in the garden, cover the roots well with soil and water thoroughly. This way you can 'hold' plants until they can be put into their permanent positions. When you have a number of roses to plant, cover them with a wet bag or stand them in a bucket

'Candy Stripe' produces nicely shaped blooms on a medium-sized bush.

of water. These days, most bare-rooted roses are sold 'packaged'; that is, their roots are protected by some moisture-holding packaging material, and this and the whole root system is wrapped in plastic. The protective material should be gently hosed off before the rose is planted. Discard the packaging material: don't put it into the planting hole.

The planting hole should be large enough to allow the roots to spread out naturally without bending them. Holes should be not less than 30 cm in diameter and about 20 cm deep. Make a mound of crumbly soil on the bottom of the hole on which to rest the plant and spread the roots. The height of the mound should be adjusted so that the bud union (where the scion is budded onto the root stock) is slightly above or at soil level. Now, cover the roots with 7–10 cm of damp crumbly soil and firm it down well to prevent pockets of air remaining around the roots. Then add half a bucket of water gently, so that soil is not washed away from the roots. Let the water drain away and then fill in the remainder of the soil without firming. The leftover soil is used to form a raised ring around the plants to help direct later watering to the plant roots. Keep the surface soil weed-free and moist by scattering compost, organic mulch or grass clippings around the plant. Later watering will depend on the weather: check the newly planted roses once a week and if the soil is dry give them about half a bucket of water. After planting,

use only a slow-release type of fertiliser (such as Dynamic Lifter pellets, blood and bone) as the plants are dormant and will not utilise it until growth commences in early spring.

GENERAL MAINTENANCE
Watering, mulching, weeding

When rose plants are established, heavy watering encourages the roots to go deeper so that plants can tolerate longer periods of dryness. This approach is preferable to frequent light sprinklings which promote shallow roots close to the surface. During the main growing period (spring to autumn) maintain a mulch of compost, leaf mould or grass clippings around the base of the plants to help conserve moisture and control weeds. When rose bushes lose their leaves in autumn, little or no watering is required except in warm, tropical climates where roses behave more or less as evergreen plants. Contact weedicides like Zero Glyphosate are also useful in controlling weeds among rose bushes if they are grown alone without annual plants. They can be sprayed around the plants, providing they do not contact leaves or green, sappy stems. Be very careful when applying, as roses are very sensitive to glyphosate.

Fertilising

Fertilisers are necessary for vigorous growth and good-sized, quality rose blooms. Immediately after planting use only slow-

English roses bred by David Austin combine the best characteristics of old and modern roses.

release fertilisers as recommended above. An application of mixed fertiliser can be given in late December or January to encourage an autumn flush of blooms. Specially formulated fertilisers, such as rose food or Dynamic Lifter PLUS Flower Food are ideal. With established plants, apply fertiliser in late winter or early spring and again in late summer. This can be scattered around the plants (not too close to the main stem) and lightly raked into the soil. If the soil is mulched, the fertiliser can remain on the surface as the nutrients will wash down to the soil below. Always apply fertilisers when the soil is evenly moist and water well afterwards to disperse the nutrients safely to the root zone. For potted roses use slow-release fertilisers such as Dynamic Lifter.

HINT

**Feed roses once a month through the leaves with a liquid seaweed fertiliser. Start at budswell and continue throughout the season.
A healthy leaf is less likely to contract black spot and powdery mildew diseases.**

MARK HAY

GARDEN CENTRE PROPRIETOR,
FORMER TV AND RADIO TALKBACK
HORTICULTURAL HOST, GARDEN ADVISER

Cutting blooms

When rose bushes are young, don't cut flowers with long stems, as the plants need as many leaves as possible to develop into vigorous bushes. Cut blooms with short stems only. With older bushes, cutting flowers with short stems leads to tall, leggy growth, so make the cut more towards the base of the stem to encourage new growth to come from eyes or buds where the stem is thicker and sturdier. Always make cuts about 6 mm above an eye and slanting back slightly behind the bud. Roses keep best if cut late in the afternoon (when it's cool). Place them in a bucket of water overnight for arranging in the morning.

Pruning

The majority of rose varieties are pruned in late July or early August in most districts but may be delayed until late August or early

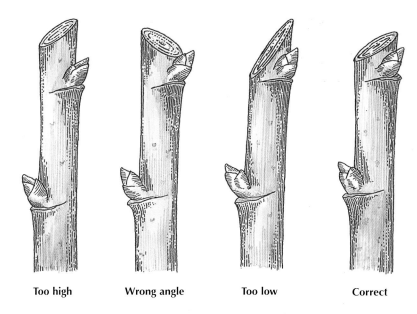

| Too high | Wrong angle | Too low | Correct |

When pruning roses, make sure the secateurs are clean and sharp to avoid bruising. The cut should be made just above a bud pointing in the direction you wish the new shoot to grow.

September in cold climates. The objectives are to remove dead, old or diseased wood, shorten healthy branches to promote new growth (flowers are borne on new wood) and to keep the bushes an appropriate size and shape. Make sure secateurs are clean and sharp and use a pruning saw for cutting thick, woody stems.

Roses that flower only in spring such as rambling or wichuriana roses, most weeping standard roses, banksia roses and Dorothy Perkins types are pruned after flowering. They bloom in spring on wood grown the previous year. Old canes are cut after flowering in spring, but if this is too severe they can be cut back halfway to stimulate new growth.

For dwarf or bush roses, cut out all dead, yellowing and diseased wood. Also discard thin or weak stems, those which rub against each other or are too crowded. Leave the strongest stems and shorten these by one-third of their length, cutting just above a bud pointing in the direction in which you wish the stem to grow. Floribunda or polyantha roses are usually cut back harder than bush roses, shortening stems by one-half. Standard roses are pruned in the same way as bush roses, but cut each stem to an outward

Step by step — pruning roses

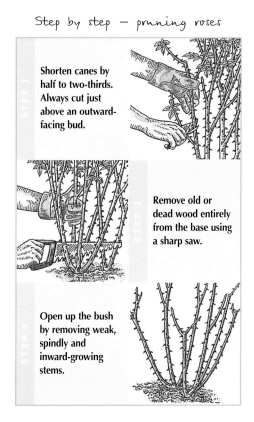

Shorten canes by half to two-thirds. Always cut just above an outward-facing bud.

Remove old or dead wood entirely from the base using a sharp saw.

Open up the bush by removing weak, spindly and inward-growing stems.

HINT

The single most important thing in pruning roses is that your secateurs must be sharp. Blunt ones don't cut, they tear, and that will do more harm to the plant than any 'wrong' pruning. Test them on a piece of heavy paper. If they cut that cleanly, they're ready for the roses. If they tear it, get them sharpened!

ROGER MANN

LANDSCAPE ARCHITECT AND AUTHOR
OF *YATES ROSES* AND *NAMING THE ROSE*

growth and retain a neat shape. Climbing roses require slightly different treatment. Some gardeners give them a light pruning in winter and their main pruning after flowering in spring, removing old canes and dead wood and shortening the canes which remain. Summer pruning is sometimes called 'summer trimming' and is usually done in late January or early February. It consists of a tidy-up, and the removal of dead branches or those showing dieback by cutting back to the bud about 5 cm below the dead section. Any unproductive stems which have not produced good flowers or new shoots can also be removed.

It is important to distinguish between 'water shoots' and 'understock shoots'. The former are tall, vigorous, sappy shoots which suddenly develop from the crown of the plant (above the bud union) or from an old cane, while the latter arise from below the bud union. Always leave the water shoots because they are important for the future framework of the bush. Shorten them in winter when the wood is fully matured. Remove understock shoots as low down as possible.

'La Reine' roses grow over a series of arches in this South Australian rose garden.

Floribunda roses, like this 'Gold Medal', with its abundant flowering, make good garden subjects and mix well with other plants in garden beds.

Pests and diseases

Rose bushes can be attacked by a number of pests and diseases. Aphids (there are several kinds which attack roses) are the worst pests. Colonies of green, brown or pink insects cluster together on young, sappy shoots and flower buds. Thrips, also sap-sucking insects, are just visible to the naked eye and damage both buds and flowers. Two-spotted or red spider, a small mite, infests the lower surface of leaves, causing yellowing or browning and premature ageing. Some caterpillars chew holes in leaves and others roll leaves together. There are also several scale insects that attack roses.

The most serious diseases of rose plants are black spot and powdery mildew. Black spot causes small blackened areas, yellowing leaves and premature leaf fall. Humid weather, moderate temperatures and heavy night dews favour its spread. Powdery mildew produces a white powdery growth on leaves, stems and buds. It is most active in warm (but not too hot), humid weather.

Pests and diseases can be effectively controlled by sprays of insecticides, miticides and fungicides. The recommended chemicals for control are given in Chapter 8. Many gardeners prefer to use an all-purpose rose spray to control both pests and diseases rather than use individual chemicals. A number of such all-purpose sprays and dusts are available. The specially formulated Rose Shield or ready-to-use Yates Rose Gun Advanced are recommended.

After winter pruning, while bushes are still leafless, spray roses with lime sulfur at winter strength. It will help control fungal spores and rose mites.

HINT

To have a good rose display over Christmas, give your plants a light prune about forty to fifty days before.

TONY FAWCETT

GARDEN WRITER — *SATURDAY HERALD SUN HOME MAGAZINE*

Types of Roses

There are many different types of roses. To observe and learn about roses in your district, visit your local public rose gardens. There you can discover landscape ideas and new introductions and smell and touch rare and unusual varieties. Look for roses you like and observe their growing habits.

Hybrid tea rose 'Saratoga'. Hybrid teas are classic long-stemmed roses that are good for picking.

Hybrid tea roses

Hybrid teas produce large, well formed flowers in a wide range of colours on upright stems. They make a good garden display and are beautiful cut flowers.

Floribunda roses

Floribunda roses produce an abundance of flowers in a wide variety of colours. Borne in clusters or trusses, the flowers are less suitable for picking than those of the hybrid teas but they provide a greater display of long-lasting garden colour.

Climbers and ramblers

There is a vast range of climbing and rambling roses. Ramblers have long, pliable stems and bear large trusses of small flowers. They produce several strong stems from their base each year. Climbers make strong stems from any part of the plant and their height potential is far greater than that of ramblers.

Floribunda rose 'Sexy Rexy'. Floribundas flower abundantly from spring through to autumn.

Climbing rose 'Contessa de Sastago'. Climbing roses may have long, arching canes or rambling, multi-branched growth.

Shrub roses

Shrub rose is a general term used to describe hybrids between wild species, hybrid tea roses and floribundas. They are extremely varied in habit, leaf shape and flower form.

Species roses

Species roses are those which are grown in their original wild form. They produce single, fine-petalled flowers, mainly in spring, followed by a display of decorative berry-like hips in autumn. They are particularly resistant to pests and diseases and require little pruning apart from the removal of soft tips and straggly growth.

Old roses

Old roses encompass a broad group including Species, Old European, Tea and China roses. In recent years there has been a great upsurge in interest in them, due to their good garden qualities. They are particularly fragrant and hardy, and have a delightful, informal character. Also called heritage roses, they are growing in popularity and there are specialist growers in most states.

Miniature roses

Miniature roses look like tiny floribundas, but have miniature leaves and flowers in perfect proportion. They normally grow between 20–50 cm high and are almost thornless. They can be used for edging, growing in containers, rockeries, window boxes or indoors as temporary houseplants.

Shrub rose 'Aotearoa'. 'Shrub rose' is a modern term for a bush rose that combines some characteristics of other rose types.

Rosa rugosa. *Rugosas are species roses which are renowned for their attractive rosehips (seed-bearing fruit). They are the best for seaside plantings.*

Moss rose Rosa centifolia muscosa. *Moss roses, like other old-style and heritage roses, have made a comeback in recent years.*

Miniature rose 'Oz Gold'. Miniature roses have small flowers and low growth (less than about 80 cm). They are useful for borders and pots.

18
Perennials, Vines and Creepers

Perennial plants are those that grow for a number of years. This definition is very general and could cover a vast array of plants including trees, shrubs, climbers, ferns, bulbs, cacti, succulents and many others – in fact, any plants which are not strictly annuals or biennials. Generally, though, the term is used to describe flowering plants that live for at least a few years.

Perennials – or, more precisely, flowering perennials – are plants that mostly have non-woody stems and branches. They burst into renewed growth every spring and repeat this cycle year after year, gradually spreading and increasing in size and number.

There are many perennials that can add interest and colour to the garden and they come in all shapes and sizes. Some grassy or strappy-leafed perennials such as Nile grass (*Cyperus papyrus*), lomandras and New Zealand flax (*Phormium tenax*) have become very popular in recent years as accent plants in modern-style gardens.

Herbaceous perennials are those plants that, after flowering in summer, die down in autumn and become dormant in winter. They usually prefer cool conditions and have been used in the traditional herbaceous border in English-style gardens. Evergreen perennials are mostly natives of warmer climates. Whether herbaceous or evergreen, perennials can complement shrubs, annual flowers and bulbs. Many provide useful flowers for indoor decoration, often at a time when annual flowers are scarce. Others have attractive, varied foliage in bronze, yellow-greens, grey and silver.

Soil preparation and planting

As most perennials will remain undisturbed for several years, it is important to prepare the soil well. Most perennials can be planted in late autumn and winter, so start preparation in early autumn. Dig the bed to spade depth and remove all roots and persistent weeds. Add organic matter in the form of animal manure or compost and a ration of mixed fertiliser. Slow-acting blood and bone, totally organic fertilisers (such as Dynamic Lifter pellets) and other slow-release fertilisers (such as Acticote), are suitable for providing nutrients over a long period. Raising the bed 10–15 cm above the surrounding level will ensure good drainage.

Select and place perennial plants according to height and size – dwarf plants in front and taller plants at the back of the bed. Make sure that each plant has sufficient space to develop without crowding or overlapping its neighbours. While a description of some popular perennials is given in this chapter, more comprehensive garden catalogues can help you plan your display. While many perennials can be started economically from seeds and cuttings, quicker results will be obtained by using established plants or divisions of good size. These can be purchased from garden suppliers (especially mail order specialists) and nurseries, or perhaps obtained from friends. Some are available in packages in winter.

Most perennials are planted with the crown (centre) slightly above soil level so that they do not collect water and rot during the dormant season. Plant the crowns so that the roots spread outwards and downwards. After planting, lightly fork the soil between clumps and water well. Be very careful when watering dry climate perennials such as gerberas, lamb's ear (*Stachys byzantina*) and Snow in Summer (*Cerastium tomentosum*) Water at the base, keeping leaves as dry as possible.

Maintaining and dividing perennials

As the plants grow, cultivate between clumps to keep down weeds, or discourage the weeds by mulching with grass clippings, compost, organic mulch or leaf litter. Taller plants may need to be staked or supported with special wire supports (available from garden stores) to protect them against wind. Remove spent flowers regularly during the summer months and cut out old shoots of herbaceous perennials as they die down. Cut back shrubby, evergreen perennials to a tidy, compact shape after

HINT

Perennial plants look great mixed in with annuals for a year-round show that doesn't need as much maintenance as an annuals-only display.

RICHARD HAWKINS

TEACHER – ILLAWARRA INSTITUTE OF TECHNOLOGY (YALLAH TAFE)

major flowering displays. Removing the spent growth will also make it easier to fork over the surface between the plants.

Apply a ration of complete fertiliser in late winter or early spring each year. Slow-release fertilisers, such as Acticote, or organic plant foods like Dynamic Lifter, are ideal. They can be scattered between plants without fear of fertiliser burn, but won't release nutrients until they are watered in. Thinning or dividing perennials is usually necessary when the clumps become overcrowded after four or five years. Often, the centre of the clump becomes old and straggly, so the best parts for replanting are on the outside. If maintaining a bed of perennials, it is best to stagger the task of lifting and dividing, and do only a few plants each year. This way, you maintain the overall effect of the bed. After lifting clumps, dig the area well, adding more organic matter and fertiliser to nourish plants for the next few years. You may have more plants than you need for replacement, but you can give leftovers to friends.

FAVOURITE PERENNIALS

Acanthus (Oyster plant)

E to D, FS to S (200–120). Large, glossy-leaved plants with white and purple snapdragon-like flowers. Watch for snails.

Achillea (Yarrow or Milfoil)

A. filipendula: D, FS (90–30). *A. tomentosa*: E, FS (20–30). Both with lacy, finely divided leaves and rounded white, yellow, pink or red flower heads in summer.

Anthemis (Chamomile)

E, FS to SS (40–30). Semi-trailing plant with fern-like foliage and yellow or white daisy-like flowers in spring and summer. Good drainage.

Arenaria (Sandwort)

E, HS or SS (10–16). Moss-like trailing plant with tiny white flowers in spring.

Armeria (Thrift)

E, FS to SS (40–20). Tufts of grassy foliage with globe-shaped heads of white or pink flowers in spring. Good drainage.

Artemisia (Wormwood or Ghost bush)

E, FS (120–60). Background plant with handsome, divided, greyish-white leaves and yellow flowers in summer. Good drainage.

Aster (Michaelmas daisy)

E, FS or HS. Tall (120–50); medium (75–50); dwarf (20–25). White, pink, mauve, lavender or blue daisies in late summer and autumn.

Astilbe (Goat's beard)

D, HS or SS (60–40). Clumps of attractive foliage with plumes of white, pink and red flowers in late spring. Moist position.

Aurinia (Golden alyssum)

(*A. saxatile*) E, FS or HS (30–30). Dwarf carpeting plant with soft mounds of foliage covered with brilliant yellow flowers in spring. Good drainage.

Bergenia (*Saxifraga*)

E, SS or S (30–40). Rosettes of large, rounded, glossy leaves with stems of waxy, pink or rose-coloured flowers in winter.

Billbergia (Queen's tears)

E, SS or S (40–75). An easy-to-grow bromeliad with clumps of thin, pointed leaves and green flowers hanging from pink-sheathed stems.

Calibrachoa

(*Calibrachoa* x *hybrida*) E, FS (20–25). Like a mini form of the closely related petunias, calibrachoas flower profusely throughout the warm weather in a wide range of colours. Good watering and feeding are essential to support this massed display. Will not tolerate frost so grow as annual in cooler areas. Trailing varieties are excellent for pots.

Campanula (Bellflower)

D or E, SS (15–20). Neat dwarf mounds of green, covered with blue or white, bell-shaped or star-shaped flowers in summer.

Cerastium (Snow in summer)

E, FS (10–50). Dwarf carpeting plant with silvery-grey foliage and masses of white, cup-shaped flowers in late spring. Plants spread rapidly. Good drainage.

Chrysanthemum

(*Leucanthemum* x *superbum*, Shasta daisy) D, FS (100–75). Large daisy flowers with white petals and golden centres in summer. Protect from strong winds.

Cineraria

(*C. maritima*, groundsel or dusty miller) E, FS or HS (60–30). Decorative, finely divided, silver foliage with brilliant yellow daisy-like flowers in late summer. Often listed as *Senecio cineraria*.

Convolvulus

(*C. sabatius*, ground morning glory) E, FS (30–100). Ground-cover and rockery plant with trailing stems and lavender-blue flowers in summer and early autumn. Good drainage.

Cyperus

(*C. papyrus*, Nile grass) E, FS to SS (250–100). Broad clump of thick stems tipped with green, pendulous, thread-like flower spikes. *C. alternifolius* (umbrella plant) is similar but shorter (120 cm), with broader leaves. Very moist conditions for both.

Refer to the front flap of this book for a key to abbreviations.

Dimorphotheca

(*D. aurantica*, African daisy) E, FS (60–100). Cheerful orange daisies in spring and summer. *D. ecklonis* has white flowers with a purple centre. *D. barberia* has mauve flowers. Good drainage for all three.

Echinops (Globe thistle)

D, FS (150–100). Background plant with spiky, grey-green leaves and tall, steel-blue, globe-shaped flowers in summer. Good drainage.

Erigeron (Fleabane)

E, FS or HS (30–50). Dwarf mat of foliage with small, daisy-like, mauve or lavender flowers in summer and autumn. Good drainage required.

Euphorbia wulfenii is valued for its unusual yellow-green flowers.

Euphorbia 'Jade Dragon' has striking blooms.

Eryngium (Sea holly)

D, FS or HS (60–40). Thistle-like plant similar to echinops with cone-shaped, blue flowers in summer. Good drainage.

Euphorbia

(*E. wulfenii*, yellow spurge) E, HS (100–100). Compact, rounded clumps of foliage covered with yellow-green or lime-green flower bracts in winter and spring. Good drainage required. Susceptible to frost.

Felicia

(*F. amelloides*, blue marguerite) E, FS or HS (50–50). Mounds of foliage with dainty, sky-blue, daisy-like flowers in most seasons. *F. bergeriana* (kingfisher daisy) is a low-growing annual that is studded with bright-blue flowers for months during the warmer part of the year. Good drainage for both.

Festuca

(*F. glauca*, blue fescue) E, FS or HS (25–25). Small, attractive grass clumps with fine, blue-grey leaves. Good sun and drainage.

Variegated markings on hosta leaves can brighten shady spots in the garden.

Luscious hosta foliage is favourite snail food.

Filipendula

D, HS or SS (100–40). Panicles of pink, mauve or white flowers with attractive, deeply cut, fern-like foliage. Prefers moist conditions.

Helianthus (Perennial sunflower)

D, FS (100–60). Bushy plants with many flowering stems with small sunflowers in autumn. Good drainage.

Helleborus (Winter Rose)

D, HS to SS (50–40). Hand-shaped leaves with lime-green, mauve or purple flowers in winter and spring. Semi-shaded moist conditions.

Heuchera (Coral bells)

E, FS or HS (50–25). Mounds of attractive, scalloped foliage with clusters of small, coral-pink bells in spring and summer. Requires moist soil and low humidity.

Hosta

(*H. plantaginea*, plantain lily) D, FS to SS (25–40). Handsome, variegated or green foliage with small, bell-shaped, white or lilac flowers in summer. Moist conditions. Protect from snails.

Hypericum

(*H. reptans*, gold flower) E, FS or HS (10–30). Trailing plant with attractive foliage and yellow, five-petalled flowers in late spring. Good drainage.

Lavandula

(*L. spica*, lavender) E, FS or HS (50–30). Attractive clumps of silver-grey, aromatic foliage and lavender-blue flower spikes in early summer. Good drainage.

Liatris (Gay feather)

D, FS or HS (60–30). Clumps of grass-like leaves with tall spikes of rose-purple flowers in summer. Good drainage.

Lychnis (Maltese cross)

D, FS or HS (60–30). Compact clumps (evergreen in mild climates) with red or white flowers on wiry stems in late spring.

Meconopsis (Blue Tibetan poppy)

D, SS or S (100–40). Beautiful, large, crepe-petalled poppies in late spring. Good drainage but regular watering. Notoriously difficult to grow. Full sun in cool areas.

Mesembryanthemum (Pig face or Ice plant)

E, FS (25–75). Drought-resistant carpeting plant with succulent leaves and silky-petalled flowers in late spring. Very wide colour range. Good drainage.

Monarda (Bergamot or Bee Balm)

D, HS or SS (60–50). Large clumps with many stems bearing pink, mauve or red flowers in summer. Moist conditions.

HINT

Why does lavender droop when picked for vases? The answer is that the stems are not fully hardened right up to the base of the flower. Feel just beneath the flowers and you will soon tell the difference between a soft stem and a mature, hard one.

FRANCES HUTCHISON
GARDENING AUTHOR AND EDITOR

Nepeta (Catmint)

D, FS or HS (25–25). Soft mounds of sage-green foliage (attractive to cats) with dainty sprays of lavender-blue flowers in late spring and summer. Good drainage.

Nierembergia (Blue cup flower)

E, HS or SS (20–25). Dwarf border or rockery plant with lacy foliage and masses of blue, cup-shaped flowers in summer.

Ophiopogon (White mondo grass)

E, SS or S (25–25). Clumps of green and white, strap-like leaves with white or cream flowers in muscari-like spikes in summer.

Bergamot can be a feature in the late-summer garden.

Paeonia (Peony Rose)

D, SS (75–50). Cool-climate plant with large, fragrant, ruffled or single flowers in spring. Flower colours in shades of pink, mauve, red and white. Good drainage.

Penstemon (Beard tongue)

D, FS (75–50). Bushy 'gloxinia-flowered' types have spikes of pink, mauve and red flowers in late spring and summer. Good drainage.

Phlox

(*P. paniculata*, perennial phlox) D, FS to SS (60–50). Good herbaceous border plant with flowers in every shade of pink, mauve, salmon and white. Flowers in late spring to early autumn.

Phormium (New Zealand flax)

E, FS or HS (150–75). Background or accent plant. Green, bronze, red-purple or variegated (green–white) strap-like leaves. Red or yellow flowers on tall spikes in summer. Handles tough conditions and salt air. Dwarf cultivars now available.

Platycodon (Balloon flower)

D, HS or SS (60–60). Herbaceous border plant with balloon-like buds which open to star-shaped, violet-blue flowers in summer. Good drainage but regular watering.

Primula obconica

E, SS or S (20–20). Evergreen perennial best suited to shady situations or for growing in pots or baskets in ferneries or shadehouses. The plants grow to 15–20 cm with large flowers in shades of rose, mauve, lavender-blue, crimson and white. The plants are excellent indoor pot plants when in flower. This type of primula is usually available as potted plants in flower. It is best to replant or re-pot obconicas in early winter. Plants can sometimes cause skin allergy problems for some people, but newer varieties are allergy-free.

Stachys (Lamb's ear)

E, FS to SS (20–30). Dwarf clumps of furry, silver-grey leaves for edging or ground cover. Spikes of small purple flowers in summer. Frost-susceptible.

Stokesia (Stokes' aster)

D or E, FS to SS (60–40). Dense clumps with large, lavender-blue daisy flowers in late spring and summer. Good drainage but adaptable to climate and soil.

Thalictrum (Lavender shower)

D, HS or SS (150–50). Mass of fern-like foliage (similar to aquilegia) with tall, shivery stems bearing tiny lavender flowers on lateral branches in summer.

Veronica (Speedwell)

D, FS to HS (30–30). Rosettes of glossy, pointed leaves and pink, mauve or blue flower spikes in spring and summer. Good drainage.

Flower spikes of veronica (speedwell).

Vinca

(*Catharanthus rosea*, Periwinkle) E, FS (35–25). This plant produces masses of five-petalled, single flowers in spring and summer, in shades of pink and white, often with a contrasting darker eye. It has been greatly improved in recent years with many compact and colourful forms being developed. The plant looks somewhat like a dwarf impatiens but will grow happily in full sun and stand up well to heat. Vincas are perennial in a frost-free climate. Cut back well in early spring to encourage bushy growth or replace plants annually.

Violet

(*Viola odorata*) E, HS or SS (20–40). Attractive clumps of rounded leaves with fragrant, purple (occasionally white) flowers in winter and spring. Good drainage but regular watering. Best replanted every few years.

Refer also to perennial plants described in Chapters 15 and 16.

CLIMBERS

Climbers – also called vines or creepers – are vertical-growing plants that need support of some kind as they grow upwards. Because of their verticality, climbing plants are good space savers in the garden. They can provide large masses of foliage that form a background to garden shrubs and annuals. Many climbers have attractive and fragrant flowers. Climbers are also useful to cover a bare wall, a fence, an old stump or a dead tree. They can soften walls and fences and add privacy to garden corners. Deciduous vines and creepers growing over a trellis or pergola are ideal for providing shade in summer while letting in the winter sun.

Types of climbers

Vines and creepers cling to their support in different ways. Some, like honeysuckle and wisteria, grow by twining their long stems around the available support – and other plants, if they are allowed to. Others develop thin tendrils or claws which grasp onto wire or timber to keep the stems upright. Good examples of this group are clematis and vitis (ornamental grape). Another group of climbers – ficus, hedera (ivy) and Virginia creeper – have aerial roots or sucker pads that cling to brick or stone walls, bark of trees and timber. The final group are the woody scramblers like bougainvillea, which lean on their supports without creating firm attachments.

Soil preparation and planting

Because most climbers will become permanent garden features, it is advisable to prepare the soil well before planting by digging to a spade depth and adding in some organic matter such as well-aged animal manure or compost. If planting a new garden check the soil in the area against the walls – it may contain builder's rubble, which should be removed and replaced with good soil. Mix some complete fertiliser into the soil before planting. Slow-release fertilisers and fertilisers based on blood and bone are often the best for supplying a pre-planting ration. Climbers, like most plants, need good drainage, so make provision for this, especially against brick or stone walls which are likely to trap water. It's a good idea to plant vines or creepers at least 20 cm from a solid wall – 30–40 cm is even better if there is room.

Many climbers can be propagated from cuttings, layers or root divisions or you can buy potted plants from garden stores or nurseries. Deciduous climbers can be planted in winter but most evergreens are best planted in early autumn or spring (spring is best for those from warm climates). Some quick-growing vines – which are often most useful in a new garden – can be raised from seed. Good examples are chain-of-hearts (*Antigonon leptopus*), cobaea (cup-and-saucer vine), mina (*Mina lobata*), sweet pea and ornamental gourds.

SELECTING VINES AND CREEPERS

It is important to choose suitable plants for your climate and for each situation in the garden. Some creepers spread quickly by self-layering and tend to take over the whole garden if not kept in check. Others, such as bougainvillea, clematis, hardenbergia and solandra, are very vigorous in warm, moist situations and may need cutting back

Refer to the front flap of this book for a key to abbreviations.

regularly. Some climbers have dangerous weed-like tendencies in certain climates. A selection of climbing plants is given below.

Akebia

(*A. quinata*) D, FS or HS. Vigorous twining creeper with divided foliage and fragrant, umbrella-shaped, lime-green to purple flowers in spring. If too vigorous, prune back after flowering and shorten the leaders. All climates.

Allamanda

(*A. cathartica*) E, FS. Sprawling climber with large, golden, trumpet-like flowers from spring to autumn. Cut back in winter to keep it within bounds. Warm–temperate, tropical.

Antigonon

(*A. leptopus*, coral creeper) D, FS. Vigorous twining creeper with clusters of small, bright-pink flowers in summer. Plants die down in winter but shoot again in spring. Sow seed in spring. Temperate, tropical.

Aristolochia

(*A. elegans*, Dutchman's pipe) Cultivation of this introduced species is discouraged because it has caused problems for the native Richmond Birdwing Butterfly in northern New South Wales. A native species (*A. proevenosa*) is worth seeking out to grow as a substitute.

Asparagus

(*A. plumosus*, asparagus fern) E, FS to SS. Dainty-looking climber with fern-like leaves but tenacious roots. Used to be in demand for bouquets and flower decoration and as a container plant with wall support or frame. Now classed as a weed.

Bauhinia

(*B. scandens*) E, FS or HS. Small tendril-climber with butterfly-like leaves and shell-pink flowers with red stamens. Temperate, tropical, but frost-susceptible.

White clematis in full bloom encloses a garden seat.

Bougainvillea

E, FS. Large, woody, scrambling creepers with hard, hooked thorns. Plants need full sun and tolerate dry conditions. The showy flower bracts make a dazzling display in spring and summer. Needs strong support and hard pruning if plants are too vigorous. Warm–temperate, tropical. The best known species are: *B. glabra* 'Magnifica Traillii' (bright purple), *B. laterita* (brick red), *B.* 'Mrs Butt' (port wine) and *B.* 'Thomasii' (dusty pink).

HINT

Many vines are vigorous climbers, especially if conditions are favourable. However, this can quickly become a significant problem. Check these plants regularly to ensure that they are not growing into gutters or under roofs and disturbing tiles.

JOHN MASON

GARDEN AUTHOR, PRINCIPAL –

ACS DISTANCE EDUCATION

There are many others, including some newer dwarf varieties that are ideal for pots.

Clematis

D, FS or HS. Tendril-climbers with showy flowers in white, pink, red or lavender-blue (depending on species and variety). Cool or temperate climates. There are some evergreen varieties.

Clerodendron

(*C. splendens*) E, FS or HS. Vigorous creeper with glossy foliage and tightly packed clusters of scarlet flowers in summer. Needs warm, sheltered position. Temperate, tropical.

Clytostoma

(*C. callistegioides*) E, FS. Was previously classified as *Bignonia lindleyi*. Vigorous creeper with masses of trumpet-shaped, lavender-blue flowers in spring or summer. Suits all climates but is susceptible to hard frosts.

Cobaea

(*C. scandens*, Cup and Saucer vine or Cathedral Bells) SD, FS or HS. Quick-growing, tendril vine often grown as an annual as plants become rather ragged in winter. Large, bell-shaped flowers (green, turning lilac or violet in summer). Sow seed in early spring. Suits temperate or tropical climates. Can be weedy.

Dipladenia (Mandevilla)

(*Mandevilla splendens*) E, HS or SS. Grown for its long-lasting display of large, pink or white, trumpet-shaped blooms, Dipladenia is best in a container and is most suited to tropical, subtropical or warm–temperate climates.

Ficus

(*F. pumila*) E, FS to SS. Aerial root-creeper with dense foliage. Must be clipped regularly. Suitable for low walls, fences or natural covering for rocks. Temperate, tropical.

Gelsemium

(*G. sempervirens*, Carolina jasmine) E, FS or HS. Small, attractive, twining creeper with pointed leaves and fragrant, bell-shaped, yellow flowers in late winter and spring. Suits all climates.

Hardenbergia

(*H. violacea*, Australian sarsparilla) E, HS to SS. Native, twining creeper with lavender-blue to violet, pea-shaped flowers in spring. All climates except coldest regions. Good ground cover.

Hedera (Ivy)

E, FS to S. Foliage creepers with aerial roots. Very adaptable to climate, soil, sun and shade. Mature foliage can become woody and develop seeds that are spread by birds. The most popular species are *H. canariensis* 'Variegata' with large, glossy, green and cream leaves, and *H. helix* (English ivy) with smaller leaves, but there are many varieties with deep-green, silver-variegated, yellow-variegated and yellow-centred leaves. All climates.

Hoya

(*H. carnosa*, wax plant) E, HS or SS. Small twining plant useful for trellises or in containers with wall support for frame in a warm, sheltered position. Clusters of pink, star-shaped flowers in summer. New buds arise from old flower spurs. Temperate, tropical.

Top five flowering climbers

ALLAMANDA

The brightest of yellow flowers are produced by this warm-climate twiner.

BOUGAINVILLEA

The papery bracts of bougainvillea are long-lasting and showy, with a range of 'almost-too-bright-to-be-real' colours.

CLYTOSTOMA

The trumpet-shaped blooms of this variety will bring a welcome patch of blue to the late-spring garden.

PANDOREA JASMINOIDES

This Australian native produces clusters of showy pink bells right throughout the warm part of the year.

CLEMATIS

Entire books have been written about the many hundreds of types of clematis. Unlike most climbers, they perform especially well in colder climates (see picture opposite).

ALLAMANDA

BOUGAINVILLEA

Top five climbers for shade

MONSTERA

Monstera has monster-sized leaves with 'Swiss cheese' perforations. It's useful for creating a tropical effect.

MANDEVILLA

M. splendens is also known as dipladenia, and its attractive flowers are seen at their best in a morning sun–afternoon shade position.

IVY

Some of the variegated and coloured-leaf ivies are very pretty and all will cope with bright, shaded conditions.

TRACHELOSPERMUM

Commonly called star jasmine, this climber has thick, waxy leaves and white, perfumed blooms. It looks wonderful in semi-shade.

FICUS PUMILA

Shade-tolerant climbing fig is grown for its flattened leaves, but must be clipped regularly to keep it under control.

MANDEVILLA

FICUS PUMILA

HINT

When planting a climber that you want to cover a fence or trellis, twine the tendrils out sideways rather than up. The plant naturally grows upwards to seek the light, so all those side laterals will become leaders, filling the width of the trellis quickly.

CAROLYN BLACKMAN
HORTICULTURIST — VIVID DESIGN

Ipomoea (Morning glory)

E, FS or HS. Vigorous vines will quickly cover walls, fences, banks and batters. Mixed packets of seed are sometimes available with an annual mixture of bright colours. Some types are bad environmental weeds. All climates except coldest regions.

Jasminum (Jasmine)

E, HS or SS. Vigorous, twining or scrambling vine with sweetly scented flowers in spring or summer (depending on species). Temperate, tropical but frost-susceptible. The most widely grown species are *J. polyanthum*, with rosy-pink buds and small, starry-white flowers in early spring; *J. grandiflorum*, with larger, white flowers produced sparsely throughout the year; *J. nitidum*, with very large, white flowers produced throughout the year and double-flowered *J. sambac* 'Grand Duke of Tuscany' that are both best suited to tropical climates.

Lonicera (Honeysuckle)

SD or E, FS to SS. Vigorous twining or scrambling creepers which are very adaptable to climate and soil. Fragrant spring flowers are creamy-white, yellow, pink, or red, depending on the species. Plants must be pruned after flowering to keep them within bounds. All climates. *L. japonica* is classed as a weed.

Macfadyena

(*M. unguis cati*, cat's claw creeper) E, FS or HS. Previously known as *Bignonia tweediana*. Vigorous creeper with claw-like tendrils and golden-yellow trumpet flowers. Frost-susceptible. Weedy in warm climates.

Mandevilla

(Chilean jasmine) ED or SD, FS or HS. Handsome vine with clusters of white, pink or red trumpet-shaped flowers in summer and autumn. Prune back after flowering to prevent overcrowding. Warm–temperate, tropical, but frost-susceptible. Other hybrids are evergreen with large flowers, e.g. 'Alice Du Pont' (pink), 'White Fantasy' (white with pink centre).

Mina

(*M. lobata*) A, FS or HS. Quick-growing vine to 2 m tall, useful for short-term cover of trellis or fence. Vines are covered with sprays of red and yellow flowers in late summer and autumn. Sow seeds in spring. All climates, but frost-susceptible.

Monstera

(*M. deliciosa*, fruit salad plant) E, FS to S. Vigorous climber with aerial roots which cling to masonry, and with large, round but deeply divided leaves. Also useful as indoor plant in large pots or tubs. Arum-type yellow flowers develop into long, cylindrical fruit with a delicious flavour. Warm–temperate, tropical climates.

Ornamental Gourd

A, FS. Quick-growing vine closely related to cucumber and pumpkin. Pick fruit with a

HINT

Use the prunings from grapevines and wisteria to make decorative wreaths. Shape them into circles or hearts and use for Christmas decorations with fresh gum leaves, gum nuts and gold ribbon.

SUSAN MONTGOMERY
GARDEN DESIGNER

Pandorea jasminoides 'Bower of Beauty'.

stem when it is ripe, and dry for indoor decoration or as ornaments. Sow seeds in spring or early summer and grow plants in the same way as trellised cucumbers. Suits all climates but very susceptible to frost.

Pandorea

E, FS or HS. *P. jasminoides* is an attractive native creeper with glossy leaves and pink, trumpet-like flowers flushed rosy-purple in spring and summer. 'Lady Di' is a white-flowering cultivar. *P. pandorana* is commonly known as wonga-wonga vine, a similar creeper but the small, creamy-white, tubular flowers are in clusters during spring. Warm–temperate, tropical climates for both species.

Parthenocissus

(*P. tricuspidata*, Boston ivy or *P. quinquefolia* Virginia creeper) D, FS or HS. Vigorous creepers, grown for their soft, deciduous leaves which colour brilliantly in autumn. Ideal for brick walls and stonework. All climates.

Passiflora (Passionfruit)

See Chapter 13.

Pelargonium (Ivy geranium)

E, FS or HS. Geraniums with long stems for training over walls and fences or for trailing over banks or batters. Also for hanging baskets. Ivy-shaped leaves and white, pink or red flowers in spring and summer. All climates.

Phaedranthus

(*P. buccinatorius*, Mexican blood trumpet) E, FS or HS. Previously known as *Bignonia cherere*. Vigorous creeper with strong stems and clusters of orange-red trumpet flowers in spring and summer. Warm–temperate, tropical.

Pyrostegia

(*P. venusta*, flame vine) E, FS. Vigorous, adaptable creeper for covering fences, trellises or outbuildings with brilliant orange, tubular flowers in late winter and spring. Temperate, tropical, but tolerates light frosts.

Rosa

(*R. wichuriana*, rambler rose) SD, FS. Spectacular spring-flowering roses for trellis, pergola or for weeping standards. All climates. For rose cultivation, see Chapter 17.

Solandra (Cup of Gold or Hawaiian lily)

E, FS to SS. Sprawling, rampant vine which needs solid support and regular cutting back to keep it under control. Large, creamy-yellow trumpet flowers to 25 cm diameter in spring. Warm–temperate, tropical. Frost-susceptible.

Stephanotis (Madagascar jasmine)

E, FS or HS. Handsome creeper which needs light support and training. Fragrant, white, trumpet-like flowers in late summer are favourites in bridal bouquets. Needs a warm, sheltered position. Temperate, tropical.

Thunbergia

E, FS. Several species are attractive climbers which flower intermittently throughout the year. The best known is *T. alata* (black-eyed Susan) with orange petals and black centres. *T. gibsonii* (golden glory vine) has masses of orange flowers. *T. grandiflora* (sky flower) has pale-blue flowers. All species prefer a warm, sheltered position. Temperate and tropical. Most can become weeds, especially in warm climates.

Trachelospermum (Star jasmine)

E, FS to SS. Sometimes available in a low growing, variegated, ground-covering form, this useful creeper has rich, glossy foliage and fragrant, lace-like, white fragrant flowers in spring and summer. All climates except coldest regions.

Vitis (Ornamental grape)

D, FS. Vigorous tendril vine with cool, green summer foliage and brilliant autumn colours. Ideal for training on a trellis or pergola, especially to let through winter sun. All climates except hot, tropical regions.

Wisteria

D, FS to HS. One of the most popular spring-flowering creepers with pendulous clusters of pea-like flowers in white, lavender and lilac (depending on species or variety). Vines may be slow to establish but become very vigorous and long-lived and therefore need strong support. Ideal for covering a pergola for summer shade, winter sun and spring blossom. All climates.

HINT

Climbers such as golden shower (*Pyrostegia venusta*) and coral vine (*Antigonon leptopus*) are wonderfully showy in bloom but unfortunately can become incredibly rampant. It is very important to cut them back hard each spring – almost to the ground – and they'll stay tame.

GEOFFREY BURNIE
GARDENING JOURNALIST

The delicate appearance of wisteria blossoms belies the vine's hardiness.

19
Trees and Shrubs

Trees and shrubs can make an important contribution to the general outline and colour of your garden. They provide an easy-care background for annuals, bulbs and perennials which change with the seasons. They can ensure privacy and protection against winds, screen unsightly views and diminish traffic noise. They provide a leafy canopy on hot summer days, and deciduous species let warm winter sun penetrate to indoor and outdoor living areas. From the hundreds of trees and shrubs available, it is essential to choose those which suit your climate, situation and soil. Plant form, shape and height when mature are very important in deciding their position in the garden, either as a single specimen or in groups. Lists of popular trees and shrubs are given in this chapter as a guide, but the best plan – especially for new gardeners – is to look at the trees and shrubs in your area and try to identify the desirable performers. Plant labels give some indication of size but these often refer to the dimensions at the end of a ten year period. Size can vary with location so it's essential to check how plants perform in your area.

PLANTING

Most shrubs and trees are sold in plastic pots. These can be planted at any time of the year, although the cooler months of autumn or spring are the best.

Before planting, check the position to make sure it is suitable for the plant when fully grown. Avoid sites close to sewerage or drainage lines which could be invaded by strong-rooting species and cause future problems – especially with trees like willows, poplars and rubber trees. Also avoid planting trees under overhead wires where they may eventually be dangerous or cause expense and trouble in keeping them pruned. Do any drainage work necessary beforehand, as many shrubs and trees resent wet, soggy conditions. If the soil is a very heavy clay, organic matter in the form of animal manure, leaf mould or compost should be incorporated to improve the structure. The addition of coarse sand or gypsum (calcium sulfate) also makes heavy soils more crumbly. Creating a raised planting bed could be a desirable option.

The potting mix in the container and the soil in the garden should be damp (but not wet) at planting time. Dig a wide but shallow hole – about twice the width of the container but not much deeper. Roots will travel faster through soil that has been well broken up. The potting mixture in the container is often of a different texture from that of the garden soil, which may cause an 'interface' problem; that is, the two soils fail to merge, creating a root barrier. Add compost or peat moss to the soil removed from the hole and mix it well. Now fill the base of the hole with the soil mixture to bring the root-ball of the plant level with the top of the hole so that the plant is not deeper in the soil than it was in the container. Take the plant from the container and set it at the correct level. If the plant is slightly root-bound (roots tangled round and round), tease the roots away gently, spread them out and cover with soil progressively. Alternatively, hose the root-ball gently to wash away the outside soil so that roots can be separated and covered. Add the rest of the soil gradually, firming it down to exclude air spaces, but avoiding heavy pressure by treading. The leftover soil should be used to form a raised ring around the plant.

Water well and then spread grass clippings, leaf mould or fibrous compost for a mulch. Keep the mulch away from the stem as it might encourage collar rot or other root rots. The mulch will prevent the surface soil from caking and will conserve moisture. Only stake if absolutely necessary; stakes should be driven in outside the root-ball to avoid damage. Tie trees or shrubs to the stake with plant ties or lengths of old rag or nylon stocking, allowing some room for stem movement. Do not use wire, as this will cut into the stem or trunk.

Water thoroughly when needed, making sure that the root-ball is wetted because it will tend to dry out more quickly than the surrounding soil. Avoid using strong powdered or granular

Planting trees and shrubs

STEP 1
Container-grown plants can be planted year round, providing the soil is not too wet. Avoid planting in extreme heat or cold conditions so as not to stress the plant.

STEP 2
Dig the planting hole twice as wide and to the same depth as the root-ball, loosening the soil at the bottom. Add compost or peat to the soil removed from the hole.

STEP 3
Take shrub out of its container. Cut away any circled or tangled roots so they radiate out from the root-ball. Plant the shrub no deeper in the soil than it was in its container.

STEP 4
Fill the hole in with enriched soil, gradually firming it down to exclude air spaces. Avoid compacting the soil through heavy treading.

STEP 5
Form a raised ring around the plant, creating a basin so that water will be concentrated in the area where it is needed most. Water thoroughly.

STEP 6
Stake if necessary, placing it on the side of prevailing winds. Drive in the stake outside of the area of the root-ball to avoid damage. Tie the plant loosely to the stake.

fertilisers, either at planting time or immediately afterwards. Slow-acting fertilisers such as blood and bone are safe to scatter on the mulched surface. Dynamic Lifter organic pellets can be placed in the planting hole. Controlled-release fertilisers may be scratched into the soil surface.

Bare-rooted, usually packaged, deciduous plants such as flowering fruit trees and other ornamental and fruit bearing varieties are available in winter. Discard packaging material around roots before planting. Plant as for roses (see pages 364–365).

PRUNING

Many trees and shrubs are more or less self-shaping, so pruning is only rarely necessary. Others can be improved by regular or occasional pruning. Briefly, the objectives of the pruning are:

- To shape the plant – especially young shrubs and trees – and ensure a balanced framework for the future. For hedges the aim is to promote a dense growth down to ground level.
- To reduce competition by thinning out crowded growth, to make room for nearby plants or to prevent obstruction of pathways and light to windows.
- To stimulate new growth and encourage flowers (and fruits). With flowering shrubs, the removal of spent blooms prevents fruits and seeds from forming and so directs plant energy into more flowering or vegetative growth.
- To remove diseased or dead wood and cut away unwanted branches such as those which have reverted from a variegated leaf to a plain leaf, or from a dwarf form to a tall form.
- To remove suckers from root stocks on which some shrubs or trees are grafted.

Only sharp tools (secateurs or pruning saws) should be used, because jagged cuts provide a resting place for disease spores and a greater area for the plant to form a callus (see Chapter 10). Always make cuts just above a bud or level with the joint to a larger branch to protect large areas from dieback.

The shaping of a tree, shrub or hedge should begin as soon as possible. If early pruning is neglected it is more difficult to achieve a balanced shape later. Shears are suitable for clipping or trimming hedges.

Pruning methods

PINCHING

The first opportunity to control or direct plant growth is to remove or to pinch out the terminal bud. This is especially useful with young plants when you want to make them bushier; for example, petunia. Conversely, if you want the plant to gain height, keep side growth pinched back so the terminal bud on the main stem continues to elongate. Nipping out the axillary laterals on tomatoes will produce a smaller crop of larger-sized fruit.

PRUNING CUTS

There is a correct way to make pruning cuts which helps direct new growth and facilitates the closure of the wound. A pruning cut should be made close to an outward-facing bud.
The lowest point of the cut should be even with the top of the bud and slanting upwards at 45 degrees. Large branches should be removed in stages to avoid unnecessary damage. Trim back to a stub of 45–60 cm which can then be removed safely, leaving a clean surface.

THINNING

Thinning removes stems or branches, opening the plant up. It enables old and unproductive wood to be removed, removes branches that are growing in awkward directions and produces a taller and more open plant. The removal of superfluous branches also allows for better air circulation within the framework of the tree or shrub, thereby minimising the likelihood of entry of disease. This leads to improved plant health and vigour.

CLIPPING BACK

Clipping back results in a stronger, more prolific growth of branches because the removal of the terminal portion of a stem destroys apical dominance and stimulates growth hormone in the lateral buds. This is particularly desirable in plants grown as hedges, which look their best when bushy and compact. To clip back, cut around the entire shape of the plant using a pair of sharp, clean secateurs.

While it is not possible to control the exact position of the cut on each stem, most hedge plants have the ability to develop new growth at almost any part of the stem and do not suffer from dieback at the cut ends.

Most slow-growing trees and shrubs need little pruning. Good examples are azalea (*Rhododendron* spp.), camellia, daphne, gardenia and frangipani (*Plumeria* spp.). As a general rule, most flowering shrubs and some flowering trees are pruned after they have flowered, although deciduous types fall into two groups. Those which flower (usually summer or early autumn) on current season's growth (new wood) are pruned in winter. Crepe myrtle is an example. Those which flower in spring on last season's growth (old wood) are pruned immediately after flowering because pruning in winter would remove much of the spring blossom. Good examples are flowering peach and weigela. Other spring-flowering trees and shrubs are best pruned back (if they need it at all) after flowering. Multi-stemmed shrubs like Japanese bamboo (*Nandina* spp.), may (*Spirea* spp.) and barberry (*Berberis* spp.) require little pruning except to remove older canes periodically at ground level to promote new growth.

REPAIRING DAMAGED TREES AND SHRUBS

Very often, a broken branch or stem, if not completely severed, can be repaired by fitting the broken section together using a splint (a piece of dowel stick for small branches or stouter hardwood for larger limbs) and then binding the break and splint firmly together with plastic budding tape. Heavy branches may be propped with stakes from below or, better still, secure the branch to the main trunk or stem with rope or garden stakes tied at each point. Pruning the foliage from the damaged branch will reduce its weight and prevent any further possible wind damage. Closely bound branches should mend in three or four months. If a break is beyond repair, saw the branch off cleanly. Make the first cut underneath to about halfway or until the saw binds. Make the second cut about 5 cm in front of the first and take it through until the branch falls. Now make a third cut right through to remove the stub, which is easily handled. In some cases it may be best to

HINT

Try planting small to medium-sized trees in groves near the house. This helps to connect the house with the garden, giving the house a complementary scale and softening strong lines of the house. Maples, crepe myrtles, birch and banksias are especially suitable.

PETER FUDGE

GARDEN DESIGNER

WWW.PETERFUDGEGARDENS.COM.AU

remove the branch entirely, cutting just outside the 'wrinkle' where the branch joins the trunk.

Trees which have been blown over can often be salvaged because usually only half the roots are broken and exposed. Trim the broken roots cleanly and paint them with a copper fungicide paste. Lift the tree upright while the soil is still moist, using one or more forked poles for extra leverage. Move them in closer to support the tree as it is raised. A permanent support of a guy wire (fencing wire or clothes line wire) fixed to one or more stakes on the windward side should be sufficient. Thread the wire through a short piece of old garden hose to prevent damage where it loops around the trunk of the tree.

Shrubs and small trees can be moved successfully if handled carefully when they are dormant. Winter is the safest time for most kinds, but warmth-loving shrubs like gardenia and hibiscus are often best moved in very early spring. Dig around the plants so that a wide, rather shallow root-ball is taken. Slide or juggle the plant onto a piece of canvas or heavy-duty plastic to carry or drag the plant to the new site. Take care that the root-ball remains intact.

TREE OR SHRUB?

Defining whether a plant is a tree or a shrub can be difficult. As a general rule, a tree grows taller (usually more than 4 m) and has a single main trunk. A shrub is usually smaller and most often has multiple shoots from the base. The line between the two can be blurred, however, and many shrubs can be grown in a tree-like shape, while many small trees can be used as shrubs. For landscaping purposes, a tree can easily be grown as a freestanding specimen in a lawn but it is far better to have shrubs in mixed garden beds, or 'shrubberies'.

On the following pages, plants have been described as either trees or shrubs, depending on their most common usage but, as discussed above, the line between the two is often blurred.

HINT

Improve your garden by selecting the appropriate plant types. For example, shady evergreen trees may be appealing in summer but will make an area cooler and damper in the winter. Choosing deciduous trees instead will give shade in the summer but let the sun shine through in the winter.

JOHN MASON

GARDEN AUTHOR, PRINCIPAL --
ACS DISTANCE EDUCATION

SELECTING TREES AND SHRUBS

The height to which a tree or shrub grows, whether it is evergreen or deciduous and whether it is grown for foliage, flowers or fruits are important factors to consider in making a selection. A summary of some of the most popular trees and shrubs is given in this chapter. It is far from being complete but may be a useful reference for the new gardener. Further information can be gathered from the internet (check local sources), nursery catalogues or reference books which deal specifically with this aspect of gardening. The most practical way of learning about trees and shrubs is to see them actually growing in your own district. Most leading nurseries employ trained horticulturists who can give valuable information to help you make your final selection. In the summary which follows, plants are listed in alphabetical order by their botanical name, followed by their common name.

Top five flowering trees

JACARANDA

This glorious South American native usually flowers when the tree is bare of leaves, which enhances the magnificent effect.

MAGNOLIA

Another tree that usually blooms on bare branches, every deciduous magnolia is a garden aristocrat.

GORDONIA

On the borderline between a tree and a shrub, but able to be pruned into a tree-like shape (which shows off its attractive bark), gordonia's 'fried egg' flowers can be close to 10 cm across.

STENOCARPUS (QUEENSLAND FIREWHEEL TREE)

At blooming time, this rainforest tree looks as if it's lit up from within by the red pinwheel flowers that cluster among its branches.

ILLAWARRA FLAME TREE

Another red-flowering native, this tree loses its leaves just before flowering and, in a good season, can be a towering pillar of red.

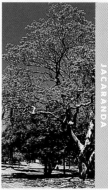

**Refer to the front flap of this book
for a key to abbreviations.**

Abelia (Glossy abelia)

E, FS or HS, H 2–3 m, W 1–2 m. Arching shrub with small leaves and white to pink, bell-shaped flowers in summer and autumn. All climates except coldest districts. Makes good specimen or hedge plant. Prune hard in late winter/early spring.

Abutilon (Japanese lantern)

E, FS to SS, H 1–2 m, W 1–2 m. Attractive, often mottled foliage and pendulous, hibiscus-like flowers in white, yellow, orange or pink (depending on variety) in summer. All climates except coldest districts.

Acacia

See Chapter 20.

Acalypha (Fiji fire plant)

SD, FS or HS, H 2–3 m, W 1–2 m. Large, attractive, multicoloured foliage plant with insignificant flowers. Another species has green leaves and drooping red flower spikes. Both are frost-susceptible and need warm–temperate or tropical conditions.

Acer (Maple)

D, FS to SS, H 2–18 m, W 1–15 m. Attractive trees with spectacular autumn foliage for cold and temperate climates. Japanese maples (*A. palmatum*) have many leaf forms and colours (some of them variegated) and are usually small to medium-sized trees. Box elder (*A. negundo*) and Norway maple (*A. platanoides*) are larger trees for cool climates. Box elder may become a weed in suitable climates.

Agonis

See Chapter 20.

Arbutus (Irish strawberry tree)

E, FS or HS, H 5–6 m, W 3–4 m. Rounded, densely foliaged tree with masses of small, white blossoms from summer to winter followed by large, rough, multicoloured (green, yellow and orange) berries. Adaptable to climate and soil except in tropical areas.

Ardisia (Coral Berry)

E, HS to S, H 60–90 cm, W 30–60 cm. An attractive small shrub with clusters of white or pink flowers in spring followed by brilliant red berries in autumn and winter. Very adaptable to climate but prefers a cool, shaded position.

HINT

Biggest is not always best when it comes to planting trees and shrubs, especially when water is scarce. Smaller plants like tubestock cost less, suffer less transplant shock and require less water to become established. Tubestock generally outgrows large-sized plants planted at the same time.

MARGARET HANKS
HORTICULTURIST

Aucuba (Gold dust tree)

E, HS to S, H 1–2 m, W 1 m. Large, oval, glossy leaves flecked with gold; may produce red berries when both male and female plants are grown together. Prefers a damp, cool, shady position and may scorch in hot, dry climates. Can also be grown as an indoor plant.

Azalea

E or SD, HS to S, H 30 cm–3 m, W 30 cm–2 m. A range of colourful spring-flowering shrubs. There are several species from dwarf (*A. kurume*) to large 'Magnifica' or 'Splendens' types (*A. indica*) with hundreds of hybrids and named varieties in single and double flowers in almost every colour. The evergreen types will grow in almost any climate except the tropics but deciduous varieties prefer cooler conditions. They must have an acid soil and will not grow in alkaline soil. They require good drainage but the shallow roots need to be cool, moist and shaded. Azaleas make excellent plants for pots or tubs.

Backhousia

See Chapter 20.

Baeckea

See Chapter 20.

Banksia

See Chapter 20.

Bauhinia (Butterfly tree)

E or SD, FS or HS, H 5–6 m, W 5–6 m. Spreading small tree or large shrub with twin, butterfly-like leaves and purple, pink or white flowers in spring. It is deciduous except in warm climates and is best suited to temperate or tropical areas, but will tolerate moderate frosts. There are several other shrub or tree species, and a creeper (*B. scandens*).

Beloperone

See Drejerella.

Berberis (Barberry)

E or D, FS or HS, H 1–2 m, W 1–2 m. Small, compact, usually spiny shrubs with yellow flowers in spring and red berries in autumn. Most deciduous species have brilliant autumn foliage. Very adaptable but prefer mild–temperate or cold climates. Those barberries with purple-bronze foliage (*B. thunbergii* 'Atropurpurea') make good accent plants. All can be used as hedge plants.

Betula (Birch)

D, FS or HS, H 6–9 m, W 3–6 m. Slender trees with graceful foliage and pendulous catkins in spring. In autumn they have brilliant foliage. Silver birch (*B. pendula*), with silvery-white bark, is the best known of all birch trees. Adapted to cool–temperate and cold climates

Boronia

See Chapter 20.

Brachychiton

See Chapter 20.

Brassaia

See under 'Schefflera' in Chapter 20.

Browallia

See Streptosolen.

Brunfelsia

E, HS or SS, H 2–3 m, W 2 m. This handsome shrub is also called yesterday, today and tomorrow because the fragrant flowers in spring open deep-blue, fade to lavender and then to white on successive days. Adaptable to all climates except the coldest districts and prefers well-drained soil in a semi-shaded situation. Prune after flowering to avoid fruiting. All parts of the plant are toxic to dogs.

Buddleia (Summer lilac or Butterfly bush)

SD, FS or HS, H 2–3 m, W 2 m. Fast-growing shrub with long sprays of slightly fragrant lilac or purple flowers in spring and summer. Attractive to butterflies. Adaptable to all climates – evergreen in warm districts and deciduous where colder. Other flower colours, too.

Buxus (Box)

E, FS or HS, H 2 m, W 1 m. Attractive, tidy, small tree or shrub with small, shiny foliage. Often used as a low hedge or as accent plants in formal gardens. Box is very adaptable to all climates. Dwarf-growing forms available.

Callistemon

See Chapter 20.

Calodendron (Cape chestnut)

E, FS, H 9–15 m, W 5–6 m. A handsome, well-shaped tree with showy clusters of pink or mauve, orchid-like flowers through summer. All climates except cold districts. Frost-susceptible and may need protection when young.

Camellia

E, HS to S, H 3–5 m, W 1–3 m. The most widely grown is *C. japonica*, which flowers in winter and early spring. There are hundreds of named varieties with single, semi-double or double flowers which range in colour from pure white through pinks and mauves to deep red. Another group, loosely called *Sasanquas*, mostly have single or semi-double flowers in late autumn and winter; useful as a background plant or trimmed as a tall hedge. The tree-like reticulata camellias are becoming better known. Like azaleas, camellias will not tolerate alkaline soils and need good drainage, plenty of organic matter and a cool root area. Camellias prefer semi-shade or shade, as strong sunlight can scorch the blooms. Sasanquas can handle more sun. Camellias make excellent tub specimens.

Cassia
See Senna.

Ceratopetalum
See Chapter 20.

Ceratostigma
D, FS, H 3 m, W 3 m. Small shrubs with pale-green, bronze-tinted leaves and bright-blue flowers in summer. Foliage colours in autumn. Cut back hard in winter to promote new growth and flowers. Very adaptable plant for most climates.

Cestrum
E, FS or HS, H 2–3 m, W 1–2 m. Fast-growing shrubs with showy, tubular flowers in light green, orange or red, according to species. The best known is the weedy night jessamine (*C. nocturnum*), which has strongly perfumed flowers on warm nights in summer. Temperate and tropical climates.

Chamaelaucium
See Chapter 20.

Chorizema
See Chapter 20.

HINT
Balling of buds on camellias is a great disappointment – all that promise of blooms but nothing to show! If this has happened to you, try this trick. Spray your camellias in late summer with a copper fungicide and also disbud the plant, reducing the number of buds in each cluster.

JENNIFER STACKHOUSE
EDITOR, *GREENWORLD* MAGAZINE

Citharexylum (Fiddlewood)
SD, FS or HS, H 6–9 m, W 5 m. Fast-growing tree with rich, green foliage that turns copper tones in spring before mostly falling. Small sprays of white flowers in summer. Excellent shade tree or suitable as a hedge or windbreak in groups. Temperate and subtropical climates.

Coleonema (Pink diosma)
E, FS or HS, H 1–2 m, W up to 1 m. Compact, delicate foliage with white or pink, star-shaped flowers in spring. Good dwarf shrub for accent and rock gardens. Prune back after flowering. All climates.

Coprosma (Looking-glass plant)
E, FS to S, H 1–2 m, W 1–2 m. Attractive shrub with glossy green or variegated foliage. Very adaptable and tolerates sea spray. All but coldest climates.

Cornus (Dogwood)
D, FS to SS, H 2–4 m, W 1–3 m. Beautiful, small trees for cool climates. Delightful flowers, foliage and handsome stems. Prefer deep, rich, well-drained, acid soils.

Cotoneaster
E or D, FS to SS, H 1–4 m, W 1–4 m. Many species and varieties, from prostrate spill-over shrubs to small trees, all of which have attractive clusters of orange or red berries. Mostly evergreen but some deciduous. Small types for rockeries. All climates. May become a weed as berries are spread by birds.

Crataegus (Hawthorn)
D, FS to SS, H 4–6 m, W 2–3 m. Thorny shrubs or small trees with white or pink, rose-like flowers in spring followed by brilliant yellow, orange or red berries according to species. All climates except very hot districts. Berries spread by birds so can be weedy.

Cuphea (Cigar plant)
E, FS to SS, H 30–60 cm, W 60 cm. Small, spreading shrubs with red, tubular flowers tipped with ash grey. Excellent for rockeries. Other varieties. Adapted to most climates.

Daphne
E, HS to SS, H 1 m, W 1 m. Charming dwarf

shrubs with glossy foliage and highly perfumed, waxy, white, pink or red flowers in winter and early spring. Needs good drainage. Mulch to keep roots cool and moist. Prefers morning sun or semi-shade. For temperate or cool climates.

Diosma
See Coleonema.

Deutzia (Wedding bells)
D, HS or SS, H 2–3 m, W 1.5 m. Attractive shrubs with long canes and clusters of white or pink flowers in late spring and early summer. Cut back after flowering. All climates except very hot districts.

Drejerella (syn. Beloperone, Shrimp plant)
E, FS or HS, H 1 m, W 1 m. Small softwood shrub with overlapping, shell-like bracts in yellow or pink, suggesting a prawn or shrimp. Very adaptable to climate but best in warm climates.

Epacris
See Chapter 20.

Erica (Heath)
E, FS, H up to 2 m, W up to 1 m. Heath-like plants in many varieties and forms with needle-like leaves and masses of tubular or bell-shaped flowers in shades of yellow, orange, pink and mauve. They need well-

HINT
Use sticky prunings as natural garden supports for climbing vegetables such as beans and peas. They can also be used for sweet peas and placed over perennials, which are then allowed to grow up and through the prunings. When pruning time comes all the organic material can be pulled up and shredded.

PETER DE WAART

HORTICULTURIST

Pure white flower bracts with a characteristic pointed tip are the most striking feature of Cornus kousa.

drained, slightly acid soils, as for azaleas, to which they are related. Best in cool–temperate or cold climates.

Escallonia
E, FS to S, H 2–3 m, W 1–2 m. Glossy foliage shrubs with rose-pink or white flowers in late spring and summer. Cut back after flowering. All climates except tropical and very cold.

Eucalyptus
See Chapter 20.

Eugenia
See Chapter 20.

Euonymus
E, FS or HS, H 1–2 m, W up to 2 m. A number of species of shrubs, mostly with attractive variegated foliage, may be clipped to any shape or size or made into a hedge. Also make useful tub specimens. All climates.

Euphorbia (Poinsettia)
D, FS or HS, H 3–5 m, W 2–3 m. Poinsettia (*E. pulcherrima*) is the most popular shrub of this huge genus. The tiny orange flowers are surrounded by showy bracts in deep crimson, pink or pale yellow. Best suited to subtropical and tropical climates but also in

The pendulous habit of fuchsias makes them suitable for hanging baskets.

warm, sheltered situations in temperate zones. Susceptible to frosts.

Exochorda (Pearl bush)

D, FS to SS, H 2–3 m, W 2–3 m. Attractive shrub with pale-green foliage and pearly white flowers like apple blossom in spring. Prune lightly after flowering. Temperate and cool climates.

Fagus (Beech)

D, FS or HS, H 9–18 m, W 9–12 m. Large but slow-growing deciduous tree. For cool–temperate and cold climates only. Magnificent foliage trees with many varied forms and colours of leaves. Silver beech and copper beech are the most widely grown.

Ficus (Fig)

E, FS or HS, H 9–15 m, W 6–15 m. Many species of medium-sized to very large trees (Port Jackson fig and Moreton Bay fig). Even the smaller species (e.g. *F. hillii*) will grow too large for most gardens. *F. pumila* is an evergreen creeper. (See Chapter 18.)

Frangipani

See Plumeria.

Fraxinus (Ash)

D, FS or HS, H 6–12 m, W 4–6 m. Fast-growing, attractive trees with brilliant autumn foliage for cool–temperate and cold climates. Golden ash, desert ash and claret ash are the most popular species. Evergreen *griffithii* is popular but seems to be developing weed tendencies.

Fuchsia

E, SS or S, H 1–2 m, W 30–60 cm. Decorative softwood shrubs which flower from late spring to early winter. Flowers are pendulous with a tubular corolla surrounded by sepals in contrasting colours. There are hundreds of named varieties. All prefer semi-shade and a friable, well-structured soil. Most are suitable for pots, tubs and hanging baskets. All climates except very cold districts.

Gardenia

E, FS or HS, H 1–2 m, W up to 1 m. Attractive shrubs or small trees with dark, glossy foliage and highly fragrant, waxy, white flowers from late spring through to summer. If necessary, prune back plants in late winter. They need a sheltered, sunny position and do well in most climates except extremely cold ones.

Garrya (Silk tassel or Curtain bush)

E, SS to S, H 3 m, W 2–3 m. Dense-foliaged shrub with pendulous clusters of greyish-yellow catkins in winter and early spring. Prefers semi-shade or shade and does best in

HINT

Gardenias grow in well-drained garden soil enriched with compost and manure, and enjoy a fairly sunny position with some shelter from the full heat of the summer sun and protection from strong wind.

SHIRLEY STACKHOUSE
GARDEN WRITER

HINT

If you don't already wear glasses, protect your eyes by wearing sunglasses when pruning or working around plants that have sharp twigs that stick out.

SUE TEMPLETON

SALVIA SPECIALIST

cool–temperate and cold climates, with low humidity.

Ginkgo (Maidenhair tree)

D, FS or HS, H 9–12 m, W 4–6 m. Pale-green, two-lobed leaves turning golden yellow in autumn. Suits cool–temperate and cold climates.

Gordonia

E, FS or HS, H 3–4 m, W 2–3 m. Tall shrub with glossy foliage and attractive bark. Autumn to spring flowering with large single white flowers with prominent yellow centres. Flowers fall stamens up, giving rise to name of 'Fried egg plant'. Best in temperate climates but has some cold tolerance.

Grevillea

See Chapter 20.

Hakea

See Chapter 20.

Hebe (Veronica)

E, FS to SS, H 1–2 m, W up to 1 m. Small, compact shrubs with dense foliage and showy racemes of white, blue or purple flowers in winter and spring. Plants can be pruned as hedges and are suitable for rockery work. Suited to temperate and cool climates.

Hibiscus

E or D, FS or HS, H 2–4 m, W 1–2 m. One of the best summer-flowering shrubs for warm–temperate and tropical climates. There are many species (most of them evergreen) and hundreds of named varieties. The magnificent large flowers (some to 20 cm across) are single or double and range in colour from pure white through to lemon, yellow, gold, orange, pink, red and maroon. All species are frost-susceptible. In cool–temperate climates select a sunny, sheltered position, preferably facing north.

Hydrangea

D, SS or S, H 0.5–3 m, W 0.5–2 m. Popular deciduous shrubs for shade and moist situations. Have large, showy flower heads in summer. Most flowers are in shades of pink or blue but colour can indicate soil pH – flowers are pink in alkaline soils and blue in acidic soils. In some varieties the flowers are white or greenish and do not change colour with soil pH. Prune after flowering or when dormant in winter, only pruning stems that have flowered.

Hypericum

E, FS to SS, H 3–5 m, W 1–2 m. Handsome shrubs or small trees with glossy foliage and yellow flowers followed by brilliant red berries in winter. Plants may be trimmed to shape and make a dense hedge. Adapted to cool–temperate and cold climates only.

Jacaranda

SD, FS or HS, H 9–12 m, W 9–12 m. Graceful tree with fine, fern-like leaves which drop just before flowering. Masses of lavender-blue flowers appear in late spring and early summer. Adapted to all climates except very cold or extreme tropical regions. Young trees may need protection from frost until established.

Kolkwitzia (Chinese beauty bush)

D, HS or SS, H 2 m, W 1.5 m. Attractive shrubs with long, arching canes covered with pale-pink, trumpet-shaped flowers in spring. Adapted to cool–temperate and cold climates.

Lagerstroemia (Crepe myrtle)

D, FS or HS, H 2–5 m, W 1–2 m. Large shrubs or small trees, often with colourful autumn leaves. They have showy clusters of pink, mauve or carmine flowers in late summer. May be pruned hard in winter. Suits all climates except the coldest districts.

Leschenaultia
See Chapter 20.

Leptospermum
See Chapter 20.

Liquidambar (Sweet gum)
D, FS or HS, H 6–12 m, W 4–9 m. Tall, conical trees with maple-like leaves in brilliant autumn colours of yellow, orange, red and purple. Adaptable but best suited to temperate and cold climates.

Liriodendron (Tulip tree)
D, FS or HS, H 9–12 m, W 4–5 m. Attractive, large tree with fiddle-shaped leaves turning bright yellow in autumn. Flowers are lime-green and tulip shaped. Cool–temperate and cold climates only.

Loropetalum (Chinese fringe flower)
E, HS or SS, H 1–2 m, W 1–2 m. Graceful shrub with rounded leaves and spidery, cream or pink flowers in spring. Temperate and cold climates, but frost-susceptible.

Deciduous magnolias make good lawn specimens and grow to a manageable size for a smaller garden.

Luculia
E, HS or SS, H 2–3 m, W 2–3 m. Attractive shrub with rounded heads of fragrant pink or white flowers in early winter. Cut back after flowering. Suits temperate climates but is susceptible to frost.

Magnolia
E or D, FS or HS, H 5–9 m, W 3–6 m. Deciduous varieties have large, tulip-shaped flowers in white, pink, mauve or purple that usually appear in early spring before the foliage. Temperate or cold climates. The evergreen tree (*M. grandiflora*) has large, fragrant, waxy, white flowers in summer. Smaller cultivars (e.g. 'Little Gem') are becoming increasingly popular. Suit all but the very coldest climates.

HINT

If you enjoy running your hand over the bark of trees, take care with fissured bark such as that of ironbarks. Huntsman spiders waiting for prey are apt to be surprised.

FRANCES SAUNDERS
HORTICULTURIST, GARDEN DESIGNER
AND WRITER

Malus (Crabapple)
D, FS or HS, H 3–5 m, W 3–5 m. A most delightful spring-flowering small tree with blossoms in white, pink or red followed by small, multicoloured apples used for jam or for decoration. Prune trees to shape and size. All climates except tropical regions.

Melaleuca
See Chapter 20.

Metrosideros (Pohutukawa or New Zealand Christmas tree)
E, FS or HS, H 5–6 m, W 4–5 m. Rounded, self-shaping large shrub or small tree with shiny leaves (grey underneath) and brilliant red, brush-like flowers in summer. Excellent shrub for exposed seaside conditions as it

tolerates salt spray, dust and city smog. Temperate and coastal climates only.

Murraya (Satin wood)

E, HS or SS, H 2–4 m, W 2–2.5 m. Dense, rounded shrub with glossy foliage and fragrant clusters of white flowers like orange blossom in spring and summer. Susceptible to frost. Suits temperate and tropical climates. Excellent clipped hedge.

Nandina (Japanese bamboo)

E, FS to SS, H 1–2 m, W 1 m. Multi-stemmed shrub with finely divided foliage, cream flowers and red berries. Attractive autumn foliage, especially in the dwarf variety (*N. domestica* 'Pygmaea' and cultivars). All climates.

Nerium (Oleander)

E, FS to SS, H 3–5 m, W 1–2 m. Adaptable shrub with lance-shaped, rather leathery leaves and masses of single or double flowers (white, cream, yellow, pink and crimson) from early summer to late autumn. Suits all but cold climates.

Nyssa

D, FS or HS, H 6–9 m, W 4–6 m. Handsome tree with horizontal branching and attractive foliage with good autumn colouring. Mild, temperate and cold climates. Prefers damp spot.

Philadelphus (Mock orange)

D, HS or SS, H 2–3 m, W 2 m. Caney shrubs with sweetly scented, white flowers in late spring. Prune back after flowering. All but tropical climates.

Photinia

E, FS to SS, H 2–5 m, W 1–3 m. Foliage plants with brilliant red new growth, often used as hedge plants. All climates except for the tropics and hot inland areas.

Pieris (Lily-of-the-valley shrub)

E, HS to SS, H 1–2 m, W 1–2 m. Small, attractive shrubs with sprays of cream flowers in spring. Well-drained soil and cool, sheltered position, similar to azaleas. Cool–temperate and cold climates.

Pimelea

See Chapter 20.

Pittosporum

E, FS to SS, H 2–6 m, W 1–4 m. Several species of handsome foliage shrubs, some variegated, others with fragrant flowers and attractive berries. Most climates.

Plumbago

E, FS to SS, H 2 m, W 1–2 m. These summer-blooming, shrubby, semi-climbers spread by clumping from the base. They flower prolifically with trusses of white or blue blooms. 'Royal Cape' is a deeper-blue cultivar. Plumbago will take only the lightest of frost and benefits from being cut back hard in early spring. Useful fast-growing screen plants.

Plumeria (Frangipani)

D, FS or HS, H 3–4 m, W 2–3 m. Small, deciduous tree with fragrant, waxy, white (or pink) flowers in summer. Frost-susceptible, warm–temperate and tropical climates only.

Poinsettia

See Euphorbia.

Polygala (Sweet pea shrub)

E, FS to SS, H 1–2 m, W 1–2 m. Small, fast-growing shrub with purple, pea-like flowers from winter to early summer. Prune after flowering to keep within bounds. Temperate and tropical climates, but dislikes excessive moisture.

Populus (Poplar)

D, FS to HS, H 9–24 m, W 3–12 m. Deciduous trees with good autumn colour, but rather large and greedy for small gardens. The tall, slender Lombardy poplar, the silver poplar and cottonwood are the best known. Very adaptable but prefer temperate and cold climates. Susceptible to rust.

Prostanthera

See Chapter 20.

Prunus

D, FS or HS, H 3–6 m, W 1–6 m. This large genus includes not only the flowering plum but also most of the spring-flowering blossoms – peaches, almonds and cherries. There are many species and varieties which differ in size, leaf and flower colour, flower form (single or double) and the time of flowering. All are pruned after flowering. Generally, this group of beautiful trees prefers full sunlight, good drainage and a cool, winter climate. Local nurseries can advise on the varieties suitable for your district.

Psoralea (Blue butterfly bush)

E, FS or HS, H 2–3 m, W 2–3 m. Fast-growing shrubs with masses of pale-blue, pea-like flowers in spring. Prune back by one-third after flowering. Frost-susceptible. Prefers temperate to warm climates. Weedy.

Pultenaea

See Chapter 20.

Pyracantha (Firethorn)

E, FS to SS, H 2–3 m, W 2–3 m. Often confused with the deciduous hawthorn, these spiny, evergreen shrubs have clusters of small, white flowers followed by yellow, orange or red berries. Good hedge plant. Temperate and cold climates. Can be spread by birds.

Quercus (Oak)

D, FS or HS, H 9–18 m, W 5–9 m. Large trees in varying shapes and sizes. English oak is round-headed and spreading. Pin oak is conical with red autumn leaves. Temperate and cold climates.

Rhaphiolepis

E, FS or HS, H 2 m, W 1–2 m. Compact shrubs with pink or white flowers in spring sometimes followed by black berries. Slow but hardy and adaptable to most climates.

Rhododendron

E, SS or S, H 3–6 m, W 2–4 m. Spectacular spring-flowering shrubs or trees for mild–temperate and cold climates. Need similar conditions (semi-shade, good drainage and acid soil) to azaleas, to which they are closely related. Many varieties and flower colours. Vireya rhododendrons are warm climate cultivars.

Rondeletia

E, HS or SS, H 2–3 m, W 1–2 m. Attractive shrub with dark-green foliage and rounded masses of pink blossoms in late winter and early spring. Frost-susceptible. Temperate to warm climates.

Rosmarinus (Rosemary)

E, FS to SS, H 1–2 m, W 1 m. Attractive, small shrub with glossy, aromatic leaves (used as a herb in cooking). Pale-blue flowers in early spring and autumn. Good hedge

Blossom trees like this Prunus 'Pink Cloud' *make a glorious display in spring.*

plant. Very adaptable to most climates, except tropics.

Russelia

E, FS or HS, H 1–2 m, W up to 1 m. A stemmy, rush-like plant with scarlet, tubular flowers in summer. Can be tied to a stake or used as spill-over plant for walls and rockeries. Temperate and warm climates.

Salix (Willow)

D, FS to SS, H 6–9 m, W 6–9 m. Weeping willow is the best known but is too big for most gardens. Willows tend to invade drains and some species infest and impede waterways. There are smaller, less vigorous species: pussy willow with silvery catkins in spring, and tortured willow with twisted stems and leaves. All climates.

Schefflera

See Chapter 20.

Senna (Cassia)

E, FS or HS, H 1–6 m, W 1–3 m. There are several species of these showy shrubs or small trees with yellow, pea-like flowers in spring, summer or autumn. Most species have yellow flowers and are fast-growing and adaptable to all climates except cold districts. A dwarf Australian species, *S. artemisioides*, is suitable for hot, dry regions. Some Sennas have weedy tendencies.

Spiraea (May)

D, FS to SS, H 1–3 m, W 1–3 m. Several species of caney shrubs with masses of white, single or double flowers in spring. Prune back after flowering to preserve shrub's compact shape. Adaptable to all except tropical climates.

Streptosolen (syn. *Browallia jamesonii*)

E, FS or HS, H 1–2 m, W 1 m. Caney shrubs with clusters of bright-orange flowers in spring and early summer. Needs occasional pruning and thinning. Frost-susceptible. Temperate and tropical climates.

Syringa (Lilac)

D, FS or HS, H 2–4 m, W 1–2 m. Attractive, suckering shrub with fragrant clumps of flowers in white, pink, red, mauve and purple. Cool–temperate and cold climates only.

Tamarix (Flowering cypress)

D or E, FS or HS, H 3–9 m, W 2–5 m. Small trees with cypress-like, pendulous foliage and feathery masses of pink flowers in spring and summer. Very adaptable and tolerates dry heat, strong winds and salty soils. All climates. Dislikes humidity.

Tibouchina

E, FS, H 1–5 m, W 60 cm–2 m. Showy, tree-shaped shrubs that bloom profusely in late summer and autumn with a glorious display of purple, mauve, pink or white flowers that can be up to more than 10 cm across. Tibouchinas have tropical origins so must be grown in frost-free conditions with rich, well-drained, loam soil. Prune back after flowering. Many cultivars: 'Alstonville' – large, purple flowers; 'Kathleen' – pink; 'Noeline' – multicoloured; 'Jules' – dwarf, purple.

Ulmus (Elm)

D or SD, FS or HS, H 9–18 m, W 9–18 m. Several species of medium to large trees with attractive foliage in spring and autumn. Golden elm and Chinese weeping elm are widely grown. Can sucker. Cool–temperate to cold climates.

Viburnum

E, D, FS to SS, H 2.5 m, W 1–3 m. More than 100 species and many more named varieties of these attractive shrubs are grown for their fragrant, hydrangea-like flowers and attractive berries. Prune both evergreen and deciduous types after flowering. Suits most climates except the tropics.

Virgilia

E, FS to SS, H 4–6 m, W 3–4 m. Fast-growing, small trees with fern-like foliage and sprays of mauve flowers in spring. Very adaptable but usually short-lived. All climates except cold districts.

Weigela

D, HS or SS, H 2–3 m, W 1–2 m. Caney shrubs with white or pink-red, trumpet-like flowers in spring. Cut back after flowering. Temperate and cold climates.

Westringia

See Chapter 20.

What can go wrong with Azaleas, Camellias and Rhododendrons?

PROBLEM	SYMPTOM	SOLUTION
Aphids	Cluster of insects on young growth.	Spray with Mavrik or Confidor when detected.
Mites	Leaves yellow (stippled or mottled) and dehydrated in hot, dry weather.	Spray with Mavrik or Natrasoap.
Thrips/lace bug	Leaves silver and dry. Brown-black specks appear on underside of leaves.	Spray with Confidor or Natrasoap when first observed.
Leaf gall	Developing leaves and flowers are thickened, fleshy and pale-green. As the thickenings enlarge, they become white or pink, with a powdery appearance during wet weather.	Remove and destroy all infected parts.
Petal blight	Earliest symptom is light-brown or whitish coloured circular spots on petals. Spots enlarge to form irregular blotches until whole flower collapses. Petals feel slimy when rubbed between fingers. Diseased flowers dry up and cling to the plant (leaves and stems are not affected).	Avoid overhead watering. Pick off diseased flowers. From expanded bud stage until end of flowering, spray at two-weekly intervals with Zaleton fungicide.
Sooty mould	Black sooty mould on leaves and twigs.	Sooty mould fungus lives on honeydew excreted from sap-sucking insects. Spray with PestOil or Confidor or use Scale Gun on scale infestation.
Lack of fertiliser	Leaves yellow and/or developing dark-purple tone. Slow, stunted growth.	Fertilise with camellia and azalea food in late spring after flowering finishes and again just before new growth starts.
Soil too alkaline	Decline in vigour and new leaves turn yellow while the veins remain green.	Fertilise with camellia and azalea food in late spring after flowering finishes; just before new growth starts apply Liquid Sulfur. Do *not* lime soil.

CONIFERS

This is the group of cone-bearing plants. Most are evergreen, grow to a definite (often symmetrical) shape and rarely need pruning. With most varieties, avoid pruning into hard wood without leaves. Conifers vary in size, shape and leaf colour from small, prostrate trees or shrubs suitable for tubs or rockeries to magnificent specimens growing to 30 m or more in height.

As a group, conifers are slow growers but respond to attention in watering, mulching and fertilising. As with other trees and shrubs, slow-acting fertilisers based on blood and bone, or slow-release fertilisers such as Acticote, are the most suitable and effective.

Conifers are best suited to temperate and cold climates where, as evergreens, they are valuable for winter effect. Very few conifers are suitable for tropical climates. There are dozens of species and hundreds of varieties and the reader is advised to consult a nursery catalogue or, better still, visit a specialist nursery where advanced specimens can be seen. The following is a brief summary of the most important conifers.

Abies (Fir trees)

Tall, pyramid-shaped trees with beautiful foliage. Best suited to cool and cold climates with high rainfall. Silver fir (*A. alba*) H 15 m: green-silver foliage. Colorado white fir (*A. concolor*) H 15 m: bluish foliage. Caucasian fir (*A. nordmanniana*) H 18 m: green-silver foliage.

Araucaria

Tall, symmetrical trees but rather too large for the average garden. Monkey puzzle (*A. araucana*) H 12–15 m: cool, moist climates. Bunya pine (*A. bidwillii*) H 8–13 m: all climates except coldest (be aware of extra large cones). Hoop pine (*A. cunninghamii*) H 24–45 m: moist coastal climates. Norfolk Island pine (*A. heterophylla*) H 18–30 m: moist coastal climates.

Callitris (Cypress pine)

Ornamental Australian native trees are useful in dry inland climates where many of them grow naturally. White cypress pine (*C. columellaris*) H 15 m: dark-green foliage. Port Jackson pine (*C. rhomboidea*) H 12 m: olive-green foliage.

Cedrus (Cedar)

Shapely, pyramidal trees with needle-like leaves and upright, barrel-shaped cones. Adaptable trees but best in cool–temperate and cold climates. Atlas cedar (*C. atlantica*) H 15–18 m: grey-green foliage; var. *glauca* with silver-blue foliage; var. *aurea* with yellow foliage. Deodar (*C. deodara*) H 15–18 m: green or grey-green foliage; var. *aurea* with yellowish foliage. Cedar of Lebanon (*C. libani*) H 12–15 m: similar to *C. atlantica* but a more flattened shape.

Chamaecyparis (syn. Retinospora, False cypress)

Shapely, ornamental, medium-sized or dwarf trees, useful for garden landscape effects. Need good drainage and do best in cool–temperate or cold climates with good rainfall. Lawson cypress (*C. lawsoniana*) H 12–15 m: pyramidal growth to ground level with many varieties and differing foliage colours. Dwarf varieties range in height from 60 cm to 3 m. Hinoki cypress (*C. obtusa*) H 9–12 m: flattened, fan-like foliage; var. *crippsii* has yellow foliage and is a smaller tree (6 m). Many dwarf varieties exist, ranging in height from 60 cm to 2 m. Sawara cypress (*C. pisifera*) H 9–12 m: similar to *C. lawsoniana* with many leaf forms and colours.

Cryptomeria (Japanese cedar, *C. Japonica*)

H 12 m. Stately tree for cool–temperate and cold climates; var. *nana* is dwarf, 1–2 m tall. Foliage turns bronze in winter.

Cupressus (Cypress)

Fast-growing, attractive conifers for screen or windbreak planting or for specimen trees. Very adaptable but prefer temperate or cold climates. Funeral cypress (*C. funebris*) H 12–18 m: grey-green, weeping foliage. Arizona cypress (*C. glabra*) H 15–18 m: fast-growing conifers for hedges and windbreaks. Smaller varieties are *C. brunniana* H 12 m, with gold foliage; Italian cypress (*C. sempervirens*) H 12–18 m, with an erect, pyramidal shape; var. *stricta*, which is more slender (often called pencil pine); Bhutan cypress (*C. torulosa*) H 12–18 m, with a tall,

A mixed display of conifers in the garden of Busker's End, Bowral, NSW, demonstrates the diversity of this plant group.

pyramidal shape, useful for screens or windbreaks. Susceptible to fungal diseases and borers.

Juniperus (syn. Sabina, Juniper)

A large group of conifers with interesting shapes and leaf colours, especially in the dwarf species and varieties. Very adaptable and suited to all climates except tropical areas. Bermuda cedar (*J. bermudiana*) H 12–15 m: frost sensitive. Chinese juniper (*J. chinensis*) H 9–12 m; var. *aurea* with yellow foliage; var. *variegata* with grey and cream foliage. Pencil cedar (*J. virginiana*) H 12–18 m: narrow column shape, very adaptable. Alligator juniper (*J. pachyphlaea*) H 3 m: erect habit, silver-blue foliage. Creeping juniper (*J. horizontalis*) H 60–90 cm: prostrate, creeping habit, blue-green foliage, good spill-over plant for rockeries and banks. Meyer juniper (*J. squamata* 'Meyeri') H 2–3 m: erect habit, blue-grey foliage. Savin juniper (*J. sabina*) H 1–2 m: spreading habit, blue-green foliage.

Leyland cypress

H 20 m: (X *Cupressocyparis leylandii*, Leyland cypress) is a popular hedging plant but can cause problems because of its dense, rapid growth that blocks light and views. 'Castlewellan Gold' is a golden- leafed form.

Picea (Spruce)

Handsome, symmetrical, cone-shaped trees. Best in cool–temperate and cold climates. Norway spruce (*P. abies*) H 9–15 m: fast-growing, green foliage. White spruce (*P. glauca*) H 9–15 m: upturned branches, grey-green foliage; var. *albertiana conica* is dwarf (1–2 m). Blue spruce (*P. pungens*) H 6–9 m: slow-growing with blue-green foliage; var. *glauca* has blue-grey foliage; var. *kosteriana* has silver-blue foliage.

Pinus (Pines)

Large, fast-growing conifers with needle-like leaves. Pyramidal in shape when young but may lose their symmetry when mature. Very adaptable to climate but generally prefer temperate regions. Canary Island pine (*P. canariensis*) H 9–15 m: pendulous, grey-green foliage, all but coldest districts. Cuban pine (*P. caribaea*) H 18–24 m: fast-growing pine for coastal and tropical areas with summer rainfall. Aleppo pine (*P. halepensis*) H 18 m: drought-resistant, suitable for poor soils in low rainfall regions. Mexican pine (*P. patula*) H 12–15 m: fast grower with pendulous, blue-green foliage, temperate and warm climates. Monterey pine (*P. radiata* syn. *P. insignis*) H 18–24 m: dense, fast-growing pine, excellent for shade, shelter or windbreaks, very adaptable to all but tropical climates but may become a weed.

Podocarpus (*P. elatus*, Illawarra plum pine)

H 12 m. Attractive, round-headed, native tree with glossy foliage, plum-coloured when young. Adaptable to all but cold and dry inland climates. Yellowwood (*P. falcatus*) is a similar tree from South Africa with blue-green foliage.

Taxodium (*T. distichum*, Swamp cypress)

H 15–18 m. Large, deciduous tree with green, feathery foliage turning russet-brown in autumn. Useful in wet situations. All climates except very cold and tropical regions.

Thuja

Ornamental conifers with attractive shapes and flattened, frond-like foliage of various colours. Best suited to cool–temperate and cold climates. American arbor-vitae (*T. occidentalis*) H 15 m: fast-growing tree with conical shape. There are many smaller and more colourful varieties including 'Fastigiata' (H 2–3 m), green foliage; 'Lutescens' (H 2–3 m), tipped foliage; 'Hoveyii' (H 1 m), green foliage; 'Rheingold' (H 1 m), golden foliage; little gem (H 60 cm), green foliage. Bookleaf cypress (*T. orientalis*) H 9–12 m: fast-growing conifer with dense, compact shape. Smaller, coloured-leaf varieties are also available. Western red cedar (*T. plicata*) H 12 m: dark-green foliage which droops at the ends; var. 'Aurea' is smaller with gold-tipped foliage and var. 'Zebrina' has striped foliage.

Wollemi pine (*Wollemia nobilis*)

H to 40m (slow). Discovered in Wollemi National Park (NSW) in 1994, these dinosaur-era trees are now available in pots. Will grow indoors or out. Prefers sheltered position. Can be pruned.

PALMS

This large family of woody, evergreen plants contains over 1000 species. In their natural habitat, most species are found in tropical and subtropical climates, but can be grown successfully in temperate climates too. They are not really suited to cold climates, unless planted in a warm, sheltered position or grown as indoor plants in containers. Some palms have a single trunk and others are multi-trunked with a distinctive crown of leaves or fronds. The fronds may be fan-shaped (palmate) or deeply divided (pinnate). Generally, palms are ornamental and easy to grow.

Archontophoenix

(*A. alexandrae*, Alexander palm) H 10–13 m: attractive specimen for garden or pot (not indoors), requires ample moisture and frost-free area. (*A. cunninghamiana*, Bangalow palm) H 9–12 m: graceful Australian native palm with smooth, grey trunk, dense crown of feathery fronds and pendulous bunches of flower spikes and fruit; good container plant when young.

Butia

(*B. capitata*, jelly or wine palm) H 6 m : short trunk with head of blue-grey fronds and orange-red bunches of fruit; sunlight or shade; good container plant.

Caryota

(*C. mitis*, fish tail palm) H 6 m: multiple trunks with long, yellow-green fronds with toothed, wedge-shaped leaflets. *Caryota urens* has a single trunk.

Chamaedorea

(*C. elegans* syn. *Neanthe elegans*, parlour palm) H 2 m: delightful pot or tub plant for patio or terrace in semi-shade or indoors; bright-green, papery fronds in a spiral around the thin, dainty stem.

Chamaerops

(*C. humilis*, European fan palm) H 5 m: clumps of several stems, bearing shiny, deeply cut, fan-like leaves; good for small gardens and containers, both indoors and outdoors;

tolerates cooler conditions more than most palms and does well in full sun or shade.

Cocos

(*C. nucifera*, coconut palm) H 12–15 m: graceful, inclined trunk with rather sparse crown of feathery, yellow-green fronds; requires tropical, high-rainfall conditions.

Golden cane palm (*Dypsis lutescens*)

H 6–8 m: multi-stemmed palm that forms a clump of up to fifty golden stems, topped with feathery, pale yellow-green leaves.

Howea (syn. Kentia)

There are two attractive species, native to Lord Howe Island: *H. belmoreana* (sentry or curly palm) H 6 m: stout-ringed trunk with feathery fronds curving inward; good container plant for indoors or outdoors; sunlight or semi-shade. *H. forsteriana* (kentia or thatch leaf palm) H 7–9 m: a more slender palm; ideal for indoors. Mature palms of both species have long spikes of green fruit turning yellow and red as they ripen.

Linospadix

(*L. monostachya*, walking-stick palm) H 3 m: attractive, mid-green fronds are broad and fringed and blend in well with other plants in a half-sun or semi-shade position; ideal container plant for a shady terrace.

Livistona

(*L. australis*, cabbage tree palm) FS to SS, H 20 m: Australian native palm with rough, ringed trunk topped with broad, fan-like fronds with spines along the edges of the stem base; fruit is orange-red turning black. *L. chinense* has broader leaves.

Phoenix (Date palms)

Several species, including the date palm (*P. dactylifera*) which is grown for its fruit. *P. canariensis* (Canary Island palm) H 6 m: arching fronds from ground level for 8–10 years. The fronds then grow from a thick, robust trunk. Heavy bunches of orange berries are produced periodically. Very adaptable but prefers full sun. *P. roebelinii* (dwarf date palm) H 4 m: very slow-growing but extremely attractive palm with glossy, finely feathered, arching fronds. A good garden palm, ideal for container growing (indoors or outdoors). Grows in sun or shade.

Rhapis

(*R. excelsa*, lady palm or ground rattan cane) H 4 m: attractive, slow growing palm with several slender trunks topped by small fan-shaped fronds; an excellent container plant for indoors or outdoors.

Syagrus (Cocos palm)

(*S. romanzoffianum* syn. *Arecastrum romanzoffianum*, cocos or queen palm)

H 12 m: slender, smooth trunk and a head of arching, blue-green fronds; prefers full sunlight or semi-shade conditions. Widely grown in late twentieth century but now out of fashion.

Trachycarpus

(*T. fortunei*, fan or Chusan palm) H 9 m: slender trunks with persistent fibres and bearing fan-shaped fronds with stout spines at base. Large clusters of fragrant yellow flowers followed by black fruit. Full sun or semi-shade. Like the European fan palm, this species tolerates cooler conditions.

The arching fronds of coconut palms dominate this fine tropical border planting.

Pruning

Plants are pruned for a variety of reasons. They will grow vigorously and look more attractive when dead, diseased or broken branches are removed.

It may be necessary to trim parts off a young plant to encourage a particular mature habit. For instance, to form a shade tree with a single trunk and elevated canopy, the regular removal of lower branches is required. Plants are also pruned for hedging, topiary or espalier where their natural habit or shape is modified in order to fulfil a particular function.

Judicious pruning of trees and shrubs can also promote greater production or better-quality flowers and fruit.

Pruning is sometimes carried out to keep a plant within bounds. However, proper selection of plants should eliminate the practice of severe annual lopping. If a plant needs to be pruned more than every five years to control its size, it is the wrong plant for the situation.

DO ALL PLANTS NEED PRUNING?

It is not necessary to prune everything annually. Some plants, like camellias, daphne and gardenias, can be left to assume their own neat habit and only need the occasional wayward stem to be corrected.

GOLDEN RULES OF PRUNING

- Never cut without good reason.
- Prune at the right time for the species concerned.
- Prune lightly, rather than severely – more can always be cut off later.
- Never prune with blunt tools.

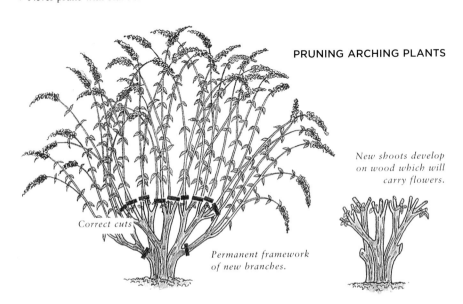

PRUNING ARCHING PLANTS

New shoots develop on wood which will carry flowers.

Correct cuts

Permanent framework of new branches.

PRUNING MADE EASY

Pruning shrubs or trees to enhance their flowering requires some knowledge of plant behaviour. Observe when growth occurs, when flowers appear and the type and age of the shoots that produce flowers. Without this information there is a tendency to prune in the wrong season, causing a complete loss of the flowering period.

FLOWERS GROW ON THREE TYPES OF WOOD

1. Flowers borne on current season's growth

Plants which flower in summer on new growth made in mid to late spring are pruned in late winter. Pruning out older wood encourages fresh new growth; the more abundant the new growth the more prolific the flowers. If plants are sensitive to frosts, delay pruning until early spring.

FIVE PLANTS PRUNED IN LATE WINTER

roses • hibiscus • crepe myrtle • murraya • fuchsia

2. Flowers borne on wood from previous year's growth

In this category new growth commences in spring, ripens through summer, becomes dormant in late autumn, rests during winter and bears flowers in spring on wood that is then one year old. Prune in spring, immediately after flowering, to allow sufficient time for the subsequent new growth to mature.

FIVE PLANTS PRUNED IN SPRING IMMEDIATELY AFTER FLOWERING

may bush • weigela • forsythia • flowering peach • many Australian natives

3. Flowers borne on one-year-old wood, older wood and short spurs

These need little pruning except to maintain their naturally tidy habit and remove any old or dying wood. Trim immediately after flowering.

FIVE PLANTS WHICH REQUIRE MINIMAL PRUNING

magnolia • crab apple • Taiwan cherry • flowering plum • Japanese flowering cherry

TRIMMING TIPS

- Retain the natural arching shape of plants like mock orange, *Weigela*, may bush, *Prunus glandulosa* and *Abelia* by removing old woody canes at the base of the plant.
- Prevent fruit from forming on ornamental flowering fruit trees by shortening the flowered shoots after blooming has finished.
- Flowering natives benefit from a light pruning of their spent flower heads.

CLEAN CUTS

Invest in good-quality tools and keep them sharpened using a whetstone. Cutting with blunt or burred blades causes bruised and torn tissue, providing an entry point for fungal diseases and insects.

Sterilise tools with household bleach after pruning to prevent transmission of diseases from one plant to another.

Cut immediately above a healthy growth bud and at an angle sloping away from the bud so that moisture is readily shed.

20
Australian
Native Plants

In recent years native plants are being grown in ever-increasing numbers in Australian gardens. Not only are native plants attractive in their own right, they have become conditioned over thousands of years to withstand the vagaries and the harsh realities of our climate. The practice of mixing natives and exotics in home gardens can produce delightful results, as both have much to contribute to garden layouts in form, colour and visual effect.

Many Australian native plants are very adaptable and are easy to grow in gardens but, because Australia is a large continent with a wide climatic range, some are difficult to grow, except in conditions close to their natural environment. For example, it is almost impossible to grow a plant from the dry, inland regions in a wet, coastal climate, and vice versa. So it is important to know the climatic and soil requirements of native plants before attempting to grow them.

Leading nurseries can give you helpful advice on the best species and varieties to grow in your garden. Also, the Australian Native Plants Society (www.anpsa.org.au) will welcome your interest and membership. The society holds meetings, discussion groups and field days to promote the preservation and cultivation of native flora. It also collects and distributes seeds of some species which may be difficult to obtain through the usual channels.

It is sometimes claimed that Australian plants need little attention. This is not true; most native plants respond to care in a well-tended garden. They can be healthier and produce more flowers than their counterparts struggling in their natural surroundings. Admittedly, some Australian plants grow naturally on rather poor soil and resent heavy applications of quick-acting fertilisers, but most will respond to slow-release, native specialist fertilisers. Another factor is root disturbance. Most Australian natives will not tolerate excessive cultivation and possible root disturbance. Many are shallow rooted, so weed around them by hand or use a shallow tool to lightly chip the surface. Mulching with grass clippings or fibrous compost will deter many weeds. Weedicides such as Zero are also useful. (See Chapter 8.)

This chapter is by no means a comprehensive work on Australian native plants. We list some of the most commonly available plants, but there are many others from which to choose.

For general notes on cultivation and care see Chapter 19.

SELECTED AUSTRALIAN TREES AND SHRUBS
Acacia (Wattle)

E, FS or HS, H 1–9 m, W 1–9 m (quite variable). There are over 600 species of this genus, ranging from small shrubs to large trees. All are evergreen with yellow flowers in late winter or spring, but the foliage may be feathery, flat or needle-like. All prefer full sun or half sun and are usually fast growing but short-lived. Reliable and adaptable species are:

- Gold dust wattle (*A. acinacea*) H 1–2 m, W 1–2 m.
- Cootamundra wattle (*A. baileyana*) H 3–5 m, W 3–5 m. Although attractive and hardy, this plant has caused problems by naturalising in some areas.
- Box-leafed wattle (*A. buxifolia*) H 2–3 m, W 2–3 m.
- Black wattle (*A. decurrens*) H 6–9 m, W 3–5 m.
- Sydney golden wattle (*A. longifolia*) H 4–5 m, W 2–3 m.
- Gossamer wattle (*A. floribunda*) H 4–8 m, W 3–5 m.
- Golden wattle (*A. pycnantha*) H 3–5 m, W 2 m. Australia's national flower.

**Refer to the front flap of this book
for a key to abbreviations.**

Acmena (Lillypilly)

E, FS or HS, H 10–12 m, W 2–4 m. Excellent medium-sized screening tree or shrub. Glossy leaves are attractive to scale insects. Fluffy white flowers are followed by berry-like fruit. A wide range of cultivars is now available. Will stand light frosts.

Agonis (Willow myrtle)

E, FS or HS, H 5–6 m, W 3–5 m. Attractive tree with willow-like branches and white, tea-tree-like flowers in spring. Frost-susceptible. Dwarf and variegated forms available.

Backhousia (Lemon-scented myrtle)

E, FS or HS, H 2–6 m, W 1–2 m. Attractive shrub with glossy, lemon-scented leaves and clusters of small, greenish-white flowers in early summer. Frost-susceptible. Temperate and warm climates.

Baeckea

E, HS or SS, H 1–2 m, W up to 1 m. Small, attractive shrub with white flowers, not unlike those of boronia, blooming in spring and summer. Temperate and warm climates.

Banksia

E, FS or HS, H 3–6 m, W 2–5 m (variable). Quaint but attractive shrubs or trees with thick, often serrated leaves and large, erect cones of stiff, wiry flowers in shades of greenish-white, yellow, orange and red. Prefer well-drained, sandy soils in warm coastal climates. Popular species are:

- Scarlet banksia (*B. coccinea*)
  H 2–3 m, W 1–2 m.
- Hairpin honeysuckle (*B. collina*)
  H 2–3 m, W 1–2 m.
- Heath banksia (*B. ericifolia*)
  H 3–4 m, W 2–3 m.

Shrubby callistemon (bottlebrush) varieties maintain a better overall appearance if trimmed immediately after blooming has finished.

Coast banksia (*B. integrifolia*)
H 3–5 m, W 2–3 m.

Swamp banksia (*B. robur*)
H 1–2m, W 1m

Boronia

E, HS or SS, H 60–90 cm, W 30–60 cm. Many species of small shrubs with spicy fragrance and attractive, delicate flowers; mostly pink, but some brown and yellow. All prefer well-drained, slightly acid, shady soils similar to those of their natural habitat. Mulch with compost or leaf mould to avoid root disturbance and hold moisture. Boronia plants tend to be short-lived.

Warm coastal climates are best. The most widely grown species are:

Sydney boronia (*B. ledifolia*)
H 90 cm, W 30 cm.

Brown boronia (*B. megastigma*)
H 90 cm, W 60 cm.

Native rose (*B. serrulata*)
H 75 cm, W 30 cm.

Brachychiton (Illawarra flame tree)

D, FS or HS, H 12–24 m, W 6–9 m. Large, pyramid-shaped tree with glossy, lobed leaves, usually deciduous in spring. Masses of brilliant red flowers in late spring and early summer. Temperate and tropical climates. Other useful trees in the genus:

Queensland lacebark (*B. discolor*)
H 9–12 m, W 6 m.

Kurrajong (*B. populneus*) E, H 6–9 m, W 4–6 m.

Buckinghamia (Ivory curl flower)

E, FS, H 3–8m. A beautiful rainforest tree that grows in a wide range of climates, decreasing in height as average temperatures become cooler. Flowers in late summer and autumn with cream-coloured pendulous spikes of tiny flowers (aptly described as 'ivory curls').

Callistemon (Bottlebrush)

E, FS or HS, H 1 m–10 m, W 1.5–4 m. Attractive shrubs or small trees with brush-like flowers in shades of cream, yellow, pink or red in spring and early summer. Very adaptable plants to both wet and dry

Banksia *'Giant Candles' is a popular cultivar with extra-large, upright-standing flowers.*

conditions with good tolerance to salty soils. Appropriate for all climates except the coldest districts. Many named varieties of the most popular species are readily available:

Crimson bottlebrush (*C. citrinus*)
H 3 m, W 2 m.

White bottlebrush or pink tips
(*C. salignus*) H 5–6 m, W 2 m.

Weeping bottlebrush (*C. viminalis*)
H 6 m, W 5 m.

Casuarina (She-oak)

E, FS, H 9–20 m, W 6–12 m. Hardy shrubs or trees, the foliage consisting of small, drooping branches. Very pleasing appearance. Casuarinas revel in poor conditions and accept salty winds. Some now *Allocasuarina* spp.

Ceratopetalum (Christmas bush)

E, FS or HS, H 3–6 m, W 2–3 m. Small, shapely tree with showy pink or red bracts in summer. Prune back after flowering. Prefers well-drained soils but water regularly from spring onwards. Temperate to warm coastal climates. Newer, cutting-grown, named cultivars give guaranteed colour.

There are hundreds of species of grevilleas, so one is sure to be right for your garden.

Chamelaucium (Geraldton wax)

E, FS or HS, H 2–3 m, W 2–3 m. Attractive Western Australian shrub or small tree with needle-like leaves and waxy flowers in pink or red. Prefers well-drained, sandy soils. Temperate or warm climate. Dislikes summer humidity.

Chorizema (Flame pea)

E, FS to SS, H 1 m, W 1 m. Compact, small shrub with heart-shaped leaves and brilliant orange-red pea flowers in winter and spring. Prefers well-drained soil but plenty of water in winter. Temperate climate.

Epacris (Native fuchsia)

E, FS to SS, H 1 m, W 30 cm. Heath-like shrub with sprays of slender, tubular, red flowers with white tips. Needs well-drained, slightly acid, sandy soil and resents root disturbance. Temperate and cold climates.

Eriostemon

See Philotheca.

Eucalyptus (Gum Tree)

E, FS to SS, H 6–90 m, W 3–12 m. Over 600 species of eucalypt trees are recorded and dominate the Australian landscape. They range in size from small trees to forest giants. Most are fast-growing and very adaptable but it is best to consult your local nursery for advice on suitable varieties for your own district. Some have showy flowers while others are suitable for windbreaks, street planting or as specimen trees. Popular species for small gardens are:

Western Australian flowering gum (*Corymbia ficifolia*) H 5 m, W 3 m. Also includes grafted hybrids such as 'Summer Red' and 'Summer Beauty'.

Dwarf sugar gum (*E. cladocalyx* 'Nana') H 6–9 m, W 5–6 m.

Lemon-scented gum (*Corymbia citriodora*) H 12–18 m, W 5–6 m.

Scribbly gum (*E. haemastoma*) H 5–6 m, W 5–6 m.

Grevillea (Spider Flower)

E, FS or HS, H 1–3 m, W 1–3 m. This is a great range of native shrubs from tropical, temperate and cold climates, about 250 species in all, so there is one to suit every garden. The spider-like flowers are usually pink or red but there are yellow and orange flowers too. Plants need good drainage, a slightly acid soil and resent root disturbance. Consult a nursery or catalogue for the best species and varieties for your district. Silky oak (*G. robusta*), the largest of the family by far, is a handsome, self-shaping tree which grows to a height of 12–15 m and has a spread of 6 m, with fern-like foliage and showy orange flowers in late spring or early summer.

Hakea

E, FS or HS, H 4–6 m, W 2–3 m. Fast-growing shrubs with thick, needle-like, leathery leaves for screening or windbreaks.

- Pin-cushion hakea (*H. laurina*) has red, globe-shaped flowers in spring.
- Willow leaf hakea (*H. salicifolia*) has bronze-tipped foliage and can be trained as a hedge. All climates except coldest districts.

Leschenaultia (Mirror of heaven)

E, FS, H 30–90 cm, W 30–60 cm. Delicate, small shrub with soft, blue flowers. Prefers well-drained, sandy or gravelly soil. Suits temperate climates.

Leptospermum (Tea tree)

E, FS, H 1–5 m, W 1–5 m. Many species and named varieties of fast-growing shrubs native to Australia. Tiny leaves and white, pink or red flowers like peach blossom in spring or summer. Plants prefer well-drained soil and resist drought, wind and salt spray. Temperate coastal climates. Some of the most widely cultivated species are:

- Coastal tea tree (*L. laevigatum*) H 3–4 m, W 3–5 m.
- Port Jackson tea tree (*L. squarrosum*) H 2–3 m, W 1–2 m.
- Lemon-scented tea tree (*L. petersonii*) H 4–5 m, W 3–4 m.

Melaleuca (Paper bark)

E, FS or HS, H 2–9 m, W 2–6 m. Shrubs or small trees noted for their showy flowers (similar to those of bottlebrush) and their decorative, papery bark. Many tolerate swampy conditions, strong winds and salt spray. All but coldest climates. Widely grown species are:

- Bracelet honey myrtle (*M. armillaris*) H 5–6 m, W 4–5 m.
- Red honey myrtle (*M. hypericifolia*) H 2–2.5 m, W 2–2.5 m.
- Broadleaf paper bark (*M. leucadendron*) H 6–9 m, W 4–5 m.

Philotheca (Waxflower)

E, HS or SS, H 120 cm, W 90 cm. Compact shrub with fragrant foliage and white or pink, star-shaped flowers showing in winter and early spring. Prefers well-drained, slightly acid, sandy soils. Suits temperate and warm climates.

Pimelea

E, FS, H 1–2 m, W 1 m. Attractive shrub with small, glossy leaves and dense clusters of cream, yellow or pink flowers in spring to early summer. Temperate climates.

Prostanthera (Mint bush)

E, FS or HS, H 2–4 m, W 2–3 m. Several species of attractive shrubs with small, aromatic leaves and masses of mauve, purple or blue flowers in spring. They prefer good drainage and resent root disturbance. Prune back after flowering to prevent bushes becoming leggy. Cool–temperate to subtropical climates.

Pultenaea (Bush pea)

E, HS or SS, H 2–3 m, W 1–2 m. Small native shrubs with yellow or orange, pea-like flowers in spring. Temperate climates.

HINT

Kangaroo paws like plenty of rain or watering from May to September. If winter is too dry for them, the flowers will turn brown before opening.

GEOFFREY BURNIE
GARDENING JOURNALIST

Australian native gardens can be filled with colour.

Schefflera (Umbrella tree)

E, FS to S, H 6–9 m, W 3–6 m. Glossy foliage resembles segments of an umbrella. Reddish flowers in spring followed by purple berries in autumn. Used as an indoor plant when small. Temperate and tropical climates. Can invade drains.

Stenocarpus (Queensland firewheel)

E, FS or HS, H 9 m, W 3–5 m. Slow-growing, upright tree with large, glossy leaves and unusual scarlet-red flowers arranged like the spokes of a wheel. Warm–temperate and tropical climates.

Syzygium (Lillypilly)

E, FS or HS, H 10–15 m, W 4–8m. A variable genus of graceful, dark-green-foliaged trees with red or pink new growth. *S. luehmannii* has a weeping habit and bright-red, pear-shaped fruit (known as 'riberries'). The trees need plenty of water and protection from severe frosts. Many cultivars. Look for psyllid-resistant varieties.

Telopea (Waratah)

E, FS or HS, H 2–3 m, W 2–2.5 m. This attractive and stately shrub has spectacular cones of vivid red flowers (the floral emblem of New South Wales) in late spring. A white cultivar is also available. Waratahs prefer well-drained, slightly acid, sandy soils but with added organic matter. Prune back plants after flowering. Temperate climates. Some hybrids are now available (e.g. 'Shady Lady').

Thryptomene (Heath myrtle)

E, FS, H 1–1.5 m, W 1 m. Several species of attractive dwarf shrubs with small leaves close to the stems and tea tree-like flowers (white, pink or lavender) in spring. Prefers well-drained, slightly acid, sandy soil. Temperate and cold climates.

Waterhousia (Weeping lillypilly, syn. *Eugenia ventenattii*)

E, FS, H 15 m, W 5–8 m. Large tree with weeping branches, white, fluffy flowers and green fruit. Because it stays branched to the ground for many years, it makes an excellent screen tree.

Westringia (Coastal rosemary)

E, FS or HS, H 1–2 m, W 1.5 m. Attractive dense shrubs with grey-green foliage and small, white or pale-lavender flowers. Very adaptable plants which tolerate strong winds, salt spray and dry conditions. Useful as low windbreak or hedge plant. All climates but coldest.

GROUND COVERS

Brachyscome multifida

E, FS or HS, H 20–40 cm, W 80 cm. Forms a low-spreading mound of fine foliage studded with small daisies mainly in blue, mauve and white shades. Flowers through spring, summer and autumn.

Brachysema lanceolatum

E, FS, H 1.5 m, W 3 m. Spreading, rounded, glaucous-foliaged shrub with red pea flowers. Needs a well-drained position.

Brachysema latifolium

E, FS, H 20 cm, W 1 m. Attractive, prostrate, trailing plant bearing orange-red, pea-shaped flowers in spring. Good drainage essential.

Correa decumbens

E, FS, H 30 cm, W 3 m. Spreading shrub carrying erect, tubular flowers, red with yellow tips for most of the year. Best flowering in winter.

Correa Dusky bells

E, FS or SS, H 80 cm, W 80 cm. An interesting plant of somewhat variable growth habit. Resilient and frost-hardy with pink flowers in winter. It will take heavy clay soils, is a vigorous grower and, like all correas, is good for attracting birds to the garden.

Dampiera diversifolia

E, FS, H 20 cm, W 1 m. An excellent native ground cover, bearing masses of dark-blue flowers over spring and summer.

Davallia pyxidata (Hare's foot fern)

E, S, H 30cm, W 1 m. A fern with long, creeping stems found in the bush on trees or rocks. Excellent for ground covering and hanging baskets.

Dichondra repens

HS to SS, H 10 cm, W 1 m. A prostrate plant producing roots at the nodes similar to grasses. Mainly grown for the dense, kidney-shaped leaves. Needs some sun and ample watering. Insignificant greenish flowers.

Grevillea juniperina

(Prostrate form) E, FS, H 60 cm, W 2 m. Excellent cover for sloping banks, large

Top five native ground covers

GREVILLEA 'POORINDA ROYAL MANTLE'

Pretty, red, brush-like flowers complement the flat mass of foliage of this ground cover.

MYOPORUM PARVIFOLIUM

A prostrate growth habit and starry, white flowers make this a good choice for a sunny, well-drained position.

SCAEVOLA

This ground cover from Western Australia has become popular because of its beautiful, mauve-blue, fan-shaped blooms.

HARDENBERGIA VIOLACEA

A hardy native climber, hardenbergia can be draped over a bank where its purple pea flowers will be easily seen. *Hardenbergia comptoniana* (native wisteria) does best in semi-shade.

BRACHYSCOME (SWAN RIVER DAISY)

Lots of little daisies dot these fine-leaved plants for months. There are perennial and annual forms, and flowers can be mauve, blue, white, purple or even pink.

Native fan flowers (Scaevola *spp.) make excellent ground covers or basket fillers.*

expanses without shrubs and for covering rock walls. Yellow, spider-like flowers in spring and summer. Dark-green, prickly leaves.

Grevillea 'Poorinda Royal Mantle'

E, FS, H 20 cm, W 3 m. Low-growing, very vigorous and hardy, carrying red, toothbrush-like flowers in winter. Tolerates drought and will accept clay soils.

Grevillea tridentifera

(Syn. *G. biternata*) E, FS, H 40 cm, W 1 m. Bright-green, dissected foliage with upright shoots bearing masses of white, perfumed flowers in spring. Suitable for sloping banks and low-maintenance areas between shrubs and trees.

Kennedia prostrata

E, FS or SS, H 15 cm, W 1.5 m. Prostrate and vigorous. Sometimes called the running postman. Free-flowering with scarlet blooms in spring and early summer. Ideal for banks and ground cover between shrubs.

Lomandra longifolia (Mat rush)

E, FS or SS, H 1 m, W 1 m. Very hardy, clump-forming plants. Named varieties available (e.g. 'Tanika', a fine-leaved form). See also Chapter 21.

Myoporum parvifolium

E, FS or HS, H 1m, W 11 m. A frost-hardy plant bearing white, star-like flowers in spring and summer. Suitable for sloping banks, cover between trees and shrubs, between paths or along driveways.

Scaevola (Fan flower)

E, FS, H 20 cm, W 1 m. A large genus of plants varying from large shrubs to perennials and ground covers. 'Purple Fanfare' and 'Mauve Carpet' are popular cultivars but there are many others used worldwide as ground covers, carrying mauve, white or purple fan-shaped flowers from late spring to early winter. Will tolerate damp conditions and has attractive, dense, bright-green leaves.

Viola hederacea

E, FS or SS, H 10 cm, W 40 cm. Commonly called the native violet, this forms an extensive mat in damp areas and carries typically violet-shaped flowers in white and purple. Suitable as a dense ground cover between shrubs, in rockeries, and will also grow indoors. Useful in baskets.

NATIVE CLIMBERS
Cissus antarctica (Kangaroo vine)

This is the best known cissus, with green, toothed, ovate leaves to 10 cm long. Bears small flowers and black, edible fruits. Suitable for pergola, fence or indoors. More attractive in shade. Requires ample moisture.

Cissus hypoglauca

Dark-green leaves with five leaflets emerging from the one point. Bears small flowers and a bluish fruit. A large, spreading foliage climber for creating a rainforest effect. Requires ample moisture.

Clematis aristata

Vigorous climber bearing creamy-white flowers 5 cm in diameter in spring. Attaches itself by twisting its petioles around supports.

Hardy in well-drained, sunny or semi-shade positions. Female plants develop attractive fluffy seed heads. Ideal for fences.

Hardenbergia comptoniana

Moderately vigorous, carrying sprays of purplish-blue, pea-shaped flowers in spring. Does well in a semi-shade position; excellent for trellises or pergolas.

Hardenbergia violacea

E, FS or SH, 20 cm–1 m. Climbing plant with generally purple flowers. However, there are some white, pink and mauve forms. Selected plants may be used as ground covers.

Hibbertia empetrifolia

Not really a climber but a lax shrub. Will grow behind wire and will produce a pillar of brilliant yellow for much of the year. Flowers are about 15 mm in diameter. Can be kept cut and grown as a shrub.

Hibbertia scandens

Rapid-growing twining plant with large, bright-green leaves and yellow flowers 5 cm in diameter. Grows well in most areas except where frosts are heavy.

Hoya australis

This rainforest native has succulent-like leaves and white or pale-pink, waxy flowers in globe-shaped clusters of about 8 cm in diameter. Hoya is suitable for outdoors in most positions and indoors in good light. Will accept salt spray.

Kennedia macrophylla

Vigorous climber with large, light-green leaves and red, pea-shaped flowers in spring and summer. Full sun to light shade; avoid frosts.

Kennedia nigricans

Very vigorous climber with large, dark-green leaves, and black and yellow flowers. The most vigorous of the kennedias, and probably one of the most rampant plants in southern Australia. Prefers full sun to light shade; will not survive heavy frosts. Gives quick cover.

Kennedia retrorsa

Vigorous plant with dark-green leaves and purple flowers. It is relatively frost-hardy, and will grow in most positions.

Kennedia rubicunda

Vigorous grower with dark-green leaves and large red flowers. Will accept most situations, but prefers full sun.

Milletia megasperma

Native wisteria from the rainforests of Queensland and northern NSW – very showy, large, white to purple, pea-shaped flowers in sprays up to 15 cm in diameter. Excellent climber for covering a fence or pergola in milder areas. Will tolerate some frost.

Pandorea spp.

Pandorea spp. See page 383

Passiflora cinnabarina

Vigorous creeper with red flowers 8 cm in diameter. Very showy for fences or pergolas and suits most aspects. Will attach to cracks in mortar between bricks. Flowers in spring.

Soliya heterophylla

Commonly called bluebell creeper. A vigorous Western Australian bushy plant with a twining habit, it produces a number of branches from ground level and carries flowers of blue and occasionally pink in spring and summer, followed by fleshy, cylindrical blue fruits. Very hardy and is suitable for all soils and aspects. Can become a weed away from its native habitat.

HINT

The best time to transplant grass trees (*Xanthorrhoea* spp.) is in July. Make a large saucer around the base of the plant and fill with a bucket of water every day during its first summer. When new growth appears, the plant has taken. This may take up to a year, so have patience.

COLIN BARLOW

GARDEN WRITER, DESIGNER AND HORTICULTURALIST, TV PRESENTER — *HOME IN WA*

Keep Bushland Free of Weeds

Many plants that have been introduced into Australia since European settlement have become weeds. Some native plants removed from their natural habitat have also developed invasive tendencies. All garden owners, but especially those living near bushland, should take responsibility for ensuring that garden plants aren't able to escape into the bush. For more information visit www.weeds.org.au.

To minimise the risk of weed invasion:
- Avoid growing plants with weed potential.
- Avoid growing weeds with fruits that attract birds.
- Don't dump garden refuse or lawn clippings in the bush.
- Don't overfertilise or allow fertiliser nutrients to run into bushland or streams.
- When walking in bushland, try to stay on the cleared pathways.
- Prune free-seeding plants (such as agapanthus) immediately after flowering.

Coreopsis.

Lantana and morning glory.

Here are examples of some garden plants that are invasive in certain climates, but there are many others with weed potential that are not included on this list. Check with local nurseries or council if in doubt.

Agapanthus	*Agapanthus* spp.
Alligator weed	*Alternanthera philoxeroides*
Arum lily	*Zantedeschia aethiopica*
Blue periwinkle	*Vinca major*
Bridal creeper	*Asparagus asparagoides*
Boneseed	*Chrysanthemoides monilifera* spp. *monilifera*
Broom	*Cytisus* ssp. and others
Camphor laurel	*Cinnamomum camphora*
Cat's claw creeper	*Macfadyena unguis-cati*
Cherry laurel	*Prunus laurocerasus*
Coreopsis	*Coreopsis lanceolata*
Cotoneaster	*Cotoneaster* spp.
English ivy	*Hedera helix*
Erigeron	*Erigeron karvinskianus*
Fishbone fern	*Nephrolepis cordifolia*
Ginger lily	*Hedychium gardnerianum*
Holly	*Ilex aquifolium*
Honeysuckle	*Lonicera japonica*
Horsetail	*Equisetum arvense, E. hyemale, E. palustre, E. ramosissimum, E. bogatensis*
Indian Hawthorn	*Rhaphiolepis indica*
Japanese knotweed	*Persicaria capitata*
Lantana	*Lantana camara, L. montevidensis*
Madeira vine	*Anredera cordifolia*
Mirror bush	*Coprosma repens*
Montbretia	*Crocosmia* x *crocosmifolia*
Morning glory	*Ipomoea indica*
Pampas grass	*Cortaderia* spp.
Passionfruit	*Passiflora edulis*
Paterson's curse	*Echium plantagineum*
Peppercorn	*Schinus* spp.
Pittosporum	*Pittosporum undulatum*
Privet	*Ligustrum* spp.
Pyracantha	*Pyracantha* spp.
Radiata pine	*Pinus radiata*
Ribbon plant	*Chlorophytum comosum* 'Variegatum'
Rubber vine	*Cryptostegia grandiflora*
Salvinia	*Salvinia molesta*
Sensitive plant	*Mimosa pigra*
Singapore daisy	*Wedelia trilobata*
Thunbergia	*Thunbergia* spp.
Tradescantia	*Tradescantia fluminensis*
Watsonia	*Watsonia* spp.
Willow	Some invasive *Salix* species

21
Plants for
Special Conditions

The most successful gardens and those easiest to maintain are those where every plant is suited to its growing conditions; the oft-repeated saying 'the right plant in the right place' sums up this principle. Before selecting plants, consider the climate, the aspect (sun or shade), exposure to wind, soil conditions and, of course, the ultimate height and spread of the plant. There are some growing conditions – such as those found by the sea, in shady areas, in fireprone areas, in courtyards and in boggy or clay soils – that are especially challenging. Selection of plants for these conditions needs more than the usual amount of thought and planning to develop a thriving, successful garden.

SEASIDE GARDENS

Strong, salt-laden wind and soil that is almost pure sand can make for difficult growing conditions. However, with careful plant selection and attention to building up the organic content of the soil, you can have an attractive, easy-care garden. First of all you need to establish a windbreak of tough, salt-tolerant plants and use soil-binding ground covers to stabilise the sandy soil. Beach spinifex (*Spinifex sericeus*) and kangaroo grass (*Themeda australis*) hold the surface sand of undisturbed or regenerated sand dunes, allowing other species to take hold.

Initially, front-line plantings may need the protection of some type of screen or barrier, such as hessian or shade cloth stretched between stakes. Don't try to plant advanced or semi-mature plants as these will require much more water and attention than small plants. Small plants require less water, are less vulnerable to wind damage and suffer less transplant shock. Plant in groups, not in lines, so that developing plants give each other protection as well as ultimately slowing wind speed. The best choices for front-line plants are usually those plants that grow naturally in your area. While these may not be your favourites, they will help modify conditions so that a wider selection of plants may be grown in their shelter. It should also be noted that those trees and shrubs that are growing in harsh, exposed conditions may be much shorter and more stunted than when they are planted in more benign situations.

Good soil preparation is essential. Prior to planting, dig in large quantities of well-decayed compost or animal manure over the whole area to be planted, not just into the planting holes. The soil will also need to be mulched. In the first few years at least use organic mulches that will break down and help to improve the water and nutrient-holding capacity of the soil. Several overlapping layers of wet newspaper placed under your chosen mulch will aid in moisture retention and will themselves break down into the soil. After planting, give the whole area a heavy watering. As with any other type of garden, less frequent deep watering will be more beneficial than frequent light sprinkling. Deep watering encourages deep rooting while light sprinkling encourages plant roots to grow close to the surface, where they are more vulnerable to wind and heat.

Once you have established some degree of protection from the full force of the salt-laden wind, you will be able to grow a much wider range of plants.

Refer to the front flap of this book
for a key to abbreviations.

Plants for seaside gardens

Acacia (Wattle)

E, FS, H 1–2 m, W 1 m. Coast wattle (*A. longifolia* var. *sophorae*), upright or semi-prostrate. Leathery, olive-green leaves, golden, rod-like flowers in spring. Coastal Myall (*A. binervia*, H 3–10 m, W 2–5 m) has grey, sickle-shaped leaves and yellow rod flowers in spring.

Banksia

E, FS, H 2–12 m, W 3+ m. Coast banksia (*B. integrifolia*) varies from a stunted shrub to a tall tree, depending on conditions. Soft yellow flowers in winter. Old man Banksia (*B. serrata*) often has twisted or leaning branches. Grey-green flowers bloom from summer to early winter.

HINT

For gardens by the sea, instead of staking new plants against gusty coastal winds, place several flat rocks over the root zone. The plant will grow stronger without a stake, and the rocks also help preserve moisture and keep the roots cool. Hose over the plants when you water, to remove accumulated salt from the foliage.

On exposed sites near the coast, consider using a mulch of gravel or pebbles instead of bark. It won't blow or wash away as easily, and lasts longer too.

HELEN YOUNG

HORTICULTURIST, GARDEN WRITER —
THE WEEKEND AUSTRALIAN,
702 ABC RADIO GARDEN TALKBACK

Carpobrotus (Pigface)

E, FS, H 15 cm, W 75 cm. *C. glaucescens* is a fast-growing, prostrate, sand-binding plant with succulent foliage and purple-pink flowers in summer.

Casuarina (She-oak)

E, FS, H 3–20 m, W 3–5 m. Beach she-oak (*C. equisetifolia*) has graceful, silvery, weeping foliage.

Convolvulus

E, FS, H 15 cm, W 70 cm. Silverbush (*C. cneorum*) is a spreading ground cover with silky silver foliage and white, trumpet-shaped flowers. It flowers from spring to early summer. *Ipomoea pes-caprae* (ssp. *Brasiliensis*) is native to dune areas in the warmer regions of eastern Australia. It has two-lobed leaves and pink to purple flowers in summer. A very useful sand-binder if available.

Coprosma (Mirror bush)

E, FS, H 15 cm, W 1.5 m. *C. x kirkii* has small, shiny leaves that form a dense mat of foliage. E, FS, H 2–3 m, W 2 m. *C. repens* is a dense shrub with glossy leaves. Good for hedges or screens.

Cupaniopsis (Tuckeroo)

E, FS, H 8–12 m, W 5–8 m. *C. anacardioides* is a fairly fast-growing tree, suitable for warmer coastal regions. Shiny foliage, small greenish flowers followed by attractive yellow-orange fruits.

Hibbertia (Guinea flower)

E, FS, H 20–30 cm (as ground cover), W 1+ m. *H. scandens* is a scrambling or climbing plant, used as ground cover and a soil-binder. Fast growing with slightly fleshy leaves and bright-yellow flowers in spring and summer.

Hibiscus

E, FS, H 5–7 m, W 3–5 m. *H. tiliaceus* is a small tree suitable for seaside gardens in warm areas. Heart-shaped or rounded leaves form a dense, shady crown. Yellow flowers with red centres appear in spring.

Leptospermum (Tea tree)

E, FS, H 3–4 m, W 3–5 m. Coastal tea tree (*L. laevigatum*) has neat, dense, grey-green foliage and small white flowers in spring and summer. A good screening plant.

Lomandra (Mat rush)
E, FS, H 1 m, W 70 cm–1 m. *L. longifolia*, a tussock-forming plant with tough, sword-shaped leaves. Cream flowers in spring, followed by creamy yellow clusters of seed capsules on female plants.

Melaleuca (Bracelet honey myrtle)
E, FS, H 3–5 m, W 3–5 m. Bracelet honey myrtle (*M. armillaris*) makes a rounded shrub with soft, narrow leaves and cream, bottlebrush-type flowers in spring or summer. Ideal as a screen or windbreak.

Metrosideros (New Zealand Christmas tree, Pohutukawa)
E, FS, H 5–10 m, W 4–6 m. *M. excelsa* develops a spreading crown. Leathery leaves, dark green above, grey underneath. Showy, bright-scarlet or crimson flowers, attractive to birds from late spring through summer.

Pandanus (Screw pine)
E, FS, H 3–6 m, W 3–5 m. *P. tectorius* (var. *Australianus*) is a small spreading tree with palm-like foliage and strong prop roots. Ideal for very warm to tropical seaside gardens.

Pittosporum
E, FS, H 4–6 m, W 2–4 m. Karo (*P. crassifolium*) is a small tree with leathery leaves that are dark green above and woolly grey beneath. Clusters of small, scented, dark red flowers appear during spring to early summer.

Scaevola (Fan flower)
E, FS, H 8–10 cm, W 1 m. *S. calendulacea* is a spreading, trailing plant ideal as a soil- and sand-binder. Small, fleshy leaves with mauve fan flowers throughout the year. Succulent purple berries follow flowers.

Vitex
E, FS, H 2–3 m, W 2–3 m. *V. trifolia* and its purple-leaved form 'Purpurea' are rounded, bushy shrubs. Small blue flowers in spring and summer are followed by blue-black fruits.

Westringia (Coastal rosemary)
E, FS, H 1–1.5 m, W 1–1.5 m. *W. fruticosa* may be grown alone or as a low hedge. Compact growth with small, grey-green leaves and white flowers in spring to early summer, this shrub responds well to shaping and clipping.

GARDENS IN THE SHADE
Many plants will grow well in shade but not in very dark, gloomy areas. Plants growing in shade are often under large trees, so they have the added problem of dealing with root competition and soil dryness. Extra care may be needed to get plants established in these conditions but it can be done if special attention is paid to watering and fertilising in the initial stages of establishment. However, it is difficult to find a wide variety of plants that will flower in these conditions so there is more reliance on foliage shape, texture and colour. This is especially true in tropical gardens where many of the plants normally thought of as indoor plants are grown outdoors in the shade of large trees.

Fortunately, there are many lovely plants that prefer to be grown in shady locations where the shade is cast by a building or more distant trees.

Potted plants can be placed into sunny spots in the garden.

Top five plants for dry shade

LIRIOPE

These strap-leaved plants can adapt readily to competitive positions under trees. Not only does liriope handle competition, but its variegated forms bring light touches to shaded garden areas.

CLIVIA

Clump-forming clivias normally produce orange flowers in spring or early summer, but newer varieties come in much-desired cream and yellow shades.

PLECTRANTHUS

Swedish ivy is the common name for the variety of plectranthus that succeeds well in the shade of large trees.

LAMIUM

Although lamium rejoices in the name 'dead nettle', it's a great ground cover for difficult shaded gardens.

IVY

Ivy is incredibly tough but it must be clipped to keep it under control. Never let it start to climb trees – it will take over.

LAMIUM AND PLECTRANTHUS

Plants for shady gardens

Acanthus (Oyster plant, Bear's breeches)

D, SS to S, H 2 m, W 1 m. *A. mollis* has dark, glossy, strongly lobed leaves with tall, stiff spikes of purple and white flowers in summer. Its leaves are the model for decoration on Corinthian columns. Protect from snails.

Ajuga (Blue bugle flower)

E, SS to S, H 20 cm, W 40 cm. Blue bugle (*A. reptans*) forms spreading rosettes of dark-green or bronze leaves. Deep-blue flower spikes appear in spring or early summer.

Alocasia (Elephant Ears)

E, SS to S, H 1–2 m, W 1–1.5 m. *A. sanderiana* has large, dark leaves that are heavily veined in silver – for tropical gardens only. *A. brisbanensis* has dark-green, wavy-edged leaves, and a cream, arum-type flower, followed by bright-red poisonous fruits.

Arthropodium (Renga renga, New Zealand rock lily)

E, HS to S, H 60 cm–1 m, W 50 cm. *A. cirrhatum* forms clumps of soft, green, recurved leaves. Sprays of tiny white flowers, standing high above the foliage, appear in late spring to early summer.

Asplenium (Bird's nest fern)

E, SS to S, H 1 m, W 1 m. *A. australasicum* (formerly *A. nidus*) forms a large, nest-shaped rosette of slightly leathery, pale-green, radiating fronds. Its shallow root system makes it ideal for growing under trees.

Begonia

E, SS to S, H 15 cm–2 m, W variable. Hundreds of species and cultivated varieties can be grown in shady gardens. Many have shallow, fibrous roots or grow from rhizomes (running roots) so that they can be established under trees. Those with cane-like stems may grow to 2 m bearing large clusters of pendulous flowers in pink, red or white. Many rhizomatous types are grown for their foliage, which is unusual both in shape and colour.

Camellia

E, HS to S, H 3–5 m, W 1–3 m. *C. sasanqua* flowers from mid-autumn through early winter while *C. japonica* flowers through winter to early spring. All camellias have handsome, glossy foliage, and flowers of various forms and colours – white, pink, red and combinations of these. Unsuitable for growing under trees because of dry soil and competition, but ideal in other shady locations, in the ground or in containers.

Cissus antarctica
(Kangaroo vine)

E, HS to S, H 20–30 cm, W 2–3 m when used as ground cover. Good for covering large areas of ground with handsome, glossy foliage, although it is a climber.

Clivia (Kaffir lily)

E, SS to S, H 35–60 cm, W 30 cm. Broad, dark-green, strappy leaves and orange or cream flowers on tall stems above foliage in late winter or spring. Ideal for dry shade under trees.

Correa

E, HS to S, H 1 m, W 1 m. Flowering during autumn through to spring, *C. alba* has felty, oval, grey-green leaves and white, starry flowers. *C. reflexa* has narrow, dark leaves and bears tubular red flowers with green tips.

Crinum

E or D, HS to SS, H 75 cm–1 m, W 50 cm. *C. moorei* is a bulbous plant with broad, recurved leaves. It bears pale-pink, trumpet-like flowers in late summer through to autumn. *C. x powellii* bears white flowers on strong stems positioned well above foliage. The leaves of the swamp lily (*C. pedunculatum*) may grow up to 2 m. Large heads of white flowers with drooping petals on strong, fleshy stems appear in summer.

Crowea

E, HS to SS, H 80 cm–1 m, W 80 cm–1 m. Long-flowering *C. exalata* and *C. saligna* both have starry flowers in different shades of pink and mid-green and linear leaves. Can be grown under trees.

HINT

Shade may be a significant problem in gardens with mature trees. Never forget that the rainforest plants selected for indoor use have enormous shade tolerance. That's exactly why we select them as indoor plants! Except in areas where frosts are heavy, you could try using *Aspidistra elatior*, *Spathiphyllum* 'Mauna Loa' and other indoor plants to offer groundcovers in the shade. They'll do the trick as well as adding an exotic look to your garden.

JOHN PATRICK
GARDENING AUSTRALIA

Ctenanthe

E, SS to S, H 1–1.5 m, W 50 cm. *C. lubbersiana* has shiny green leaves splashed with yellow. *C. oppenheimiana* has dark-green leaves, patterned in silver with burgundy undersides. The variety 'Tricolor' has dark leaves patterned with pink and cream. Can be grown under trees in warm or tropical gardens.

Cyathea (Rough tree fern)

E, SS to S, H 4–15 m, W (crown) 6–8 m. *C. australis*, *C. cooperi* and *C. dealbata* are fairly fast-growing tree ferns with slender trunks and wide canopies of lacy fronds. Silver fern (*C. dealbeata*) is the New Zealand national emblem.

Dicksonia (Soft tree fern)

E, SS to S, H 4–12 m, W (crown) 6–8 m. *D. antarctica* forms a massive trunk covered with brown, fibrous roots and old frond bases. Long arching fronds to about 4 m.

Eupomatia (Bolwarra)

E, SS to S, H 2–6 m, W 1–2 m. *E. laurina* has glossy, dark foliage with pink new growth. It bears unusual flowers and edible fruit. Grow under trees as a specimen or elsewhere as a hedge.

Farfugium (Leopard plant)

E, SS to S, H 40–60 cm, W 30 cm. Also known as *Ligularia*, *F. tussilagineum* (and especially var. 'Aureo-maculatum', which is gold-spotted) is best planted in groups for effect. Grow as a feature, tall ground cover or edging plant.

Hedera (Ivy)

E, SS to S, H (as ground cover) 15–20 cm, W 1–2+ m. Many cultivated varieties of *H. helix* make great ground cover under trees if kept in control. Good cover for banks and trailing over walls.

Helleborus (Lenten rose, winter rose)

E, SS to S, H 30–60 cm, W 30 cm. *H. orientalis* has toothed finger-like leaves and white, green, pink or mottled flowers in winter through to spring. *H. niger* does well in cooler areas.

Hosta

D, SS to S, H 25–40 cm, spreading. Many species and varieties are grown for their outstanding foliage. Large leaves that are green, variegated or blue-grey. White or mauve flowers in summer. Watch for snails.

Hydrangea

D, SS to S, H 0.5 m–3 m, W 0.5–2 m. Best in shady, moist situations. Large mop-heads of flowers in white, various shades of pink, red or blue. Some newer varieties have stable flower colour.

Impatiens (Busy Lizzie)

E, SS to S, H 30–50 cm, W 20–40 cm. Single and double flowers in white and shades of pink, red and purple, appear almost year round. New Guinea hybrids are most colourful and disease-resistant.

Justicia

E, SS to S, H 1.5 m, W 70 cm–1 m. Cane-like stems bear dark, strongly veined leaves. Large heads of old-rose-pink flowers. Var. 'Alba' has white flowers.

Kohleria

E, SS to S, H 30 cm–70 cm, W 15 cm. Soft-stemmed, velvety green leaves with red margins, orange-scarlet tubular flowers in spring. Spreads by underground rhizomes. Ideal under trees or in pots.

Lamium (Dead nettle)

E, SS to S, H 15–20 cm, W 15 cm. Soft-leaved ground cover spread by running stems. Many variegated forms include 'Beacon Silver', 'White Nancy' and others. Flowers are pink, purple, cream or yellow depending on variety.

Liriope

D, HS to S, H 30 cm, W 15 cm. *L. muscari* has strappy leaves which may be dark green or variegated cream or yellow. Deep violet flowers in late summer through to autumn. Excellent ground cover or edging plant.

Macrozamia (Burrawang)

E, HS to SS, H 1.5–2 m, W 1–1.5 m. *M. communis* fairly fast-growing cycad with long, dark green, arching fronds. Ideal under trees.

Nandina (Sacred bamboo)

E, HS to SS, H 1–2 m, W 1 m. *N. domestica* has multi-stemmed, fine, divided leaves. Cream flowers in summer followed by decorative red berries. Forms attractive clumps.

Ophiopogon (Mondo grass)

E, SS to S, H 15–25 cm, W 20 cm. *O. jaburan* has dense, dark green, grassy foliage that forms clumps. White flowers in summer. Ideal edging or ground cover plant in shade.

Plectranthus

E, SS to S, H 20–30 cm, W 75 cm. These soft-stemmed plants are ideal spreading ground cover. *P. graveolens* has silvery, aromatic foliage and bears pale-blue flowers in spring through to summer. *P. oertendahlii* has burgundy undersides to green leaves and soft, pink-lilac flowers in early autumn.

GARDENING IN FIRE-PRONE AREAS

All plants will burn if a fire is hot enough, but there are many plants that are slower to ignite than others. Plants with a high water or salt content in their leaves and those with a low oil or resin content tend to be slow to ignite. It is important to avoid trees with loose, dangling, stringy bark and those that retain dead leaves or twigs throughout the summer. Australian eucalypts, in particular, contain large amounts of volatile oils in their leaves which burst into flame once conditions are hot enough. Many conifers such as cypresses and pines not only have a high resin content in their leaves but they also tend to retain old, dead foliage within their canopies. Cypress hedges are a good example of this. These trees are not, therefore, a wise choice for planting near dwellings in fire-prone areas.

Trees and shrubs with thick bark may regenerate after fire if dormant buds beneath the bark survive. Many Australian plants have evolved with fire and even if they have been so badly burned that they fail to regenerate, there is a strong likelihood that seed has been released. This should germinate after the first good rain. Some trees and shrubs survive because they have lignotubers – specialised storage units at, or below, soil level. These, too, bear dormant buds that may regenerate if all top growth is burnt. Many Australian trees and shrubs, including rainforest species, burn slowly and may regenerate after fire while introduced species on the whole will be even slower to ignite but will ultimately be killed by the fire.

Proper planning and good garden maintenance will help give you some protection. In fact, if your garden area is large enough, planting trees of the recommended types will help control fire by slowing wind speed, increasing humidity and acting as the first line of defence against flying embers. However, any tree should be planted a minimum of 5 m from the house. Very tall trees should be planted at an even greater distance from buildings. Never have trees of any kind overhanging a house. It is best not to have a continuous tree canopy in any section but rather to plant in groups, with adequate spacing in between. It also makes sense to have an open lawn, play area or pool on the side of the house from which fire is likely to come. This not only gives free access to the building in case of emergency but also increases the distance between fire and house.

Good housekeeping in the garden is essential, especially during hot summers.

Don't allow leaf litter to build up under trees but rake it up and add to the compost heap. Certainly keep your garden well mulched but use only non-flammable mulches such as compost; decayed animal manure; large, chunky pine-bark chips or even pebbles. Resins in pine-bark chips will leach out in a couple of weeks with constant wetting or soaking. Avoid all loose mulches such as straw, lucerne hay and sugar-cane waste.

Ground covers for fire-prone areas

Agapanthus
E, FS to HS, H 60–90 cm, W 30 cm, dwarf forms H 30 cm. Vigorous, strap-leaved plants with fleshy roots. Large heads of blue or white flowers in summer.

Ajuga (Blue bugle flower)
E, SS to S, H 15 cm, W 20 cm. Both *A. reptans* and *A. australis* form dense ground cover. Both have blue flowers in spring and form spreading rosettes of leaves.

Dianthus.

Clivia (Kaffir lily)

E, HS to S, H 35–60 cm, W 30 cm. Broad, dark-green, strap-shaped leaves with orange or cream flowers from late winter to spring.

Coprosma

E, FS to HS, H 15 cm, W 1.5 m. *Coprosma* x *kirkii* forms a dense mat of small, shiny leaves. Good as ground cover or for trailing over walls or banks.

Dianthus (Pinks)

E, FS, H 10–30 cm, W 30–50 cm. Species and hybrid dianthus tolerate dry conditions. Its foliage is grey-green and its flowers are mostly scented and in tones of pink, red and white.

Dichondra (Kidney weed)

E, HS to SS, prostrate. Forms roots at the nodes and makes a good lawn substitute.

Hardenbergia (False sarsparilla)

E, FS, W 1–2 m. *Hardenbergia violacea* is a climbing plant that makes excellent ground cover. Leathery dark leaves and masses of purple pea flowers in spring.

Hedera (English ivy)

E, SS to S, H 15–20 cm, W 1–2 m. A climber that makes great ground cover in shade. Don't allow it to climb into trees.

Hibbertia (Guinea flower)

E, FS to HS. H 20–30 cm (as ground cover), W 1+ m. This plant scrambles or climbs and has slightly fleshy leaves and yellow flowers in spring and summer.

Mesembryanthemum (Pigface, ice plant)

E, FS, H 25 cm, W 75 cm. Succulent-leaved spreading ground cover, silky flowers in many

The fleshy leaves of canna lilies burn with difficulty.

colours in late spring. Drought-resistant. *Carpobrotus* spp. and *Lampranthus* spp. are equally suitable.

Myoporum (Creeping boobialla)

E, FS to HS, H 15 cm, W 1 m. Spreading growth, narrow leaves and white, starry flowers through late spring into summer.

Scaevola (Fan flower)

E, FS to SS, prostrate, W 50 cm–1 m. *S. aemula* and other cultivated varieties. They are spreading and trailing with neat, light-green foliage and pale-blue to purple fan flowers in spring and summer.

Vinca (Periwinkle)

E, HS to S, H 15–20 cm, W 1+ m. Vigorous, spreading growth, rooting at nodes, with plain green or variegated leaves and mauve-blue flowers in spring.

Shrubs and perennials for fire-prone areas

Atriplex (Saltbush)

E, FS, H 1–3 m, W 1–2 m. Drought-resistant shrubs with a high salt content in their leaves. These shrubs have a range of leaf shapes and sizes, mostly insignificant flowers and some have colourful fruits.

Bursaria (Blackthorn)

E, FS to SS, H 3 m, W 1.5–2 m. Thorny shrub with wiry branches and small, dark, shiny leaves. This plant provides a good habitat for small birds. Small, fragrant, cream flowers mainly in summer are rich in nectar and attract insects.

Canna

E or SD, FS, H 90–150 cm, W 25–30 cm. Broad, green or bronze leaves, large, showy flowers in a great colour range: red, yellow, orange, pink and white to cream. Tolerates most conditions but does well in damp soil. Plant in bold clumps.

Coprosma (Mirror bush)

E, FS, H 2–3 m, W–2 m. Its shiny, rounded leaves form dense growth. Good for screens and hedges.

Crinum (Darling lily, Swamp lily)

E, FS to HS, H 1 m, W 80 cm. Darling lily (*C. flaccidum*) has drooping leaves to 50 cm and white trumpet flowers on thick stems from spring to summer. Swamp lily (*C. pedunculatum*) has stiff, broad, upright leaves and open, starry, white flowers on sturdy stalks in late spring and summer.

Elaeagnus (Japanese oleaster)

E, FS to HS, H 3–4 m, W 3–4 m. *E. pungens* has leathery leaves with wavy margins which are dark green above and silver-grey beneath. Scented cream flowers dotted brown appear in early autumn. Variegated forms are showier. Makes a good windbreak or hedge.

Euphorbia (Spurge)

E, FS, H 1 m, W 1 m. *E. characias* ssp. *wulfenii* is an upright, rounded shrub with blue-green foliage and large heads of sharp, lime green flower bracts in late winter through to spring. Stems contain milky latex. Other shrubby or succulent species of Euphorbia are useful in fire-prone areas.

Eupomatia (Bolwarra)

E, SS to S, H 2–6 m, W 1–2 m. Glossy, dark foliage and pink new growth. Bears unusual flowers and edible fruits. May be grown under trees.

Lavandula (Lavender)

E, FS, H 50 cm, W 40 cm. Rounded shrubs densely covered in silver-grey, aromatic foliage. Pale-lavender to purple flowers appear mainly in late winter through to spring. *L. angustifolia*, *L. dentata* and *L. stoechas* vary in foliage and flowers. Likes dry, hot summers.

Limonium (Perennial statice, Sea lavender)

E, FS, H 40 cm, W 60 cm. *L. latifolium*. Broad, rounded, slightly fleshy leaves form a large rosette. Tall stems of purple and white papery flowers stand high above foliage in spring and remain through summer and sometimes into autumn. Drought-tolerant.

Photinia

E, FS to HS, H 2–5 m, W 1–3 m. *P. glabra* 'Rubens' and *P. serratifolia*. Slightly leathery, dark foliage, with flushes of bright-pink new growth. Fluffy cream flowers in spring. Often used for hedging. Unsuitable for very hot areas.

Rosmarinus (Rosemary)

E, FS, H 60 cm–1 m, W 60 cm–1 m. *R. officinalis*. Highly aromatic, narrow foliage forms a rounded shrub. Blue flowers in spring. Decorative herb with culinary use. A prostrate form makes good ground cover.

Sedum (Stonecrop)

D, FS to SS, H 40–60 cm, W 40 cm. *S. spectabile*. Fleshy, soft, green scalloped leaves and large heads of pink to red flowers in late summer to autumn. Numerous other species of succulent sedums are suitable for use as ground covers.

Trees for fire-prone areas

Most fruit and nut trees are suitable for fire-prone areas, as well as introduced deciduous trees such as oak, maple, elm and beech. Australian native figs are also good choices for fire-prone areas but only if they can be planted at least 10 m from pipes or buildings. These trees are usually considered too large for the average garden but include Port Jackson fig (*Ficus. rubiginosa*), Moreton Bay fig (*F. macrophylla*) and Hill's fig (*F. microcarpa* var. *hillii*).

Acacia (Wattle)

E, FS to SS, H 8–20 m, W 5–15 m. Fast growing, with grey or green foliage that may be feathery, flat or needle-like. Many species are short-lived. Fluffy yellow flowers in rods or balls bloom mainly in winter through to spring but there is a wattle in flower every month of the year. Large but long-lived are cedar wattle (*A. elata*, H 15–20 m) and blackwood (*A. melanoxylon*, H 15–30 m). Other suggestions are Cootamundra wattle (*A. baileyana*, H 7 m), white sallow wattle (*A. floribunda*, H 8 m), sticky wattle (*A. howittii*, H 6 m) and Australian golden wattle (*A. pycnantha*, H 4–10 m), the national floral emblem.

Acmena (Lillypilly)

E, FS to HS, H 10–12 m, W 5–8 m. *A. smithii*. Attractive glossy leaves, white fluffy flowers in summer followed by round pink fruits during autumn and winter.

Brachychiton

E or D, FS to HS, H 10–20 m, W 5–15 m. Trees with variable leaf shapes and bell-shaped flowers in late spring or summer. Illawarra flame tree (*B. acerifolius*) is semi-deciduous, H 10–15 m with scarlet flowers. Lace bark (*B. discolor*) D, H 15–20 m, pink flowers. Kurrajong (*B. populneus*) E, H 10–15 m, cream flowers spotted crimson on the inside.

Buckinghamia (Ivory curl tree)

E, FS to SS, H 8–15 m, W 5–8 m. *B. celsissima*. Dark-green leaves of variable shape, curly cream flowers in late summer to autumn. Flowers attract birds.

Callicoma (Black wattle)

E, HS to S, H 6 m, W 3 m. *C. serratifolia*. Unrelated to wattle despite the common name, this tree has dark-green, toothed leaves and cream, ball-shaped flowers in spring. Plant stems were used in wattle-and-daub construction by early European settlers.

Ceratonia (Carob)

E, FS, H 10–12 m, W 6–8 m. *C. siliqua*. Tough, adaptable tree with shiny, leathery leaves. Green flowers appear on female trees in spring or summer. Insignificant male flowers appear on separate trees, although some may have both. Pollinated flowers form large pods of edible seeds which are used as a chocolate substitute.

Ceratopetalum (Christmas bush)

E, FS or HS, H 3–6 m, W 2–3 m. *C. gummiferum*. Pretty, shiny foliage. Its true flowers are cream but the decorative bracts are red or pink. In its natural habitat may reach 8–10 m tall.

Cercis (Judas tree)

D, FS, H 5–8 m, W 3–5 m. *C. siliquastrum*. Blue-green, round to heart-shaped leaves. Rosy-lilac pea flowers appear on the bare wood of branches, late winter to spring.

Elaeocarpus (Blueberry ash)

E, FS to SS, H 8–10 m, W 5 m. *E. reticulatus*. New growth is pink, maturing to dark-green, leathery leaves. Fringed, white, bell-shaped flowers are followed by small, rich-blue berries. Pink-flowered forms are also available.

Glochidion (Cheese tree)

E, FS to HS, H 6–10 m, W 4–7 m. *G. ferdinandi*. Broad, shiny leaves and insignificant flowers, which develop into distinctive flattened, cheese-like fruits that are on the tree most of the year. Flowers mid-spring.

Hymenosporum (Native frangipani)

E, FS to HS, H 8–10 m, W 3–6 m. *H. flavum*. Fairly pyramidal in shape with distinctly layered branches. Glossy foliage and scented cream spring flowers that age to yellow.

Ilex (Holly)

E or D, FS to HS, H 5–10 m, W 6–8 m. *I. aquifolium* and *I.* x *altaclarensis* are the evergreen varieties most often grown. Glossy leaves with spined wavy margins. Male and female flowers are borne on separate trees; both are needed to obtain berries. The berries are usually red. Several hundred species and cultivars of holly are in cultivation, some with variegated leaves and yellow or orange berries.

Laurus (Bay)

E, FS, H 8–10 m, W 3–5 m. *L. nobilis*. Dark-green, leathery leaves used as food flavouring. Small creamy-yellow flowers in spring. Male and female flowers are carried on separate trees. Green berries form on female trees (if the flowers are pollinated), maturing to black.

Melia (White cedar)

D, FS, H 10 –15 m, W 8–10 m. *M. azederach*. Fast-growing, adaptable and drought-tolerant tree with compound green leaves that turn deep yellow in autumn. Pale-lilac flowers in spring are followed by clusters of dull-gold berries. Fruit is toxic if eaten. Trees are sometimes defoliated by processional caterpillars.

Podocarpus (Brown pine)

E, FS, H 10–15 m, W 8–10 m. *P. elatus*. Narrow, lance-shaped leaves with a sharp point. Unusual blue-black edible fruits. Moderately slow to grow but adaptable to a wide range of conditions.

Schinus (Pepper tree)

E, FS, H 8–15 m, W 8–10 m. *S. areira*. Graceful, weeping foliage almost to ground level. Small creamy flowers in spring or summer, followed by small, decorative, bright-pink berries. Adaptable and drought-tolerant.

Stenocarpus (Firewheel tree)

E, FS to SS, H 10–15 m, W 5–8 m. *S. sinuatus*. Upright-growing tree with interesting wavy-edged foliage. Scarlet to orange flowers in a wheel shape late summer to autumn. Fairly slow to grow but very decorative.

Syzygium (Lillypilly)

E, FS, H 8–20 m, W 6–10 m. Glossy leaves, fluffy cream flowers in spring to summer followed by decorative, edible fruit which ripens in late summer to autumn. Small-leaf lillypilly (*S. luehmannii*) H and W 6–8 m, bright coral-red, pear-shaped fruit. S. *paniculatum*, H 15 m, W 10 m, also known as brush cherry. Its round fruits are cerise pink.

Tamarix (Tamarisk, Flowering cypress)

E or D, FS to HS, H 3–9 m, W 2–5 m. Fast-growing, small trees with narrow, pendulous foliage and feathery pink flowers. Adaptable, tolerating drought, saline soil and strong wind.

Tristaniopsis (Water gum)

E, FS to SS, H 8–15 m, W 6–8 m. *T. laurina*. Glossy, dark, occasionally red leaves. Clusters of small yellow flowers from late spring. Adaptable but likes regular water.

HINT

Be very wary of Coral trees (*Erythrina variegata* or *E. indica*) as they drop huge limbs without any apparent cause. An enormous Coral tree wiped out the power to our suburb when it fell over without warning. These weedy trees are spread by bird droppings.

DON BURKE

BURKE'S BACKYARD

GARDENING IN PERMANENTLY WET OR BOGGY SOIL

Some gardens encompass an area of permanently wet or boggy soil where many plants will not thrive. These areas include what are sometimes known as 'hanging swamps', where there is a layer of soil overlying sandstone and almost permanent seepage. However, many garden areas like this can be turned into an attractive feature with the right choice of plant. Bear in mind that the planting itself will dry out the soil in this area to an extent, and in extremely dry summers there may even be the need to give occasional supplementary water.

Perennials for wet and boggy soil

Acorus

H or E, FS to SS. Sweet flag (*A. calamus* 'Variegatus'), H 60 cm, W 40–60 cm. Broad, green, sword-shaped leaves striped cream or white form a spreading clump. Flowers insignificant. Japanese rush (*A. gramineus*), H 10–20 cm, W 10–15 cm. Fans of narrow green leaves form clumps. Variegated forms widely grown. Good edging plant.

Astilbe (Goat's beard)

H, HS or SS, H 60 cm, W 30–40 cm. Astilbe species and hybrids. Attractive foliage, tall, graceful plumes of soft flowers in white, crimson, pink or mauve appear in late spring or early summer in cool areas. Many named varieties. Looks best when mass-planted.

Blandfordia (Christmas bell)

E, FS, H 30–50 cm, W 10 cm. *B. grandiflora*, *B. nobilis*. Sparse, reedy leaves in small clumps. Yellow-tipped, scarlet bells held on stems high above foliage. Not easy to cultivate but worth trying in suitable conditions.

Blechnum (Water fern)

E, SS to S, H 30–60 cm, W 30+ cm. Several species of ferns with slightly leathery fronds that are variable in habit. New growth is often pink. Fishbone water fern (*B. nudum*) grows in a wide range of conditions. This is not the weedy fishbone fern *Nephrolepis cordifolia*.

Other species to try include *B. cartilagineum*, *B. penna-marina* and *B. wattsii*.

Canna

E or SD, FS, H 90–150 cm, W 25–30 cm. Broad, green or bronze leaves. Large, showy flowers in shades of red, pink, yellow, orange, cream or white. Plant in clumps for best effect.

Carex (Sedge)

E or H, FS to SS, H 50 cm–1 m, W 25–60 cm. *Carex* spp. A great range of species and cultivars ranging from compact clumps to large tussocks. Foliage colour may be brown, gold, variegated, green, grey-blue or silver. Some species may become invasive in warm regions.

Crinum (Darling lily, Swamp lily)

E, FS to HS, H 1 m, W 80 cm. Darling lily (*C. flaccidum*) has drooping leaves to 50 cm. White, trumpet-shaped flowers on thick stems through spring and summer. Swamp lily (*C. pedunculatum*) has stiff, broad, upright leaves. White, open, starry flowers are carried on strong stalks in late spring to summer.

Gunnera

H, HS to S, H 2.5 m, W 2–4 m. *G. manicata* is a very large plant suitable only for large gardens. Huge, strongly veined, lobed leaves are prickly underneath, as are the stems. A stiff, cone-shaped flower appears in early summer but is often not seen beneath the foliage. This is a magnificent feature plant for cooler climates.

Hosta

H, SS to S, H 25 cm, W 40 cm. Wide range of cultivars available. Attractive foliage may be various shades of green, variegated or blue-grey. White or mauve flowers appear in summer.

Iris

E or H, FS to HS, H 40 cm–1 m, W 25+ cm. *I. ensata* (formerly *I. kaempferi*) is summer-flowering with flattish flowers of lilac, purple, white or pink, many with lovely feathering on the flowers. Louisiana hybrids, with a huge range of named varieties, also have fairly flat flowers in rich colours, mainly from spring to early summer. *I. pseudacorus* (known as yellow flag) has tall, sword-like leaves and bright-yellow flowers in spring.

Lobelia (Cardinal flower)

H, FS to SS, H 60 cm–1 m, W 25 cm. *L. cardinalis* has dark-green leaves and tall spikes of scarlet flowers throughout summer. Named varieties with burgundy foliage are available.

Lysichiton (Skunk cabbage)

H, FS to SS, H 40 cm–1 m, W 30+ cm. *L. americanum* is a rich-yellow, arum-type flower with an unpleasant odour. *L. camschatensis* is a Japanese species with white, arum-like, sweet-smelling flowers. Both have large, wrinkled leaves. Both form dense colonies over time. Best grown in cool regions.

Primula

H, FS to SS, H 30 cm–1 m, W 30+ cm. Known as candelabra primulas, these lovely perennials are best in cool climates. Oval, crinkly, mid-green leaves, flowers in whorls on tall stems rise from the centres of leaf rosettes. Flower colour range includes white, yellow, orange, pink, purple and red. Many species include *P. bulleyana*, *P. denticulata*, *P. florindae*, *P. japonica*, *P. sikkimensis* and *P. viali*, which differs in having poker-like flowers in purple and red.

Rheum (Ornamental rhubarb)

H, FS to SS, H 1.5–2 m, W 1 m. Large, crinkled leaves with prominent veins. Flowering stems carry masses of cream flowers above the leaves in summer. Some cultivars have crimson to purple foliage. Best in cool areas.

Zantedeschia (Arum lily)

E or H, FS to S, H 50–75 cm, W 30+ cm. *Z. aethiopica* has dark, arrow-shaped leaves, pure white flowers with yellow spadix from late winter to spring. Very adaptable, this has become weedy in some areas. The variety 'Green Goddess' has white flowers edged and streaked with green.

Shrubs and trees for wet and boggy soil

Alnus (Alder)

D, FS, H 10–15 m, W 5–8 m. Common alder

Callistemon.

(*A. glutinosa*) has slightly pendulous branches bearing almost round leaves. Flowering catkins appear in late winter to spring, before the leaves. Woody, cone-like summer fruits ripen to brown and persist on trees to the following year. Best in cooler areas.

Banksia (Swamp banksia)

E, FS, H 3–4 m, W 1–3 m. *B. robur*. Large, toothed, leathery leaves, yellow-green flowers late summer through winter. Old flowers and large cones persist for some years. Plants sometimes prostrate.

Bauera (Dog rose)

E, HS to SS, H 70 cm–2 m, W 50 cm–2 m. *B. rubioides*. Tiny leaves on wiry stems. Plants may be upright or sprawling. Pink flowers from late winter to spring. White-flowered forms may also be available.

Callistemon (Bottlebrush)

E, FS, H 1 m–10 m, W 1.5–4 m. *C. citrinus* (red flowers) and its cultivars, *C. linearis*, (red flowers), *C. paludosus* (cream to yellow flowers) and *C. salignus* (cream to yellow flowers), should all do well in wet soils.

Casuarina (She-oak)

E, FS, H 5–20 m, W 3–8 m. Swamp she-oak (*C. glauca*), H 15–20 m. Grows well in wet soils, including saline soils.

Colocasia (Taro)

E or D, FS to SS, H 1–2 m, W 50+ cm. *C. esculenta* has large, arrow- or heart-shaped leaves on tall stems, an arum-type flower and edible tubers. *C. esculenta* 'Fontanesii' (grown as an ornamental only) has purple-black stems and dark veins on its leaves.

Epacris (Heath)

E, FS to HS, H 30 cm–1 m, W 20–50 cm. *E. impressa* (1 m) is Victoria's floral emblem. It's often straggly but has pink, red or white flowers in flushes throughout the year, peaking in spring. Coral heath (*E. microphylla*, H 30–60 cm) has pink buds opening to white flowers in mid-winter through to spring.

Eucalyptus (Gum tree)

E, FS, H 10–30 m, W 5–15 m. Bangalay (*E. botryoides*, 10–20 m) is a shade tree that also tolerates saline soils. Swamp mahogany (*E. robusta*, 10–15 m) has thick, reddish, spongy bark. Both have similar foliage, dark green above, paler beneath.

Hakea

E, FS to HS, H 2–8 m, W 2–4 m. Willow-leaf hakea (*H. salicifolia*, 3–6 m) has bushy growth suitable for screening, leathery, lance-shaped leaves and small white flowers in spring.

Melaleuca.

Lomatia

E, HS to SS, H 2–20 m, W 1–10 m. *L. myricoides* (H 2–5 m, W 2–3 m) has long, slender leaves and fragrant clusters of small cream flowers in summer.

Melaleuca (Paperbark)

E, FS, H 1–20 m, W 1–10 m. *M. leucadendron* and *M. quinquenervia* are both large trees (10–20 m), with thick, creamy, spongy bark, leathery leaves, and pale-yellow, bottlebrush-type flowers from late summer to early winter. Shrubs and small trees include *M. hypericifolia*, H 2–5 m, red flowers spring to summer; *M. linariifolia*, H 5–8 m, feathery white flowers in mid-spring to early summer; *M. nodosa*, H 3 m, yellow flowers in spring; *M. squarrosa*, H 2 m, yellow flowers in spring; and *M. thymifolia*, H 1 m, mauve to pink flowers mid-spring to summer.

Nyssa (Tupelo, Sour gum)

D, FS, H 15–20 m, W 6–10 m. *N. sylvatica* is a pyramid-shaped tree with almost horizontal branches and glossy green foliage that turns bright scarlet in autumn. The most brilliant autumn colour is seen in cool areas but these trees colour well even in fairly mild regions.

Salix (Willow)

D, FS, H 1–20 m, W 50 cm–10 m. Willows are unsuitable for the average home garden but are ideal for larger areas where wet soil exists. Best known are weeping willow (*S. babylonica*), white willow (*S. alba*) and its weeping form 'Tristis', tortured willow (*S. matsudana* 'Tortuosa') and pussy willow (*S. caprea*), which is also known as goat willow. In cool climates some of the shrubby willows may be available.

Sprengelia (Pink swamp heath)

E, FS, H 1 m, W 50 cm. Small, stem-clasping leaves, masses of pink, starry flowers from mid-winter to spring.

Tristianopsis (Water gum)

E, FS to HS, H 8–12 m, W 5–8 m. *T. laurina* has dark, glossy foliage and clusters of rich yellow flowers late spring to mid-summer. Adaptable to most conditions.

Courtyard designed by Eckersley/Stafford Design

This courtyard brilliantly combines furniture, paving, pots and plants.

PLANTS FOR COURTYARDS

Many courtyards are in shade for a good deal of the day so plants that rely on foliage colour and form are often a good choice. Seasonal colour can be provided by pots of flowering annuals or bulbs, but the bones of the planting should rely on foliage. However, there is often a difficult south-facing side that is in total shade for six months of the year, partial shade for another couple of months and full sun during the hottest months. There are plants that will cope with these conditions but they will need extra mulching, watering and attention during summer. Climbing plants should not be overlooked as they provide a decorative, softening effect for bare walls and fences and take up very little space at ground level. Support in the form of lattice, wires, plastic climbing net, wire mesh or poles must be provided.

Where a courtyard is enclosed on three sides by walls or fences, as is common in terrace houses, townhouses and some villas, it may be possible to build raised planting beds or boxes around the perimeter. If this is not an option, then large troughs or pots can be used. It is better to use a few large

containers of plants in a confined area rather than a large collection of small pots. Large numbers of small pots not only look fussy but require much more attention to watering and general maintenance.

Your choice of containers for courtyard planting will be influenced by the style of your house. Coloured glazed pots tend to suit modern homes while terracotta pots can be used in either modern or older, more traditional, settings. Real or mock sandstone containers are another possible choice. There are also many plastic pots, shaped and coloured to resemble classic terracotta containers. Plastic pots are, of course, lighter and easier to move around. If you are using large pots of stone, ceramic or terracotta, make sure you know where you want to position them before filling with potting mix, as they can be extremely heavy once filled.

Climbing plants for courtyards

Climbing plants are not self-supporting and use various methods to reach up into the sunlight. Tendril climbers have fine, curling tendrils that coil around thin supports like wire or string. Twining climbers twine their new shoots around a support while scramblers use downward curving hooks or prickles to grasp on to other plants or supports to pull themselves upwards. Self-clingers cling on to walls and fences with supplementary roots known as *adventitious* roots. Boston ivy, however, has a double set of climbing aids. Its tendrils wind around supports as well as using adhesive discs that are on the end of each tendril.

Clematis

D, FS or HS. For cool or temperate regions, twining clematis are a must. They like their roots in the shade and their heads in the sun. Spring to early summer flowers are large with a great range of colours in shades of blue, purple, pink, red and white. Some are two-toned.

Hedera (Ivy)

E, FS to S. English ivy (*H. helix*) is a self-clinging ivy, excellent for covering ugly masonry walls or rough paling fences. The species has dark-green, lobed leaves but there are varieties with leaves that are spotted, splashed, edged or streaked with cream or

HINT

Create the best show of potted plants in a small courtyard by making a collection of plants of different sizes, foliage colours and textures and flowering times. Keep some that love shade and some that love sun. You can rotate, mix and match them every few months for a continuous source of colour and variety. Use the cool-climate lovers for your winter show and rest them in a cool position out of the way with shelter over summer, and vice versa for the plants that love heat.

ROSEMARY DAVIES

GARDEN MEDIA PERSONALITY
AND CONSULTANT

yellow. Canary Islands ivy (*H. canariensis*) and its variegated forms have much larger leaves than English ivy.

Pandorea

E, FS to HS. *P. jasminoides*, a glossy-leaved twiner, is attractive even out of flower. Trumpet-shaped flowers are white with a crimson throat while the variety 'Rosea' has pink flowers with a crimson centre. Long-flowering, from spring to mid-summer.

Parthenocissus (Virginia creeper or Boston ivy)

D, FS or HS. *P. quinquefolia* and *P. tricuspidata* are vigorous, self-clinging climbers, ideal for covering masonry walls. They have large-lobed leaves that produce brilliant autumn colour. Sometimes attacked by vine-moth caterpillar.

Pyrostegia (Flame vine)

E, FS. A tendril climber prized for its winter display of bright-orange, tubular flowers. Growth is vigorous but easily controlled. Protect from frost.

Rosa (Rose)

E, FS to HS. Banksia rose (*R. banksiae*). Thornless stems, bright, pretty foliage, with large clusters of small yellow roses in spring. There is a pink form and a white-flowered form, too. Prune after flowering, not in winter. Few climbing roses are suitable for courtyards as they are too vigorous and thorny.

Solanum (Potato vine)

E, FS to HS. Vigorous, quick-growing, twining climber that flowers from late spring through to autumn. Small, white, starry flowers have yellow centres. May be deciduous in cool areas.

Trachelospermum (Star jasmine)

E, FS to SS. *T. jasminoides*. Probably the pick of all climbers for courtyards, this has strong, glossy foliage and masses of highly scented white flowers from mid-spring to early summer.

Vitis (Ornamental grape)

D, FS. *V. coignetiae*. Vigorous tendril climber with large-lobed leaves that display brilliant autumn colour. Often used to cover pergolas for summer shade and winter sun.

Wisteria
D, FS to HS. *W. sinensis*, *W. floribunda*. Vigorous twining climber that needs strong support. Scented, pendulous flowers in spring are usually lavender-blue but pink, white or purple varieties are available. Should be container-grown to restrict vigour.

Shrubs and perennials for courtyards

Agapanthus
E, FS to HS, H 60–90 cm, dwarf forms H 30 cm. Strong grower with strap-shaped leaves and large heads of blue or white flowers in summer.

Alocasia (Cunjevoi, Elephant ears)
E, SS to S, H 1 m, W 80+ cm. *A. brisbanensis* (formerly *A. macrorrhizos*). Large, arrow-shaped leaves and a cream, arum-type flower in summer followed by decorative, bright-red, berry-like fruit. Fruit is poisonous if eaten.

Asplenium (Bird's nest fern)
E, SS to S, H 1 m, W 1 m. *A. australasicum* (syn. *A. nidus*). Its large, nest-shaped rosette of light-green, slightly leathery fronds makes a good foil for other ferns and foliage plants.

Begonia (Cane-stemmed begonia)
E, SS to S, H 1.5–2 m, W 70+ cm. The many named varieties of cane-stemmed begonias have large, slightly succulent leaves with wavy edges. Many are patterned with spots or splashes of silver and may be red on the underside. Large trusses of flowers in pink, white, red or orange bloom from mid-spring through summer.

Camellia
E, HS to S, H 2–5 m, W 1–3 m. Ideal for screening or background planting, *C. sasanqua* and its numerous varieties are perfect for courtyards. Growth may be upright, pendulous or spreading. Easily shaped if a formal look is wanted. Dark, glossy foliage and flowers through autumn into mid-winter. Flowers are single or double in white and many shades of pink and red. Popular *C. japonica* and its varieties make

lovely specimen plants but are not so suitable for pruning and training. A huge range of flower types and colours is available.

Chamaedorea (Parlour palm)
E, SS to S, H 2 m, W 1 m. *C. elegans* is ideal for container growing. Slightly papery fronds are bright green. It bears small yellow flowers on orange-scarlet stems.

Clivia (Kaffir lily)
E, HS to S, H 35–60 cm. Broad, dark, strap-shaped leaves with orange or cream flowers in late winter to spring.

Cyathea (Tree fern)
E, HS to S, H 5–12 m, W trunk 15 cm, canopy 3–8 m. *C. cooperi* and the New Zealand national emblem *C. dealbata* are probably the best-known species. Rough brown trunks covered in silky hairs are topped with spreading crowns of long, lacy fronds. Lovely to look at, they also provide pretty patterns of light and shade. Soft tree fern (*Dicksonia antarctica*) has a thick, sometimes massive, trunk but its fronds appear very similar to those of the *Cyathea* species.

Clivia 'Cream Dalby'.

Escallonia

E, FS to SS, H 2–3 m, W 1–2 m. Small, shiny leaves, neat growth and white, pink or red flowers late spring through summer. May be clipped for hedging. New compact forms are available.

Fortunella (Cumquat)

E, FS to HS, H 1.5–2 m, W 70 cm–1 m. Attractive tub specimen with shiny foliage, scented cream blossoms and decorative orange fruit. 'Nagami' has oval fruit; 'Meiwa' or 'Marumi' have round fruit.

Gardenia

E, HS to FS, H 30 cm–1.5 m, W 50 cm–1 m. Dark, glossy foliage and heavily scented white flowers from late spring through summer. 'Radicans' is a low-growing, spreading ground cover. 'Florida', 'Grandiflora', 'Magnifica' and 'Professor Pucci' are tall growing.

Laurus (Bay tree)

E, FS to HS, H 8–10 m, W 3–5m. *L. nobilis* has dark, leathery leaves that are used in food flavouring. Bay trees grown in containers as standards make ideal accent plants for formal courtyards. They are too large for growing in open ground in this situation.

Lonicera (Honeysuckle)

E, FS to HS, H 1–2 m, W 50+ cm. Small-leaf or Box-leaf honeysuckle (*L. nitida*). Ideal for hedging or shaping. Can be hedged as low as 50 cm.

Nandina (Sacred bamboo)

E, HS to SS, H 1–2 m, W up to 1 m. *N. domestica.* Multi-stemmed with finely divided leaves and cream flowers in summer that are followed by decorative red berries. Suitable for pots or open ground.

Ophiopogon (Mondo grass)

E, SS to S, H 15–25 cm, W 20 cm. *O. jaburan.* Dense, dark-green, grassy foliage forms dense clumps. White flowers, occasionally lilac in summer. Ideal as edging or ground cover.

Phormium (New Zealand flax)

E, FS to HS, H 30 cm–2 m. *P. tenax* and *P. cookianum* and their numerous colourful varieties make strong accent plants. Stiff or weeping sword-shaped leaves in plain or mixed shades of bronze, burgundy, green, red, yellow, cream and pink. Grown for their striking foliage effects, the summer flower spikes are not outstanding but attract nectar-feeding birds.

Rhaphiolepis (Indian hawthorn)

E, FS to HS, H 1.5–3 m, W 1+ m. *R. indica.* Dark-green leathery leaves, white flowers with crimson throats from late winter to spring. Neat compact growth. Good in exposed windy sites. *R.* x *delacourii* has pretty pink flowers.

Rhapis (Lady palm)

E, HS to S, H 1.5–3 m, W 1 m. *R. excelsa* is a multi-stemmed, clumping palm that can be grown in containers or in the ground. The divided leaves are fan-shaped and dark green when grown in the shade. Slender lady palm (*R. humilis*) has narrower leaflets but is similar in other respects.

Syzygium (Lillypilly)

E, FS to HS, dwarf forms H 50 cm–2–3 m, W 50+ cm. Attractive dwarf forms of these rainforest trees are 'Bush Christmas', 'Lilliput', 'Aussie Compact', 'Blaze' and 'Tiny Trev'. All have glossy, dark foliage, pink new growth, fluffy cream flowers in summer followed by red or pink fruits. The species *S. wilsonii* (about 2 m) has pendulous pink new growth and deep-pink, powder-puff flowers from spring to early summer. 'Cascade' is an attractive hybrid to 3 m. Suitable for containers or open ground. All are suitable for clipping and shaping.

CLAY SOILS

Clay soils, even those that have been improved, often have an impervious layer of subsoil below. This can lead to drainage problems, a lack of air in the soil and the subsequent death of plants through root rot. Most clay soils can be improved by the addition of gypsum, which helps open up the soil, and all clay soils can be improved by the regular addition of well-decayed compost and animal manure. Mulching the soil surface is a must, as this helps to stop the surface soil from caking in dry weather. It is important to carefully select plants that have been found to tolerate these often difficult growing conditions.

Ground covers and climbers for clay soils

Akebia

D, FS to HS. *A. quinata*. Vigorous twining climber with divided leaves and brownish-purple flowers in spring. Flower fragrance is said to resemble chocolate.

Cissus (Kangaroo vine)

E, HS to S, W 2–3 m. *C. antarctica*. Covers large area when used as ground cover. Handsome glossy foliage and small greenish flowers in spring.

Grevillea

E, FS to HS. *G. juniperina*. Prostrate form of this species covers 1–2 m with dark, prickly foliage and yellow, spidery flowers. The 'Molonglo' form has apricot-coloured

> **HINT**
>
> No one ever thinks of planting natives in clay soil, or the damper parts of the garden, but bottlebrushes, most melaleucas and the swamp banksia (*Banksia robur*) flourish in heavy clay or moist soils. Another plant that grows happily in clay is the lillypilly (*Acmena smithii* var. minor).
>
> **DON BURKE**
> *BURKE'S BACKYARD*

flowers. *G*. 'Poorinda Royal Mantle' is a prostrate grower with lobed leaves and red toothbrush-style flowers from late winter to spring. Spreads 2–5 m.

Hardenbergia (False sarsparilla)

E, FS. *H. violacea* is a twining climber often used as ground cover. Dark, leathery leaves and masses of purple, pea-shaped flowers in spring. Another species *H. comptoniana* is known in its Western Australian home as native wisteria.

Jasminum (Jasmine)

E, FS to HS. *J. polyanthum* is an extremely vigorous (sometimes invasive) twining climber with glossy foliage and clusters of white, heavily scented flowers that emerge from bright-pink buds from late winter to spring. *J. officinale* 'Grandiflorum' is a loose, scrambling plant with scented white flowers that blooms in summer through to autumn and erratically at other times.

Solanum (Potato vine)

E, FS to HS. Blue potato vine (*S. crispum*) is a scrambling, fast-growing twiner with dark leaves. It bears clusters of blue flowers in summer. Grows 3–5 m tall.

Sollya (Bluebell creeper)

E, FS to HS. *S. heterophylla*. Twining climber grows to about 3 m, bearing small clusters of sky-blue, bell-shaped flowers from spring to summer. Good for wire fences, small trellises or for covering stumps or unsightly structures.

Shrubs and trees for clay soils

Acacia (Wattle)

E, FS to HS, H 5–15 m, W 5–15 m. Black wattle (*A. decurrens*, H 15 m) has a green trunk, very fine, dark foliage and showy, golden, ball-shaped flowers in spring. Cedar wattle (*A. elata*, H 15–20 m) has dark-green, divided leaves and cream, ball-shaped flowers in summer; Sticky wattle (*A. howittii*, H 3–6 m) has pendulous, spreading foliage and pale-yellow rod flowers in spring; Sydney golden wattle (*A. longifolia*, H 3–6 m) has light-green, lance-shaped leaves and yellow rod flowers in spring. These wattles all tolerate clay.

Acer (Maple)

D, FS to HS, H 2–20 m, W 1–10 m. Trident maple (*A. buergeranum*, H 6–10 m) has three-lobed leaves and a good autumn colour; Box elder (*A. negundo*, H 10–12 m) has unlobed leaves in threes and yellow autumn tones. It is a vigorous grower.

Acer.

Brachychiton (Kurrajong)

E, FS to HS, H 10–20 m, W 5–15 m. *B. populneus* has a massive trunk, variable leaf shape and cream, bell-shaped flowers with spotted throats in late spring to summer.

Callistemon (Bottlebrush)

E, FS to HS, H 60 cm–10 m, W 50 cm–6 m. Many species and cultivated varieties can be grown successfully in clay soils. These range from 'Little John' (H 60 cm) through to *C. citrinus* (H 3–4 m), *C. viminalis* (H 3–5 m) and the many varieties of these species through to *C. salignus* (H about 10 m).

Chaenomeles (Flowering quince, Japonica)

D, FS, H 2–3 m, W 1–1.5 m. *C. speciosa* and its varieties are multi-stemmed shrubs with woody, thorned stems that bear pretty blossoms in mid to late winter, or spring in cool areas. Blossoms may be white, pink, scarlet or apricot.

Crataegus (Hawthorn)

E, FS, H 3–6 m, W 2–3 m. Tall shrubs or small trees with spiny branches and lobed leaves that colour well in autumn. White or pink blossoms in spring; red, berry-like fruits in autumn.

Cupressus (Cypress)

E, FS, H 10–20 m, W 2–6 m. Arizona cypress (*C. glabra*) has reddish bark and dense, blue-grey foliage that forms a pyramidal tree of 12–15 m. Drought-tolerant once established.

Cydonia (Quince)

D, FS, H 5 m, W 5 m. *C. oblonga* is a small tree with a rounded form, dark-green leaves that are silvery beneath and large, pale-pink flowers in spring followed by pale-gold fruit that matures in autumn. Fruit subject to fruit fly and codling moth attack. If grown for ornament, prune after flowering to avoid fruit set.

Eucalyptus (Gum tree)

E, FS, H 10–30 m, W 5–15 m. Bangalay (*E. botryoides*, H 10–20 m); Tallow-wood (*E. microcorys*, H 15–20 m); Grey gum (*E. punctata*, H 10–20 m); Willow gum, Wallangarra white gum (*E. scoparia*, H 10–12 m); Mugga ironbark (*E. sideroxylon*, H 12–20 m); Forest red gum (*E. tereticornis*, H 15–25 m). These are a few of the species known to do well in clay soils. Local suppliers should be able to give further advice.

Fraxinus (Ash)

D, FS to HS, H 6–15 m, W 5–8 m. Fairly fast-growing ornamental trees have compound leaves that provide lovely autumn colour in cool areas. Desert ash (*F. oxycarpa*, H 10–12 m), yellow autumn tones; Syrian ash (*F. syriaca*, H 12–15 m), yellow in autumn.

Gleditsia (Honey Locust)

D, FS, H 10–20 m, W 6–10 m. *G. triacanthos* is a large tree covered in savage thorns that make it unsuitable for the garden; however, thornless varieties 'Sunburst' and 'Ruby Lace' are ideal. 'Sunburst', H 8–10 m, bright lime-green, feathery foliage becomes gold in autumn. 'Ruby Lace', H 8–10 m, reddish-bronze foliage deepens to burgundy in autumn.

Hydrangea

D, SS or S, H 0.5–3 m, W 0.5–2 m. Large, showy mop-heads of flowers in summer. Flowers may be white, pink, red or blue. Likes ample moisture in dry months.

Lagerstroemia (Crepe myrtle)

D, FS to HS, H 2–6 m, W 1–3 m. *L. indica* is a small vase-shaped shrub or tree with attractive mottled trunk. Ruffled summer flowers may be white, lavender, cerise and other shades of pink or red. Powdery mildew common in humid areas but the 'Indian Summer' range of varieties has resistance to this fungal disease.

Liquidambar (Sweet gum)

D, FS to HS, H 10–20 m, W 4–9 m. One of the few trees to produce glorious autumn colour even in mild areas. Large pyramidal tree with lobed, almost star-shaped, leaves.

Malus (Crabapple)

D, FS or HS, H 3–5 m, W 3–5 m. Ideal small tree for home gardens, providing abundant spring blossom, shade, decorative fruit and colourful autumn foliage. Many lovely species and varieties.

Nerium (Oleander)

E, FS to HS, H 3–5 m, W 2–4 m. *N. oleander* is a tough shrub that adapts to most conditions with the exception of very cold climates. Long, lance-shaped leathery leaves and masses of flower from late spring through to summer and sometimes into autumn. Flowers may be white, pink, crimson or apricot. Some attractive dwarf forms grow less than 2 m high.

Phormium (New Zealand flax)

E, FS to HS, H 1.5–2 m, W 1–2 m. *P. tenax* has stiff, sword-shaped leaves and a brownish-red flower spike that stands high above the foliage during summer. There are many varieties with colourful foliage now available.

Prunus

D, FS or HS, H 1.5–6 m, W 1–6 m. Many lovely, spring-flowering shrubs and trees are included in this group. *P. glandulosa* forms a clump of upright woody stems to 1.5 m and bears pink or white flowers in late winter to spring. Flowering cherry plum (*P. x blireana*, H 5 m) is a vase-shaped tree with slightly bronze foliage, which appears after the double, pink blossoms have fallen.

Tristaniopsis (Water gum)

E, FS to HS, H 8–12 m, W 5–8 m. *T. laurina* is a round-headed tree with dark, glossy foliage and clusters of yellow flowers from late spring to mid-summer.

Ulmus (Elm)

D or SD, FS to HS, H 9–20 m, W 9–25 m. Chinese elm (*U. parvifolia*) is a broad-domed tree with an attractive mottled trunk. Graceful weeping branches carry small, neat, shiny foliage.

22
Designer Plants

What are designer plants? The term 'designer plants' can mean many different things to different gardeners, but in this chapter we've looked at plants with strong structure that are used as features to make design statements in the garden. Plants may be classed as 'designer' because they have striking shapes, such as bromeliads, cacti or succulents, showy flowers such as proteas or, as with ornamental grasses, they create garden accents. They might also be called designer plants because they are beloved – and much used – by garden designers. Place these plants wisely and you will immediately create points of interest in the garden that will increase its overall visual impact.

BROMELIADS

Bromeliads are unusual and attractive plants that are easy to cultivate. Many species are grown outdoors successfully in the tropics, subtropics and generally mild areas. They can also be grown indoors although flowering rarely occurs unless there are ideal conditions of light, temperature and humidity.

Most bromeliads are epiphytes, growing on trees, rocks or cliff faces – although they are not parasites. Some are ground dwellers. Most have leaves arranged in a rosette of spiralling leaves that channel water into a central 'tank'. Many have microscopic water-absorbing scales on their leaves too. Leaves may be green, silver, maroon or red, some are multicoloured. Many have bands, spots or stripes of contrasting colour. Leaf margins may be smooth or spiny. Flowers may be tall and spectacular, held high above the foliage on strong stems, or they may be small and almost hidden in the centre of the plant rosette. Some have flowers that last a very short time while others give a showy display over many weeks. The flower bracts generally provide the most brilliant colour as the true flowers they enclose are often fairly small.

These lovely plants can be cultivated in several ways but free drainage is their prime requisite. Whether grown in containers or in the ground, the growing medium must be very coarse. Growing media could include gravel, coarse bark, charcoal, leaf mould, aged compost or mixtures of these. When growing in plastic pots, it may be necessary to place a layer of stones in the pot base to provide stability, as plants are sometimes top-heavy. Terracotta pots can be useful as they have extra weight.

When growing bromeliads in the ground, it is best to build up an area so that it is higher than the surrounding soil. Pockets in a lightly shaded rockery can also be used to great advantage. Thoroughly mix some coarse material (such as orchid compost) into the soil before planting. Make a hole for the roots then, holding the plant in one hand, backfill the hole, pushing the soil under and around the roots so that the plant is sitting high on the ground. If the plant wobbles or is unstable, then push a couple of stones under the plant sides to hold it until the roots take hold.

Vase-shaped plants are best watered by filling the central cup and allowing it to overflow down to the root area. Plants growing on boards or logs are best watered with a hose giving a gentle spray. Through the warm months, plants may need watering every couple of days while in winter this may be reduced to once a week depending on conditions.

Bromeliads can also be grown on boards, stumps (especially old tree fern stumps) or artificial logs. You can make a log by forming a cylinder of plastic or galvanised mesh and packing this with sphagnum moss and bark. Plant roots can be carefully pushed through holes in the mesh into the growing medium and tied on with plastic-coated wire or budding tape. Once the roots have taken hold, the ties can be removed. These 'logs' are light and can be suspended from fences, balcony rails or the roof of a pergola or shadehouse. Most of these plants do well in filtered sunlight, although some can be grown in full sun.

Top five bromeliads

NEOREGELIA

One of the common names for this bromeliad group is 'Heart of Flame'. This aptly describes the way the plant's centre colours in order to attract pollinating insects to the insignificant flowers.

PINEAPPLE

The best-known bromeliad, pineapple, grows in humid, frost-free climates. It can take two years for the fruit to develop and ripen. In cool climates, the pineapple can be grown as a scene-stealing indoor plant.

BILLBERGIA NUTANS

Billbergia Nutans is one of the easiest bromeliads to grow. 'Nutans' means 'nodding', and is used to describe the drooping flower stems. It will grow indoors or out and, as long as the soil is well drained, is tough enough to handle light frosts.

SPANISH MOSS

Spanish moss, or old man's beard, can exist on the moisture and oxygen it captures from the surrounding air. It doesn't need any soil and can be draped from any convenient position in a warm, humid, lightly shaded position. The greatest threat it faces is from passing birds – they love to steal sections of the soft plant to line their nests!

AECHMEA

The most popular aechmeas have blue-grey leaves and a central clump of jewel-like mauve flowers that hide themselves amongst pink bracts.

NEOREGELIA

PINEAPPLE

Bromeliad groups

Alcantarea

Alcantarea imperialis 'Rubra', is a striking designer bromeliad that is popular for providing an eye-catching accent in frost-free gardens. Its clump of shiny leaves with red/purple undersides grows slowly to about 1.2m tall and 1.5m across but the central flower spike can reach up to 3m. This large bromeliad looks good in a raised garden bed or a large container where it can be seen at its best.

Aechmea

Originating from Central and South America, this is possibly the most widely grown group. There is a very large number of species and cultivated varieties that can be grown. Best in areas with mild winters, they need to be kept frost-free. Leaves form vase-shaped rosettes with an open central cup. Plants vary in height from 15 cm to about 2 m, but their flowering stems are often much taller than the foliage. Foliage may be green, burgundy, silvery, variegated with yellow or pink on a green background, or streaked, banded or spotted in a contrasting colour. Flowering spikes stand clear of the foliage and come in a great range of colours including red, yellow, purple, blue, pink, orange and white. Flowering times vary, but many flower in late summer through autumn while others bloom through winter. *A. fasciata* is a popular species with silvery-grey foliage banded in silver. The flower developing in the centre of the rosette is a large pyramid of pink bracts enclosing small blue flowers. *A. chantinii* has dark-green foliage heavily banded in silvery white. A tall red stem holds the red and yellow flowers high above the foliage. 'Foster's Favorite' has deep-burgundy foliage and deep-blue flowers displayed on a pendulous stem. *A. weilbachii* has bright-green foliage and bright-red and purple flowering stems that last for many weeks.

Ananas (Pineapple)

The pineapple, *A. comosus*, grows as a rosette of very stiff, spiny, grey-green leaves. It is a terrestrial (or ground) grower. Purple-blue flowers with red bracts appear on a central stem. After the flowers fade, large fruits form. These are topped with a tuft of leaves that can be used to propagate a new plant. The fruit is slow to mature, especially in cooler areas. There is also a form with cream-striped leaves that may take on pink tones in strong light.

Billbergia

Easily grown, this group of plants is very adaptable to a wide range of growing conditions and is not even fussy about soil. Most will take some direct sun although midday sun, especially in summer, tends to scorch leaf tips. The best known is probably Queen's tears (*B. nutans*) with narrow, grey-green leaves and small blue and green flowers surrounded by bright-pink bracts. *B. pyramidalis* has spiny, light-green leaves that form a rosette. Its flower is a bright orange-scarlet pyramid of bracts; the small flowers are red with violet tips. *B. zebrina* has prickly dark leaves spotted and banded in silvery-white with a drooping flower spike of bright-pink bracts surrounding small green to yellowish flowers.

Guzmania

This group of bromeliads is grown mainly for its lovely rosettes of generally spineless foliage although some have very attractive flowers. This group has been widely hybridised with the *Vriesea* group to produce some spectacular cultivated varieties. Foliage may be a plain, bright glossy green, striped with pink or gold, or sometimes cross-banded in a contrasting colour. *G. sanguinea* has flattish rosettes of shiny green, which are sometimes spotted in a darker colour. As flowering time nears, the centre of the rosette becomes flushed red or sometimes yellow to orange. Flowers, which are held low in the rosette, are yellow or white and surrounded by red bracts. *G. musaica* is grown for its spreading rosettes of dark leaves patterned in beige to brown, purple or darker green. Flowers are yellow with pink bracts. *G. lingulata* has narrow, shiny green leaves and a striking flower head of bright-red bracts surrounding white flowers.

Neoregelia

This popular group is definitely grown for its foliage alone as its flowers are small and sunk

This hybrid guzmania has stunning flowers.

into the central cup of the plant rosette. This group has often been referred to as 'heart of flame' or 'blushing bromeliads' because so many in the group undergo a strong colour change in the rosette centre at flowering time. *N. carolinae* is by far the most commonly grown species. The centre of the plain green rosette becomes bright red before tiny purple flowers develop in the rosette. The cream and green variegated form *N. carolinae* 'Tricolor' also develops the strong red centre at flowering. *N. concentrica* has broad, green leaves blotched dark purple. The plant centre becomes a dull violet at flowering time. *N. marmorata* has broad leaves marbled in dark red and consequently is known as marble plant. *N. spectabilis* is known as the painted fingernail, as the broad, glossy leaves are tipped in bright red. Leaf undersides are banded in greyish white. Small blue flowers with red bracts form low in the rosette.

Puya

Most plants in this group are more cold-tolerant than the majority of bromeliads as many have their origins in the high Andes. The largest of all known bromeliads is *P. raimondii* that may grow 3–4 m high. Few

HINT

Most premium Australian Standard potting mixes work well. There is a catch though. A mix might claim to contain enough fertiliser for three months' growth. However by the time you purchase the mix, some or all of the three months will have passed, and the fertiliser might support adequate growth for only about one month. I suggest adding a controlled release fertiliser at the recommended rate either at the time of potting or shortly after.

BRIAN SAMS

HORTICULTURIST, TOOWOOMBA

WWW.WATTLETREEHORTICULTURE.COM.AU

species are generally available, but those worth seeking out are *P. berteroniana* and *P. venusta*. *P. berteroniana* forms a spiny plant about 1 m high, bearing a tall stem of metallic blue-green flowers in summer. *P. venusta* makes a silver-grey rosette of spiny leaves from which a strong pink stem emerges, bearing purple flowers.

Tillandsia

This is a varied group of epiphytes, the best known being Spanish moss, *T. usneoides*, which with its thread-like foliage is seen hanging from trees and overhead wires in the southern United States and many parts of South America. However, most species form rosettes of fairly stiff foliage that may be green, grey or even reddish. Species from fairly arid regions have silvery-grey foliage while those from humid forest areas have soft green leaves. The true flowers are small and tubular. They appear from floral bracts that often form flattish, paddle-shaped heads. *T. cyanea* is the most commonly grown species, having small violet flowers that appear from strong pink bracts.

Vriesea

This group has been widely hybridised and contains some large and very attractive species. The so-called king of bromeliads, *V. hieroglyphica*, has broad, spreading leaves that form a rosette up to 1 m high and wide. The arching mid-green leaves are banded in dark-green to purple-brown squiggles, thought to resemble the hieroglyphs of the ancient Egyptians. The flowering stem has greenish-yellow bracts surrounding yellow flowers. Parrot feather (*V. psittacina*) forms a rosette of pale-green leaves while the upright flower spike has yellow-tipped red bracts and yellow-green flowers.

CACTI AND SUCCULENTS

A cactus is a succulent plant with the capacity to store water in its swollen stems and roots. Not all succulent plants are cacti. Cactus plants have some special characteristics. Cactus plants are mainly round or cylindrical in shape with a ribbed surface. The ribbing exposes less surface area to the sun, thus cutting down on moisture loss. They also have sharp spines that are actually modified leaves that have evolved as part of their defence against their natural arid environment. All cactus have areoles that are small woolly cushions from which both spines and flower buds emerge. Cactus flowers are short-lived but very beautiful. Flowers have a satiny texture and come in every colour except blue. Many have pink, red or yellow flowers that after pollination form brightly coloured berry-like fruits. All cacti are native to the Americas with the greatest number having their origins in the low-rainfall areas of the southwestern United States and Mexico.

Cactus can be successfully grown outdoors in regions of low rainfall and low humidity. In wetter or more humid regions winter rain will kill the plants unless you can provide covering. They may be grown in pots or in the ground close to the house if there is protection from overhanging eaves. They can also be grown indoors in very bright light or on balconies and terraces. Cactus do not generally blend in well with most other types of garden plants but do mix very attractively with most succulents.

Potted plants should be grown in a sharp draining mix of coarse sand, crushed sandstone, fine gravel and compost or coir peat. Use slow-release fertiliser during the warmer months of the growing season, and water only as the mix dries out. In winter, restrict watering. Some growers never water in winter at all.

Avoid injury when handling cactus by wearing sturdy gloves and using a band made of folded cardboard, paper or bubble wrap to hold the plant. Wrap the band around the plant and hold it firmly where the pieces come together. Kitchen tongs or wooden spoons can also be used to lift and move cactus or to hold plants while repotting.

Cactus species

Astrophytum (Bishop's cap)
The most popular species in this group have very few spines. *A. myriostigma* has an overall shape like a bishop's mitre. It may be green, dull purple or blue-green with some spines along the ribs, but the body is speckled all over with small white scales. Flowers are bright yellow. In cultivation it is slow growing but may eventually reach melon size after many years. *A. ornatum* may also be called bishop's cap but is more often called star cactus. Its growth is cylindrical; its ribs are heavily spined.

Cephalocereus (Old man cactus)
Requiring minimal attention, this is a favourite of both children and adults alike. *C. senilis* is covered in long white hair that almost obscures the finely-ribbed, grey-green, column-shaped body. It is slow growing and may only reach a height of 30 cm in a pot but up to 1–2 m in the open ground. In its native Mexico it can reach heights of 15 m.

Cleistocactus (Silver torch)
Although there are many species in this group, only one is common in cultivation. *C. straussii* grows 1–2 m high and looks its best planted in groups. Branching from the base, clumps may eventually spread 1–2 m. Ribbed upright columns are densely covered in fine spines, giving plants a woolly appearance. Red tubular flowers emerge almost at right angles from the column. Fruit rarely forms, as these plants are pollinated by humming-birds in their native South America.

Echinocactus (Golden barrel)
Common in cultivation, *E. grusonii* is rare and threatened in its native Mexico. Slow-growing, it may, after many years, reach its maximum size of about 1 m high and wide. It is unlikely to bear its yellow flowers until it is 40–60 cm wide. The spherical, ribbed body is dark green and covered in fierce golden-yellow spines. In time, plants produce offsets that can be separated from the parent plant during spring or summer.

Ferocactus (Fish hook or Barrel cactus)
Reasonably fast-growing, these cacti form flattened spheres with well-defined ribs that are covered with fierce spines, which are hooked in some species. In the wild some grow 1–3 m high, although many never exceed 40 cm. They are very much smaller in cultivation. The colourful spines are most decorative, especially in species like *F. acanthodes* and *F. latispinus* where the spines are red. *F. wislizenii* is known as candy cactus in Mexico where its succulent fruits are stewed and candied. Most species are solitary growers but some form clumps over the years.

Gymnocalycium (Chin cactus)
This is a popular group of cactus for beginners as they are not difficult to cultivate and most produce plenty of offsets from an early age. They are mostly small and globular and it is the protrusion below each spined areole that gives it the name 'chin'. Few grow higher than 10 cm although some reach 25 cm. Popular species are *G. andreae*, which bears yellow spring flowers, and *G. bruchii*, which has pale-pink flowers. Both produce plenty of offsets to form little colonies. Flowers in the various species may be white, cream, yellow, pink or a deep wine-red.

Mammillaria (Pincushion or Strawberry cactus)
This is a very large group of cacti, possibly the most popular of all those in cultivation. Most are easy to grow and produce offsets readily, thus forming attractive groups. Most are small, rounded plants, densely covered in spines, but some species have fat finger-like stems. From a young age plants produce rings

Mammillaria.

of flowers around the crown of the plant from spring to early summer. Some, like *M. prolifera* (sometimes called little candles), form large colonies that have cream flowers followed by small red fruits. Plants rarely grow more than 6 cm high. *M. hahniana* produces a neat ring of cerise flowers on the crown of the plant. These are followed by the red fruits that give it the name of birthday cake cactus. Some species are covered in white wool below their spines so that they are sometimes referred to as snowballs or powder puffs. These include *M. bocasana*, *M. plumosa* and *M. sempervivi*.

Opuntia (Prickly pear)

Several species of prickly pear are known as devastating weeds in Australia, Africa and India, but there are a number of small, non-invasive species that are most decorative. Many people enjoy the fruit of Indian fig (*O. ficus-indica*) which is widely grown. It is a large, tree-like cactus that may grow to a 5 m height and width. All species of *Opuntia* have flattened, padded joints dotted with areoles. Known as chollas in south-western United States, one popular species, *O. bigelovii*, is known as teddy bear cholla, as its spines are so dense they resemble fur. It grows 1–2 m high. Bunny ears (*O. microdasys*) grows only 40–60 cm high and has dark-green pads dotted with white

areoles from which emerge masses of white, yellow or brown spines. Beaver tail (*O. basilaris*) branches from the base with sparsely spined pads that are grey-purple. It is generally less than 40 cm high.

Pereskia (Leafy cactus)

Despite its appearance this plant is classified as a cactus. *P. aculeata* is a leafy shrub that becomes a vine with large recurved spines that allow it to climb as high as 8–10 m.

Outside the tropics, it most often remains shrub-like. It is cultivated for its edible fruit known as the Barbados gooseberry.

Rebutia (Crown cactus)

Easy to cultivate, plants in this group of cacti stay small, readily produce offsets and generally flower freely. Round or barrel-shaped with fairly soft spines, their flowers develop on the lower half of the plant. Flowers may be yellow, orange, pink, violet or red, with white flowers being found in some hybrids. Many popular varieties grow only 5–10 cm high, making them ideal for pot culture, especially indoors.

Schlumbergera (Crab cactus, Zygocactus)

These popular plants are now available in a great range of colours. Ideal in pots or hanging baskets, they are greatly enjoyed for their autumn to winter flowering and ease of culture. Their flat, segmented stems have an arching habit which is quite graceful. The species *S. truncata* and *S. x buckleyi* are the parents of many modern varieties. Flowers are mainly in the pink to red shades, but white, salmon and violet shades are now seen often. These plants prefer to be grown in filtered sunlight or with morning sun and afternoon shade.

SUCCULENT PLANTS

Succulents are water-retaining plants that are currently enjoying a surge of popularity. They are easy-care, drought-tolerant and attractive. Some are frost-tolerant while others are very sensitive to cold. Unlike cacti, which all belong to the same botanical family, there are succulent plants in many families, including the daisy family and the lily family. There is an amazing diversity of form and foliage type that can be teamed with a range of garden plants and, of course, cacti. Generally, except for the larger species of *Euphorbia*, they make excellent container plants.

Succulents are best grown in an open sunny situation with free-draining soil. If there is any doubt about the drainage it is best to raise the planting area above the existing soil level or plant on mounds. Before planting, dig in some well-rotted compost or manure. Plants like to be watered fairly regularly during the warm months of the year but kept much drier in winter. Potted plants should be allowed to dry out between waterings. In areas of high winter rainfall it is best to grow plants in containers that can be moved under cover to avoid waterlogging and rotting of plants. Use slow-release fertiliser from spring through summer but don't overdo feeding, as this can result in soft, sappy growth that will not stand up to periods of tough weather conditions.

Aeonium

E, FS, H 5 cm–2 m, W 10 cm–1 m. This group of succulents forms flat, saucer-shaped rosettes of shiny foliage. Some, like *A. tabuliforme*, grow almost flat to the ground while *A. arboreum* becomes a branched shrub up to 2 m high. This species has pale-green rosettes on sturdy stems but a popular variety of this is 'Schwarzkopf', which has dark-mahogany to burgundy foliage. Both

Top five succulents

AGAVE ATTENUATA

Because of its sculptured shape, this popular succulent features prominently in many modern gardens. Its fleshy grey-green leaves are spineless so the plant doesn't present any danger to passers-by.

ALOE VERA

Grow an aloe vera and you'll have an on-hand remedy for burns and scalds. Simply snap off a small section and smear the juice over the affected area.

SEDUM 'AUTUMN JOY'

This plant combines an amazingly tough constitution with soft and pretty autumn flowers. These start off in pink shades but gradually change to coppery tones as the flower ages. It dies down completely in winter.

JADE (PORTULACARIA)

Jade is said to bring good fortune. Grow it near the front door and good luck will follow you inside. Jade plants will grow in sun or full shade but must have good drainage and a frost-free position.

KALANCHOE

While winter/spring-flowering *Kalanchoe blossfeldiana* will grow and bloom outdoors in frost-free climates, it also makes a successful indoor plant.

Balconies can typically be hot and dry places for plants. Plunge small pots into a bucket of water for a few minutes to give them a good soak. This is good way of getting water to the whole root area, and to prevent soil from drying out and becoming hydrophobic.

LOUISE McDAID

EDITOR, GARDEN WRITER AND DESIGNER

the species and its variety can be grown equally well in the ground or in containers. While all species need a well-drained growing medium, *A. tabuliforme* must be protected from excessive rain or irrigation as it will rot rapidly if water lodges in its crown. In its native Canary Islands, it grows in crevices on vertical cliff faces.

Agave

E, FS, H 1–1.5 m, W to 1 m. Agaves make great feature plants and can be grown in the ground or in containers. Their stiff leaves

Agave.

form large rosettes that may be up to 1 m across. Most have spiky margins although the popular, fast-growing *A. attenuata* has smooth grey-green leaves. Flower spikes of agaves emerge from the centre of the plant, often reaching several metres high. Once an agave has flowered, the plant will slowly die but not before it has produced numerous offsets or suckers that can be detached to start afresh. *A. americana* was named 'century plant' because it was thought to live that long before producing a flower. However, the real time is more like twenty to thirty years. This species is plain green but there are some attractive forms striped cream or yellow. Creamy-yellow flower spikes may reach 4–6 m in height. An outstanding feature plant is the slow-growing *A. victoriae-reginae*. Its dark-green leaves are attractively patterned in white, but the tips are very sharp. Some agaves are frost-tolerant while others need warm conditions.

Aloe

E, FS, H 40 cm–6–8 m, W 30 cm–2 m. There are over 300 species of aloe, the best known being *A. vera*, which is used in cosmetics, shampoos and in burn treatments. It is a suckering plant, growing 30–50 cm high, which forms clumps of thick, fleshy, pale-green leaves that are flecked white. Tubular yellow flowers appear on a branched stem. Candelabra plant (*A. arborescens*) grows to about 3 m and forms a multi-branched shrub topped with rosettes of fleshy leaves that bear showy pink-orange flowers in winter. Fan aloe (*A. plicatilis*) grows up to 5 m. Its flat, succulent leaves are arranged in one plane. Vivid red flowers stand high above the foliage. Aloe flowers are tubular and mostly in shades of red or yellow; all attract nectar-feeding birds.

Crassula

E, FS to HS, H 15 cm–2 m, W 10 cm–1 m. This is another large group of succulents of about 200 species, but few are common in cultivation. Most often grown is shrubby *C. arborescens* that reaches about 1.5 m in a container or more in the ground. Almost circular, grey-green leaves are neatly edged in red and it produces masses of pink, starry flowers in late autumn through to winter.

HINT

Once established in the right situation, succulents thrive with little care. But the very fact they are such tough plants leads some people to imagine nothing can harm them.

Surprisingly then, succulents – in particular tall columnar cacti – can suffer burns if you bring them from a nursery's shadehouse and plant them straight out in mid-summer sun. The sunburn will not kill them but it produces scars which, given these plants' longevity, could remain unsightly for years.

Avoid sunburn by buying succulents in autumn or winter, so they have several months to get accustomed to ever-increasing sunshine, before summer peaks.

JULIA BERNEY

HORTICULTURAL–AGRICULTURAL
FREELANCE EDITOR

C. *ovata* is very similar to C. *arborescens* but its fleshy leaves are plain green and its flowers white to very pale pink. A very different species is London pride (*C. multicava*), a vigorous, semi-prostrate plant with dark, round or oval leaves sometimes used as ground cover. Its small, pink and white, star-like flowers appear in spring.

Echeveria (Hen and chickens)

E, FS to HS, H 5–15 cm, W spreading 20–50 cm. Popular in Victorian times and enjoying a great resurgence of interest is this group of neat, rosette-forming plants. The overlapping leaves may be green, blue to grey, or silver, many with pink flushes. Leaves may be smooth or covered in fine silky hairs. Their growth habit is neat and formal and they look attractive in containers or in the ground.

Flowering times vary but most bloom during late winter or spring through to summer. Flowers are held on tall stems high above the foliage and are bell-shaped, mostly red, yellow or orange They tend to multiply readily, forming decorative clumps. *E. elegans* forms a neat rosette of silvery-blue, fleshy leaves that may take on pink tones in cold weather. Species covered with fine, velvety hairs include *E. setosa*, ('Mexican firecracker'), *E. pilosa* and *E. pulvinata*. Some hybrid varieties are known as painted ladies, as their leaf margins are deep pink to red and crinkled or wavy.

Haworthia

E, FS to HS, H 5–10 cm, W 10–20 cm. These rosette-forming succulents are generally stemless but show a great range of variation in form and colour. They are easy-care but while they can take regular water in the warm months, they must be kept dry while dormant or they will rot. *H. attenuata* has dark leaves with a line of white spots down both leaf surfaces while its form *clariperla* has rows of tiny white dots that are very heavy on the outer surface. *H. cymbiformis* has pale-green, translucent leaves forming a neat rosette. Some forms of this species are pink-flushed. *H. truncata* produces two rows of fat, upright leaves that look like stepping stones. *H. tessellata* has blue-green, fleshy foliage finely chequered with pale lines.

Kalanchoe

E, FS to HS, H 10 cm–2+ m, W 10 cm–1 m. This is an extremely diverse group of plants ranging from small neat species ideal for pot culture to shrub- or tree-like species like the striking felt bush, *K. beharensis*. Capable of growing up to 5–6 m in its native Madagascar, it rarely exceeds 1.5–2 m in cultivation. Its large, wavy-edged leaves are covered in fine hairs that have a distinctly felty texture. Flaming Katy (*K. blossfeldiana*) is probably the most familiar member of this group. It is a pretty garden or pot plant with dark, scalloped leaves. Masses of small flowers in red, yellow, bright pink or white appear in late winter to spring. It is best grown in dappled sunlight or with morning sun and afternoon shade. *K. fedtschenkoi* is popular for its blue-green, scalloped foliage and its masses of pinky-red,

Blue chalk sticks (Senecio serpens) *is a hardy ground cover.*

bell-shaped flowers in summer. Different named varieties have cream leaf margins or the whole leaf may be flushed pink or cream. Lavender scallops (*K. pumila*) is another small plant, good for pots or hanging baskets. Its leaves have a silvery bloom and its small bright-cerise flowers stand well above the foliage in spring. *K. tomentosa*, known as panda or plush plant, has brown-tipped, furry, grey leaves that form upright rosettes. In cultivation it is rarely more than 30–40 cm high but it may grow to 1 m high in its habitat.

Portulacaria (Jade)
E, FS to HS, H 2–3 m, W 1.5 m Jade (*P. afra*) can be found with plain green or variegated leaves. It has thick brown stems and small, round, succulent leaves. It may be grown in a container or in the garden. It adapts well to tough, dry conditions but its appearance will be improved with regular watering in warm weather.

Sedum (Stonecrop)
E or D, FS to HS, H 5 cm–50 cm, W 10+ cm. This very large group of succulents contains a number of familiar plants. *S. acre* is a small, mat-forming succulent with tiny pale-green leaves and bright-yellow flowers through summer. Burro's tail (*S. morganianum*) is best displayed in hanging baskets where its long trails of blue-green, fleshy leaves can be seen to advantage. Display it where it cannot be knocked, as it is very brittle. Jellybean plant (*S. rubrotinctum*) is a popular pot plant as its small, swollen, succulent leaves grow in pretty rosettes. Its green leaves take on red hues in cold weather or when it is very dry. *S. sieboldii* has round blue-green leaves and a spreading habit. It bears its starry pink flowers in late summer. The cream variegated form is very pretty. *S. spectabile* and its varieties are most often grown amongst other garden plants, especially perennials. Growing 40–60 cm high it has soft green leaves and large heads of late summer to autumn flowers, ranging from soft mauve-pink in the species to named varieties that may be white, brick-red or strong pink. It is herbaceous, dying down completely during winter.

Sempervivum (Houseleek)
E, FS to HS, H 8–15 cm, W to 30 cm. Rosette-forming succulents with pointed leaves that form dense mats, houseleeks were once planted on roof tops primarily to hold tiles or slates in place but they were also believed to give protection from lightning. *S. tectorum*, the common houseleek, was usually employed for this purpose. Some species have smooth leaves while others are covered with soft hairs (*S. ciliosum*), or cobwebbed with white, thread-like hairs (*S. arachnoideum*). Leaves may be various shades of green but some have burgundy foliage or green leaves that may be tipped in dark red. Flowers are carried on sturdy stems high above the rosettes. These may be red, purple, yellow or white. After flowers fade the flowered rosette will die but numerous offsets will take its place. Plants must have perfect drainage. They are best suited to cooler areas.

Senecio (Blue chalk sticks)
E, FS to HS, H 10–20 cm, W 40–60 cm. Foliage of this succulent is a most distinctive shade of frosted blue. It makes a spreading ground cover, its foliage being a great foil for other green-leaved plants. In summer it bears small cream flowers but these add nothing to its effect and are probably best cut off.

Surprisingly, this is a member of the daisy family.

Yucca

E, FS, H 75 cm–8 m, W 50 cm–3 m. These are bold, striking plants that make a strong impact on the landscape. Most have stiff, upright, sharply pointed foliage. Flowers are commonly white and held on strong stems well above the foliage. Plants must be carefully sited so that passers-by are not accidentally stabbed! *Y. whipplei*, known as 'Our Lord's Candle', grows into a large rosette of very stiff blue-green leaves that after many years bears white flowers. Spineless *Y. elephantipes* in both its plain and variegated forms has become popular for its architectural shape and is used both indoors and out. It may grow to 8 m in its natural habitat but in cultivation it is more usually 1.5–3 m high. Adam's needle (*Y. filamentosa*) is widely grown, especially its yellow- or white-margined varieties. It rarely grows more than 1 m high. The tallest growing yuccas are Spanish bayonet, *Y. aloifolia*, which reaches 8 m, and the Joshua tree from the southwestern United States, *Y. brevifolia*, that can grow to 12 m tall.

PROTEAS

Proteas are members of a large botanical family, but the name is most often given to those native to South Africa. Banksia, grevillea and waratah are some of the best-known Australian members of the Protea family. Each of the plant groups described below contain a very large number of species of which only a very few are in general cultivation. Proteas have become very popular as cut flowers, as most are spectacular or unusual to look at and have a long vase life. They are attractive garden shrubs, although many do well in containers, and their long-lasting flowers attract nectar-feeding birds. Proteas have been extensively hybridised so that there is an amazing range of flower shape and colour from which to make your selection. Home gardeners in many areas have tried these plants but given up when the first one died. Their needs are simple but there are a few general rules that help lead to success.

Proteas do best in mild climates with low humidity, although some are tolerant of light frost. In regions where frost is likely, plant them where they have protection from early-morning sun. Although they like good air

Leucadendrons make long-lasting cut flowers.

Proteas have long-lasting flowers.

movement, young plants should be protected from very strong wind. Plants will usually bloom one or two years after planting out.

Proteas like to be grown in an open sunny position with good air circulation. They must have very well-drained soil and generally do well in sandy soils. On clay soils they should be grown in raised beds. They do not like to be fertilised as they are extremely sensitive to phosphorus and do not like more than tiny amounts of nitrogen and potassium either. Their root zones should be mulched but mulch must be kept completely clear of plant stems. Newly planted shrubs must be watered in thoroughly and watered regularly until they are well established. Once established, a good heavy soaking once a week is better than frequent light sprinklings. Water around the base of the plant only and avoid overhead watering as this increases humidity around plants.

Some proteas are self-shaping but most benefit from light pruning after flowering. Flowering times may vary with both the

selected strain of the particular plant and district. Young plants can be tip-pruned in late autumn or winter to encourage bushy growth. Established plants can be pruned quite hard after flowering but never cut into bare, leafless stems. Plants that produce many branches from the base need only tip-pruning but those that bear a single flower on a single stem should have the spent flower removed with a good length of stem.

Leucadendron

E, FS, H 1.5–10 m, W 1–3 m. The name 'leucadendron' literally means 'white tree'. Most species have leathery leaves that vary in shape, although most are lance-shaped. Flowers carried on stem tips are formed into small cones surrounded by colourful, leaf-like bracts. Flowers and bracts are in a range of colours and there are many named varieties to choose from. Some have citrus-yellow or green flowers and bracts but there are also varieties with deep-red to burgundy flowers and bracts. Flowering times vary but many bloom in autumn or winter. Cones that contain seed may persist on trees for years if not pruned off. The best known species is probably *L. argenteum* which is known as the 'silver tree' because its leathery leaves are covered in silky silver hairs. Flowers are yellowish green. In its natural habitat it may grow up to 10 m high but is much smaller in cultivation. Most of the varieties are grown for the cut-flower trade and those most suitable for the garden grow only 1.5–2 m high. *L. laureolum*, known as 'yellow tulip' or 'gold tips', has both yellow flowers and bracts.

Leucospermum (Pincushion)

E, FS, H 1.5–3 m, W 1–2 m. Leaves of plants in this group are leathery but variable in shape and may be narrow or broad or spoon-shaped. Flowers are open and spidery and form into large, spherical or cone-shaped heads. Most are in the red, orange or yellow colour range. The main flowering period is through spring into early summer. Plants are usually multi-stemmed and the majority grow 1.5–3 m high. *L. cordifolium* and *L. reflexum* are the two species most often grown. Both have red, yellow or orange flowers but there are several named varieties which are still in the same colour range but with more intense colour or variation in shades.

Protea

E, FS, H 1–5 m, W 1+ m. This is the best-known group of proteas both as garden shrubs and cut flowers. They too have leathery leaves but their flowers come in an amazing diversity of form and colour. Most outstanding is the king protea (*P. cynaroides*), with flowers that may be up to 30 cm across. Silvery-pink bracts encircle a central dome of petals creating a spectacular effect. Plants are open and spreading, growing 1–2 m high and wide. Mink protea or feather tip protea (*P. neriifolia*) is probably the species most often seen as a cut flower. Selected varieties have pink, red, white or cream flowers with feathery, dark tips. The species grows about 3 m high. Honey protea (*P. repens*) bears masses of red and white flowers that produce copious amounts of nectar, which accounts for the common name. There are both winter and summer flowering strains available. Duchess protea (*P. eximia*) grows about 2 m high and has a very long flowering period during which it bears a succession of rosy-pink flowers with darker centres. There are many new, named varieties on the market.

Serruria

E, FS, H 1.5–2 m, W 1–1.5 m. Only one species of this quite large group is common in cultivation. This is known as blushing bride (*S. florida*). It forms a fairly open shrub with fine, almost needle-like, grey-green foliage. Plants are generally fairly short-lived, lasting from three to five years. In late winter and spring they bear cup-shaped flowers. The outer pointed bracts are cream flushed with pink and surround the soft pink centre.

ORNAMENTAL GRASSES AND FOLIAGE PLANTS

Plants grown for their foliage effects can be incorporated into any style of garden. Most do not depend on season for their effect but look good year round as they rely on shape, colour and texture to add interest to the garden. Even an all-green garden can be very attractive when one considers the range of tones of green in addition to the diversity of plant foliage. Fine-foliaged ferns can be contrasted with large, heavy-leaved plants like philodendrons or elephant ears. Grass trees, cycads, dracaenas and cordylines make outstanding features on their own. Cardoon, a relative of artichokes, makes an outstanding feature both in its leaf shape and silvery colour. Apart from ferns and cycads, most plants grown for their foliage produce some kind of flower but these are generally secondary to the foliage. Most foliage plants need little maintenance beyond the occasional removal of dead or yellowing leaves and the removal of any spent flowering stems.

Ornamental grasses can be grown in all climatic zones although most are unsuitable for fire-prone areas. Although they have become increasingly popular in Europe and North America over the past few decades, many gardeners here are less likely to use them. However, they are certainly worth trying as there is a grass to suit just about any garden. Grasses introduce a different texture and form to garden plantings and provide movement in the lightest breeze. They can look very effective planted near a water feature. Grasses may be shades of green or variegated in cream, yellow or silver. There are also decorative grasses in red, russet, purple and yellow, plus shades of blue to blue-green. Many have attractive, flowering plumes that add interest to the late summer or autumn garden. Some die back in winter so should have their old growth slashed in winter or early spring. This ensures that every year the growth is fresh and at its best. Gardeners in cold areas like to leave plumes on the plant to enjoy the pretty effect of frosted stems and flowers.

HINT

For very damp, shady spots there's nothing better than the stream lily (*Helmholtzia glaberrima*). I grow mine in fishponds, where they happily produce their sprays of creamy-white flowers.

DON BURKE

BURKE'S BACKYARD

Acorus (Japanese rush)

E to H, FS to SS, H 10–25 cm, W 8–15 cm. *A. gramineus*. A small plant with fans of stiff green leaves most often seen in the form 'Variegatus' that has green leaves striped yellow and cream. This makes a good edging plant but is also effective when mass planted.

Alpinia (Native ginger)

E, SS to S, H 1.5 m, W 50+ cm. *A. caerulea*. Grown mainly for its graceful arching foliage, this ginger bears sprays of white flowers in late spring that are followed by small, bright-blue berries.

Calamagrostis (Feather reed grass)

E, FS to HS, H 45–90 cm, W 30–50 cm. C. x *acutiflora* is a clump-forming grass with narrow, green, slightly arching leaves. In late summer it produces silvery to buff-brown feathery flowers on tall stems. The variety 'Overdam', with leaves striped and edged in creamy yellow, is a most decorative feature plant.

Carex (Sedge)

E or H, FS to HS, H 40 cm–1.3 m, W 30+ cm. Within this group there are sedges with foliage colour ranging from green, through to reds and browns, blue-green, yellow, silver and striped. Some are neat, compact growers while others form tall tussocks. Some sedges can be invasive, especially in mild to warm climates. Bowles golden sedge (*C. elata* 'Aurea') is a favourite for foliage contrast, as its leaves are rich yellow. Leatherleaf sedge (*C. buchananii*) from New Zealand forms dense stands of orange-brown leaves that are curled at the tips. 'Frosted Curls' is an unusual grass, as it has silvery foliage that also curls at its tips. Weeping sedge (*C. pendula*) has mid-green leaves that are blue on the underside. It produces long, drooping catkins in late spring to early summer. Most sedges bear small, crowded spikes of flowers similar to those of many grasses.

Codiaeum (Croton)

E, FS, H 1–2.5 m, W 70+ cm. *C. variegatum* var. *pictum*. These handsome foliage shrubs provide a colourful show in warm to tropical gardens. Leaves vary greatly in shape and may be straight or twisted, narrow, lobed or broad. There seems an almost infinite variety of splashed, spotted or striped patterns on leaves which range from darkest green to yellow, orange, pink or red. Crotons are often used as hedges in the tropics and can be mass planted, used as specimens or even grown in containers.

Cordyline

E, FS to SS, H 3–6 m, W 2–4 m. *C. australis*. Known as cabbage palm, this New Zealand native is not related to palms. This plant makes a striking focal point in the garden with its stiff, spiky leaves which become pendulous as they age. Upright when young, as it matures it develops a branching habit. Mature plants bear sprays of small cream flowers in summer. These are followed by whitish or mauve berries. Several coloured-leaf varieties are grown, including 'Variegata' with its cream-striped green leaves, 'Purpurea' with broad purple foliage, and 'Albertii' that is cream-striped, with red midribs and leaf margins. 'Red Fountain' forms a trunkless clump. *C. stricta* is native to moist forests of eastern Australia. Good for growing under tall trees, it has arching leaves, pale violet summer flowers and small black berries. *C. fruticosa* (formerly *C. terminalis*) can be grown in warm to tropical gardens only. Its broad leaves may be green, deep red or striped.

Cycas (Sago palm)

E, FS to HS, H 1–3 m, W 1–2m. *C. revoluta*. Of the many species of cycads grown, this is the most common in cultivation. Slow-growing, this can be cultivated in a container or in the ground. It has stiff, dark-green leaves that are palm-like (although cycads are unrelated to palms). As it ages it develops a thick trunk but this can take many years. This is not a flowering plant but produces a type of cone. Male and female cones are borne on separate plants.

Cynara (Cardoon)

H, FS, H 1.5–2 m, W 1+ m. *C. cardunculus*. This striking accent plant is closely related to globe artichoke. It has large, spiny, silvery-grey leaves that may be lobed or dissected. It produces purple, thistle-like flowers like an artichoke, although it is grown for its foliage effect, not its flowers. It does best in cooler areas.

Dracaena

E, FS to SS, H 2–10 m, W 1–6 m. Dracaenas create bold, architectural effects in the garden. Many species are familiar as indoor plants but can be a great asset in the garden. They can be grown in any warm, frost-free area but prefer temperatures over 12°C. *D. marginata* has red-edged, dark-green, glossy leaves. Outdoors they will grow 5–7 m over many years, branching as they mature. *D. draco*, the dragon's blood tree, makes an imposing feature in the larger garden. In cultivation it may reach over 10 m after many years. It is slow-growing with a thick trunk, and its upswept branches bear large tufty rosettes of sword-shaped leaves. Grown in an open sunny position, it will develop a broad umbrella shape over the years. *D. fragrans* has sturdy, cane-like stems, topped with a rosette of broad, arching leaves. The variety 'Massangeana' with its yellow-striped leaves is sold as 'happy plant' for indoor use. In a warm garden it may grow to about 3 m.

Festuca (Fescue)

E, FS to HS, H 15–25 cm, W 15–20 cm. *F. glauca*, blue fescue and its many named varieties is a small, tufty grass ideal for edging or for pockets in a rockery. It does best in cooler areas and may partly or fully die off in summer in warm, humid regions.

Foeniculum (Fennel)

E, FS, H 1–2 m, W 50+ cm. Purple fennel (*F. vulgare*, 'Purpureum'). The bronze-leaved form of the common fennel provides lovely colour and foliage contrast. The fine, feathery foliage gives a misty effect. It is best grown in cooler areas. As it produces flowers and seeds like the common fennel, spent flower heads should be cut off as they fade to avoid spread of unwanted seedlings.

Hedychium (Ginger lily)

E, HS to SS, H 1–3 m, W 500 cm–1 m. Although these plants all bear quite striking flowers, none of them has a long flowering period while their foliage provides a permanent backdrop year round. They grow from fleshy rhizomes, a type of running root that sends up canes on which the foliage develops. All have broad, tapering, lance-shaped leaves. Kahili Ginger (*H. gardnerianum*) is probably best avoided as it tends to be quite invasive. Garland ginger (*H. coronarium*) grows to about 1.5 m but to 3 m in the tropics, bearing its short-lived but sweetly scented white flowers in summer. *H. coccineum*, red ginger

Phormium (New Zealand Flax) comes in a range of attractive leaf colours.

lily, grows 2–3 m high and bears pale-red to orange flowers in late summer.

Imperata (Japanese blood grass)

H, FS to HS, H 30–50 cm, W 10–20 cm. *I. cylindrica* 'Rubra' is an upright grower with narrow, sword-shaped leaves. In spring the new growth emerges green and rapidly turns bright scarlet. Colour intensity increases in autumn before fading and dying back to the ground. This does best in cooler areas.

Lomandra (Mat rush)

E, FS to SS, H 1 m, W to 1 m. Although there are many species in this group only spiny mat rush (*L. longifolia*) is commonly grown. This is a tough plant that will tolerate poor growing conditions and a wide range of climates. It is fast-growing, forming tussocks of flat leathery leaves. Small cream-coloured flowers, followed by rounded yellow fruits, develop on stems that stand well clear of the foliage. Many cultivars are now available.

Macrozamia (Burrawang)

E, FS to SS, H 1–2 m, W 2–3 m. *M. communis*. This fairly fast-growing cycad occurs naturally in coastal areas of New South Wales where it forms an understorey in open eucalypt forest. It has dark-green, arching fronds of foliage that resemble palms, although it is not related. This is a great feature plant that can be grown in the ground or in a container.

Melianthus (Honey flower)

E, FS, H 1–2 m, W 1+ m. *M. major* is a South African native with outstanding blue-green foliage. It does sucker to form large clumps if left alone, but it can be contained or divided if it gets too large. It bears dark-red, nectar-rich flowers on tall spikes in summer but the unusual colour and form of its leaves are its main decorative asset.

Miscanthus

E or H, FS, H 1–2 m, W 1–1.5 m. *M. sinensis*. The plain green species of this grass is less often seen than its variegated leaf forms. Zebra grass (*M. sinensis* 'Zebrinus') makes a fine feature grown alone or massed to form a low screen. Bright-green leaves are transversely banded in bright yellow. Gold banding may not appear on the new growth in spring until the weather is consistently warm. Eulalia grass(*M. sinensis* 'Variegatus') has soft green foliage striped creamy white. Both these varieties and other forms of miscanthus look attractive when planted near a water feature. In late summer to autumn, tall plumes of creamy-beige flowers appear high above the foliage. Cut these off as they begin to look untidy. Ideally the whole plant should be cut back to the ground during winter or very early spring to allow for fresh new growth.

Pennisetum (Fountain grass)

E or H, FS, H 60 cm–1.5 m, W 50 cm–1 m. Although these grasses will grow in all climates, some varieties should be avoided in warm climates as they seed heavily and may become weedy. To avoid this, in any climate, cut off the flower heads before seeds ripen fully and disperse. A colour change will usually indicate this. *P. alopecuroides* is a clump-forming grass that grows to about 1.5 m, bearing cream to pink, foxtail flowers that mature to a red-brown. Its variety, 'Hameln', grows only 30–60 cm high. *P. villosum* sometimes called 'Feathertop,' has plumes of soft creamy flowers that mature to deep pink or purple in late summer or autumn. These grasses are related to kikuyu, well known as a lawn grass.

Philodendron

E, SS to S, H 40+ cm, W 30+ cm. Known to most people as indoor plants, there are many species and varieties of philodendron that are ideal for growing in shady spots in the garden. *P. bipinnatifidum* (formerly *P. selloum*) has dark-green, lobed leaves that may grow 50 cm–1 m long. This is an ideal filler for a shady corner or for growing under trees. Aerial roots will develop in time but these can be removed if containment is wanted. A small-growing variety (reaching about 40 cm) is sold as either 'Xanadu' or 'Winterbourn'. *P.* x Redwings has a similar growth habit to *P. bipinnatifidum* but its large, heart-shaped leaves have red undersides. There are several well-known climbers in this group including *P. cordatum* and *P. scandens*, both of which are referred to as heartleaf.

Phormium (New Zealand flax)

E, FS to HS, H 60 cm–2 m, W 1–2 m. *P. tenax* and *P. cookianum* plus their large range of cultivated varieties may be used as accent plants, as screens or in mixed shrub plantings. Foliage is stiff and sword-shaped and may be upright or arching in habit. The large range of lovely varieties now available include those with leaves in one colour only or striped in several shades. Foliage may be green, bronze, red, yellow, pink or cream or various mixtures of these shades.

Poa (Tussock grass)

E, FS, H 30–50 cm, W 20–40 cm. *P. labillardieri* forms a neat clump of very slender, grey-blue to grey-green leaves. It can be used as an accent plant amongst annuals, perennials or small shrubs or used as a feature edging. Thin spikes of purplish flowers appear in autumn. Like most grasses its appearance is improved if it is cut back to the ground in late winter so that the new season's growth is not spoiled by old leaves. This grass occurs naturally in many regions of Australia so it is suited to most garden conditions.

Stipa (Spear grass)

E or H, FS to SS, H 1–2 m, W 1–1.5 m. Many of these handsome ornamental grasses are native to Australia and New Zealand. All bear decorative plumes of soft fluffy seed heads in autumn that continue into winter. *S. arundinacea*, which is native to New Zealand, forms a large clump of fine, arching stems of green leaves that change to shades of orange and brown in autumn and winter. *S. ramosissima*, known as bamboo grass, is native to eastern New South Wales, where it grows on forest margins. It forms upright clumps of canes to about 2 m, the softer foliage weeping from the top of the clump. Smaller-growing species include feather spear grass (*S. elegantissima*) and corkscrew grass (*S. setacea*).

Xanthorrhoea (Grass tree)

E, FS to HS, H 40 cm–6 m, W 50 cm–3 m. These distinctive-looking, slow-growing plants range from those without visible trunks to tree-like specimens 6 m high. Stiff or arching grassy leaves may form large rosettes (in trunkless species) or produce tufts of upright foliage on top of dark, solid trunks. Flower spikes are borne on top of long stems that stand high above the foliage. The tiny flowers are crowded and often surrounded by dense matted hairs. Species flower at different times of the year. Grass trees occur naturally in many varied climates and conditions in different parts of Australia. It makes good sense to choose a species that suits your local area. Grass trees grow readily from seed and although slow, a reasonable specimen can be growing within three to five years. Trunks may take many years to develop. Established plants are difficult to move successfully and loss rate is high. Always buy from a reputable supplier.

HINT

If ants are a problem, boil up a handful pennyroyal in water, allow to steep for an hour, strain and spray around the affected area.

JUNE TAYLOR
GARDEN WRITER

Clump-forming grasses make striking accent plants.

23

Gardening in Containers

Plants are grown in containers for many reasons. The increasing number of people who live in flats or home units must, by necessity, do their gardening on windowsills or balconies. But even gardeners with plenty of outdoor space find potted plants are very decorative, especially if they are grown in attractive containers. They can be used to soften and beautify large paved areas like patios and courtyards or can create focal points in the garden. One of the best things about container-grown plants is that they can be moved about from one place to another, providing the containers are not too heavy. This way you can give plants a suitable microclimate or show them off when they're looking their best.

There are, of course, many other reasons why the popularity of this form of gardening is growing. Garden centres now offer a much bigger range of attractive tubs, pots, troughs, hanging baskets, vertical garden kits and window boxes and an even greater variety of plants to grow in them. Moreover, there are new, efficient potting mixtures these days which greatly reduce the chances of failure, and plant breeders have developed plants more suitable for tub culture.

However, the two outstanding advantages of gardening in containers are that they are portable and that almost any plant can be grown in them – flowering annuals, bulbs, ferns, creepers, herbs, shrubs and trees. There are even specially bred compact forms of fruiting plants for confined spaces.

SITUATION AND POTTING MIX

To be a successful container gardener you must choose the right plant for your situation. Balconies are often windy, so anything you plant should be able to stand up to the breezes. The amount of sunlight is very important and will also influence your choice of plants. Sun-loving plants – which includes vegetables – need at least four to five hours of sunlight each day to grow successfully, so check the amount of sunshine before spending money on plants that may not be suitable.

Containers must have free drainage, otherwise your plants will drown. Most pots and tubs have one or several drainage holes 1–2 cm in diameter.

Ordinary garden soil is usually unsuitable for pot culture because it does not drain well and tends to set hard. Proprietary potting mixtures, which are available from garden stores and nurseries, are open, porous mixes which are very satisfactory and have the added advantage of being free from weed seeds, soil pests and plant diseases. Special potting mixes like orchid compost, African violet mix, cactus mix and bulb mix are available too. For the best quality potting mixtures look for those that meet the Australian Standard, usually shown as a 'five ticks' logo. This guarantees that the potting mix has been produced to the highest possible quality. Cheap potting mixtures are just that: cheap. They are rarely a bargain.

When potting up most plants, don't be tempted to put a small plant into a large pot with the idea of saving yourself some work. Plants do not thrive in over-large containers – some even prefer to be crowded. It is best to move a plant into a slightly larger pot when the previous one fills with roots.

WATERING AND FEEDING

Whatever you decide to grow in your pots, remember that container-grown plants have a restricted root system and cannot forage for moisture as they would do in the open garden. On hot summer days, daily watering may be needed – perhaps twice a day if the plants are in full sunlight. Always water thoroughly – not just a sprinkle. Use a water-breaker or a watering wand rather than a hose nozzle. A water-breaker delivers a large volume of water gently onto the potting

Before you begin, water the pot thoroughly and allow to drain. The potting mix should be moist but not over-wet.

Spread your opened fingers over the top of the mix before inverting the pot. Tap gently on the base to loosen root-ball. Ease plant out of the pot.

Carefully remove some of the old potting mix, either by hand or with a jet of water from a hose. Gently tease out the outermost roots.

With sharp secateurs, trim off any diseased, dead or over-long roots. When finished, make sure you clean the secateurs to remove any potting mix residue.

Repot into a slightly larger container using fresh potting mix. The top of the root-ball should be at the same level as it was in the previous pot.

Firm the mix gently into place. Water well. Add some controlled-release fertiliser. When finished, wash your hands well with soap and water.

mix and causes minimum disturbance.

When potting, leave a margin between the soil level and the rim of the container. When watering, fill this space slowly with water until it weeps out of the drainage holes. A mulch of grass clippings, compost, coarse gravel, pebbles or pine bark helps to reduce evaporation and cools the surface soil.

Good drainage and frequent watering also means loss of plant nutrients. Regular, small amounts of fertiliser are needed to keep plants growing strongly. Always apply fertilisers to moist soil to avoid burning young roots. The

HINT

To stop potted plants from drying out, use plastic or glazed pots that lose less water from evaporation. Paint the inside of terracotta pots with a sealer or place a plastic pot inside and disguise the edges with mulch or a trailing ground cover.

DEBBIE McDONALD
GARDEN WRITER, EDITOR
AND HORTICULTURIST

water-soluble fertilisers, such as Thrive or Aquasol, are suitable for regular liquid feeds. Use at half-strength for tender plants. Slow-acting and controlled-release fertilisers (such as Acticote) or organic pellets (such as Dynamic Lifter) are also suitable to provide nutrients over a long period. Whatever fertiliser you choose, always use it according to the manufacturer's directions. Too much fertiliser for potted plants can be disastrous, especially if the mix becomes dry, and salty granular fertilisers are best avoided for potted plants.

PESTS AND DISEASES

Container-grown plants are not immune to attack by pests and diseases. Grubs, bugs, blights and mildews must always be guarded against. A few plants on a balcony can often be kept clear of caterpillars, snails and other leaf-eating pests by picking them off by hand or spraying with low-toxic insect sprays which are suitable for controlling pests of potted and indoor plants. Pyrethrum-based sprays such as Bug Gun or insecticidal soaps such as Natrasoap are ideal. A few pellets of snail bait at the base of potted plants will control snails and slugs.

FAVOURITE SHRUBS FOR TUBS

Camellias and azaleas with all-year-round foliage and exquisite flowers in season make excellent tub specimens. They do best in partial shade or filtered sunlight. They prefer acidic potting mix, so proprietary mixes that are marked as being suitable for azaleas and camellias are the best choice for growing these plants successfully. Growing these acid-loving plants in tubs is a good solution if your garden soil is alkaline, which it may well be in some districts.

Hydrangeas make magnificent tub plants for shady situations, although they do look rather bare in winter. They give a wonderful flower display in summer and can be brought indoors when flowering. Flower colour depends on whether the mix is acid or alkaline – blue in acid soil, pink in alkaline. If you want your hydrangeas to be a particular colour, grow them in a tub and treat the mix accordingly. (See Chapter 5.)

Fuchsias – and there are dozens of varieties – are dependable flowering shrubs for tubs, pots or hanging baskets in cool and temperate climates. Flowers in white, pink, red and purple are produced over a long period. Gardenias, with handsome glossy leaves and waxy, white, fragrant flowers, make good tub specimens. Gardenias prefer full sun or half sun in a warm, sheltered spot. In the right position (especially in warm climates) some varieties of gardenias will flower from spring to autumn. Daphne is another neat, evergreen shrub with exquisitely perfumed pink, red or mauve flowers in late winter and spring. Plants need good drainage and are often more reliable in a large pot or tub than in the open garden. They prefer morning sun but shade for the rest of the day.

Geraniums will provide a bright patch of colour on a sunny terrace or patio. Grow them in tubs, large pots or window boxes; with plenty of sun they will flower from early spring to late autumn. The ivy-leaf trailing

HINT

Create easy-care potted gardens by choosing a large pot and a single evergreen or deciduous tree or shrub and underplant different annuals in the base of the pot to match the season. You will have twice the value and easy colour all year round.

ROSEMARY DAVIES

GARDEN MEDIA PERSONALITY AND CONSULTANT

varieties are ideal for hanging baskets. Bougainvillea is another sun-lover, especially for warm, northern climates, and dwarf varieties are now readily available. These are best for containers and give a magnificent, long-lasting display of flower bracts.

Citrus trees are both ornamental and useful tub plants for outdoor living areas. The smaller citrus trees like cumquats and limes are easy to grow in tubs, but potted lemons, oranges and mandarins may need pruning to keep them within bounds. Choose citrus grafted onto dwarfing rootstocks. (See Chapter 13 for more information.)

Japanese bamboo (*Nandina*), with its lacy foliage, makes a good container plant and can be kept in bounds by pruning. True bamboo, which belongs to the grass family, gives an oriental effect for tub culture but only dwarf varieties up to 2–3 m tall should be chosen.

ROSES

Roses do well in tubs and pots and they are easy to grow, though obviously the miniature varieties and small floribundas will perform best. They are not fussy about climate and can withstand hot summers as well as freezing winters – provided you don't let the container dry out.

Full-sized roses need a pot at least 50 cm or more in diameter to allow room for the roots to develop properly. Fertilise with controlled-release fertiliser in early spring, as new growth begins, and again in early autumn. Your display will last longer if

A bowl-shaped container effectively displays flowering annuals and bulbs.

you keep removing dead flower heads to encourage the formation of new buds. Never allow rose hips (fruits) to develop because they drain energy from the plant and inhibit the growth of more flowers. Here is a list of some roses suitable for container growing – and remember that roses generally look better massed than as single specimens. Try to group several pots together.

Floribunda types: 'Apricot Nectar', 'Confetti', 'Friesia', 'Iceberg', 'Love Potion', 'Marlena', 'Red Gold', 'Regensberg', 'Saratoga' and 'Sonoma'. Miniatures: 'Amorette', 'Chameleon', 'Foxy Lady', 'Green Ice', 'Holy Toledo',

HINT

Seal the inside of terracotta pots with a polyurethane sealer. It reduces water evaporation through the earthenware pots and keeps your plants happier in summer, saving your water and time as well.

CAROLYN BLACKMAN

HORTICULTURIST — VIVID DESIGN

'Hopscotch', 'Guletta', 'Kaikoura', 'Ko's Yellow', 'Lavender Lace', 'Little Red Devil', 'Magic Carrousel', 'Mary Marshall', 'Ocarina', 'Otago', 'Over the Rainbow', 'Petite Folie', 'Royal Salute', 'Snow Carpet', 'Starina', 'Sunspray', 'Wanaka'.

FLOWERING BULBS FOR POTS

Bulbs are easy plants to grow in pots. Favourite spring-flowering bulbs for this treatment are daffodils, jonquils, hyacinths, bluebells, lachenalias, freesias, triteleias and tulips. Daffodils, hyacinths and tulips are ideal for growing indoors.

In cool districts, lily-of-the-valley can be planted several bulbs to the pot and will be a great source of enjoyment either indoors or outdoors. Permanent plantings of large evergreen bulbous plants like agapanthus are suitable for large tubs around swimming pools, barbecue areas or on sunny patios. The strap-like leaves are attractive all year round, with large clusters of blue or white flowers in summer when outdoor living areas are most used.

Clivia, with orange-red or cream blooms in winter followed by attractive berries, is a good substitute for shady areas. Hippeastrums are popular container-grown bulbs in Europe and favourites for their large pink, white or red, lily-like flowers in spring. They are ideal for pots on balconies, patios and in courtyards and can be brought inside as temporary house plants when they flower. Many other bulbs and bulbous plants can be grown in this way. Hymenocallis (one of the many spider lilies), eucharis, eucomis (pineapple flower) and liliums are good examples. Gloriosa (climbing lily) can be grown in a hanging basket. For further information on flowering bulbs refer to Chapter 16.

HINT

Protect the soil on the top of containers with coarse gravel mulch for small plant pots or large pebbles for larger pots. This looks great, protects the soil from heat and drying out, stops birds scratching out the soil and making a mess and it adds extra weight to stabilise the plant during windy weather.

ROSEMARY DAVIES

GARDEN MEDIA PERSONALITY
AND CONSULTANT

COLOURFUL ANNUALS

Annual flowers make a colourful display in pots or hanging baskets and are invaluable for brightening a balcony, terrace or patio. Potted annuals are also useful for special occasions like parties or weddings, which are planned well ahead.

For spring flowers, plant cineraria, lobelia, nemesia, pansy, polyanthus, primrose, primula, schizanthus, dwarf sweet pea and violas. These can all be raised from seed or seedlings planted in late summer to autumn. Annuals for summer pots include petunia (especially colourful for hanging baskets), phlox, nasturtium ('Jewel Mixed' is a good trailing basket plant) and verbena. All need a sunny position but one which is sheltered from wind. Marigolds flower over a long period in containers – use dwarf varieties for small pots and troughs and larger ones for

Top five container plants for full sun

CITRUS

Citrus grafted onto dwarfing rootstocks grow well in pots. Their glossy leaves are green year round, the flowers have a delightful fragrance, and the fruits are decorative. In Asia, potted citrus are given as 'good luck' tokens at New Year.

HEBE

These neat, small-growing New Zealand plants are not particularly fussy about conditions, but will always maintain a better profile if they're given a light haircut after flowering.

NEW ZEALAND CHRISTMAS BUSH

Almost unkillable (but no heavy frosts, please) and, if you're lucky, you'll get a good show of red blooms at Christmas. The pretty, variegated form is notoriously reluctant to flower.

GREVILLEA

There are hundreds of grevillea species around but *G. juniperina*, *G. intricata* and *G.* 'Robyn Gordon' are particularly attractive.

BOX

Renowned for their hardiness and their small, neat leaves, box plants are very popular for topiary work. Begin clipping when the plant is young to maintain a dense foliage cover.

tubs where they will make a dazzling display. Celosia makes a striking pot plant for hot summer weather. Dwarf varieties in scarlet or gold can be combined or planted separately. Bedding begonias are delightful in quite small pots and make a good show in semi-shade planted in a strawberry pot. New Guinea impatiens is an excellent pot plant for shady areas and flowers for months in colours of pink, salmon and mauve, often with multi-coloured foliage. The more glamorous hybrids with large, butterfly-like flowers or handsome variegated foliage make delightful features on balconies or patios.

As a change from annual flowers in pots, ornamental chilli has interesting, multi-coloured fruits, and coleus, which has colourful leaves, is another attractive foliage plant which is ideal for container growing, even in shade. Most herbs, except the very tall ones, can be grown successfully in pots, as can many of the smaller vegetables.

Refer to Chapter 11 for information on vegetables and Chapter 12 for information on suitable herbs.

HINT

If you haven't room for a vegetable garden, liven up a small space with a variety of easily grown herbs and vegetables that have colourful and unusual foliage or fruit. Miniature capsicums and chillies, silver beet varieties, chard, purple basil, golden thyme, and dwarf tomatoes all look great planted in containers.

JOHN MASON

GARDENING AUTHOR, PRINCIPAL — THE AUSTRALIAN CORRESPONDENCE SCHOOLS

Plants in hanging baskets (like these tuberous begonias) can look stunning but must be in a suitable situation. Exposed baskets can heat up and dry out quickly.

HERBS FOR POTS

Many herbs are both decorative and useful in pots or tubs. Most herbs need some sunshine each day and an ideal place is a window box as close to the kitchen as possible. Herbs also need fresh air to thrive – they do not grow well indoors for any length of time. Although they are not as fussy as some ornamental plants, herbs should be planted in a good potting mix to encourage lush, attractive growth. The best herb plants to grow in pots are the low or dwarf varieties, like chives, parsley, thyme, tarragon, basil, geraniums, savory, mint, marjoram, oregano, thrift, pennyroyal, prostrate rosemary and dwarf lavender. A sprinkling of slow or controlled-release fertiliser (such as Acticote), or regular applications of soluble fertilisers like Thrive and Aquasol, will improve plant growth, particularly if you are picking the leaves for cooking or infusions. Apart from chives (which can be cut to the ground when ready for harvest), never remove more than one-fifth of the plant in one cut, and let the plant start growing again before harvesting any more leaves. Herbs with strong roots like mint, tarragon and lemon balm should be contained in pots and not mixed in with other plants. Dill, fennel, borage and sage are larger-growing plants which tend to grow smaller when restricted in a pot. Don't grow these in amongst the more prostrate herbs as they will soon overwhelm the smaller plants. Grow aromatic herbs where they can be touched, brushed against or walked on. The fragrance is always pleasing and often wards off insects. Scented-leaf geraniums are among the easiest to grow and come in a variety of perfumes, such as peppermint, nutmeg, rose, lemon and a number of other spicy flavours.

Growing Vegetables in Containers

VEGETABLE	MOST SUITABLE VARIETIES	RECOMMENDED MIN. DEPTH OF CONTAINER
Cabbage	Sugarloaf	25 cm
Capsicum	All	40 cm
Carrot	Baby	25 cm
	Chantenay	25 cm
Chilli	Burke's Backyard Thai	25 cm
Cress	Curled Cress	10 cm
Cucumber	Lebanese	40 cm
Eggplant	All	40 cm
Herbs	Many types	20 cm
Lettuce	Cos	25 cm
	Mignonette	25 cm
	Buttercrunch	25 cm
Onion	Spring or Straight Leaf	20 cm
Pumpkin	Golden Nugget	30 cm
Radish	All	20 cm
Rocket	All	30 cm
Silver beet	Fordhook Giant	25 cm
	Compact	25 cm
Tomato	Small Fry	30 cm
	Tiny Tim	30 cm
	Roma	30 cm
Zucchini	Blackjack	40 cm
	Greyzini	40 cm
	Lebanese	40 cm

Epiphytic cacti will flower in a well-lit indoor position.

INDOOR PLANTS

After a period out of favour, indoor plants are gradually making a return to popularity. And few offices, foyers, hotels or restaurants are without indoor plants to soften the atmosphere. The early Victorians grew plants indoors, but their choice was limited and the introduction of gaslighting and regular winter heating killed so many that only the aspidistra survived to become the most remembered plant feature of the late nineteenth-century home. It wasn't until after the Second World War that indoor plants became popular again.

Although millions of plants are sold to be grown indoors, there is really no such thing as an indoor plant. The natural place for plants is outdoors but certain species can adapt to growing indoors. The most successful indoor plants are those from tropical rainforests that grow in the shade of large trees. When you grow these plants in your home you should try to duplicate these conditions.

Indoor plants need good light, but should never be placed in direct sunlight. If there is enough light to cast a shadow (test by holding your hand against a piece of white paper), there is enough for most indoor plants. Temperature should be fairly even (about 20°C), without extremes, if possible. In warm, dry weather, the humidity they need can be created by standing the pots on pebbles above a tray of water, and mist-spraying the foliage regularly. Plants grouped together are better off than a single plant because the massed leaves will create a microclimate to produce higher humidity. This point is easily demonstrated in nurseries which specialise in selling indoor plants; they often create a mini-jungle of plants in tubs or hanging baskets.

The easiest plants to grow indoors are those with thick, glossy leaves, such as

HINT

Recent research has shown that plants in pots growing indoors have the ability to absorb toxic vapours. It appears that pollutants are absorbed both by the plants themselves and the micro-organisms in the potting mix. So, stay healthy and keep indoor plants.

MICHÈLE ADLER

LECTURER, AUTHOR, TOUR LEADER –
ADLAND HORTICULTURAL

Zanzibar Gem (*Zamioculcas*), Philodendrons (e.g. 'Xanadu'), umbrella plant (*Schefflera*), cast iron plant (*Aspidistra*), dragon plant (*Dracaena*), prayer plant (*Maranta*), Swiss cheese plant (*Monstera deliciosa*), mother-in-law's tongue (*Sansevieria*), dumb cane (*Dieffenbachia*), bromeliad (*Aechmea*) and fatsia (*Fatsia japonica*).

Other plants well adapted to growing indoors are spider plant (*Chlorophytum*), madonna lily (*Spathiphyllum*), aglaeonema, arrowhead (*Syngonium*), grape ivy and kangaroo vine (*Cissus* spp.), aluminium plant (*Pilea*), coleus, peperomias, pelargoniums or geraniums, Kentia palm (*Howea*) parlour palm and brake ferns.

These are some of the most reliable indoor plants, so begin with these before graduating to the more exotic kinds available from specialist nurseries.

There are many flowering indoor plants, too: African violet (*Saintpaulia*), anthurium tuberous and elatior begonias, calceolaria, cyclamen, gloxinia, *Primula obconica* and polyanthus are popular and readily available in nurseries in season.

These require more light and care than the hardier foliage plants listed above. Most of them are described in Chapter 15. Flowering chrysanthemums and dwarf poinsettias will produce long-lasting indoor blooms but should never be regarded as permanent indoor fixtures.

Most indoor plants will grow better if they are rested outside in a shady, sheltered spot periodically (although never in full sun or cold conditions) – three weeks indoors and three weeks outdoors is a good timetable. If you have no sheltered place outside, rotate the plants to the best growing spot beside a well-lit window. Plants dislike dark, closed rooms. They need fresh air and light to grow. If you are away all day and your home is closed, try to arrange ventilation for your plants. Don't pull down the blinds or draw the curtains, but let in the light.

Indoor plants also need regular watering. This may mean daily watering in dry weather, but perhaps only once a week when it is cooler. In cold weather it is best to use tepid water because cold water will chill the soil and damage the roots. Don't water pots if the mix feels damp. More plants are lost through

HINT

Look for dark-green leaves, strong, well-developed stems and new shoots when purchasing indoor plants. These are all better indicators of healthy growth than lush, tender leaves and bright-green shoots.

JOHN MASON

GARDENING AUTHOR, PRINCIPAL – THE AUSTRALIAN CORRESPONDENCE SCHOOLS

over-watering than under-watering – the soil becomes clogged and the roots drown or suffocate. Always use your index finger to check the potting mix at least 3 cm below the surface. Gadgets which can measure the degree of soil moisture are particularly useful to anyone with lots of potted plants.

Most indoor plants react to stress by dropping their leaves. This can mean they are too dry, too wet, too hot, too cold or too dark. You will have to assess the situation to decide what the problem may be.

Fertilise indoor plants in the warm growing season. Small doses of liquid feed (Thrive, Aquasol, fish emulsion) at half-strength every three to four weeks should be sufficient. Otherwise use slow or controlled-release plant food such as Acticote according to directions.

Dust plants regularly and gently with a clean cloth or duster for glossy-leafed plants or a soft paintbrush for those with furry leaves. Spray-on Leaf Shine will give indoor plants a remarkable facelift. Milk is also good for shiny leaves and should be wiped on with a thick wad of cotton wool.

It can be helpful to put your plants outside when it rains. Rain washes the leaves and helps leach the soil of any build-up of salts from tap water (but don't leave them outside to be burnt when the sun comes out).

Some plants which grow too big for their containers can often be rejuvenated by cutting off the tops and letting them shoot again from the base. Dracaena, dieffenbachia and umbrella plants can be treated this way.

Houseplant Ailments

PROBLEM	PLANT RESPONSE
Aphids	New leaves curl and become distorted. Presence of small, soft insects on buds, young stems and leaves. To control, spray with Mavrik or Natrasoap.
Mealybug	White cottony or waxy insect on the underside of leaves and leaf axils. Infested plants become unthrifty. Control is difficult. If only a few present, wipe off with a damp cloth. Otherwise take outside and spray with Confidor. Severely infested plants should be discarded.
Scale insects	Stems and leaves become covered with flattened reddish, grey or brown scaly bumps. To control, spray with PestOil. Repeat applications may be necessary.
Mites	Leaves yellow, become stippled and may fall. There may also be spider-webbing present. To control, spray with Natrasoap at regular intervals and mist-spray leaves.
Botrytis	Brown spots and blotches appear on leaves and sometimes stems. Under humid conditions infected portions may be covered with a fuzzy grey growth. Diseased and dead plant material should be removed promptly, particularly flowers. Avoid splashing water on foliage and growing plants in crowded conditions where the air is damp and still.
Powdery mildew	Faint white spots appear on leaves and gradually enlarge until the whole leaf surface is covered with white powder. Spray with Rose Gun Advanced (outdoors in shade).
Too little light	Leaves smaller and paler than normal. Flowers poor or absent. Lower leaves turn yellow, dry and fall. Spindly growth with long spaces between leaves. Variegated leaves turn green.
Too much water	Leaves limp. Soft areas may appear. Poor growth. Leaves curl. Leaves yellow and wilt, tips may brown.
Too cold	Leaves curl, brown and fall.
Too hot	Spindly growth when in good light conditions. Flowers short-lived. Lower leaves wilt, brown and fall.
Sudden change in temperature	Leaves fall after rapid yellowing.
Too little humidity	Leaf-tips brown and shrivelled. Leaf edges yellow. Buds and flowers shrivel and fall.
Draughts	Leaves turn yellow and fall. Leaves curl and fall. Brown tips or edges on leaves.

ORCHIDS

Orchids make lovely container plants. They thrive in warm, subtropical and tropical areas but need glasshouse conditions in cold districts. When growing orchids in containers it is best to use proprietary orchid potting mixes. These special mixes do not contain any soil and the roots of the plants can move through them freely. Many orchids are epiphytes (a plant attached to another plant but not a parasite) and under natural conditions they grow in the debris of bark and dead leaves of trees. It is a good idea to place a layer of crocks or pine bark at the bottom of the container before adding the orchid mix.

Some species of orchid are very easy to grow. The crucifix orchid (*Epidendrum*) can usually be grown in the open garden in mild climates but also makes an attractive pot plant for a sunny position. There are hundreds of species of tree orchids (*Dendrobium*), many of them Australian natives. The Sydney rock lily (*D. speciosum*) and tongue orchid (*D. linguiforme*) are some of the best known and are very adaptable to climates which are frost-free. Other tree orchids do best in warm, tropical areas but need glasshouse treatment where the climate is cooler. Cymbidiums are the most popular orchids for mild climates where the temperature does not drop below 5°C. In mild–temperate, frost free climates, pots or tubs of cymbidium orchids can be placed under trees in filtered light. They make ideal plants for large pots and tubs which can be moved to a favoured position for flowering. They need light shade in summer but full sun in winter when the flower spikes are forming. Flower spikes last for many weeks. There are hundreds of varieties, coming in shades of white, yellow, pink, red, brown and green. Moth orchids (*Phalaenopsis*) are becoming

The spectacular pink and cream blooms of a Cattleya *orchid.*

much more readily available. They will grow indoors in bright light. After flowering the flower stem should be left in place to bloom again or produce aerial plantlets. Only cut back stems that are clearly dead. Slipper orchid (*Paphiopedilum*) is a reliable orchid for a small pot (they like to be crowded). It blooms in winter or early spring. Dancing ladies (*Oncidium*) are also delightful orchids for pots or hanging baskets. Natives of Brazil, they need a warm, subtropical climate but can be grown in a shadehouse or glasshouse in cool areas. Angel orchid (*Coelogyne*) has pure white flowers with golden throats in autumn and winter. They are very adaptable to climate, providing there are no frosts. They like to be crowded in pots and prefer rather dry conditions when flowering. Chinese ground orchid (*Bletilla*) is another adaptable orchid for pot culture. It is dormant in winter and flowers in spring. *Vanda* and *Cattleya* are probably the showiest of all the orchids, but they need a warm, humid, tropical climate or glasshouse conditions in cooler areas. *Stanhopeas* are fascinating orchids for hanging baskets. Their vanilla-scented flowers bloom through the bottom of the basket. They are best potted using a natural liner (e.g. bark or unlined coco fibre) so that the new spikes can easily force their way through.

Most orchids respond to supplementary feeding in addition to the compost in which they are growing. Use soluble orchid foods, Dynamic Lifter pellets or liquid feeds of Thrive

or Aquasol every two to three weeks during the growing period. Do not fertilise orchids when they are dormant.

POTTED CACTUS AND OTHER SUCCULENT PLANTS

Cactus plants and other succulents make ideal pot plants for a sunny windowsill, balcony or patio. They are easy to grow and require very little attention. They prefer a dry atmosphere so they need access to plenty of fresh air in humid climates. For pot culture, a suitable mixture consists of coarse sand or fine gravel, compost and leaf mould or peat moss. This mixture holds water but also drains well. Although these fleshy plants can go for long periods without water in their natural habitat, the pots should be watered when the mixture is dry to the touch, especially during the warmer months. Avoid heavy feeding because this promotes rapid, soft growth and plants may rot. A scattering of Acticote (used according to directions) is probably the most suitable fertiliser to use.

The spines of cactus plants are very sharp and may be difficult to remove from the skin, so care must be taken in handling the plants. People with sensitive skins are advised to stick to those succulents without spines, such as *Kalanchoe*, hen and chickens (*Echeveria*), stonecrop (*Sedum*), jade plant (*Crassula*) and sempervivum. Most of these quaint, fleshy plants have attractive flowers. Crab cactus (*Zygocactus*) and orchid cactus (*Epiphyllum*) are also spineless with jointed, flattened stems and showy flowers in winter and spring. Both are ideal for pots or hanging baskets but prefer semi-shade. See also Chapter 22.

FERNS FOR POTS AND BASKETS

Some of the smaller ferns of the dozens of different species available can be grown in containers indoors, or more often in a sheltered patio or courtyard. Most are grown in pots or hanging baskets but some, like staghorns and elkhorns, can be wired to wooden uprights or boards.

Ferns as a group require cool, moist conditions. When indoors, they are best in full light from a window facing south or where summer sunlight can be excluded by curtains.

Free air movement is essential as ferns resent still, dry air and are prone to attack by insects (aphids, mealybug and scale) under poorly ventilated conditions. (See Chapter 8.) It is best to bring potted ferns indoors for decoration for short periods only (one or two weeks) and then return them to a shady, sheltered spot for the same length of time.

A suitable mix for pots and baskets of ferns consists of equal parts of premium potting mix and peat moss or leaf mould. Potting up is best done in late winter or early spring when new fronds appear. Pots or baskets should not be too large as the plants prefer to be crowded. Wire baskets are usually lined with moisture-retaining liner or sphagnum moss. Ferns must be kept damp at all times, although they require less water in winter when growth is slower. Ferns need little feeding and do not like concentrated fertilisers. The safest method is to use water-soluble fertilisers. Apply them at half-strength every three or four weeks during warm weather. Maidenhair fern (*Adiantum*) is one of the most popular and widely grown ferns for pots and baskets. The fronds are finely cut and come on long wiry stems. There are over 200 species of maidenhair fern which differ in leaf shape and size. Hare's-foot fern (*Davallia*) has lacy fronds curving downwards and furry, creeping rhizomes. It is an ideal plant for baskets and tolerates warm conditions providing it is kept moist. Brake fern (*Pteris*) is easily propagated from new crowns which develop from the rhizomes. It is a handsome fern with curled or crimped, many-lobed fronds. Bird's nest fern (*Asplenium*) is a clump of shiny, undivided fronds which may grow to 1 m long. It is an epiphyte that may be grown on pieces of old tree or timber, but is equally at home in a pot filled with sand and leaf mould or peat moss. Propagate by quartering the plant and repotting each section, which will eventually regain its rosette shape. Staghorn or elkhorn ferns (*Platycerium*) are epiphytes that can be attached to a number of surfaces, including stone or brickwork, cork or timber – and are popular in courtyards and ferneries where there is semi-shade. Tree ferns (*Cyathea*) are the giants of the fern family and are best grown in shady positions out of doors. They can be potted into large tubs or sited in a shaded corner bed. Several species are popular, including black tree fern (*C. medullaris*), New Zealand or silver tree fern (*C. dealbata*), the coin spot tree fern (*C. cooperi*) and the Tasmanian tree fern (*Dicksonia australis*). All species are best in semi-shade and like plenty of moisture.

PALMS

Many palms are suitable indoor plants given the correct growing conditions. Palms do not mind root restriction so it is best to put them in a larger pot only when the previous one is filled to capacity with roots. Good drainage and an open, porous soil mixture are essential. Water regularly and feed with water-soluble fertilisers or slow or controlled-release pellets. Palms hate low humidity, so rooms with heaters or air-conditioners are not suitable. If the air is too dry, leaf tips will brown off. Draughts, too, are damaging. Mist spraying the foliage several times a day when the weather is dry and hot helps prevent lasting damage.

Do not stand potted palms in a tray of water because most varieties of palms loathe wet feet. To increase humidity around the palm, fill a shallow tray with pebbles and almost cover with water. Then stand the potted palm on top of the pebbles. Good indirect light is necessary for healthy growth. If a window is not close by, palms will absorb some light from an ordinary electric light placed 40–50 cm above the foliage. Wipe fronds regularly to remove dust. Use commercial leaf wipes, or a weak solution of soap in water.

Indoor palms are often attacked by scale insects and red spider mites. Spider mites usually only occur when the atmosphere is dry. Increase the humidity by mist spraying with water for effective control. Scale is easily removed by scrubbing with a toothbrush and soapy water. Avoid spraying with chemicals indoors.

Palms most suited to growing indoors include: kentia palms (*Howea* spp.); parlour palm (*Chamaedorea*); fish tail palm (*Caryota*); European fan palm (*Chamaerops*); triangle palm (*Neodypsis*) and golden cane palm (*Dypsis*); walking stick palm (*Linospadix*); window palm (*Reinhardtia*); and lady palm or ground rattan cane (*Rhapis*). See detailed information on selected palms in Chapter 19.

24
Gardening for Kids

Gardening is a skill that used to be readily passed on from one generation to the next but, with changing lifestyles, many children grow up without learning any basic gardening skills. Children who don't garden are less likely to gain an appreciation of the importance of plants and of the natural world in our lives. And, just as some children never learn that milk comes from a cow, others fail to understand that the peas, broad beans and sweet corn they eat are seeds, that they are not made in a factory and packed into plastic bags, but that they come from living plants. Introducing children to these and other aspects of their surrounding world can be valuable outcomes from learning to garden.

GARDEN BASICS

The best way to teach children about gardening is for parents to show the way by gardening themselves. Try to make gardening a family activity.

GETTING STARTED

Giving children responsibility for a few potted plants will start them on the path to learning valuable lessons about nurturing other living things. Younger children are seldom successful in maintaining their own part of the garden – their enthusiasm rarely lasts for the required length of time – but plants in pots require far less of an overall commitment. It is important that the basic gardening equipment is at hand – hat, sunscreen, trowel (lightweight but sturdy), pots, potting mix and a small watering can – before the fun can begin.

Flowering annuals may be the best plants to grow in a pot. Because they don't last all that long, a child can grow them then have a break at the end of the season and come back to gardening further down the track. Make sure, though, that children realise that annual plants are short-lived so they're prepared for the plant to come to the end of its life. Choose plants with lots of colour, like petunias; hardiness, like marigolds (although some children don't like their smell); good smells, such as sweet peas; or shade tolerance, like impatiens. Nasturtium seeds are relatively easy to handle and the plants are also straightforward to cultivate. They make a good choice for container growing or garden beds.

If it is difficult to grow a pot outdoors, hardy indoor plants, like madonna lily (*Spathiphyllum* sp.), arrowhead (*Syngonium* sp.) or a kentia palm can be placed in a well-lit spot, out of direct sunlight, in a child's bedroom and even given a name. Teach the child to judge when the plant needs watering by feeling the top of the potting mix, or by using a self-watering pot. Make sure that the water can drain away and that the roots are not sitting in moisture all the time. If necessary, put a layer of fine pebbles in the saucer – this will raise the base of the pot above the residue of water in the saucer.

Feed the plant during the growing season with a long-lasting, slow or controlled-release fertiliser such as Acticote.

GARDEN RULES AND SAFETY

Throughout their growing years children are learning the rules of life. This learning process applies just as much to gardening as to any other activity.

Some commonsense rules are:

1. Don't touch someone else's garden unless you have their permission.
2. Never eat anything in the garden unless you know it is okay.
3. Ask before you pick flowers.
4. Wear sunscreen and a hat as a routine when you are outside in the garden.
5. Wear gloves when handling soil or potting mix, when moving anything rough or sharp or when working where spiders may lurk.
6. Wear boots or solid footwear.
7. Always check inside boots before putting them on, especially if they have been stored outdoors.
8. Garden in suitable old clothes.
9. Wash hands well after handling potting mix, soil or compost.

Most children would love to 'adopt a pot' – especially if the fruit can be used to make lemonade!

POISONOUS PLANTS

Some common garden plants are poisonous and their planting should, if possible, be avoided in kids' gardens. This list is by no means exhaustive, but the inclusion of many commonly grown plants reinforces how important it is that children are taught never to eat anything in the garden unless they know it is safe. All parts of the following plants are poisonous:

✗ Caladium – coloured-leaf indoor plant
✗ Datura and Brugmansia – angel's trumpet
✗ Delphiniums
✗ Foxgloves
✗ Helleborus species – also known as Christmas roses
✗ Lily-of-the-valley
✗ Lobelia
✗ Rhododendrons and azaleas
✗ *Thevetia peruviana* – known as yellow oleander or be-still tree

The leaves of the following plants are poisonous:

✗ Box (*Buxus* spp.)
✗ Calendula
✗ Elephant ears
✗ Rhubarb
✗ Tomato

The flowers of the arum lily are poisonous.

The milky sap of the following is poisonous:

✗ Frangipani
✗ Oleander
✗ Poinsettia

The fruits and seeds of the following are poisonous:

✗ *Cestrum nocturnum* – night-scented jessamine
✗ Clivias
✗ Cycads
✗ Duranta – pigeon berry
✗ Laburnum
✗ *Melia azederach* – white cedar
✗ Moreton Bay chestnut – black bean
✗ Peppercorn tree
✗ Privet
✗ Sweet peas
✗ Wisteria
✗ Yew

These tubers and bulbs are poisonous:

✗ Daffodils
✗ Gloriosa lily
✗ Hyacinth bulbs

Kids can have a face-to-face meeting with a sunflower.

EASY-TO-GROW GARDEN PLANTS

A child can be given responsibility for their 'own' plant in the garden but make sure that the plant chosen is not particularly temperamental or fragile. Geraniums (pelargoniums) are almost indestructible. Clumping plants like agapanthus (there are some wonderful, smaller-growing cultivars) and liriope, lavender, cuphea, abelia and citrus are hard to kill if they are given basic care.

EASY-TO-GROW SEEDS

Growing plants from seed gives a child a chance to understand the very basics of nature. But, in order to achieve success, a child will need some help and guidance. Here are a few tips for successful seed-raising:

1. Read the packet. If it says sow in seed trays or pots, then do so.
2. Sow at the right time of year. Germination is very temperature-dependent.
3. Sow into seed-raising mix.
4. Keep seed trays in bright light, but out of direct sunlight.
5. Keep seeds moist. Water gently with a watering- can or a very soft water-breaker.

Some seeds are easy for beginners as long as you follow basic instructions on the packet.

EASY FLOWERS FROM SEED

Flowers that children will like to grow include nasturtiums, sweet peas, sunflowers, Mexican sunflowers (*Tithonia*), marigolds, cosmos, rudbeckia, pansies and violas. Always sow in the right season. Avoid plants with tiny seeds, such as petunias and lobelias. These can be difficult for the inexperienced seed grower.

Mixed packets of flower seeds (some of them especially labelled for children) can be scattered onto flower beds. Keep moist and something is bound to come up.

HINT

Make a child's garden of golden treasures. Plant a background stand of sunflowers – be sure to give them space as they don't like crowding – then plant little yellow pear tomatoes, golden zucchinis, golden sweet peppers, yellow alpine strawberries, yellow nasturtiums and clumps of stripy yellow French marigolds.

FRANCES HUTCHISON

GARDENING AUTHOR AND EDITOR

GARDENS KIDS CAN EAT

Most children like to have a productive garden but it is essential that the fruits and vegetables they grow are varieties they are likely to eat. For example, radishes give satisfyingly fast results, but very few children enjoy eating them. Some vegies that are popular with kids are sweet corn, cherry tomatoes, beans straight off the plant (not cooked) and snow peas.

Easy-to-grow fruits include strawberries (which can even be grown in a hanging basket), citrus trees of most kinds (especially mandarins), blueberries, passionfruit, and raspberries in colder climates.

Productive plants need a sunny position, compost-enriched soil (or potting mix), and regular watering and fertilising.

HINT

Keep your strawberry punnets – the clear plastic ones with holes – for raising seeds to show children how the roots of plants grow. Plant a big seed, bean or pea, in Yates Seed Raising mix next to the edge of the punnet, and as the seed germinates and grows, the roots will be seen as well as the shoot. From little things big things grow!

TIM JACKSON
FREELANCE GARDEN WRITER

If given some encouragement, children will love learning the joys of cultivating their own garden plot.

Create parts of the garden that are secret or enclosed, for a good game of Hide-and-Seek.

CONTAINER GARDENING

Gardening in pots or containers is a good way to kick-start a child's interest in gardening. There are many interesting pots available or children can enjoy painting and decorating plastic containers. The basics for success are:

1. Don't have too small a pot – it will dry out too quickly and will need to be watered often.
2. Use a good-quality potting mix. Look for the Australian Standards mark on the bag.
3. Water with a water-breaker (not a nozzle) attached to the end of a hose.
4. Don't allow the base of the pot to sit in water.
5. Remember potting mixes need more fertiliser than soil. Feed regularly during the growing season with a soluble plant food, such as Thrive or Aquasol, or slow- or controlled-release pellets.
6. Wear gloves if possible and wash hands after handling potting mix.

HINT

Are your kids too big for their boots? Don't throw away their old shoes. Fill them with potting mix and grow some small treasures, like mini cyclamens or African violets. Paint the shoes in matching colours for a boot-iful display.

MICHÈLE ADLER

LECTURER, AUTHOR, TOUR LEADER – ADLAND HORTICULTURAL

Top five trees for climbing

PLANE TREE

Platanus x hybrida Though rather large for the suburban garden, plane trees have excellent, well-spaced branches. The round seed balls are just right for squashing underfoot.

KAFFIR PLUM

Harpephyllum caffrum Really only suitable for frost-free areas, the dense canopy of this African tree provides a perfect hiding place.

CEDAR WATTLE

Acacia elata A fast-growing and long-lived wattle that can be ready for climbing after a relatively short period of time.

BRUSH BOX

Lophostemon confertus A favourite street tree that is hardy enough to withstand difficult conditions. It has lovely smooth bark and reasonably broad branches. An attractive, slightly smaller-growing variagated variety is available.

MULBERRY

Morus alba Every child's dream and a parent's nightmare! A tree you can sit in and feast from at the same time. Everyone can be happy if the child knows to wear old clothes – then the stains won't matter.

PLANE TREE

SECRET GARDENS

One of the most famous twentieth-century children's stories, *The Secret Garden* by Frances Hodgson Burnett, surely owes much of its enduring popularity to the fact that every child fantasises about having a secret outdoor place to escape to.

Children love parts of the garden that are secretive and enclosed – where they can feel alone but secure.

If your garden can be designed with some slightly hidden or separate sections, it will have a special appeal for children.

GARDEN ACTIVITIES FOR KIDS

1. Use stalks from dead agapanthus flowers to build a 'cubby' around a simple frame.
2. Collect cicada shells, ask an adult to help you spray-paint them gold or silver, and use them as decorations on next year's Christmas tree.
3. Using a small, sharp stick or a ballpoint pen, write your name on a baby zucchini and watch it grow as the fruit expands into a giant marrow.
4. Have a competition to grow the biggest pumpkin.
5. Under supervision, make a Jack-o'-lantern out of a pumpkin (or a ripe orange).
6. Make poppy dolls out of poppy flowers by pulling down the petals and tying a ribbon or piece of grass around the 'waist'.
7. Make pictures on the ground or in the sandpit by using round wattle flowers.
8. Gather winged maple seeds. They make fantastic helicopters if dropped from a height and allowed to corkscrew to the ground.
9. Pop any flower buds that are ready to open. Fuchsias and poppies are good.
10. Stick rose thorns onto a friend's forehead with a bit of moisture, and turn the child into an instant 'devil'.

Another activity for kids is to grow a hyacinth bulb in the top of a bottle. All they will need is a good-sized bulb and a jar or bottle whose top is just about the right diameter for the bulb to sit on top. Fill the jar with water until it is just below the base of the bulb, and keep it topped up by carefully lifting the bulb and pouring more water in. The roots of the bulb will grow down where they can be clearly seen in the water. Eventually the bulb will produce a flower.

Hyacinth bulbs can also be grown in an indoor pot. In order to develop a good flower stem, it's helpful to keep the pot in a dark cupboard, or cover it with an upside-down pot until the shoot emerges. Gradually introduce the hyacinth to more light as its shoot develops.

Never place the indoor bulb into direct sunlight or subject it to indoor heating. These stresses will spoil the flowering before it even starts to happen.

One word of warning: hyacinth bulbs have a special irritant in their scaly outer skin that can cause itchiness. Always wash hands well after touching hyacinth bulbs or, better still, handle the bulbs with gloves.

FASCINATING PLANTS FOR KIDS' GARDENS

Strelitzia (bird of paradise). This plant has colourful flowers that look like exotic birds on top of stiff stems.

Sensitive plant (*Mimosa pudica*). This plant has become a dreadful weed in northern Australia but can be a fun, potted plant in cooler climates. When touched, the leaves fold up and can take some time before they unfurl again.

Tortured willow (*Salix matsudana* 'Tortuosa') and twisted hazelnut (*Corylus avellana* 'Contorta') have curiously curled and twisted stems that children love. They can be cut during their dormant winter season, dried and used as floral decorations or for displaying light ornaments, especially for Christmas.

Pussy willows are also loved for the fluffy catkins that decorate their stems in spring. All willows should be planted with care and never where there is any risk of these water-hungry plants invading drains.

Chain of hearts (*Ceropegia woodii*) is a delightful basket plant with leaves that do indeed resemble tiny hearts.

Making a scarecrow is a fun garden activity.

Try planting drifts of bulbs over part of the lawn. Plant clumps of freesias, sparaxis, ixia, tritonia and gladiolus species as the backbone of your display. Add clumps of paper-white narcissus, jonquils and daffodils here and there as highlights.

SHIRLEY STACKHOUSE
GARDEN WRITER

If you don't want your lawn to look too formal, include a path and plant dwarf mondo grass, brachyscome daisy or thyme in the strips between the paving.

SHIRLEY STACKHOUSE
GARDEN WRITER

For romance, plant three silver birch trees in the lawn. Add some summer- and autumn-flowering bulbs (belladonna, nerines, zephyranthes).

SHIRLEY STACKHOUSE
GARDEN WRITER

Thatch is an enemy of the dedicated lawn cultivator because it makes a spongy surface, invites turf diseases and shows up as brown marks within a day of mowing. This thatch consists of a layer of brown-coloured grass stems and roots between the soil and the green foliage. Couch lawns are the main sites of thatch but it can be present in buffalo and kikuyu lawns too.

Verticutting is the traditional means of removing this layer and this has now become an annual job, not only for turf professionals but for home gardeners as well.

Recent work, however, has shown that using organic fertilisers, together with fish- and kelp-based plant tonics, seems to encourage soil-borne microbes to go to work and eat up the thatch. In effect these organic materials promote a natural composting process.

NEVILLE PASSMORE
WA GARDENING MEDIA PERSONALITY

If you have a very weedy lawn, rather than spraying with a weedicide, try placing sheets of Masonite or black plastic over the lawn. This is called solar sterilisation. After a few weeks remove the sheets, rake the soil over, water, let the bulk of the seeds come up, then again apply the sheets. After this, lay your lawn.

MEREDITH KIRTON
HORTICULTURIST, AUTHOR OF *DIG AND PLOT*, *HARVEST* AND *AN HOUR IN THE GARDEN*

Where flowerbeds intersect the lawn, trim lawn edges by hand. Whipper-snippers are noisy and don't allow fine detail . . . and it's amazing how many small seedlings you find when you're on your knees and close to the action.

ANNE LATREILLE
GARDEN WRITER

Plants with sharp spines or serrated leaf margins can wreak havoc with your skin. Get yourself a pair of pruning gauntlets that go almost to the elbows or if your favourite gloves do not have long sleeves, cut the foot out of a pair of footy socks and slide them up your forearms for protection.

KAREN SMITH
EDITOR, *HORT JOURNAL*

Before dividing large clumping plants like New Zealand flax, bird of paradise or wild iris, run a dripping hose on the root-ball for two to three hours. This loosens the dirt and the hold that those tenacious rhizomes have on it. It makes your job (almost) as easy as cutting cake.

MICHÈLE ADLER
LECTURER, AUTHOR, TOUR LEADER – ADLAND HORTICULTURAL

When transplanting bulbous plants, lift soon after dying down to avoid damaging any new season roots, then plant as advised for each kind of bulb.

GEORGE JONES, H.L.M.
HORTICULTURAL MEDIA ASSOCIATION

To help cut flowers last longer, take half a bucket of water with you when picking flowers (rather than a basket) and place flowers immediately into the water. Cut stems on a slant, as they will absorb more water through the wider cut.

GRAEME PURDY
GARDENING WRITER

At bulb-planting time use a waterproof marker pen to write two labels, one for sticking in the ground where the bulbs are planted, the other to keep. When the bulbs go in, drop one of the labels in alongside them. When you come to dig the bulbs up at the end of the season you have positive identification of the variety and a ready-made label to pop in the bag for storage.

JOHN 'GREENFINGERS' COLWILL
GARDENING WRITER AND BROADCASTER

So you know exactly which way up to plant ranunculi corms, place moistened cottonwool on a saucer and then rest your corms on top. In a few days white roots will appear. By doing this you also make sure that you only plant healthy corms.

PETER DE WAART
HORTICULTURIST

After your bulbs have died down, avoid tying the foliage in knots. This damages the foliage and reduces the amount of nutrients returning to the bulb for future use.

PETER DE WAART
HORTICULTURIST

To achieve stronger rose plants and more flowers, use seaweed solution fortnightly, deep-soak roses to deliver 20 litres of water per rose, weekly (roses are drought-tolerant plants); support standard roses with a metal stake and remove spent flowers continually to give massive displays of roses throughout the season.

GRAHAM SARGEANT
SILKIES ROSE FARM & ROSESALESONLINE, CLONBINANE, VICTORIA

Plants sitting in a garden centre are usually in immaculate condition. Don't expect the perfection to continue immediately after you put them in your garden. Be prepared for a temporary setback when these pampered children are introduced to the real world. When you're buying in summer, even the species that are tolerant of full sun may suffer burnt foliage if they've been protected in the production nursery and kept in a shady area of the garden centre. Wind can also damage the foliage of a shrub which has spent its infancy sheltered by nursery walls. Just give the plants time to adjust to their new location.

JULIA BERNEY
HORTICULTURAL–AGRICULTURAL FREELANCE
EDITOR

The simple act of adding temporary shade in the garden holds the key to preventing significant plant damage caused by summer heatwaves. Shading can drop air temperatures in and around the plant's canopy by 15°C to 20°C and drop topsoil temperatures (where most roots grow) by 10°C to 15°C. When mulching is added to shading, you can drop topsoil temperatures a further 5°C to 10°C. Collectively, these measures will go a long way to preventing plant stress.

JON LAMB
SOUTH AUSTRALIAN GARDEN WRITER AND ABC 891
SATURDAY TALKBACK GARDENER

Most South African bulbs, including freesias, lapeirousias, babiana, gladiolus, agapanthus and many others, are so well suited to Australian conditions they can easily become weeds in the garden from their own seeds. Stop this happening by always removing the seed capsules that form straight after flowers finish.

GEOFFREY BURNIE
GARDENING JOURNALIST

To encourage constant flowering from climbing roses, tie canes down flat so they shoot and flower the length of the branch. When they have flowered, cut back to one or two shoots for repeat flowering. Tip-prune the water shoots in the autumn or winter.

HOLLY KERR FORSYTH
GARDEN WRITER, PHOTOGRAPHER –
THE WEEKEND AUSTRALIAN

In most areas of Australia, David Austin roses flower better if pruned reasonably hard in spring and summer after their main flush of flowers. In particular, prune the growth that has flowered by at least one-third, feed with Dynamic Lifter Plus Flower Food for Roses and mulch carefully. You'll be rewarded with masses of flowers and perfume.

LEIGH SIEBLER
DAVID AUSTIN ROSES
SIEBLER PUBLISHING SERVICES

Species hydrangeas are easy to grow, more sun-hardy and need no special pruning. Prune only in winter for shape. There is no need to prune to plump buds as you do for the common hydrangeas.

TEENA CRAWFORD
GARDEN WRITER AND CONSULTANT

If you have a black spot problem on your roses, be sure to collect all the infected leaves that fall to the ground and spray surrounding soil with fungicide. The dead leaves can easily harbour the dormant fungal spores and reinfect your roses as soon as conditions are favourable.

CAROLYN BLACKMAN
HORTICULTURIST — VIVID DESIGN

To have roses flower for months and months of the year, give them a good hard prune after each flush of flowers (as if you were picking them for a tall vase), plus a handful of pelletised manure and a spread of lucerne hay.

SANDRA ROSS
THE GARDEN CLINIC

Prune spent flowers of helleborus before seed pods form to prevent self-seeding in the garden. Alternatively leave the spent flowers until the seed pods develop fully (when the seed turns black), harvest and scatter where you want them to grow.

TEENA CRAWFORD
GARDEN WRITER AND CONSULTANT

When pruning a tall hedge, make sure the base is wider than the top. This allows light to reach all parts of the hedge.

PETER DE WAART
HORTICULTURIST

For best results prune self-clinging climbers such as Boston ivy to about 10–15 cm, before planting flush with the wall. This encourages the plant to produce new growth which will adhere to the supporting structure and establish itself quickly.

TEENA CRAWFORD
GARDEN WRITER AND CONSULTANT

Many gardeners grow New South Wales Christmas bush (Ceratopetalum gummiferum) to use in indoor arrangements over the festive season. Another equally attractive Christmas native to grow with it is Baeckea virgata, an elegant, arching shrub about 3 m tall. At Christmas it covers itself with masses of tiny white flowers that cut well.

GEOFFREY BURNIE
GARDENING JOURNALIST

There's no better way to clear the head than by visiting the mountains. When the mountain mists swirl through the trees, the droplets of water hang on the leaves and a glimmer of sunlight hits mist-laden cobwebs, it is simply magic. This light is also perfect for garden photography. I leave the mountains totally invigorated to face the real world.

CEDRIC BRYANT
GARDEN DESIGNER AND GARDEN WRITER CITY NEWS CANBERRA

Plants with succulent rather than woody stems, such as impatiens, geraniums, begonias and many others, will often form new roots in a month or less just by placing a cutting in a jar of water in bright light. It's an easy and free way to make more of the same plant.

GEOFFREY BURNIE
GARDENING JOURNALIST

One of the best products country people can use for their garden is sheep dags – do not waste them, they are great starter pack for plant roots. The wool has keratin (a wonderful protein source) and of course there is the attached slow release fertiliser in the form of poo. What more could a plant want! Wool also has good water retention qualities, so bag those dags and take them into the garden.

SABRINA HAHN
ABC RADIO GARDENING PRESENTER AND JOURNALIST.

Looking for a lightweight climber that flowers for months but doesn't get out of hand? Go straight for a Dipladenia, sometimes also sold as Mandevilla.

They start blooming in spring and, in frost-free areas, can still be flowering the following June. Flowers are 7cm-wide trumpets in white, pink or red.

GEOFFREY BURNIE
GARDENING JOURNALIST

When planting trees and shrubs from pots into the ground the general rule is to remove about half the potting mix and tease the roots to expose any kinked or circling roots, which you should cut out. Back fill the hole with soil you dug out so that the exposed roots come in direct contact with the soil. Do not put compost or fertiliser into the hole, instead place mulch (compost) and any fertiliser on top of the soil once you have finished planting. Firm the tree or shrub with fingers not the heel of your shoes – this avoids compaction.

ROD McMILLAN
PUBLISHER, TOUR LEADER, DIRECTOR – ADLAND
HORTICULTURAL

For cut flowers to last their full lives, their water must be perfectly clean, so rinse out the vase with bleach to kill off any fungi or bacteria lurking from last time and then filling with fresh water. Don't worry if a touch of bleach remains.

ROGER MANN
LANDSCAPE ARCHITECT AND AUTHOR
OF YATES ROSES AND NAMING THE ROSE

To achieve an interesting multi-trunked effect in specimen trees such as *Corymbia haemastoma* (Scribbly gum), plant three or five tubestock in the one hole.

ROS ANDREWS
HORTICULTURAL CONSULTANT

Do your bit to keep fallen leaves out of stormwater drains by raking up leaves from nature strips and gutters and either putting them directly on your garden or adding them to your compost heap. Encourage neighbours to collect and use this free autumn bounty.

MARGARET HANKS
HORTICULTURIST

If bushwalking is a favourite pastime, before you head home check for weed seeds on your shoes and clothing, particularly the legs of your pants. If you take your pets with you, check them too. Seeds are the perfect stowaways and would be very happy to hop on the coat of your dog and hitch a ride back to your beautiful garden where conditions may suit them nicely.

KAREN SMITH
EDITOR, *HORT JOURNAL*

When planting trees and large shrubs in poor-quality soils, add a slice of lucerne hay in the bottom of the planting hole. It won't burn the roots and as it rots it acts as a slow-release organic fertiliser. Worms love it, too.

ROSEMARY DAVIES
GARDEN MEDIA PERSONALITY AND CONSULTANT

What to do about that gardenia that will not thrive in your garden?
I was about to give up on a gardenia in my garden and in desperation I placed some magnesium-rich fertiliser close to its roots. Within a couple of weeks the leaves started to turn green (instead of sickly yellow) and now I have flowers for the first time in years.

MORRIS HOLMES
HORTICULTURAL CONSULTANT AND GARDEN
DESIGNER

It is encouraging to see plants grow quickly but watch that your plants don't become top-heavy if the stem and roots are not yet developed well enough to support such growth. A little shortening and/or thinning of branches can help to reduce the stress. Always try to maintain the growth character of the plant as you undertake the removal of foliage.

RODGER ELLIOT AM
CO-AUTHOR *ENCYCLOPAEDIA OF AUSTRALIAN PLANTS*

If you are not sure whether a plant can be successfully pruned back into leafless stems, cut one or two branches and wait for a few weeks to see if new growth develops. If new buds and leaves appear you can then confidently proceed with further pruning of the plant.

GWEN ELLIOT AM
GARDEN WRITER AND BROADCASTER

Passionfruit and hibiscus can be pruned and fertilised in August in frost-free areas. In cold districts wait until September. Winter-flowering peach should be pruned when blossoms finish.

SHIRLEY STACKHOUSE
GARDEN WRITER

Clematis like to keep their roots in the shade and to grow towards the sun. To ensure that roots are kept cool, cut a piece of shade cloth to fit around the stem and over the root area. Then cover with mulch.

HOLLY KERR FORSYTH
GARDEN WRITER, PHOTOGRAPHER – *THE WEEKEND AUSTRALIAN*

When staking a tree, put a small piece of carpet or a wad of hessian against the trunk so the stake does not damage the bark. Do not use wire, wire tie or twine – these do not rot and are likely to cause damage over time. Nylon stockings or Velcro tape are among the best ties.

PAMELA JANE 1936–2012
GARDEN WRITER

Digging a planting hole can become a major hassle if you strike rock (or large roots). So before you start digging, test the soil depth by hammering a length of heavy-gauge wire into the ground and measuring the result.

ROGER FOX
GARDEN EDITOR – *BETTER HOMES AND GARDENS* MAGAZINE

Cardboard toilet-roll inners and the like, when laid on their sides in garden beds, make wonderful hiding places for snails. Check regularly and stand on any hiding culprits. If you don't like the sound of that, poke your fingers in your ears and wear shoes!

DAVID YOUNG OAM
FORMER WRITER, TV AND RADIO PRESENTER

To remove a medium-sized tree or shrub, dig a circular trench around it about a metre away from the trunk. Using a sharp spade, dig vertically all the way around to cut cleanly any surface roots. Fill the trench with water several times and then rock the tree. This will loosen other roots and should make removal easier.

PAMELA JANE 1936–2012
GARDEN WRITER

Tree ferns often outgrow their garden space and need to be moved. Dicksonias, the tree ferns with fat hairy trunks, can be cut off and replanted. The other common tree ferns, cyatheas, have thinner trunks, grow more quickly and are difficult to transplant because they must be moved with their root systems intact. Whatever the variety, cut off most of the leaves at transplanting time and keep the trunk moist while the fern is settling into its new home.

JUDY HORTON
GARDEN WRITER, BROADCASTER AND HORTICULTURIST

Many large camellia blooms fall from their stems before they have lost their glory. A long florist pin, poked through the calyx at the base of the flower, will hold it in place for a few more days.

PAMELA JANE 1936–2012
GARDEN WRITER

Many gardeners grow NSW Christmas bush (*Ceratopetalum gummiferum*) to use in indoor arrangements over the festive season. Another equally attractive Christmas native to grow with it is *Baeckea virgata*, an elegant, arching shrub with masses of tiny white flowers.

GEOFFREY BURNIE
GARDENING JOURNALIST

Callistemons or Australian bottlebrushes are among the most adaptable of plants for so many situations. Most are happy to be waterlogged in winter but can also tolerate extended dry periods. They are ideal for screening purposes and provide a wonderful display of colourful flower-heads. Try planting two different-coloured bottle-brushes in the same hole; they will thrive with such

treatment and the flowers are eye-catching.

RODGER ELLIOT AM
CO-AUTHOR ENCYCLOPAEDIA OF AUSTRALIAN PLANTS

Clump-forming liriopes are hardy, versatile plants for semi-shade or shaded areas of the garden. Grow them as borders, drifts, ground covers or even as a substitute for lawn. They also make excellent container plants. Liriopes have dark-green strap leaves and numerous spikes of small purple flowers appear in the beginning of summer through to the middle of autumn. Once established, they tolerate periods of dryness and grow well even under large trees.

TEENA CRAWFORD
GARDEN WRITER AND CONSULTANT

The antiseptic action of tea-tree oil has long been known. Used by the Australian Aborigines, particularly those in the north of Australia to treat coral cuts or abrasions, tea-tree oil can also be used to relieve mosquito and insect bites, muscular aches and pains and minor burns.

ROSS McKINNON AM
RETIRED CURATOR – BRISBANE BOTANIC GARDENS

If your cymbidium orchid has failed to flower this year you may need to re-pot it. Over the years potting mix breaks down and the plants stop flowering. The best time to re-pot is spring. Choose a pot your orchid just fits into – they prefer being slightly root-bound. If they have too much space they'll grow lots of roots instead of flowers.

DEBBIE McDONALD
GARDEN WRITER, EDITOR AND HORTICULTURALIST

There's nothing better to give house plants a boost than a shower in the rain. Take them outside and let the rain wash the dust off the leaves and drench the soil. They will shine until next time.

MARK HAY

GARDEN CENTRE PROPRIETOR, FORMER TV
AND RADIO TALKBACK HORTICULTURAL HOST,
GARDEN ADVISER

Rejuvenate indoor containerised plants that have dried out and are too heavy or awkward to move outside by watering thoroughly with warm (not hot) water, or if you prefer, ice blocks left to slowly penetrate the potting medium. When the plant has perked up, give it a good dose of soil wetter to prevent future drying-out problems.

VALERIE AND GERRY ZWART

GARDEN WRITERS, QUEENSLAND

If moving indoor plants temporarily outside, be extremely careful about the environmental conditions they are exposed to. Never place plants in direct sunlight. They have not developed the capability to protect themselves and can receive very significant UV damage. Also beware of cool temperatures. Even without frosts, some 'tropical' indoor plants may be damaged by temperatures of 5°C.

JOHN MASON

GARDENING AUTHOR, PRINCIPAL – THE
AUSTRALIAN CORRESPONDENCE SCHOOLS

Use old terracotta flowerpots, tucked between plants and half-buried on their sides, to provide a cool, safe retreat for the frogs, lizards and invertebrates which keep the garden's ecosystem in balance. While hollow logs are sometimes used for this purpose, their disadvantage is that they may also attract termites.

JULIA BERNEY

HORTICULTURAL–AGRICULTURAL FREELANCE
EDITOR

Check the drainage holes of vigorously growing pot plants at the end of summer. Sometimes the roots will have blocked the holes, which can give rise to water-logging problems in winter. If the holes are blocked, use a sharp knife to cut them away and restore good drainage.

JOHN 'GREENFINGERS' COLWILL

GARDENING WRITER AND BROADCASTER

Chillies grown in a hydroponic container placed in a bright, light spot make a dramatic decoration for a dining room. Potted peppers will heat up table talk and stimulate taste buds.

SUSAN PARSONS

KITCHEN GARDEN WRITER

Roses love a feed. For longer flowering and hardier plants, apply the recommended dose of a dedicated rose fertiliser (e.g. Dynamic Lifter for Flowers) in early September then monthly, at half the recommended rate, finishing in April. Your roses will be blooming brilliant!

KIM SYRUS

GARDEN GURUS TV

Modern potting mixes are terrific but a little hard to re-wet if allowed to dry out. When watering a dry pot, you'll usually find the water runs through quickly and does not soak the plant. Either add a soil-wetter like Waterwise or stand your pot overnight in a trough of water to allow water uptake. Don't leave the pot sitting in water after that though.

LEIGH SIEBLER
SIEBLER PUBLISHING SERVICES

Make an instant portable hedge with potted plants or fast-growing plants with short internodes (such as *Plectranthus saccatus*). It is preferable to put them into square green pots so that you can place them close together. The pots can be moved every time you need an outline in your garden.

LORNA ROSE M.A.I.H.
HORTICULTURAL PHOTOGRAPHER

You can grow a feast of fruit and vegetables in small spaces. Make the most of a tight spot with compact growing vegies, herbs and mini fruit trees, which are tailor made for growing in decorative containers.

MELISSA KING
HORTICULTURALIST, TV PRESENTER AND AUTHOR

Indoor plants often suffer in the cooler months from being over-watered. The most sophisticated moisture-sensing device is literally on hand. Poke your finger into the soil to the first joint. If the soil feels damp or grains of soil stick to your fingertip, the plant does not need watering.

JOHN 'GREENFINGERS' COLWILL
GARDENING WRITER AND BROADCASTER

Plan an out-of-sight resting area in your garden where pot plants not in bloom can be placed. Once they begin to flower, put them back on show.

TONY FAWCETT
GARDEN WRITER – SATURDAY *HERALD SUN* *HOME* MAGAZINE

Introduce children to the joys of growing from seed by letting them write their names in a patch of soil with fast-germinating species such as radish, cosmos or cornflowers. Pre-mixing the seed with sugar will make it easier to see them on the ground.

MERILYN KUCHEL
GARDEN ADVISER

Older children can grow spuds in a courtyard or small garden space by planting seed potatoes into composty soil in a deep, green plastic pot with saucer. As leaves emerge, keep covering them with composty soil, then place a second pot on top with its bottom cut out. Top the lot with lucerne hay and harvest new potatoes four months later.

SUSAN PARSONS
KITCHEN GARDEN WRITER

When kids go on an Easter egg hunt, give them a basket of bulbs. At each spot where an egg is found, encourage the child to plant a bulb in its place. This doesn't just apply to kids, either – Easter is also a great time for adults to plant bulbs and spring seedlings. Much better for the waistline than eating chocolate eggs!

SHIRLEY STACKHOUSE
GARDEN WRITER

As long as you have the space for them to sprawl across the ground in sun, watermelons and rockmelons are fun summer crops to grow that are cheap and easy to raise from seed.

GEOFFREY BURNIE
GARDENING JOURNALIST

Egg cartons (use a pencil to make a drainage hole) make an ideal substitute for mini peat pots when sowing larger seeds such as sunflowers, peas or beans. A few weeks later, little fingers can easily break apart the soggy cartons and pop the seedlings into the soil without damaging the roots.

MERILYN KUCHEL
GARDEN ADVISER

Place a broad bean seed in a glass jar filled with potting mix. Children will be intrigued to see how the fibrous roots develop.

PETER DE WAART
HORTICULTURIST

I believe the greatest advance we will see in successful gardening and growing food this century will come from an understanding of the role of humified carbon (we know this as humus) in enhancing soil biology leading to true soil fertility. We can add this vital by incorporating mature composted material to all forms of soil. While it does have some nutrient content its chief role is to build soil carbon levels and feed the biology that is the real driver of plant success.

NEVILLE PASSMORE
WA GARDENING MEDIA PERSONALITY

If you are prone to attack by mozzies and like to garden at dusk when they are out in droves, rub a bit of eucalyptus oil onto your skin. Mosquitoes hate it and you can garden for hours mossie-free.

KAREN SMITH
EDITOR, *HORT JOURNAL*

There are many plants that bees will love but it is important for them to have diversity for their pollen and nectar gathering. Check when your local native plant will be flowering, and when they might be lacking in flowers, plant annuals or perennials that will flower at that time. Daisies, Cosmos, Sunflowers etc all have high pollen counts for example.

As a new beekeeper, I have become more aware that there are many plants that bees will love but it is important for them to have diversity for their pollen and nectar gathering. Check when your local native plant varieties will be flowering and consider planting exotic species that will fill the gaps. There is a great book to help you choose the right plant for your area all around Australia: Bee Friendly by Mark Leech and available from the Rural Industries publishing house.

TIM JACKSON
FREELANCE GARDEN WRITER

Use pheromone traps to attract pests like citrus leaf miner or fruit fly. Home-made traps will also capture the good bugs like lacewings and lady beetles. Also pick up any fallen fruit that might attract fruit fly.

MARIANNE CANNON
PRESENTER, REAL WORLD GARDENER ON 2RRR
AND ACROSS AUSTRALIA ON THE COMMUNITY
RADIO NETWORK

Twelve-month Gardening Calendar

JANUARY

In cold climates

1 Prepare bulb beds and order new bulbs from catalogues.

2 Grow new plants for free by taking cuttings from favourite shrubs.

3 Spray apples, pears and hawthorns with Success Ultra to control pear and cherry slug. Success Ultra will also control codling moth.

4 Pick strawberries regularly and make sure they're well watered during dry periods.

5 Sow or plant hollyhocks, stocks and forget-me-nots.

In temperate climates

1 For a wonderful autumn rose display (in 6–8 weeks' time), cut back now and fertilise with a good quality rose food.

2 Spray a film of Yates DroughtShield over tender plants to protect them from sunburn and heatwaves.

3 Harvest beans, zucchinis and other summer vegetables regularly so they'll produce more crops.

4 Use Nature's Way Fruit Fly Control in fruit fly areas.

5 Sow or plant broccoli, silver beet and basil around tomatoes.

In tropical/subtropical climates

1 Pinch out the growing tips of poinsettias. The plants will be bushier, which will mean more winter blooms.

2 Feed avocadoes with Dynamic Lifter PLUS Fruit Food. Spray with Anti Rot to prevent root rot.

3 Prune bougainvilleas and other climbers that are threatening to take over the whole garden.

4 Use a garden fork to aerate lawns after heavy rains. Top up mulch on garden beds.

5 Sow or plant sunflowers, vincas and zinnias.

FEBRUARY

In cold climates

1 Prune stone fruit after harvest.

2 Keep dahlias blooming by removing dead flowers.

3 Powdery mildew spoils roses, begonias and many other plants. Control with Rose Gun Advanced.

4 Buy new season's bulbs but don't plant until the ground cools down.

5 Sow or plant calendulas and forget-me-nots.

In temperate climates

1 Water, water, water during dry periods. Deep watering trains roots to grow down, making plants less vulnerable to heat and drought.

2 Put cold-climate bulbs – tulips, daffodils, hyacinths, crocus – into the refrigerator. Chill them for at least six weeks.

3 Treat scale pests with PestOil or Scale Gun. Any sooty mould will gradually flake away after treatment.

4 Repot cyclamens into fresh potting mix. Feed with Acticote or begin a program with a soluble fertiliser like Thrive.

5 Sow or plant nigella and dwarf marigolds.

In tropical/subtropical climates

1 Cobwebby dead patches on lawns are usually caused by fungal diseases. Spray with Mancozeb Plus or Zaleton and feed with disease-resistant, high-potash Thrive Flower & Fruit.

2 Remove diseased flowers and leaves regularly. Bin them; don't put them in the compost.

3 Sow cucurbits (squash, zucchinis, etc) now that there's less chance of mildew. Treat with Lime Sulfur if it does appear.

4 Feed fruit trees with Dynamic Lifter PLUS Fruit Food and top up mulch over root systems.

5 Sow beans and cucumbers for a fast-maturing crop.

MARCH

In cold climates

1 March is caterpillar time. Control by spraying with Nature's Way Caterpillar Killer Dipel, a natural bio-insecticide that is non-toxic to humans.

2 This is a good month to divide and plant perennials like alpine phlox, campanulas, bergenias, shasta daisies, asters and hostas.

3 Harvest pumpkins and leave them in an open sunny position to dry out before storing.

4 Continue spraying roses for black spot and pests with Rose Gun Advanced or Rose Shield.

5 Sow or plant some true English spinach. It's really at its best in a cooler climate.

In temperate climates

1 Twisted and curled young leaves on citrus are caused by citrus leaf miner. Spray regularly with PestOil to prevent further damage. Use Success Ultra if the problem's severe.

2 Prune hedge plants such as box, coast rosemary, grevilleas and murrayas.

3 Thicken up tired lawns with Yates All Season blend or another fast-germinating grass blend.

4 Keep a Rose Gun Advanced on hand to treat powdery mildew as soon as it appears on ornamentals.

5 Sow sweet peas next to a sunny fence on St Patrick's Day (17 March). Wait a few weeks if weather's still warm.

In tropical/subtropical climates

1 Stop weeds from seeding by pulling them out, smothering them with mulch or spraying with Zero 1-Hr Rapid.

2 Take leaf cuttings of African violets and begonias.

3 Pots of New Guinea impatiens will give bright autumn colour.

4 Lawn grubs can eat entire lawns at this time of year. Complete Lawn Insect Control can be applied as an easy hose-on.

5 Feed hibiscus and gardenias with Dynamic Lifter PLUS Flower Food.

APRIL

In cold climates

1 Prune and tidy day lilies, Easter daisies, lavender, phlox and other perennials that have finished flowering.

2 Plant the rest of the spring-flowering bulbs.

3 Sow Flanders poppies to commemorate Anzac Day.

4 Select and plant trees for autumn colour while you can see them at their best.

5 Sow broad beans, peas and onions.

In temperate climates

1 Feed shrubs and trees with organic Dynamic Lifter. Make holes down through the lawn and fill with Dynamic Lifter to avoid greedy grass getting all the nutrients.

2 Mix some compost or old manure into the soil to get it ready for new roses.

3 Feed lawns with a good-quality lawn food such as Dynamic Lifter Concentrated. Afterwards, water well to carry the fertiliser down to the roots.

4 Take daffodil, tulip and hyacinth bulbs out of the fridge and plant into pots or garden beds.

5 Sow or plant sweet peas, cinerarias (in frost-free areas) and primulas.

In tropical/subtropical climates

1 This is one of the best months for planting trees and shrubs.

2 Bulbs that have the best chances of success in warm climates are freesias, jonquils, ixias and babianas.

3 Cut back geraniums with spotty, diseased leaves. Spray with a Rose Gun Advanced.

4 Start a new lawn by laying turf. Prepare soil well, adding some

Dynamic Lifter Turf Starter.

5 Sow or plant lettuces, beans and cherry tomatoes.

MAY

In cold climates

1 A pot filled with garden goodies makes a great Mother's Day gift.

2 After their leaves fall, give deciduous fruit trees a clean-up spray with lime sulfur.

3 Move cold-sensitive container plants into more sheltered positions or begin to spray with DroughtShield to give frost protection

4 Collect fallen autumn leaves. They're ideal for composting.

5 Sow or plant lilium bulbs, baby's breath and carnations.

In temperate climates

1 Choose a cyclamen in full flower to brighten up a cool, well-lit indoor spot.

2 May's the last-chance month for planting spring bulbs.

3 Continue feeding lettuce, cabbages and silverbeet with Thrive All Purpose to encourage as much growth as possible.

4 New season's packaged roses appear in the shops. Purchase early for the best selection.

5 Sow or plant primulas, spring onions and radishes.

In tropical/subtropical climates

1 Transplant runners (sideways-growing pieces with some roots) from couch, kikuyu or Durban (sweet smother) grass lawns to fill bare patches.

2 This is a good month for planting citrus. The leaves of the kaffir lime add a special flavour to Asian dishes and native finger limes make a great garnish.

3 Protect emerging orchid flower spikes with a sprinkling of Blitzem or Baysol snail pellets.

4 In warm climates, there's still plenty of time to plant sweet peas. Pots provide best drainage.

5 Sow or plant spider flowers (cleome), calendulas, beetroot and carrots.

JUNE

In cold climates

1 Plant new roses. A thick layer of straw around the base will protect the young stems in very cold areas.

2 Prune hydrangeas and take cuttings to grow new plants, only cutting back stems that flowered last season.

3 Feed winter vegetables with soluble Thrive or Aquasol to keep them growing strongly.

4 Before the sun hits their leaves in the morning, spray water generously over frost-sensitive plants. This may help prevent frost burn.

5 Plant asparagus and rhubarb crowns.

In temperate climates

1 Liliums, with their exotic flowers and gorgeous perfume, are worth a place in any garden. Plant bulbs now.

2 Petal blight is a fungal disease that causes azalea flowers to rot on the bush. Pick off affected flowers and control with Zaleton.

3 Reduce watering of indoor plants. Most come from warm climates, so bring water to room temperature before you start.

4 Crab-apples, crepe myrtles and other ornamental deciduous trees can be planted this month.

5 Sow or plant calendulas, snap-dragons, broad beans and lettuce.

In tropical/subtropical climates

1 Get rid of lawn weeds with Yates BuffaloPro or BuffaloPro Weed 'n' Feed.

2 Split up established day lily clumps and spread to other parts of the garden.

3 Plant hippeastrum bulbs with the top of the bulb protruding from the soil.

4 Prune sasanqua camellias after flowering has finished.

5 Sow or plant nasturtiums, salvias, potatoes and sweet potatoes.

JULY

In cold climates

1 Plant or transplant deciduous trees now while they're dormant.

2 Begin applying Hydrangea Blueing or Pinking Liquid to change flower colour.

3 Exquisitely beautiful paeony roses are at their best in cool climates. Plant now.

4 Spray Yates White Oil to control sap-sucking pests such as aphids, mites and scale.

5 Plant new raspberries in a sunny spot where the prickly canes won't catch passers-by.

In temperate climates

1 July is the main month for rose pruning. Use sharp secateurs and a good quality saw. Spray with Lime Sulfur after pruning.

2 Winter lawns can become infested with bindi. Get rid of it now at the fern leaf stage (with selective bindi killer) or suffer from its barbed seeds later in the season.

3 Check plantings of spring annuals and replace any casualties. Buy advanced seedlings for the quickest results.

4 Towards the end of the month, feed citrus with Dynamic Lifter PLUS Fruit Food.

5 Sow or plant English daisies, delphiniums and dianthus.

In tropical/subtropical climates

1 Fertilise mangoes by putting some Dynamic Lifter PLUS Fruit Food into a series of holes in the soil beneath the outer foliage.

2 Tidy dead flowering stems from cymbidium orchids and feed plants with Dynamic Lifter organic pellets.

3 Moist weather encourages snails and slugs. Sprinkle Blitzem pellets among clumps of foliage.

4 Check roses for suckers coming from below the ground. Use a sharp tug to remove these as cleanly as possible.

5 Plant summer-flowering bulbs such as gladioli and hippeastrums.

AUGUST

In cold climates

1 Cut or pluck dead flowers from bulbs, but leave foliage to die down naturally.

2 August's a good month to plan and prepare a new vegie bed.

3 Spray Liquid Copper or Leaf Curl Copper Fungicide onto peach and nectarine trees when their new buds start to swell.

4 Prune roses and transplant deciduous trees and shrubs while they're still dormant.

5 Plant paeonies, lily-of-the-valley and raspberries.

In temperate climates

1 Finish rose pruning and prune crepe myrtles if desired

2 Spray weedy lawns with bindi killer or BuffaloPro Weed 'n' Feed.

3 Sow tomatoes indoors, ready to plant out once the soil is warmer.

4 New season's dahlia tubers can start to go into well-prepared, sunny garden beds.

5 Feed camellias and azaleas after they finish blooming. Any trimming should be done at this time.

In tropical/subtropical climates

1 Repot indoor and outdoor container plants into fresh, good-quality potting mix.

2 Prune hibiscus, abutilons (Chinese lantern), acalyphas and poinsettias.

3 Fertilise everything in the garden, and top up layers of organic mulch.

4 Pinch back and feed geraniums and gardenias to encourage bushy growth.

5 Plant marigolds, petunias, zinnias and asters in pots and flowerbeds.

SEPTEMBER

In cold climates

1 Feed azaleas as they finish blooming with Acticote or Dynamic Lifter PLUS Flower Food.

2 Four weeks after full bloom, begin a spray program to control codling moth in apples, pears and quinces.

3 Give a garden-minded dad a great plant or garden book for Father's Day.

4 After bulbs finish flowering, continue watering weekly with soluble Thrive or Aquasol until leaves die down completely.

5 Sow or plant peas, lettuce, beetroot, carrots and silver beet.

In temperate climates

1 Sow seed or transplant runners into bare patches in lawns. Topdress hollows.

2 Visit open gardens in your area to be inspired and gather ideas.

3 Plant a gorgeous native gymea lily in your garden. It will take some time to bloom but when it does, the 6 m-tall flower spike will look like a giant torch.

4 Prune spring-flowering shrubs and roses as soon as their flowering has finished.

5 Sow or plant sunflowers, petunias, tomatoes and beans.

In tropical/subtropical climates

1 Plant crotons, caladiums, iresine gingers and coleus to brighten shady parts of the garden.

2 Feed all established fruit trees with Dynamic Lifter PLUS Fruit Food.

3 Spray hibiscus with Confidor to control hibiscus beetle.

4 Separate young bromeliad suckers from the mother plant when they're about one-third the mature size.

5 Apply Yates Complete Lawn Insect Control to lawns to give season-long control of curl grubs and black beetles.

OCTOBER

In cold climates

1 October's a wonderful month for planting. Shrubs that go in now will make maximum growth over the next few months.

2 Fertilise potted plants with Acticote and repot if the roots are crowded.

3 Begin a program with Success Ultra to protect apples and pears from codling moth. Wrap cloth around trunks to trap migrating grubs.

4 When you're sure that frosts are finished for the year, prune frost damaged parts of plants.

5 Plant tomatoes, beans and sweet corn. Start indoors if soil's still too cold.

In temperate climates

1 Divide and repot congested clumps of cymbidium orchids. Feed with Dynamic Lifter pellets.

2 Feed lawns with an organic-based food like Dynamic Lifter Concentrated.

3 Rejuvenate tired old citrus trees by pruning hard, renewing mulch and feeding with Dynamic Lifter PLUS Fruit Food. If cut back severely, the plant may not fruit again for a couple of seasons.

4 Plant a pot of mixed salad greens (e.g. lettuce, rocket, spring onion and parsley) just outside the kitchen door where they're easy to harvest.

5 Plant marigolds, salvias and nasturtiums.

In tropical/subtropical climates

1 Climbing plants are especially at home in warmer climates. This month plant mandevilla, allamanda and bougainvillea.

2 Basil grows well with tomato plants. It repels pests and promotes healthy growth.

3 Water hydrangeas every two weeks with soluble Thrive Flower & Fruit to encourage larger blooms.

4 Use a garden fork to aerate the lawn (push and pull the fork in and out of the soil) then follow up by feeding with a good-quality lawn fertiliser.

5 Sow or plant tropical fruits such as lychees, mangoes and custard apples.

NOVEMBER

In cold climates

1 Mix dampened peat moss and compost to make an ideal mulch for azaleas and camellias.
2 Replace tired spring annuals with some bright summer colour.
3 Fertilise roses with a good-quality rose food, such as Dynamic Lifter PLUS Flower Food.
4 Pear and cherry slug numbers are increasing. Control with Success Ultra, or dust with wood ash or lime.
5 Sow or plant tomatoes, zucchinis and sweet corn.

In temperate climates

1 Pot up containers with colourful annuals for decorating summer entertaining areas.
2 Lift bulbs after leaves have died down, dry and store for next year.
3 Prune spring-blooming rambling roses (such as banksias) after they finish flowering.
4 Apply Confidor Tablets to azaleas and lillypillies to protect from sucking insects.
5 Sow or plant ageratum, geraniums, salvias and portulacas.

In tropical/subtropical climates

1 Feed bananas and pawpaws every six weeks with Dynamic Lifter PLUS Fruit Food.
2 Take cuttings of favourite bougainvilleas.
3 Hand-prune side shoots from tomatoes. Dust regularly with Yates Tomato & Vegetable Dust.
4 A Nature's Way Fruit Fly Control program is essential for good crops. Infested fruit should be sealed in a plastic bag and left to 'cook' in the sun.
5 Plant day lilies for their tough constitutions and generous blooming – they'll open a new flower every day.

DECEMBER

In cold climates

1 Watering in the morning and watering at the base of the plant reduces risk of fungal diseases.
2 Mulch tomatoes with old compost or manure. Keep dusting with Yates Tomato & Vegetable Dust.
3 Continue spraying apple and pear trees with Success Ultra to control codling moth.
4 Harvest strawberries regularly and make sure they're protected from snails and slugs with Blitzem or Baysol. Remove excess runners.
5 Sow or plant phlox, cosmos and nasturtiums.

In temperate climates

1 Clear away garden rubbish and clean out gutters to reduce fire risk.
2 Water has a cooling effect in the garden. Think of installing a garden pond or fountain.
3 Raise the mower height during warm weather – longer grass means cooler soil at root level.
4 Whitefly is a nuisance on tomato plants. Try pyrethrum or Natrasoap applied under leaves.
5 Sow or plant dwarf beans, spring onions and carrots.

In tropical/subtropical climates

1 Re-apply mulch to garden beds to protect soil during heavy downpours.
2 Feed mangoes with Dynamic Lifter PLUS Fruit Food to encourage production of healthy fruit. In humid weather, use Liquid Copper to control the fungal disease anthracnose.
3 Check drainage. In heavy soils use a liquid claybreaker.
4 Hibiscus flower beetle can cause flower drop. Control with Confidor or Yates Rose Gun Advanced.
5 Sow or plant salvias, ageratum, sweet corn and zucchini.

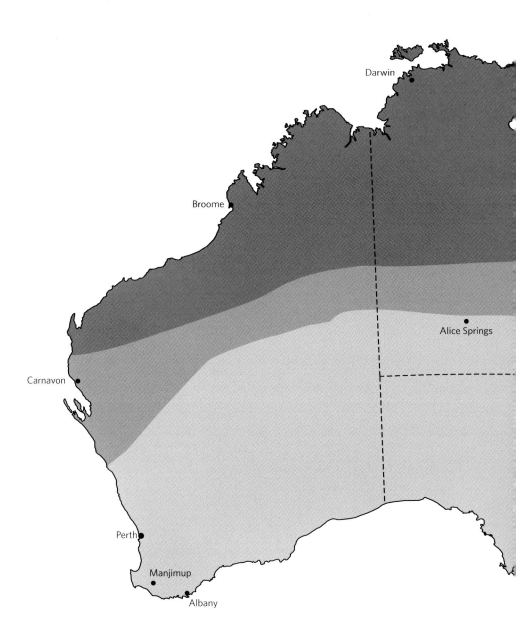

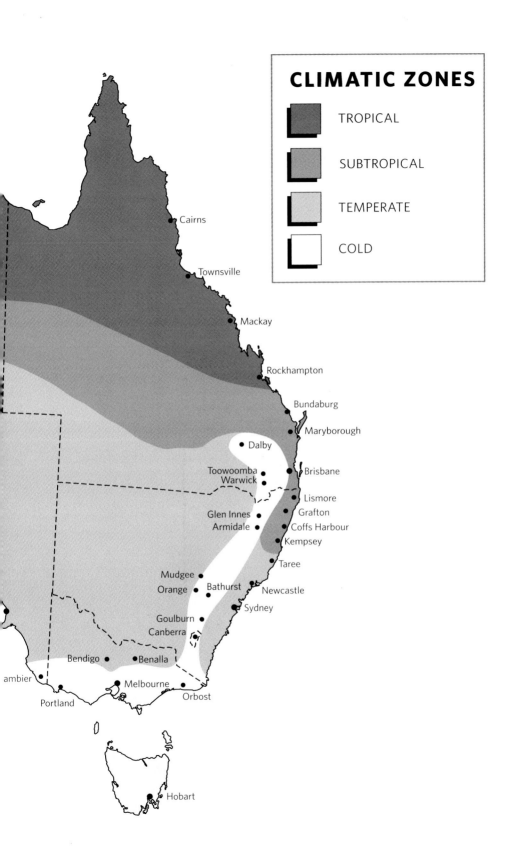

CLIMATIC ZONES

- TROPICAL
- SUBTROPICAL
- TEMPERATE
- COLD

Cairns

Townsville

Mackay

Rockhampton

Bundaburg

Maryborough

Dalby

Toowoomba
Warwick

Brisbane

Lismore

Glen Innes
Armidale

Grafton
Coffs Harbour
Kempsey

Taree

Mudgee
Orange

Bathurst

Newcastle

Sydney

Goulburn
Canberra

Bendigo

Benalla

ambier

Melbourne

Portland

Orbost

Hobart

Picture Credits

t = top   b = bottom   c = centre   l = left   r = right

Alamy 62, 180, 372

Auscape International 46r, 75b, 101, 115, 130, 132, 189br, 220t, 220b, 246t, 255, 285, 327, 349, 355, 357, 365, 370t, 370b, 371b, 381b, 391bl, 396, 417tr, 467r, 480

Esther Beaton 412, 414, 420l

Jennifer Blau 47, 100, 111

Donna Brown 370c, 371cb

Leigh Clapp viii, xii-xiii, 9, 11, 12, 13, 14t, 14b, 15t, 15b, 17t, 17b, 23t, 36, 38, 45, 48, 49, 67br, 75t, 81, 92, 96, 103, 105, 107, 110, 112, 121r, 131, 139, 150-151, 164t, 164b, 168, 171, 178-179, 184, 216, 220t, 220b, 229, 230, 238, 266-267, 282, 311, 329, 335, 338, 343t, 343m, 343b, 346, 398, 404, 409, 410, 418, 420r, 422, 462, 476, 478, 481

Nancy Cohen 141t

Michael Cook 44

DW Stock Picture Library 40, 41l, 41r, 64, 69, 73b, 114b, 119, 120l, 122, 124l, 126, 129l, 129r, 154, 155, 157, 159, 160, 162, 233br, 381t

Getty Images front cover (main photo), 16, 76, 98, 116, 152, 268, 344, 362, 386, 444

Denise Greig 120r, 124r, 127, 161, 274l, 274r, 391t, 417tl, 417b

HS Photography 21, 35, 43, 67l, 67t, 68t, 102, 113, 123r, 141b, 172m, 172b, 189t, 233bl, 246bl, 246br, 256, 275l, 305, 321, 331, 375t, 376b, 382b, 391br, 407, 413, 435

Jack Hobbs 104, 121l, 281b, 324, 350, 353, 375b, 376t, 377, 382t, 400, 467l, 468

iStock 206, 228, 320, 369

Judy Horton, Yates 73t, 114t, 235, 258, 383

Cheryl Maddocks 352

Keith A. McLeod 51, 68b, 123l, 125, 133, 167t, 189bl, 233t, 251, 358, 366, 380, 479, 483

National Archives of Australia (A12111, 1/1959/21/9) 7b

National Library of Australia (Australian Womens Weekly Aug 1944) 7t

National Library of Australia (Wolfgang Sievers vn 4186475) 10

Stuart Read 5, 6

Tony Rodd 172t, 175, 275r, 281t, 309, 371ct, 378, 395, 470, 482

Lorna Rose 20, 22t, 22b, 23b, 24, 28, 90, 91, 93, 94, 253, 270, 364, 368, 473

Shutterstock front cover (three smaller photos), back cover, 46l, 87, 197, 244

State Library of Queensland (Charles Huet neg.10002-0001-0001) 8

State Library of Queensland (neg 86902) 2

Claire Takacs 60-61, 88, 97

Claire Takacs/Fiona Brockhoff, Sorrento home garden 18

Claire Takacs/Phillip Johnson Design 25, 26

Gerry Whitmont 50, 385, 416, 466

Adam Woodhams 199

Yates Archives v, ix, x, xit, xib, 134, 167, 234, 347

Your Garden 425, 426, 429, 430, 436, 437, 440, 442, 446l, 446r, 447, 450, 451l, 451r, 452, 454, 455, 456, 459, 461

Index

NOTE: Because of space limitations not every botanical and common name is included, and where only a Genus name is given, several species can often be found on the pages indicated. The reader can also search under main headings e.g. Palms

European plum, 251
evergreen trees, planting, 25
everlasting daisy, 286–7, 309, 322
Exochorda, 396
exotic ground covers, 281

F

Fagus, 396
fairy rings, 133
false cypress, 403
false sarsparilla, 430, 441
fan flower, 418, 425, 431
Farfugium, 428
feather reed grass, 458
Federation gardens, 4, 12
Feijoa sellowiana, 255
Felicia, 376
fennel (*Foenicum vulgare*), 92, 234, 240–1, 459
fern spores, treatment before sowing, 148
ferns, 340, 474–5
Ferocactus, 449
fertilisers
    applying before sowing seed, 155–6
    buying, 79
    granular, 80
    inorganic, 80–2
    on lawns, 271–2, 277, 278
    for roses, 365–6
    for vegies, 183
fescue (Festuca), 376, 459
feverfew, 234, 240–1
fiddlewood, 46, 394
fig trees (Ficus), 249, 381, 382, 396, 432
Fiji fire plant, 392
Filipendula, 376
final garden plans, 30–3
fine fescue grass, 276
fineleaf weeds, 140–1
fir trees, 403
fire-prone areas, gardening in, 428–33
firethorn, 400
fish hook cactus, 449
flame pea, 414
flame vine, 384, 438
fleabane, 375
floribunda roses, 370
floss flower, 296

flowering bulbs, 345–8, 359–61, 466–7
flowering cypress, 401, 433
flowering gums, 101
flowering plants, types, 283–4
flowering plum, 399–400
flowering quince, 442
flowers
    choosing, 30
    cutting, 342–3
    growing from seed, 161
    pest and disease control, 339–41
    place in overall plan, 58
    sowing guide for, 286–95
focal points in garden design, 27
Foeniculum vulgare, 92, 234, 240–1, 459
foliage plants, 457
foliage selection, 29
forget-me-not, 288–9, 310
form in gardens, 26
formal gardens, 11–13
Fortunella, 440
fountain grass, 460
fowls *see* chooks
foxglove, 288–9, 310, 340
frangipani, 399
Fraxinus, 396, 443
Freesia, 350, 360
French beans, 186
French marigolds, 290–1, 317–18
Fritillaria, 350–1, 360
fruit, selection and cooking, 259–61
fruit fly, 120, 131
fruit salad plant, 383
fruit trees
    citrus, 245–7
    deciduous, 247–8
    pest and diseases of, 131–2
    sprays for, 135
fruit vines, 251–2
fruits
    berries, 256–7
    tropical, 253–4
Fuchsia, 396
fun, having, 52–3
funeral cypress, 403
fungal disease control, 125–7

G

Gaillardia, 288–9, 310
Galanthus, 353, 361
gall wasp, citrus, 132
Galtonia, 355, 360
garden design
    concepts, 24–7
    hard landscapes, 27–8
    low-allergen, 34–5
    plans, 30–3
    principles, 19
    soft landscapes, 28–9
    style selection, 20–4
garden maintenance
    considerations in design, 26
    time involved in, 54
garden styles, 3–17, 20–4
Gardenia, 396, 440
garlic, 90, 235, 240–1
Garrya, 396
gay feather, 376
Gazania, 288–9, 310
Gelsemium, 381
Georgian Revival period gardens, 6
Geraldton wax, 100, 414
geranium, 288–9, 310–11, 341
Gerbera, 288–9, 311–12, 341
germination problems with seeds, 165
gherkins, 203
ghost bush, 374
ginger, 235, 240–1
ginger lily, 459–60
Ginkgo, 397
Gladiolus, 340, 355–6, 360
glasshouses, 51
Gleditsia, 443
globe amaranth, 290–1, 312
globe thistle, 375
Glochidion, 433
Gloriosa, 356, 360
glory of the snow, 348, 359
glossy abelia *see* Abelia
Gloxinia, 290–1, 312, 356, 360
goat's beard, 374, 434
Godetia, 290–1, 313
gold dust tree, 392
golden alyssum, 374
golden barrel cactus, 449
golden cane palm, 406
golden glory vine, 384

K

Kaffir lily, 56, 348, 359, 427, 430
Kaffir plum trees, 482
Kalanchoe, 451, 453–4
kale, 203–4, 224–5, 314
kangaroo grass, 105
kangaroo paw, 105, 290–1, 314–15, 415
kangaroo vine, 418, 427, 441
Kennedia spp., 418, 419
Kentucky bluegrass, 276
kidney weed, 430
kikuyu grass, 274–5
kim chee, 202–3
kiwi fruit, 252
Kniphofia, 356, 360
Kochia, 315
kohl rabi, 205, 224–5
Kohleria, 428
Kolkwitzia, 397
kurrajong, 102, 442

L

lace bugs, 123, 136
Lachenalia, 352, 360
lady palm, 440
Lagerstroemia, 397, 443
lamb's ear, 105, 378
lamb's tongue, 140
Lamium, 428
larkspur, 290–1, 315, 340
Laurus nobilis, 104, 232, 240–1, 433, 440
Laurustinus, 104
lavender (*Lavandula* spp.), 103, 236, 240–1, 376, 431
lavender shower, 378
lawn grass mixtures, 277
lawns *see also* ground covers
  adding strawberry clover, 271
  care of new, 277
  fertilising, 271
  in garden design, 29
  maintaining, 278–9
  pests and disease, 133–4
  pests in, 280
  planning, 269
  planting sprigs and runners, 272
  renovating, 279
  selecting grass for, 273–7

site preparation, 269–72
sowing seed, 272
sprays for, 134
turf laying, 272–3
weeds in, 139, 279
Lawson cypress, 403
layering, propagating by, 169–70
leaf cuttings, 173
leaf hoppers, 122
leaf miners, 120
leaf mould, making, 143
leaf nematodes, 128
leaf spots, 126
leafy cactus, 450
Lebanese cucumber, 204
leeks, 204–5, 226–7
lemon balm, 236, 240–1
lemon grass, 236, 240–1
lemon scab, 133
lemon verbena, 236, 242–3
lemon-scented myrtle, 412
lemons, 247, 260
Lenten rose *see* Helleborus
leopard plant, 428
Lepidozamia, 105
Leptospermum, 415, 424
Leschenaultia, 415
lettuce, 186, 193, 206–7, 226–7, 469
Leucadendron, 456
Leucojum, 353, 361
Leucospermum, 456–7
Leyland cypress, 405
Liatris, 376
lighting, 57, 59
lilac, 67, 401
Lilium, 141, 356–7, 360
lillypilly, 412, 416, 432, 433, 441
lily-of-the-valley, 352, 360, 466
lily-of-the-valley shrub, 399
lime
  and pH, 84–6
  use, 71, 183, 271, 278
limes, 247
Limonium, 431
Linaria, 290–1, 315
Linospadix, 406
Linum, 316
liquid organic fertilisers, 82–3
Liquidambar, 398, 443
Liriodendron, 398

Liriope, 428
litchi, 255
little leaf, 131
Livingstone daisy, 290–1, 316
Livistona, 406
loams, 64
Lobelia, 290–1, 316, 435
local conditions, planting for, 58
local materials, using, 27
loganberries, 257
Lomandra longifolia, 418, 425, 460
Lomatia, 436
long-standing crops, placement, 185
Lonicera, 382, 440
looking-glass plant, 394
Loropetalum, 398
lovage, 236–7, 242–3
love-in-a-mist, 292–3, 320
low-allergen gardens, 34–5
low-water use gardens, 13
Luculia, 398
Lunaria, 290–1
Lupin, 316–17
lychee nut, 255
Lychnis, 376
Lycoris, 357, 361
Lysichiton, 435

M

macadamias, 258
Macfadyena, 383
Macrozamia, 428, 460
Madagascar jasmine, 384
magnesium (Mg) in soil, 79
Magnolia, 398
maidenhair fern, 56
maidenhair tree, 397
Malope, 290–1, 317
Maltese cross, 376
Malus, 398, 443
Mammillaria, 449–50
mandarins, 247, 260
Mandevilla, 381, 382, 383
manganese (Mn) in soil, 79
mangos, 254
manures, organic, 83
maple tree, 392, 442
marigolds, 286–7, 300–1, 317–18, 339, 340
marjoram, 237, 242–3